LOEB CLASSICAL LIBRARY
FOUNDED BY JAMES LOEB 1911

EDITED BY
JEFFREY HENDERSON

PLAUTUS

I

LCL 60

PLAUTUS

AMPHITRYON · THE
COMEDY OF ASSES · THE
POT OF GOLD · THE TWO
BACCHISES · THE CAPTIVES

EDITED AND TRANSLATED BY

WOLFGANG DE MELO

HARVARD UNIVERSITY PRESS
CAMBRIDGE, MASSACHUSETTS
LONDON, ENGLAND
2011

Copyright © 2011 by the President and Fellows
of Harvard College
All rights reserved

First published 2011

LOEB CLASSICAL LIBRARY® is a registered trademark
of the President and Fellows of Harvard College

Library of Congress Control Number 2010924480
CIP data available from the Library of Congress

ISBN 978-0-674-99653-3

*Composed in ZephGreek and ZephText by
Technologies 'N Typography, Merrimac, Massachusetts.
Printed on acid-free paper and bound by
The Maple-Vail Book Manufacturing Group*

CONTENTS

To my wife

PREFACE

The last decade has seen several new Loeb editions replacing older ones. The edition I am presenting here also has a predecessor, in Paul Nixon's Plautus. Nixon's work has helped many generations of students and scholars to understand Plautus, but after almost a century, a new edition, reflecting the progress made in Plautine studies, was overdue. Times have changed; these days one cannot assume universal familiarity with ancient drama any longer. For this reason I have been more generous with introductions than Nixon was. This volume contains a general introduction providing the reader with basic background information on various aspects of Plautine scholarship and with a minimum of bibliography. In addition, each play is preceded by a brief introduction outlining the principal problems the reader is likely to encounter there.

While the text of Loeb editions has to be reliable, the series has aims different from those of the major critical collections, such as the Oxford Classical Texts or the Teubner editions. The Latin text of my Plautus edition is based on the latest critical works, but I have not considered it necessary to follow them slavishly. There are places where I would mark the text as corrupt if I were to write a Teubner edition, but where the sense is nevertheless clear I have followed emendations and conjectures by earlier scholars that make the text more readable. I have added notes where I deviate from the standard critical editions or where there are major textual problems. My notes are not meant to replace a critical apparatus. Readers who desire more detailed information on these or other problems are advised to consult the critical texts listed in the bibliography. At the end of the volume there is a metrical appendix that should enable any reader with a basic knowledge of Latin to scan the plays.

Nixon's translation was a child of its time. I have profited much from working through it, but it must be said that its archaic ring and the bowdlerization of a number of passages make it less accessible and less helpful for today's readers. I have striven for accuracy as well as a more modern idiom, though not for uniformity of language, since Plautus himself is a chameleon when it comes to registers and styles. I have supplemented my translation with stage directions. My hope is that these will help readers understand how the action is developing. But even where the stage action is clear, there are occasionally obscure passages. This is not surprising given that we are separated from Plautus by more than two millennia. I have tried to elucidate such passages through footnotes. Readers who require more information should consult the commentaries listed in my bibliography.

I have received generous help with this edition. My colleagues at Oxford, J. N. Adams and Peter Brown, commented extensively on the general introduction; they have also read parts of the *Asinaria* and *Aulularia* and have helped me with English idiom as well as with linguistic and metrical questions. Peter Kruschwitz also answered various queries on metre. I am much indebted to Plautine scholars in Urbino, in particular Cesare Questa, Roberto Danese, and Alba Tontini; they have sent me the latest critical editions and many splendid articles on individual problems. Walter Stockert in Vienna has sent me his excellent edition of and commentary on the *Aulularia*; I am very much looking forward to his *Cistellaria*.

When Terence wrote his comedies a generation after Plautus' death and was criticized for receiving help from distinguished members of the Scipionic Circle, he replied that he was proud to have received such help (*Ad.* 15–21). I am equally proud to have received much help from John Trappes-Lomax, who read the entire manuscript and commented on the introduction, the Latin text, and especially the English translation. Without him, the volume would not be what it is.

As always, my family and friends have been very supportive. Since space does not allow me to mention every name, I prefer not to name anyone. There must, however, be one exception: my wife, Sally, has always had more confidence in my ability to finish this project than I had myself, and she has supported me very much even though she was pregnant during most of the time in which I worked on this volume. To her, then, this volume is dedicated with much love.

GENERAL INTRODUCTION

While it would be difficult to understand Cicero's letters without detailed knowledge of the history of the late Republic, Plautine comedy seems very different, at least at first sight: the characters are fictional and live in a fictional world that is called Greece but has little to do with the Greece of reality. Political and historical allusions are few. But this simplicity of Roman comedy is deceptive. In order to get a real understanding of it, some background information is necessary; for instance, Plautus' plays are all adaptations of Greek comedies, and it is essential to know something about these in order to see why Plautus is more than a translator. There are excellent monographs covering all aspects of Plautine comedy, in particular Duckworth (1952) and Beare (1964) in English, Lefèvre (1973) in German, and Paratore (1957) in Italian. In this introduction, my aim is more modest: I shall deal with essential issues but cannot go into much detail. I look at Plautus' life, his Greek sources, and the content of his plays. Since Plautine comedies are said to owe much to native Italian traditions of entertainment, I examine what we know about such traditions and to what extent we can speak of real influence. I also give a brief outline of Plautine language and meter and its differences from classical Latin. After this, I discuss how plays were staged. As the text of

Plautus is not always unproblematic, I give an overview of the ancient and medieval manuscripts as well as of the history of Plautine textual emendation. A topic I can only touch upon is the influence Plautus has had on European literature.

PLAUTUS' LIFE

Very little is known about Plautus.[1] He is usually referred to as Titus Maccius Plautus, but scholars have suspected for a long time that this was not his real name.[2] Titus is a common first name, while Maccius and Plautus are attested more rarely. What gives rise to the suspicions is the combination of names and the fact that they belong to a writer of comedy. *Maccus* is the standard name of the clown in a type of comedy called the Atellan farce, and Plautus, a hypercorrect form of *plotus*, means "flat-footed"; the latter may or may not be a reference to the actors of mime, who normally performed barefoot. Given that the possession of three names was more or less restricted to the nobility in Plautus' day, it is possible that Plautus' real name was simply Titus and that Maccius and Plautus are stage names.

Sextus Pompeius Festus (second century CE) wrote a dictionary, which is an abridged version of a work by Marcus Verrius Flaccus, who lived in the Augustan period. Verrius Flaccus' has been lost, and some parts of Festus' are now fragmentary. But in the eighth century Paul the Deacon, who still had access to the complete Festus,

[1] See Leo 1912: 63–86 for a discussion of ancient sources.
[2] On this question see Gratwick 1973.

abridged him in turn, which makes Paul an invaluable source for Plautine scholarship. Paul (p. 275 Lindsay) informs us that Plautus was an Umbrian from Sarsina. However, in the same passage he tells us that Plautus got this name because he had flat feet, which is pure speculation. We may wonder whether Paul, or rather Festus or Verrius Flaccus, based this statement about Plautus' Umbrian origins on some ancient source or it was extrapolated from a pun in *Most*. 769–70, where *umbra* (shadow) is deliberately misunderstood as *Umbra* (woman from Umbria) by a witty slave, who then goes on to ask about a woman from Sarsina. If Plautus was an Umbrian, Latin would not have been his first language, and his complete mastery of so many registers and meters of Latin would be even more astonishing than Joseph Conrad's skill as a nonnative English novelist.

We do not know when Plautus was born, but we learn from Cicero that he died in 184 (*Brut*. 60).[3] Cicero also tells us that as a *senex* (an old man) Plautus took pleasure in his *Truculentus* and *Pseudolus* (*Cato* 50). The term *senex* is normally reserved for men over sixty, and the *Pseudolus* was first staged in 191, seven years before his death. If we assume that Plautus died at the age of seventy—and this is a mere assumption—he would have been born in 254, which is the date usually given in histories of Latin literature.

According to Gellius (3. 3), Plautus worked for the stage, then did business with the money he had earned, lost it all, and worked in a mill, where he wrote the plays *Saturio* and *Addictus* (The Bondsman). It is indeed highly

---

[3] All dates are BCE unless otherwise noted.

likely that Plautus worked for the stage before beginning
to write his own plays, although it is unclear in what ca-
pacity. However, the rest of the story looks apocryphal.[4] It
may be based on what we find in Plautus' comedies: they
abound in young men doing business abroad and slaves be-
ing threatened with being sent to the mill, which meant ar-
duous work.

In the same essay, Gellius states that around 130 come-
dies ascribed to Plautus were in circulation. How many of
these were genuine has to remain unclear. According to
Varro, twenty-one plays were genuine and were accepted
as such by everyone, and it is these which have come down
to us through the direct manuscript tradition. However,
Varro believed other plays to be genuine as well, for in-
stance the *Boeotia*, even though there was no scholarly
consensus on them. Varro's criteria, like those of his col-
leagues, were impressionistic, and there is no guarantee
that the remaining plays considered genuine by Varro or
others were really all written by Plautus. There was much
disagreement. One generation after Plautus, for instance,
Terence (*Ad.* 7) speaks of a Plautine comedy called *Com-
morientes* (Men Dying Together), while Gellius informs us
that Accius did not believe this play to be genuine (Gell. 3.
3. 9). Of these other plays ascribed to Plautus, only isolated
fragments survive, usually cited by ancient grammarians
and lexicographers.

Most of Plautus' plays are difficult to date. Because
of *didascaliae*, that is production notices transmitted to-
gether with the plays, we know that the *Stichus* was first
performed in 200 and the *Pseudolus* in 191. Elsewhere

---

[4] For a different opinion see Norwood 1932: 15–17.

we need to rely on internal evidence, which is rare since Plautus does not often allude to contemporary events and new institutions. Such internal evidence is usually not very precise. Thus Ergasilus says in *Capt.* 90 that he might have to go to the *Porta Trigemina* to earn money, presumably as a porter. There was no market at this place before 193 CE, and we can infer that the *Captiui* was performed after that date. In *Bacch.* 214 Plautus speaks of his play *Epidicus*, which means that the *Bacchides* was written after this play. Since allusions to historical events in Plautus are few and far between, scholars have tried to supplement our information with linguistic and stylistic evidence. There is, for example, a general consensus that Plautus wrote fewer songs for his earlier plays than for the later ones.[5] But the metrical method can only supplement other information and will never replace it. For most plays the best we can do is to come up with rough dates. In the introductions to the individual plays I present all information relevant to their dating and try to assess its quality.

PLAUTUS' GREEK SOURCES

Plautus was undoubtedly the greatest writer of Roman comedy, but he did not invent comedy in general or Roman comedy in particular. Rather, he stands in two long traditions. The first is that of Greek comedy, which has to be discussed before we can look at Plautine comedy as such. Greek comedy, in the centuries since its first attestation in fifth-century Athens and Sicily, had become an internationally popular and constantly developing form; the

5 For early work in this area see Sedgwick 1925 and 1930.

more recent plays were adapted by Roman playwrights such as Naevius and then Plautus. As far as the plots are concerned, Plautus is not original at all. But Plautus is also heir to native Italian traditions of farce and entertainment. He introduced many such Italian elements into his plays and developed them further, and it is this achievement that allows us to speak of Plautus as an original genius. We can thus distinguish between two influences on Plautus, a direct Greek one and an indirect Italian one. I shall turn to native Italian elements in a later section, once I have discussed the themes and characteristics of Plautine comedy. But now let us examine Greek comedy.

Greek Comedy

Comedy in the sense of humorous impersonation of others may be a cultural universal. The Greek word *komoidia* originally just meant "song in the company of men behaving in a festive way," but became a dramatic art form early on.[6] At Athens, comedy was performed during two festivals in honor of Dionysus, a god of both vegetation and artistic inspiration. These festivals are the Lenaea, held in January, and the City Dionysia, held in March. The religious character of these festivals was never lost; on the contrary, it was reinforced by processions and hymns.

The Athenians took comedy very seriously. It was staged in the Theatre of Dionysus, where probably up to six thousand people could attend in the classical period and up to seventeen thousand later on. The organizational

[6] For the texts see Kassel and Austin 1983–.

side was quite complex and lay in the hands of the state. The dramatists competed, and at the end of the festival there was a vote by judges, after which one of the officials would award a prize, a wreath, to the best producers, dramatists, and (later) actors.

The topics Greek comedy dealt with are not easy to summarize, but there are clear developments, to which I shall now turn.

Old Comedy

Comedy is attested in Sicily in the early fifth century. Its principal composer was Epicharmus, from whom only fragments remain: apparently mythological plots were an emphasis, and many plural titles suggest that there was a chorus as well as actors. But because the influence of Sicilian comedy on the later development of the genre seems to be negligible, for us the first stage is Old Comedy, essentially the Athenian comedy of the fifth century. The first official presentation of comedy at Athens was during the City Dionysia of 486, but the earliest writers of Old Comedy, Chionides, Ecphantides, and Magnes, are mere names to us. The greatest talents of the fifth century were Cratinus, Eupolis, and above all Aristophanes, the only comic writer of the period from whom we have complete plays.[7]

How much we know about Old Comedy depends to a large extent on how representative Aristophanes is. Aris-

---

[7] For a general introduction see Dover 1972; for a text and translation, Henderson 1998–2007; for a linguistic study, Willi 2003.

tophanes was born ca. 446 and died around 386, so he belongs to the latest phase of Old Comedy and could be argued already to mark the transition to Middle Comedy.[8] Eleven plays survive complete. We have thirty-three titles in addition, but some of these are probably alternate titles of other plays, and some clearly belong to other authors.

The plots of the plays are bizarre and eccentric, sometimes fantastic, often featuring nonhuman characters and choruses. In the *Lysistrata*, for example, the women of two Greek states force their husbands to make peace with each other by refusing to have sex with them otherwise. In the *Birds* an Athenian creates a city in the sky, becomes a birdman, and usurps the power of gods. And in the *Clouds* the great philosopher Socrates is ridiculed as a corrupt teacher of rhetoric. Thus Old Comedy draws heavily on contemporary events and satirizes them. No attempt at realistic plots is made, and masks and large phalli worn by the actors further contributed to an artificial atmosphere of jest and fun.

Structurally, Old Comedy is rather complex. It often begins with a prologue in which the protagonist presents the topic of the play by proposing a utopian solution to a crisis. The *parodos* is the entrance of the chorus. In the *proagon* and the *agon* the protagonist and his opponent debate the topic of the play with each other and the chorus. Then the chorus steps forward (*parabasis*) and addresses the audience. This is followed by three to five episodes alternating between actors and chorus. Finally, the *exodos* is the exit song of the chorus.

[8] For a different opinion see Nesselrath 1990: 334.

Middle Comedy

Middle Comedy can be argued to begin around 404, when Athens became a subject of Sparta and the oligarchic Thirty Tyrants came to power. A clear demarcation, however, cannot be established. Political topics continued to be discussed, albeit less routinely and in a more subdued fashion, whereas scenes of private life became more prominent, as did love affairs, tricks, and the stock characters we know from later Greek comedy and Roman adaptations. Mythological travesties also became increasingly popular. In terms of structure, Middle Comedy is also a transition period. The parabasis was given up and the chorus became less prominent and less involved in the plot. A five-act structure emerged, with the chorus merely providing a convenient means of separating the individual acts.

Much less survives of Middle Comedy than of Old Comedy. The only two complete plays we have are Aristophanes' late works, the *Ecclesiazusae* (Assembly-women) and the *Plutus* (Wealth), if indeed they should be regarded as Middle Comedy rather than late Old Comedy. Of the three most prominent exponents of Middle Comedy, Antiphanes (first play in 385), Anaxandrides (died after 349), and their younger contemporary Alexis (ca. 375–275), we have only fragments.

New Comedy

The development of Middle Comedy into New Comedy was a gradual one, so again there is no clear date when the latter began. In 336 Philip II of Macedon died and Alexander the Great became his successor, and it is around this time that one can speak of New Comedy. Its foremost exponents are Diphilus, Philemon, and above all Menander. Plautus adapted plays of all three, but also used comedies by less well-known playwrights, such as Demophilus, whose *Onagos* (The Ass-Driver) was the model for Plautus' *Asinaria* (The Comedy of Asses).

Diphilus and Philemon are only known to us through fragments and adaptations by Roman dramatists. Diphilus was born in Sinope on the Black Sea some time between 360 and 350 and died at the beginning of the third century. He wrote about a hundred plays, and we know about sixty titles. His *Kleroumenoi* (Men Casting Lots) was the basis for Plautus' *Casina,* and his *Synapothneskontes* (Men Dying Together) was the model for Plautus' *Commorientes*, a play of which less than one line survives, and a scene in Terence's *Adelphoe* (The Brothers). Philemon lived from 368/60 till 267/63; he became an Athenian citizen later, but by birth he was either a Sicilian from Syracuse or a Cilician from Soli. In his long life he wrote ninety-seven comedies, of which we know more than sixty titles. Slightly less than two hundred fragments survive, but we know that Plautus' *Mercator* is based on Philemon's *Emporos* (The Merchant) and that the *Trinummus* is modelled on the *Thesauros* (The Treasure).

Yet however important Diphilus and Philemon were, it is Menander of Athens who is generally considered to be the leading light of New Comedy.[9] Menander lived from

---

[9] The literature on Menander is enormous; for general introductions see Webster 1974 and Brown's part in Balme and Brown 2001, for a critical edition see Sandbach 1990, for a commentary

ca. 344/43 until 292/91, and even though he took up writ-
ing young, it is astonishing that he managed to write 108
plays. Nearly a hundred titles survive, but some are simply
alternate titles for one and the same play. Over nine hun-
dred quotations are preserved in other authors, and for a
long time this was all we had of Menander. But in 1905
remnants of a papyrus codex were found, the so-called
Cairo Codex. It contains more than half of the *Epitrepon-
tes* (Men at Arbitration), long sections of the *Perikeiro-
mone* (The Girl with Her Hair Cut Short) and the *Samia*
(The Woman from Samos), and part of the *Heros* (The
Guardian Spirit). Later, the Bodmer Codex was found,
which contains more of the *Samia*, the entire *Dyscolos*
(The Grumpy Man), and parts of the *Aspis* (The Shield). In
1968 part of the recently discovered *Dis exapaton* (The
Double Deceiver) was published, a find of extraordinary
importance for Plautine studies because this play is the ba-
sis of the *Bacchides*.

New Comedy has moved away from the sphere of pub-
lic life into the domain of the household. Its topics are by
and large domestic: love triumphs over obstacles consist-
ing of tensions between parents and children, rich and
poor, or men and women. The exuberant satire of Old
Comedy has to a large extent been replaced by calmer
smiles, the ancient aggression has mostly given way to po-
lite, bourgeois conversation. The general attitude writers
of New Comedy exhibit toward their characters is one of
refined humanity, reflected in Menander's dictum "what a

Gomme and Sandbach 1973, and for clear translations Arnott
1979–2000 and again Balme and Brown 2001.

pleasant thing man is, if only he is a man" (fr. 707 Kassel-Austin). New Comedy does not contain many truly bad people; most characters are essentially good, though sometimes misguided. The texts are nevertheless not bland: the stage action is typically very lively and the characterizations finely observed and lifelike.

Plautus' plays mainly have stock characters. He took them over from New Comedy, where we find a set of stock characters, like hangers-on and boastful soldiers, a set of stock situations, for instance the rediscovery of long-lost children, and a set of stock routines, for instance door-knocking scenes. It is the skillful combination of such stock characters, situations, and routines that leads to elegant and new plots. Interestingly, stock characters also have stock names. Typically, slaves are called Daos or Parmenon, and prostitutes often have the name Thais. Laches and Demeas are the names of old men, while Moschion and Sostratos are youngsters.

The techniques of New Comedy have also become more or less standardized. Most of the conversation is in relatively neutral but refined language in iambic trimeters. The action is divided into five acts, separated by interludes from the chorus, which is now completely detached from the plot. Actors wear type-masks, but not the phalli or special costumes of Old Comedy.

Plautus as Translator and Adapter

Plautine comedy belongs to the genre *fabula palliata* (comedy in Greek dress) because it is based on Greek plays. Naturally, this raises the question to what extent Plautus simply translated such comedies and to what extent he adapted them, in other words, the question of his originality.[10]

For a long time, scholars were in a better position to answer such questions with regard to the comedians Terence (185–159) and Caecilius (died in 168). Terence is generally regarded as a more faithful translator, but even he occasionally takes great liberties. Thus he informs us in the prologue to the *Andria* (The Woman from Andros) that he based this play on two originals by Menander, the *Andria* and the *Perinthia* (The Woman from Perinthos) (ll. 9–14).

Caecilius is usually considered to be closer to Plautus than to Terence. Gellius (2. 23) gives us three passages of Menander's *Plokion* (The Necklace) and Caecilius' adaptation. All three of the Greek passages are in iambic trimeters and relatively neutral language. Caecilius has turned the first passage into a song but left the others in iambic senarii, the Latin equivalent of the trimeter. More important, Caccilius has changed the content considerably. The first passage is full of Roman ritual terminology; the second contains some slapstick humor about the speaker's wife's bad breath, absent in the Greek original; and the third passage has been shortened and given a tragic ring.

In the early twentieth century substantial portions of Menander were found; later, in 1959, the entire *Dyscolos* (The Grumpy Man) became available to scholarship. But when Fraenkel in 1922 published his important study on Plautine originality, *Plautinisches im Plautus*,[11] direct

---

10 For a brief introduction see Arnott 1975; the classic in this field is Fraenkel 2007, see below.

11 Now translated into English and updated as Fraenkel 2007.

comparison was still impossible because there were no Greek fragments of any considerable length that corresponded to any passage in Plautus. Fraenkel had to rely on internal evidence, such as allusions to Roman institutions and Latin puns, to show what types of expression were Plautine rather than Greek. He reached interesting conclusions; for example, he argued that many references to Greek myths could not have been in the Greek originals, but were inserted by Plautus.[12] The same goes for many references to Greek customs and places.[13] For example, Plautus writes:

> *praeterea tibicinam,*
> *quae mi interbibere sola, si uino scatat,*
> *Corinthiensem fontem Pirenam potest* (*Aul.* 557–59)

(Then there's the flute-girl, who could drink dry the fountain of Pirene at Corinth without any help if it gushed with wine).

The play is said to take place in Athens, and Fraenkel (2007: 59–60) argues that for this reason a Greek playwright would have used a reference to an Athenian fountain. But for Plautus any Greek fountain is as good as another, so long as it is a well-known one.

Also very typical of Plautus are jokes and puns involving what Fraenkel calls "transformation and identification":

> *musca est meus pater: nil potest clam illum haberi*
> (*Merc.* 361)

[12] For mythological hyperbole see Zagagi 1980: 15–67.
[13] On Plautine geography see Blackman 1969.

(My father is a fly: nothing can be kept secret from him).

A writer of Greek New Comedy would probably have restricted himself to the complaint or perhaps said "my father is like a fly," but Plautus regularly goes one step further and identifies object and means of comparison.

Although Plautus' plays are situated in the Greek world, references to Roman institutions and customs, obviously his own additions, are frequent. Plautus even introduces Roman cuisine to his plays.[14] For the ancient Greeks the main source of animal protein was fish, and this is reflected in their comedies, where meat is rare. But Plautus exhibits an entirely Roman obsession with pork throughout his plays. Thus when the hanger-on Ergasilus is allowed to help himself to whatever food he wants, he immediately launches into an unremitting description of the various cuts of pork he will devour (*Capt.* 901–8).

Perhaps the most Plautine feature of all is the expansion of the role of the clever slave.[15] Naturally, slaves play an important part in Greek comedy as well, but Plautus gives a prominence to his slaves that is rare in Greece. Figures like the impertinent (albeit not very clever) Sosia in the *Amphitruo*, the unwaveringly loyal Palaestrio in the *Miles gloriosus*, or the brilliant Chrysalus in the *Bacchides* have no real counterpart in the Greek originals; of course Chrysalus is based on the clever Syros in the original by

14 Fraenkel 2007: 398–99.
15 On this topic and the saturnalian overthrow of norms see also Segal 1987; on the issue of a social code, norms, and their violations in comedy see Konstan 1983.

Menander, but trickery for the sake of trickery is as alien to the Greek playwright as it is standard for the Roman writer. Some slaves are in fact so important that Plautus named entire plays for them; this is the case for the *Epidicus*, *Pseudolus*, and *Stichus*.

But Fraenkel went much further. He even considered certain Greek puns as Plautine additions, for instance *opus est chryso Chrysalo* (Chrysalus needs gold) (*Bacch.* 240), which contains the Greek name Chrysalus and the Greek noun *chrysos* (gold): according to Fraenkel (2007: 21) no slave in Menander would ever be called Chrysalus because this is not a stock name.

Fraenkel died in 1970, two years after Handley published a new papyrus fragment, which contains some sixty lines of Menander's *Dis exapaton* (The Double Deceiver), the Greek original of Plautus' *Bacchides*.[16] Fraenkel's conclusions turned out to be essentially correct. The pun just mentioned, for example, cannot have been in Menander because we now know that Menander called his slave Syros rather than Chrysalus.

It may be worthwhile to dwell on the differences between the two passages for a bit longer.[17] Plautus changes certain names: Syros becomes Chrysalus, Sostratos is turned into Mnesilochus, and Moschos ends up as Pistoclerus. The old tutor's name Lydus is taken over from Menander, but the pun between his name and *ludus* (school) in l. 129 must be Plautine because it involves a Latin word. Yet such changes are minor. What is more important is that Plautus did not hesitate to shorten his

16 Greek text and discussion in Handley 1968.
17 For more details see Bain 1979.

model: while in the Greek text Sostratos confesses his
slave's trick to his father and goes away with him to return
the gold (ll. 47–63), Plautus has deleted the scene and
merely reports that this event took place offstage (l. 530).
Where the Greek and Latin text have the same content,
Plautus can be very literal on occasion; Sostratos says
that he is "empty-handed" after handing over the money
(*kenos*) (l. 92), literally "empty," and Plautus uses the word
inanis (l. 531), which also means "empty." Elsewhere,
however, Plautus is an adapter rather than a translator.
Compare ll. 102–12 in Menander. In this short scene in
iambic trimeters, Moschos wonders where Sostratos is, the
latter appears, there is a brief greeting, and then Sostratos
accuses Moschos of cheating on him. The language is col-
loquial, but elegant. No word is superfluous. By contrast,
the Plautine scene is four times as long (ll. 526–61). It is
written in trochaic septenarii in an elevated register; com-
pare the unmarked *akousas* (having heard) (l. 102) and the
elaborate *tetigit nuntius* (my message has reached him) (l.
528), or the military metaphors *hostis* (enemy) and *contol-
lam gradum* (I'll confront him) (ll. 534–35). Plautus has
drawn out the recognition scene between the two friends,
but the main reason why his scene is so long is that
Mnesilochus does not accuse Pistoclerus immediately; in-
stead he dwells on the bad character of a certain false
friend before revealing that he means Pistoclerus. The
Menandrean Sostratos had referred to Moschos as a fool
(ll. 98–99) taken in by the woman's seductive charms and
had pitied him; the Plautine Mnesilochus is resentful and
does not feel sorry for Pistoclerus.

Fraenkel's study is still the most important work on
Plautine originality; others, like Jachmann (1931), had

similar aims, but never achieved what Fraenkel did. The majority of scholars nowadays accept his conclusions, but there has also been some disagreement. Zwierlein (1990–92), for instance, believes that Plautus stayed quite close to the Greek originals and made no fundamental changes to the plots and characters he found in his models. What Fraenkel would regard as Plautine additions, Zwierlein considers interpolations of a reviser who lived not much later than Plautus himself. Zwierlein deletes many lines as later additions: 42 out of 729 in the *Curculio*, 277 out of 1,335 in the *Pseudolus*, and so on. Zwierlein's work, though full of interesting insights, is ultimately unsatisfactory:[18] for it is generally assumed that adaptations after Plautus strove for ever greater faithfulness to the Greek originals, and it would be strange to have a reviser making plays less faithful at that time; besides, if the reviser wrote so many lines, why did he not simply write his own plays? In this edition, I have put those passages that I believe to be interpolations in square brackets, but since there is often disagreement on such issues, I have left them in the Latin text and have translated them on the facing pages (again in square brackets; only interpolations that do not exceed two or three words in length have been left untranslated).

The opposite extreme is exemplified by the so-called Freiburg School, for example Lefèvre, Stärk, and Vogt-Spira 1991. Adherents of its theories believe that Plautus was far more original than Fraenkel would give him credit for and that not only Fraenkel's Plautine elements but also many seemingly Greek features are all based on a tradition of native Italian drama (on this issue see below).

[18] See Jocelyn 1993 and 1996.

Structural Problems and Contaminatio

Plautus does not tell us how he went about writing plays. Terence is more explicit in his prologues, which he mainly uses to defend his procedures against criticism. In his prologues, he uses the verb *contaminare* twice; elsewhere it occurs once: *nunc est profecto interfici quom perpeti me possum, ne hoc gaudium contaminet uita aegritudine aliqua* (*Eun.* 551–52) (Yes, now is the time when I could suffer death so that life doesn't spoil this joy with some sorrow). *Contaminare* here has the meaning "to ruin" or "to spoil." From the prologues we learn that the verb with its negative connotations was used by Terence's critics to describe what he did with the Greek originals. It is unlikely that the verb had any technical meaning in Terence's lifetime, even though today the term has special connotations. In *Haut.* 16–19 Terence states that his enemies say that he has spoiled many Greek plays while producing few Latin ones, and he admits that he has done so and will do so again. In *Andr.* 13–16 he says that for his play he used the *Andria* as his model, but inserted elements from the *Perinthia* (both are by Menander); his critics argue that one should not *contaminare* plays in this way: again the verb probably just means "to ruin."

Nowadays literary critics call a play "contaminated" if it is based on more than one source; in other words, the term *contaminatio* is used to refer to what happened to the Latin play. But this is not how Terence's opponents used the term. For them it was the Greek plays that suffered "contamination." The Greek plays were presumably "spoiled" by such adaptations for two reasons. The first is obvious: the structure of the Greek original which pro-

vided the main story line was distorted. The second reason
has to do with Roman concepts of plagiarism. For the
Romans, adaptations of Greek plays counted as Latin liter-
ature and were not considered plagiarized as long as there
was at least tacit acknowledgment of the Roman author's
debt to the author of the original.[19] But it was unaccept-
able to produce a Latin play based on a Greek source if that
Greek source had already been used by someone else, and
Terence apologized for accidentally doing so in *Eun.* 23–
28. If a playwright added a scene from a second Greek play
to his translation of another Greek play, he "spoiled" this
second text by making it unusable for other translators.

Did Plautus ever graft scenes from one Greek play onto
another? When Terence replies to the charge of *contam-
inatio*, he states that Naevius, Plautus, and Ennius fol-
lowed the same procedure (*Andr.* 18–19). Terence may
simply have made this up in order to defend himself; but it
is equally likely that he is correct. The question then arises
to what extent Plautus used this strategy.

In the absence of further fragments of New Comedy,
the question has traditionally been tackled by looking at
the Plautine comedies themselves. Inconsistencies and
structural problems could arguably point to the insertion
of alien passages. A typical kind of inconsistency can be
found in *Capt.* 147: Hegio has two sons, but one was kid-
napped as a small child, and the other is now a prisoner of
war; yet when Hegio is talking about the latter, he refers to
him as *unicus*, his only son. Can this problem be solved by
assuming that Plautus used two Greek plays, one in which

19 For ancient views on plagiarism see Russell 1979: 11–12.

an old man recovers a son who was kidnapped as a child and another one in which he recovers a son who was taken prisoner? This is one possibility, but other solutions to the problem are equally possible. We know that Plautus, even when using only one play, made extensive changes by shortening some passages and expanding others. The inconsistency could have been introduced by Plautus while he was expanding the dialogue. We could go further: Plautus may even have been conscious of the inconsistency, but tolerated it because it enabled him to create a witty remark in l. 150. It is perhaps also possible to assume that the inconsistency already existed in Plautus' Greek model, although the witticism in l. 150 bears all the hallmarks of Plautine humor.

The traditional approach is also open to criticism. To begin with, the text of Terence's *Andria* is internally consistent, and one cannot easily detect traces of *contaminatio* in the modern sense of the word. If Plautus was equally skilful in concealing such textual maneuvers, at least sometimes, many cases of grafting will be impossible to recover. Second, it would be a mistake to assume that the Greek originals were always entirely consistent. But which types of inconsistency go back to the Greek originals and which were introduced by Plautine insertions from other plays? Some inconsistencies will also be found in passages that Plautus made up himself without recourse to a Greek text. And finally, one should not forget that not all inconsistencies are equally problematic. Modern scholars reading plays in quiet offices and working through them with pen and paper in their hands are likely to find inconsistencies that ancient spectators in a crowded audience were bound to miss. *Contaminatio* did certainly exist, but in the absence of more New Comedy, the extent to which it was practised must remain unclear.

THEMES AND CHARACTERISTICS OF PLAUTINE COMEDY

Those who regularly watch romantic comedies on television can usually predict after a few minutes how the plots are going to develop. The situation is essentially the same with Plautine comedy: after reading a few plays, one normally gets a feel for what is going to happen. This does not mean that the plays become boring; but it is the variations on common themes, rather than exuberant originality, that make them interesting.

Common Themes

We tend to think of Roman comedies as love stories in which a young man falls for a girl, but as the course of true love never did run smooth, there is usually an obstacle that needs to be overcome with the help of a cunning slave. Yet romantic love does not figure in every comedy, and even in those where it does play a role, love is never at the heart of the action. Plautus often prefers to emphasize the cunning slave's deceptions. In the most extreme cases, the slave even warns his victim beforehand that he will deceive him (*Pseud.* 517) but nevertheless manages to carry out his tricks and gets away unpunished.

Such deceptions may have taken place in real life, but certainly very rarely. A situation equally rare in real life is what is often called *anagnorisis* (recognition). In comedies where recognition is an element, a young girl or more rarely a boy was abandoned or kidnapped but finds her parents or his relatives in the comedy, usually through some "tokens" that he or she received as a child. In the *Poenulus*, Hanno eventually finds his daughters and their nurse, but before that he also finds his nephew Agorastocles, whose recognition token is unusual: it is a scar on his left hand, the result of a monkey bite (ll. 1072–76).

Another of Plautus' favorite themes is mistaken identity. It can be accidental, as in the *Menaechmi*, where we find twins with the same name separated as children. One of them goes on a long journey to find his brother, and when he finally arrives in Epidamnus, where his brother lives, everybody mistakes him for his twin, which leads to many scenes of confusion. In the *Amphitruo*, however, the mistaken identity is not accidental at all. Jupiter, the king of gods, falls in love with Amphitruo's wife and deliberately assumes Amphitruo's looks so that he can sleep with her.

Plays in which certain aspects of character are the central theme are rarer. Here Plautus' masterpiece is the *Aulularia*, a comedy portraying Euclio, a man who has found a hoard of gold but cannot handle the situation appropriately. Euclio eventually comes close to a nervous breakdown, but in the end he realizes that money cannot make him happy, and he gives it to his daughter as a dowry.

Stock Characters

When Plautus praises the *Captiui* as a play that improves morals, he states:

> *hic nec periurus leno est nec meretrix mala*
> *nec miles gloriosus (Capt. 57–58)*

(Here there's no pimp perjuring himself, no bad
prostitute, no boastful soldier).

The pimp perjuring himself, the bad prostitute, and the
boastful soldier are typical roles that occur in play after
play. What entertains us in a Plautine comedy is not so
much a novel character as the usual stock characters in
somewhat novel situations. We regularly find the role of
adulescens (the young man) in Plautus' plays. The young
man is normally portrayed as a lover with financial or other
predicaments that prevent him from union with the girl
he loves. Plautus shows a certain sympathy for the young
lover, but to modern readers this character does not al-
ways appeal because of his weak, spineless, and some-
times brainless behavior. Most young men in Plautus come
from well-to-do families and need not worry about work.
When Nicodemus asks the old man, Dinia, for employ-
ment, Dinia points out that people like him are not used to
hard work:

talis iactandis tuae sunt consuetae manus (*Vid.* 33)

(Your hands are only used to throwing dice).

The young man's father is usually referred to as the
senex (the old man). Old men are more varied than the
young lovers. We find harsh ones and mild ones, but both
types normally act in what they believe to be their sons'
best interests. The harsh ones are typically stingy and do
not want their sons to spend money on love affairs; the
young men then have to trick them out of their money with
the help of their slaves. The mild fathers can be hypocrites,
such as Demaenetus in the *Asinaria*, who claims that he
wants to help his son but in the end just wants to enjoy his

son's prostitute. Not all the old men in comedy are as faithless as Demaenetus, but even the righteous ones are notorious misogynists. Thus Callicles says that he does not want a different wife because

nota mala res optuma est (*Trin*. 63)

(a bad thing you know is the bad thing that's best).

Slavery was a ubiquitous feature of the ancient world, and naturally slaves appear in Plautus as well. How slaves were treated in real life depended on their masters. Their legal status was clear: they were the property of their masters and hence could not sue or be sued, own money, or marry;[20] a master could also put a slave to death without breaking the law.[21] Often, however, masters would allow a slave to have some private funds, the *peculium*, and to enter into a quasi marital relationship, the *contubernium* (note *Amph*. 659: the master has a wife, the slave only an *amica*, a "girlfriend"). Plautine slaves are constantly threatened with beatings and savage punishments, ranging from breaking the shinbones (*Asin*. 474) to working in the mill in fetters (*Most*. 17–19; incidentally, this passage shows that mills in Plautus' day were not rotary mills, but pushing-mills).[22] But such threats are part and parcel of Plautine humor and do not necessarily reflect the Roman world in general. Plautine slaves are by and large cunning creatures, unwaveringly loyal to their young masters, and proud of their intelligent tricks. When their strategies suc-

20 Johnston 1999: 43.
21 Watson 1971: 44–45.
22 Moritz 1979: 67.

ceed, these larger-than-life figures invariably incur the hatred of the ones they have fooled out of their money, but despite all the talk of punishment, the slaves typically get away scot-free.[23] Of all the stock characters in Plautus, the cunning slave is perhaps the most entertaining, if the least true to life.

Women play several roles in Plautus: there are prostitutes (*meretrices*), marriageable young women (*uirgines*), married women (*matronae*), and slave girls (*ancillae*). The last category can be dealt with swiftly: female slaves typically have subordinate roles. The prostitutes are always presented as physically attractive. Some of them have a good character despite growing up in brothels; they are still virgins and regularly turn out to be free-born Athenian citizens, thus actually belonging to the category "marriageable young women." But others are mercenary, evil characters, for instance Astaphium in the *Truculentus*. The noncitizen prostitute of noble character, so typical of Terence, does not exist in Plautus.

Young, marriageable women of good family, for instance Lesbonicus' sister in the *Trinummus*, do not normally appear on stage. Married women do occasionally appear. Their portrayal tends to be negative. Alcumena in the *Amphitruo* is a virtuous matron, but even she is presented as self-righteous. The remaining matrons are constantly nagging battleaxes.

Other stereotyped characters are the cook, the pimp, and the soldier. All three are disagreeable. The cook has a

[23] On the rarity of slave beatings in Plautus see Spranger 1985: 47–51.

tendency to steal and boast.[24] The pimp is always immoral, a liar whose only concern is money. And the soldier is pompous and vain, typically (though not always) an outsider,[25] and when action is needed he turns into a coward. Arrogant soldiers typically speak along the lines of the unnamed soldier in the *Epidicus*:

> *uirtute belli armatus promerui ut mihi*
> *omnis mortalis agere deceat gratias (Epid.* 442–43)

(Through valor in war I have in arms earned the right that all mortals should give me thanks).

When the soldier Stratophanes appears, he seems to be an exception:

> *ne exspectetis, spectatores, meas pugnas dum*
> *   praedicem:*
> *manibus duella praedicare soleo, haud in sermonibus*
> *   (Truc.* 482–83)

(Spectators, don't wait for me to tell you about my fights; I normally tell about my battles with my hands, not in speeches).

He continues his invective against braggarts for a bit longer. But not much later he shows his true colors: in ll. 505–10 he reveals himself to be no better than those he was reproaching.

A category without a true modern equivalent is the hanger-on (*parasitus*). The hanger-on is a free man without money but with an immense appetite. A typical

24 Lowe 1985.
25 Brown 2004.

hanger-on is complaining about his hunger in Plautus'
Boeotia; he dislikes the new sundial for one particular rea-
son:

> *nam <unum> me puero uenter erat solarium,*
> *multo omnium istorum optumum et uerissumum.*
> *ubi is te monebat, esses, nisi quom nil erat.*
> *nunc etiam quom est non estur nisi Soli lubet* (*Boeotia*
>   fr. i. 4–7)

(Yes, when I was a boy the only sundial was your
belly, by far the best and most reliable of them all.
When it reminded you, you'd eat, except when there
was nothing to eat. Now even when there *is* some-
thing to eat, you don't eat unless Sun likes it).

The hanger-on never does any real work. By cracking jokes
and through barely concealed flattery he manages to
hang on to a young man, who rewards him with food and
drink. Just as with the slave's role, Plautus gives the hanger-
on a far greater prominence than he had in the Greek orig-
inals.

Attitudes Toward Women, Sex,
Prostitution, and Rape

Plautine comedies, just like their Greek models, present
relationships mainly from the male perspective. The old
man Daemones in the *Rudens* is portrayed very positively,
and the audience is clearly expected to side with him. But
when he talks about his wife, he refers to her as *scelesta*
(wretched) (l. 895), and when she is overjoyed at finding

their long-lost daughter, he is not sympathetic to her emotional outbursts:

> *uxor complexa collo retinet filiam.*
> *nimis paene inepta atque odiosa eius amatio est* (*Rud.*
> 1203–4)

(My wife is embracing our daughter's neck and clinging to her. Her fondling is almost unbearably silly and repulsive).

Other old men are even more misogynistic. We hardly ever hear women complain about their husbands, and where they do, they are typically portrayed in such a way that the audience cannot be expected to sympathize with them, even if the wife has a point. Thus in the *Menaechmi* the wife of the Epidamnian twin has every reason to be upset at her husband's behavior: he admits to having a mistress (l. 124) and in addition hands over his wife's possessions as presents to this other woman (ll. 133–34). But Plautus presents the wife rather than her husband as an awful person. Her husband's hanger-on has shown her what her husband is doing and asks what reward he will get (l. 663). She answers rudely:

> *opera reddetur, quando quid tibi erit surruptum*
> *domo* (*Men.* 664)

(I'll return the favor when something has been stolen from your home).

But the focus is normally on young men's love affairs rather than on their parents' generation. Like everyone else in Roman comedy, young men are always heterosexual. References to homosexuality are few and far between, and where they occur, the homosexual is always the butt of a joke. When Curculio tells a banker not to insult him, he uses the verb *incomitiare* (revile), which seems to be based on *comitium* (assembly place) (l. 400). The banker facetiously asks if at least *inforare* is allowed, a verb which puns on *forum* (market place) but also has the meaning "drill a hole into" (l. 401). In this way the banker ridicules Curculio as someone who takes the passive role in homosexual intercourse. Similar ridicule of nonnormative sexual behavior is found in *Pseud.* 1177–89:[26] in ll. 1177–78 it is insinuated that Harpax masturbated when he was still a baby, in ll. 1179–81 it is said that he took the passive role in homosexual acts with his master, and in l. 1188 Harpax is described as a male prostitute. Harpax feels deeply insulted.

Young men in comedy fall in love with two types of women: prostitutes, who are often mercenary, and citizen girls of good character. The men always treat these women inappropriately: they adore the prostitutes and rape the citizen girls. Going to prostitutes was not necessarily frowned upon. Horace (*Sat.* 1. 2. 31–35) tells us that Cato the Elder, the guardian of Roman morals, praised a young man for visiting the brothel, because it is better to sleep with a prostitute than with another man's wife. The reason why fathers in Plautine comedy are so opposed to their sons' having affairs with prostitutes is not moral but financial, for the prostitutes are adept at extracting large sums of money from the naive young men.

While young men from good families had considerable sexual freedom, young women from equally good families were expected to remain virgins until marriage. But in

---

[26] Discussed by Jocelyn 2000: 456.

many Plautine plots a pregnant girl is required, otherwise
there would be no need for the young man to marry her, at
least not so urgently. But neither a Greek nor a Roman
playwright could portray a citizen girl willingly sleeping
with a lover, for such an act would immediately make her
unsuitable for marriage. The only way out for the play-
wright was to have the young man rape the girl. Even
though rape was a serious offense, it was not considered as
bad as a woman having consensual premarital sex. Roman
law did not put the blame for rape on the woman: officially
her reputation remained unstained, and she was still free
to marry.[27] In practice, however, the situation would be
more difficult for a woman who had been raped, especially
if she had become pregnant.

Rape was regarded as shocking in the ancient world, so
that the rape itself is never staged but always happens be-
fore the play begins. What is more, the young men never
plan to rape the girls but usually do it after drinking too
much (cf. *Aul.* 745) and consistently want to marry the girls
they have raped, which was considered to make their of-
fenses less offensive. Whether their victims love them or
not is deemed immaterial; what matters is that the mar-
riage removes the stain from both families involved. Nev-
ertheless, modern readers cannot help feeling uneasy
about the fact that the young men Greek and Roman play-
wrights want them to sympathize with are rapists.

Jokes and Humor

After this dark side of Roman comedy, let us return to its
more pleasant aspects. Roman comedy is of course sup-

27 Harries 2007: 88.

posed to be funny. Many jokes in Plautus follow patterns similar to their English counterparts, but there are occasions where the modern reader is baffled. It is very difficult to pin down why this is the case because humor still defies definition despite countless modern studies on the subject. What Cicero has to say about the ancient equivalents of these studies on humor rings true even today:

> *sed qui eius rei rationem quandam conati sunt artemque tradere, sic insulsi exstiterunt, ut nihil aliud eorum nisi ipsa insulsitas rideatur* (Cic. *de orat.* 2. 217)

> (But those who have tried to give some sort of theory and method of it have shown themselves to be so humorless that their lack of humor is the only thing one can laugh about).

This passage comes from a long discussion on humor (*de orat.* 2. 216–90), which is the basis for Quintilian's more systematic treatment. Like Cicero, Quintilian discusses Roman humor at length (*inst.* 6. 3) but restricts himself to categories appropriate for an orator, who should not use the humor of the stage (6. 3. 29) or make himself the butt of jokes, as this is only appropriate for professional comedians (6. 3. 82). Even though Quintilian's discussion is detailed, he has to admit that humor is difficult to define: *tum uaria hominum iudicia in eo quod non ratione aliqua, sed motu animi quodam nescio an enarrabili iudicatur* (moreover, people's judgments differ over something which is judged not on a rational basis, but by a certain emotion which perhaps cannot be put into words) (Quint. *inst.* 6. 3. 6).

Certain types of humor are particularly frequent in Plautus. An important category consists of the so-called *para prosdokian* (against expectation) jokes; Cicero translates the Greek phrase as *praeter expectationem* (*de orat.* 2. 284), while Quintilian uses the phrases *expectationem decipere* and *opinionem decipere*, both meaning "to defy expectation" (*inst.* 6. 3. 24 and 64, respectively). There are two types:

> *ne illa illud hercle cum malo fecit . . . meo;*
> *nam mihi diuini numquam quisquam creduat,*
> *ni ego illam exemplis plurumis planeque . . . amo*
>   (*Bacch.* 503–5)

> (Seriously, there will be a price to pay for doing that . . . and I'll pay it. Yes, let no one ever believe me when I swear by the gods if I don't pay her back in every conceivable way by . . . loving her).

> SOSIA   *sed, mulier, postquam expberrecta es, te*
>   *prodigiali Ioui*
>   *aut mola salsa hodie aut ture comprecatam oportuit.*
> ALCVMENA   *uae capiti tuo!*
> SOSIA *tua istuc refert . . . si curaueris* (*Amph.* 739–41)
> (SOSIA   But, woman, after getting up you ought to have invoked Jupiter with salted flour or incense today, since he's in charge of prodigies.
> ALCVMENA   Bad luck to you!
> SOSIA   To you . . . this is important, if you see to it).

In the first example Mnesilochus believes that he has been treated unfairly by a prostitute and talks of revenge. We expect the last word to be *perdo* (I annihilate), but this expectation is not fulfilled; instead, Mnesilochus says the opposite and reveals his true feelings. In the second example Alcumena's slave insults her and she is angry with him. He makes a saucy reply but then gives his words an unexpected and innocent turn, presumably to avoid punishment.

Some jokes involve minute changes in pronunciation and spelling. Cicero (*de orat.* 2. 256) reports that Cato the Elder called Fulvius Nobilior (Fulvius the Noble) Fulvius Mobilior (Fulvius the Fickle). This type of joke occurs in Plautus as well. In *Rud.* 1304–6 Gripus asks Labrax whether he is a *medicus* (doctor). Labrax replies that he has one letter more, which enables Gripus to draw the correct conclusion that Labrax is a *mendicus* (beggar).

Plautus also loves deliberate misunderstandings, sometimes involving obscene double meanings:

EVCLIO   *pone.*
SERVOS   *id quidem pol te datare credo consuetum,*
    senex. (*Aul.* 637)
(EUCLIO   Let me have it.
SLAVE   I'm sure you've learnt to love providing that
    service, old boy).

Euclio is using *pone* as the imperative of *ponere* (put down); but the slave interprets it as an adverb meaning "behind" and thus regards the old man's words as an invitation to anal sex. However, Plautus, and with him all other adapters of Greek comedy, eschew obscenities that were considered too offensive.[28] Words like *futuere* (to fuck), *mentula* (dick), or *cunnus* (cunt), so common in inscriptions from Pompeii, are avoided entirely. Cicero (*off.* 1.

---

[28] Fraenkel 2007: 424 n. 268.

104), after stating that jokes can be vulgar and obscene or urbane and elegant, says that Plautus' jokes belong to the second category. In fact, there are clear cases where Plautus actually removed obscenities. Otto 1890: 52 points out that in antiquity it was widely believed that seeds of mistletoe, from which birdlime was produced, could only germinate once they had passed through the digestive tract of birds. This is what is behind the Plautine fragment (*fab. inc.* fr. lix) *ipsa sibi auis mortem creat* (the bird creates its own death). As Adams 1982: 137–38 points out, Isidore quotes the same proverb with the verb *cacare* (to shit) (*etym.* 12. 7. 71). Plautus chose a verb with the same initial consonant and the same number of syllables to make clear what he is alluding to, but avoids direct mention of the obscene word.

Nevertheless, Plautus does occasionally delight in exaggerated insults.[29] In the *Pseudolus*, an entire eight lines are taken up by insults against a pimp and his nonchalant replies (ll. 360–67). And we find such entertaining vocatives as *ex sterculino effosse* (you man dug out from a dung heap) (*Cas.* 114). Hardly less comical are exaggerated endearments. One such list can be found in *Poen.* 365–67, where there are terms of endearment such as *meus molliculus caseus* (my soft little cheese).

Behavior and statements that are completely over the top are another common source of laughter. We expect military types to boast, but when Antamoenides in *Poen.* 470–87 informs us about his expedition against flying men, pathos quickly turns into bathos.

Humor regularly arises when idiomatic expressions are

---

[29] See Dickey 2002: 163–85 and Lilja 1965.

taken literally. Cicero offers a particularly good example:
*ridicule etiam illud L. Nasica censori Catoni, cum ille "ex
tui animi sententia tu uxorem habes?," "non hercule," in-
quit, "ex mei animi sententia"* (Lucius Nasica also gave a
funny reply to the censor Cato when he asked, "On your
conscience, are you satisfied that you are married?" Nasica
said, "On my conscience, yes, I am married, but certainly
not satisfied") (Cic. *de orat.* 2. 260). Cato uses the phrase *ex
tui animi sententia* to elicit an honest reply, but Nasica
takes it literally and interprets it as an enquiry about his
happiness. Examples of this type abound in Plautus. The
Latin way of saying "how are you" is *quid agis* (what are you
doing) or its passive equivalent. Just as in English this is not
a real enquiry after someone's health, in Latin this is not an
enquiry after someone's activities. That is why the follow-
ing example is funny:

> SIMO   *salue. quid agitur?*
> PSEVDOLVS   *statur hic ad hunc modum* (*Pseud.* 457)
> (SIMO   Hello. How are you?
> PSEUDOLUS   Standing here in this way).

Formulaic phrases can of course be played with in
other ways as well. When a friend returns from abroad, the
exchange can contain up to five elements: the recognition,
greetings, an expression of joy at the traveler's safe return,
inquiries about his well-being throughout, and an invita-
tion to dinner. But when Chrysalus on his return from
Ephesus is greeted by Pistoclerus, he cuts him short:

> *compendi uerba multa iam faciam tibi.*
> *uenire tu me gaudes: ego credo tibi;*
> *hospitium et cenam pollicere, ut conuenit*

peregre aduenienti: ego autem uenturum annuo
  (*Bacch*. 184–87)

(I'll save you a lot of words now. You're happy I've
returned. I believe you. You're promising me hospi-
tality and a dinner, as is appropriate for someone ar-
riving from abroad. And I nod in approval that I'll
come).

By complimenting himself on his safe return and inviting
himself to dinner, Chrysalus is behaving in an outrageous
way.

Much of Plautine humor is linguistic; I have already
mentioned double entendres and other phenomena. But
not every type of humor involves a punch line. Sometimes
we laugh because the register of a passage does not suit its
content. When asked about his name, the slave Sosia re-
plies:

Sosiam uocant Thebani, Dauo prognatum patre
  (*Amph*. 365)

(The Thebans call me Sosia, son of Davus).

Slaves occupy the lowest possible social and legal status,
and yet Sosia presents himself in a way more appropriate
for his master, the victorious general Amphitruo. The free-
born Athenian Lyconides says *ego uocor Lyconides* (I'm
called Lyconides) (*Aul*. 779); the passive is normal here,
whereas by using the active with the Thebans as subject,
Sosia is not just being more elaborate, but presents himself
as if he were a citizen. The same is true of the second part
of the sentence: slaves were considered property and as
such their parents did not matter. Again Sosia behaves like

li

a freeborn citizen, because he mentions his father's name, and what is more, he does so by using the most solemn term possible in this context, *prognatus*.[30]

Unlike Greek, Latin is relatively restricted in the formation of compounds. Roman writers of tragedy formed many artificial compounds in imitation of their Greek models. Plautus is also fond of such compounds with their mock-solemn tone.[31] A pimp's old servant, Leaena, is referred to as *multibiba atque merobiba* (a heavy drinker of undiluted wine) (*Curc.* 77). Both words are calques on Greek, and the second even has the Greek link vowel *-o-* rather than the Latin *-i-*. The high register associated with such compounds is in stark contrast to their ridiculous content.

Elsewhere, Plautus gives Latin words new meanings. *Oppugnare* in *Cas.* 412 is a case in point. The simple verb *pugnare* is derived from *pugnus* (fist) and originally meant "to fight with the fists," but it is mostly used in the sense "to fight (in battle)"; the deverbative noun from *pugnare* is *pugna*, which means "battle" and has lost all connections with "fist."[32] *Pugnare* in the meaning "to fight in battle" can take a prefix and become *oppugnare*, "to attack a fortified position," such as a city. But in *Cas.* 412 Chalinus, who has just received a blow to his face, uses the verb as if it were still connected with *pugnus* and meant "to hit someone with the fist."

Perhaps the most subtle sort of humor results from the spectators' superior knowledge not shared by the charac-

[30] On the register of this term see Fraenkel 1957: 82 n. 4.
[31] For a complete list see Oniga 1988: 278–83.
[32] Ernout and Meillet 1951: 961.

ters on stage, who suffer from temporary misunderstandings. One of the best-known scenes of this kind is *Aul.* 731–70. Euclio's gold has been stolen and he is wailing. Lyconides believes that Euclio has found out that he raped his daughter and approaches him to confess his guilt. But Euclio does not know what happened to his daughter at all and thinks that Lyconides is admitting theft. The ensuing misunderstandings are easy to understand only for the spectators. In *Aul.* 755–56, for example, Lyconides says that he is prepared to keep what he has touched, meaning that he wants to marry the girl. But Euclio understands that Lyconides wants to keep the gold.

It is impossible to do justice to all types of Plautine humor. I have given examples of the most frequent types, but Quintilian's statement remains true:

> *sed repetam necesse est (sc. species) infinitas esse tam salse dicendi quam seuere* (Quint. *inst.* 6. 3. 101)

(But I have to repeat that the types of humorous speech are as infinite as those of earnest speech).

Nonrealistic Drama

One of the most striking differences between ancient theater and some forms of modern theater is that the former does not consistently aim at realism. Realism in drama is a comparatively recent development. Plays by Plautus should perhaps be called "nonrealistic" rather than "unrealistic" because "unrealistic" has the negative connotation that realism was intended but that the playwright was incapable of achieving it. Yet this is not the case with Plautus, who is happy to adopt features that make his plays less realistic if he can make his audience laugh. For instance, his characters regularly acknowledge the presence of the audience in order to achieve some effect; thus when Charinus wants to take things slowly, Acanthio does not hesitate to ask him

> *dormientis spectatores metuis ne ex somno excites?*
> (*Merc.* 160)

(Are you afraid that you might stir the sleeping spectators from their slumber?).

The dramatic illusion, the pretence that we are watching something happening in real life, is often ruptured in this way.

No pretence of realism is made in asides either, unlike the asides of Greek New Comedy.[33] Asides are directed at the audience during a dialogue between two people on stage. In the *Aulularia*, for instance, we find a long conversation between Euclio and Megadorus (ll. 182–263), interrupted briefly when Euclio goes into his house. Megadorus tries to be as polite as possible and then asks Euclio for his daughter's hand. In this dialogue Euclio often turns away from Megadorus and tells the audience that he cannot trust a rich man like Megadorus and that Megadorus simply wants to steal his money. The asides can be quite lengthy; one extends over five entire lines (ll. 194–98). It is normal practice in Plautus that the interlocutor does not realize that anything is being said. In this dialogue, however, Megadorus does notice occasionally that Euclio is speaking to himself, even though he does not hear what is being said (see l. 190).

[33] On these see Bain 1977.

Eavesdropping is similar. It is quite common in Plautus to find one or two eavesdroppers listening in on a conversation and commenting on it. During the comments the conversation stops, but the pair talking to each other do not realize that they are being overheard. In Menander, many of whose plays were models for Plautus, such constellations are not unusual, but there the comments are typically short and the scenes maintain a certain realism. In Plautus the comments can be rather long. A typical case is the conversation between Philematium and Scapha, overheard by Philolaches (*Most.* 157–292). Philolaches makes various comments and even addresses the audience when remarking on Scapha's clever ways:

ut perdocte cuncta callet! nihil hac docta doctius.
uerum illuc est: maxuma adeo pars uostrorum
    intellegit,
quibus anus domi sunt uxores, quae uos dote
    meruerunt (*Most.* 279–81)

(How cleverly she's smart in everything! Nothing is more intelligent than this intelligent woman. What she says is true; and the majority of you realize it, those who have old women at home as their wives, women who bought you with their dowries).

Monologues are an element in drama that may or may not be realistic. In Plautus we find monologues very frequently, and often they are so long that they cannot be deemed realistic.[34]

---

[34] On metatheater and moralizing soliloquies see Moore 1998: 67–90.

The Roman stage also imposed restrictions on how realistically events could be portrayed. Since the stage represented a street, the audience could not see what was happening inside the houses. All the action had to take place outside. For this reason, speakers often leave the house and then shout their orders through the door instead of giving their commands before leaving (e.g., *Capt.* 398). But other scenes are much more artificial. In *Asin.* 828 Argyrippus, his girlfriend, and his father come out of the procuress's house in order to continue their banquet, where the father wants to enjoy the attentions of his son's girlfriend; enduring this banquet is the price the son has to pay in order to get his father's money needed for the girl. Outdoor banquets were not unusual in Athens, but obviously the father wants to keep his doings secret because he is afraid that his wife might find out. But since indoor scenes could not be shown, the banquet has to take place outside despite the risks involved.

Another convention that requires getting used to is the regular announcement of a character's arrival: speakers typically say that character *x* or *y* is coming or that they can see him just before this person actually arrives. Arrivals from a house instead of a side entrance are regularly announced by phrases such as "but the door is creaking, look, *x* is coming out."

Finally, dramatic time is not real time. Again Plautus is uninterested in creating a realistic atmosphere. In *Men.* 875 an old man who says of himself that he cannot walk fast states that he is going to fetch a doctor. But only a few lines later (ll. 882–83) he returns, complaining that the doctor made him wait for a long time.

The Prologue

Plautus' plays often, though not always, begin with a prologue.[35] Prologues can contain up to five elements, though usually not all five are used: (1) a *captatio beneuolentiae* (an attempt to secure the audience's goodwill), (2) the naming of the Greek author and original play, (3) the specification of which city the stage represents, (4) the narration of the *argumentum* (plot/background to the plot), and (5) a formula of valediction.

Plautus knows how to make his audience well-disposed. In his prologues he cracks jokes but also uses the more direct methods of flattering the audience or praising his own writings. The *captatio beneuolentiae* is not confined to the beginning of the prologue; rather, there are usually several such elements scattered throughout. Even the formula of valediction at the end of the prologue is often combined with flattery:

> *ualete, bene rem gerite, uincite*
> *uirtute uera, quod fecistis antidhac (Cas.* 87–88)

> (Farewell and be successful and victorious through true valor, as you have been before).

The author and title of the Greek original are often not mentioned at all. Plautus tells us that the *Asinaria* goes back to Demophilus' *Onagos* (The Ass-Driver) (*Asin.* 10–11), but for plays like the *Aulularia* we can only guess. In

---

[35] A good typology of such prologues can be found in Abel 1955.

INTRODUCTION

the prologue to Terence's *Heauton timorumenos* (The Self-Tormentor), we find a startling statement:

> *nunc qui scripserit*
> *et quoia Graeca sit, ni partem maxumam*
> *existumarem scire uostrum, id dicerem* (*Haut.* 7–9)

(Now if I didn't believe that the majority of you knows who wrote it and who the author of the Greek play is, I'd tell you that).

Presumably these details were posted on notice boards by the organizers of the plays. We can assume a similar practice in Plautus' day, which would account for the frequent absence of information. But it is also possible that Plautus simply did not consider this information important.

The default location for Plautine comedies is Athens. Only if the stage represents a different city does a location have to be mentioned. The prologue to the *Menaechmi* is instructive in this respect:

> *atque hoc poetae faciunt in comoediis:*
> *omnes res gestas esse Athenis autumant,*
> *quo illud uobis Graecum uideatur magis;*
> *ego nusquam dicam nisi ubi factum dicitur* (*Men.*
>   7–10)

(And this is what writers do in comedies: they claim that everything is done in Athens, intending that it should seem more Greek to you. *I* shall say what happened nowhere except where it is said to have happened).

Plays usually take place in Athens because as adaptations of Greek originals they should have a Greek air, and Athens is the quintessential Greek city, just as Attic Greek is considered the purest Greek dialect; in the phrase *Athenis Atticis* (in Attic Athens) the adjective emphasizes the culture and refinement associated with Athens. The action of the *Menaechmi* takes place in Epidamnus, so Plautus needs to make this explicit (l. 72, probably to be transposed behind l. 10).

The narration of the plot, or at least of the background to the plot, is normally considered to be the most important element of the prologue. Knowing what is going to happen does not spoil the fun; on the contrary, misunderstandings between the figures on stage are more amusing for an audience that understands what is really going on. But even though a narration of the plot is arguably the central element of most prologues, some do not contain one. In the *Asinaria*, for example, the short prologue lacks any information about the action of the play, and the important expository material is presented in the subsequent dialogue between Demaenetus and his slave Libanus.

This strategy of delaying the presentation of expository material is actually quite common and certainly taken over from the Greek models; we find it in both Euripides (e.g., *Iphigenia in Aulis*) and Menander (e.g., *Aspis*, "The Shield"). The *Mostellaria* does not have a prologue at all but begins with a spectacular duel of words between the slaves Grumio and Tranio. Grumio does not appear again in the play; his main function is to argue with Tranio, the hero of the comedy, so as to enable a characterization of the latter as a clever and witty but also reckless slave. Grumio does furnish us with some background to the play (ll. 78–83), and expository elements had come up in the preceding fight as well, but much important information is delayed until the next scene, in which Philolaches delivers a lengthy monologue.

Some prologues are delivered by deities or allegorical personifications. Thus the prologue to the *Aulularia* is delivered by Euclio's *Lar familiaris*, a guardian spirit watching over the house and its inhabitants, and the prologue to the *Trinummus* is delivered by *Luxuria*, the personification of extravagant spending, who is accompanied by her daughter *Inopia* (Poverty). But all the agents in Plautus' comedies are human, and the prologue deities do not appear again with the exception of the *Amphitruo*, in which Jupiter and Mercury, who is the speaker of the prologue, play important roles.

PLAUTUS AND NATIVE ITALIAN TRADITIONS

Italian Drama

Although Greek New Comedy provided Plautus with his plots, much of Plautus' humor is rather atypical of Greek plays, and however much one wishes to stress Plautus' originality, the types of jokes he uses cannot be entirely of his own devising. In fact we find similar jokes in his predecessor Naevius. Plautus must have been influenced by native Italian traditions of humor, to which we can now turn, although it must be said that the extent to which this is the case is difficult to assess, since most of these native traditions were oral and/or not preserved in written form.

This is particularly true of the Fescennine verses, a type of coarse songs named after the town Fescennia, close to Falerii, the main city of the Faliscans. Duckworth 1952:

16–17 believed that they exerted some influence on Roman comedy. According to Horace (*epist.* 2. 1. 145–46), they were sung at harvest festivals, but they were also associated with weddings and were given a literary form in Catullus (61. 119–48). A few lines can illustrate their nature:

> *nupta, tu quoque quae tuus*
> *uir petet caue ne neges,*
> *ne petitum aliunde eat.*
> *io Hymen Hymenaee io,*
> *io Hymen Hymenaee* (Catull. 61. 144–48)

(And you, bride, don't refuse what your husband seeks so he doesn't go and seek it from someone else. Io Hymen Hymenaeus io, io Hymen Hymenaeus!).

Although Catullus had earlier referred to this as Fescennine verse (l. 120), one notices the Greek meter—the poem is in glyconics and pherecrateans—and the reference to the Greek marriage god, Hymenaeus. Despite Duckworth's suggestions, the link between the Fescennine verses and Plautine comedy remains unproven. Such a link may well have existed, but the remains of these verses are so scanty that it is no longer visible. We should not assume that any oral or literary genre exerted influence on Plautus simply because it was coarse or farcical.

The *satura* is a genre cultivated by some of the greatest poets Rome produced, for instance Horace.[36] Although the English word "satire" is derived from it and later *sat-*

---

36 For a general overview see Knoche 1975.

urae were quite satirical in the modern sense, the earliest forms had mixed content and were not necessarily biting. Thus the few lines that survive from Ennius' books of *saturae* are not particularly aggressive. Much more survives of Lucilius' thirty books of satires in various meters; he could be quite aggressive but also varied the tone and style of his work. At any rate, it remains open to doubt how typical a representative of early satire Lucilius is. He was born in 180, after Plautus' death, and was clearly influenced by the Greek poet Archilochus.

There is tangible influence of comedy on satire; Muecke 2005: 45 notes a shared fondness for racy colloquialisms and comic coinages as well as for popular moralizing and proverbs. Less clear is to what extent satire influenced comedy. All we can do is note similarities. Thus we find a passage in Plautus' *Curculio* (ll. 467–84) in which the leader of the troupe describes where in Rome particular sorts of crooks can be found. Lucilius may have had this passage in mind when he wrote

> *nunc uero a mani ad noctem, festo atque profesto*
> *totus item pariterque die populusque patresque*
> *iactare indu foro se omnes, decedere nusquam,*
> *uni se atque eidem studio omnes dedere et arti,*
> *uerba dare ut caute possint, pugnare dolose,*
> *blanditia certare, bonum simulare uirum se,*
> *insidias facere, ut si hostes sint omnibus omnes*
> (Lucil. 1252–58 Krenkel)

(But now both the entire populace and the senators alike go about the market place, from morning till night, on feast days as well as on workdays, and never leave it. They dedicate themselves to one and the same profession and art, how they can carefully trick others, attack with guiles, fight with flattery, pretend to be good men, lay ambushes, as if all people were enemies to all others).

If the influence of Fescennine verse and satire on Plautus remains elusive, can we say more about other types of drama?[37] Little is known about the *fabula Atellana* (Atellan farce),[38] a genre named for Atella, a town in Campania, though it was common in other Oscan cities as well and was also performed in Rome. Actors wore masks and had stock roles: we know of Dossennus, a glutton and possibly a hunchback; Bucco, a fool; Pappus, an old man; and Manducus, a bogeyman, though his name (the chewer) suggests that this might simply be an alternative name for Dossennus. The most famous role is that of Maccus, the clown, from whom Plautus may have got his name. Atellan farce long remained oral; we have about three hundred lines from a scripted version of it by Pomponius and Novius, both from the early first century.

Influence of the *fabula Atellana* on Plautus has been claimed on general stylistic grounds but also for two very specific reasons: Plautus' name Maccius looks suspiciously like the name of the clown Maccus, and the ending of the *Casina* is so farcical that scholars found it hard to believe that it had a Greek origin. It is indeed possible that Plautus began his career as an actor in the Atellan farce and that he learned some tricks of the trade there, but what precise

37 For the fragments see Ribbeck 1871–73.

38 Fragments in Frassinetti 1967, commentary Frassinetti 1953.

form this influence took is hard to pin down. As for the ending of the *Casina*, it makes no sense to explain away a difficulty by reference to a genre that remains obscure; we are on safer ground if we assume, with Frassinetti 1953: 90 and Fraenkel 2007: 214, that the ending of this play goes back to one or more Greek texts. This brings us to the stylistic similarities, or rather the lack thereof, between the *fabula Atellana* and the *fabula palliata*: the fragments of Atellan farce that have come down to us frequently involve obscenities Plautus would not have accepted; two examples from Pomponius' *Prostibulum* (The Prostitute) should suffice:

> *continuo ad te centuriatim current qui penem petent*
> (Pompon. *com.* 149 Frassinetti = *Prostibulum* ii)

(Immediately a large number of people will run to you seeking out your penis).

> *ego quaero quod comedim; has quaerunt quod cacent;*
> *contrarium est* (Pompon. *com.* 150 = *Prostibulum* iii)

(I'm looking for something to eat up; these women are looking for something to shit out; it's the exact opposite).

Plautus is certainly not prudish, but words like *penis* (dick, penis) and *cacare* (to shit) are taboo for him.[39] Moreover, Atellan farce, at least in the Empire, was not averse to ridiculing politicians. Suetonius tells us that Mallonia was

[39] For an excellent discussion of this semantic field see Adams 1982.

brought to the emperor Tiberius to sleep with him, but
that she refused to submit to his requests; Tiberius was rid-
iculed in a subsequent Atellan farce, where it was claimed
hircum uetulum capreis naturam ligurire (that the old goat
licked the private parts of roes) (Suet. *Tib.* 45). In contrast,
Plautus, though he does allude to contemporary events
and criticizes the Roman public, never picks on individu-
als; his plays have no political dimension.

There was also a type of comedy called the *fabula
togata*. Plautine comedy belongs to the genre of *fabula
palliata* because some of the actors wore the *pallium*, a
Greek cloak, and the plays are set in Greece. The *fabula
togata* is the Italian equivalent; some of the actors were
clad in the *toga*, the Roman national dress, and the plays
are set in Italy. The three main authors are Titinius, per-
haps an older contemporary of Terence;[40] Lucius Afranius,
who lived in the late second century; and T. Quinctius Atta,
who died in 77. If Daviault 1981: 18 is correct in stating
that the *togata* existed before Titinius, it is not unlikely that
it partly influenced Plautus; there are clear linguistic simi-
larities, and the themes seem similar to those of the *palli-
ata*. But Afranius apparently liked pederastic topics (see
Quint. *inst.* 10. 1. 100), which were practically excluded
from the *palliata*. The *fabula togata* may have influenced
the *palliata* to a certain extent, and again the exact extent is
hard to pin down, but it must be said that the influence was
probably much stronger in the opposite direction because
the *togata* began as an offshoot of the *palliata* invented in
reaction to it.

[40] Dated to the early second century by Guardì 1985: 19 and
to the second half of the third century by Daviault 1981: 18.

From early times there also existed at Rome the *mimus*, or mime, a performance of improvised sketches. Common themes were love affairs or changes of fortune. Mime became literary only in the late Republic.[41] The best-known authors of literary mime are Gnaeus Matius, Decimus Laberius, and Publilius Syrus, all of whom lived in the first century. Mime continued to be practiced throughout the Empire and was eventually reborn as the Italian commedia dell'arte. Not much is known about early mime. Mime actors were barefoot and without masks. Staging of drama will be discussed in more detail below, but here it should be pointed out that in contrast to all other types of Greco-Roman drama, in mime there were also actresses, some of whom became famous, or rather notorious. The bad reputation of mime continued, and when the emperor Justinian married the former actress Theodora some time after 523 CE, it was still considered scandalous. Later mime may well have had masks, like the commedia dell'arte, which incidentally also has the stock characters so typical of ancient comedy; an otherwise unidentified character, for instance, is simply called *Zanni* (the Venetian form of *Giovanni*), hence our term "zany."

The importance of mime for Roman comedy remains problematic. The adjective *planipes* (barefoot) is used for mime actors, and scholars have tried to connect this with the name Plautus (flatfoot), assuming that "flatfoot" can mean "not wearing the shoes typical of tragedy or comedy," but it is evident how tenuous such connections are. Far more important is the fact that some mimes had names identical to *fabulae palliatae*: Laberius wrote an *Aulula-*

---

41 Bieber 1961: 159.

ria and a *Colax* (Flatterer), the former also the title of a
Plautine comedy and the latter a title used by both Naevius
and Plautus, and Lucius Valerius wrote a mime called
Phormio, also the title of a comedy by Terence. Duckworth
1952: 16–17 pointed out that mime is farcical rather than
sentimental, like Plautine comedy but unlike Plautus'
Greek models. But it does not follow that Plautus was in-
fluenced by mime; indeed several of the fragments contain
vocabulary too indecent for Plautus, for instance the fol-
lowing from Laberius:

A *numne aliter hunce pedicabis?*
B   *quo modo?*
A *uideo, adulescenti nostro caedis hirulam* (Laber.
      mim. 34–35 Bonaria = *Catularius* ii)

(A Are you going to bugger him in another way?
B How do you mean?
A I can see you're cutting our young fellow's
      intestines to pieces).

Other Italian Elements

Not all Italian elements one finds in Plautus are theatrical.
Plautus enjoys giving his plays a truly Roman coloring by
adding the jargon of Roman customs, religion, and law.
Thus the *di penates* (household gods) and the *Lar pater*
(Father Lar) (*Merc*. 834) are Roman deities, but not too
much should be made of phrases such as *di te perdant*
(may the gods destroy you), which are so formulaic that
any religious connotations have been lost.[42] Plautus also

---

[42] Jocelyn 2001: 270.

parodies augury in *Epid*. 183–84, where "the bird to the left" signifies good luck.[43] Plautus pokes fun at the language of the senate when he has the slave Trachalio constantly reply to his master with the word *censeo* (I think so/ I decree) (*Rud*. 1269–79); in the last line the master makes it explicit that his slave was using legal idiom.[44] Another typical instance of a Roman legal institution can be found in a passage of the *Mostellaria* in which a money-lender, who is shouting very loudly (l. 576), tries to get his dues:

> *cedo faenus, redde faenus, faenus reddite.*
> *daturin estis faenus actutum mihi?*
> *datur faenus mi?* (*Most*. 603–5)

> (Give me my interest, return my interest, you two should return my interest. Are you not going to give me my interest this instant? Am I given my interest?).

Here we are dealing with what Usener (1901) called *Volksjustiz* (popular justice): a man who felt that he was being treated unfairly could make his demands by voicing his feelings loudly so that the neighbors would hear and the opponent would feel ashamed. This *flagitatio*, or "demand," was repetitive in nature, but the repetitions typically contained some variation, for instance of word order, as in the first line of our example. Fraenkel 1961: 48 calls such reversals of word order a "stylistic device of

---

43 In both Greece and Rome birds in the east brought good luck, those in the west bad luck; a Roman augur faced south but a Greek north, so that the birds to the left indicated good luck in Rome and bad luck in Greece; see Gulick 1896: 241–42.

44 On the nuances of *censeo* see Daube 1956: 87.

popular eloquence" and compares a similar example from
Catullus:

> *moecha putida, redde codicillos,*
> *Redde, putida moecha, codicillos* (Catull. 42. 11–12)

(Dirty drab, give back my tablets, give back my tab-
lets, dirty drab).

Just before this passage, Catullus had also used the term
reflagitare (demand back), which makes even clearer the
genre with which we are dealing.

Other Writers of Palliatae

The first *palliata* was performed in Rome in 240 by Lucius
Livius Andronicus, a Greek by birth and a freedman of the
Livii, who produced both a comedy and a tragedy for the
Ludi Romani of that year. Little is known of Livius An-
dronicus as a writer of comedy, since only three titles of
plays have come down to us.

Gnaeus Naevius was a Campanian who served in the
last years of the first Punic War, which ended in 241. He is
therefore slightly older than Plautus. Naevius continued
the tradition begun by Andronicus by writing epic as well
as tragedy and comedy. Thirty-two titles of *palliatae* are
known to us.

Caecilius Statius was a very popular author. He was an
Insubrian Gaul from northern Italy and came to Rome as a
slave but was subsequently freed. He died in 168, meaning
that he was a younger contemporary of Plautus. Forty-two
titles and around 280 lines survive. Caecilius' style is re-
markably similar to that of Plautus.

Apart from Plautus, the only writer of Roman comedy from whom we have complete plays is Publius Terentius Afer, now known as Terence.[45] Terence was born around 185 and died during a visit to Greece in 159. Suetonius' *Life of Terence*, transmitted through Donatus, tells us that he was born in Carthage and came to Rome as a slave, but that he was soon freed because of his talents and his good looks. It is impossible to verify this account: the Carthaginian birth may or may not be a mere inference from Terence's cognomen *Afer* (the African). Terence's six plays were performed between 166 and 160. Their names are *Andria* (The Woman from Andros), *Heauton timorumenos* (The Self-Tormentor), *Eunuchus* (The Eunuch), *Phormio*, *Hecyra* (The Mother-in-Law), and *Adelphoe* (The Brothers).

Terence is very different from Plautus. His plots are smoother and more consistent and his characters more realistic, even though the rarity of any thoroughly bad and despicable figures is rather unnatural; in Terence even the prostitutes are likeable. Terence has given up much of Plautus' ribaldry, and there are other noticeable stylistic differences. Terence's language is far more modern, which is partly the result of diachronic change but also partly due to his adoption of a more natural, colloquial idiom. He all but abolished the sung passages so characteristic of Plautus, while enjambement, relatively rare in Plautus, has become frequent and gives his verse a more natural feel.[46]

[45] Critical edition by Kauer and Lindsay 1926, translations by Barsby 2001 and Brown 2006.

[46] See Deufert 2007 for data and Danese 2008 for general discussion.

Terence's enduring success is partly due to his colloquial yet relatively tame language, which made him an ideal school author. Throughout antiquity and the Middle Ages he was much read, and even today he is occasionally read in schools.

PLAUTINE LANGUAGE

Plautine comedy used to be viewed as a mirror of everyday speech, but no longer: while Plautine comedy does contain many colloquialisms, it is also highly artificial. Plautus loves to play with sounds, and every page bristles with numerous alliterations, assonances, and other figures of speech. Modern scholarship has developed a more clearly differentiated picture of Plautine language. We now recognize, for example, that Plautus can be solemn and archaic in certain places, especially in recitatives and sung passages.[47]

The use of Greek in the comedies deserves special attention. Plautus' Greek, even where it is in the Attic dialect, for instance *apage* (go away) or *euge* (hurray), was not necessarily taken from the original comedies: *apage* is also used by Afranius (*com.* 383 Ribbeck), a writer of *comoedia togata*, which of course is not based on Greek originals (although there may be indirect influence from Greek plays via the *fabula palliata*); and *euge* is also attested as expressing surprise (*Bacch.* 991), a usage alien at least to Attic Greek. Often Plautus' Greek has Doric characteristics and

---

[47] For the higher frequency of some figures of speech in such passages see Haffter 1934; for archaic morphology in song see Happ 1967.

thus reflects the Greek spoken in Italy; in addition, it also contains idiosyncratic, purely Plautine features.

Archaism

In *de orat*. 3. 45, Cicero tells us that his mother-in-law's old-fashioned way of speaking reminded him of Plautus' *incorrupta antiquitas* (unspoiled archaism). A modern student who has mainly read authors from the classical period will form the same impression. But much of what may seem archaic to us was not archaic in Plautus' day. Imperfects like *audibam* (I was hearing), for example, were still the norm, with *audiebam* being a later formation. Similarly, Plautus regularly uses the indicative in *quom*-clauses, even in those cases where later writers would use the subjunctive. A telling example is *Aul*. 178 and the way the line is quoted by Cicero (*div*. 1. 65): in Plautus the speaker says *quom exibam domo* (when I was leaving the house), but when Cicero cites the line, he accidentally changes it to *quom exirem domo*, conforming to the usage of his own time.

Plautus' language does, however, contain elements that were already old-fashioned when he was writing. Since most contemporary documents of the same period are formal, a comparison with them does not always enable us to define what Plautus' spectators would have considered archaic. But a close look at variation within Plautus can often help us. For example, Plautus uses both *sit* and the older *siet* (he may be), but the latter form is virtually restricted to line-end, where it is a convenient metrical variant of the former. The same is true of the medio-passive infinitives in *-ier*, like *conuortier* (turn into), which are practically confined to line-end. Archaic features of nouns, adjectives, and pronouns are the genitive in -*ai* (*magnai rei publicai*, "of the state," in *Mil.* 103), the genitive plural in -*um* rather than -*orum* (although *nummum*, "of coins," is regular), and the prevocalic accusative/ablative forms *med* (me/from me) and *ted* (you/from you).[48] All of these were already archaic in Plautus' day. Among the verbs, Plautus uses a number of archaic futures like *faxo* (I shall do) and *amasso* (I shall have loved), as well as corresponding subjunctives like *faxim* (I may do), *amassim* (I may love), *duim* (I may give), *attigas* (you may touch). Most of these archaic verb forms were already old-fashioned in Plautus and are used for special effects.[49]

Colloquialism

Plautine comedy presents us with dialogues between young men, slaves, prostitutes, and a spectrum of others, so it is natural that his language is rich in low-register colloquialisms. However, we should be careful not to describe every feature of spoken rather than written language as being of low register.[50] A typical feature of spoken language is that it is rich in primary interjections like *ah*, *attat*, *ei*, and *o*. Secondary interjections, based on lexemes, are also fre-

48 For other archaisms in nominal morphology see Gerschner 2002.

49 de Melo 2007*b*.

50 A good discussion of such problems with special emphasis on Plautus is Hofmann and Ricottilli (1985); the introductory chapter of Lindsay 1907 is also useful, though in places too simplistic.

quent, to cite only *ecastor*, *hercle*, and *pol*, originally invocations of Castor, Hercules, and Pollux. It is often said that pleonasm, that is, the use of more words than is necessary to convey a concept, is colloquial. Pleonasm is extremely common in Plautus. The plays abound in phrases like *propere celeriter* (fast [and] quickly) (*Rud.* 1323) or *nemo . . . homo* (nobody) (*Amph.* 566), literally "nobody man." The latter is instructive because *nemo* is a contraction of a phrase containing a form of *homo*. But we must be very careful with labels such as "colloquial." It is true that pleonasm is a feature of colloquial registers in many languages, but it is also typical of Roman religious language, where one type, the so-called *asyndeton bimembre*, is frequent. Here two synonyms (or antonyms, in which case we are not dealing with pleonasm) are placed next to each other without coordination.

Ellipsis is common in all registers, but particularly so in the more colloquial ones. In general, Terence is more elliptical than Plautus. For instance, "a few words" is *pauca uerba* or *pauca* in Plautus, and "in a few words" is *paucis uerbis* or *paucis*. Plautus uses the fuller phrases eight times and the ellipsis sixteen times, while Terence uses only the ellipsis (nine times). Again, not every ellipsis is colloquial per se, and sometimes there are good morphosyntactic reasons for leaving out words. In the accusative and infinitive construction, for example, the subject accusative is often absent when it can be inferred from the context. This has often been regarded as a colloquialism, but wrongly so, because such ellipses are typical of tragedy as well, and a closer analysis reveals that the subject accusative is more often left out if the infinitive is in the future active or the perfect passive.[51] The reason is that these two infinitives are formed with participles, which mark gender and number, so the subject accusative can be inferred more easily if it is not made explicit.

Many studies argue that diminutives are colloquial. This is true only in part. Where a diminutive form fulfills the function of indicating small size, it is certainly not colloquial. But not all diminutives in Plautus mark size. Sometimes the diminutive is affectionate, for example when Olympio imagines being called *mi animule* (my little soul) (*Cas.* 134), and sometimes the diminutive carries an overtone of contempt, for example when Mercury refers to the role of the running slave with the term *seruolus* rather than *seruos* (*Amph.* 987). One could speak of colloquialism here, although the term is better reserved for cases in which the diminutive morphology carries no function at all; thus *seruolus* does not have any affective connotations in *Cist.* 182, nor does it refer to a small or young slave. But even here we have to be cautious. *Asinus* and *asellus* both occur in Plautus and refer to the same animal, the donkey. The second form, a diminutive, is neither restricted to small animals nor is it affectionate or contemptuous. Nevertheless, *asellus* is not colloquial: as Housman 1930 demonstrated, it is the more refined term, while *asinus* is a rustic word.

Studies of colloquialisms in Plautus typically focus on the lexicon or morphology. But spoken language also has its own constructions. Genuinely long sentences are rare in Plautus, who prefers coordination of main clauses to

51 de Melo 2006.

subordination: where sentences are long, they are long because many main or subordinate clauses have been coordinated, not because there are particularly complex patterns of subordination.[52] In fact, certain types of subordination, for instance the ablative absolute, are exceedingly rare in Plautus[53] and restricted to battle reports and the like; interestingly, the construction already shows certain signs of fossilization: we find *praesente nobis* (in our presence) in *Amph.* 400, with irregular number agreement (singular participle and a plural pronoun), presumably formed on the basis of fossilized *me praesente* (in my presence). But while sentence complexity is a question of degree, we do find certain phrases that are not supposed to occur in higher registers:

> *numero mihi in mentem fuit*
> *dis aduenientem gratias pro meritis agere atque*
> *alloqui? (Amph.* 180–81)

(When I arrived, it didn't occur to me too quickly to thank the gods for their good turns and to address them, did it?")

suo sibi suco uiuont (Capt. 81)

(They live on their own juice)

tu si te di amant, agere tuam rem occasio est (Poen. 659)

(You, if the gods love you, there is an opportunity to do what's good for you).

---

[52] Blänsdorf 1967: 6–41 and de Melo 2007*a*.
[53] Data in Bennett 1910–14. ii: 368–72.

In the first example we find *in mentem fuit* instead of *in mente fuit* or *in mentem uenit*; that is, we find the accusative of direction with a verb that is not normally regarded as describing motion. Here, however, *fuit* must mean "it came" rather than "it was." As Adams 2007: 348 points out, the phenomenon is well known from English as well, where we can say "I've been to America," combining "to be" with a prepositional phrase indicating direction. Petersmann 2002–3: 99–100 shows that in Plautus this construction is restricted to lower-class speakers, such as slaves. The same construction existed throughout the history of Latin in colloquial registers; Spanish then went one step further: *fui* is the simple past of both *soy* (I am) and *voy* (I am going).[54] In the second example *sibi* does not modify *uiuont*. The reflexive pronoun strengthens the possessive *suo* and gives it particular emphasis ("their own" rather than just "their"). This construction type is often regarded as colloquial. It is better classified as unmarked in Plautus, although later on a purist like Cicero avoided it.[55] And in the third example there is an anacoluthon: the speaker begins with a nominative pronoun, as if to say "you can do" but then switches to the impersonal construction in mid-sentence by saying "there is an opportunity." But such dangling nominatives are not necessarily always colloquial; they do at least sometimes have the function of emphasizing the agent, as is the case here.

54 We find the opposite phenomenon in the type *in lustra iacuisti* (*Cas.* 242), "you lay in the brothel," where we might expect the ablative; here *iaceo* effectively functions as the passive of *iacio* "throw."

55 de Melo 2010.

INTRODUCTION

Greek Influence

A Roman living in the third century would be exposed to much Greek from many sources. If he belonged to the upper class, he would read Homer, Attic tragedies, and oratory at school. And a Roman of any class would come into contact with Greeks in Rome, whether they were slaves, teachers of philosophy, or traders. Plautus expected his audiences to understand a great deal of Greek, since Greek words and phrases appear frequently. But the Greek in Plautus' comedies is not the Greek of the originals he adapted but rather the Greek spoken in Rome and the rest of Italy, and its connotations are not prestige and education but servile status and frivolity.[56] Thus the word for "trick" is *machina* in Plautus, not the Attic form *mechane*. The vowel weakening in the middle syllable shows that this word was not a Plautine borrowing, but goes back some way. Such adaptations are common: at *Persa* 394 the word for "witticisms" is *logi*, with the Latin ending, not *logoi*. "Blows with the fist" are transmitted as *colaphos* (accusative plural) in *Capt.* 88, again with a Latin ending. This word, incidentally, originated in Sicily and spread from there to Greece on the one hand and to Italy on the other.[57] The spelling in our editions corresponds nicely to Greek *kolaphoi*, but we should not forget that the Greek aspirate was probably pronounced as a plain stop in Plautus (and certainly written -*p*-), a state of affairs reflected in the Romance continuations Italian *colpo* (blow) and French *couper* (to cut) (in *coup* the *p* is no longer pronounced).

[56] Shipp 1953: 112.
[57] Shipp 1979: 326–27.

Plautus also loves the Greek verbal suffix -*izein*, rendered as -*issare*. Some of his coinages look quite Greek, for instance *cyathissare* (ladle out wine) (cf. *Men.* 303), while others are clearly formed by Plautus himself, such as *graecissare* (assume Greek airs) (cf. *Men.* 11); Greeks did not refer to themselves as *Graeci* when speaking Greek. Plautus can also adapt Greek adjectives and adverbs and give them Latin endings. The Greek adjective *basilikos* (royal) has *basilikōs* as its adverb, but Plautus prefers the Latin endings and says *basilicus* and *basilice*. The meaning of this word in Plautus is interesting. In *Persa* 462 *exornatu's basilice* means "you're dressed up magnificently," not as a king but as a Persian merchant. And in *Epid.* 56 *interii basilice* means "I've perished completely," with the adverb being little more than an intensifier. Such usages have no parallels in formal Greek. Fraenkel 2007: 130–32 points out that they are typical of slaves, Plautus' favorite role, and that we therefore seem to be dealing with a purely Plautine mannerism.

Plautus also makes up his own Greek puns. In *Mil.* 436 Philocomasium, pretending to be her own twin sister, calls herself Dicea, that is, *Dikaia* (the just one). Sceledrus does not believe her and says:

adikos es tu, non dikaia (*Mil.* 438)

(You're unjust, not Justine).

Other jokes are truly bilingual. In *Pseud.* 210–11 the pimp speaks of *oliui dunamin*, which must mean "a vast amount of oil." But *dunamis* does not have the meaning "vast amount" in Greek. The puzzle can be solved if we translate into Latin: *dunamis* normally means "power" and in this sense corresponds to Latin *uis*, but the Latin word also means "vast amount," and this is what is behind the Greek *dunamis* here. Another case of translator's Greek can be found at *Cas.* 728–29a.[58] The slave says πράγματά μοι παρέχεις (you're annoying me), a normal Greek phrase; but his master answers *dabo tibi* μέγα κακόν (I'll give you a big thrashing), which is a calque on *magnum malum*. There is one instance where a Greek phrase in Plautus means the opposite of what it would mean in normal Greek. In *Capt.* 880 μὰ τὸν Ἀπόλλω means "yes by Apollo," while in Greek written by Greeks (and also in *Most.* 973) it means "no by Apollo." But perhaps this is not a Plautine feature of Greek but simply a piece of textual corruption.[59] At any rate, usages deviating from standard Greek are not always facetious; *andron* means "men's quarters" in Greek, but in Vitruvius the meaning "corridor" is found (6. 7. 5), clearly a technical term not intended to amuse.

Particularly interesting are concepts for which Plautus uses both Latin and Greek words.[60] For instance, Plautus refers to a banker as either *argentarius* or *tarpezita* (Greek τραπεζίτης), and to a sword as either *gladius* or *machaera* (Greek μάχαιρα). At first sight, one could think that the Greek terms have been taken directly from the Greek plays. But the situation is more complicated. The Plautine Greek word for "banker" is *tarpezita* (probably spelled *tarpessita* by Plautus), not *trapezita* or *trapessita*, as one

---

58 Discussed by Shipp 1953: 106.

59 Thesleff 1960: 51–52 would emend to ναὶ τὸν Ἀπόλλω "yes by Apollo."

60 For an excellent discussion see Shipp 1955.

might expect from Attic τραπεζίτης. Presumably the Plautine form comes from Italian Greek. Plautus uses this Greek form to give his plays a Greek atmosphere, whereas *argentarius* occurs in passages in which Plautus talks about Roman life. *Machaera* (an Attic form) is used by Plautus to refer to the sword of Greek mercenaries, while *gladius* is used elsewhere. Nevertheless, Plautus seems to have taken this word from the Greek he heard in Italy rather than from the Greek comedies he was adapting, for the word for sword in Greek comedy is σπάθη (borrowed later as *spatha*).

The Greek influence I have discussed so far always can and often must be explained without recourse to the Greek comedies that Plautus adapted. I have looked at loanwords common throughout Italy and at Plautine idiosyncrasies. But is Plautine language sometimes directly influenced by the Greek of the original comedies? Such influence could be lexical and also syntactic. Lexical influence is more difficult to pin down, since we could be dealing with loans common outside Plautus as well; in general, a translator like Plautus will avoid directly taking over words from the source he is using, which means that lexical influence from his sources will typically manifest itself in more subtle ways, for instance in calques or "loan translations." Loan syntax is more likely to come directly from the Greek originals than loan words because a translator can escape the latter without much effort.

We have seen that Plautus does not shy away from using Greek words but that these are usually not from his originals. What calques does he have? The following passage contains a clear case: *sibi sua habeant regna reges, sibi diuitias diuites, sibi honores, sibi uirtutes, sibi pugnas, sibi proelia* (Let the kings have their kingdoms, the rich their riches; let them have their honors, their feats, their fights, their battles) (*Curc.* 178–79). In this context *uirtutes* must refer not to a personal quality or characteristic but to something more concrete, "feats" or "accomplishments" as the result of some personal quality or characteristic. But *uirtus* is an abstract noun. The concrete meaning that *uirtutes* has here seems to be calqued on Greek ἀρεταί, which has both abstract and concrete meanings. This process of transferring another meaning from a Greek noun to a Latin noun with fewer meanings is the opposite of the bilingual joke above involving *uis* ("power" and "large amount") and *dunamis* (only "power" outside Plautus).

Plautus' syntax looks thoroughly Latin. But there is one clear instance where it could be argued that the Latin syntax is influenced by Greek: *argenti uiginti minae med ad mortem appulerunt, quas hodie adulescens Diabolus ipsi daturus dixit* (Twenty silver minas have driven me to my death; young Diabolus said he'd give them to her today) (*Asin.* 633–34). After *dixit* (he said) one would expect the accusative and infinitive construction. The accusative is often left out, but the participle constituting the nonfinite element should be in the accusative. Here *daturus* (going to give) is in the nominative, as is customary in Greek when the subject of the finite verb and the subject of the infinitive are identical. We find a similar case in Catullus:

> *phaselus ille quem uidetis, hospites,*
> *ait fuisse nauium celerrimus* (Catull. 4. 1–2)

> (That pinnace you see, my friends, says she was once the fastest of ships).

But in Catullus such a phenomenon is not unexpected, since he consciously imitates the language of Hellenistic poetry.

Elsewhere Greek influence can be detected, but without violations of Latin syntactic rules. Adams 2003: 518 points out that demonstrative pronouns, mainly *hic* (this) and *ille* (that), are remarkably frequent in the delayed narration of the plot of the *Miles gloriosus* (from line 88 onwards); typically they accompany nouns indicating character roles. This seems to reflect Greek usage. Since in Greek plays the characters often have standard names associated with them, prologues typically mention the roles, in combination with the article, rather than the actual names attached to the roles. Thus Plautus has translated the Greek article with demonstrative pronouns. But these demonstrative pronouns have not lost their deictic qualities: in this prologue *hic* is still used for people near the speaker and *ille* for those further away.

Excursus: Terms for Greek Currency

Plautine money is essentially Greek money, but there are complications because different currency systems were used in Greece, and of course Romans would mainly be familiar with their own type of money. It is clear that Plautus did not know his Greek money only from Greek comedy; Shipp 1955: 145–46 pointed out that the Macedonian stater, called χρυσοῦς, στατήρ, or Δαρεικός in Greek, typically has the name *Philippus* or *Philippeus*, "Philippic" in Plautus, a name never used for this coin in Greek comedy and probably known to Plautus from the Greek spoken in southern Italy. Interestingly, *Philippus* when referring to a person always has a heavy second syllable, but when referring to a coin always has a light second syllable, because of iambic shortening.[61] Since accented syllables cannot be made light by iambic shortening, we have to assume that the name of the Greek coin *Philippus* was borrowed with the accent on the first syllable, against the Latin rules of pronunciation, but in full accord with standard Greek accentuation.

The highest monetary unit in Plautine comedy is the talent. When Plautus wants to refer to the Attic talent, he uses the terms *talentum magnum* (great talent), *talentum argenti* (talent of silver), or *talentum auri* (talent of gold); *talentum* without modifier refers to the southern Italian talent, which is of lesser value.[62] Thus when *talentum* is used on its own, we are dealing with a south Italian and hence Plautine element, not with the talent of the Greek originals. A talent is worth sixty *minae*. The Greek word is μνᾶ, but an initial *mn*-cluster would violate the phonotactic rules of Latin, hence the insertion of *i*. Plautus has a similar kind of anaptyxis in the next smallest monetary unit: Greek δραχμή corresponds to Latin *drachuma*. One *mina* is worth one hundred *drachumae*. And one *drachuma* is worth six *oboli*.

In Plautus we also find references to the Macedonian monetary system. I have already mentioned the stater, called *Philippus*, *Philippeus*, or *nummus aureus* by Plautus. One stater is worth four drachmas or twenty-four obols. Apart from the stater, the most important Macedonian coins are the didrachma (double drachma) and the tetrobol (four-obol piece). How does Plautus refer to these

---

[61] Questa 2007: 88–89; on iambic shortening see below.
[62] Shipp 1955: 143.

two coins? Shipp 1955: 144 points out that Greek mercenaries would get a tetrobol per day and that a soldier's pay in *Most.* 357 is three *nummi*; *nummus* is a vague term and simply means "coin," but if *nummus* here refers to the *sestertius*, we have a good equivalent, because one sesterce piece is worth one and a half obols, so that the tetrobol of the Greek mercenary is worth practically as much as the three coins of the Roman. In fact, it seems that the default value of the *nummus* is one sesterce piece.[63] It is possible that the *trinummus*, the coin after which Plautus named one of his plays, corresponds to three sesterces, in which case it would be the closest equivalent to the Greek tetrobol.

As for the didrachma, *drachuma* is a firmly established loan, so it is easy for Plautus to translate sums given in didrachmas in the Greek originals. But in *Truc.* 561–62 Plautus renders the Greek didrachma as *nummus*; he speaks of one *mina*, that is, one hundred drachmas, of which 10 percent or five *nummi* are subtracted, which shows that the term *nummus* stands for the didrachma here. Such passages are not really problematic, for *nummus* is an inherently vague term, and even though its default value is one sesterce piece, it can stand for other coins so long as the context makes it clear which type of coin is meant.

Varieties of Speech

The language of Plautine comedy is not uniform. Young men do not speak like their fathers, and slaves do not speak like their masters. In recent years, much work has been

---

63 Shipp 1955: 148, *pace* Mattingly and Robinson 1935: 230.

done on the linguistic differences between men and women.[64] Among other differences, Adams 1984 examined the use of certain oaths with emphatic functions and noted that only men use *hercle* and *mehercle*, while only women use *ecastor* and *mecastor*. *Pol* and *edepol*, by contrast, are used by both sexes. Women also use more markers of politeness than men do, for instance *opsecro* (I beg you), and *amabo* (please, literally "I'll love you") is almost exclusively employed by women. Similarly, women are far more likely than men to modify a vocative by adding the intimate *mi* (my dear). This tendency is especially noticeable with personal names (Dutsch 2008: 55).

Variation is not restricted to differences between speakers. One and the same speaker can adopt vastly different styles and cover anything from neutral, unmarked speech to tragic pathos. An example of religious language can be found in Epignomus' short prayer:

> *quom bene re gesta saluos conuortor domum,*
> *Neptuno gratis habeo et Tempestatibus;*
> *simul Mercurio, qui me in mercimoniis*
> *iuuit lucrisque quadruplicauit rem meam* (*Stich.*
>   402–5)

(I give thanks to Neptune and the Weather-goddesses for letting me return home successful and safe; and also to Mercury, who helped me in my business affairs and increased my possessions fourfold with profit).

One immediately notices the formal ablative absolute *bene re gesta*, also found in battle reports, and the religious term

---

64 See Gilleland 1980.

for "thanks" (*gratis*; the nonreligious equivalent would be *gratias*). The register is usually elevated when Plautus imitates formal genres. Particularly frequent is legal language, as in the "edict" in *Mil.* 160–65; parodies of tragedy, as in *Pseud.* 702–6; and "running slaves' speeches," as in *Curc.* 280–98, which originate in the typical messengers' speeches of tragedy.

PLAUTINE VERSE

Practically every commentary on Plautus contains an introduction to his meters; this section is merely intended as an overview and an explanation of principles adopted in this edition.[65]

Prosody

Plautus' comedies are entirely in verse. His verse, like that of the classical period, is quantitative, that is, its rhythm is created by the orderly sequence of light and heavy syllables. A syllable minimally consists of a vowel or diphthong but can in addition contain consonants as syllable onset and coda. A syllable is light only if it ends in a short vowel. Syllables ending in a long vowel or diphthong and/or a consonant are heavy.

But while these fundamental principles are the same in Plautus and the classical period, there are numerous finer

[65] The best book on Plautine meter in recent years is Questa's *La metrica di Plauto e di Terenzio* 2007. Lindsay 1922 is still useful. Soubiran 1988 is an excellent introduction to the two most common meters in Plautus, the iambic senarius and the trochaic septenarius.

points in which Plautine prosody differs from that of later periods. For instance, *patrem* (father) (accusative) can be syllabified in two ways in Ovid: as *pat.rem* with a heavy first syllable and as *pa.trem* with a light first syllable. Ovid has this freedom when the first of the two intervocalic consonants is a *muta* (stop consonant: *p, b, t, d, c, g*) and the second is a *liquida* (*r* or *l*). In Plautus, only the second type of syllabification exists, unless there is a morpheme boundary between *muta* and *liquida*, in which case the first type of syllabification is obligatory (*ob.loquere*, "speak against," never *o.bloquere*; incidentally, classical Latin also allows only the first type of syllabification here).

It is important to note that Plautus has preserved many heavy final syllables which became light later on. Thus we find an inherited long vowel in the second syllable of *amat* (he loves), and *miles* (soldier) still has a heavy final syllable because it was pronounced *miless* with a final geminate consonant (from earlier **milet-s*). All long vowels in final syllables that were followed by a single consonant were shortened after Plautus, unless the word was a monosyllable ending in *s*, *r*, or *l*, or a polysyllable ending in *s*; *res* (thing), *fur* (thief), *sol* (sun), and *amas* (you love) all still have long vowels in their final syllables in classical Latin. And final geminate consonants were simplified unless the word was monosyllabic. Plautus' prosody is thus more archaic.

If one word ends in a vowel and the next begins with one, the two typically coalesce.[66] Words ending in vowel + *m* or beginning with *h* + vowel behave in the same way, as final *m* and initial *h* were not always pronounced. In classi-

[66] The most important study on this subject is Soubiran 1966.

cal poetry one normally speaks of elision of the final vowel of the first word, because for metrical purposes it is treated as if it were lost completely. If the second word is *es* (you are) or *est* (he is), it is this second word which is said to lose its vowel (cf. English "you're" and "he's"). This phenomenon, called prodelision, does not really involve loss of a vowel; rather, we are dealing with inherited clitic by-forms which never had a vowel to begin with.

In Plautus, prodelision can also occur after a word ending in *-us* or *-is*, so that we find both *bonus es* and *bonu's* (you are good) and both *amabilis est* and *amabilest* (she is lovable).[67] In this edition, prodelision is marked in such cases because here it is not obligatory in Plautus and writing *bonus est* for *bonust* can be confusing, whereas marking prodelision is a real aid to scansion. But I write *bonum est* rather than *bonumst* (it is good) because here prodelision is the rule throughout Latin, and nothing is gained from making explicit what is obligatory anyway.

Elision is also frequent, though not as regular as in classical poetry. To some extent the reason is that Plautine comedy reflects everyday pronunciation somewhat more realistically than later poetry does. Thus monosyllables often retain their vowels in Plautus as they no doubt would in normal speech as well. And after interjections, at major syntactic breaks, at the regular pauses in verse (the so-called *caesurae* and *diaereseis*), and when there is a change of speaker, Plautus also readily admits hiatus.

Similar to elision in some respects is the loss of final

---

[67] *Amabilest*, the typical spelling in editions, somewhat obscures the fact that there is no elision of *-is*, but the addition of a clitic *-st*.

phonemes before words beginning with a consonant, where short *e* is often lost. In classical Latin doublets like *atque/ac* (and) or *neue/neu* (nor) remain, but in Plautus the phenomenon also affects words such as *nempe*. In such cases this edition regularly writes *nemp'*. Final *s* is also often lost after short vowels: in *magis quam* (more than), for example, the first word can count as two light syllables. As meter often allows both scansions, I have preferred not to mark this phenomenon.

Iambic shortening, sometimes referred to as *brevis brevians*, is perhaps the most intriguing feature of early Latin prosody. We speak of iambic shortening when an iambic sequence, that is a light syllable followed by a heavy one, counts as a sequence of two light syllables. Iambic shortening definitely has its basis in everyday speech. Many originally iambic words admit both scansions even in the classical period, for instance *ego* (I) or *mihi* (to me). But where the affected syllable is heavy because it ends in one or more consonants, we are probably justified in regarding iambic shortening as a metrical license rather than a reflection of speech; after all, long vowels can be shortened, but consonant clusters could only become light if consonants were lost completely.

Iambic shortening is subject to certain restrictions. The heavy syllable that is affected may not carry the word accent; there must not be word-end between the light and the heavy syllable (unless the light syllable is a word in its own right rather than part of a longer word); and the new light-light sequence must form a single metrical element, that is, it must be metrically legitimate to replace this sequence by a single heavy syllable. In addition, iambic shortening is not equally frequent across meters: it often occurs in spoken verse, is very rare in certain sung verses (bacchiacs and cretics), and is most frequent in anapaests.

Finally, there is shortening through enclisis. This can affect long vowels in certain words when followed by certain clitics like *quidem*. Thus the combination *si quidem* can scan as a heavy-light-heavy sequence or as a light-light-heavy sequence. In the latter case we have shortening through enclisis, and I write the sequence as a single word.

Meters

Plautus' poetry consists of verses in a number of different meters, whose variety is so great that most of them cannot be discussed here. Most can be divided into smaller units, the following are the most important ones ($\cup$ stands for a light syllable, – for a heavy one):

$\cup$ –	iamb (ia)
– $\cup$	trochee (tr)
– –	spondee (sp)
$\cup\cup$ –	anapaest (an)
– $\cup$ –	cretic (cr)
$\cup$– –	bacchiac (ba)

A common meter is the iambic senarius (ia^6), which makes up around 40 percent of Plautus' lines. The iambic senarius consists of six iambs or units that can substitute for iambs. Each of the first five iambs can be replaced by various other units; the light element can be replaced by one heavy or two light syllables, and the heavy element can be replaced by two light syllables. This means that each of the five iambs can be replaced by five other units (– –, $\cup\cup$–, $\cup\cup\cup$, –$\cup\cup$, or $\cup\cup\cup\cup$). The sixth iamb has to be pure, that is, it has to consist of two syllables, the first of which has to be light; but as in most meters, the last syllable may be either light or heavy. A typical iambic senarius looks like this:

petunt fullones, sarcinatores petunt (*Aul.* 515)

(The launderers are demanding pay, and the menders of clothes are demanding pay).

The metrical structure of this line is ∪– –– –– ∪– –– ∪– (iamb, spondee, spondee, iamb, spondee, iamb).

Many substitutions are possible. In theory this pattern gives us over fifteen thousand possibilities of forming an iambic senarius, and one may wonder whether under these circumstances it still makes sense to speak of one single meter, and if so, how one can recognize it. The answer is that much of what is possible in theory is excluded in practice; for instance, the proceleusmatic (∪∪∪∪) is a fairly uncommon substitute for an iamb, and two proceleusmatics never occur immediately next to each other, because this would obscure the rhythm too much. In addition, most verse types regularly have some sort of incision, traditionally called caesura if it divides a metrical unit and diaeresis if it comes immediately after one.[68] The iambic senarius typically has a caesura after the fifth element, dividing the third metrical unit. Such incisions help the hearer to perceive the rhythm of the verse more clearly. We normally find word end here, sometimes with hiatus, but occasionally the caesura is obscured because even though it comes immediately before a new word, the preceding

[68] On such incisions in the senarius and the trochaic septenarius, discussed below, see Ceccarelli 1990: 11–52.

word merges with this new word by means of elision. But complete absence of caesura is rare and can normally be accounted for in some other way. For example, *Aul.* 510 *flammarii, uiolarii, carinarii* (those who dye garments in flaming red, violet, and brown) contains the names of three related professions, each of which occupies two metrical units. The rhythm is clear despite the absence of a regular caesura.

Plautine senarii follow a number of rules. These rules are not random but rather enable the audience to follow the rhythm more easily. Two examples should suffice. The rule of Bentley-Luchs states that if there is word-end after the fifth metrical unit, the first element of this fifth unit must be – or ∪∪ but not ∪. Thus a senarius may end *mater dedit* (– – ∪) (mother gave it) or *Blepharo dedit* (∪∪– ∪–) (Blepharo gave it) but not *pater dedit* (∪– ∪–) (father gave it). The ending ∪– ∪– is not excluded so long as there is no word-end before the final iamb; we find *coloniam* (*Aul.* 576) as well as *(face-)re ludicram* (*Aul.* 626). Why is *pater dedit* excluded? The reason seems to be that an inattentive listener might believe that the line ends with *pater* rather than *dedit*. Such confusion cannot arise if the fifth metrical unit is not iambic or, in case it is iambic, if there is no word end after it.

A second example of metrical rules comprises two rules with similar effects. Ritschl's law states that if a metrical element is disyllabic (two light syllables), it may not be divided by the word end of a polysyllable. And the law of Hermann and Lachmann states that if a metrical unit is disyllabic (again two light syllables), the end of this metrical unit may not coincide with the end of a polysyllabic word. Two examples will make this clear. "Now he is coming here" could be translated as *nunc ille uenit huc*; but if this sequence were supposed to form the first five elements of a senarius, the scansion – – ∪∪ – – would be impossible because (*il*)*le ue*(*nit*) is a disyllabic element divided by a word-end and thereby breaking Ritschl's law. However, *ille* has a monosyllabic by-form *ill'*; if this by-form were used here, the scansion would be –– ∪ ––, so there would be no divided element, and the half-line would be acceptable. The law of Hermann and Lachmann is similar. In the prologue to the *Asinaria* (l. 11) we find the following senarius: *Demophilus scripsit, Maccus uortit barbare* (Demophilus wrote it and Maccus translated it into barbarian language). *Maccus*, the "Clown," stands for Maccius, Plautus' middle name, literally "son of the clown." Ritschl, who was the first modern scholar to see that Plautus was called Titus Maccius rather than M(arcus) Accius, wanted to change Maccus to Maccius (the final -*s* cannot count in that case). But that would violate the law of Hermann and Lachmann, because (*Macc-*)*ius* would be a disyllabic element whose end coincides with the word-end of a polysyllable. Ritschl was a true scholar: he was humble enough to acknowledge the existence of this rule in later years and to admit that his emendation had been faulty.

The raison d'être behind these two laws is the same. Disyllabic elements, though relatively frequent, constitute a divergence from the "ideal" scheme of the senarius. For a listener it is important to grasp immediately whether a disyllabic sequence constitutes one element or whether each syllable belongs to a separate element. If word-end intervenes, the second interpretation is more natural. In order not to mislead his audience over rhythmical patterns, Plautus allows only the second interpretation if the disyllabic sequence is split by word end.

Plautus uses another meter, the trochaic septenarius (tr^7), even more often than the iambic senarius. The name trochaic septenarius and the abbreviation tr^7 are traditional, but not ideal, since the meter does not consist of seven trochees, but of seven and a half; we are really dealing with a catalectic trochaic octonarius, that is, eight trochees, the last of which lacks its final syllable (hence also the abbreviation $tr^{8\wedge}$, where $\wedge$ marks a missing final element; $\wedge$ stands for Λ, the abbreviation of λείπεται, "is missing").

There is another way of looking at the trochaic septenarius, which ultimately goes back to the first-century CE grammarian Caesius Bassus (Keil vi. 267. 6–8): we can analyse this meter as a cretic followed by an iambic senarius. In the cretic, – can be replaced by ∪∪, and ∪ can be replaced by – or ∪∪. The senarius is entirely regular and follows the rules outlined above. This analysis has a clear advantage: the cretic was felt to be a separate part of the verse, as is clear from the fact that its third element is a *locus Jacobsohnianus*, that is, it can behave like an element at line end: hiatus is allowed, and so is a light syllable instead of the heavy one.

A special type of trochaic septenarius is the so-called *uersus quadratus*, a septenarius that falls into four parts separated by word-end. The first three parts contain four elements each, the last part contains three elements, for example *Men.* 859 *osse fini dedolabo assulatim uiscera* (I'll hew away his flesh, bit by bit, down to the bone), where part 1 is *osse fini*, part 2 *dedolabo* (with hiatus), part 3 *assulatim*, and part 4 *uiscera*.

Other meters are much less common. Plautus is fond of cretics and bacchiacs, particularly cr⁴ and ba⁴, which are essentially four cretics or four bacchiacs in succession. Again there are catalectic versions of such verses, and syncopated versions in which an internal element is missing are often called cola. A bacchiac colon can, for example, look like this: *plus aegri ex abitu* (more grief from going away) (*Amph.* 641), essentially a syncopated dimeter. The first bacchiac is syncopated and consists of two heavy syllables (*plus aeg-*); the first syllable of the second bacchiac is heavy (a common licence), and the second element consists of two light syllables rather than one heavy syllable.

Recitation

Given the wealth of Plautine meters, it would be surprising if all of them were recited in the same way. The Palatine manuscripts often contain the marks *DV* and *C*. *DV* stands for *deuerbium* (spoken verse), while *C* stands for *canticum* (song). Donatus *de com.* 8. 9 tells us that the sung passages were accompanied by music. But which verses were normally spoken and which were normally sung? The ancient evidence is presented and discussed in detail by Moore 2008; here a rough outline has to suffice. According to Pseudo-Marius Victorinus (Keil vi. 2. 2), iambic senarii were spoken, whereas everything else was sung. The comedies themselves also contain indications that this is correct:

> tene, tibicen, primum; postidea loci
> si hoc eduxeris, proinde ut consuetu's antehac,
> celeriter

lepidam et suauem cantionem aliquam occupito
  cinaedicam,
ubi perpruriscamus usque ex unguiculis. inde huc
  aquam (*Stich.* 758–61)

(Piper, take this first; then, when you've drunk it up,
quickly play us some nice and sweet lewd tune, just
as you used to before, a tune where we itch all over
down to our fingertips. Put some water in here).

This passage in trochaic septenarii is accompanied by a
piper. But after this line the musician is drinking, and the
meter accordingly changes to iambic senarii. At the end of
the iambics (ll. 767–68) the speaker says *age iam infla
buccas, nunciam aliquid suauiter redd' cantionem ueteri
pro uino nouam* (Go on, now puff out your cheeks, play
something sweet now. Give us a new tune for the old wine).
After these words the song continues in different meters.

Modern scholarship normally distinguishes between
two types of sung verse. On the one hand, there are the so-
called long verses, that is, trochaic septenarii and iambic
septenarii and octonarii. One generally assumes that pas-
sages in these meters were recitatives rather than songs.
And on the other hand, there are all other verses, except
for the spoken senarii. These so-called *mutatis modis can-
tica* (songs in changing meters) (Don. *de com.* 8. 9) are
lyric passages that were sung. Plautus does not use these
three different types of verse indiscriminately. There is of-
ten a sequence of spoken verse, followed by song, followed
by recitative, which can be repeated several times. Some-
times recitative is followed by song again, and sometimes
spoken verse is followed by recitative rather than song, but

song is not normally followed by spoken verse immediately.

Prologues are normally in senarii, whereas the end of a play is always in trochaic septenarii; the *Poenulus* has two endings, one of which is in senarii (ending at *Poen.* 1371), but this alternative ending was written after Plautus' death. One should also note that not every type of verse is suitable for every speaker or passage. Unsympathetically portrayed characters, for example, are rarely given song; since women typically sing, Menaechmus' wife, whose first appearance is in senarii (*Men.* 559–68, with Peniculus as second speaker), can immediately be classified as a bad character. Letters are always read out in iambic senarii.

The Structure of Plautine Songs

Plautus uses iambic senarii and long verses in so-called stichic fashion: an entire passage exclusively in iambic senarii, octonarii, or the like. Monotony never becomes a problem, because each meter can be realized in so many different ways. Plautine songs have much more variety. Bacchiacs can be followed by iambics, cretics by trochees, and so on. To the modern reader this variety is bewildering. Especially if a passage is corrupt, it is vital to know what meter was intended, otherwise emendation is impossible. But even where the text is secure, a line can often be analysed in more than one way, and being able to interpret the verse as Plautus intended is helpful for a deeper understanding of the passage. Here the Plautine scholar's work would be much easier if we knew what the music underlying the texts was like; but that has been lost for good.

Despite the great variety in Plautine songs, some remarks about their structure are possible.[69] Plautus generally tries to make content and meter coincide. Sentence- or clause-end typically coincides with verse-end. A major change in content will be marked by a change in meter as well. A longer song can thus consist of several sections, each characterized by its own meter. The end of such a section is typically marked in some way: the last line may be catalectic or syncopated, or it may be in an entirely different meter, and often a line shortly before the last will differ from the rest of the section in a similar way.

A question that has exercised scholars for a long time is the origin of the *mutatis modis cantica*, a very prominent feature of Plautus' plays but absent in the dialogues of New Comedy. The question remains difficult, but there seem to be two not mutually exclusive answers to it. First, it is likely that preliterary farce in Rome was musical. Plautus and also his predecessor Naevius were of course familiar with these genres and took over music to keep the Roman audiences entertained. Second, while Greek New Comedy had no arias, Greek tragedy contained elaborate music, including arias. Roman authors took over the Greek meters and with them the music. Roman writers before Plautus normally adapted both genres, tragedy and comedy, and comedy was much influenced by tragedy. It is thus highly likely that a poet like Naevius, who used song in his tragedies, realized what effect this had and extended the sphere of song to comedy as well.

[69] Maurach 1964 and Braun 1970.

STAGING

Today Plautus has a readership rather than an audience. But in his lifetime and for some time after, his comedies were mainly intended for performance. Although many details escape us, we still know a reasonable amount about how Plautus was actually staged.

Occasions for Performance

Comedies were performed during festivals that were religious at least in their origins. In Plautus' day there were at least four such festivals per year.

The oldest was the *ludi Romani* (Roman games) held in September in honor of Jupiter. According to Livy (1. 35. 9), the Roman games were already celebrated on an annual basis under Tarquinius Priscus, that is, in the seventh or sixth century; yet this seems unlikely. The first dramatic performances at these games were introduced in 364, but the first regular tragedy and the first regular comedy were performed in 240, when Livius Andronicus translated plays from the Greek for performance.

The *ludi plebeii* (plebeian games) were named for the plebeian aediles, the magistrates who organized them. They were held in November, also in honor of Jupiter. These games are attested for the first time in 220, when the place where they were held, the Circus Flaminius, was built. But the games may have existed earlier. Plautus' *Stichus* was performed at the *ludi plebeii* of 200.

The *ludi Apollinares* were held in July in honor of Apollo. They were a more recent invention and took place for the first time in 212 (Liv. 27. 23. 5).

Finally, there were the *ludi Megalenses*, celebrated in

April in honor of the *Megale Meter* (Great Mother) and introduced in 204 together with her cult; Plautus' *Pseudolus* was first staged during the *ludi Megalenses* of 191, when her temple was dedicated.

After Plautus' death, the number of festivals, and thus the opportunities to perform plays, increased considerably. Plays were also performed on other special occasions. As the stage records preceding Terence's comedies tell us, his *Adelphoe* and his *Hecyra* were both presented at Lucius Aemilius Paullus' funeral games in 160.

A phenomenon that may seem curious to us is the frequency with which *instaurationes* (repetitions of festivals) took place. An *instauratio* had to happen if an element of the ceremony went wrong. Thus it was a religious matter, at least officially. But *instaurationes* took place so regularly that one suspects that the officials in charge deliberately looked for pretexts for repeat festivals. They may have done so because festivals with their dramatic and other performances were extremely popular, and the more they could be prolonged, the more the people would favor the politicians putting on the games.

From the Script to the Stage

At Rome the dramatic festivals were normally organized by the aediles. Aediles were minor officials, who used these opportunities to gain popularity and votes. The aediles would approach an *actor* (actor-manager).[70] The *actor* would buy a script from a playwright and sell its pro-

---

[70] In the older literature typically referred to as the *dominus gregis*, the "manager of the troupe," but the ancient evidence for such a term is slim, to say the least; see Jory 1966.

duction to the aediles; the manager would put on the play with his own troupe of actors and take part in it himself. We know that the *actor* of at least some of Plautus' plays was a certain Titus Publilius Pellio (see *Bacch.* 215).

The actors were slaves or low-class freedmen. It is often claimed, on the basis of *Cist.* 784–85 that they could be punished for bad acting: *ubi id erit factum, ornamenta ponent; postidea loci qui deliquit uapulabit, qui non deliquit bibet* (When this is done, they'll put down their costumes. Then anyone who made a mistake will get a beating and anyone who made no mistake will get a drink). But this passage cannot necessarily be taken as evidence for what an actor's life was like; the statement is jocular and the mistakes referred to could be the misbehavior of the characters whom the actors were playing.[71]

It is generally assumed that, as in Greek drama, each actor played more than one role per play, a state of affairs facilitated by the use of masks (see below). But a manager needed a minimum number of actors in his troupe. Occasionally four or more speaking actors were required on the stage at the same time, and there was normally a need for nonspeaking extras.

The stages in Plautus' day were simple wooden open-air structures. Pompey was the first to build a permanent theatre in Rome in 55. The stage represents a street, and all the action takes place on it. There are at most three house fronts with doors, though some plays can make do with only one, for instance the *Amphitruo*. In the street there is regularly an altar. The street leads to side entrances to the right and left, one side entrance leading to

71 Brown 2002: 235.

the city center, the other to a more remote location, the harbor or the countryside.

It is not clear whether the same side entrance by convention always led to the city center.[72] In *Men.* 555 Menaechmus takes his garland and throws it to his left (our right); then he goes in the opposite direction to the harbor. In this play, then, the harbor can be reached by the left entrance and the city center by the right. *Amph.* 333 points in the same direction. Sosia is coming from the harbor and Mercury, standing in front of Amphitruo's house in the city, says that a voice coming from his right is hitting his ears: if he is facing us, the harbor entrance is to our left. Similarly, in *Rud.* 156–57 Daemones says that there are people swimming on the right-hand side, which is our left, the beach. In all these cases the city must be to our right. The situation is different in Terence, where in *Andr.* 734–35 Davus says that he will pretend to come from the right, our left; from *Andr.* 744–46 it appears that this is where the market is situated.

The audiences were mixed. Both men and women attended, children and old people, and officials of high rank and slaves.

Dress

The different stock characters wore different stock dresses, emphasizing their roles rather than their individuality. All actors wore a *tunica*, a kind of undergarment common to both sexes. On top of that actors wore cloaks; a man's cloak is called a *pallium*, a woman's a *palla*. Soldiers

[72] For discussion see Rosivach 1970.

would wear the shorter *chlamys* instead of the regular *pallium*. Shoes were a type of sandal called *soccus* or *solea*. Old men usually had a *scipio*, a walking-stick that was also convenient for beating unruly slaves (see *Persa* 816–17). Actors typically wore wigs, black for young men, white for old men. There is some evidence that slaves had red wigs: in Plautus, Leonida and Pseudolus have red hair (*Asin.* 400 and *Pseud.* 1218), and in Terence, Davus is described as red-haired (*Phorm.* 51).

The ancient evidence concerning masks is not clear-cut. Some believe that actors in Plautus' day did not wear masks,[73] but in Greek New Comedy and also in Atellan farce, masks were the norm, and the same is true of Rome in the classical period; Cicero, for example, informs us that Roscius, who portrayed the pimp Ballio in Plautus' *Pseudolus*, wore a mask (*de orat.* 3. 221). The most natural assumption is that from the beginning Roman actors took over the masks of Greek comedy and that the classical practice is merely a continuation of what went on before as well. Gratwick 1982: 83 is right to doubt arguments against masks based on references to characters being pale or blushing; similar references occur in Greek drama as well, where we know that actors wore masks. Besides, one should not forget that some plays contain look-alikes (the *Amphitruo* even contains two pairs); masks make it easier for the audience to envisage two characters as look-alikes, although it would be wrong to assume that for this reason masks are necessary.[74]

[73] See Saunders 1911.
[74] Marshall 2006: 127.

INTRODUCTION

Acts and Scenes

Menander's plays were divided into five acts, with a chorus providing entertainment between them. Roman comedy was not divided in this way: the plays do not naturally fall into five sections, and there was no chorus for the intervals during which the stage was empty. Still, under Greek influence, Roman grammarians began discussing act divisions in Terence.[75] Modern editions, including this one, mark acts not because they are a useful concept but simply because some of the older literature refers to individual passages by acts and scenes. The act division of all modern editions follows that of G. B. Pio from 1500; but as is clear today, Pio was not the first to introduce such divisions, for similar ones can be found at least fifty years earlier.[76]

Division into scenes goes back to antiquity and is already found in the Ambrosian Palimpsest of the fourth or fifth century CE. Here the criterion is the entrance or the exit of a speaker. But even such divisions are not entirely natural and do not derive from the playwrights themselves. In the *Bacchides*, for instance, there is a scene where the soldier's hanger-on is knocking on the door. Pistoclerus opens the door in the middle of l. 583 and addresses him. For this reason, the new scene begins in the middle of a line, surely an unlikely arrangement.[77]

75 E.g. Donatus, *Andr. praef.* 2. 3, who is by no means the first.
76 See Questa 1962 for details.
77 For more details see Bader 1970.

THE TEXT OF PLAUTUS

The text of Plautus is fraught with difficulties, not only because many mistakes have crept into the text during centuries of manual copying but also because the manuscripts are often defective and have lost pages. But even if there were no copying errors and missing pages, we could not simply assume that the text we have derives from Plautus in its entirety. The following paragraphs outline how the text of Plautus was altered and modified by generations of copyists and scholars and how it deteriorated and improved by turns.[78]

Manuscripts

In antiquity, many more Plautine plays were known than have come down to us. But Varro tells us which plays were generally considered authentic without doubts, and it is these twenty-one "Varronian" plays that were transmitted together in ancient Plautus editions. But that does not mean that there was a uniform text. Plautine comedies were not just performed once. Revivals were frequent, and the texts were altered to suit each performance. The prologue of the *Casina*, for instance, was clearly written not very long after Plautus' death:

> *nos postquam populi rumore intelleximus*
> *studiose expetere uos Plautinas fabulas,*
> *antiquam eius edimus comoediam,*

[78] For an introduction to these issues see Tarrant 1983 and especially Lindsay 1896.

quam uos probastis qui estis in senioribus;
nam iuniorum qui sunt non norunt, scio;
uerum ut cognoscant dabimus operam sedulo (Cas.
11–16)

(Since we learned from popular rumor that you strongly desire Plautine plays, we are putting on an old play of his, which those of you have come to love who are among the older people. Well, those who are among the younger people are not familiar with it, I know that; but we will do our best to familiarize them with it).

The addition of a prologue is a comparatively minor change. In other places we find more radical alterations. Occasionally, entire scenes were deleted or replaced by others. This explains why the *Poenulus* has an alternative ending (ll. 1372–1422).

Our manuscripts go back to two ancient texts. Of the two manuscript families, one consists of a single manuscript, the Ambrosian palimpsest, abbreviated A. This manuscript was written in the fourth or fifth century and was rediscovered in Milan in 1815. It is now in the Ambrosian Library in Milan, shelf-mark G. 82 sup. (S.P. 9/13–20). A originally contained all Varronian plays, but the original Plautine text was effaced and replaced by Old Testament texts, and in addition many leaves have been lost, so that A is not available for a number of plays, such as the *Amphitruo*. Moreover, A was treated with chemicals in the nineteenth century to make it more legible, but these agents had the opposite effect, making it difficult to decipher. An apograph of the text was published by Wilhelm

Studemund in 1890, who lost his eyesight in the process of deciphering the text.

A few details about the layout of A are worth mentioning. The manuscript is written in rustic capital letters. Each page contains nineteen lines. A has preserved metrical, nonacrostic plot summaries for the *Persa*, *Pseudolus*, and *Stichus*. They were certainly not composed by Plautus; rather, they seem to go back to the second century CE, when C. Sulpicius Apollinaris was composing metrical plot summaries for the plays of Terence. A regularly marks the beginning of new scenes. Speakers were indicated by single letters in red ink. These letters were certainly not abbreviations of the speaker's names, since many characters have the same initials. Presumably A had an algebraic notation, so that A, B, Γ, etc. were used for the speakers in order of appearance in the play.[79] The red ink is no longer legible; now all we can see is a gap within a line, and indications of change of speaker at the beginning of lines have been lost entirely. A has the sung passages arranged according to the "Alexandrinian" method of colometry; where A is preserved well, this layout greatly helps us to understand how scholars of the Varronian period analysed Plautine meter, a skill largely lost soon after.

The second manuscript family is the Palatine family, so named because two of its most important manuscripts were once in the library of the Elector Palatine (*Kurfürst der Pfalz*) in Heidelberg. The lost archetype of this family is designated by Π or P^A. From this archetype two copies were made, the Codex Turnebi (T) and the now lost archetype of the remaining manuscripts (P). T was a manuscript

[79] For such notations see Jory 1963.

of the ninth or tenth century used by the French scholar
Adrien de Tournebu in the sixteenth century. The manu-
script no longer exists, but we do have various quotations
by de Tournebu, a full collation of the *Persa* and *Poenulus*,
and partial collations of the *Bacchides*, *Pseudolus*, and
Rudens.[80]

To some extent, later manuscripts allow us to recon-
struct how the archetype must have looked. Like A, it was
presumably written in rustic capitals, but of course its
daughter manuscripts are in the minuscules common in
the Middle Ages. A page of the archetype contained be-
tween nineteen and twenty-one lines; we know this be-
cause occasionally scribes failed to copy a folio, and in such
cases the number of missing lines is fairly consistent. The
archetype contained metrical, acrostic plot summaries for
all the plays and in addition metrical, but nonacrostic plot
summaries for the *Amphitruo*, *Aulularia*, *Mercator*, and
Miles gloriosus. Again these summaries probably go back
to the second century CE. The archetype contained scene
divisions. Speakers were indicated in algebraic notation, of
which traces have survived in the daughter manuscripts,
but later copyists typically changed these Greek letters to
fuller designations.[81] The Palatine archetype followed a
method of line division similar to what we find in A. In the
daughter manuscripts this system was by and large aban-
doned in order to save space, but traces remain.

For ease of copying, P was divided into two halves, but
only two of the daughter manuscripts, B and D, contain
both halves. The first half contained the first eight plays,

80 For a more detailed discussion of T see Lindsay 1898.
81 See Lindsay 1904: 91–92.

excluding the *Bacchides*, in alphabetical order according to the first letter, and the second half contained the remaining plays, also in alphabetical order according to the first letter. Thus P had the *Bacchides* immediately after the *Epidicus*, presumably because in the *Bacchides*, the *Epidicus* is referred to in l. 214, which showed the copyist that the *Epidicus* is a chronologically earlier play. We do not know when the *Bacchides* were placed after the *Epidicus*, but it is clear that they were not always in this position: the beginning of the *Bacchides* is lost, just as the ending of the *Aulularia*; the simplest explanation is that one group of folios was lost in an ancestor of P that still had the plays in a more strictly alphabetical order.

Among the manuscripts of the P family, the Codex uetus Camerarii, abbreviated B, occupies a special place. B is a manuscript of the tenth or early eleventh century, now in the Vatican (shelf-mark Vat. Pal. lat. 1615). It was edited by J. Kammermeister (Camerarius) in the sixteenth century. This manuscript is important for two reasons. First, it has preserved more of the original colometry than the other Palatine manuscripts, and the colometry often agrees with that of the Ambrosian palimpsest, which is of great help for understanding Plautine songs.[82] And second, the quality of the text as such is superior to other Palatine manuscripts. The first half containing eight plays is a copy of a text that is also the basis for the Codex Ursinianus, but B is special because it contains a number of excellent corrections (the writer of these is usually referred to as B[3] in editions). The second half of B, containing the remaining twelve plays, comes from a better source

[82] For details see Questa 1984: 23–78.

than the basis of the Codex Ursinianus; perhaps B is a direct copy of P here.

The Codex Ursinianus referred to just now is abbreviated D. It is a manuscript of the tenth century discovered in Cologne in 1426 by Nicholas of Kues (Cusanus, 1401–64), then owned by Cardinal Orsini (died 1438), and now in the Vatican Library (shelf-mark Vat. lat. 3870). The second half of D contains all twelve plays, but the first half has the text only until the middle of the *Captiui*.

C, called the Codex decurtatus (mutilated codex) because it contains only the twelve plays of the second half in an incomplete state, is a tenth-century manuscript, now in Heidelberg (Pal. lat. 1613). It derives from the same source as D.

For the eight plays constituting the first half of P, we do not have to rely on B and D alone in order to reconstruct the archetype. For these eight plays, B and D go back to the same manuscript, which was a copy of P. Another manuscript derived from that one must have existed, but has been lost. It was the basis for E, V, and another manuscript, again lost, which in turn was the basis for the *Itala recensio* of these eight plays.

E, the Codex Ambrosianus, is a twelfth-century manuscript, now in Milan (shelf-mark Ambros. I. 257 inf.).

V, the Codex Vossianus Leidensis, is a manuscript of the eleventh century, now in Leiden (shelf-mark Voss. Lat. Q. 30). It lacks the *Amphitruo* and *Asinaria* completely, and the beginning of the *Aulularia* and the second half of the *Epidicus* are also missing. V contains a number of corrections (designated V^2) by someone who had access to the same family of manuscripts that J and O belong to.

J and O belong to the so-called *codices minores* of Plautus.[83] J, the Codex Londiniensis, dates to the twelfth century and contains the first eight plays, but it has unfortunately been damaged by damp. It is now in the British Library in London (Royal 15. C. XI). Thomson (1986) was able to identify the scribe as someone from Salisbury with a limited command of Latin. O, the Fragmentum Ottoboniense, contains only a section of the *Captiui* (ll. 400–555). It is now in the Vatican (Ottob. lat. 687) but originated in central France and may be the direct ancestor of J.

Also from France is K, a manuscript now in Paris (Bibl. Nat., lat. 7890). It also contains the first eight plays. Interestingly, J and K often have readings superior to those of the other Palatine manuscripts; there are occasions where J and K agree with A, while the rest of the Palatine tradition is corrupt. Questa 2001 refers to J and K as the *Gallica recensio* and assumes that the superior readings are the conjectural work of a learned French editor; but while medieval scholars have often been underestimated, the quality of some readings is high enough that these manuscripts may actually go back to an independent branch of the Palatine tradition. Interestingly, the *Florilegium Cantabrigense* (thirteenth century, Ca, Cambridge, Gonville and Caius College 225/40[84]) and the lexicographers Osbern of Gloucester (1123–1200) and Hugh of Pisa (died in 1210) preserve Plautine quotations linked to the *Gallica recensio*.[85]

Later manuscripts of Plautus have often been ne-

---

[83] For the term see Chelius 1989.

[84] For a description see Thomson 1974.

[85] For the latter two see Tontini 1992. Despite Chelius'

glected: unfortunately, since the humanist tradition has much to contribute to Plautine scholarship. But all manuscripts produced after the discovery of D reproduced its text for the second half of the plays, or, more precisely, they reproduced the text of an edited form of D called the *Itala recensio* (ς);[86] before the discovery of D, only the first eight plays were available. For the first eight plays there are more than a hundred humanist codices.[87] Only a handful of the most important humanist manuscripts can be mentioned here. S, an Italian manuscript of the fifteenth century, now in Spain (El Escorial, R. Bibl. del Monasterio, T. II. 8), is an important humanist manuscript containing all twenty plays, though not all by the same hand. W, the Codex Vindobonense (Vienna, Österr. Nationalbibl., lat. 3168), is a copy of S, though not a direct one,[88] and the Codex Lipsiensis (F, Leipzig, Universitätsbibl., Repositorium I fol. 5) is an indirect copy of W. Both F and W have now mostly disappeared from critical editions. Other important manuscripts of the humanist period are G and M. G (Vat. lat. 1629) is interesting because it contains corrections by Poggio. M (Florence, Bibl. Medicea Laurenziana, San Marco 230) contains important corrections that anticipate S.

---

claims, the fragment Fo (Foligno, Biblioteca Comunale, 10. 3. 32-XVII) is not connected with the *Gallica recensio* and goes back to the fifteenth century; see Tontini 2000.

[86] For details on this Italian humanist text see Tontini 2002*b*: 71–85.

[87] For a description of those in the Vatican library see Tontini 2002*a*.

[88] For details see Tontini 1996.

Ultimately the Ambrosian palimpsest and the archetype of the Palatine manuscripts go back to the same ancient edition (Ω), perhaps of the second century CE, a time when interest in archaic authors was flourishing. This common ancestry can be seen in a number of shared errors difficult to explain otherwise. The question then arises why sometimes A and the Palatine manuscripts have entirely different lines. Presumably this is a consequence of what ancient scholarly editions were like, with alternative readings deriving from revival performances kept in the margins next to the more ancient variants. Later copyists either copied both variants in the main text or eliminated one, and not necessarily the later version.

Plautus was widely read and quoted in antiquity. Such quotations, while often merely confirming the direct manuscript tradition for the Varronian plays, are sometimes invaluable for restoring their original text. However, it must be said that for instance Nonius Marcellus (fourth century) did not have a Plautus edition that was of the same value as Ω; rather, it is clear from his quotations of the Varronian plays that Ω was not only the source of A and P^A, but also of Nonius' edition.[89] As for plays outside the Varronian canon, quotations by literary authors and grammarians are all we have. The lexicographers Sextus Pompeius Festus (second century CE) and Nonius are particularly rich sources, but by no means the only ones; their often important etymologies are collected in Maltby 1991.

[89] Deufert 2002: 320–29.

Textual Emendation

When we read Plautus in a modern edition, we often fail to realize that any such edition is the work of many generations of scholars, each improving the text or occasionally changing it for the worse. To give just one example of the many improvements that have been made, it is clear to us that Plautus used the classical first-declension genitive in -*ae* but also the older disyllabic form in -*ai*. But while the form in -*ai* occurs in our editions, it is only attested once in the manuscripts, in *Poen.* 51.[90] Elsewhere the manuscripts have -*ae* or various corruptions of -*ai*. Without the work of editors, we would have an unmetrical text.

The first printed edition of Plautus (Venice 1472) was edited by Giorgio Merlani (Merula, c. 1424–94), who based his text on the Codex Ursinianus. The next edition (Milan 1490) was edited by a scholar upset at the loss of so many Roman comic writers, Eusebio Scutario (Scutarius). An edition by Bernardo Saraceno (Saracenus) soon followed (Venice 1499), with a commentary by himself and Giovanni Pietro della Valle (Valla). The following year an edition by Giovanni Battista Pio (Pius, died in 1540) appeared in Milan. There followed an edition by Filippo Beroaldo (Beroaldus, 1453–1505) in Bologna in 1503 and another one by Gianfrancesco Boccardo (Pylades) in Brescia in 1506, one year after the editor's death.

More serious attempts at emendation began with the edition by Joachim Kammermeister (Camerarius, 1500–74), who also used what is now known as the Codex uetus Camerarii and the Codex decurtatus (Basel 1552). His

---

90 See Leo 1912: 342–43.

contemporary Adrien de Tournebou (Turnebus, 1512–65) collated the now lost Codex Turnebi, a manuscript from Sens that was probably destroyed when the Calvinists burnt down the monastery in 1567. Many valuable emendations go back to Denis Lambin (Lambinus, 1520–72), who unfortunately fell ill while emending the thirteenth play; his later comments reveal that he had lost energy and acumen due to his ailments, and his edition appeared posthumously (Paris 1576).

In the next generation we find such scholars as Johan van der Does (Dousa, 1545–1604), who wrote four books of comments and emendations of Plautus. His son, also called Johan van der Does (1571–97), continued his father's work; his own Plautus edition appeared posthumously in Leiden in 1598. Their contemporary Jan Gruyter/Gruytère (Gruterus, 1560–1627) was interested in manuscript readings but appealed to regular Latin usage as the most important authority in emendation; his edition was published in Wittemberg in 1621. Johann Wilhelm (Janus Gulielmus, 1555–84) wrote a book of Plautine emendations. Friedrich Taubmann (1565–1613) edited the entire text of Plautus (Wittemberg 1612), as did his French colleague François Guyet (1575–1655; edition Paris 1658). Another edition of Plautus (Leiden 1645) was that of Marcus Zuerius Boxhorn (1612–53), perhaps better known as one of the precursors of modern Indo-European philology. Many conjectures by Johann Philipp Pareus (1576–1648) are still useful; his edition appeared in Frankfurt in 1610. But perhaps the most brilliant Plautine scholar of that period was Valens Havekenthal (Acidalius, 1567–95), many of whose observations and comments definitively improved the text. Another important editor of

Plautus was Johann Friedrich Gronov (Gronovius, 1611–71), who particularly valued meter as the basis of emendation; his edition was published in Leiden in 1664.

Not much further progress was made until the nineteenth century. Johann Gottfried Jakob Hermann (1772–1848), perhaps the greatest scholar of Plautine meter, ushered in a new era in Plautine studies. Still useful today are the editions by Friedrich Heinrich Bothe (1770–1855; text Berlin 1810) and Karl Eduard Geppert (1811–81; text Berlin 1845). But Plautine scholarship in the nineteenth century is associated most strongly with the name of Friedrich Wilhelm Ritschl (1806–76), who examined the Ambrosian palimpsest and made important contributions to Plautine meter. Ritschl, when working on the palimpsest, was the first to realize that Plautus was not called Marcus (= M.) Accius, but Titus Maccius. He was also the first to see that only the senarii were spoken verse, the rest recitative or song. Ritschl did not manage to edit the entire Plautine corpus, but his groundbreaking work was continued by Georg Goetz (1849–1932) and Friedrich Schoell (1850–1919). A close colleague of Ritschl was Carl Friedrich Wilhelm Alfred Fleckeisen (1820–99), who worked on Plautine language and meter; his edition (Leipzig 1850–51) is incomplete.

The standard editions today are those of Friedrich Leo and Wallace Martin Lindsay. Leo (1851–1914) was an all-round classicist and is generally acknowledged to have been one of the greatest in the field. He edited Plautus for the Teubner series (1895–96). Lindsay (1858–1937) was renowned as a palaeographer and scholar of early Latin meter; he also edited Nonius and Festus, both of whom contain much important material for Plautine scholars.

His Plautus edition is part of the Oxford Classical Texts series (1904–5).

A specific problem of emendation was tackled after these editions: Andreas Thierfelder (1903–86) discussed in more detail and more systematically than his predecessors which lines should be regarded as genuine and which should be treated as interpolated; his work appeared in 1929. Like Leo and Lindsay, Alfred Ernout (1879–1973) edited the entire Plautine corpus for the Budé series (first edition 1932–40). His text, though in places better than those of Leo and Lindsay, is on the whole less good and his critical apparatus not very detailed.

New critical editions of individual plays are still being produced. The most important editor of Plautus today is Cesare Questa, an outstanding expert on Plautine meter and manuscripts. He has edited the *Bacchides* (Urbino 2008) and *Casina* (Urbino 2001), but more importantly, the sung passages of all the plays (Urbino 1995). These are fraught with difficulties, and the critical text by this unrivalled scholar of meter is extremely useful. Questa's pupils are continuing his work and will eventually replace the older critical editions with their Urbino texts.

Work on Plautus is now much easier than in the past, and not just because of improved editions. For instance, the concordance to Plautus published by Lodge between 1924 and 1933 has greatly advanced our ability to produce stylistic and other analyses. New commentaries on individual plays appear regularly.[91] In fact, the amount of scholar-

---

[91] The era of commentaries covering the whole of Plautus is over, but Ussing 1875–86 is still useful.

ship has been such that today Plautus has his own bibliographies.[92] Scholarship on Plautus has not come to an end, and this edition will not be the last one to be produced; but by now a consensus has been reached on many issues, and at least as far as the text of Plautus is concerned, we are unlikely to see any improvements as dramatic as those produced in the nineteenth century.

Spelling Conventions

The spellings found in Plautine manuscripts do not reproduce the spellings Plautus would have used himself.[93] The spelling in the Ambrosian palimpsest on the whole reflects conventions current in Varro's day. Thus the digraph *ei* is used for long *i* regardless of whether this long vowel represents a diphthong or an original long vowel. Plautus would have written *ei* (or perhaps *e*) and *i* respectively, for in his lifetime the diphthong *ei* had not yet been monophthongized or at least not yet merged with long *i*. So Plautus would have said and written *captiuei* or *captiue* (both nominative plural), while the acrostic argument of a later century, preserved in the Palatine manuscripts, has nine lines because it uses the pseudo-archaic spelling *capteiuei*. Varro would still write *seruos* and *quom* instead of *seruus* and *cum*, as is also the case in the palimpsest; it is not clear whether such spellings indicate that the older pronunciation -*uo*- was still in use or whether they were simply used

[92] Fogazza 1976, Hanson 1965–66, Hughes 1975, Lowe 2007, Segal 1980–81.

[93] For a more detailed discussion of changes than can be given here see Redard 1956.

in order to avoid the graphemic sequence -*VV*-. Plautus would render Greek v, ζ, ϕ, θ, χ as *u*, *s* (or *ss* within words), *p*, *t*, *c*, but Varro and the palimpsest already used *y*, *z*, *ph*, *th*, *ch*. Aspirate spellings did not appear before the middle of the second century,[94] and unaspirated pronunciations persisted even longer; Cicero (*orat.* 160) explicitly tells us that they were not used by his predecessors and that he began to use aspirate pronunciations only later in his career. Occasionally the later spellings obscure puns, for example when Chrysalus, called Crusalus by Plautus, says that he will change his name to Crucisalus, one who jumps onto the cross (*Bacch.* 362); but in most cases a more modern presentation of the Plautine text has no ill effects.

The archetype of the Palatine manuscripts seems to have followed the same spelling conventions as the Ambrosian palimpsest, but many of the first-century spellings were modernized further by the copyists. Occasionally, however, the Palatine manuscripts or the Ambrosian palimpsest preserve traces of pre-Varronian spellings. Thus at *Pseud.* 688 the Ambrosian palimpsest has the ancient form *auricalco* instead of *aurichalco*, and at *Trin.* 425 the reading *drahcumarum* found in *C* and *D* points to an earlier *dracumarum*, which a copyist was supposed to modernize but failed to modernize correctly.

An issue where archaic and modern spellings diverge from the classical norm concerns geminate or "long" consonants like -*ll*-. Latin always had geminate consonants in pronunciation, but these were spelled like their simple counterparts in the archaic period. The first geminate

---

94 Biville 1990: 139.

spellings are found toward the end of the third century,[95] yet even in the *Senatus consultum de Bacchanalibus* of 186, we still find *habuise* for *habuisse*. It is unclear whether Plautus used geminate spellings, and if so, whether he did so consistently. In Varro's day such geminates were written consistently, hence spellings like *caussa* and *aiio* (the latter attested for Cicero by Quintilian, *inst.* 1. 4. 11). In the postclassical period, geminates were simplified in pronunciation under certain circumstances, hence the spellings *causa* and *aio*. Copyists confronted with a form like *aiio* were often at a loss. At *Cas.* 71 we find the archaic/postclassical spelling *aio* in A and J, while B has *alio*, and V and E have *alia*, both obviously "corrections" of earlier *aiio*.

The final consonants of prefixes were commonly assimilated to the initial consonant of a word stem in pronunciation, though perhaps not for every prefix.[96] This enables Plautus to pun on *adsum/assum* (I am here) and to treat it as if it were a form of *assus* (roasted) in *Poen.* 279. But whether Plautus wrote *adsum* or *assum* is a different question. Inscriptions of the time use both spellings, and Lucilius 375–76 Marx states that one can write *accurrere* as well as *adcurrere*. It should also be noted that Plautine manuscripts frequently write *obsonium* for *opsonium* (provisions); since the word goes back to Greek ὀψώνιον, the spelling with a *b* is the result of a false etymology involving the Latin prefix *ob-*.

In this edition I use modern (postclassical) spellings, for instance *i* for long *i*, regardless of origin, because that is

95 Meiser 1998: 49.

96 For details see Leumann 1977: 193–95; for an ancient testimony see Quint. *inst.* 1. 7. 7.

what most readers will find familiar. But I have preferred *seruos* and *quom* over their modern forms. No manuscript is entirely consistent and often old and new spellings are found side by side. I have aimed at consistency, even where it meant eliminating old spellings or introducing modern ones. I have also tried to use assimilated spellings consistently, except where it would lead to a confusion between the prefixes *ad-* and *ab-*.

Modernization in manuscripts has also affected archaic morphology. Plautus used both disyllabic *siet* and monosyllabic *sit* (and probably spelled both *siet*), but the manuscripts often have the monosyllabic form where the meter requires two syllables. Similarly, Plautus could use *med* and *ted* alongside *me* and *te*, but manuscripts tend to contain the more modern forms, even where this leads to hiatus in unacceptable places. And Plautus knew a nominative *illic* next to *ille* (that one) and a locative *illi* next to *illic* (there). Much of this variation has been eliminated in the manuscript tradition, where we typically find the nominative *ille* and the locative *illic*, even where such forms are unmetrical. I have not hesitated to introduce more archaic morphology where we are dealing with semantic doublets of which only one will scan. Where scansion is not an issue, I have also used the more archaic morphology if at least one manuscript has preserved it, thus *feruont* as in A in *Pseud.* 840 rather than *feruent* as in the Palatine family, or *faxint* as in A in *Pseud.* 315 rather than *faciant* as in P.

PLAUTUS' INFLUENCE ON
EUROPEAN LITERATURE

Although Terence, being more suitable as a school author than Plautus, was far more widely known than the latter in the Middle Ages, Plautus exerted an enduring influence on European literature. It is impossible to present this Plautine heritage here even in broad strokes; von Reinhardstoettner (1886) gives an excellent overview of imitations and adaptations before the twentieth century, and today the online Archive of Performances of Greek and Roman Drama is even more useful, since it contains current information on performances of ancient plays or adaptations from the Renaissance to the present day. Even today Plautus has lost nothing of his importance. I shall merely mention some of the most striking adaptations here.

A curious piece of work is the *Querolus* (The Moaner), a Latin comedy based on the *Aulularia*. Nothing is known of its author, but since the text is also called *Aulularia*, this play was for a long time attributed to Plautus. It was written in Gaul in the late fourth or early fifth century and not intended for performance on stage. The text is in prose, with certain metrical features. The main character is Querolus, a miser and misanthrope. The Guardian Spirit of the house, who spoke the prologue in Plautus' play, has a bigger role in this late piece; the conversation between him and Querolus is reminiscent of an examination of conscience.

The most famous adaptation of the *Aulularia* is that by Molière (1622–73). His play *L'Avare* (The Miser) has Harpagon as its main character, who is clearly modelled on Plautus' Euclio; but in the French play Harpagon has a son and not a daughter as in Plautus.

The *Amphitruo* has been adapted and translated many times.[97] Luiz Vaz de Camões (1524–80), the greatest

97 For an overview see Shero 1956.

Portuguese writer, is perhaps best known for his epic *Os Lusíadas*, but he also wrote a play based on Plautus' *Amphitruo*, called *Os Enfatriões* (The Amphitruos). One of its entertaining features is that while everyone else speaks Portuguese, the slave Sosia speaks Spanish as an outward sign of his low status.

English readers will probably be most familiar with an adaptation of Plautus' *Menaechmi* written by William Shakespeare, *The Comedy of Errors*. One of the perennial questions arising from this play and other texts is how literally one should take Ben Jonson's claim that Shakespeare knew "small Latine and lesse Greeke." But Baldwin 1944. i: 1–18 has convincingly shown that Jonson wants to say that Shakespeare has greater natural talent than training. He certainly had the traditional grammar school training and read at least some Plautus and Terence in the original.[98]

Plautus continues to inspire modern drama in all its forms. Even musicals are sometimes based on Plautine comedy. A good example is *A Funny Thing Happened on the Way to the Forum*, a Broadway musical based on the *Miles*, *Mostellaria*, and *Pseudolus*, with music and lyrics by Stephen Sondheim and book by Burt Shevelove and Larry Gelbart. The musical has been enduringly successful, and to date there have been hundreds of performances and a film version.

[98] Jones 1977: 91; on Plautine echoes in Shakespeare see Miola 1994.

SELECT BIBLIOGRAPHY

Abel, K. (1955), *Die Plautusprologe* (diss. Frankfurt am Main).

Adams, J. N. (1982), *The Latin Sexual Vocabulary* (London).

——— (1984), "Female speech in Latin comedy," *Antichthon* 18: 43–77.

——— (2003), *Bilingualism and the Latin Language* (Cambridge).

——— (2007), *The Regional Diversification of Latin: 200BC–AD 600* (Cambridge).

Archive of Performances of Greek and Roman Drama, *APGRD Database*, University of Oxford, ed. Amanda Wrigley. Online.

Arnott, W. G. (1975), *Menander, Plautus, Terence* (Oxford).

——— (1979–2000), *Menander: Edited with an English Translation*, 3 vols. (Cambridge, MA).

Bader, B. (1970), *Szenentitel und Szeneneinteilung bei Plautus* (diss. Tübingen).

Bain, D. (1977), *Actors & Audience: A Study of Asides and Related Conventions in Greek Drama* (Oxford).

——— (1979), "*PLAVTVS VORTIT BARBARE*: Plautus, *Bacchides* 526–61 and Menander, *Dis exapaton* 102–12," in West and Woodman (eds.), 17–34.

BIBLIOGRAPHY

Baldwin, T. W. (1944), *William Shakspere's Small Latine and Lesse Greeke*, 2 vols. (Urbana).

Balme, M., and P. G. McC. Brown (2001), *Menander: The Plays and Fragments* (Oxford).

Barsby, J. A. (2001), *Terence*, 2 vols. (Cambridge, MA).

Beare, W. (1964), *The Roman Stage*, 3rd ed. (London).

Bennett, C. E. (1910–14), *Syntax of Early Latin*, 2 vols. (Boston).

Bieber, M. (1961), *The History of the Greek and Roman Theater*, 2nd rev. ed. (Princeton).

Biville, F. (1990), *Les emprunts du latin au grec: approche phonétique*, 2 vols. (Louvain).

Blackman, D. J. (1969), "Plautus and Greek Topography," *Transactions of the American Philological Association* 100: 11–22.

Blänsdorf, J. (1967), *Archaische Gedankengänge in den Komödien des Plautus* (Wiesbaden).

Bonaria, M. (1965), *Romani Mimi* (Rome).

Braun, L. (1970), *Die Cantica des Plautus* (Göttingen).

Brown, P. G. McC. (2002), "Actors and Actor-Managers at Rome in the Time of Plautus and Terence," in P. Easterling and E. Hall (eds.), *Greek and Roman Actors: Aspects of an Ancient Profession* (Cambridge), 225–37.

——— (2004), "Soldiers in New Comedy: Insiders and Outsiders," in *Leeds International Classical Studies* 3. 08.

——— (2006), *Terence: The Comedies* (Oxford).

Ceccarelli, L. (1990), *Due studi di metrica latina arcaica* (Rome).

Chelius, K. H. (1989), *Die Codices minores des Plautus: Forschungen zur Geschichte und Kritik* (Baden-Baden).

Danese, R. (2008), "*Enjambement* e stile in Plauto e Terenzio," in G. C. Baiardi, L. Lomiento, and F. Perusino (eds.), *Enjambement: Teoria e tecniche dagli antichi al Novecento* (Pisa), 127–44.

Daube, D. (1956), *Forms of Roman Legislation* (Oxford).

Daviault, A. (1981), *Comoedia togata: fragments; texte établi, traduit et annoté* (Paris).

de Melo, W. D. C. (2006), "If in Doubt, Leave It in: Subject Accusatives in Plautus and Terence," *Oxford University Working Papers in Linguistics, Philology & Phonetics* 11: 5–20.

——— (2007a), "Zur Sprache der republikanischen *carmina Latina epigraphica*: Satzumfang, Satzkomplexität und Diathesenwahl," in P. Kruschwitz (ed.), *Die metrischen Inschriften der römischen Republik* (Berlin), 97–120.

——— (2007b), *The Early Latin Verb System: Archaic Forms in Plautus, Terence, and Beyond* (Oxford).

——— (2010), "Possessive Pronouns in Plautus," in E. Dickey and A. Chahoud (eds.), *Colloquial and Literary Latin* (Cambridge), 71–99.

Deufert, M. (2002), *Textgeschichte und Rezeption der plautinischen Komödien im Altertum* (Berlin).

——— (2007), "Terenz und die altlateinische Verskunst: Ein Beitrag zur Technik des Enjambements in der Neuen Komödie," in P. Kruschwitz, W.-W. Ehlers, F. Felgentreu (eds.), *Terentius Poeta* (Munich), 51–71.

Dickey, E. (2002), *Latin Forms of Address: From Plautus to Apuleius* (Oxford).

Dover, K. J. (1972), *Aristophanic Comedy* (London).

Duckworth, G. E. (1952), *The Nature of Roman Comedy: A Study in Popular Entertainment* (Princeton).

BIBLIOGRAPHY

Dutsch, D. M. (2008), *Feminine Discourse in Roman Comedy: On Echoes and Voices* (Oxford).

Ernout, A. (1932–40), *Plaute: Comédies*, 7 vols. (Paris).

—— and Meillet (1951), *Dictionnaire étymologique de la langue latine: Histoire des mots*, 3rd ed. (Paris).

Fogazza, D. (1976), "Plauto 1935–1975," *Lustrum* 19: 79–295.

Fraenkel, E. (1957), *Horace* (Oxford).

—— (1961), "Two poems of Catullus," *Journal of Roman Studies* 51: 46–53.

—— (2007), *Plautine Elements in Plautus (Plautinisches im Plautus)*, transl. of the German edition (Berlin 1922) and the Italian addenda (Florence 1960) by T. Drevikovsky and F. Muecke (Oxford).

Frassinetti, P. (1953), *Fabula Atellana: Saggio sul teatro popolare latino* (Genoa).

—— (1967), *Atellanae fabulae* (Rome).

Gerschner, R. (2002), *Die Deklination der Nomina bei Plautus* (Heidelberg).

Gilleland, M. E. (1980), "Female Speech in Greek and Latin," *American Journal of Philology* 101: 180–83.

Gomme, A. W., and F. H. Sandbach (1973), *Menander: A Commentary* (Oxford).

Gratwick, A. S. (1973), "'Titus Maccius Plautus,'" *Classical Quarterly* NS 23: 78–84.

—— (1982), "Drama," in E. J. Kenney and W. V. Clausen (eds.), *The Cambridge History of Classical Literature*, vol. 2: *Latin Literature* (Cambridge), 77–137.

Guardì, T. (1985), *Titinio e Atta: Fabulae togatae; i frammenti: introduzione, testo, traduzione e commento* (Milan).

Gulick, C. B. (1896), "Omens and Augury in Plautus," *Harvard Studies in Classical Philology* 7: 235–47.

Haffter, H. (1934), *Untersuchungen zur altlateinischen Dichtersprache* (Berlin).

Handley, E. W. (1968), *Menander and Plautus: A Study in Comparison; An Inaugural Lecture Delivered at University College London 5 February 1968* (London).

Hanson, J. A. (1965–66), "Scholarship on Plautus since 1950," *Classical World* 59: 103–7, 126–29, 141–48.

Happ, H. (1967), "Die lateinische Umgangssprache und die Kunstsprache des Plautus," *Glotta* 45: 60–104.

Harries, J. (2007), *Law and Crime in the Roman World* (Cambridge).

Henderson, J. (1998–2007), *Aristophanes*, 5 vols. (Cambridge, MΛ).

Hofmann, J. B., and L. Ricottilli (1985), *La lingua d'uso latina*, 2nd ed. (Bologna).

Housman, A. E. (1930), "The Latin for *Ass*," *Classical Quarterly* 24: 11–13.

Hughes, J. D. (1975), *A Bibliography of Scholarship on Plautus* (Amsterdam).

Jachmann, G. (1931), *Plautinisches und Attisches* (Berlin).

Jocelyn, H. D. (1993), review of Zwierlein (1990), *Gnomon* 65: 122–37.

——— (1996), review of Zwierlein (1991), *Gnomon* 68: 402–20.

——— (2000), "The Unpretty Boy of Plautus' *Pseudolus* (767–789)," in E. Stärk and G. Vogt-Spira (eds.), *Dramatische Wäldchen: Festschrift für Eckard Lefèvre zum 65. Geburtstag* (Zürich), 431–60.

——— (2001), "Gods, Cult and Cultic Language in Plautus' *Epidicus*," in U. Auhagen (ed.), Studien zu Plautus' *Epidicus* (Tübingen), 261–96.

Johnston, D. (1999), *Roman Law in Context* (Cambridge).

Jones, E. (1977), *The Origins of Shakespeare* (Oxford).

Jory, E. J. (1963), "'Algebraic' Notation in Dramatic Texts," *Bulletin of the Institute of Classical Studies* 10: 65–78.

——— (1966), "*Dominus gregis?*," *Classical Philology* 61: 102–5.

Kassel, R., and C. Austin (1983–), *Poetae Comici Graeci (PCG)*, 8 vols. (Berlin).

Kauer, R., and W. M. Lindsay (1926), *P. Terenti Afri Comoediae* (Oxford) (repr. with additions by O. Skutsch, 1958).

Knoche, U. (1975), *Roman Satire*, transl. by E. S. Ramage (Bloomington).

Konstan, D. (1983), *Roman Comedy* (Ithaca).

Lefèvre, E. (ed.) (1973), *Die römische Komödie: Plautus und Terenz* (Darmstadt).

Lefèvre, E., E. Stärk, and G. Vogt-Spira (1991), *Plautus barbarus: Sechs Kapitel zur Originalität des Plautus* (Tübingen).

Leo, F. (1895–96), *Plauti Comoediae*, 2 vols. (Berlin).

——— (1912), *Plautinische Forschungen zur Kritik und Geschichte der Komödie*, 2nd ed. (Berlin).

Leumann, M. (1977), *Lateinische Laut- und Formenlehre*, 6th ed. (Munich).

Lilja, S. (1965), *Terms of Abuse in Roman Comedy* (Helsinki).

Lindsay, W. M. (1896), *An Introduction to Latin Textual Emendation Based on the Text of Plautus* (London).

——— (1898), *The Codex Turnebi of Plautus* (Oxford).

——— (1904), *The Ancient Editions of Plautus* (Oxford).

——— (1904–5), *T. Macci Plauti Comoediae*, 2 vols. (Oxford).

——— (1907), *Syntax of Plautus* (Oxford).

——— (1922), *Early Latin Verse* (Oxford).

Lodge, G. (1924–33), *Lexicon Plautinum*, 2 vols. (Stuttgart).

Lowe, J. C. B. (1985), "Cooks in Plautus," *Classical Antiquity* 4: 72–102.

Lowe, N. J. (2007), *Comedy*, Greece & Rome Survey 37 (Cambridge).

Maltby, R. (1991), *A Lexicon of Ancient Latin Etymologies* (Leeds).

Marshall, C. W. (2006), *The Stagecraft and Performance of Roman Comedy* (Cambridge).

Mattingly, H., and E. S. G. Robinson (1935), "Nummus," *American Journal of Philology* 56: 225–31.

Maurach, G. (1964), *Untersuchungen zum Aufbau plautinischer Lieder* (Göttingen).

Meiser, G. (1998), *Historische Laut- und Formenlehre der lateinischen Sprache* (Darmstadt).

Miola, R. S. (1994), *Shakespeare and Classical Comedy: The Influence of Plautus and Terence* (Oxford).

Moore, T. J. (1998), *The Theater of Plautus: Playing to the Audience* (Austin).

——— (2008), "When Did the *tibicen* Play? Meter and Musical Accompaniment in Roman Comedy," *Transactions of the American Philological Association* 138: 3–46.

Moritz, L. A. (1979), *Grain-Mills and Flour in Classical Antiquity* (New York).

Muecke, F. (2005), "Rome's First 'Satirists': Theme and

Genre in Ennius and Lucilius," in K. Freudenburg (ed.), *The Cambridge Companion to Roman Satire* (Cambridge), 33–47.

Nesselrath, H.-G. (1990), *Die attische Mittlere Komödie: Ihre Stellung in der antiken Literaturkritik und Literaturgeschichte* (Berlin).

Norwood, G. (1932), *Plautus and Terence* (London).

Oniga, R. (1988), *I composti nominali latini: Una morfologia generativa* (Bologna).

Otto, A. (1890), *Die Sprichwörter und sprichwörtlichen Redensarten der Römer* (Leipzig; *Nachträge* by R. Häussler, Darmstadt 1968).

Paratore, E. (1957), *Storia del teatro latino* (Milan).

Petersmann, H. (2002–3), "Bedeutung und Gebrauch von lateinisch *fui*: Eine soziolinguistische Analyse," *Die Sprache* 43: 94–103.

Questa, C. (1962), "Plauto diviso in atti prima di G. B. Pio (Codd. Vatt. Latt. 3304 e 2711)," *Rivista di cultura classica e medioevale* 4: 209–30.

———— (1984), *Numeri innumeri: Ricerche sui* cantica *e la tradizione manoscritta di Plauto* (Rome).

———— (1995), *Titi Macci Plauti Cantica* (Urbino).

———— (2001), "Per un'edizione di Plauto," *Giornate Filologiche «Francesco Della Corte» II* (Genoa), 61–83.

———— (2007), *La metrica di Plauto e di Terenzio* (Urbino).

Redard, G. (1956), "Le rajeunissement du texte de Plaute," in *Hommages à Max Niedermann* (Brussels), 296–306.

Ribbeck, O. (ed.) (1871–73), *Scaenicae Romanorum poesis fragmenta*, 2nd ed., 2 vols. (Leipzig).

BIBLIOGRAPHY

Rosivach, V. J. (1970), "Plautine Stage Settings (*Asin.*, *Aul.*, *Men.*, *Trin.*)," *Transactions of the American Philological Association* 101: 445–61.

Russell, D. A. (1979), "*De imitatione*," in West and Woodman (eds.), 1–16.

Sandbach, F. H. (1990), *Menandri reliquiae selectae*, 2nd ed. (Oxford).

Saunders, C. (1911), "The Introduction of Masks on the Roman Stage," *American Journal of Philology* 32: 58–73.

Sedgwick, W. B. (1925), "The *cantica* of Plautus," *Classical Review* 39: 55–58.

——— (1930), "The Dating of Plautus' Plays," *Classical Quarterly* 24: 102–6.

Segal, E. (1980–81), "Scholarship on Plautus since 1965–1976," *Classical World* 74: 353–433.

——— (1987), *Roman Laughter: The Comedy of Plautus*, 2nd ed. (New York).

Shero, L. R. (1956), "Alcmena and Amphitryon in Ancient and Modern Drama," *Transactions of the American Philological Association* 87: 192–238.

Shipp, G. P. (1953), "Greek in Plautus," *Wiener Studien* 66: 105–12.

——— (1955), "Plautine Terms for Greek and Roman Things," *Glotta* 34: 139–52.

——— (1979), *Modern Greek Evidence for the Ancient Greek Vocabulary* (Sidney).

Soubiran, J. (1966), *L'élision dans la poésie latine* (Paris).

——— (1988), *Essai sur la versification dramatique des romains: sénaire iambique et septénaire trochaïque* (Paris).

Spranger, P. P. (1985), *Historische Untersuchungen zu den Sklavenfiguren des Plautus und Terenz*, 2nd ed. (Stuttgart).

Studemund, W. (1890), *T. Macci Plauti Fabularum reliquiae Ambrosianae: Codicis rescripti Ambrosiani apographum* (Berlin).

Tarrant, R. J. (1983), "Plautus," in L. D. Reynolds (ed.), *Texts and Transmission: A Survey of the Latin Classics* (Oxford), 302–7.

Thesleff, H. (1960), *Yes and No in Plautus and Terence* (Helsingfors).

Thierfelder, A. (1929), *De rationibus interpolationum Plautinarum* (Leipzig).

Thomson, R. (1974), "A Thirteenth-Century Plautus Florilegium from Bury St. Edmunds Abbey," *Antichthon* 8: 29–43.

——— (1986), "British Library Royal 15 C. XI: A Manuscript of Plautus' Plays from Salisbury Cathedral (c. 1100)," *Scriptorium* 40: 82–87.

Tontini, A. (1992), "Citazioni plautine in Osberno Uguccione Perotti," in S. Troiani and A. Grilli (eds.), *Studi Umanistici Piceni XII* (Sassoferrato), 243–53.

——— (1996), "Il codice escorialense T. II. 8: un Plauto del Panormita e di altri?," in C. Questa and R. Raffaelli (eds.), *Studi latini in ricordo di Rita Cappelletto* (Urbino), 33–69.

——— (2000), "Tre frammenti di codici plautini," *Scrittura e Civiltà* 24: 283–94.

——— (2002*a*), *Censimento critico dei manoscritti plautini*, vol. 1: *Biblioteca Apostolica Vaticana* (Rome).

——— (2002*b*), "La tradizione manoscritta umanistica di Plauto: novità e problemi," in C. Questa and R. Raffaelli (eds.), *Due seminari plautini: la tradizione del testo; i modelli* (Urbino), 57–88.

Usener, H. (1901), "Italische Volksjustiz," *Rheinisches Museum für Philologie* 51: 1–28.

Ussing, J. L. (1875–86), *T. Macci Plauti Comoediae*, 5 vols. (Copenhagen).

von Reinhardstoettner, K. (1886), *Plautus: Spätere Bearbeitungen plautinischer Lustspiele* (Leipzig).

Watson, A. (1971), *Roman Private Law around 200 BC* (Edinburgh).

Webster, T. B. L. (1974), *An Introduction to Menander* (Manchester).

West, D., and T. Woodman (eds.) (1979), *Creative Imitation and Latin Literature* (Cambridge).

Willi, A. (2003), *The Languages of Aristophanes: Aspects of Linguistic Variation in Classical Attic Greek* (Oxford).

Zagagi, N. (1980), *Tradition and Originality in Plautus: Studies of the Amatory Motifs in Plautine Comedy* (Göttingen).

Zwierlein, O. (1990–92), *Zur Kritik und Exegese des Plautus*, 4 vols. (Stuttgart).

AMPHITRVO,

OR

AMPHITRYON

INTRODUCTORY NOTE

Doubles are not uncommon in Plautine comedy. In the *Bacchides* Plautus presents us with two sisters sharing the same name and profession. In the *Menaechmi* we find twin brothers separated at a young age, again with the same name. Only one fragment of the *Lenones Gemini* (The Twin Pimps) survives, but it is not difficult to imagine the humorous confusion staged in that play.

In the *Amphitruo* we encounter two doubles: Jupiter, king of gods and men, is impersonating Amphitruo in order to have an affair with his wife, Alcumena, and Mercury, Jupiter's divine but also very worldly son, plays Amphitruo's slave Sosia in order to support Jupiter in his affair. Sosia and his impersonator achieved such fame that even today the Italian word for a double is *sosia*.

The plot of the *Amphitruo* is complex. The eponymous hero is leader of the Theban army. While he is abroad fighting against the Teloboians, Jupiter falls in love with his wife, Alcumena, who is already pregnant by Amphitruo. By pretending to be Amphitruo, Jupiter gains access to Alcumena. He tells her of his successful expedition and presents her with the golden bowl from which the Teloboian king used to drink and which was given to Amphitruo in recognition of his valor. The two eat and sleep together, and Alcumena is impregnated a second time.

3

Meanwhile, Mercury is playing Sosia and keeping away potential intruders. The comedy begins when the real Amphitruo and Sosia arrive in Thebes. Amphitruo sends Sosia home to announce his arrival. On his way, Sosia is practicing his battle report, a difficult task since he himself hid in a tent during the action. Nonetheless, his famous speech, which resembles epic more than comedy, is considered accurate by Mercury, who can overhear everything. When Sosia arrives, he finally meets Mercury. Mercury not only prevents him from going inside but also convinces him with arguments and brute force that he, Mercury, is the true Sosia. In a last attempt to hold on to his identity, Sosia states what is almost a comical anticipation of Descartes's *cogito ergo sum*: "but when I think about it, I'm certainly the same person I've always been" (l. 447). Yet in the end Sosia reaches the conclusion that he has been bewitched and lost his own self. Bewildered, he returns to Amphitruo.

By now it should be obvious that the *Amphitruo* is not a typical doubles comedy. In the *Menaechmi*, confusion ends and normality is restored when the twins finally meet. In the *Amphitruo*, confusion begins when Sosia encounters his double and reaches its climax when Amphitruo encounters his. In the *Menaechmi*, the Sicilian brother had always hoped to meet his twin. In the *Amphitruo*, Sosia and Amphitruo had never even expected to have doubles. Moreover, these doubles are trying to take away the identities of the real Sosia and Amphitruo.

When Sosia sees Amphitruo he reports what has happened. Naturally, Amphitruo thinks that Sosia is trying to make a fool of him. While the two are approaching Amphitruo's house, Alcumena says goodbye to Jupiter and

Mercury, who claim that they need to return to the army. Alcumena reflects on her loneliness and the value of bravery and then sees her real husband with his slave. She feels ridiculed and addresses them harshly. Amphitruo feels that he has been treated unjustly and demands an explanation. When he hears how Alcumena spent the last night, he believes that she has cheated on him. Alcumena cannot understand what wrong she did and why Amphitruo is denying having spent the night with her. In order to prove that she is not inventing things, she has the Teloboian king's bowl brought out. Amphitruo had this bowl in a sealed box, and when that box turns out to be empty, he is astonished. He leaves in order to find Naucrates, a relative of Alcumena's, to prove to her that he spent the night on his ship.

Alcumena is so upset that she wants a divorce. Jupiter returns and apologizes so that he can enjoy her body again. Alcumena quickly forgives her husband. Jupiter then sends the real Sosia away to find Blepharo, the captain of Amphitruo's ship.

Now Amphitruo returns, without Naucrates, whom he could not find. The door is locked and Amphitruo cannot get in. On the rooftop he sees Mercury, whom he believes to be Sosia. Mercury is rude and refuses to let him in.

At this point some pages in the archetype of the Palatine manuscripts are missing (the Ambrosian palimpsest is not available for this play). The lacuna can to some extent be filled with quotations by grammarians. Most editors arrange them more or less like Schroeder, who discusses them extensively. We can assume that the argument between Mercury and Amphitruo continues for some time until Alcumena comes out. Amphitruo renews his accusations. Alcumena, who believes that she had made peace with him, gets angry. Now the real Sosia arrives with Blepharo. Amphitruo is upset about the treatment he was given by Mercury and verbally attacks the slave. Jupiter appears on stage, and he and Amphitruo try to detain each other. Blepharo cannot decide who the real Amphitruo is and leaves.

Here our manuscripts continue. Jupiter goes inside because Alcumena is about to give birth. Amphitruo is at the height of his anger when suddenly there is loud thunder, a sign of Jupiter's presence. Amphitruo collapses. His maid Bromia leaves the house and tells him that Alcumena has given birth to twins. She convinces him that Alcumena is innocent because the other Amphitruo is Jupiter himself. Amphitruo wants to consult the seer Tiresias about what he should do now, but Jupiter himself appears and reveals what has happened. He promises Amphitruo future glory on account of Hercules, the twin begotten by Jupiter. Amphitruo is happy with this turn of events.

The *Amphitruo* is Plautus' only extant comedy covering a mythological theme. In what is left of Greek New Comedy, there is nothing comparable. But the theme of Amphitryon and Alcmene was a common one. In the fifth century it is covered by Sophocles in tragedy and by Archippus and Platon in comedy, and probably also by Aeschylus, Ion of Chios, and Euripides. In the fourth century the theme has lost nothing of its popularity and occurs in Astydamas and Dionysius of Syracuse. In the west the topic became popular in Rhinthon's phylax plays and was also dealt with in Latin by Accius. Thus some scholars believe that Plautus may have reworked an earlier piece, either from Middle Comedy or a burlesque from the Greek-speaking south of Italy, while others, for instance Lefèvre and Stärk, believe that Plautus may have worked directly on a tragedy, perhaps Euripides' *Alcmene*. This latter hypothesis is particularly attractive, because if one leaves out those parts which appear to be Plautine additions rather than translated from a Greek source, no humor remains. Given how little is left of New Comedy, however, it seems best not to be too dogmatic on these issues, especially since all the other Plautine plays we have are based on New Comedy.

It should be noted that there are some obvious inconsistencies in the play. The most important of these concern the times of various events. Jupiter is said to have slept with Alcumena three months after Amphitruo impregnated her, which is just before Amphitruo returns. Jupiter is also present the night before Alcumena gives birth seven months later, and again we are told that this is when Amphitruo returns. Of course one would not imagine Plautus' audience to calculate exactly when everything happened, but this inconsistency is so striking that it cannot go unnoticed. It could be explained—but this is only one of many possible explanations—by assuming that the first four acts are based on a tragedy in which Jupiter slept with Alcumena but was not present when she gave birth. The fifth act, in which Alcumena gives birth and which is clearly a parody of tragedy, would then be a purely Plautine addition.

We do not know exactly when the *Amphitruo* was first put on stage. The large amount of sung verse points to a later date in Plautus' career. In l. 703 Alcumena is described as a Bacchant, which has led several scholars to believe that the play was written around the same time as the

Senatus consultum de Bacchanalibus (186). However, not too much should be made of such a fleeting reference. There is mention of another play in ll. 91–92. This play, which unfortunately remains unnamed, was performed the year before the *Amphitruo*, and Jupiter played a part in it. The next line says, "What is more, he certainly appears in tragedy," a verse deleted by many editors because it appears pointless after what precedes. However, the line would have a point if the play referred to were not a tragedy. It has been argued by Arcellaschi that this other play was Ennius' *Ambracia*, a *fabula praetexta* rather than a tragedy. If this is correct, the *Amphitruo* was first performed in 187, because Fulvius Nobilior was on his military expedition in 189, and Ennius finished his laudatory composition the year after. Whether or not we believe in Arcellaschi's theory, the *Amphitruo* is certainly a late creation, and it is reasonably safe to say that it was composed between 190 and 185.

SELECT BIBLIOGRAPHY

Editions and Commentaries

Christenson, D. M. (2000), *Plautus: Amphitruo* (Cambridge).

Oniga, R. (1991), *Tito Maccio Plauto: Anfitrione* (with an introduction by M. Bettini) (Venice).

Paratore, E. (1959), *Plauto: Amphitruo (Anfitrione), testo latino con traduzione a fronte* (Florence).

Criticism

Arcellaschi, André (1982), "*Amphitryon* 187, ou: influences pythagoriciennes sur l'*Amphitryon* de Plaute," *Revue des Études Latines* 60: 128–38.

Lefèvre, E. (1982), *Maccus vortit barbare: vom tragischen Amphitryon zum tragikomischen Amphitruo* (Wiesbaden).

Oniga, R. (1985), "Il canticum di Sosia: forme stilistiche e modelli culturali," *Materiali e discussioni per l'analisi dei testi classici* 14: 113–208.

Raffaelli, R., and A. Tontini (eds.) (1998), *Lecturae Plautinae Sarsinates I: Amphitruo (Sarsina, 13 settembre 1997)* (Urbino).

Schroeder, J. (1891), "De fragmentis Amphitruonis Plautinae" (diss.), in W. Studemund (ed.), *Studien auf dem Gebiete des archaischen Lateins* (vol. 2, Berlin), 1–46.

Stärk, E. (1982), "Die Geschichte des Amphitryonstoffes vor Plautus," *Rheinisches Museum für Philologie* NS 125: 275–303.

AMPHITRVO

ARGVMENTVM I

In faciem uersus Amphitruonis Iuppiter,
dum bellum gereret cum Telobois hostibus,
Alcmenam uxorem cepit usurariam.
Mercurius formam Sosiae serui gerit
5 apsentis; his Alcmena decipitur dolis.
postquam rediere ueri Amphitruo et Sosia,
uterque deluduntur [dolis] in mirum modum.
hinc iurgium, tumultus uxori et uiro,
donec cum tonitru uoce missa ex aethere
10 adulterum se Iuppiter confessus est.

ARGVMENTVM II

Amore captus Alcumenas Iuppiter
Mutauit sese in formam eius coniugis,
Pro patria Amphitruo dum decernit cum hostibus.
Habitu Mercurius ei subseruit Sosiae.
5 Is aduenientis seruom ac dominum frustra habet.
Turbas uxori ciet Amphitruo atque in uicem
Raptant pro moechis. Blepharo captus arbiter
Vter sit non quit Amphitruo decernere.
Omnem rem noscunt. geminos illa enititur.

AMPHITRYON

PLOT SUMMARY 1

While Amphitruo was waging war against the Teloboians, Jupiter assumed his appearance and took a loan of his wife, Alcumena. Mercury takes on the form of his absent slave, Sosia. Alcumena is deceived by these tricks. After the real Amphitruo 6 and Sosia have returned, they are both made fun of in a fantastic fashion. This leads to a quarrel between husband and wife, until Jupiter sends his voice from the skies, accompanied by a peal of thunder, and confesses to having been the adulterer. 10

PLOT SUMMARY 2

Jupiter fell in love with Alcumena and changed his form into that of her husband, while he, Amphitruo, was fighting with the enemy in defense of his country. Mercury, in the guise of Sosia, acts as Jupiter's servant. He deceives master and slave on their 5 return. Amphitruo gives his wife a hard time, and he and Jupiter seize each as adulterers. Blepharo is called on as judge but cannot decide which one is Amphitruo. Amphitruo and Alcumena learn the whole truth. She gives birth to twin sons.

---

arg. 1. 7 dolis *del.* ς
arg. 2. 9 Alcumena *P*, illa *Bothe*

PERSONAE

MERCVRIVS deus
SOSIA seruos
IVPPITER deus
ALCVMENA matrona
AMPHITRVO dux
BLEPHARO gubernator
BROMIA ancilla

SCAENA

Thebis

AMPHITRYON

CHARACTERS

MERCURY a god; in a slave's outfit
SOSIA a slave; serves Amphitruo
JUPITER a god; in a general's outfit
ALCUMENA a married woman; pregnant
AMPHITRUO a general; Alcumena's husband
BLEPHARO a captain; Amphitruo's friend
BROMIA a slave-girl; works for Amphitruo and his wife

STAGING

The stage represents a street in Thebes. In the middle we can
see Amphitruo's house. To the left, the street leads to the har-
bor; to the right, to the city center.

PROLOGVS

MER   ut uos in uostris uoltis mercimoniis
      emundis uendundisque me laetum lucris
      afficere atque adiuuare in rebus omnibus,
      et ut res rationesque uostrorum omnium
5   bene expedire uoltis peregrique et domi,
      bonoque atque amplo auctare perpetuo lucro
      quasque incepistis res quasque inceptabitis,
      et uti bonis uos uostrosque omnis nuntiis
      me afficere uoltis, ea afferam, ea ut nuntiem
10   quae maxume in rem uostram communem sient
      (nam uos quidem id iam scitis concessum et datum
      mi esse ab dis aliis, nuntiis praesim et lucro):
      haec ut me uoltis approbare, annitier
      lucrum ut perenne uobis semper suppetat,
15   ita huic facietis fabulae silentium
      itaque aequi et iusti hic eritis omnes arbitri.
      nunc quoius iussu uenio et quam ob rem uenerim
      dicam simulque ipse eloquar nomen meum.
      Iouis iussu uenio; nomen Mercurio est mihi.
20   pater huc me misit ad uos oratum meus;
      tam etsi pro imperio uobis quod dictum foret
      scibat facturos, quippe qui intellexerat
      uereri uos se et metuere, ita ut aequom est Iouem;
      uerum profecto hoc petere me precario
25   a uobis iussit leniter dictis bonis.
      etenim ille quoius huc iussu uenio, Iuppiter

PROLOGUE

Enter MERCURY, *dressed as a slave, wearing a hat with little wings.*

MER As you wish me to give you rich gain in the buying and selling of goods and to support you in everything, and as you wish me to advance the business matters and speculations of all of you abroad and at home and to prosper with good and large profit for ever what you have begun and what you will begin; and as you wish me to bring you and all your family members good news and to bring and announce what's most profitable for your common good (for you already know that I was put in charge of messages and profit by the other gods); as you want me to bless you in these matters and to try my best so that you always have constant profit, you will keep silence during this play and you will all be fair and just judges. Now I'll tell you on whose command and for what reason I've come, and at the same time I'll tell you my name. I've come on Jupiter's command. My name is Mercury. My father's sent me here to plead with you. He did know that you were going to do what you were told by way of command, since he realized that you revere and fear him, as one should Jupiter; still, he's told me to ask you for this by way of entreaty, mildly, with kind words. Well, that Jupiter[1] on whose command I'm coming here is no less

6

11

15

20

26

---

[1] I.e., the actor, not the god.

non minus quam uostrum quiuis formidat malum:
humana matre natus, humano patre
mirari non est aequom sibi si praetimet;
30 atque ego quoque etiam, qui Iouis sum filius,
contagione mei patris metuo malum.
propterea pace aduenio et pacem ad uos fero:
iustam rem et facilem esse oratam a uobis uolo,
nam iustae ab iustis iustus sum orator datus.
35 nam iniusta ab iustis impetrari non decet,
iusta autem ab iniustis petere insipientia est;
quippe illi iniqui ius ignorant nec tenent.
nunc iam huc animum omnes quae loquar aduortite.
debetis uelle quae uelimus: meruimus
40 et ego et pater de uobis et re publica;
nam quid ego memorem (ut alios in tragoediis
uidi, Neptunum, Virtutem, Victoriam,
Martem, Bellonam commemorare quae bona
uobis fecissent) quis benefactis meus pater,
45 deorum regnator, architectust omnibus?
sed mos numquam ⟨ille⟩ illi fuit patri meo
ut exprobraret quod bonis faceret boni;
gratum arbitratur esse id a uobis sibi
meritoque uobis bona se facere quae facit.
50 nunc quam rem oratum huc ueni primum proloquar;
post argumentum huius eloquar tragoediae.
quid? contraxistis frontem quia tragoediam
dixi futuram hanc? deus sum, commutauero.
eandem hanc, si uoltis, faciam ⟨iam⟩ ex tragoedia
55 comoedia ut sit omnibus isdem uorsibus.

46 ille *add. Ussing*   49 fecit *P,* facit *edd.*
54 iam *add. Lachmann*   55 omni[bu]s *Mueller*

16

afraid of a thrashing than any of you. He's born of a human mother and a human father; so it wouldn't be fair to be surprised if he's afraid for himself. And I too, who am Jupiter's son, have caught the fear of a thrashing from my father. Therefore I'm coming in peace and bringing peace to you. I want to ask you for a just and small favor: I was appointed as a just pleader pleading with the just for a just cause. For it wouldn't be right to obtain what's unjust from the just; but it would be stupidity to demand what's just from the unjust since those who are unjust don't know or keep justice. Now, all of you, pay attention to what I'm saying. *You* must wish for what *we* wish for. We, my father and I, have acquired a claim to your gratitude and that of the state. Well, why should I mention— as I've seen other deities mention in tragedies what good things they'd done for you, namely Neptune, Courage, Victory, Mars, and Bellona[2]—well, why should I mention the good deeds my father, the king of gods, has devised for all of you? But my father never had the habit of casting in good people's teeth what good turns he's doing them. He believes that you're grateful to him for that and that you deserve that he should do you the good turns he's doing you. Now I'll first tell you what I've come here to ask you for; then I'll tell you the plot of this tragedy. (*looks at people in the audience*) What? You're frowning because I said this was going to be a tragedy? I'm a god, I'll change it. If you want, I'll immediately turn this same play from a tragedy into a comedy with all the same

30

35

41

46

50

---

[2] Neptune is the sea god; Mars and Bellona are the god and goddess of war.

utrum sit an non uoltis? sed ego stultior,
quasi nesciam uos uelle, qui diuos siem.
teneo quid animi uostri super hac re siet:
faciam ut commixta sit; ⟨sit⟩ tragico[co]moedia;
nam me perpetuo facere ut sit comoedia,
reges quo ueniant et di, non par arbitror.
quid igitur? quoniam hic seruos quoque partis habet,
faciam sit, proinde ut dixi, tragico[co]moedia.
nunc hoc me orare a uobis iussit Iuppiter
ut conquistores singula in subsellia
eant per totam caueam spectatoribus,
si quoi fauitores delegatos uiderint,
ut is in cauea pignus capiantur togae;
†siue qui† ambissint palmam ⟨his⟩ histrionibus
seu quoiquam artifici (seu per scriptas litteras
seu qui ipse ambissit seu per internuntium),
siue adeo aediles perfidiose quoi duint,
sirempse legem iussit esse Iuppiter,
quasi magistratum sibi alteriue ambiuerit.
uirtute dixit uos uictores uiuere,
non ambitione nec perfidia: qui minus
eadem histrioni sit lex quae summo uiro?
uirtute ambire oportet, non fauitoribus.
sat habet fauitorum semper qui recte facit,
si illis fides est quibus est ea res in manu.
hoc quoque etiam mihi in mandatis ⟨is⟩ dedit

60

65

70

75

80

59 sit *add. Leo* tragicocomoedia *P*, tragicomoedia *edd.*
63 tragicocomoedia *P*, tragicomoedia *Pareus*
69 *uersus corruptus* ambissent *P*, ambissint *edd.* his *add. Lindsay*
71 ambisset *P*, ambissit *edd.*
81 is *add. Lindsay*

verses. Do you want it to be one or not? But I'm being 56
silly, as if I didn't know that you want it; after all, I'm a
god. I know what your feelings in this matter are: I'll
make sure it's a mixed play; it'll be a tragicomedy. Well, I 60
don't think it would be appropriate to turn completely
into a comedy a play where kings and gods come on stage.
What then? Since a slave has a role here as well, I'll make
it, as I said, a tragicomedy. Now Jupiter has told me to ask 64
you for this favor:[3] inspectors should go to each and every
seat, to the spectators throughout the entire theatre; if
they see any claqueurs appointed for anyone, their togas
should be taken as security[4] in the theatre; or if any peo- 69
ple should try to canvass the palm for these actors or any
artist, through letters written, or if anyone should can-
vass himself, or through an intermediary, or for that mat-
ter, if the aediles[5] should give it to anyone unfairly, Jupi-
ter has decreed that the same law should apply as if he'd
canvassed for an office for himself or another party. He 75
said that you live as winners on account of your capability,
not of canvassing or unfair behavior. Why shouldn't the
same law apply to an actor as to a man of high rank? One
ought to canvass through one's capability, not through
claqueurs. A man who always acts correctly has enough
supporters, if those can be trusted in whose hands this is.
Among his instructions Jupiter also gave me the follow- 81

[3] What follows is a parody of a law against corrupt practices, such as
the *lex Poetelia* of 358.

[4] A reference to the *pignoris capio*: a pledge is taken until an obliga-
tion is fulfilled.

[5] The magistrates supervising games, but also buildings and mar-
kets.

ut conquistores fierent histrionibus:
qui sibi mandasset delegati ut plauderent
quiu' quo placeret alter fecisset minus,
85   eius ornamenta et corium uti conciderent.
mirari nolim uos quapropter Iuppiter
nunc histriones curet; ne miremini:
ipse hanc acturust Iuppiter comoediam.
quid? ammirati estis? quasi uero nouom
90   nunc proferatur Iouem facere histrioniam;
etiam, histriones anno quom in proscaenio hic
Iouem inuocarunt, uenit, auxilio is fuit.
praeterea certo prodit in tragoedia.
hanc fabulam, inquam, hic Iuppiter hodie ipse aget
95   et ego una cum illo. nunc ⟨uos⟩ animum aduortite,
dum huius argumentum eloquar comoediae.
haec urbs est Thebae. in illisce habitat aedibus
Amphitruo, natus Argis ex Argo patre,
quicum Alcumena est nupta, Electri filia.
100   is nunc Amphitruo praefectust legionibus,
nam cum Telobois bellum est Thebano poplo.
is prius quam hinc abiit ipsemet in exercitum,
grauidam Alcumenam fecit uxorem suam.
nam ego uos nouisse credo iam ut sit pater meus,
105   quam liber harum rerum multarum siet
quantusque amator sit quod complacitum est semel.
is amare occepit Alcumenam clam uirum
usuramque eius corporis cepit sibi,
et grauidam fecit is eam compressu suo.
110   nunc de Alcumena ut rem teneatis rectius,
utrimque est grauida, et ex uiro et ex summo Ioue.

89 admirati⟨n⟩ *Lindsay*   95 uos *add. Pylades*

ing: inspectors should be appointed for the actors; should
anyone have given instructions that claqueurs should ap-
plaud him, or should anyone have caused another to be
unsuccessful, they should beat his costume and his skin
to pieces. I wouldn't want you to be surprised that Jupiter   86
cares about actors now. Don't be surprised: Jupiter him-
self is going to act a part in this comedy. What? You *are*
surprised? As if something new were brought on now,
Jupiter taking up the dramatic art. Last year, when the   91
actors called upon Jupiter here on stage, he also came
and brought them help. What's more, he certainly ap-
pears in tragedy. This play, then, Jupiter will act himself   94
here today, and I together with him. Now pay attention
while I'm telling you the plot of this comedy. This city is
Thebes. In that house there (*points*) lives Amphitruo,
born in Argos of an Argive[6] father. His wife is Alcumena,
daughter of Electrus. This Amphitruo is now in com-   100
mand of the legions because the Theban people is at war
with the Teloboians.[7] Before he himself went away to the
army, he made his wife Alcumena pregnant. Well, I be-   104
lieve you already know what my father's like, how liberal
he is in many things of this sort, and what a great lover he
is of anything that's taken his fancy. He fell in love with
Alcumena behind her husband's back, enjoyed her body,
and made her pregnant through his embrace. Now you   110
should understand this about Alcumena quite clearly:
she's pregnant from both, from her husband and from

[6] I am following Nonius' interpretation here, who regards *Argus* as a
by-form of *Argiuos* (p. 783 Lindsay).

[7] The Teloboians, or Teleboians, are a mythical people on Taphos
(Plin. *nat. hist.* 4. 53).

21

et meus pater nunc intus hic cum illa cubat,
et haec ob eam rem nox est facta longior,
dum ‹cum› illa quacum uolt uoluptatem capit;
115   sed ita assimulauit se, quasi Amphitruo siet.
nunc ne hunc ornatum uos meum ammiremini,
quod ego huc processi sic cum seruili schema:
ueterem atque antiquam rem nouam ad uos proferam,
propterea ornatus in nouom incessi modum.
120   nam meus pater intus nunc est eccum Iuppiter;
in Amphitruonis uortit sese imaginem
omnesque eum esse censent serui qui uident:
ita uorsipellem se facit quando lubet.
ego serui sumpsi Sosiae mi imaginem,
125   qui cum Amphitruone abiit hinc in exercitum,
ut praeseruire amanti meo possem patri
atque ut ne qui essem familiares quaererent,
uorsari crebro hic quom uiderent me domi;
nunc, quom esse credent seruom et conseruom suom,
130   hau quisquam quaeret qui siem aut quid uenerim.
pater nunc intus suo animo morem gerit:
cubat complexus quoius cupiens maxume est;
quae illi ad legionem facta sunt memorat pater
meus Alcumenae: illa illum censet uirum
135   suom esse, quae cum moecho est. ibi nunc meus pater
memorat legiones hostium ut fugauerit,
quo pacto sit donis donatus plurumis.
ea dona quae illic Amphitruoni sunt data
apstulimus: facile meus pater quod uolt facit.
140   nunc hodie Amphitruo ueniet huc ab exercitu
et seruos, quoius ego hanc fero imaginem.
nunc internosse ut nos possitis facilius,
ego has habebo usque in petaso pinnulas;

great Jupiter. And my father's now lying with her inside
the house, and for that very reason this night's been made
longer, while he's enjoying himself with the one he wants.
But he's pretending to be Amphitruo. Now don't be sur-   115
prised about this outfit of mine, since I've come here like
this in slave's dress: I'll bring to you an old and ancient
tale anew, hence I've come here clothed in a new way.
Well, you see, my father Jupiter is inside now, he's turned   120
himself into Amphitruo's image, and all the slaves who
see him believe that he's the real thing. He changes ap-
pearances like that whenever he wants. I've taken on the
slave Sosia's image, who went away to the army with   125
Amphitruo, so that I can be in attendance on my father
during his love affair and so that the family servants won't
ask who I am when they see me spend a great deal of time
here in the house. Now when they believe that I'm a
slave, their fellow slave in fact, no one will ask me who I
am or what I've come for. My father's now enjoying him-   131
self inside. He's lying there, embracing the woman he de-
sires most. My father's telling Alcumena what he did dur-
ing the campaign. She believes he's her husband, while   135
she is with an adulterer. In there my father's now telling
how he put the enemy's legions to flight and how he
was presented with a great many gifts. We took away the
gifts Amphitruo was given there: my father does what he
wants with ease. Now today Amphitruo will come here   140
from the army, and also his slave, whose likeness I bear.
Now in order that you can tell us apart more easily, I'll
have these little wings here on my hat throughout. And   144

---

114 cum *add. Lindemann*

tum meo patri autem torulus inerit aureus
145   sub petaso: id signum Amphitruoni non erit.
ea signa nemo horum familiarium
uidere poterit: uerum uos uidebitis.
sed Amphitruonis illi[c] est seruos Sosia:
a portu illic nunc ⟨huc⟩ cum lanterna aduenit.
150   abigam iam ego illum aduenientem ab aedibus.
adeste: erit operae pretium hic ⟨in⟩spectantibus
Iouem et Mercurium facere ⟨hic⟩ histrioniam.

ACTVS I

I. i: SOSIA. MERCVRIVS

SOS qui me alter est audacior homo aut qui confidentior,
iuuentutis mores qui sciam, qui hoc noctis solus ambu-
lem?
155   quid faciam nunc si tresuiri me in carcerem compege-
rint?
ind' cras quasi e promptaria cella depromar ad flagrum,
nec causam liceat dicere mi, neque in ero quicquam
auxili
siet, nec quisquam sit quin me omnes esse dignum depu-
tent.
159   ita quasi incudem me miserum homines octo ualidi cae-
–60   dant:
ita peregre adueniens
hospitio puplicitus accipiar.
haec eri immodestia coegit me,

148 illic *P*, illi *Lindsay*   149 huc *add. Camerarius*
151 spectantibus *P*, inspectantibus *scripsi* (*cf. 998*)
152 hic *add. Hermann ex 151 ubi* hic *deleuit*

my father will have a golden ribbon under his hat; Amphitruo won't have this mark. No one of the household here will be able to see these marks, yet you will see them. (*looks down the street*) But there is Amphitruo's slave Sosia; he's coming here from the harbor with a lantern now. This instant I'll drive him away from the house, 150 as soon as he gets here. Pay attention: it'll be worthwhile for you to see Jupiter and Mercury take up the histrionic art.

ACT ONE

SOSIA enters from the left, holding a lantern; he does not see MERCURY, who is standing in front of the house.

SOS   Who is braver or bolder than me? I know the ways of young people and still I'm walking around alone at this time of night. What would I do now if the Board of 155 Three[8] were to put me into prison? From there I'd be taken out for a flogging tomorrow, just like from a store room. I wouldn't be allowed to defend myself; there wouldn't be any help from my master and there wouldn't be anyone who didn't think that I fully deserved it. Eight 160 strong men[9] would hit me, a poor wretch, just like an anvil. So on my arrival from abroad I'd get a state reception. My master's lack of restraint has forced me into it. He

[8] The *tresuiri capitales*, magistrates responsible for maintaining order in the city; they supervised prisons and are responsible for executions.

[9] The lictors accompanying officials.

164		qui hoc noctis a portu
164a		ingratiis excitauit.
165		nonne idem huc luci me mittere potuit?
		opulento homini hoc seruitus dura est,
		hoc magis miser est diuitis seruos:
		noctesque diesque assiduo satis superque est
		quod facto aut dicto adeo est opus, quietus ne sis.
170		ips' dominus diues operis, [et] laboris expers,
		quodquomque homini accidit lubere, posse retur:
		aequom esse putat, non reputat laboris quid sit,
		neque aequom anne iniquom imperet cogitabit.
		ergo in seruitute expetunt multa iniqua:
175		habendum et ferundum hoc onust cum labore.
	MER	satiust me queri illo modo seruitutem:
		hodie qui fuerim liber,
		eum nunc potiuit pater seruitutis;
		hic qui uerna natust queritur.
180	SOS	sum uero uerna uerbero: numero mihi in mentem fuit
		dis aduenientem gratias pro meritis agere atque alloqui?
		ne illi edepol si merito meo referre studeant gratiam,
		aliquem hominem allegent qui mihi aduenienti os occil-
		let probe,
		quoniam bene quae in me fecerunt ingrata ea habui
		atque irrita.
185	MER	facit ille quod uolgo hau solent, ut quid se sit dignum
		sciat.
	SOS	quod numquam opinatus fui neque alius quisquam
		ciuium
		sibi euenturum, id contigit, ut salui poteremur domi.
		uictores uictis hostibus legiones reueniunt domum,

routed me out of the harbor against my will at this time of
night. Couldn't he have sent me here by daylight? This is   165
why being a wealthy man's slave is hard, this is why a rich
man's slave is worse off: night and day there's always
more than enough that needs to be done or said, so that
you can't rest. The rich master himself is without work or   170
toil. He believes that anything he takes a fancy to is possi-
ble. He thinks it's fair, he doesn't consider how much
hard work it is, and he won't consider whether what he
orders is fair or unfair. Well then, many unfair things hap-
pen when you're a slave. You must take up and bear this   175
wearisome burden.

MER (*aside*) I am the one who should complain like that about
being a slave: even though I was free this very day, my fa-
ther enslaved me; *he* is complaining, and he was born a
slave!

SOS I really am a slave fit for a beating: when I arrived, it   180
didn't occur to me too quickly to thank the gods for their
good turns and to address them, did it? Seriously, if they
were keen to thank me for my good turns, they'd send
somebody to smash up my face properly on my arrival,
since I felt no gratitude for the good they did me and
didn't appreciate it.

MER (*aside*) That man does what people don't normally do: he   185
knows what he deserves.

SOS What neither I nor anyone else of our citizens ever be-
lieved would happen to us has taken place: we've reached
home safely. The enemy's been conquered and our le
gions return home as conquerors, now that a mighty war's

---

169 adest *P*, adeost *Lachmann*   170 et *del. Havet*
187 domi *Nonius*, domum *P*

duello exstincto maxumo atque internecatis hostibus.
190 quod multa Thebano poplo acerba obiecit funera,
id ui et uirtute militum uictum atque expugnatum oppi-
    dum est
imperio atque auspicio mei eri Amphitruonis maxume.
praedaque agroque adoriaque affecit popularis suos
regique Thebano Creoni regnum stabiliuit suom.
195 me a portu praemisit domum ut haec nuntiem uxori suae,
ut gesserit rem publicam ductu, imperio, auspicio suo.
ea nunc meditabor quo modo illi dicam, quom illo adue-
    nero.
si dixero mendacium . . . solens meo more fecero.
nam quom pugnabant maxume, ego tum fugiebam
    maxume;
200 uerum quasi affuerim tamen simulabo atque audita elo-
    quar.
sed quo modo et uerbis quibus me deceat fabularier,
prius ipse mecum etiam uolo hic meditari. sic hoc pro-
    loquar.
principio ut illo aduenimus, ubi primum terram tetigi-
    mus,
continuo Amphitruo delegit uiros primorum principes;
205 eos legat, Telobois iubet sententiam ut dicant suam:
si sine ui et sine bello uelint rapta et raptores tradere,
si quae asportassent reddere, se exercitum extemplo do-
    mum
redducturum, abituros agro Argiuos, pacem atque otium
dare illis; sin aliter sient animati nec dent quae petat,

192 eri mei *P, transp. Fleckeisen*
193 praeda atque agro *P,* praedaque agroque *Lindsay*
207 redderent *BDEVJO,* reddere *B2*

28

been brought to an end and the enemy's been extermi-
nated. The city that has inflicted many an untimely death   190
on the Theban people has been conquered and crushed
through the strength and courage of our soldiers, and
chiefly under the command and auspices of my master
Amphitruo. He's enriched his countrymen with booty,
land, and fame and has secured the kingship for the
Theban king, Creon. As for me, he's sent me ahead home   195
from the harbor so that I could report to his wife how he
managed affairs of state through his leadership, com-
mand, and authority. I'll now think over how I'm going to
speak to her when I get there. If I tell a lie . . . I'll be acting
in my usual way, in keeping with my custom: when they
were fighting most intensely, I was running away most in-
tensely. Anyway, I'll pretend that I was there and I'll tell   200
what I've heard. But first I want to rehearse here by my-
self in what way and with what words I ought to speak. I'll
tell her like this: first, when we arrived there, when we
touched the shore, Amphitruo immediately chose the
leading men among those of high rank. He sent them as   205
legates and ordered them to tell the Teloboians his deci-
sion: should they wish to hand over the pillage and the
pillagers without violence and without war, and to return
what they had taken away, he would immediately take his
army back home, the Argives[10] would leave their terri-
tory, and they would give them peace and quiet; but
should they be otherwise disposed and not comply with

[10] Amphitruo is an Argive, but his army actually consists of
Thebans.

210   sese igitur summa ui uirisque eorum oppidum oppugnas-
          sere.
      haec ubi Telobois ordine iterarunt quos praefecerat
      Amphitruo, magnanimi uiri freti uirtute et uiribus
      superbe nimis ferociter legatos nostros increpant,
      respondent bello se et suos tutari posse, proinde uti
215   propere suis de finibus exercitus deducerent.
      haec ubi legati pertulere, Amphitruo castris ilico
      producit omnem exercitum. contra Teloboae ex oppido
      legiones educunt suas nimis pulchris armis praeditas.
      postquam utrimque exitum est maxuma copia,
220   dispertiti uiri, dispertiti ordines,
      nos nostras more nostro et modo instruximus
      legiones, item hostes contra legiones suas instruont.
      deinde utrique imperatores in medium exeunt,
      extra turbam ordinum colloquontur simul.
225   conuenit, uicti utri sint eo proelio,
      urbem, agrum, aras, focos seque uti dederent.
      postquam id actum est, tubae contra utrimque occanunt,
      consonat terra, clamorem utrimque efferunt.
      imperator utrimque, hinc et illinc, Ioui
230   uota suscipere, ‹utrimque› hortari exercitum.
      pro se quisque id quod quisque ‹et› potest et ualet
      edit, ferro ferit, tela frangunt, boat
      caelum fremitu uirum, ex spiritu atque anhelitu
      nebula constat, cadunt uolnerum ui [et] uiri.
235   denique, ut uoluimus, nostra superat manus:
      hostes crebri cadunt, nostri contra ingruont.

215 de suis *P, transp. Bothe*   227 utrimque canunt contra *P,*
contra utrimque occanunt *Bergk*   230 utrimque *add. Spengel*
231 ‹et› potest *Bothe,* ‹tum› pro *Leo (sed* quisq' *displicet)*

his demands, then he would attack their city with all   210
his might and men. When Amphitruo's ambassadors re-
peated this message to the Teloboians word for word,
those bold men, trusting in their valor and strength, up-
braided our envoys very haughtily and aggressively. They   214
replied that they could protect themselves and their fam-
ilies by war; so our men had better remove their troops
from their territory quickly. As soon as the envoys had
delivered this message, Amphitruo led the entire army
out of the camp. On the other side the Teloboians took
their troops out of the city, equipped with magnificent
arms. After both sides had come out in full force, the men   219
were arrayed, the lines were arrayed. We drew up our le-
gions according to our usual method and manner; on the
other side, the enemy also drew up their legions. Then
the two commanders came forward into the center and
held a parley outside the serried ranks. It was agreed that   225
whichever side was defeated in battle should surren-
der its city, land, altars, homes, and themselves. After
that was settled, the trumpets blared on either side, the
ground echoed, and the people raised a din on either
side. On either side, in both armies, the commanders of-   229
fered vows to Jupiter; on either side they encouraged
their forces. Each man inflicted for himself what he
could and struck with his sword; lances broke, the heav-
ens resounded with the uproar of men, a mist arose from
their breathing and gasping, men fell under the force of
their wounds. Finally our side prevailed, as we wished.   235
The enemy was falling in heaps, our men were advancing

---

234 uolneris ui et uirium (uirum *D*[1]) *P*, uolnerum ui uiri *Luchs*

ui‹n›cimus ui feroces.
sed fugam in se tamen nemo conuortitur
nec recedit loco quin statim rem gerat;
240   animam amittunt prius quam loco demigrent:
quisque ut steterat iacet optinetque ordinem.
hoc ubi Amphitruo erus conspicatus est,
ilico equites iubet dextera inducere.
equites parent citi: ab dextera maxumo
245   cum clamore inuolant impetu alacri,
foedant et proterunt hostium copias
iure iniustas.
MER   numquam etiam quicquam adhuc uerborum est prolocu-
        tus perperam:
namque ego fui illi in re praesenti et meus quom pugna-
        tum est pater.
250 SOS perduelles penetrant se in fugam; ibi nostris animus ad-
        ditust:
uortentibus Telobois telis complebantur corpora
ipsusque Amphitruo regem Pterelam sua optruncauit
        manu.
haec illi est pugnata pugna usque a mani ad uesperum
(hoc adeo hoc commemini magis quia illo die impransus
        fui),
255   sed proelium id tandem diremit nox interuentu suo.
postridie in castra ex urbe ad nos ueniunt flentes princi-
        pes:
uelatis manibus orant ignoscamus peccatum suom,
deduntque se, diuina humanaque omnia, urbem et libe-
        ros
in dicionem atque in arbitratum cuncti Thebano poplo.
260   post ob uirtutem ero Amphitruoni patera donata aurea
        est,

against them. We were winning, wild with might. But
nonetheless no one turned in flight or deserted his place,
but instead fought at his post. They lost their lives sooner   240
than desert their places. As everybody had stood, so he
lay and kept his position. When my master Amphitruo
saw this, he instantly gave orders to lead the cavalry to
the charge on the right. The cavalry obeyed swiftly. In an   244
eager assault they rushed in from the right, shouting
frantically. They rightly mangled and crushed the en-
emy's unrighteous troops.

MER   (*aside*) Up till now he's never spoken even a single word
amiss: my father and I were there at the scene of action
when the fighting took place.

SOS   The enemy took to flight; at this point our men gained   250
courage. When the Teloboians turned their backs, their
bodies were filled with spears, and Amphitruo himself
slew King Pterela with his own hand. This fight was
fought there without interruption from morning till eve-
ning—I remember this all the more clearly because that
day I went without lunch. But finally night settled the   255
battle through its intervention. The next day their leaders
came from the city to our camp, crying, and with covered
hands[11] they asked us to forgive them their transgression.
They all surrendered themselves, all their sacred and
profane possessions, their city and their children, into
the power and sway of the Theban people. Afterwards   260
my master Amphitruo was presented with a golden bowl

[11] In Greece suppliants carried olive branches or wreaths in their
hands.

---

237 uicimus *del. Spengel* ui<n>cimus *Christenson*

qui Pterela potitare rex est solitus. haec sic dicam erae.
nunc pergam eri imperium exsequi et me domum capes-
sere.

MER attat, illic huc iturust. ibo ego illic obuiam,
neque ego hunc hominem ⟨huc⟩ hodie ad aedis has si-
nam umquam accedere;

265 quando imago est huius in me, certum est hominem elu-
dere.
et enim uero quoniam formam cepi huius in med et sta-
tum,
decet et facta moresque huius habere me similis item.
itaque me malum esse oportet, callidum, astutum admo-
dum,
atque hunc telo suo sibi, malitia, a foribus pellere.

270 sed quid illuc est? caelum aspectat. opseruabo quam rem
agat.

SOS certe edepol [scio], si quicquam est aliud quod credam
aut certo sciam,
credo ego hac noctu Nocturnum obdormiuisse ebrium.
nam nec se Septentriones quoquam in caelo com-
mouent,
nec se Luna quoquam mutat atque uti exorta est semel,

275 nec Iugulae nec Vesperugo nec Vergiliae occidunt.
ita statim stant signa, nec nox quoquam concedit die.

MER perge, Nox, ut occepisti; gere patri morem meo:
optumo optume optumam operam das, datam pulchre
locas.

SOS neque ego hac nocte longiorem me uidisse censeo,

280 nisi item unam, uerberatus quam pependi perpetem;
eam quoque edepol etiam multo haec uicit longitudine.

34

for his valor, the one from which King Pterela used to drink. That's how I'll tell my mistress the story. Now I'll continue to carry out master's command and go home.

MER (*aside*) Oho, he's going to come here. I'll go and meet him. I'll never let him come here to this house today. Now that I'm his double, I'll definitely make a fool of him. And since I took on his looks and dress, I also ought to have similar ways and habits. So I should be very malicious, sly, and tricky, and I should drive him away from the door with his own weapon, malice. But what's that? He's looking at the sky. I'll observe what he's up to.

SOS If there's anything I believe or know for sure, I certainly do know that this night Nocturnus[12] has fallen asleep drunk: the Great Bear isn't moving anywhere in the sky, the Moon isn't going to any place different from where it was when it first rose, and Orion, the Evening Star, and the Pleiades aren't setting either. The constellations are standing still and there's no sign anywhere that night is giving way to day.

MER (*aside*) Continue, Night, as you've begun. Oblige my father. You're doing an excellent job for an excellent god in an excellent way, you're investing your effort beautifully.

SOS I don't think I've seen a longer night than this, except the one when I got beaten and was left hanging for as long as it lasted. But lengthwise this one has outdone even that

265

270

275

279

---

[12] The god of night.

261 potare *P*, potitare ς rex solitus est *P*, rex est solitus *Bothe*, solitus est rex *Ussing*
264 huc hominem *P*, hunc hominem huc *Studemund*
271 scio *del. Bothe* quid *P*, quod ς

		credo edepol equidem dormire Solem atque appotum probe;
		mira sunt nisi inuitauit sese in cena plusculum.
	MER	ain uero, uerbero? deos esse tui similis putas?
285		ego pol te istis tuis pro dictis et male factis, furcifer,
		accipiam; modo sis ueni huc: inuenies infortunium.
	SOS	ubi sunt isti scortatores qui soli inuiti cubant?
		haec nox scita est exercendo scorto conducto male.
	MER	meus pater nunc pro huius uerbis recte et sapienter facit,
290		qui complexus cum Alcumena cubat amans, animo opsequens.
	SOS	ibo ut erus quod imperauit Alcumenae nuntiem.
		sed quis hic est homo quem ante aedis uideo hoc noctis? non placet.
	MER	nullust hoc metuculosus aeque.
	SOS	mi in mentem uenit
		illic homo ⟨hodie⟩ hoc denuo uolt pallium detexere.
295	MER	timet homo: deludam ego illum.
	SOS	perii, dentes pruriunt;
		certe aduenientem hic me hospitio pugneo accepturus est.
		credo misericors est: nunc propterea quod me meus erus
		fecit ut uigilarem, hic pugnis faciet hodie ut dormiam.
		oppido interii. opsecro hercle, quantus et quam ualidus est!
300	MER	clare aduorsum fabulabor, ⟨ut⟩ hic auscultet quae loquar;

294 hodie *add. Goetz et Loewe*
300 hic auscultet *P, transp. Lindsay,* ⟨ut⟩ hic auscultet *Leo*

36

one by far. I think Sol[13] is asleep, after some heavy drinking. It would be strange if he hasn't drunk his own health a bit much at dinner.

MER (*aside*) Do you really say so, you thug? Do you think the gods are similar to you? Well, for those words and for that 285
bad behavior of yours I'll give you a reception, you criminal. Just come here, will you, and you'll meet trouble.

SOS Where are those lechers who are lying alone against their will? This night is perfect for exhausting a prostitute hired for a lot of money.

MER (*aside*) According to this chap's words, my father's now 289
doing the right and clever thing; he's lying with Alcumena in his arms, full of passion and enjoying himself.

SOS I'll go and tell Alcumena what master ordered. (*stops and looks around*) But who's this man I can see in front of our house at this time of night? I'm not happy about it.

MER (*aside*) No one's as timid as him.

SOS (*aside*) It looks to me as if he wants to weave my cloak again today.[14]

MER (*aside*) He's scared; I'll fool him. 295

SOS (*aside*) I'm done for, my teeth are tingling. He's definitely going to give me a fisty welcome[15] on my arrival. I think he's merciful: since my master made me stay up, he'll now put me to sleep with his fists today. I'm completely dead. Just look at him, how big and strong he is!

MER (*aside*) I'll speak loudly in his direction so he can hear 300

13 The sun god.

14 Weaving is a metaphor for beating; the shuttle will be Mercury's fist.

15 Pun on *hospitium publicum* (state welcome).

igitur magis multo maiorem in sese concipiet metum.
agite, pugni, iam diu est quod uentri uictum non datis:
iam pridem uidetur factum heri quod homines quattuor
in soporem collocastis nudos.

SOS   formido male

305   ne ego hic nomen meum commutem et Quintus fiam e
       Sosia;
     quattuor uiros sopori se dedisse hic autumat:
     metuo ne numerum augeam illum.

MER   em nunciam ergo: sic uolo.

SOS   cingitur: certe expedit se.

MER   non feret quin uapulet.

SOS   quis homo?

MER   quisquis [homo] huc profecto uenerit, pugnos edet.

310 SOS   apage, non placet me hoc noctis esse: cenaui modo;
     proin tu istam cenam largire, si sapis, esurientibus.

MER   hau malum huic est pondus pugno.

SOS   perii, pugnos ponderat.

MER   quid si ego illum tractim tangam, ut dormiat?

SOS   seruaueris,
     nam continuas has tris noctes peruigilaui.

MER   pessume est,

315   facimus nequiter, ferire malam male discit manus;
     alia forma ⟨eum⟩ esse oportet quem tu pugno legeris.

SOS   illic homo me interpolabit meumque os finget denuo.

MER   exossatum os esse oportet quem probe percusseris.

SOS   mirum ni hic me quasi murenam exossare cogitat.

---

301 modum maiorem D^2, modum morem *cett.*, multo maiorem
Redslob, modum ⟨in⟩ maiorem *Camerarius*

309 homo *del. Redslob*

316 eum *add. Lindsay in apparatu*

what I'm saying. Then he'll get still more frightened. (*loudly*) Go on, fists, you haven't provided food for my stomach for ages. It seems a long time since yesterday when you stripped four men and put them to sleep.

SOS   (*aside*) I'm terribly afraid that I might change my name here and turn from Sosia into Sosia the Fifth.[16] He says 306 he's put four men to sleep. I'm afraid I might increase that number.

MER   (*hitching up his cloak*) There, now then; I like it like this.

SOS   (*aside*) He's girding himself: he's clearly getting ready.

MER   He won't get away without getting a thrashing.

SOS   (*aside*) Who?

MER   Yes, whoever comes here will eat fists.

SOS   (*aside*) Away with you! I don't like eating at this time of 310 night. I've just had my dinner; so if you have any sense, donate that dinner to those who are hungry.

MER   This fist doesn't have a bad weight.

SOS   (*aside*) I'm done for, he's weighing his fists.

MER   What if I touch him slowly into sleep?

SOS   (*aside*) You'll save me: these three nights running I've stayed awake.

MER   That's awful! We're doing a terrible job! My hand is bad 315 at learning how to strike a cheek. Someone you merely skim with your fist ought to have a different shape.

SOS   (*aside*) That man will do some plastic surgery on me and remodel my face.

MER   Someone you strike properly ought to have a filleted face.

SOS   (*aside*) It would be odd if he isn't thinking about filleting

---

16 *Quintus* (born in the fifth month) is a common first name.

320		ultro istunc qui exossat homines! perii si me aspexerit.
	MER	olet homo quidam malo suo.
	SOS	ei, numnam ego obolui?
	MER	atque hau longe abesse oportet, uerum longe hinc afuit.
	SOS	illic homo superstitiosust.
	MER	gestiunt pugni mihi.
	SOS	si in me exercituru's, quaeso in parietem ut primum domes.
325	MER	uox mi ad auris aduolauit.
	SOS	ne ego homo infelix fui
		qui non alas interuelli: uolucrem uocem gestito.
	MER	illic homo a me sibi malam rem arcessit iumento suo.
	SOS	non equidem ullum habeo iumentum.
	MER	onerandus est pugnis probe.
	SOS	lassus sum hercle e naui, ut uectus huc sum: etiam nunc nauseo;
330		uix incedo inanis, ne ire posse cum onere existumes.
	MER	certe enim hic nescioquis loquitur.
	SOS	saluos sum, non me uidet:
		"nescioquem" loqui autumat; mi certo nomen Sosiae est.
	MER	hinc enim mi dextra uox auris, ut uidetur, uerberat.
	SOS	metuo, uocis ne uicem hodie hic uapulem, quae hunc uerberat.
335	MER	optume eccum incedit ad me.
	SOS	timeo, totus torpeo.
		non edepol nunc ubi terrarum sim scio, si quis roget,
		nec miser me commouere possum prae formidine.
		ilicet: mandata eri perierunt una et Sosia.

---

[17] Pun on the two meanings of *alae*: he did not pluck his "armpits" or the "wings" of his voice—the latter is a reference to the "winged words" in Homer (*Iliad* 1. 201 and elsewhere).

	me like a lamprey. Away with that man who fillets people! I'm dead if he sets eyes on me.	320
MER	Someone's smelling here, and it won't do him any good.	
SOS	(*aside*) Dear me, did I emit that smell?	
MER	And he shouldn't be far away now, but he was far away from here before.	
SOS	(*aside*) That man's a clairvoyant.	
MER	My fists are losing patience.	
SOS	(*aside*) If you're going to exercise them on me, please tame them on the wall first.	
MER	A voice has flown to my ears.	325
SOS	(*aside*) I really was an unlucky fellow—I didn't depilate my wings;[17] now I have a voice that flies to another's ears.	
MER	He's asking me to give a thrashing to his beast of burden.	
SOS	(*aside*) Well, *I* don't have any beast of burden.	
MER	He needs to be loaded up with fists properly.	
SOS	(*aside*) I'm tired from coming here by ship. I'm still feeling sea-sick. I can barely walk empty-handed, so don't think I can walk with a burden.	330
MER	Certainly someone's speaking here.	
SOS	(*aside*) I'm safe, he can't see me. He says "Someone" is speaking; *I* certainly have the name Sosia.	
MER	Yes, from here from the right a voice is hitting my ear, as it seems.	
SOS	(*aside*) I'm afraid that I might get a thrashing here today instead of my voice, which is hitting him.	
MER	Excellent, look, he's coming toward me.	335
SOS	(*aside*) I'm scared, I'm completely paralysed. If anyone were to ask, I don't know where on earth I am, and I can't move for fear, poor chap that I am. It's over: master's commands have perished together with Sosia. (*pauses*	

uerum certum est confidenter hominem contra colloqui,
340 [igitur] qui possim uideri huic fortis, a me ut apstineat
manum.

MER quo ambulas tu qui Volcanum in cornu conclusum geris?
SOS quid id exquiris tu qui pugnis os exossas hominibus?
MER seruosne ⟨es⟩ an liber?
SOS   utquomque animo collibitum est meo.
MER ain uero?
SOS   aio enim uero.
MER   uerbero.
SOS   mentire nunc.
345 MER at iam faciam ut uerum dicas dicere.
SOS   quid eo est opus?
MER possum scire quo profectus, quoius sis aut quid ueneris?
SOS huc eo. eri sum seruos. numquid nunc es certior?
MER ego tibi istam hodie, sceleste, comprimam linguam.
SOS   hau potes:
bene pudiceque asseruatur.
MER   pergin argutarier?
350 quid apud hasce aedis negoti est tibi?
SOS   immo quid tibi est?
MER rex Creo uigiles nocturnos singulos semper locat.
SOS bene facit: quia nos eramus peregri, tutatust domi;
at nunc abi sane, aduenisse familiaris dicito.

---

340 igitur *del. Camerarius*   343 ⟨es⟩ *add.* ς

---

[18] The god of fire, standing for fire itself in tragic language.
[19] Lanterns were made of horn.   [20] Sosia puns on the two
meanings of *uerbero*: "whipping post" as a noun, "I'm beating" as a verb.
[21] Pun on the two meanings of *comprimere*; Mercury means "re-strain," Sosia understands "have sex with."

for a moment) But I'm resolved to address him boldly, in   339
the hope that somehow I may manage to appear coura-
geous to him, so that he keeps his hands off me. (*ap-
proaches him*)

MER   Where are you going, you who are carrying Vulcan[18]
locked up in your horn?[19]

SOS   Why do you ask this, you who fillet people's faces with
your fists?

MER   Are you a slave or free?

SOS   Whichever I like.

MER   Do you say so?

SOS   Yes, I say so indeed.

MER   You're a whipping post.

SOS   You're lying now.[20]

MER   But in a second I'll make sure that you tell me I'm telling   345
the truth.

SOS   What's that necessary for?

MER   Can I know where you are bound, whose slave you are, or
what you've come for?

SOS   I'm coming here. I'm my master's slave. Are you better
informed now?

MER   I'll violate that tongue of yours today, you thug.

SOS   You can't: she's kept carefully and chastely.[21]

MER   Are you continuing with your witticisms? What business   350
have you at this house?

SOS   Well, what business have *you*?

MER   King Creon always posts individual sentries for the night.

SOS   Quite rightly so. As we were abroad, he kept guard at
home. But now do go away and say that the family ser-
vants have arrived.

	MER	nescio quam tu familiaris sis: nisi actutum hinc abis,
355		familiaris, accipiere faxo hau familiariter.
	SOS	hic, inquam, habito ego atque horunc sum seruos.
	MER	at scin quo modo?
		faciam ego hodie te superbum, nisi hinc abis.
	SOS	quonam modo?
	MER	auferere, non abibis, si ego fustem sumpsero.
	SOS	quin med esse huius familiae familiarem praedico.
360	MER	uide sis quam mox uapulare uis, nisi actutum hinc abis.
	SOS	tun domo prohibere peregre me aduenientem postulas?
	MER	haecin tua domust?
	SOS	ita inquam.
	MER	quis erus est igitur tibi?
	SOS	Amphitruo, qui nunc praefectust Thebanis legionibus,
		quicum nupta est Alcumena.
	MER	quid ais? quid nomen tibi est?
365	SOS	Sosiam uocant Thebani, Dauo prognatum patre.
	MER	ne tu istic hodie malo tuo compositis mendaciis
		aduenisti, audaciai columen, consutis dolis.
	SOS	immo equidem tunicis consutis huc aduenio, non dolis.
	MER	at mentiris etiam: certo pedibus, non tunicis uenis.
370	SOS	ita profecto.
	MER	nunc profecto uapula ob mendacium.
	SOS	non edepol uolo profecto.

356 seruos sum *P, transp. Camerarius*

44

MER	I don't know how you are a family servant; if you don't go away from here this instant, family servant, I'll make sure that you'll get a reception that's not in family style.	354
SOS	I live here, I assure you, and I'm the slave of these people.	
MER	But you know what? I'll exalt you today unless you go away from here.	
SOS	How so?	
MER	You won't *walk* away, you'll be *carried* away, if I take my club.	
SOS	But I'm telling you, I'm a family servant of this family.	
MER	Do consider how soon you want to get a thrashing, unless you go away from here this instant.	360
SOS	Do you want to keep me away from my home, now that I've arrived from abroad?	
MER	Is this your home?	
SOS	Yes, I assure you.	
MER	Then who's your master?	
SOS	Amphitruo, who's in command of the Theban legions now and who Alcumena is married to.	
MER	What do you say? What's your name?	
SOS	The Thebans call me Sosia, son of Davus.	365
MER	You there, you really will pay today for coming here with your premeditated lies, you peak of audacity, and with your patched up tricks.	
SOS	No, I'm coming here with a patched up tunic, not with patched up tricks.	
MER	You're lying; you're certainly coming with your feet, not with a tunic.	
SOS	Yes, indeed.	370
MER	Now, indeed, get a thrashing for your lie.	
SOS	Indeed, I don't want to.	

MER	at pol profecto ingratiis.
	hoc quidem "profecto" certum est, non est arbitrarium.
SOS	tuam fidem opsecro.
MER	tun te audes Sosiam esse dicere,
	qui ego sum?
SOS	perii.
MER	parum etiam, praeut futurum est, praedicas.

375 quoius nunc es?
SOS   tuos, nam pugnis usu fecisti tuom.
     pro fidem, Thebani ciues!
MER   etiam clamas, carnufex?
     loquere, quid uenisti?
SOS   ut esset quem tu pugnis caederes.
MER quoius es?
SOS   Amphitruonis, inquam, Sosia.
MER   ergo istoc magis,
     quia uaniloquo's, uapulabis: ego sum, non tu, Sosia.
380 SOS ita di faciant, ut tu potius sis atque ego te ut uerberem.
MER etiam muttis?
SOS   iam tacebo.
MER   quis tibi erust?
SOS   quem tu uoles.
MER quid igitur? qui nunc uocare?
SOS   nemo nisi quem iusseris.
MER Amphitruonis te esse aiebas Sosiam.
SOS   peccaueram,
     nam Amphitruonis socium memet esse uolui dicere.
385 MER scibam equidem nullum esse nobis nisi me seruom So-
       siam.
     fugit te ratio.

384 neme *P*, memet *Lindemann*, sane me *Palmer*

MER Then, indeed, against your wishes. This "indeed" is certain, it's not optional. (*hits him*)

SOS Please spare me!

MER You dare say that you are Sosia, the one I am? (*hits him again*)

SOS It's over with me.

MER (*continues to beat him*) Compared with what's coming you're still saying too little. Whose are you now?   375

SOS Yours: with your fists you've made me yours by prescription.[22] (*very loudly*) Help, citizens of Thebes!

MER You're shouting, villain? Tell me, what did you come for?

SOS So that there'd be someone you could cut down with your fists.

MER Whose slave are you?

SOS I'm Amphitruo's Sosia, I'm telling you.

MER Well then, you'll get a thrashing all the more because you're an airbag: *I* am Sosia, not *you*. (*hits him again*)

SOS May the gods do so, so that *you* are him instead and so   380 that *I* am beating *you*.

MER You're still muttering?

SOS I'll be quiet now.

MER Who's your master?

SOS Anyone you want.

MER What then? What are you called now?

SOS Only what you tell me to be called.

MER You said you're Amphitruo's Sosia.

SOS I made a mistake: I wanted to say I'm Amphitruo's associate.

MER I knew we had no slave Sosia other than myself. You took   385 leave of your senses.

---

[22] Joke about the law of *usucapio*: continuous possession of another's property leads to transfer of ownership.

	SOS	utinam istuc pugni fecissent tui.
	MER	ego sum Sosia ille quem tu dudum esse aiebas mihi.
	SOS	opsecro ut per pacem liceat te alloqui, ut ne uapulem.
	MER	immo indutiae parumper fiant, si quid uis loqui.
390	SOS	non loquar nisi pace facta, quando pugnis plus uales.
	MER	dic si quid uis, non nocebo.
	SOS	tuae fide credo?
	MER	meae.
	SOS	quid si falles?
	MER	tum Mercurius Sosiae iratus siet.
	SOS	animum aduorte. nunc licet mi libere quiduis loqui.
		Amphitruonis ego sum seruos Sosia.
	MER	etiam denuo?
395	SOS	pacem feci, foedus feci. uera dico.
	MER	uapula.
	SOS	ut lubet quid tibi lubet fac, quoniam pugnis plus uales;
		uerum, utut es facturus, hoc quidem hercle hau reticebo
		tamen.
	MER	tu me uiuos hodie numquam facies quin sim Sosia.
	SOS	certe edepol tu me alienabis numquam quin noster siem;
400		nec praesente nobis alius quisquam est seruos Sosia.
		qui cum Amphitruone hinc una iueram in exercitum.
	MER	hic homo sanus non est.
	SOS	quod mi praedicas uitium, id tibi est.
		quid, malum, non sum ego seruos Amphitruonis Sosia?

391 dicito si *P*, dic si *Lindemann*, dicito [si] *Camerarius*

SOS I wish you'd done that to your fists.

MER I am that Sosia you claimed to be a while ago.

SOS Please allow me to speak to you in peace, without getting a thrashing.

MER Not in peace, but for a short time there can be a truce if you want to say anything.

SOS I won't speak unless peace has been made, since you have 390 more strength in your fists.

MER Say what you want, I won't harm you.

SOS Can I trust your promise?

MER Yes.

SOS What if you deceive me?

MER Then may Mercury be angry with Sosia.

SOS Pay attention. Now I can say anything freely. *I* am Amphitruo's slave Sosia.

MER What, again?

SOS I've made peace with you, I've made an agreement. I'm 395 telling the truth.

MER Get a thrashing. (*beats him*)

SOS Do what you like as you like, since you have more strength in your fists; but however you're going to treat me, still, I shan't be silent about this.

MER So long as I'm alive you'll never bring it about today that I'm not Sosia.

SOS And *you* will certainly never change my identity so that I don't belong here; and when the two of us are present, 400 there's no other slave Sosia. I went to the army together with Amphitruo.

MER This man isn't in his right mind.

SOS *You* have the fault you say *I* have. (*half aside*) What, the hell! Aren't I Amphitruo's slave Sosia? Didn't our ship

49

nonne hac noctu nostra nauis ⟨huc⟩ ex portu Persico
405 uenit, quae me aduexit? nonne me huc erus misit meus?
nonne ego nunc sto ante aedis nostras? non mi est lanter-
na in manu?
non loquor, non uigilo? nonne hic homo modo me pugnis
contudit?
fecit hercle, nam etiam ⟨mi⟩ misero nunc malae dolent.
quid igitur ego dubito, aut quor non intro eo in nostram
domum?
410 MER quid, domum uostram?
SOS   ita enim uero.
MER   quin quae dixisti modo
omnia ementitu's: equidem Sosia Amphitruonis sum.
nam noctu hac soluta est nauis nostra e portu Persico,
et ubi Pterela rex regnauit oppidum expugnauimus,
et legiones Teloboarum ui pugnando cepimus,
415 et ipsus Amphitruo optruncauit regem Pterelam in proe-
lio.
SOS egomet mihi non credo, quom illaec autumare illum au-
dio;
hicquidem certe quae illic sunt res gestae memorat me-
moriter.
sed quid ais? quid Amphitruoni a Telobois est datum?
MER Pterela rex qui potitare solitus est patera aurea.
420 SOS elocutus est. ubi patera nunc est?
MER   ⟨est⟩ in cistula;
Amphitruonis opsignata signo est.
SOS   signi dic quid est?

---

404 huc *add. Pylades*   408 mi *add. Pylades*
418 est datum *P, transp. Lindsay,* ⟨doni⟩ a Ussing (*qui* est datum
scribit)   420 est *add. Dousa*

come here from Port Persicus[23] this night, the one that
brought me here? Didn't my master send me here?
Aren't I standing in front of our house now? Haven't I a   406
lamp in my hand? Aren't I speaking, aren't I awake?
Didn't this man here beat me up with his fists just now?
Yes, he did: my jaws are still hurting, dear me. Then why
am I hesitating and why don't I go into our house?

MER   What, your house?   410

SOS   Yes indeed.

MER   No, you lied about everything you just said: *I* am Am-
phitruo's Sosia: this night we set sail from Port Persicus;
we've seized the city where King Pterela reigned, we've
conquered the Teloboian legions by force of arms, and   415
Amphitruo himself has killed King Pterela in battle.

SOS   (*aside*) I don't believe myself when I hear him speak;
he's certainly telling what happened there accurately.
(*loudly*) But what do you say? What was Amphitruo given
by the Teloboians?

MER   The golden bowl King Pterela used to drink from.

SOS   (*aside*) He's said it. (*loudly*) Where's the bowl now?   420

MER   It's in a little chest; it's sealed with Amphitruo's signet.

SOS   Tell me, what kind of signet is it?

---

[23] We do not know where this is. Festus (p. 238 Lindsay) thinks that
it is in the Euboean sea, near Thebes, where the Persian army had been.
That would be an anachronism. Stephanus of Byzantium (519. 8–9)
mentions a city and port called Perseus, and some derive Port Persicus
from this.

MER cum quadrigis Sol exoriens. quid me captas, carnufex?
SOS argumentis uicit, aliud nomen quaerundum est mihi.
    nescio unde haec hic spectauit. iam ego hunc decipiam
        probe;
425   nam quod egomet solus feci, nec quisquam alius affuit,
    in tabernaclo, id quidem hodie numquam poterit dicere.
    si tu Sosia es, legiones quom pugnabant maxume,
    quid in tabernaclo fecisti? uictus sum si dixeris.
MER cadus erat uini, inde impleui hirneam.
SOS   ingressust uiam.
430 MER eam ego, ut matre fuerat natum, ‹tum› uini eduxi meri.
SOS factum est illud, ut ego illic uini hirneam ebiberim meri.
    mira sunt nisi latuit intus illic in illac hirnea.
MER quid nunc? uincone argumentis te non esse Sosiam?
SOS tu negas med esse?
MER   quid ego ni negem, qui egomet siem?
435 SOS per Iouem iuro med esse nec me falsum dicere.
MER at ego per Mercurium iuro tibi Iouem non credere;
    nam iniurato scio plus credet mihi quam iurato tibi.
SOS quis ego sum saltem, si non sum Sosia? te interrogo.
MER ubi ego Sosia esse nolim, tu esto sane Sosia;
440   nunc, quando ego sum, uapulabis, ni hinc abis, ignobilis.
SOS certe edepol, quom illum contemplo et formam cognos-
      co meam,
    quem ad modum ego sum (saepe in speculum inspexi),
    nimis similest mei;
    itidem habet petasum ac uestitum: tam consimilest atque
    ego;

430 tum *add. Palmer*   439 nolim esse *P, transp. Gruterus*

---

[24] Drinking wine undiluted was considered bad style.

MER   Sol rising in his four-horse chariot. Why are you trying to catch me out, you criminal?

SOS   (*aside*) He's won through evidence. I have to find myself another name. I don't know where he saw this from. Now I'll trick him properly: what I did alone in the tent, when 425 no one else was around, that he'll never be able to tell to-day. (*aloud*) If you're Sosia, what did you do in the tent when the armies were fighting bitterly? I'm defeated if you can tell me.

MER   There was a jar of wine; from there I filled a jug.

SOS   (*aside*) He's on the right track.

MER   I drained the jug of wine as pure as it had come from its 430 mother.[24]

SOS   (*aside*) That did happen: yes, I did empty a jug of pure wine there. He must have hidden in that jug.

MER   Well then, have I convinced you with my evidence that you aren't Sosia?

SOS   You deny that *I* am Sosia?

MER   Why shouldn't I deny it? I myself am him.

SOS   I swear by Jupiter that *I* am Sosia and that I'm not lying. 435

MER   But I swear by Mercury that Jupiter doesn't believe you; I know he'll believe *me* even without taking an oath more than he'll believe *you* after taking one.

SOS   Then who am I if I'm not Sosia? I'm asking you.

MER   When I don't want to be Sosia, you can be Sosia, by all means; now that I am him, you'll get a thrashing unless 440 you go away from here, you unknown creature.

SOS   (*aside*) Yes, definitely, when I look at him and consider my own looks, what I'm like (I've often looked into the mirror), he's extremely similar to me; he has a hat and clothes just like me. He's as similar to me as I am. Leg,

sura, pes, statura, tonsus, oculi, nasum uel labra,
445　malae, mentum, barba, collus: totus. quid uerbis opust?
si tergum cicatricosum, nihil hoc similist similius.
sed quom cogito, equidem certo idem sum qui semper
　　fui.
noui erum, noui aedis nostras; sane sapio et sentio.
non ego illi optempero quod loquitur. pultabo fores.
450　MER　quo agis te?
SOS　　　　　　　domum.
MER　　　　　　　　　　　quadrigas si nunc inscendas Iouis
atque hinc fugias, ita uix poteris effugere infortunium.
SOS　nonne erae meae nuntiare quod erus meus iussit licet?
MER　tuae si quid uis nuntiare: hanc nostram adire non sinam.
nam si me irritassis, hodie lumbifragium hinc auferes.
455　SOS　abeo potius. di immortales, opsecro uostram fidem,
ubi ego perii? ubi immutatus sum? ubi ego formam per-
　　didi?
an egomet me illic reliqui, si forte oblitus fui?
nam hic quidem omnem imaginem meam, quae antehac
　　fuerat, possidet.
uiuo fit quod numquam quisquam mortuo faciet mihi.
460　ibo ad portum atque haec uti sunt facta ero dicam meo;
nisi etiam is quoque me ignorabit: quod ille faxit Iup-
　　piter,
ut ego hodie raso capite caluos capiam pilleum.

461 faxit *Seruius*, faciat *P*

foot, height, haircut, eyes, nose, lips, cheeks, chin, beard,   445
neck: the whole lot. What need is there for words? If his
back's full of scars, there's nothing more similar than this
similarity. (*pauses*) But when I think about it, I'm cer-
tainly the same I've always been. I know my master, I
know our house. I'm clearly in my right senses. I'm not
following what he says. I'll knock at the door. (*makes a
move*)

MER   Where are you going?   450

SOS   Home.

MER   If you should get onto Jupiter's four-horse chariot now
and flee from here, even so you'll hardly be able to escape
misfortune.

SOS   Can't I tell my mistress what my master ordered?

MER   You can, if you want to tell *yours* anything; but I won't let
you go to *ours* here. If you provoke me, you'll carry away
broken hips from here today.

SOS   I'd rather leave. (*aside*) Immortal gods, I implore you,   455
where did I get lost? Where did I change? Where did I
lose my looks? Did I by chance forget myself and leave
myself behind? Well, this man has my complete image,
the one I had before. What no one will ever do to me
when I'm dead is happening to me while I'm still alive.[25]
I'll go to the harbor and tell my master how this hap-   460
pened; that is, unless he doesn't know me either. May
Jupiter up there do so, so that today I can shave my head
and take the freeman's cap as a bald man.[26]

[25] Sosia refers to the Roman tradition of carrying wax masks of the
ancestors during funerals.

[26] Those who had just become free went to the temple of Feronia,
shaved their heads, and put on a felt cap.

I. ii: MERCVRIVS

MER   bene prospere[que] hoc hodie operis processit mihi:
amoui a foribus maxumam molestiam,
465   patri ut liceret tuto illam amplexarier.
iam ille illuc ad erum quom Amphitruonem aduenerit,
narrabit seruom hinc sese a foribus Sosiam
amouisse; ille adeo illum mentiri sibi
credet, nec credet huc profectum, ut iusserat.
470   erroris ambo ego illos et dementiae
complebo atque omnem Amphitruonis familiam,
adeo usque satietatem dum capiet pater
illius quam amat. igitur demum omnes scient
quae facta. denique Alcumenam Iuppiter
475   rediget antiquam coniugi in concordiam.
nam Amphitruo actutum uxori turbas conciet
atque insimulabit eam probri; tum meus pater
eam seditionem illi in tranquillum conferet.
nunc de Alcumena dudum quo dixi minus,
480   hodie illa pariet filios geminos duos:
alter decumo post mense nascetur puer
quam seminatus<t>, alter mense septumo;
eorum Amphitruonis alter est, alter Iouis:
uerum minori puero maior est pater,
485   minor maiori. iamne hoc scitis quid siet?
sed Alcumenae huius honoris gratia
pater curauit uno ut fetu fieret,
uno ut labore apsoluat aerumnas duas
et ne in suspicione ponatur stupri
490   et clandestina ut celetur consuetio.
quamquam, ut iam dudum dixi, resciscet tamen

463 que *del. Acidalius*   482 seminatus *P*, seminatust *Fleckeisen*

Exit SOSIA to the left.

MER This job went well and successfully for me today. I re-
moved a terrible nuisance from the door so that my fa- 465
ther can embrace that woman in safety. In a moment,
when that chap gets there and meets his master Am-
phitruo, he'll say the slave Sosia drove him away from the
door. Amphitruo will believe that he's telling lies, and
he won't believe that he came here as he'd ordered.
I'll fill both of them and Amphitruo's entire household 470
with misunderstandings and madness until my father
gets enough of the woman he's in love with. Then, and
only then, will all know what's happened. In the end Jupi-
ter will bring Alcumena back into her old harmony
with her husband. Well, Amphitruo will start a row with 476
his wife in a moment, and he'll accuse her of adultery.
Then my father will quell this quarrel there. Now about
Alcumena, something I didn't say earlier: today she'll
give birth to two twin sons. One boy will be born in the 481
tenth month[27] after he was conceived, the other in the
seventh; one of them is Amphitruo's, the other Jupiter's.
But the younger boy has the greater father and vice
versa. Do you know what I mean now? But out of consid- 486
eration for Alcumena here, my father's taken care that it
would happen in one go, so that she could complete two
arduous tasks in one labor, so that she wouldn't be sus-
pected of adultery, and so that the secret affair would be
concealed. Still, as I've said already, Amphitruo will find 491

[27] These are lunar months.

Amphitruo rem omnem. quid igitur? nemo id probro
profecto ducet Alcumenae; nam deum
non par uidetur facere, delictum suom
495   suamque ut culpam expetere in mortalem ut sinat.
orationem comprimam: crepuit foris.
Amphitruo subditiuos eccum exit foras
cum Alcumena, uxore usuraria.

     I. iii: IVPPITER. ALCVMENA. MERCVRIVS

IVP   bene uale, Alcumena, cura rem communem, quod facis;
500   atque imperce quaeso: menses iam tibi esse actos uides.
     mihi necesse est ire hinc; uerum quod erit natum tollito.
ALC quid istuc est, mi uir, negoti quod tu tam subito domo
     abeas?
IVP   edepol hau quod tui me nec domi distaedeat;
     sed ubi summus imperator non adest ad exercitum,
505   citius quod non facto est usus fit quam quod facto est
     opus.
MER nimis hic scitust sycophanta, qui quidem meus sit pater.
     opseruatote <eum> quam blande mulieri palpabitur.
ALC ecastor te experior quanti facias uxorem tuam.
IVP   satin habes si feminarum nulla est quam aeque diligam?
510 MER edepol ne illa si istis rebus te sciat operam dare,
     ego faxim ted Amphitruonem esse malis quam Iouem.
ALC experiri istuc mauellem me quam mi memorarier.
     prius abis quam lectus ubi cubuisti concaluit locus.

495 ut[1] *del. Acidalius*
507 quam *P, ut Donatus*, ut quam *Lindsay*, <eum> quam *Bothe*

---

[28] Unless a child is lifted up (normally by the father), it will be exposed.

out the whole thing all the same. What then? Certainly
no one will hold Alcumena guilty: it wouldn't seem the
right thing to do for a god to let *his* misdeed and *his* guilt
fall on a mortal. (*looks at the door*) I'll stop talking: the   496
door's creaked. Look, the counterfeit Amphitruo is com-
ing out with Alcumena, his borrowed wife.

*MERCURY steps aside so that he can hear the pair without be-
ing overheard himself.*
Enter JUPITER and ALCUMENA from the house.

JUP   Goodbye, Alcumena, look after our common interest, as
you're doing now, and please don't exert yourself too   500
much: you can see that your months are up already. I
have to leave. But when the time comes, lift up your off-
spring.[28]

ALC   What business is that, my dear husband? You're going
away from home so suddenly.

JUP   Well, not because I'm fed up with you or our home. But
when the chief commander isn't with the army, what   505
shouldn't happen happens more quickly than what
should happen.

MER   He's a terribly clever impostor; after all, he's my father.
Watch how coaxingly he'll soothe the woman.

ALC   Seriously, I'm experiencing how much you value your
wife.

JUP   Aren't you satisfied if there's no other woman I love as
much?

MER   Honestly, if your wife above knew you're doing this sort   510
of thing, I bet you'd rather be Amphitruo than Jupiter.

ALC   I'd prefer experiencing this to being told. You're leaving
before the place on the bed where you lay got warm. Yes-

heri uenisti media nocte, nunc abis. hoccin placet?
515   MER   accedam atque hanc appellabo et supparasitabor patri.
numquam edepol quemquam mortalem credo ego uxo-
        rem suam
sic efflictim amare, proinde ut hic te efflictim deperit.
    IVP   carnufex, non ego te noui? abin e conspectu meo?
quid tibi hanc curatio est rem, uerbero, aut muttitio?
520   quoi ego iam hoc scipione—
    ALC   ah noli.
    IVP   muttito modo . . .
    MER   nequiter paene expediuit prima parasitatio.
    IVP   uerum quod tu dicis, mea uxor, non te mi irasci decet.
clanculum abii: a legione operam hanc surrupui tibi,
ex me primo prima ‹ut› scires rem ut gessissem publi-
        cam.
525   ea tibi omnia enarraui. nisi te amarem plurumum,
non facerem.
    MER   facitne ut dixi? timidam palpo percutit.
    IVP   nunc, ne legio persentiscat, clam illuc redeundum est
        mihi,
ne me uxorem praeuortisse dicant prae re publica.
    ALC   lacrumantem ex abitu concinnas tu tuam uxorem.
    IVP   tace,
530   ne corrumpe oculos, redibo actutum.
    ALC   id "actutum" diu est.
    IVP   non ego te hic lubens relinquo neque abeo aps te.
    ALC   sentio,
nam qua nocte ad me uenisti, eadem abis.
    IVP   quor me tenes?
tempus ‹est›: exire ex urbe prius quam lucescat uolo.

    524 ut *add. Havet hic, alii alibi*   533 est *add.* ς

terday you came at midnight, now you're leaving. Is that what you want?

MER I'll go to them, address her, and play my father's hanger- 515
on. (*approaches Alcumena*) I don't think any mortal ever loves his wife as madly as *he* dotes on you.

JUP You good-for-nothing, don't I know you? Won't you get out of my sight? Why are you interfering in this matter, you whipping stock, or why are you breathing one word about it? I'll take my cane this instant and you— 520

ALC Ah, don't.

JUP (*to Mercury*) Just breathe one word . . .

MER (*aside*) My first attempt at being a hanger-on almost ended in disaster.

JUP But as for what you're saying, my darling wife, it's not fair of you to be angry with me. I went away secretly. I have withdrawn my services from the legion for you, so that you'd be the first to know from me how I served our country. I've told you about all this. If I didn't love you 525
most, I wouldn't have done it.

MER (*aside*) Isn't he behaving as I said? She's apprehensive and he's buttering her up.

JUP Now I have to get back there secretly so that the army doesn't realize; they shouldn't say I put my wife ahead of our country.

ALC You're making your wife cry because you're going away. (*starts sobbing*)

JUP Do be quiet, stop spoiling your eyes. I'll return immedi- 530
ately.

ALC This "immediately" is a long time.

JUP I'm not happy about leaving you here and going away.

ALC I can feel that: the same night you've come to me you're going away. (*holds him tight*)

JUP Why are you holding me? It's time: I want to leave the

nunc tibi hanc pateram, quae dono mi illi ob uirtutem
    data est,

535   Pterela rex qui potitauit, quem ego mea occidi manu,
       Alcumena, tibi condono.

ALC   facis ut alias res soles.
       ecastor condignum donum, quale est qui donum dedit.

MER   immo sic: condignum donum, quale est quoi dono datum
       est.

IVP   pergin autem? nonne ego possum, furcifer, te perdere?

540 ALC noli amabo, Amphitruo, irasci Sosiae causa mea.

IVP   faciam ita ut uis.

MER   ex amore hic admodum quam saenos est.

IVP   numquid uis?

ALC   ut quom apsim me ames, me tuam te apsenti tamen.

MER   eamus, Amphitruo. lucescit hoc iam.

IVP   abi prae, Sosia;
       iam ego sequar. numquid uis?

ALC   etiam: ut actutum aduenias.

IVP   licet,

545   prius tua opinione hic adero: bonum animum habe.
       nunc te, nox, quae me mansisti, mitto ut concedas die,
       ut mortalis illucescat luce clara et candida.
       atque quanto, nox, fuisti longior hac proxuma,
       tanto breuior dies ut fiat faciam, ut aeque disparet;

550   i, dies e nocte accedat. ibo et Mercurium supsequar.

550 et P, ei Havet subsequar P, sequar Leo

city before dawn. (*produces a golden bowl*) Now I'll give   534
you this bowl as a present, Alcumena. It was given to me
there as a token for my valor; King Pterela, whom I slew
with my own hand, used to drink from it.

ALC   That's so like you. Honestly, a worthy gift, matching the
one who gave it.

MER   No: a worthy gift, matching the one it has been given to.

JUP   Are you continuing? Can't I get rid of you, you good-for-
nothing?

ALC   Please, Amphitruo, don't be angry with Sosia, for my   540
sake.

JUP   I'll do as you wish.

MER   (*aside*) How very wild he is because of his love!

JUP   (*turning to go*) Do you want anything?

ALC   Yes: love me when I'm not around, me, the woman be-
longing to you, whether you're around or not.

MER   Let's go, Amphitruo. Day's dawning already.

JUP   Go ahead, Sosia; I'll follow in a moment.

Exit MERCURY to the left.

JUP   Do you want anything?

ALC   Yes: come here soon.

JUP   Yes, I'll be here earlier than you think. Cheer up.   545

Exit ALCUMENA into the house.

JUP   Night, you've waited for me, but now I let you give way to
Day, so that he may shine upon the mortals with clear and
bright light. And, Night, as much as you were longer than
the last, so much shorter shall I let Day become so as to
compensate. Go, let Day issue forth from Night. I'll go   550
and follow Mercury.

Exit JUPITER to the left.

ACTVS II

II. i: AMPHITRVO. SOSIA

AMPH age i tu secundum.

SOS   sequor, supsequor te.

AMPH scelestissumum te arbitror.

SOS   nam quam ob rem?

AMPH quia id quod neque est nec fuit nec futurum est
mihi praedicas.

SOS   eccere, iam tuatim
555   facis, ut tuis nulla apud te fides sit.

AMPH quid est? quo modo? iam quidem hercle ego tibi istam
scelestam, scelus, linguam apscidam.

SOS   tuos sum,
proinde ut commodum est et lubet quidque facias;
tamen quin loquar haec uti facta sunt hic,
560   numquam ullo modo me potes deterrere.

AMPH scelestissume, audes mihi praedicare id,
domi te esse nunc qui hic ades?

SOS   uera dico.

AMPH malum quod tibi di dabunt, atque ego hodie
dabo . . .

SOS   istuc tibi est in manu, nam tuos sum.

565 AMPH tun me, uerbero, audes erum ludificari?
tun id dicere audes, quod nemo umquam homo antehac
uidit nec potest fieri, tempore uno
homo idem duobus locis ut simul sit?

SOS profecto ut loquor res ita est.

AMPH   Iuppiter te
570   perdat.

SOS   quid mali sum, ere, tua ex re promeritus?

ACT TWO

Enter AMPHITRUO from the left, followed by SOSIA with slaves carrying the luggage.

AMPH Come on, walk behind me.

SOS I'm following you, I'm following you closely.

AMPH I think you're a hardened criminal.

SOS But why?

AMPH Because you're telling me something that doesn't exist, hasn't existed, and won't exist.

SOS Look, now you're behaving in your typical way, not trusting your servants at all.

AMPH What's that? How so? I'll cut out this villainous tongue of   556
yours this instant, you villain.

SOS I'm yours; you can do anything that's convenient and to your taste; still, you can never deter me in any way from saying what really happened.

AMPH You hardened criminal, you dare tell me that you, who   561
are here, are at home now?

SOS I'm telling the truth.

AMPH The bad time which the gods will give you today, and I too . . .

SOS That's in your hand: I'm yours.

AMPH You whipping post, do you dare to poke fun at me, your   565
master? Do you dare to tell me a thing which no one's ever seen before and which is impossible, namely that one and the same man can be in two places simultaneously at the same time?

SOS Yes, it's just as I'm telling you.

AMPH May Jupiter destroy you.

SOS With regard to you, I haven't deserved punishment, have I, master?

	AMPH	rogasne, improbe, etiam qui ludos facis me?
	SOS	merito maledicas mihi, si id ita factum est.
		uerum hau mentior, resque uti facta dico.
	AMPH	homo hic ebrius est, ut opinor.
575	SOS	utinam ita essem.
	AMPH	optas quae facta.
575a	SOS	egone?
	AMPH	tu istic. ubi bibisti?
576		nusquam equidem bibi.
	AMPH	quid hoc sit
576a		hominis?
	SOS	equidem deciens dixi:
577		domi ego sum, inquam, ecquid audis?
577a		et apud te assum Sosia idem.
578		satin hoc plane, satin diserte,
578a		ere, nunc uideor tibi locutus
579		esse?
	AMPH	uah,
580		apage te a me.
	SOS	quid est negoti?
	AMPH	pestis te tenet.
	SOS	nam quor istuc
		dicis? equidem ualeo et saluos
583		sum recte, Amphitruo.
	AMPH	at te ego faciam
583a		hodie proinde ac meritus es,
584		ut minus ualeas et miser sis,
584a		saluos domum si rediero: iam
585		sequere sis, erum qui ludificas
585a		dictis delirantibus,
586		qui quoniam erus quod imperauit neglexisti persequi,
		nunc uenis etiam ultro irrisum dominum: quae nec fieri

AMPH Are you asking me, you rascal, when you are still derid- 571
ing me?

SOS You'd be right to abuse me if it happened like this. But
I'm not lying, and I'm telling you the matter as it really
happened.

AMPH This man's drunk, I think.

SOS I wish I were. 575

AMPH You're wishing for what's happened.

SOS I?

AMPH Yes, you there. Where have you been drinking?

SOS I haven't drunk anywhere.

AMPH What sort of a man is this?

SOS I've told you ten times over: I'm at home, I'm telling
you, can't you hear me? And I, the same Sosia, am here
with you. Don't you think now that I've said this clearly
enough and eloquently enough, master?

AMPH Bah, go away from me.

SOS What's the matter?

AMPH You have the plague. 581

SOS Why are you saying that? I'm perfectly well and healthy,
Amphitruo.

AMPH But if I return home safe and sound, I'll make sure today
that you're unwell and wretched, as you've deserved.
Follow me now, will you? You're poking fun at your mas-
ter with your crazy claims. Now that you've neglected to 586
carry out what your master ordered, you're coming of
your own accord to ridicule him. You good-for-nothing,

---

572 si non id *J*

possunt nec fando umquam accepit quisquam profers,
 carnufex;

quoius ego hodie in tergum istaec faxo expetant menda-
 cia.

590 SOS   Amphitruo, miserruma istaec miseria est seruo bono,

apud erum qui uera loquitur, si id ui uerum uincitur.

AMPH quo id, malum, pacto potest nam—mecum argumentis
 puta—

fieri, nunc uti tu ⟨et⟩ hic sis et domi? id dici uolo.

SOS   sum profecto et hic et illic. hoc quoiuis mirari licet.

595   nec tibi istuc mirum ⟨mirum⟩ magis uidetur quam mihi.

AMPH quo modo?

SOS   nihilo, inquam, mirum magis tibi istuc quam mihi;

neque, ita me di ament, credebam primo mihimet
 Sosiae,

donec Sosia illic egomet fecit sibi uti crederem.

ordine omne, uti quidque actum est, dum apud hostis se-
 dimus,

600   edissertauit. tum formam una apstulit cum nomine.

nec lact' lactis magis est simile quam ille ego similest mei.

nam ut dudum ante lucem a portu me praemisisti do-
 mum—

AMPH quid igitur?

SOS   prius multo ante aedis stabam quam illo adueneram.

AMPH quas, malum, nugas? satin tu sanus es?

SOS   sic sum ut uides.

589 faxo ista *P*, istaec faxo *Schmidt*
593 et *add. Loman*
595 mirum *add. Spengel*
598 ille egomet ⟨me⟩ *Kaempf*, illic egomet *Lindemann*

you're dishing up what cannot happen and what no one's ever heard tell of. I'll take care that those lies of yours will fall back on your back today.

SOS   Amphitruo, it's the most miserable misery for a good   590
slave who's speaking the truth in front of his master if this truth is subdued by force.

AMPH   Damn it, how is it possible—discuss it with me in a rational way—that you're both here and at home now? This is what I want to be told.

SOS   I really am both here and there. Anyone may be surprised at this. And that surprise doesn't seem any more   595
surprising to you than to me.

AMPH   How's that?

SOS   I'm telling you, this is no more surprising to you than to me. And as truly as the gods may love me, at first I didn't believe my own self, Sosia, until that other Sosia made me believe him. He told me all from first to last, just how everything happened while we were in the field with the enemy. He's stolen my looks along with my name. Milk   601
doesn't resemble milk more than that me resembles this me: when you sent me ahead home from the harbor, a while ago, before sunlight—

AMPH   (*interrupting*) Yes? What?

SOS   I was already standing in front of the house way before I got there.

AMPH   Damn it, what sort of rubbish is this? Are you in your right mind?

SOS   I'm just as you see me.

605 AMPH huic homini nescioquid est mali mala obiectum manu,
        postquam a me abiit.
    SOS   fateor, nam sum optusus pugnis pessume.
    AMPH quis te uerberauit?
    SOS   egomet memet, qui nunc sum domi.
    AMPH caue quicquam, nisi quod rogabo te, mihi responderis.
        omnium primum iste qui sit Sosia, hoc dici uolo.
610 SOS tuos est seruos.
    AMPH   mihi quidem uno te plus etiam est quam uolo,
        nec postquam sum natus habui nisi te seruom Sosiam.
    SOS at ego nunc, Amphitruo, dico: Sosiam seruom tuom
        praeter me alterum, inquam, adueniens faciam ut offen-
            das domi,
        Dauo prognatum patre eodem quo ego sum, forma, ae-
            tate item
615   qua ego sum. quid opust uerbis? geminus Sosia hic fac-
            tust tibi.
    AMPH nimia memoras mira. sed uidistine uxorem meam?
    SOS quin intro ire in aedis numquam licitum est.
    AMPH   quis te prohibuit?
    SOS Sosia ille quem iam dudum dico, is qui me contudit.
    AMPH quis istic Sosia est?
    SOS   ego, inquam. quotiens dicendum est tibi?
620 AMPH sed quid ais? num obdormiuisti dudum?
    SOS   nusquam gentium.
    AMPH ibi forte istum si uidisses quendam in somnis Sosiam.
    SOS non soleo ego somniculose eri imperia persequi.

AMPH This man's suffered some evil through the evil hand[29] af- 605
ter he left me.

SOS I admit it: I was beaten up horribly with fists.

AMPH Who hit you?

SOS I hit myself, the I that is at home now.

AMPH Mind you don't give me any reply except to what I ask
you. First of all I want to be told who that Sosia is.

SOS He's your slave. 610

AMPH In you I have one more than I want already, and ever
since I was born I haven't had a slave Sosia other than
you.

SOS But now I'm telling you, Amphitruo: I assure you, I'll
make sure that when you get there you'll find another
slave Sosia of yours at home; he's a son of the same father,
Davus, as I am, and he also has the same appearance and
age that I have. What need is there for words? You've re-
ceived a twin Sosia.

AMPH You're telling strange things indeed. But did you see my 616
wife?

SOS No, I was never allowed to go inside the house.

AMPH Who forbade you?

SOS That Sosia I've been talking about all this time, the one
who beat me up.

AMPH Who is that Sosia?

SOS It's me, I say. How often do you have to be told?

AMPH But what do you say? Did you fall asleep a while ago? 620

SOS Nowhere at all.

AMPH If by chance you'd seen that certain Sosia there, in your
dreams.

SOS I'm not in the habit of carrying out master's commands

---

29 Reference to black magic.

uigilans uidi, uigilans nunc ⟨ut⟩ uideo, uigilans fabulor,
uigilantem ille me iam dudum uigilans pugnis contudit.

625 AMPH quis homo?

SOS   Sosia, inquam, ego ille. quaeso, nonne intellegis?

AMPH qui, malum, intellegere quisquam potis est? ita nugas
blatis.

SOS uerum actutum nosces, quom illum nosces seruom So-
siam.

AMPH sequere hac igitur me, nam mi istuc primum exquisito
est opus.
sed uide ex naui efferantur quae imperaui iam omnia.

630 SOS et memor sum et diligens, ut quae imperes compareant;
non ego cum uino simitu ebibi imperium tuom.

AMPH utinam di faxint infecta dicta re eueniant tua.

II. ii: ALCVMENA. AMPHITRVO. SOSIA

ALC satin parua res est uoluptatum in uita atque in aetate
agunda

634 praequam quod molestum est? ita quoiqu' comparatum
est

634a in aetate hominum;

635 ita dis est placitum,

635a uoluptatem ut maeror comes consequatur:
quin incommodi plus malique ilico assit, boni si optigit
quid.
nam ego id nunc experior domo atque ipsa de me scio,
quoi uoluptas

623 ut *add. Lindsay,* te *add. Camerarius*
629–31 *secl. Ussing*

72

sleepily. I saw him wide awake, as I'm seeing wide awake now and talking wide awake. And that man was wide awake when he beat me up with his fists a while ago, and I was wide awake too.

AMPH Who beat you up? 625

SOS I'm telling you, Sosia, that other me. Please, won't you understand?

AMPH How on earth can anyone understand? You're waffling such nonsense.

SOS But you'll get to know it in a moment when you get to know that slave Sosia.

AMPH (*moving toward the house*) Then follow me this way: I need to get to the bottom of this first. (*stops*) But mind that everything I ordered is taken out of the ship now.

SOS I'm mindful and careful that what you order should ap- 630 pear. (*aside*) I didn't drink up your command together with the wine.

AMPH May the gods take care that your words are rendered null and void by reality.

AMPHITRUO and SOSIA are slowly walking toward the house, the latter directing the slaves with the luggage.
Enter ALCUMENA from the house; she cannot see Amphitruo and Sosia yet.

ALC Aren't the enjoyments in the course of one's life and age few compared with what's disagreeable? Yes, this is ev- eryone's lot, this is the gods' will: grief should follow en- 635 joyment as its companion, yes, and there should immedi- ately be more discomfort and trouble if anything good has happened. Well, I'm learning this at first hand now and I know it from my own experience: I was given enjoy-

638	parumper data est, dum uiri [mei] mi potestas
638a	uidendi fuit
639	noctem unam modo; atque is repente abiit a me
639a	hinc ante lucem.
640	sola hic mi nunc uideor, quia ille hinc abest quem ego amo praeter omnis.
641	plus aegri ex abitu
641a	uiri, quam ex aduentu uoluptatis cepi.
641b	sed hoc me beat
	saltem, quom perduellis uicit et domum laudis compos reuenit:
	id solacio est.
	apsit, dum modo laude parta
645	domum recipiat se; feram et perferam usque
645a	abitum eius animo
	forti atque offirmato, id modo si mercedis
647	datur mi, ut meus uictor uir belli clueat.
647a	satis mi esse ducam.
	uirtus praemium est optumum;
	uirtus omnibus rebus anteit profecto:
650	libertas, salus, uita, res et parentes,
650a	patria et prognati
	tutantur, seruantur:
	uirtus omnia in sese habet, omnia assunt
	bona quem penest uirtus.
AMPH	edepol me uxori exoptatum credo aduenturum domum,
655	quae me amat, quam contra amo, praesertim re gesta bene,
	uictis hostibus: quos nemo posse superari ratust,
	eos auspicio meo atque [in]ductu primo coetu uicimus.
	certe enim med illi expectatum optato uenturum scio.
SOS	quid? me non rere expectatum amicae uenturum meae?

ment only for a short time, as long as I had the opportunity to see my husband, for a single night only. And now he left me suddenly before sunlight. I feel alone now because the one I love more than all others is away from here. I've received more grief from my husband's going away than I've received joy from his coming. But there's one thing at least that makes me happy: he's won a victory over the enemy and returned home a hero. That gives me comfort. Let him be away, so long as he comes home in glory. I'll bear and keep bearing his departure with a firm and strong heart, if only my reward is that my husband is renowned as winner in war. I'll consider this enough for me. Courage is the best reward. Courage does indeed outdo everything: freedom, safety, life, possessions and parents, home and relatives are protected and preserved. Courage has all goods within itself, all goods are with the man who has courage.

AMPH I really believe my wife will be waiting eagerly for my arrival. She loves me and I love her in return. Especially after this success, after our victory over the enemy. No one believed they could be overcome, and yet we conquered them in the first encounter under my auspices and leadership. Yes, I know for sure that my wife will be waiting eagerly for my arrival.

SOS Well, don't you think my girlfriend will be waiting for *my* arrival?

640

644

650

655

---

638 mei *del. Lindsay*
657 inductu *P*, ductu *s*

660 ALC meus uir hicquidem est.

AMPH   sequere hac tu me.

ALC   nam quid ill' reuortitur
      qui dudum properare se[se] aibat? an ille me temptat
           sciens
      atque id se uolt experiri, suom abitum ut desiderem?
      ecastor med haud inuita se domum recipit suam.

SOS   Amphitruo, redire ad nauem meliust nos.

AMPH   qua gratia?

665 SOS   quia domi daturus nemo est prandium aduenientibus.

AMPH   qui tibi nunc istuc in mentem est?

SOS   quia enim sero aduenimus.

AMPH   qui?

SOS   quia Alcumenam ante aedis stare saturam intellego.

AMPH   grauidam ego illanc hic reliqui quom abeo.

SOS   ei perii miser.

AMPH   quid tibi est?

SOS   ad aquam praebendam commodum adueni domum,
670   decumo post mense, ut rationem te ductare intellego.

AMPH   bono animo es.

SOS   scin quam bono animo sim? si situlam [iam] cepero,
      numquam edepol tu mihi diuini [quicquam] creduis post
           hunc diem,
      ni ego illi puteo, si occepso, animam omnem intertraxe-
           ro.

     661 sese aiebat *P*, se aibat *Guyet Pylades*
     666 in mentem uenit *P*, in mentem est *Lindemann* qui *P*, quia ς
     670 dictare *P*, ductare *Lambinus*
     671 iam *del. Camerarius*
     672 quicquam *del. Bothe*
     673 occepso *Nonius*, occepto *P*

ALC (*spotting the two*) This is my husband.   660

AMPH Follow me this way. (*moves toward the house*)

ALC Why is he returning? A while ago he said he was in a rush.
Is he deliberately testing me and does he want to find out
how much I miss him when he's away? Well, I'm happy
he's returning home.

SOS (*seeing Alcumena*) Amphitruo, it's better if we return to
the ship.

AMPH Why?

SOS Because at home no one's going to give us a lunch on our   665
arrival.

AMPH How did that idea occur to you now?

SOS Well, because we've come too late.

AMPH How so?

SOS Because I can see that Alcumena is standing in front of
the house, with a well-fed look.

AMPH I left her pregnant here when I went away.

SOS Oh no, I'm done for, poor me.

AMPH What's the matter with you?

SOS As I understand your reckoning, I've come home in the
nick of time, to fetch water, ten months later.

AMPH Cheer up.   671

SOS Do you know how cheerful I am? If I take a bucket, you
shall never trust me after this day when I swear by the
gods unless I drain away all breath from that well once
I've begun.[30]

---

[30] Sosia is personifying the well and treating his work as a fight
with it.

AMPH sequere hac me modo; alium ego isti rei allegabo, ne
   time.

675 ALC magis nunc <me> meum officium facere, si huic eam
   aduorsum, arbitror.

AMPH Amphitruo uxorem salutat laetus speratam suam,
   quam omnium Thebis uir unam esse optumam diiudicat,
   quamque adeo ciues Thebani uero rumiferant probam.
   ualuistin usque? exspectatun aduenio?

SOS   hau uidi magis.

680   exspectatum eum salutat magis hau quicquam quam ca-
   nem.

AMPH et quom [te] grauidam et quom te pulchre plenam aspi-
   cio, gaudeo.

ALC opsecro ecastor, quid tu me deridiculi gratia
   sic salutas atque appellas, quasi dudum non uideris,
   quasi qui nunc primum recipias te domum huc ex hosti-
   bus,

685   atque me nunc proinde appellas quasi multo post uide-
   ris?

AMPH immo equidem te nisi nunc hodie nusquam uidi gen-
   tium.

ALC quor negas?

AMPH   quia uera didici dicere.

ALC   haud aequom facit
   qui quod didicit id dediscit. an periclitamini
   quid animi habeam? sed quid huc uos reuortimini tam
   cito?

690   an te auspicium commoratum est an tempestas continit
   qui non abiisti ad legiones, ita uti dudum dixeras?

AMPH dudum? quam dudum istuc factum est?

AMPH Just follow me this way. I'll give this job to someone else, stop being afraid.

ALC I think it's more in keeping with my duty now if I go toward him. (*does so*)

AMPH Amphitruo is happy to greet his longed-for wife, whom her husband judges to be the absolutely best of all in Thebes, and whom the citizens of Thebes truly celebrate as virtuous. Have you been well throughout? Are you happy that I'm coming?

SOS (*aside*) I don't think so. She's as happy to greet him as she would be to greet a dog.

AMPH I'm pleased to see you pregnant and beautifully round.

ALC Please, why are you making fun of me by greeting and addressing me like this, as if you hadn't seen me for a long time and as if you were coming home here from the enemy just now? Why are you addressing me now as if it was 685
ages since you saw me?

AMPH Well, I haven't seen you at all except for now today.

ALC Why are you denying it?

AMPH Because I've learnt to speak the truth.

ALC Anyone who unlearns what he's learnt isn't doing the right thing. Are you two testing what feelings I have? But why are you coming back here so quickly? Did the aus- 690
pices delay you or did the weather detain you since you didn't go away to the army as you'd said not long ago?

AMPH Not long ago? How long ago was that?

---

675 me *add. Lindemann*   678 rumiferant *Nonius*, rumificant *P*
681 te *del. Pylades*   685 *uersum secl. Muretus*
690 continet *P*, continit *Luchs*

ALC   temptas. iam dudum [pridem], modo.

AMPH qui istuc potis est fieri, quaeso, ut dicis: iam dudum,
       modo?

ALC   quid enim censes? te ut deludam contra lusorem meum,
695   qui nunc primum te aduenisse dicas, modo qui hinc abie-
       ris.

AMPH haec quidem deliramenta loquitur.

SOS   paullisper mane,
       dum edormiscat unum somnum.

AMPH   quaene uigilans somniat?

ALC   equidem ecastor uigilo et uigilans id quod factum est fa-
       bulor.
       nam dudum ante lucem et istunc et te uidi.

AMPH   quo in loco?
700 ALC hic in aedibus ubi tu habitas.

AMPH   numquam factum est.

SOS   non taces?
       quid si e portu nauis huc nos dormientis detulit?

AMPH etiam tu quoque assentaris huic?

SOS   quid uis fieri?
       non tu scis? Bacchae bacchanti si uelis aduorsarier,
       ex insana insaniorem facies, feriet saepius;
705   si opsequare, una resoluas plaga.

AMPH   at pol qui certa res
       hanc est obiurgare, quae me hodie aduenientem domum
       noluerit salutare.

SOS   irritabis crabrones.

AMPH   tace.
       Alcumena, unum rogare te uolo.

ALC   quiduis [rogare] roga.

692 pridem *del. Brunck*   708 rogare[2] *del. Aldus*

80

ALC You're testing me. Not long ago at all, just now.

AMPH How can that happen the way you're telling me, I won-
der: not long ago, just now?

ALC What do you think then? That I am making fun of you,
because you are making fun of me and claiming that 695
you've now arrived for the first time? Just now you went
away from here.

AMPH (*to Sosia*) She's talking nonsense.

SOS Wait for a bit until she sleeps off one slumber.

AMPH What, she's awake and dreaming?

ALC *I* am awake and awake I'm telling you what happened:
not long ago, before sunlight, I saw both him (*points to
Sosia*) and you.

AMPH In what place?

ALC Here in the house where you live. 700

AMPH That's never happened.

SOS Won't you be quiet? What if the ship brought us here
from the harbor while we were asleep?

AMPH Are even you agreeing with her?

SOS What do you want to be done? Don't you know? If you
want to oppose a Bacchant in her frenzy, you'll turn her
from mad into madder and she'll hit you all the more. If 705
you humor her, you can settle it by receiving just one
blow.

AMPH But I've decided to scold her, since she didn't want to
greet me today on my arrival.

SOS You'll stir up hornets.

AMPH (*to Sosia*) Be quiet. (*to his wife*) Alcumena, I want to ask
you one thing.

ALC Ask anything you like.

AMPH num tibi aut stultitia accessit aut superat superbia?
710 ALC qui istuc in mentem est tibi ex me, mi uir, percontarier?
AMPH quia salutare aduenientem me solebas antidhac,
   appellare itidem ut pudicae suos uiros quae sunt solent.
   eo more expertem te factam adueniens offendi domi.
ALC ecastor equidem te certo heri aduenientem ilico
715   et salutaui et ualuissesne usque exquisiui simul,
   mi uir, et manum prehendi et osculum tetuli tibi.
SOS tune heri hunc salutauisti?
ALC   et te quoque etiam, Sosia.
SOS Amphitruo, speraui ego istam tibi parituram filium;
   uerum non est puero grauida.
AMPH   quid igitur?
SOS   insania.
720 ALC equidem sana sum et deos quaeso ut salua pariam filium.
   uerum tu malum magnum habebis si hic suom officium
    facit:
   ob istuc omen, ominator, capies quod te condecet.
SOS enim uero praegnati oportet et malum et malum dari
   ut quod obrodat sit, animo si male esse occeperit.
725 AMPH tu me heri hic uidisti?
ALC   ego, inquam, si uis deciens dicere.
AMPH in somnis fortasse.
ALC   immo uigilans uigilantem.

710 in mente est *P Nonius*, in mentem est ς
726 misero *del. Pylades*

---

[31] A pun involving vowel quantities: *malum* with a light first syllable means "beating," *malum* with a heavy first syllable, "apple." "Punic apples," i.e., pomegranates, were given to pregnant women against nausea (Plin. *nat. hist.* 23. 107).

AMPH Have you put some foolish notion into your head or is
your pride getting out of control?

ALC How can it occur to you to ask me such a question, my 710
husband?

AMPH Because you used to greet me on my arrival before and
to address me the way modest wives normally greet their
husbands. On my arrival I've found you at home without
that habit.

ALC I certainly did greet you here on your arrival yester- 714
day and asked you at the same time if you'd been well
throughout, my husband, and I took your hand and gave
you a kiss.

SOS You greeted him yesterday, did you?

ALC And you too, Sosia.

SOS Amphitruo, I hoped that woman would bear you a son;
but she's not pregnant with a son.

AMPH Then what is she pregnant with?

SOS With madness.

ALC *I* am sane and I ask the gods that I may safely give birth to 720
a son. But *you* will have a big thrashing if *he (points to her
husband)* is doing his duty. You'll get what you deserve
for that omen, you speaker of omens.

SOS *(to Amphitruo)* Really, a pregnant woman ought to be
given a boot and a fruit[31] so she has something to chew
when she begins to feel seedy.

AMPH *(to Alcmena)* You saw me here yesterday? 725

ALC Yes, I did, I assure you, if you want me to tell you ten
times over.

AMPH In your sleep perhaps.

ALC No, while both of us were awake.

AMPH   uae [misero] mihi!

SOS   quid tibi est?

AMPH   delirat uxor.

SOS   atra bili percita est.

nulla res tam delirantis homines concinnat cito.

AMPH ubi primum tibi sensisti, mulier, impliciscier?

730 ALC equidem ecastor sana et salua sum.

AMPH   quor igitur praedicas

te heri me uidisse, qui hac noctu in portum aduecti su-
mus?

ibi cenaui atque ibi quieui in naui noctem perpetem,

nec meum pedem huc intuli etiam in aedis, ut cum exer-
citu

hinc profectus sum ad Teloboas hostis eosque ut uicimus.

735 ALC immo mecum cenauisti et mecum cubuisti.

AMPH   quid [id] est?

ALC uera dico.

AMPH   non de hac quidem hercle re; de aliis nescio.

ALC primulo diluculo abiisti ad legiones.

AMPH   quo modo?

SOS recte dicit, ut commeminit: somnium narrat tibi.

sed, mulier, postquam experrecta es, te prodigiali Ioui

740   aut mola salsa hodie aut ture comprecatam oportuit.

ALC uae capiti tuo!

SOS   tua istuc refert . . . si curaueris.

ALC iterum iam hic in me inclementer dicit, atque id sine
malo.

735 id *del. Aldus*

AMPH Bad luck to me!

SOS What's the matter with you?

AMPH My wife's mad.

SOS She's been stirred up by black bile.[32] Nothing drives people mad so quickly.

AMPH When did you first feel seizures, woman?

ALC Honestly, *I* am sane and sound.   730

AMPH Then why do you say you saw me yesterday? We only reached the harbor last night. There I had dinner and there I rested the entire night on the ship. I haven't set foot here into this house ever since I and the army went away from here to our enemy, the Teloboians, and defeated them.

ALC No, you had dinner with me and went to bed with me.   735

AMPH What's that?

ALC I'm telling the truth.

AMPH Not about this matter; about others I don't know.

ALC At the crack of dawn you went to the troops.

AMPH How's that?

SOS She's speaking correctly, as she remembers; she's telling you her dream. But, woman, after getting up you ought to have invoked Jupiter with salted flour or incense today, since he's in charge of prodigies.[33]

ALC Bad luck to you!   741

SOS To you . . . this is important, if you see to it.

ALC (*to Amphitruo*) He's abusing me the second time already, and without punishment.

---

[32] One of the four humors, responsible for depression and madness.

[33] The Romans believed that bad dreams could be predictive of bad luck. To avert this danger, they sacrificed *mola salsa*, i.e., spelt groats with brine, prepared by the Vestal virgins.

AMPH   tace tu. tu dice: egone aps te abii hinc hodie cum dilucu-
       lo?

ALC   quis igitur nisi uos narrauit mi illi ut fuerit proelium?

745 AMPH an etiam id tu scis?

ALC   quipp' qui ex te audiui, ut urbem maxumam
      expugnauisses regemque Pterelam tute occideris.

AMPH egone istuc dixi?

ALC   tute istic, etiam astante hoc Sosia.

AMPH audiuistin tu me narrare haec hodie?

SOS   ubi ego audiuerim?

AMPH hanc roga.

SOS   mequidem praesente numquam factum est, quod sciam.

750 ALC   mirum quin te aduorsus dicat.

AMPH   Sosia, age me huc aspice.

SOS   specto.

AMPH   uera uolo loqui te, nolo assentari mihi.
      audiuistin tu hodie me illi dicere ea quae illa autumat?

SOS   quaeso edepol, num tu quoque etiam insanis, quom id
      me interrogas,
      qui ipsus equidem nunc primum istanc tecum conspicio
      simul?

755 AMPH quid nunc, mulier? audin illum?

ALC   ego uero . . . ac falsum dicere.

AMPH nec tu illi nec mihi uiro ipsi credis?

ALC   eo fit quia mihi
    plurumum credo et scio istaec facta proinde ut prolo-
      quor.

AMPH tun me heri aduenisse dicis?

ALC   tun te abiisse hodie hinc negas?

AMPH *(to Sosia)* Be quiet, you. *(to his wife)* You tell me: I went away from you from here at dawn today, did I?

ALC Well, then who told me how the battle went there, if not you?

AMPH You know about it? 745

ALC Of course! I heard from you how you conquered the great city and slew King Pterela yourself.

AMPH Did I tell you about this?

ALC Yes, you there, and Sosia here was standing right next to you.

AMPH *(to Sosia)* Did you hear me tell her about this today?

SOS Where should I have heard it?

AMPH Ask *her*.

SOS This never happened in my presence, as far as I know.

ALC *(to Amphitruo)* Oh yes, it's so surprising that he doesn't 750 speak against you.

AMPH Sosia, come on, look here at me.

SOS Yes, I'm looking.

AMPH I want you to tell the truth, I don't want you simply to agree with me. Have you heard me say to her today what she's telling?

SOS Please, are you also crazy, asking me about this? I'm now seeing her for the first time myself, together with you.

AMPH What now, woman? Can you hear him? 755

ALC I can indeed hear him . . . tell a lie.

AMPH You won't believe him or me, your husband?

ALC Precisely, for the simple reason that I believe myself most and that I know that these things happened the way I'm telling you.

AMPH Are you saying that I arrived yesterday?

ALC Are you denying that you went away from here today?

AMPH nego enim uero, et me aduenire nunc primum aio ad te
        domum.

760 ALC opsecro, etiamne hoc negabis, te auream pateram mihi
        dedisse dono hodie, qua te illi donatum esse dixeras?

AMPH neque edepol dedi nec dixi; uerum ita animatus fui
        itaque nunc sum ut ea te patera donem. sed quis istuc tibi
        dixit?

ALC   ego equidem ex te audiui et ex tua accepi manu
765   pateram.

AMPH   mane, mane, opsecro te. nimis demiror, Sosia,
        qui illaec illi me donatum esse aurea patera sciat,
        nisi tu dudum hanc conuenisti et narrauisti haec omnia.

SOS neque edepol ego dixi neque istam uidi nisi tecum simul.

AMPH quid hoc sit hominis?

ALC   uin proferri pateram?

AMPH   proferri uolo.

770 ALC   fiat. <i> tu, Thessala, intus pateram proferto foras,
        qua hodie meus uir donauit me.

AMPH   secede huc tu, Sosia.
        enim uero illud praeter alia mira miror maxume,
        si haec habet [pateram] illam.

SOS   an etiam credis id, quae in hac cistellula
        tuo signo opsignata fertur?

AMPH   saluom signum est?

SOS   inspice.

775 AMPH recte, ita est ut opsignaui.

      770 i *add.* ς
      773 pateram *del.* Brix

88

AMPH Yes, I am denying it indeed, and I'm telling you that I've arrived home at your place for the first time now.

ALC Please, will you also deny that you gave me the golden 760 bowl as a gift today, the one you'd said you were presented with there?

AMPH I didn't give it and I didn't say so; but I did have it in mind to present you with this bowl, and I still do. But who told you that?

ALC I heard it from you and I received the bowl from your own hand.

AMPH Wait, wait, please. (*to Sosia*) I'm highly surprised, Sosia, how she knows I was presented with a golden bowl there, 766 unless you met her before and told her about all this.

SOS I haven't told her and I haven't seen her except together with you.

AMPH (*half aside*) What sort of a man is this?

ALC Do you want the bowl to be produced?

AMPH Yes, I do.

ALC Very well, (*calling a maid inside the house*) Go, Thessala, 770 bring out the bowl my husband presented me with today.

AMPH Step aside here, Sosia. (*they withdraw a little*) Honestly, I am astonished if she has that bowl more than I am astonished about the other astonishing things.

SOS Do you really believe that? It's being carried in this little chest (*produces it*), sealed with your own signet.

AMPH Is this seal unbroken?

SOS (*shows the chest*) Check.

AMPH Yes, it's as I sealed it. 775

SOS   quaeso, quin tu istanc iubes
        pro cerrita circumferri?

AMPH   edepol qui facto est opus;
        nam haec quidem edepol laruarum plena est.

ALC   quid uerbis opust?
        em tibi pateram, eccam.

AMPH   cedo mi.

ALC   age aspice huc sis nunciam
        tu qui quae facta infitiare; quem ego iam hic conuincam
        palam.

780   estne haec patera qua donatu's illi?

AMPH   summe Iuppiter,
        quid ego uideo? haec ea est profecto patera. perii, Sosia.

SOS   aut pol haec praestigiatrix multo mulier maxuma est
        aut pateram hic inesse oportet.

AMPH   agedum, exsolue cistulam.

SOS   quid ego istam exsoluam? opsignata est recte, res gesta
        est bene:

785   tu peperisti Amphitruonem ⟨alium⟩, ego alium peperi
        Sosiam;
        nunc si patera pateram peperit, omnes congeminauimus.

AMPH certum est aperire atque inspicere.

SOS   uide sis signi quid siet,
        ne posterius in me culpam conferas.

AMPH   aperi modo;
        nam haec quidem nos delirantis facere dictis postulat.

785 alium *add. Guyet*

SOS   Please, why don't you have an exorcism done for this madwoman?[34]

AMPH   Yes, that needs to be done: honestly, she's possessed by evil spirits.

Enter Thessala with a golden bowl, which she gives to Alcumena.

ALC   What need is there for words? Here's the bowl for you, look.

AMPH   Give it to me.

ALC   *(handing it over to him)* Go on, look here now, will you, you who deny what's happened. Now I'll refute you openly here. Isn't this the bowl you were presented with there?   780

AMPH   Great Jupiter, what do I see? That is indeed the bowl. I'm done for, Sosia.

SOS   Either this woman is by far the greatest trickster or the bowl ought to be in here. *(points to the chest)*

AMPH   Go on, open the chest.

SOS   What should I open it for? It's sealed correctly, everything's perfect. You've given birth to another Amphitruo,   785 I've given birth to another Sosia. Now if the bowl's given birth to a bowl, we've all doubled.

AMPH   I'll definitely open and check.

SOS   Please look what seal it is, so that you can't put the blame on me afterwards.

AMPH   *(examining the chest)* Just open it; this woman wants to drive us crazy with her words.

---

[34] *Cerritus*, a form influenced by Oscan, means "driven mad by Ceres." Madmen were in need of purification; in the relevant ritual, torches were carried round the possessed person (Serv. *ad Aen.* 6. 229).

790 ALC   unde haec igitur est nisi aps te quae mihi dono data est?

AMPH opus mi est istuc exquisito.

SOS   Iuppiter, pro Iuppiter!

AMPH quid tibi est?

SOS   hic patera nulla in cistula est.

AMPH   quid ego audio?

SOS   id quod uerum est.

AMPH   at cum cruciatu iam, nisi apparet, tuo.

ALC   haec quidem apparet.

AMPH   quis igitur tibi dedit?

ALC   qui me rogat.

795 SOS me captas, quia tute ab naui clanculum huc alia uia

      praecucurristi, atque hinc pateram tute exemisti atque
        eam

      huic dedisti, post hanc rursum opsignasti clanculum.

AMPH ei mihi! iam tu quoque huius adiuuas insaniam?

      ain heri nos aduenisse huc?

ALC   aio, adueniensque ilico

800   me salutauisti, et ego te, et osculum tetuli tibi.

AMPH iam illud non placet principium de osculo. perge exse-
      qui.

ALC   lauisti.

AMPH   quid postquam laui?

ALC   accubuisti.

SOS   eugae optume!

      nunc exquire.

AMPH   ne interpella. perge porro dicere.

ALC   cena apposita est; cenauisti mecum, ego accubui simul.

805 AMPH in eodem lecto?

     797 post hac *P*, post hanc *Spengel*
     801 iam . . . osculo *dat Sosiae Bothe* pergam *P*, perge *Muret*

ALC   Then where's the bowl I was given as a gift from, if not   790
from you?

AMPH I need to examine that matter.

SOS   (*opening the chest*) Jupiter, o Jupiter!

AMPH What is it?

SOS   There's no bowl in the chest here.

AMPH What do I hear?

SOS   The truth.

AMPH But you'll pay heavily this instant unless it appears.

ALC   Well, it does appear; here it is (*points to "her" bowl*).

AMPH Who gave it to you then?

ALC   The one who's asking me.

SOS   (*to Amphitruo*) You're trying to catch me out, because   795
you secretly ran ahead here from the ship on another
route, and you yourself took the bowl out from here and
gave it to her; afterwards you secretly resealed it.

AMPH Dear me! Do you also support her in her madness now?
(*to Alcumena*) Do you claim that we arrived here yester-
day?

ALC   I do, and on your arrival you immediately greeted me,
and I you, and I gave you a kiss.

AMPH I already dislike that first point about the kiss. Continue   801
your story.

ALC   You washed.

AMPH What after I washed?

ALC   You reclined at table.

SOS   (*to Amphitruo*) Fantastic, perfect! Question her now.

AMPH (*to Sosia*) Stop interrupting. (*to Alcumena*) Continue
speaking.

ALC   Dinner was served. You dined with me and I reclined at
table with you.

AMPH On the same couch?   805

ALC   in eodem.

SOS   ei, non placet conuiuium.

AMPH sine modo argumenta dicat. quid postquam cenauimus?

ALC te dormitare aibas; mensa ablata est, cubitum hinc abii-
    mus.

AMPH ubi tu cubuisti?

ALC   in eodem lecto una tecum in cubiculo.

AMPH perdidisti.

SOS   quid tibi est?

AMPH   haec me modo ad mortem dedit.

810 ALC quid iam, amabo?

AMPH   ne me appella.

SOS   quid tibi est?

AMPH   perii miser,
   quia pudicitiae huius uitium me hinc apsente est addi-
    tum.

ALC opsecro ecastor, quor istuc, mi uir, ex ted audio?

AMPH uir ego tuos sim? ne me appella, falsa, falso nomine.

SOS haeret haec res, si quidem haec iam mulier facta est ex
    uiro.

815 ALC quid ego feci qua istaec propter dicta dicantur mihi?

AMPH tute edictas facta tua, ex me quaeris quid deliqueris.

ALC quid ego tibi deliqui, si quoi nupta sum tecum fui?

AMPH tun mecum fueris? quid illac impudente audacius?
   saltem, tute si pudoris egeas, sumas mutuom.

808 tecum una *P, transp. Lindemann*

ALC Yes, on the same.

SOS Dear, dear, I don't like the dinner.

AMPH (*to Sosia*) Just let her state her case. (*to Alcumena*) What after we had dinner?

ALC You said you were feeling sleepy. The table was removed, we went away from there to sleep.

AMPH Where did you sleep?

ALC Together with you, in the same bed, in the same bedroom.

AMPH You've killed me.

SOS What's the matter with you?

AMPH This woman has just handed me over to death.

ALC Please, what do you mean?   810

AMPH Stop speaking to me.

SOS What's the matter with you?

AMPH Poor me, I'm done for because her chastity's been violated during my absence from here.

ALC Good heavens, please, why must I hear that from you, my man?

AMPH I should be your man? Stop calling me by a false name, false woman.

SOS (*half aside*) There's a problem here: if he's not a man, he must be a woman.

ALC What have I done to be talked to like that?   815

AMPH You yourself are reporting your actions, and you're asking me what you've done wrong.

ALC What wrong have I done to you if I was with you, the one I'm married to?

AMPH You were with me? What's bolder than that shameless woman? If you lack shame, you could at least borrow some.

95

820   ALC   istuc facinus quod tu insimulas nostro generi non decet.
            tu si me impudicitiai captas, capere non potes.
    AMPH pro di immortales, cognoscin tu me saltem, Sosia?
    SOS   propemodum.
    AMPH   cenauin ego heri in naui in portu Persico?
    ALC   mihi quoque assunt testes qui illud quod ego dicam as-
            sentiant.
825   SOS   nescio quid istuc negoti dicam, nisi si quispiam est
            Amphitruo alius, qui forte ted hinc apsenti tamen
            tuam rem curet teque apsente hic munus fungatur tuom.
            nam quom de illo subditiuo Sosia mirum nimist,
            certe de istoc Amphitruone iam alterum mirum est ma-
            gis.
830   AMPH nescioquis praestigiator hanc frustratur mulierem.
    ALC   per supremi regis regnum iuro et matrem familias
            Iunonem, quam me uereri et metuere est par maxume,
            ut mi extra unum te mortalis nemo corpus corpore
            contigit, quo me impudicam faceret.
    AMPH   uera istaec uelim.
835   ALC   uera dico, sed nequiquam, quoniam non uis credere.
    AMPH mulier es, audacter iuras.
    ALC   quae non deliquit, decet
            audacem esse, confidenter pro se et proterue loqui.
    AMPH satis audacter.
    ALC   ut pudicam decet.
    AMPH   enim uerbis proba's.
    ALC   non ego illam mi dotem duco esse quae dos dicitur
840   sed pudicitiam et pudorem et sedatum cupidinem,

        838 in uerbis probas *P*, enim uerbis proba's *Lachmann*

ALC The deed you're accusing me of doesn't become our fam- 820
ily. If you're trying to catch me in immoral conduct, you
won't succeed.

AMPH Immortal gods, can at least you recognize me, Sosia?

SOS Just about.

AMPH Didn't I have dinner on the ship yesterday, in Port
Persicus?

ALC I also have witnesses to corroborate what I'm saying.

SOS (to Amphitruo) I can't say what's the matter, unless 825
there's some other Amphitruo who happens to look after
your business even when you're away from here and
who's doing your job here in your absence. Well, even
though it's a very odd business with that substitute Sosia,
that other business with that other Amphitruo is cer-
tainly even odder.

AMPH Some trickster is deceiving this woman. 830

ALC I swear by the kingdom of the king on high and by the
matron Juno, whom I must honor and fear above all oth-
ers, that apart from you no mortal touched my body with
his body in a way that would make me unchaste.

AMPH I wish that were true.

ALC I'm telling the truth, but in vain, since you don't want to 835
believe me.

AMPH You're a woman, you swear boldly.

ALC A woman who hasn't done anything wrong ought to be
bold and speak confidently and daringly in her own de-
fense.

AMPH Boldly enough.

ALC As an honorable woman ought to.

AMPH Yes, you're immaculate, but only in your words.

ALC I don't consider that to be my dowry which is called
a dowry, but chastity, modesty, self-control, fear of the 841

97

deum metum, parentum amorem et cognatum concor-
diam,
tibi morigera atque ut munifica sim bonis, prosim probis.

SOS   ne ista edepol, si haec uera loquitur, examussim est optu-
ma.

AMPH delenitus sum profecto ita ut me qui sim nesciam.

845 SOS Amphitruo es profecto, caue sis ne tu te usu perduis:
ita nunc homines immutantur, postquam peregre adue-
nimus.

AMPH mulier, istanc rem inquisitam certum est non amittere.

ALC   edepol me lubente facies.

AMPH   quid ais? responde mihi,
quid si adduco tuom cognatum huc a naui Naucratem,

850   qui mecum una uectust una naui, atque is si denegat
facta quae tu facta dicis, quid tibi aequom est fieri?
numquid causam dicis quin te hoc multem matrimonio?

ALC   si deliqui, nulla causa est.

AMPH   conuenit. tu, Sosia,
duc hos intro. ego huc ab naui mecum adducam Naucra-
tem.

855 SOS nunc quidem praeter nos nemo est. dic mihi uerum se-
rio:
ecquis alius Sosia intust qui mei similis siet?

ALC   abin hinc a me, dignus domino seruos?

gods, love for my parents, friendship with relatives, obedience to you, generosity to the good, and help for the honorable.

SOS (*to Amphitruo*) Well, if she's telling the truth, she's a model of excellence.

AMPH I've really been so bewitched that I don't know who I am.

SOS You really are Amphitruo, watch out that you don't lose 845 yourself as a result of alien occupation, given the rate people get changed now after we came back from abroad.

AMPH Woman, I'm resolved not to let this matter go uninvestigated.

ALC Well, I'm happy for you to do so.

AMPH What do you say? Answer me, what if I bring your relative Naucrates over from the ship, who travelled together 850 with me on one and the same ship? What would be fair to be done to you if he denies that what you said has happened has in fact happened? Do you have any objection to me divorcing you?

ALC If I did anything wrong, I have no objection.

AMPH Agreed. You, Sosia, take those people in (*points to the slaves carrying the luggage*). I'll bring Naucrates along with me from the ship.

Exit AMPHITRUO to the left; SOSIA takes the slaves to the door and they go in without him.

SOS Now there isn't anyone here apart from us. Tell me the 855 honest truth: is there another Sosia inside, who resembles me?

ALC Will you go away from me, a slave worthy of his master?

99

SOS   abeo, si iubes.

ALC   nimis ecastor facinus mirum est qui illi collubitum siet
       meo uiro sic me insimulare falso facinus tam malum.

860   quicquid est, iam ex Naucrate cognato id cognoscam
          meo.

ACTVS III

III. i: IVPPITER

IVP   ego sum ille Amphitruo, quoi est seruos Sosia,
       idem Mercurius qui fit quando commodum est,
       in superiore qui habito cenaculo,
       qui interdum fio Iuppiter quando lubet;

865   huc autem quom extemplo aduentum apporto, ilico
       Amphitruo fio et uestitum immuto meum.
       nunc huc honoris uostri uenio gratia,
       ne hanc incohatam transigam comoediam.
       simul Alcumenae, quam uir insontem probri

870   Amphitruo accusat, ueni ut auxilium feram:
       nam mea sit culpa, quod egomet contraxerim,
       si id Alcumenae in innocentiam expetat.
       nunc Amphitruonem memet, ut occepi semel,
       esse assimulabo atque in horum familiam

875   frustrationem hodie iniciam maxumam;
       post igitur demum faciam res fiat palam
       atque Alcumenae in tempore auxilium feram
       faciamque ut uno fetu et quod grauida est uiro
       et me quod grauida est pariat sine doloribus.

872 Alcumenae innocenti *P*, Alcumenae in innocentiam *Havet*

SOS I'm going if you tell me to.

Exit SOSIA into the house.

ALC It really is a very strange thing how my husband could
     think fit to accuse me falsely of such a bad deed like this.
     Whatever it is, I'll find out from my relative Naucrates in   860
     a moment.

Exit ALCUMENA into the house.

ACT THREE

Enter JUPITER from the left.

JUP I am that Amphitruo who has a slave Sosia who becomes
     Mercury when it's convenient; I live in the upper attic
     (*points heavenward*) and from time to time become Jupi-
     ter when I feel like it. But as soon as I make my appear-   865
     ance here, I become Amphitruo immediately and change
     my clothes. Now I'm coming here out of regard for you,
     so as not to bring this comedy to a premature end. At the   869
     same time I've come to bring help to Alcumena, whom
     her husband Amphitruo is accusing of adultery, even
     though she's innocent; I'd deserve blame if what I myself
     have stirred up should fall on innocent Alcumena. Now
     I'll pretend to be Amphitruo, continuing as I have begun,
     and I'll cast their household into utter confusion today.
     Then afterwards I'll eventually have the matter revealed;   876
     I'll bring Alcumena help in the nick of time and I'll make
     sure that she can painlessly give birth in one go to both
     the child she's conceived with her husband and the one

880   Mercurium iussi me continuo consequi,
        si quid uellem imperare. nunc hanc alloquar.

                 III. ii: ALCVMENA. IVPPITER

ALC   durare nequeo in aedibus. ita me probri,
        stupri, dedecoris a uiro argutam meo!
        ea quae sunt facta infecta re esse clamitat,
885   quae nec sunt facta neque ego in me ammisi arguit;
        atque id me susque deque esse habituram putat.
        non edepol faciam, nec me perpetiar probri
        falso insimulatam, quin ego illum aut deseram
        aut satis faciat mi ille atque adiuret insuper
890   nolle esse dicta quae in me insontem protulit.
IVP   faciundum est mi illud fieri quod illaec postulat,
        si me illam amantem ad sese studeam recipere:
        quando ego quod feci id factum Amphitruoni offuit
        atque illi dudum meus amor negotium
895   insonti exhibuit, nunc autem insonti mihi
        illius ira in hanc et maledicta expetent.
ALC   sed eccum uideo qui ‹modo› me miseram arguit
        stupri, dedecoris.
IVP   te uolo, uxor, colloqui.
        quo te auortisti?
ALC   ita ‹ingeni› ingenium meum est:
900   inimicos semper osa sum optuerier.
IVP   heia autem inimicos?
ALC   sic est, uera praedico;
        nisi etiam hoc falso dici insimulaturus es.

884 infectare est at *P*, infecta re esse *Lindemann*
897 modo *add. Goetz Schoell*
899 ingeni *add. Seyffert*

she's conceived with me. I told Mercury to follow me im- 880
mediately in case I wanted to give him any orders. Now
I'll address her.

Enter ALCUMENA, not yet seeing Jupiter.

ALC   I can't endure staying in the house. To be accused of
scandal, adultery, and disgrace like this by my husband!
He's shouting that what *has* happened has *not* happened,
and he's accusing me of what hasn't happened and what 885
I haven't become guilty of. He believes I'll consider
this immaterial. But I won't, and I won't tolerate be-
ing wrongly accused of indecent behavior. No, either I'll
leave him or he has to apologize to me and in addition
swear that he wished the things hadn't been said which
he brought up against an innocent woman.

JUP   (*aside*) I have to do what she demands to be done, if I 891
want her to receive me as her lover again. Since the deed
I did was bad for Amphitruo, and since my love created
trouble for him a while ago, even though he was inno-
cent, his anger toward her and his bad words will fall on
me now, even though I am innocent.

ALC   (*aside*) But look, I can see the man who just accused his 897
poor wife of adultery and disgrace.

JUP   I want to speak to you, my dear wife. (*she turns her back*)
Where did you turn away to?

ALC   This is the nature of my nature: I've always hated looking
at my enemies.

JUP   Dear, dear; enemies? 901

ALC   Yes, correct, I'm telling the truth; unless you're going to
allege that this is also a lie.

103

	IVP	nimis iracunda es.
	ALC	potin [est] ut apstineas manum?
		nam certo, si sis sanus aut sapias satis,
905		quam tu impudicam esse arbitrere et praedices,
		cum ea tu sermonem nec ioco nec serio
		tibi habeas, nisi sis stultior stultissumo.
	IVP	si dixi, nihilo magis es neque ego esse arbitror,
		et id huc reuorti ut me purgarem tibi.
910		nam numquam quicquam meo animo fuit aegrius
		quam postquam audiui ted esse iratam mihi.
		quor dixisti? inquies. ego expediam tibi.
		non edepol quo te esse impudicam crederem;
		uerum periclitatus sum animum tuom
915		quid faceres et quo pacto id ferre induceres.
		equidem ioco illa dixeram dudum tibi,
		ridiculi causa. uel hunc rogato Sosiam.
	ALC	quin huc adducis meum cognatum Naucratem,
		testem quem dudum te adducturum dixeras
920		te huc non uenisse?
	IVP	si quid dictum est per iocum,
		non aequom est id te serio praeuortier.
	ALC	ego illum scio quam doluerit cordi meo.
	IVP	per dexteram tuam te, Alcumena, oro, opsecro,
		da mihi hanc ueniam, ignosce, irata ne' sies.
925	ALC	ego istaec feci uerba uirtute irrita;
		nunc, quando factis me impudicis apstini,
		ab impudicis dictis auorti uolo.
		ualeas, tibi habeas res tuas, reddas meas.
		iuben mi ire comites?

903 uerecunda *P*, iracunda *Lambinus* est *del. Camerarius*
926 abstines *P*, abstinei *Luchs*

JUP   *(trying to take her hand)* You're too hot-tempered.

ALC   Can't you keep your hands off? If you were sane or had   904
any sense at all, you certainly wouldn't hold a conversa-
tion, either in jest or in earnest, with a woman you con-
sider or call unchaste, unless you're more stupid than the
most stupid man.

JUP   If I said so, that doesn't make you unchaste, and I don't
think you are, and I've come back here to apologize to
you. Well, never have I been more upset about anything   910
than after hearing that you're angry with me. Why did
you say it, you'll ask. I'll explain it to you. Well, not be-
cause I believed you're unchaste. But I was testing your
attitude, what you'd do and how you'd take it. I said those   916
things as a joke to you a while ago, for fun. Ask Sosia here
if you like. *(points to the house)*

ALC   Why aren't you bringing my relative Naucrates here? A
while ago you said you'd bring him as a witness that you
hadn't come here.

JUP   If something was said as a joke, it isn't fair for you to take   921
it seriously.

ALC   I know how that joke hurt my heart.

JUP   *(grasping her hand)* I ask, I entreat you by your right
hand, Alcumena, give me this pardon, forgive me, don't
be angry.

ALC   I made your words invalid through my virtuous conduct.   925
Now that I've stayed away from unchaste actions, I want
to turn away from unchaste words. Farewell, have your
things for yourself, and return mine.[35] Are you ordering
my attendants to come with me?[36]

---

[35] This is the standard divorce formula.   [36] It was considered
inappropriate for a matron to leave the house on her own.

	IVP	sanan es?
	ALC	si non iubes,
930		ibo egomet; comitem mi Pudicitiam duxero.
	IVP	mane. arbitratu tuo ius iurandum dabo
		me meam pudicam esse uxorem arbitrarier.
		id ego si fallo, tum te, summe Iuppiter,
		quaeso Amphitruoni ut semper iratus sies.
935	ALC	a, propitius sit potius.
	IVP	confido fore;
		nam ius iurandum uerum te aduorsum dedi.
		iam nunc irata non es?
	ALC	non sum.
	IVP	bene facis.
		nam in hominum aetate multa eueniunt huius modi:
		capiunt uoluptates, capiunt rursum miserias;
940		irae interueniunt, redeunt rursum in gratiam.
		uerum irae si quae forte eueniunt huius modi
		inter eos, rursum si reuentum in gratiam est,
		bis tanto amici sunt inter se quam prius.
	ALC	primum cauisse oportuit ne diceres,
945		uerum eadem si idem purgas mi, patiunda sunt.
	IVP	iube uero uasa pura adornari mihi,
		ut quae apud legionem uota uoui si domum
		rediissem saluos, ea ego exsoluam omnia.
	ALC	ego istuc curabo.
	IVP	euocate huc Sosiam;
950		gubernatorem qui in mea naui fuit
		Blepharonem arcessat qui nobiscum prandeat.
		is adeo impransus ⟨lepide⟩ ludificabitur,
		quom ego Amphitruonem collo hinc opstricto traham.

952 lepide *add. Lindemann*

106

JUP   Are you sane?

ALC   If not, I'll go by myself. I'll take Chastity as my attendant.   930
(*turns to go*)

JUP   Wait. I'll swear an oath on your own terms that I believe
my wife to be chaste. If I deceive you in this, then I ask
you, great Jupiter, to be angry with Amphitruo for ever.

ALC   No no, let him rather be well-disposed.   935

JUP   I trust he will be: I gave a truthful oath in your presence.
You aren't angry any longer, are you?

ALC   No, I'm not angry.

JUP   Thank you. In human life many things of this sort hap-
pen: they reap enjoyment, and they reap misery again.
Arguments come up between them, and they're recon-   940
ciled again. But if by chance any argument of this sort
arises between them, and if they're reconciled again,
they're twice as fond of each other as before.

ALC   You ought to have been careful not to say such a thing in   944
the first place, but if you apologize to me for it, I'll have to
bear it.

JUP   But have clean vessels prepared for me so that I can fulfill
all the vows I made while on active service if I should
return home safe and sound.

ALC   I'll take care of that.

JUP   (*to those inside*) Call Sosia out here. He is to fetch our pi-   950
lot Blepharo, who was on my ship, so that he can have
lunch with us. (*aside*) He'll be made fun of without get-
ting lunch when I'm holding Amphitruo by the neck and
dragging him out from here.

	ALC	mirum quid solus secum secreto ille agat.
955		atque aperiuntur aedes. exit Sosia.

III. iii: SOSIA. IVPPITER. ALCVMENA

	SOS	Amphitruo, assum. si quid opus est, impera, imperium exsequar.
	IVP	‹Sosia,› optume aduenis.
	SOS	iam pax est inter uos duos?
		nam quia uos tranquillos uideo, gaudeo et uolup est mihi.
		atque ita seruom par uidetur frugi sese instituere:
960		proinde eri ut sint, ipse item sit; uoltum e uoltu comparet:
		tristis sit, si eri sint tristes; hilarus sit, si gaudeant.
		sed age responde: iam uos rediistis in concordiam?
	IVP	derides qui scis haec [iam] dudum me dixisse per iocum.
	SOS	an id ioco dixisti? equidem serio ac uero ratus.
965	IVP	habui expurigationem; facta pax est.
	SOS	optume est.
	IVP	ego rem diuinam intus faciam, uota quae sunt.
	SOS	censeo.
	IVP	tu gubernatorem a naui huc euoca uerbis meis
		Blepharonem, ut re diuina facta mecum prandeat.
	SOS	iam hic ero quom illic censebis esse me.
	IVP	actutum huc redi.
970	ALC	numquid uis, quin abeam iam intro, ut apparentur quibus opust?

957 Sosia *add. Leo*
963 iam *del. Camerarius*
968 ut *P*, uti *Lindemann*, qui *Loewe Goetz*

108

ALC   (*aside*) I wonder what he's talking about to himself alone
and in secret. (*looks around*) The door's opening. Sosia's 955
coming out.

Enter SOSIA from the house.

SOS   Amphitruo, here I am. If you need anything, command
me, I'll carry out your command.

JUP   Sosia, it's very good of you to come.

SOS   Is there peace between you two now? Well, I'm happy
and pleased to see you calm. And it seems right for a de-
cent slave to stick to this principle: just as his masters are, 960
so he too should be himself; he should model his expres-
sion on theirs: he should be unhappy if his masters are
unhappy and he should be cheerful if they are happy. But
go on, answer me: have you returned to harmony now?

JUP   You're mocking me; you know that I said this as a joke a
while ago.

SOS   You said it as a joke? *I* thought you said it in earnest and
seriously.

JUP   I've apologized. Peace has been made. 965

SOS   That's excellent.

JUP   I'll make the offerings I vowed.

SOS   Very good.

JUP   As for you, call our pilot Blepharo here from the ship on
my behalf to have lunch with me after the offerings have
been made.

SOS   I'll already be back here when you think I'm still there.

JUP   Come back here immediately.

Exit SOSIA to the left.

ALC   Is there anything you want? Otherwise I'll go in now so 970
that what's needed is prepared.

IVP   i sane, et quantum potest parata fac sint omnia.

ALC   quin uenis quando uis intro? faxo hau quicquam sit
       morae.

IVP   recte loquere et proinde diligentem ut uxorem decet.

       iam hisce ambo, et seruos et era, frustra sunt duo,

975   qui me Amphitruonem rentur esse: errant probe.

       nunc tu diuine huc fac assis Sosia,

       (audis quae dico, tam etsi praesens non ades),

       face iam Amphitruonem aduenientem ab aedibus

       ut abigas; quouis pacto fac commentus sis.

980   uolo deludi illunc, dum cum hac usuraria

       uxore nunc mi morigero. haec curata sint

       fac sis, proinde adeo ut uelle med intellegis,

       atque ut ministres mi, mihi quom sacruficem.

III. iv: MERCVRIVS

MER   concedite atque apscedite omnes, de uia decedite,

985   nec quisquam tam au‹i›dax fuat homo qui obuiam opsis-
       tat mihi.

       nam mihi quidem hercle qui minus liceat deo minitarier

       populo, ni decedat mihi, quam seruolo in comoediis?

       ill' nauem saluam nuntiat aut irati aduentum senis:

       ego sum Ioui dicto audiens, eius iussu nunc huc me af-
       fero.

990   quam ob rem mi magis par est uia decedere et conce-
       dere.

       pater uocat me, eum sequor, eius dicto, imperio sum
       audiens;

       ut filium bonum patri esse oportet, itidem ego sum patri.

       amanti supparasitor, hortor, asto, ammoneo, gaudeo.

980 illum edum *P*, illunc dum *Pareus*
985 au‹i›dax *Skutsch*

110

JUP   Do go and make sure that everything is prepared as quickly as possible.

ALC   Why don't you come in as soon as you wish? I'll make sure that there won't be any delay.

JUP   You speak properly and just as is appropriate for a diligent wife.

Exit ALCUMENA into the house.

JUP   Now both of them, slave and mistress, are fooled; they 974 think I'm Amphitruo. They're completely wrong. Now, divine Sosia, do come here (you can hear what I'm saying, even if you're not physically present); drive Amphitruo away from the house when he comes. Come up with something in any way you like. I want him to be fooled 980 while I'm enjoying myself with this borrowed wife. Do make sure that this is taken care of just the way you know I want it, and that you assist me when I'm sacrificing to myself.

Exit JUPITER into the house.
Enter MERCURY from the left.

MER   Get away and get out, all of you, get off the street; let no 985 one be so bold as to stand in my way. Why should I, a god, not be allowed to threaten people if they don't get out of my way just as much as some paltry slave in comedies? *He* announces that the ship's safe or that the angry old man's coming. But *I* obey Jupiter, I'm now betaking myself here on his command. For this reason it's more ap- 990 propriate to get off the street for *me* and to get out of *my* way. My father calls me; I follow him and obey his word and command. I behave toward my father as a good son ought to. I play the hanger-on for him while he's in love, I encourage him, stand by him, advise him, rejoice with

111

si quid patri uolup est, uoluptas ea mi multo maxuma est.

995 amat: sapit; recte facit, animo quando opsequitur suo,

quod omnis homines facere oportet, dum id modo fiat bono.

nunc Amphitruonem uolt deludi meus pater: faxo probe

iam hic deludetur, spectatores, uobis inspectantibus.

capiam coronam mi in caput, assimulabo me esse ebrium;

1000 atque illuc sursum escendero: inde optume aspellam ui-rum

de supero, quom huc accesserit; faciam ut sit madidus so-brius.

deinde illi actutum sufferet suos seruos poenas Sosia:

eum fecisse ille hodie arguet quae ego fecero hic. quid <id> mea?

meo me aequom est morigerum patri, eius studio seruire addecet.

1005 sed eccum Amphitruonem, aduenit; iam ille hic delude-tur probe,

siquidem uos uoltis auscultando operam dare.

ibo intro, ornatum capiam qui potis decet;

dein sursum ascendam in tectum ut illum hinc prohi-beam.

ACTVS IV

IV. i: AMPHITRVO

AMPH Naucratem quem conuenire uolui in naui non erat,

1010 nec domi neque in urbe inuenio quemquam qui illum ui-derit.

998 spectantibus *P*, inspectantibus *Pylades*

him. If my father enjoys something, that's by far the greatest enjoyment for me. He's in love: he's wise. He's 995 doing the right thing when he's having a good time. All humans ought to do so, as long as it's done in moderation. Now my father wants Amphitruo to be made fun of: I'll make sure that he'll be made fun of properly this instant, spectators, while you're watching. I'll put a garland[37] on my head and pretend to be drunk. I'll climb up there 1000 (*points to the roof*): from up there I'll drive the chap away gloriously when he comes here. I'll take care that he's soaked even when sober. Then his slave Sosia will immediately pay the price. Today Amphitruo will accuse him of doing what *I* will have done here. So what? It's appropriate for me to be obedient to my father, it's proper for me to serve his desire. But look, Amphitruo's coming. 1005 He'll be made fun of properly this instant, if you're willing to make the effort to listen. I'll go inside and pick an outfit suitable for those who're drunk. Then I'll go up onto the roof in order to keep him away from here.

Exit MERCURY into the house.

ACT FOUR

Enter AMPHITRUO from the left.

AMPH I wanted to meet Naucrates, but he wasn't on the ship, and neither at home nor in town can I find anyone who's 1010

---

[37] Garlands are worn at banquets.

1003 id *add. Camerarius*

nam omnis plateas perreptaui, gymnasia et myropolia;

apud emporium atque in macello, in palaestra atque in foro,

in medicinis, in tonstrinis, apud omnis aedis sacras

sum defessus quaeritando: nusquam inuenio Naucra-
tem.

1015 nunc domum ibo atque ex uxore hanc rem pergam exqui-
rere,

quis fuerit quem propter corpus suom stupri compleue-
rit.

nam me quam illam quaestionem inquisitam hodie amit-
tere

mortuom satiust. sed aedis occluserunt. eugepae,

1020 pariter hoc fit atque ut alia facta sunt. feriam fores.

aperite hoc. heus, ecquis hic est? ecquis hoc aperit os-
tium?

IV. ii: MERCVRIVS. AMPHITRVO

MER quis ad fores est?

AMPH   ego sum.

MER   quid "ego sum"?

AMPH   ita loquor.

MER   tibi Iuppiter

dique omnes irati certo sunt qui sic frangas fores.

AMPH quo modo?

MER   eo modo, ut profecto uiuas aetatem miser.

AMPH Sosia.

MER   ita: sum Sosia, nisi me esse oblitum existumas.

1025 quid nunc uis?

AMPH   sceleste, at etiam quid uelim, id tu me rogas?

MER ita, rogo. paene effregisti, fatue, foribus cardines.

an fores censebas nobis publicitus praeberier?

seen him: I crept through all the streets, sports grounds, and perfume shops; I was at the bazaar and in the meat market, in the wrestling school, and in the square, at the doctors', at the barbers', at all the temples. I'm tired from searching; I can't find Naucrates anywhere. Now I'll go 1015 home and continue questioning my wife about this matter, who it was she filled her body with shame for. Yes, I'd rather be dead than let this question go unexamined. (*tries to open the door*) But they've locked the house. Splendid! This is being done the same way as the rest. I'll knock at the door. (*does so*) Open up. Hello, is anyone 1020 here? Is anyone opening this door?

MERCURY appears on the roof-top, wearing a garland.

MER   Who's at the door?

AMPH   It's me.

MER   What, "it's me"?

AMPH   That's what I'm saying.

MER   Jupiter and all the gods are definitely angry with you for breaking the door like this.

AMPH   What do you mean?

MER   I mean that you'll live your life miserably indeed.

AMPH   Sosia!

MER   Yes, I am Sosia, unless you think I've forgotten. What do 1025 you want now?

AMPH   You criminal, you're even asking me what I want?

MER   Yes, I am asking. You almost broke the hinges off the doors, you thickhead. Did you think we get doors at pub-

quid me aspectas, stolide? quid nunc uis tibi? aut quis tu
es homo?

AMPH uerbero, etiam quis ego sim me rogitas, ulmorum Ac-
cheruns?

1030 quem pol ego hodie ob istaec dicta faciam feruentem
flagris.

MER prodigum te fuisse oportet olim in adulescentia.

AMPH quidum?

MER quia senecta aetate a me mendicas . . . malum.

AMPH cum cruciatu tuo istaec hodie, uerna, uerba funditas.

1034 MER sacrufico ego tibi.

AMPH qui?

MER quia enim te macto infortunio.

---

³⁸ Fr. i: Non. p. 540 Lindsay, *mactare* means "give someone some-
thing bad." Fr. ii: Non. p. 562 L., *occupatus* means "busy." Fr. iii: Prisc.
ii. 564 Keil, *abiendi* instead of *abeundi*. Fr. iv: Non. p. 871 L., an *aula* is a
very spacious vessel. Fr. v: Non. 871 L., a *matella* is a vessel for water.
Fr. vi and viii: Non. p. 64 L., *cerritus* and *laruatus* both mean "insane,"
the former because of the deity Ceres, the latter because of *laruae* (evil
spirits). Fr. vii: Non. p. 150 L., *exiurare* means "swear much." Fr. ix:
Non. p. 353 L., *autumare* means "say." Fr. x: Non. p. 268 L., *uolgare*
means "hold cheap and give to the people." Fr. xi: Non. p. 759–60 L.,
minitari can have active endings. Fr. xii: Non. p. 333 L. and Prisc. ii. 168
Keil, *scrobis* can be masculine. Fr. xiii: schol. in Verg. *Aen*. 8. 127,
precari can take the dative. Fr. xiv: Non. p. 347 L., *anima* can mean "an-
ger." Fr. xv: Non. p. 727 L., *furtum* can refer to anything done in secret.
Fr. xvi: Non. p. 520 L., *impedire* can mean "make dirty, bring into dis-
grace," and p. 731 L., *thesaurus* can also refer to a large amount of
something bad. Fr. xvii: Non. p. 727 L., *ingredi* can mean "come and
show oneself." Fr. xviii: gloss. Plaut. Ritschelii, between *susque deque*
(l. 886) and *perniciter* (l. 1116). Fr. xix: Non. p. 440 L., *decernere* can
mean "say."

lic expense? What are you looking at me for, you idiot?
What do you want now? Or who are you?

AMPH You thug, you even ask me who I am, you burial ground
for elm rods? For those words I'll warm you up with   1030
whips today.

MER You must have been a spendthrift back in your youth.

AMPH How so?

MER Because in your old age you're begging me . . . for a
thrashing.

AMPH You'll suffer for pouring out these words today, slave.

MER I'm making a sacrifice to you.

AMPH How?

MER Because I'm giving you an offering of blows.

*At this point a few pages must have been lost in the archetype of
the Palatine manuscripts because all of them have a gap here.
The Ambrosian palimpsest is not available for this play. How-
ever, the lacuna can partly be filled because Roman scholars
quote our comedy extensively to illustrate grammatical points,
and a number of their quotations come from the lost passage.*[38]
*Fragments i–vi are from the immediately preceding, incomplete
scene. Here Mercury continues to insult Amphitruo. Fragments
vii–x present another quarrel between Alcumena and Amphi-
truo. Presumably Alcumena heard the noise, came out, and
was immediately confronted by her husband. Mercury seems to
have left by now. Then Sosia comes back, bringing with him
Blepharo, as Jupiter had ordered. The ensuing exchange can be
seen in fragments xi–xiv. Amphitruo does not understand why
Blepharo has been brought along, and he is furious with Sosia,
whom he accuses of Mercury's rude behavior. Blepharo tries to
calm Amphitruo down. We can assume that Alcumena is back in
the house by now. Amphitruo goes in and meets Jupiter. The re-*

FRAGMENTA

i	AMPH	at ego te cruce et cruciatu mactabo, mastigia.
ii	MER	erus Amphitruo⟨st⟩ occupatus.
iii (xv G)	MER	abiendi nunc tibi etiam occasio est.
iv (iii)	MER	optumo iure infringatur aula cineris in caput.
v (iv)	MER	ne tu postules matulam unam tibi aquai infundi in caput.
vi (vii)	MER	laruatu's. edepol hominem miserum! medicum quaerita.
vii (xi)	ALC	exiurauisti te mihi dixe per iocum.
viii (xii)	ALC	quaeso aduenienti morbo medicari iube:
		tu certe aut laruatus aut cerritus es.
ix (xiii)	ALC	nisi hoc ita factum est, proinde ut factum esse autumo,
		non causam dico quin uero insimules probri.
x (xvi)	AMPH	quoius? quae me apsente corpus uolgauit suom.
xi (v)	AMPH	quid minitabas te facturum, si istas pepulissem fores?
xii (vi)	AMPH	ibi scrobes effodito ⟨tu⟩ plus sexagenos in dies.
xiii (xvii)	AMPH	noli pessumae precari.
xiv (xviii)	BLE	animam comprime.
xv (ix)	IVP	manufestum hunc optorto collo teneo furem flagiti.
xvi (x)	AMPH	immo ego hunc, Thebani ciues, qui domi uxorem meam
		impudicitia impediuit, teneo, thesaurum stupri.
xvii (viii)	AMPH	nilne te pudet, sceleste, populi in conspectum ingredi?
xviii (xix)	AMPH	clandestino.

fr. ii est *add. Hoffmann*   fr. v aquam (aqua) *P*, aquai *Lindsay*
fr. x cuiusque *P*, quoius? quae *Stowasser* uulga *P*, uolgauit *edd.*
    fr. xii tu *add. Hertz*   fr. xiii nobili pessime *Nonius*, noli pessu-
mae *Lindsay*, noli pessumo *alii edd.*
    fr. xv furem *Nonius in textu, sed* furtum *in lemmate*, furti *Loewe
Goetz*

maining fragments show the two of them coming out again, grappling with each other. Blepharo is asked to decide which is the true Amphitruo, but is unable to do so. Then the manuscripts continue.

AMPH	But I shall give you an offering of a cross and crucifixion, you whipping post.	i
MER	My master Amphitruo is busy.	ii
MER	You still have a chance to leave now.	iii (xv G)
MER	It would serve you right if a pot of ashes were smashed on your head.	iv (iii)
MER	You'd certainly ask to have one jar of water emptied on your head.	v (iv)
MER	You're possessed. A wretched man! Look for a doctor.	vi (vii)
ALC	You swore that you'd said it to me as a joke.	vii (xi)
ALC	Please, have the disease treated at the outset; you have definitely been afflicted by evil spirits or Ceres.	viii (xii)
ALC	If it didn't happen as I'm telling you, I really have no objection to you accusing me of immoral behavior.	ix (xiii)
AMPH	Whose? She prostituted her body in my absence.	x (xvi)
AMPH	What did you threaten to do if I knocked at that door?	xi (v)
AMPH	There you shall dig more than sixty ditches a day.	xii (vi)
AMPH	Don't intercede for the horrible woman.	xiii (xvii)
BLE	Keep your temper in check.	xiv (xviii)
JUP	I'm holding him in flagrante, his neck in a noose, that secret perpetrator of a shameful act.	xv (ix)
AMPH	No, *I* am holding *him*, citizens of Thebes, the man who's debased my wife with debauchery at home, this storehouse of indecency.	xvi (x)
AMPH	Don't you feel any shame, you criminal, to come into public view?	xvii (viii)
AMPH	secretly	xviii (xix)

_{xix}
_(xiv) IVP/AMPH qui nequeas nostrorum uter sit Amphitruo decer-
          nere.

IV. iii: BLEPHARO. AMPHITRVO. IVPPITER

1035 BLE uos inter uos partite; ego abeo, mihi negotium est;
          neque ego umquam usquam tanta mira me uidisse cen-
          seo.

  AMPH Blepharo, quaeso ut aduocatus mi assis neue abeas.
  BLE   uale.
          quid opust me aduocato qui utri sim aduocatus nescio?
  IVP intro ego hinc eo: Alcumena parturit.
  AMPH   perii miser.
1040   quid ego ‹faciam›, quem aduocati iam atque amici dese-
          runt?
          numquam edepol me inultus istic ludificabit, quisquis est;
          [nam] iam ad regem recta me ducam resque ut facta est
          eloquar.
          ego pol illum ulciscar hodie Thessalum ueneficum,
          qui peruorse perturbauit familiae mentem meae.
1045   sed ubi ille est? intro edepol abiit, credo ad uxorem
          meam.
          qui me Thebis alter uiuit miserior? quid nunc agam,
          quem omnes mortales ignorant et ludificant ut lubet?
          certum est, intro rumpam in aedis: ubi quemque homi-
          nem aspexero,
          si ancillam seu seruom siue uxorem siue adulterum
          seu patrem siue auom uidebo, optruncabo in aedibus.
          nec me Iuppiter nec di omnes id prohibebunt, si uolent,
          quin sic faciam uti constitui. pergam in aedis nunciam.

    1040 faciam *add. Guyet, alii alia*   1042 nam *del. Gruterus*

---

  [39] Throughout antiquity, Thessaly was considered a place full of
witches.

JUP/AMPH you who cannot decide which of us is Amphitruo

BLE You can share her between you. I'm going away, I'm busy. 1035
(*aside*) I don't think I've ever seen such strange goings-on
anywhere. (*turns to go*)

AMPH Blepharo, please help me as an advocate and don't go
away.

BLE Bye. What do you need me as an advocate for? I don't
know which of you I should be an advocate for.

Exit BLEPHARO to the left.

JUP (*aside*) I'll go inside; Alcumena is in labor.

Exit JUPITER into the house.

AMPH I'm dead, poor me. What should I do? Advocates and 1040
friends are already leaving me in the lurch. That man will
never ridicule me without paying for it, whoever he is.
This instant I'll go to the king directly and tell him how
this happened. I'll take revenge on that Thessalian[39] sor-
cerer today, who's made my household lose their heads
completely. But where is he? He went inside, to my wife I 1045
believe. What other man in Thebes is more wretched
than me? What should I do now? All mortals disown and
ridicule me as they like. (*pauses*) I'm resolved to burst
into the house. Anyone I see there, maid or slave, wife or
adulterer, father or grandfather, I'll slay in the house. 1050
Neither Jupiter nor all the gods will prevent me, if they
want to, from doing as I'm resolved to. I'll continue on
my way into the house now.

*He rushes to the door, but there is a peal of thunder and he col-
lapses.*

121

ACTVS V

V. i: BROMIA. AMPHITRVO

BRO spes atque opes uitae meae iacent sepultae in pectore,
neque ulla est confidentia iam in corde, quin amiserim;
1055 ita mi uidentur omnia, mare, terra, caelum, consequi
iam ut opprimar, ut enicer. me miseram, quid agam nes-
cio.

ita tanta mira in aedibus sunt facta. uae miserae mihi,
animo male est, aquam uelim. corrupta sum atque ap-
sumpta sum.

caput dolet, neque audio, neque oculis prospicio satis,
1060 nec me miserior femina est neque ulla uideatur magis.

ita erae meae hodie contigit. nam ubi parturit, deos [sibi]
inuocat,

strepitus, crepitus, sonitus, tonitrus: ut subito, ut prope,
ut ualide tonuit!

ubi quisque institerat, concidit crepitu. ibi nescioquis
maxuma

uoce exclamat: "Alcumena, adest auxilium, ne time:
1065 et tibi et tuis propitius caeli cultor aduenit.

exsurgite," inquit, "qui terrore meo occidistis prae
metu."

ut iacui, exsurgo. ardere censui aedis, ita tum confulge-
bant.

ibi me inclamat Alcumena; iam ea res me horrore afficit.

erilis praeuortit metus: accurro, ut sciscam quid uelit.

1061 sibi *del. Pylades*

ACT FIVE

Enter BROMIA from the house, not seeing Amphitruo.

BRO My hopes and chances of keeping my life lie buried in my
breast. There's not a bit of courage left in my heart, I've
lost it all: everything, sea, earth, and heaven, seem to pur- 1055
sue me in order that I should be crushed and killed. Dear
me, I don't know what to do. Such strange things have
happened in the house. Poor me, poor me! I'm feeling
sick, I'd like some water. I'm destroyed and I'm ruined.
My head's in pain, I can't hear, I can't see well with my
eyes, and there isn't a more wretched woman than me, 1060
nor could there seem to be one. The experience my
mistress had today! Well, when her labor began, she im-
plored the gods. There's crashing and smashing, rum-
bling and grumbling: how sudden, how close, how strong
that thunder was! Everybody fell down at the peal where
he stood. Then someone called out very loudly: "Alcu-
mena, help is at hand, stop being afraid. The one who 1065
dwells in heaven is coming, well-disposed toward you
and your family. Rise," he said, "you who have fallen
down in terror of me, out of fear." Lying as I was, I stood
up. The house was so bright at the time that I thought it
was on fire. Then Alcumena called for me. The previous
events were already filling me with terror, but the fear of
my mistress prevailed. I ran to her to find out what she

1070   atque illam geminos filios pueros peperisse conspicor;

        nec nostrum quisquam sensimus, quom peperit, nec pro-
           uidimus.

        sed quid hoc? quis hic est senex qui ante aedis nostras sic
           iacet?

        numnam hunc percussit Iuppiter?

        credo edepol, nam pro Iuppiter sepultust quasi sit mor-
           tuos.

1075   ibo et cognoscam, quisquis est. Amphitruo hic quidem
           ⟨est⟩ erus meus.

        Amphitruo.

AMPH   perii.

BRO   surge.

AMPH   interii.

BRO   cedo manum.

AMPH   quis me tenet?

BRO   tua Bromia ancilla.

AMPH   totus timeo, ita med increpuit Iuppiter.

        nec secus est quasi si ab Accherunte ueniam. sed quid tu
        foras

        egressa es?

BRO   eadem nos formido timidas terrore impulit

1080   in aedibus tu ubi habitas. nimia mira uidi. uae mihi,

        Amphitruo; ita mihi animus etiam nunc abest.

AMPH   agedum expedi:

        scin me tuom esse erum Amphitruonem?

BRO   scio.

AMPH   uide etiam nunc.

BRO   scio.

AMPH   haec sola sanam mentem gestat meorum familiarium.

1075 et *P*, ut *Acidalius* est *add. Camerarius*

wanted. I could see that she'd given birth to twin sons.   1070
When she gave birth none of us noticed or foresaw it.
(*seeing Amphitruo*) But what's this? Who's this old man
lying in front of our house like this? Has Jupiter struck
him?[40] Yes, I do believe so: by Jupiter, he's buried as if he
were a corpse. I'll go and check, whoever it is. (*examining*   1075
the man) This is my master Amphitruo. (*calling*) Am-
phitruo!

AMPH   I'm dead.

BRO   Get up.

AMPH   I'm gone.

BRO   Give me your hand. (*takes it*)

AMPH   Who's holding me?

BRO   Your maid Bromia.

AMPH   I'm all in fear, the way Jupiter struck me. It's just as if I
were coming from the Underworld. But why did you
come out?

BRO   The same fear struck us timid women with fright in the
house where you live. I have seen very strange things.
Dear me, Amphitruo: I'm beside myself even now.   1081

AMPH   Go on, tell me: do you know that I'm your master Am-
phitruo?

BRO   I do.

AMPH   Have another look now.

BRO   I do know it.

AMPH   (*half aside*) Of my household members only this one is
sane.

---

40 I.e., has he been struck down by lightning; lightning and thunder
are controlled by Jupiter.

BRO   immo omnes sani sunt profecto.

AMPH   at me uxor insanum facit

1085   suis foedis factis.

BRO   at ego faciam tu idem ut aliter praedices,

Amphitruo, piam et pudicam esse tuam uxorem ut scias.

de ea re signa atque argumenta paucis uerbis eloquar.

omnium primum: Alcumena geminos peperit filios.

AMPH   ain tu, geminos?

BRO   geminos.

AMPH   di me seruant.

BRO   sine me dicere,

1090   ut scias tibi tuaeque uxori deos esse omnis propitios.

AMPH   loquere.

BRO   postquam parturire hodie uxor occepit tua,

ubi utero exorti dolores, ut solent puerperae,

inuocat deos immortalis ut sibi auxilium ferant,

manibus puris, capite operto. ibi continuo contonat

1095   sonitu maxumo; aedis primo ruere rebamur tuas.

aedes totae confulgebant tuae quasi essent aureae.

AMPH   quaeso, apsoluito hinc me extemplo, quando satis delu-
         seris.

quid fit deinde?

BRO   dum haec aguntur, interea uxorem tuam

nec gementem nec plorantem nostrum quisquam au-
         diuimus;

1100   ita profecto sine dolore peperit.

AMPH   iam istuc gaudeo,

utut me erga merita est.

BRO   mitte istaec atque haec quae dicam accipe.

postquam peperit, pueros lauere iussit nos. occepimus.

1102 lauare *P*, lauere *Nonius*

BRO No, all are sane indeed. 1084

AMPH But my wife is driving me insane with her shameful actions.

BRO But I'll make you speak differently, Amphitruo, and I'll make you realize that your wife is pious and chaste. I'll tell you the signs and evidence for this in a few words. First of all: Alcumena has given birth to twin sons.

AMPH Do you say so, twins?

BRO Yes, twins.

AMPH The gods are saving me.

BRO Let me speak, so that you know that all the gods are well- 1090 disposed toward you and your wife.

AMPH Yes, speak.

BRO After your wife began to be in labor today, when the pains were starting in her womb, she invoked the immortal gods to bring her help, as women in labor do, with clean hands and covered head. Then immediately it thundered with a frightful sound. At first we thought your house was 1095 collapsing. Your entire house was shining as if it were made of gold.

AMPH Please free me from this anxiety immediately, now that you've had fun enough with me. What happened next?

BRO Meanwhile, while this was going on, none of us heard your wife groaning or weeping. In fact, she gave birth like 1100 this without pain.

AMPH I'm happy about that now, no matter how she behaved toward me.

BRO Stop that and take in what I'm telling you. After she gave birth, she told us to wash the boys. So we began. But the

        sed puer ille quem ego laui, ut magnust et multum ualet!
        neque eum quisquam colligare quiuit incunabulis.

1105 AMPH nimia mira memoras; si istaec uera sunt, diuinitus
        non metuo quin meae uxori latae suppetiae sient.

    BRO magis iam faxo mira dices. postquam in cunas conditust,
        deuolant angues iubati deorsum in impluuium duo
        maxumi: continuo extollunt ambo capita.

  AMPH   ei mihi!

1110 BRO ne paue. sed angues oculis omnis circumuisere.
        postquam pueros conspicati, pergunt ad cunas citi.
        ego cunas recessim rursum uorsum trahere et ducere,
        metuens pueris, mihi formidans; tantoque angues acrius
        persequi. postquam conspexit anguis ille alter puer,

1115   citus e cunis exsilit, facit recta in anguis impetum:
        alterum altera prehendit eos manu perniciter.

  AMPH mira memoras, nimis formidolosum facinus praedicas;
        nam mihi horror membra misero percipit dictis tuis.
        quid fit deinde? porro loquere.

    BRO   puer ambo anguis enicat.

1120   dum haec aguntur, uoce clara exclamat uxorem tuam—
  AMPH quis homo?

    BRO   summus imperator diuom atque hominum Iuppiter.
        is se dixit cum Alcumena clam consuetum cubitibus,
        eumque filium suom esse qui illos anguis uicerit;
        alterum tuom esse dixit puerum.

1108 iuuati *P codd. schol. Aen.*, iubatae *Nonius* (*sed* duo *feminini
generis in textu Nonii displicet; fortasse* iubatei > iubate, *quam formam
Nonius in* iubatae *correxit*)

boy I washed, how big and strong he is! No one could strap him down in his cradle.

AMPH You're telling an absolutely astonishing tale. If that is true, I have no doubt that divine help was brought to my wife. 1105

BRO I'll make you call it stranger still. After he was put into the cradle, two huge crested snakes glided down into the fountain basin.[41] Immediately both lifted up their heads.

AMPH Dear me!

BRO Stop being afraid. But the snakes were looking at all of us with their eyes. After setting eyes on the boys, they quickly made for the cradles. I dragged and shoved the cradles backwards, afraid for the boys, scared for myself. The snakes followed all the more angrily. When that one boy set eyes on the snakes, he quickly jumped out of the cradle and attacked the snakes directly. He swiftly grabbed them, one with each hand. 1110 / 1116

AMPH You're telling me astonishing things, you're speaking of an absolutely horrifying event: fright seizes my limbs at your very words, poor me. What happened next? Go on speaking.

BRO The boy killed both snakes. While this was going on, your wife's name was called out in a clear voice— 1120

AMPH (interrupting) By what man?

BRO By the greatest commander of gods and men, Jupiter. He said that he'd slept with Alcumena in secret, and that the son who'd crushed those snakes was *his*; he said that the other was *your* boy.

---

[41] The *impluuium* is a basin in the floor of the atrium, used to collect rainwater.

AMPH   pol me hau paenitet,
1125   si licet boni dimidium mihi diuidere cum Ioue.
     abi domum, iube uasa pura actutum adornari mihi,
     ut Iouis supremi multis hostiis pacem expetam.
     ego Teresiam coniectorem aduocabo et consulam
     quid faciundum censeat; simul hanc rem ut facta est elo-
          quar.
1130   sed quid hoc? quam ualide tonuit. di, opsecro uostram
     fidem.

V. ii: IVPPITER

IVP   bono animo es, assum auxilio, Amphitruo, tibi et tuis:
     nihil est quod timeas. hariolos, haruspices
     mitte omnis; quae futura et quae facta eloquar,
     multo adeo melius quam illi, quom sum Iuppiter.
1135   primum omnium Alcumenae usuram corporis
     cepi, et concubitu grauidam feci filio.
     tu grauidam item fecisti, quom in exercitum
     profectu's: uno partu duos peperit simul.
     eorum alter, nostro qui est susceptus semine,
1140   suis factis te immortali afficiet gloria.
     tu cum Alcumena uxore antiquam in gratiam
     redi: hau promeruit quam ob rem uitio uorteres;
     mea ui subacta est facere. ego in caelum migro.

V. iii: AMPHITRVO

AMPH faciam ita ut iubes et te oro promissa ut serues tua.
1145   ibo ad uxorem intro, missum facio Teresiam senem.
     nunc, spectatores, Iouis summi causa clare plaudite.

AMPH Well, I'm not upset if I can share half of the good with 1125
     Jupiter. Go home and have clean vessels prepared for me
     immediately so that I can seek great Jupiter's favor with
     many victims.

Exit BROMIA into the house.

AMPH I'll call the soothsayer Tiresias here and consult him as to
     what he thinks should be done. At the same time I'll tell
     him how this came about. But what's this? (*it thunders*) 1130
     How strong that thunder was. O gods, I implore your
     mercy.

JUPITER appears on the roof-top.

JUP Take heart, I'm here with help for you and your fam-
     ily, Amphitruo: there's no reason to be afraid. Forget
     about all seers and soothsayers. I'll tell you what's going
     to happen and what has happened much more reliably
     than they; after all I'm Jupiter. First of all I enjoyed 1135
     Alcumena's body and made her pregnant with a son by
     sleeping with her. You also made her pregnant when you
     left for the army. In one go she gave birth to both. The
     one of them who was conceived of my seed will give you
     immortal fame through his deeds. You should make up 1141
     with your wife Alcumena: she hasn't deserved that you
     should consider her at fault. She was forced to do it by my
     might. I'm departing to heaven.

AMPH I'll do as you tell me and I ask you to keep your promises.
     I'll go inside to my wife; I give up on the idea of old 1145
     Tiresias. (*turns to the audience*) Now, spectators, give us
     a big hand for the sake of great Jupiter.

ASINARIA,

OR

THE COMEDY OF ASSES

INTRODUCTORY NOTE

The humor we find in the *Asinaria* is more biting and more satirical than the jokes of almost any other play written by Plautus. Argyrippus and the courtesan Philaenium are in love with each other, but Philaenium's mother, Cleareta, disapproves of the liaison because Argyrippus cannot pay. Argyrippus has an equally impecunious rival, Diabolus. Cleareta announces that Philaenium will spend the next year with whoever pays first. Diabolus is confident that he will be able to get hold of the money required.

Argyrippus confesses his problem to his father, Demaenetus. Demaenetus seems to be a selfless and indulgent man whose only wish is to be loved by his son, but he lives under the thumb of his wife, Artemona, who would not tolerate an expensive affair. The only way Demaenetus can help his son financially is to trick his wife out of the money. He orders his slave Libanus to do the job for him together with Leonida, another slave.

Artemona has a steward called Saurea. He does not make an appearance in the play, but we learn that he is pompous and has more power in the house than Demaenetus does. Some time ago, he sold Arcadian donkeys to a man from Pella. This man has now sent someone to deliver the money. This unnamed character meets Leonida and asks where he can find Saurea. Leonida immediately claims that he himself is Saurea and asks for the money, but in vain; the man says that he does not know Saurea and wants to hand over the money in the presence of Demaenetus, whom he does know.

Leonida informs Libanus of what has happened and then rushes off to find Demaenetus. When the man with the money arrives at Demaenetus' door, he encounters Libanus and soon thereafter Leonida. Libanus also pretends that Leonida is Saurea, but the messenger is suspicious and insists on handing the money over in Demaenetus' presence. In the end the slaves take him to Demaenetus, who backs up the two slaves, who finally get the cash.

The slaves now meet Argyrippus and Philaenium, who are forced to separate because of Cleareta's greed. They hand over the money, but not before they have humiliated the two lovers by forcing Argyrippus to give Libanus a piggyback and Philaenium to embrace the slaves as if she were in love with them. Yet this is less trying than what is still in store for the couple. Demaenetus, who in the beginning had seemed rather charming, now shows his true face. The slaves are allowed to give Argyrippus the money only if Demaenetus can spend a night with Philaenium. Since the lovers have no choice, they agree to this condition. They now go to Cleareta's house, where Demaenetus is already waiting for them.

In the meantime, Diabolus has also got hold of money. With the help of his hanger-on, he has created an elaborate contract regulating every detail of Philaenium's and Cleareta's behavior. But when he goes to deliver the money, he finds out that his rival was faster and sees the party Demaenetus is having with Philaenium and a very depressed Argyrippus.

After a short discussion with Diabolus, his hanger-on

goes to Artemona to inform her of what is going on. She drags her husband out of the brothel. Argyrippus and Philaenium are now free to enjoy each other for the rest of the year. It is not clear what is going to happen to Diabolus. His hanger-on hopes to come to terms with Argyrippus and arrange some sort of prostitute-sharing, but it seems rather unlikely that this plan will materialize.

Partly due to its less than edifying content, the *Asinaria* has not received as much scholarly attention as other plays. However, there are a number of problems that would merit discussion. I can merely mention two. In ll. 127–52 a young man is standing outside Cleareta's house and shouting abuse. In ll. 153–248 she comes out and talks to him. Who is this man? The Palatine manuscripts ascribe the verses to Argyrippus; the Ambrosian palimpsest is not available for our play. At first sight this attribution seems to make good sense. One expects the young man who appears first to be the protagonist, not his rival. Yet the angry outbursts seem more in keeping with Diabolus' character, whereas Argyrippus is presented as a man prone to tears. Perhaps more importantly, Cleareta tells the young man to write a contract (l. 238). Argyrippus never mentions a contract, while Diabolus and his hanger-on come up with a lengthy document. For this reason Havet argued that the passages in question should be given to Diabolus. Speaker assignment is notoriously unreliable in our manuscripts. Like Danese, I follow Havet's suggestions here.

The second problem has to do with stage conventions. Roman comedy does not present indoor scenes. All the action takes place outside, in the street. In most comedies, this leads to a certain lack of realism, for instance when people are shouting commands into their houses af-

ter leaving them instead of saying what they want to say in-
side and then leaving. In the *Asinaria* this lack of realism is
even more striking. Demaenetus is having his party with
the courtesan and his son inside, but in l. 828 all three of
them come out and continue outside the house. To us this
seems bizarre because Demaenetus is of course afraid that
his wife might find out. However, such an oddity is perhaps
tolerable if we bear in mind that indoor scenes were im-
possible because of the stage set-up.

We know very little about the background to the *Asin-
aria*. As Plautus tells us, the play is based on the *Onagos*, or
"Ass-Driver," by Demophilus, an author of New Comedy
who is a mere name to us. As far as the first performance of
the Latin play is concerned, we also have little to rely on.
Since the play is almost devoid of sung passages, we can as-
sume that it belongs to Plautus' earliest works. In l. 307, a
verbal fight is called a *uerbiuelitatio*, a neologism achiev-
ing its comical effect by referring to the *uelites* (light-
armed and fast soldiers). Such a joke would have had the
greatest impact when the *uelites* had just been introduced.
According to Livy (26. 4. 4–10), this special force was first
deployed in 211, but presumably their training had started
somewhat earlier. *The Comedy of Asses* was probably first
staged around the same time. Some scholars try to be more
precise. In l. 124 Demaenetus says that he can see his
scipio. A *scipio* is the walking stick characteristic of old
men in comedy, often doing double duty as a cane. How-
ever, several scholars believe that Plautus is punning on
the Scipio family here and assume that a member of this
family was the magistrate who had undertaken the con-
tract to produce the play. Many members of this family
became important magistrates, but around the time the

uelites were introduced, there were only two years in which a Scipio could have produced plays as magistrate: in 212 Scipio Africanus the Elder became curule aedile, and in the following year he was made proconsul of Hispania. However, we will never know for certain whether *scipio* in l. 124 had a double meaning or not.

SELECT BIBLIOGRAPHY

Editions and Commentaries

Bertini, F. (1968), *Plauti Asinaria cum commentario exegetico* (2 vols.) (Genoa).

Danese, R. M. (2004), *Titus Maccius Plautus: Asinaria* (Sarsina).

Gray, J. H. (1894), *T. Macci Plauti Asinaria: From the Text of Goetz and Schoell, with an Introduction and Notes* (Cambridge).

Criticism

Havet, L. (1905), "Études sur Plaute, *Asinaria*, I: La seconde et la troisième scènes et la composition générale," *Revue de Philologie* 29: 94–103.

Hough, J. N. (1937), "The Structure of the *Asinaria*," *American Journal of Philology* 58: 19–37.

Lowe, J. C. B. (1992), "Aspects of Plautus' Originality in the *Asinaria*," *Classical Quarterly* 42: 152–75.

———— (1995), "Plautus' 'Indoor Scenes' and Improvised Drama," in L. Benz, E. Stärk, and G. Vogt-Spira (eds.), *Plautus und die Tradition des Stegreifspiels: Festgabe für Eckard Lefèvre zum 60. Geburtstag* (Tübingen), 23–31.

Raffaelli, R., and A. Tontini (eds.) (1999), *Lecturae Plautinae Sarsinates II: Asinaria (Sarsina, 12 settembre 1998)* (Urbino).

ASINARIA

ARGVMENTVM

Amanti argento filio auxiliarier
Sub imperio uiuens uolt senex uxorio.
Itaque ob asinos relatum pretium Saureac
Numerari iussit seruolo Leonidae.
5 **A**d amicam id fertur. cedit noctem filius.
Riualis amens ob praereptam mulierem
Is rem omnem uxori per parasitum nuntiat.
Accurrit uxor ac uirum e lustris rapit.

arg. 6 riumus *BDE*[1], ruimus *JK*, riuinus *ME*[3]*G*, primus *S*, riualis
Pylades

140

THE COMEDY OF ASSES

PLOT SUMMARY

An old man living under his wife's thumb wants to help out his
lovesick son with money. That is why he ordered that cash
in payment for donkeys, which was brought back for Saurea,
should be paid out to the slave Leonida. It is brought to the girl- 5
friend. The son concedes a night with her to his father. His rival
is furious because the woman has been snatched away under his
nose. Through his hanger-on he lets the wife know about the
whole affair. The wife rushes to the scene and drags her hus-
band out of the brothel.

PLAUTUS

PERSONAE

LIBANVS seruos
DEMAENETVS senex
DIABOLVS adulescens
CLEARETA lena
LEONIDA seruos
MERCATOR
PHILAENIVM meretrix
ARGYRIPPVS adulescens
PARASITVS
ARTEMONA matrona

SCAENA

Athenis

THE COMEDY OF ASSES

CHARACTERS

LIBANUS a slave; serves Demaenetus and his lovesick son
  Argyrippus
DEMAENETUS an old man; unhappily married
DIABOLUS a young man; Argyrippus' rival
CLEARETA a madam; prostitutes her daughter Philaenium
LEONIDA a slave; Libanus' colleague, serves Demaenetus
  and Argyrippus
MERCHANT carrying money
PHILAENIUM a prostitute; in love with Argyrippus
ARGYRIPPUS a young man; Demaenetus' son, loves
  Philaenium
HANGER-ON dependent on Diabolus
ARTEMONA a married woman; Demaenetus' wealthy wife

STAGING

The stage represents a street in Athens. In the middle are the
houses of Demaenetus and Cleareta. To the left, the street
leads to the countryside; to the right, to the city center.

PROLOGVS

hoc agite sultis, spectatores, nunciam,
quae quidem mihi atque uobis res uortat bene
gregique huic et dominis atque conductoribus.
face nunciam tu, praeco, omnem auritum poplum.
5   age nunc reside, caue modo ne gratiis.
nunc quid processerim huc et quid mi uoluerim
dicam: ut sciretis nomen huius fabulae;
nam quod ad argumentum attinet, sane breue est.
nunc quod me dixi uelle uobis dicere
10   dicam: huic nomen Graece Onago est fabulae;
Demophilus scripsit, Maccus uortit barbare;
Asinariam uolt esse, si per uos licet.
inest lepos ludusque in hac comoedia,
ridicula res est. date benigne operam mihi
15   ut uos, item <ut> alias, pariter nunc Mars adiuuet.

ACTVS I

I. i: LIBANVS. DEMAENETVS

LIB   sicut tuom uis unicum gnatum tuae
superesse uitae sospitem et superstitem,
ita ted optestor per senectutem tuam

15 item *P*, item <ut> *Guyet*, ut *Bothe*

THE COMEDY OF ASSES

PROLOGUE

Enter the SPEAKER OF THE PROLOGUE with a herald.

Spectators, pay attention now if you please. May this turn out
well for me, you, this troupe, our managers, and those who have
hired us. (*turning to the herald*) You, herald! Make the entire
crowd all ears now. (*the herald proclaims silence*) Go on, now sit　5
down; just make sure you don't do so for free.[1] Now I'll tell you
why I've come out here and what my purpose was: the purpose
was that you should know the name of this play; as far as its plot
is concerned, I'm keeping things pretty brief. Now I'll tell you
what I told you I wanted to tell you: the name of this play is
Onagos[2] in Greek. Demophilus wrote it and Maccus translated　11
it into barbarian language. He wants it to be "The Comedy of
Asses," if that is all right by you. There's wit and humor in this
comedy, it's a funny one. Do oblige me by being attentive so that　15
Mars may support you now just as he has at other times.

Exit the SPEAKER OF THE PROLOGUE with the herald.

ACT ONE

Enter DEMAENETUS from his house together with LIBANUS.

LIB　(*solemnly*) Just as you want your only son to survive you
　　safe and sound, I implore you by your old age and by the

---

[1] A joke at the herald's expense. He has to be paid not only to speak
but also to shut up.　　[2] "The Ass-Driver."

		perque illam quam tu metuis uxorem tuam,
20		si quid med erga hodie falsum dixeris,
		ut tibi superstes uxor aetatem siet
		atque illa uiua uiuos ut pestem oppetas.
	DEM	per Dium Fidium quaeris: iurato mihi
		uideo necesse esse eloqui quicquid roges.
25		ita me opstinate aggressu's ut non audeam
		profecto percontanti quin promam omnia.
		proinde actutum istuc quid sit quod scire expetis
		eloquere: ut ipse scibo, te faciam ut scias.
	LIB	dic opsecro hercle serio quod te rogem,
30		caue mi mendaci quicquam.

DEM   quin tu ergo rogas?
LIB   num me illuc ducis ubi lapis lapidem terit?
DEM quid istuc est? aut ubi istuc est terrarum loci?
LIB   ubi flent nequam homines qui polentam pinsitant,

apud fustitudinas, ferricrepinas insulas,

35   ubi uiuos homines mortui incursant boues.

DEM modo pol percepi, Libane, quid istuc sit loci:

ubi fit polenta, te fortasse dicere.

LIB   ah,

neque hercle ego istuc dico nec dictum uolo,

teque opsecro hercle ut quae locutu's despuas.

40 DEM fiat, geratur mos tibi.

LIB   age age, usque exscrea.

DEM etiamne?

LIB   age quaeso hercle usque ex penitis faucibus.

etiam amplius.

25–26 *secl. Leo*

---

[3] A god sworn by in oaths, possibly a title of Jupiter.

one you are afraid of, your wife: if you tell me any lie to- 20
day, then may your wife outlive you by a lifetime and may
you, while she is still alive, meet a living death.

DEM *(laughing)* It's by the God of Truth[3] you're asking me: I
can see that I have to tell you under oath whatever you
ask. You've accosted me so stoutly that I really wouldn't 25
dare not to bring it all out as you interrogate me. So tell
me at once what it is you want to know; anything I know
myself I'll let you know.

LIB *(in a serious tone)* Please, tell me in earnest what I'm ask-
ing you, no lies for me. 30

DEM Then why don't you ask?

LIB *(anxiously)* You won't take me to the place where stone
wears down stone, will you?

DEM What's that? Where on earth is that place?

LIB Where worthless people weep, pounding barley meal, on
the Isles of Club-Drubbing and Iron-Clanking, where 35
dead oxen[4] assault living beings.

DEM Libanus, only now have I grasped what this place of yours
is: perhaps you're mentioning the place where barley
meal is made.[5]

LIB *(in fear)* No, no! I'm not mentioning that, and I don't
want it to be mentioned, and I implore you, spit out what
you've said.

DEM All right, I'll humor you. *(spits out)* 40

LIB Come on, come on, keep on spitting it out.

DEM *(spits again)* Still more?

LIB Go on, will you; from the bottom of your throat. *(Demae-
netus spits again)* Even more.

---

[4] Jocular reference to ox-hide whips.

[5] Slaves are often punished by being sent to the mill.

	DEM	nam quo usque?
	LIB	usque ad mortem uolo.
	DEM	caue sis malam rem.
	LIB	uxoris dico, non tuam.
44–5	DEM	dono te ob istuc dictum ut expers sis metu.
	LIB	di tibi dent quaequomque optes.
	DEM	redde operam mihi.

DEM redde operam mihi.
quor hoc ego ex te quaeram? aut quor miniter tibi
propterea quod me non scientem feceris?
aut quor postremo filio suscenseam,
50 patres ut faciunt ceteri?

LIB quid istuc noui est?
demiror quid sit et quo euadat sum in metu.

DEM equidem scio iam filius quod amet meus
istanc meretricem e proxumo Philaenium.
estne hoc ut dico, Libane?

LIB rectam instas uiam.
55 ea res est. sed eum morbus inuasit grauis.

DEM quid morbi est?

LIB quia non suppetunt dictis data.

DEM tune es adiutor nunc amanti filio?

LIB sum uero, et alter noster est Leonida.

DEM bene hercle facitis, [et] a me initis gratiam.
60 uerum meam uxorem, Libane, nescis qualis sit?

LIB tu primus sentis, nos tamen in pretio sumus.

DEM fateor eam esse importunam atque incommodam.

LIB posterius istuc dicis quam credo tibi.

DEM omnes parentes, Libane, liberis suis,
65 qui mi auscultabunt, facient obsequentiam

59 et *del. Fleckeisen*   65 obsequellam *P*, obsequentiam
Gruterus, obsequelam ⟨eam⟩ *Acidalius*

DEM How far?

LIB As far down as death, that's what I want.

DEM Watch out for trouble.

LIB I mean your wife's, not yours.

DEM For that remark I grant you immunity from fear. 44–5

LIB May the gods give you whatever you wish for.

DEM Give me your attention. Why should I ask you about this? Why should I threaten you because you didn't inform me? And lastly, why should I be angry with my son like 50 other fathers?

LIB (*aside*) What new thing is this? I wonder what this means and I'm fearful of the outcome.

DEM Well, I already know that my son is in love with that prostitute from next door, Philaenium. Isn't that so, Libanus?

LIB You're on the right track. That's how it is. But a grave dis- 55 ease has come over him.

DEM What's this disease?

LIB It's that what he gives cannot match what he says.

DEM Are you now an accomplice of my son in his affair?

LIB I am indeed, and the other is our Leonida.

DEM That's very good of you; you're earning my gratitude. But 60 my wife, Libanus, don't you know what she's like?

LIB You are the first to feel the pain, but we still get a fair share.

DEM I admit that she's harsh and difficult.

LIB I believe you before you even say it.

DEM (*with an air of profound moral conviction*) Libanus, all 64 parents who listen to my advice will oblige their children

quipp' qui mage amico utantur gnato et beneuolo.
atque ego me id facere studeo, uolo amari a meis;
uolo me patris mei similem, qui causa mea
nauclerico ipse ornatu per fallaciam
70   quam amabam abduxit ab lenone mulierem;
nec puduit eum id aetatis sycophantias
struere et beneficiis me emere gnatum suom sibi.
eos me decretum est persequi mores patris.
nam me hodie orauit Argyrippus filius
75   uti sibi amanti facerem argenti copiam;
et id ego percupio opsequi gnato meo:
uolo amori †obsecutum† illius, uolo amet me patrem.
quamquam illum mater arte contenteque habet,
patres ut consueuerunt: ego mitto omnia haec.
80   praesertim quom is me dignum quoi concrederet
habuit, me habere honorem eius ingenio decet;
quom me adiit, ut pudentem gnatum aequom est pa-
          trem,
cupio esse amicae quod det argentum suae.

LIB   cupis id quod cupere te nequiquam intellego.
85   dotalem seruom Sauream uxor tua
adduxit, quoi plus in manu sit quam tibi.

DEM   argentum accepi, dote imperium uendidi.
nunc uerba in pauca conferam quid te uelim.
uiginti iam usust filio argenti minis:
90   face id ut paratum iam sit.

LIB   unde gentium?

DEM   me defrudato.

77 amori *P*, amari *Nonius*   obsecutum *P*, obsecutam *Nonius*, ob-
seculum *Gratwick*

85 Sauream *P*, Sauream ⟨huc⟩ *Havet hiatum fugiens*

150

because they then have a more friendly and affectionate son. And I am eager to do so myself. I want to be loved by my offspring. I want to be like my father, who for my sake put on a shipmaster's outfit himself and by a trick abducted the woman I was in love with from a pimp. And he 71 was not ashamed to play tricks at his age and to buy the affection of me, his son, with these acts of kindness. I'm resolved to follow these ways of my father. Today my son Argyrippus has asked me to supply him with money for 75 his affair. And I'm very keen to oblige my son in this. I want him to love me, obliging him in his love; I want him to love me, his father. But his mother has a firm and tight grip on him, just as fathers usually do; I'm having none of that. It's only fair that I should respect his inclinations, 80 especially since he felt that I deserved his confidence. Since he approached me the way a respectful son should approach his father, I wish that he should have money to give to his girlfriend.

LIB You're desiring something that I can see you're desiring in vain. Your wife brought the slave Saurea as part of her 85 dowry; even he might well have more in his pocket than you.

DEM (*bitterly*) I took the money and sold my authority for the dowry. (*after a pause*) Now I'll be short and sweet about what I want from you. My son needs twenty silver minas at once. Make sure that this sum is ready at once. 90

LIB Where on earth should it come from?

DEM Cheat me.

LIB	maximas nugas agis:
	nudo detrahere uestimenta me iubes.
	defrudem te ego? age sis tu, sine pennis uola.
	ten ego defrudem, quoi ipsi nihil est in manu
95	nisi quid tu porro uxorem defrudaueris?
DEM	qua me, qua uxorem, qua tu seruom Sauream
	potes, circumduce. aufer; promitto tibi
	non offuturum, si id hodie effeceris.
LIB	iubeas una opera me piscari in aere,
100	reti autem iaculo uenari in medio mari.
DEM	tibi optionem sumito Leonidam,
	fabricare quiduis, quiduis comminiscere:
	perficito argentum hodie ut habeat filius
	amicae quod det.
LIB	quid ais tu, Demaenete?
105 DEM	quid ⟨uis⟩?
LIB	si forte in insidias deuenero,
	tun redimes me, si me hostes interceperint?
DEM	redimam.
LIB	tum tu igitur aliud cura quidlubet.
DEM	eo ego ad forum, nisi quid uis.
LIB	i, bene ambula.
DEM	atque audin etiam?
LIB	ecce.
DEM	si quid te uolam,
110	ubi eris?
LIB	ubiquomque lubitum erit animo meo.
	profecto nemo est quem iam dehinc metuam mihi
	ne quid nocere possit, quom tu mi tua

100 uenari autem rete iaculo *BD*, uenari autem iaculo *JEK*, reti
autem iaculo uenari *Hermann*

152

LIB You're talking absolute nonsense. You're ordering me to
remove the clothes from someone who's naked. I should
cheat you? Come on, will you, and fly without wings. Am
I to cheat you? You yourself have nothing in your pocket
unless there's something you in turn have cheated your 95
wife out of.

DEM As much as you can, deceive me, my wife, the slave
Saurea; take it away. I promise you that it won't be to your
disadvantage if you achieve this today.

LIB You might as well order me to go fishing in the air, and to 100
go hunting with a casting-net in the middle of the sea.

DEM Take Leonida as your adjutant. Devise anything you like,
dream up anything you like. Just make sure that today my
son has the money to give to his beloved.

LIB What do you say, Demaenetus?

DEM What is it? 105

LIB Suppose I fall into a trap; will you ransom me if the
enemy catches me?

DEM I will.

LIB In that case you needn't worry about it.

DEM I'm going to the market, unless you want anything.

LIB Go ahead, have a good walk. (*turns away*)

DEM Are you still listening?

LIB Yes.

DEM If I want anything from you, where will you be? 110

LIB Wherever it suits me. As a matter of fact, I won't be afraid
any longer that anyone could harm me, now that you've

---

105 quid *P*, quid ⟨uis⟩ *Vahlen Demaeneto attribuens*, quid ⟨tum⟩
Niemeyer Libano attribuens

108 eo ego *DJEK*, ego eo *B*   fietne *P*, ei bene *Fleckeisen*

		oratione omnem animum ostendisti tuom.
		quin te quoque ipsum facio hau magni, si hoc patro.
115		pergam quo occepi atque ibi consilia exordiar.
	DEM	audin tu? apud Archibulum ego ero argentarium.
	LIB	nempe in foro?
	DEM	ibi, si quid opus fuerit.
	LIB	meminero.
	DEM	non esse seruos peior hoc quisquam potest
		nec magis uorsutus nec quo ab caueas aegrius.
120		eidem homini, si quid recte curatum uelis,
		mandes: moriri sese misere mauolet
		quam non perfectum reddat quod promiserit.
		nam ego illuc argentum tam paratum filio
		scio esse quam me hunc scipionem contui.
125		sed quid ego cesso ire ad forum quo inceperam?
		⟨ibo⟩ atque ibi manebo apud argentarium.

I. ii: DIABOLVS

	DIA	sicine hoc fit? foras aedibus me eici?
		promerenti optume hoccin preti redditur?
		bene merenti mala es, male merenti bona es;
130		at malo cum tuo, nam iam ex hoc loco
		ibo ego ad trisuiros uostraque ibi nomina
		faxo erunt, capitis te perdam ego et filiam,
133		perlecebrae, permities,
133ª		adulescentum exitium.

126 ibo *add. Camerarius*
127–52 *Havet attribuit Diabolo, non Argyrippo*

---

⁶ Possibly a pun on a member of the Scipio (= "stick") family; cf. introduction.

⁷ A commission responsible for prisons and executions.

shown me the depths of your soul in your speech. What's
more, I won't even care much about you yourself if I
carry this through. I will go where I had set out to go and   115
I'll begin my plans there.

DEM Are you listening? I'll be at the banker Archibulus'.

LIB You mean in the market?

DEM Yes, there, if any need arises.

LIB I'll remember.

Exit LIBANUS to the right.

DEM There can't be a worse slave than this one, or one cleverer
and more difficult to be on one's guard against. But if   120
you want anything sorted out well, you should give it to
this same man. He'll prefer dying a miserable death to
not fulfilling his promise perfectly. I am as certain that
this money is waiting for my son as I am certain that I'm
looking at this stick.[6] But why am I delaying going to the   125
market where I'd set out? I'll go and stay there at the
banker's.

Exit DEMAENETUS to the right.
Enter DIABOLUS from Cleareta's house.

DIA *(shouting)* So this is what's happening? I'm being thrown
out of the house? Is this the reward given to someone
who's done you so many good turns? You're bad to the
one who does you a good turn, you're good to the one
who does you a bad turn. But you'll suffer for it! I'll im-   130
mediately go from here to the Board of Three[7] and make
sure your names are with them. I'll destroy you and your
daughter utterly, you allurements, you ruins, you de-
structions of young men; compared to you, the sea is no

nam mare haud est mare, uos mare acerrumum;

135   nam in mari repperi, hic elaui bonis.

ingrata atque irrita esse omnia intellego

quae dedi et quod bene feci, at posthac tibi

male quod potero facere faciam, meritoque id faciam
tuo.

ego pol te redigam eodem unde orta es, ad egestatis ter-
minos,

140   ego edepol te faciam ut quae sis nunc et quae fueris scias.

quae prius quam istam adii atque amans ego animum
meum isti dedi,

sordido uitam oblectabas pane in pannis inopia,

atque ea si erant, magnas habebas omnibus dis gratias;

eadem nunc, quom est melius, me quoius opera est igno-
ras mala.

145   reddam ego te ex fera fame mansuetem, me specta
modo.

nam isti quid suscenseam ipsi? nihil est, nil quicquam
meret;

tuo facit iussu, tuo imperio paret: mater tu, eadem era es.

te ego ulciscar, te ego ut digna es perdam atque ut de me
meres.

at scelesta uiden ut ne id quidem, me dignum esse existu-
mat

150   quem adeat, quem colloquatur, quoique irato supplicet?

atque eccam illecebra exit tandem; opinor hic ante
ostium

meo modo loquar quae uolam, quoniam intus non lici-
tum est mihi.

156

sea: you are the wildest sea. At sea I found goods, here   135
they went overboard. I realize that all I gave you and did
for you is without thanks and without effect, but from
now on I'll do to you everything bad I can, and it'll serve
you right. I'll bring you back to where you came from, the
utmost poverty. Seriously, I'll make sure you know who   140
you are now and who you were before. Before I came to
her, fell in love, and gave her my heart, you used to lead
your life with coarse bread, in rags because of your pov-
erty, and if you had that, you were very grateful to all the
gods. Now that you're better off, you don't know me, you
crook, me, through whose efforts this is the case. But I'll   145
turn you from a wild beast into a tame one through hun-
ger, just look at me. Well, why should I be angry with
the girl herself? It's nothing, she's not to blame at all;
she does it on your order, she's obeying your command:
you're her mother, you're also her mistress. You are the
one I'll take revenge on, you are the one I'll annihilate as
you deserve and as your behavior toward me merits. (*af-*
ter a pause) But watch how this criminal doesn't even   149
think I'm worth coming to, worth addressing, and worth
apologizing to while I'm angry! (*Cleareta's door opens*)
Look here, at last the seductress is coming out. I think I'll
say in my own way what I want here in front of the door
since I didn't get a chance inside.

I. iii: CLEARETA. DIABOLVS

CLE   unum quodque istorum uerbum nummis Philippis aureis
      non potest auferre hinc a me si quis emptor uenerit;
155   nec recte quae tu in nos dicis, aurum atque argentum
        merum est:
      fixus hic apud nos est animus tuos clauo Cupidinis.
      remigio ueloque quantum poteris festina et fuge:
      quam magis te in altum capessis, tam aestus te in portum
        refert.

DIA   ego pol istum portitorem priuabo portorio;
160   ego te dehinc ut merita es de me et mea re tractare exse-
        quar,
      quom tu med ut meritus sum non tractas ⟨quom⟩que
        eicis domo.

CLE   magis istuc percipimus lingua dici quam factis fore.

DIA   solus solitudine ego ted atque ab egestate apstuli;
      solus si ductem, referre gratiam numquam potes.

165 CLE   solus ductato, si semper solus quae poscam dabis;
      semper tibi promissum habeto hac lege, dum superes
        datis.

DIA   qui modus dandi? nam numquam tu quidem expleri
        potes;
      modo quom accepisti, hau multo post aliquid quod pos-
        cas paras.

CLE   quid modi est ductando, amando? numquamne expleri
        potes?
170   modo remisisti, continuo iam ut remittam ad te rogas.

DIA   dedi equidem quod mecum egisti.

153–248 *Havet attribuit Diabolo et Clearetae potius quam
Argyrippo et Clearetae*
    161 quom[2] *add. F. Skutsch*

Enter CLEARETA from her house.

CLE (*cheerfully*) If any buyer comes, he can't take a single one
of your words away from me for gold Philippics. Your 155
abuse against us is pure silver and gold: your heart is fas-
tened here at our place with Cupid's spike. Hurry and
flee with oar and sail as fast as you can: the more you put
out to sea, the more the tide brings you back to the har-
bor.

DIA (*angrily*) I'll deprive that customs officer of the import
tax; from now on I'll persist in treating you the way you 160
merit of me and my property since you don't treat me as
I've merited of you and since you're throwing me out of
your house.

CLE We are aware that you say this with your tongue rather
than that you'll do it with your actions.

DIA I was the only one to rescue you from loneliness and pov-
erty. Even if I were the only one to take her home, you
could never make a sufficient return for my kindness.

CLE You alone shall take her if you alone will always give what 165
I demand. You can always rely on this promise, on this
condition, that you keep the upper hand in your gifts.

DIA What limit is there to giving? You can never be satisfied.
As soon as you've received something, you get ready to
demand something else not much later.

CLE What limit is there to taking her and making love? Can
you never be satisfied? Just now you've sent her back, yet 170
immediately you ask me to send her back to you.

DIA I gave you what you arranged with me.

CLE   et tibi ego misi mulierem:
par pari datum hostimentum est, opera pro pecunia.

DIA   male agis mecum.

CLE   quid me accusas, si facio officium meum?
nam nec fictum usquam est nec pictum nec scriptum in poematis

175   ubi lena bene agat cum quiquam amante quae frugi esse uolt.

DIA   mihi quidem te parcere aequom est tandem, ut tibi durem diu.

CLE   non tu scis? quae amanti parcet, eadem sibi parcet parum.

quasi piscis itidem est amator lenae: nequam est nisi recens;

is habet sucum, is suauitatem, eum quouis pacto condias

180   uel patinarium uel assum, uorses quo pacto lubet:
is dare uolt, is se aliquid posci, nam ibi de pleno promitur;

neque ille scit quid det, quid damni faciat: illi rei studet.

uolt placere sese amicae, uolt mihi, uolt pedisequae,
uolt famulis, uolt etiam ancillis; et quoque catulo meo

185   subblanditur nouos amator, se ut quom uideat gaudeat.

uera dico: ad suom quemque hominem quaestum esse aequom est callidum.

DIA   perdidici istaec esse uera damno cum magno meo.

CLE   si ecastor nunc habeas quod des, alia uerba praehibeas;
nunc quia nil habes, maledictis te eam ductare postulas.

190 DIA   non meum est.

CLE   nec meum quidem edepol ad te ut mittam gratiis.

uerum aetatis atque honoris gratia hoc fiet tui,

CLE And I sent you the girl. A fair return has been given for a fair price, service for money.

DIA You're treating me badly.

CLE Why do you accuse me if I do my duty? It has never been 174 recorded in sculpture or picture or poetry that a madam who wants to be any good treats any lover well.

DIA It's only fair if you spare me, though, so that I last for a long time.

CLE Don't you know? A woman who is generous to her lover is not being generous enough to herself. For a madam a lover is just like a fish: if he's not fresh, he's worthless. A 179 fresh one has juice, a fresh one has sweetness, a fresh one you can prepare any way you wish, done in a pan or baked, you can turn it any way you like. A fresh one wants to give, a fresh one wants to be asked for something, because then you take it from a full store. And he doesn't know what he's giving and what loss he's making; he's put his heart into it. He wants to please his girlfriend, he wants to please me, he wants to please the waiting-woman, he wants to please the servants, he even wants to please the maids; and a new lover even tries to make friends with my little dog so that it's happy when it sees him. I'm telling you the truth: everyone ought to be cle- 186 ver at his trade.

DIA I've learnt that this is true by making a great financial loss.

CLE Seriously, if you had something to give now, you'd be using other words; now that you don't have anything you demand to take her off in exchange for abuse.

DIA That's not my style. 190

CLE And it's not *my* style to send her to you free of charge. But on account of your youth and our regard for you the fol-

quia nobis lucro fuisti potius quam decori tibi:
si mihi dantur duo talenta argenti numerata in manum,
hanc tibi noctem honoris causa gratiis dono dabo.

195 DIA   quid si non est?

CLE   tibi non esse credam, illa alio ibit tamen.

DIA   ubi illaec quae dedi ante?

CLE   abusa. nam si ea durarent mihi,
mulier mitteretur ad te, numquam quicquam poscerem.
diem, aquam, solem, lunam, noctem, haec argento non
    emo:
cetera quae uolumus uti Graeca mercamur fide.

200   quom a pistore panem petimus, uinum ex oenopolio,
si aes habent, dant mercem: eadem nos discipulina uti-
    mur.
semper oculatae manus sunt nostrae, credunt quod ui-
    dent.
uetus est: "nihili coactio est"; scis quoius. non dico am-
    plius.

DIA   aliam nunc mi orationem despoliato praedicas,

205   longe aliam, inquam, ⟨iniqua⟩, praebes nunc atque olim
quom dabam,

205 ⟨iniqua⟩ *Danese*, ⟨linguam⟩ *Vahlen*

---

[8] I.e., 120 minas, a ridiculously high price. The girl is later on prosti-
tuted for a whole year for twenty minas.

[9] Nonius says that *abusa* is passive here (p. 107 Lindsay). Although
abutor can be used passively (Prisc. *gramm*. 2. 381. 10–12), I prefer an
active interpretation. Plautus never uses *utor* or *abutor* passively, and
omission of the copula is not unusual (cf. *Amph*. 964, where *ratus* is
short for *ratus sum*).

[10] I.e., no goods without cash.

lowing will be done, since you produced profit for us rather than a good reputation for yourself: if two silver talents[8] are handed over to me in cash, I'll give you this night with her as a gift, free of charge, on account of our regard for you.

DIA What if I don't have them? 195

CLE Then I'll believe you that you don't have them, but she'll still go elsewhere.

DIA Where's what I gave you before?

CLE I've used it up;[9] if it had lasted, the woman would have been sent to you and I'd never have demanded anything. Daylight, water, sunlight, moonlight, night, these I don't buy for money. The other things we want to use we buy on Greek credit.[10] When we want bread from the baker 200 or wine from the wineshop, they give the goods if they get the money; we have the same policy. Our hands always have eyes: they believe what they see. There's an old proverb: "there's no point in collecting"—you know what.[11] I say no more.

DIA Now that you've robbed me you are using a different 204 kind of rhetoric on me; I say, now you give me a kind of rhetoric far different from when I was providing for you, you criminal, different from the time when you were en-

---

11 An unknown proverb. I follow Ussing's interpretation, which regards *quoius* as neuter and referring to something worthless, like sand or wind (and empty promises). *Quoius* could also be masculine. If it is an object genitive, the meaning is "there's no point in forcing someone (sc. who can't pay)"; if it is a subject genitive, the meaning is "there's no point in someone (sc. blind) collecting money (sc. because he won't get it)."

aliam atque olim quom illiciebas me ad te blande ac be-
  nedice.

tum mi aedes quoque arridebant quom ad te ueniebam
  tuae;

me unice unum ex omnibus te atque illam amare aibas
  mihi;

ubi quid dederam, quasi columbae pulli in ore ambae
  meo

210 usque eratis, meo de studio studia erant uostra omnia,

usque adhaerebatis: quod ego iusseram, quod uolueram

faciebatis, quod nolebam ac uotueram, de industria

fugiebatis, nec conari id facere audebatis prius.

nunc nec quid uelim nec nolim facitis magni, pessumae.

215 CLE non tu scis? hic noster quaestus aucupi simillimust.

auceps quando concinnauit aream, offundit cibum;

[aues] assuescunt: necesse est facere sumptum qui quae-
  rit lucrum;

saepe edunt: semel si captae sunt, rem soluont aucupi.

219–
20 itidem hic apud nos: aedes nobis area est, auceps sum
  ego,

esca est meretrix, lectus illex est, amatores aues;

bene salutando consuescunt, compellando blanditer,

osculando, oratione uinnula, uenustula.

si papillam pertractauit, haud ‹id› est ab re aucupis;

225 sauium si sumpsit, sumere eum licet sine retibus.

haecin te esse oblitum in ludo qui fuisti tam diu!

DIA tua ista culpa est, quae discipulum semidoctum aps te
  amoues.

217 aues *del. Reiz*, aues suescunt *Boldrini*
218 sunt captae *P, transp. Gruterus*
224 id *add. Camerarius*, re‹d› *Lindsay item hiatum fugiens*

164

ticing me to you with flattery and kind words. Then even your house was smiling at me when I came to you. You used to say to me that out of all people you and she loved me and me only; whenever I gave you something, both of you were at my lips all the time, like chicks of a dove,[12] all your interests were in line with mine, you were clinging on to me all the time. You did whatever I ordered and whatever I wished, you deliberately avoided whatever I didn't wish and forbade, and you didn't dare try this earlier. Now you don't give a damn about what I like and what I dislike, you crooks.   209

CLE Don't you know? This trade of ours is very similar to   215
catching birds. When a fowler prepares a clearing, he spreads food there; they get used to it. He who seeks profit must make an investment. They eat often; but once they're caught they give the fowler his reward. It's the   220
same at our place here: our house is our clearing, I'm the fowler, the prostitute is the bait, the bed is the decoy, and the lovers are the birds. They get used to us through nice greetings, sweet addresses, kissing, tender[13] and delightful speech. If he's fondled her breast, that suits the fowler's interests. If he's snatched a kiss, you can snatch   225
him without nets. How could you forget that, you, who spent so much time at school!

DIA That's your fault, sending your pupil away when he's halfway through the syllabus.

12 I.e., waiting to be fed.

13 The meaning of *uinnulus* is not clear. I have followed the interpretation given by Paul the Deacon (p. 519 Lindsay).

CLE   remeato audacter, mercedem si eris nactus: nunc abi.

DIA   mane, mane, audi. dic, quid me aequom censes pro illa
      tibi dare,

230   annum hunc ne cum quiquam alio sit?

CLE   tene? uiginti minas;
      atque ea lege: si alius ad me prius attulerit, tu uale.

DIA   at ego est etiam prius quam abis quod uolo loqui.

CLE   dic quod lubet.

DIA   non omnino iam perii, est relicuom quo peream magis.
      habeo unde istuc tibi quod poscis dem; sed in leges meas

235   dabo, uti scire possis, perpetuom annum hunc mihi uti
      seruiat

      nec quemquam interea alium ammittat prorsus quam me
      ad se uirum.

CLE   quin, si tu uoles, domi serui qui sunt castrabo uiros.
      postremo ut uoles nos esse, syngraphum facito afferas;
      ut uoles, ut tibi lubebit, nobis legem imponito:

240   modo tecum una argentum afferto, facile patiar cetera.
      port[it]orum simillumae sunt ianuae lenoniae:
      si affers, tum patent, si non est quod des, aedes non
      patent.

DIA   interii si non inuenio ego illas uiginti minas,
      et profecto, nisi illud perdo argentum, pereundum est
      mihi.

245   nunc pergam ad forum atque experiar opibus, omni co-
      pia,
      supplicabo, exopsecrabo ut quemque amicum uidero,

241 portitorum *P*, portorum *Lindsay* (*genetiuus* porti *inuenitur in*
Turpilio)

CLE Come back with confidence if you find the fees: now go
away.

DIA Wait, wait, listen. Tell me, what do you think would be a   229
fair price for me to give you for her so that she won't be
with anyone else this year?

CLE For you? Twenty minas. And on these terms: if anyone
else brings it to me earlier, it's good-bye to you. (*turns
away*)

DIA But before you go away, there's still something I want to
say.

CLE (*stops and turns back to Diabolus*) Say what you like.

DIA I'm not yet completely ruined, there's still something left
that allows me to be ruined even more. I have the means   234
to give you what you demand; but I'll give it on my own
terms. Just so that you know: she has to give me her ser-
vices for this entire year and cannot let any man other
than me come near her in the meantime.

CLE If you want me to do so, I'll even castrate the male slaves
at home. In short, do bring along a contract that states
how you want us to be; as you wish, as you please, impose
your terms on us. Just bring along the money with you,   240
I'll easily put up with the rest. The doors of a madam's
house are very similar to harbors: if you bring something,
the house stands open, if you don't have anything to give,
it remains closed.

Exit CLEARETA into her house.

DIA I'm dead if I don't find those twenty minas; in fact, unless
I lose that money, I am lost. Now I'll go to the market and   245
try my luck with all means, with every resource. I'll en-
treat and implore every friend I see; I've decided to ap-

dignos, indignos adire atque experi[ri] certum est mihi,
nam si mutuas non potero, certum est sumam faenore.

ACTVS II

II. i: LIBANVS

LIB   hercle uero, Libane, nunc te meliust expergiscier
250   atque argento comparando fingere fallaciam.
     iam diu est factum quom discesti ab ero atque abiisti ad
       forum,
     igitur inueniundo argento ut fingeres fallaciam.
     ibi tu ad hoc diei tempus dormitasti in otio.
     quin tu aps te socordiam omnem reice et segnitiem
       amoue
255   atque ad ingenium uetus uorsutum recipe te tuom.
     serua erum, caue tu idem faxis alii quod serui solent,
     qui ad eri fraudationem callidum ingenium gerunt.
     unde sumam? quem interuortam? quo hanc celocem
       conferam?
     impetritum, inauguratum est: quouis ammittunt aues,
260   picus et cornix [est] ab laeua, coruos, parra ab dextera
     consuadent; certum hercle est uostram consequi senten-
       tiam.
     sed quid hoc quod picus ulmum tundit? hau temerarium
       est.
     certe hercle ego quantum ex augurio eius pici intellego,
     aut mihi in mundo sunt uirgae aut atriensi Saureae.

247 experiri *BD*, experire *JE*, experi *F. Skutsch*
255 te recipis *P*, recipe te *Scaliger*
260 est *del. Guyet*

proach the deserving and the undeserving and to try my luck: if I can't borrow it without interest, I've decided to take up a loan at interest.

Exit DIABOLUS to the right.

ACT TWO

Enter LIBANUS from the right.

LIB   Good god, Libanus, it's better to wake up now and to think up a trick for procuring the money. It's already a   251 long time since you left your master and went to the market to think up a trick for procuring the money there. There you dozed in idleness until this time of the day. Shake off all sluggishness from you, get rid of your laziness, and get back to your old clever ways! Save your mas-   256 ter, don't do the same as other slaves do, who have cunning ways only in order to cheat master. (*after a pause*) Where should I take it from? Whom should I swindle? Where should I steer this speed-boat? (*looks around*) I have a favorable omen, a favorable sign: the birds let me go in any direction. The woodpecker and the crow on the   260 left and the raven and the owl on the right recommend it;[14] I've decided to follow *your* advice. But what's this? A woodpecker is tapping an elm?[15] That cannot be due to chance. As far as I can see from the omen of this woodpecker, rods are certainly in store either for me or for the

---

14 Originally, birds on the left meant good luck. Under Greek influence, birds on the right began to mean good luck. In Plautus' time, there is confusion between the two systems.

15 Parody of an augury.

265   sed quid illuc quod exanimatus currit huc Leonida?
        metuo quom illic opscaeuauit meae falsae fallaciae.

II. ii: LEONIDA. LIBANVS

LEO ubi ego nunc Libanum requiram aut familiarem filium,
        ut ego illos lubentiores faciam quam Lubentia est?
        maxumam praedam et triumphum is affero aduentu
           meo.
270   quando mecum pariter potant, pariter scortari solent,
        hanc quidem quam nactus praedam pariter cum illis par-
           tiam.
LIB illic homo aedis compilauit, more si fecit suo.
        uae illi qui tam indiligenter opseruauit ianuam.
LEO aetatem uelim seruire, Libanum ut conueniam modo.
275 LIB mea quidem hercle liber opera numquam fies ocius.
LEO etiam de tergo ducentas plagas praegnatis dabo.
LIB largitur peculium, omnem in tergo thesaurum gerit.
LEO nam si occasioni huic tempus sese supterduxerit,
        numquam edepol quadrigis albis indipiscet postea;
280   erum in opsidione linquet, inimicum animos auxerit.
        sed si mecum occasionem opprimere hanc quae obuenit
           studet,
        maxumas opimitates, gaudio effertissumas
        suis eris ille una mecum pariet, gnatoque et patri,
        adeo ut aetatem ambo ambobus nobis sint obnoxii,
285   nostro deuincti beneficio.

275 opera liber *P, transp. Reiz*

---

[16] White horses were considered the fastest.

steward Saurea. (*looks to the right*) But what's that? Why   265
is Leonida running here all out of breath? I'm worried
because he's given me a bad omen for my deceitful de-
ceit.

Enter LEONIDA from the right.

LEO   Where should I now look for Libanus or for our young
master so that I can make them more joyful than Joy is
herself? With my coming I'm bringing them the greatest
booty and triumph. Since they drink together with me   270
and hang out with prostitutes together with me, I'll share
the booty I've got hold of together with them.

LIB   (*to the audience*) That man has plundered a house if he's
acted in character. Bad luck to the man who watched his
door so carelessly.

LEO   I'd be willing to be a slave all my life if only I can meet
Libanus.

LIB   (*aside*) You'll never be freed any sooner through *my* help.   275

LEO   I'll even give two hundred blows ready to multiply from
my back.

LIB   (*to the audience*) He's generous with his property; he car-
ries his entire treasure on his back.

LEO   If the time for this opportunity slips past, he'll never
catch it afterwards, not even with a team of four white
horses.[16] He'll leave master under siege and will increase   280
the enemy's courage. But if along with me he strives to
snatch this opportunity which is coming our way, then
along with me he'll bring forth the greatest prosperity,
brim-full with joy, for his masters, both son and father, so
much so that both of them will be indebted to both of us
for life, chained down by our good deed.   285

LIB   uinctos nescioquos ait;
non placet: metuo in commune ne quam fraudem frausus sit.

LEO perii ego oppido nisi Libanum inuenio iam, ubiubi est gentium.

LIB illic homo socium ad malam rem quaerit quem adiungat sibi.
non placet: pro monstro extemplo est quando qui sudat tremit.

290 LEO sed quid ego hic properans concesso pedibus, lingua largior?
quin ego hanc iubeo tacere, quae loquens lacerat diem?

LIB edepol hominem infelicem, qui patronam comprimat.
nam si quid sceleste fecit, lingua pro illo peiierat.

LEO approperabo, ne post tempus praedae praesidium parem.

295 LIB quae illaec praeda est? ibo aduorsum atque electabo, quicquid est.
iubeo te saluere uoce summa, quoad uires ualent.

LEO gymnasium flagri, salueto.

LIB   quid agis, custos carceris?

LEO o catenarum colone.

LIB   o uirgarum lasciuia.

LEO quot pondo ted esse censes nudum?

LIB   non edepol scio.

300 LEO scibam ego te nescire, at pol ego qui ted expendi scio:
nudus uinctus centum pondo es, quando pendes per pedes.

LIB quo argumento istuc?

LIB   (*to the audience*) He's talking about people in chains. I'm not happy about it: I'm afraid he might have got into some mischief involving the two of us.

LEO   (*shaking with excitement*) I'm done for completely if I don't find Libanus immediately, wherever he is.

LIB   (*to the audience*) That man is looking for a comrade he can attach to himself for a bad deed. I'm not happy about it: it's immediately an omen when someone who's sweating is shivering.

LEO   But now that I'm in a hurry, why am I dawdling here with   290 my feet, being generous with my tongue? Why don't I tell her to be quiet? She's wagging the day to pieces with her talk.

LIB   (*to the audience*) He's an ill-fated man since he's subduing his protectress: if he's committed any crime, his tongue gives a false oath in his favor.

LEO   I'll hurry up so that I won't procure protection for the booty when it's too late.

LIB   (*to the audience*) What sort of booty is that? I'll go to-   295 ward him and worm it out, whatever it is. (*to Leonida, loudly*) I greet you at the top of my voice, with all my strength.

LEO   Greetings to you, exercise-ground for the whip.

LIB   How do you do, guard of the gaol?

LEO   O you chain farmer.

LIB   O you rod tickler.

LEO   How many pounds do you think you weigh naked?

LIB   I really don't know.

LEO   I knew you didn't know, but I know, who weighed you: 300 naked and tied you're a hundred pounds, when you're being weighed hanging from your feet.

LIB   How so?

LEO   ego dicam, quo argumento et quo modo.
ad pedes quando alligatum est aequom centumpondium,
ubi manus manicae complexae sunt atque adductae ad
    trabem,

305   nec dependes nec propendes . . . quin malus nequamque
    sis.

LIB   uae tibi!

LEO   hoc testamento Seruitus legat tibi.

LIB   uerbiuelitationem fieri compendi uolo.
quid istuc est negoti?

LEO   certum est credere.

LIB   audacter.

LEO   licet,
sis amanti subuenire familiari filio:

310   tantum adest boni improuiso, uerum commixtum malo:
omnes de nobis carnuficum concelebrabuntur dies.
Libane, nunc audacia usust nobis inuenta et dolis.
tantum facinus modo ego inueni, ut nos dicamur duo
omnium dignissumi esse quo cruciatus confluant.

315 LIB   ergo mirabar quod dudum scapulae gestibant mihi,
hariolari quae occeperunt sibi esse in mundo malum.
quicquid est, eloquere.

LEO   magna est praeda cum magno malo.

LIB   si quidem omnes coniurati cruciamenta conferant,
habeo opinor familiarem . . . tergum, ne quaeram foris.

320 LEO   si istam firmitudinem animi optines, salui sumus.

LIB   quin si tergo res soluenda est, rapere cupio publicum:
pernegabo atque obdurabo, peiierabo denique.

313 inueni ego *P*, *transp. Bothe*
319 familiare *P*, familiarem *Nonius*

---

[17] The weight, tied to the hanging slave's feet, is intended to make

LEO I'll tell you how and in what way. When an equal weight
of a hundred pounds has been tied to your feet and
when handcuffs have embraced your hands and have
been brought to the beam, then you hang neither too 305
high nor too low . . . to stop you being bad and useless.[17]

LIB Bad luck to you!

LEO That's what Slavery bequeaths to you in her will.

LIB I want to cut short our word duel. What's that business of
yours?

LEO I've decided to entrust it to you.

LIB You can do so with confidence.

LEO Okay, if you want to help our young master in his love af-
fair. So much good is here unexpectedly, but it's mixed 310
with evil: all the days of the year will be celebrated as tor-
turers' days at our expense. Libanus, now we need to find
boldness and tricks. I've just hit upon so great a deed that
the two of us may be said to deserve more than anyone to
have tortures streaming together on us.

LIB So that's why I was wondering why my shoulder blades 315
were tickling not long ago; they began to prophesy that
trouble was in store for them. Whatever it is, speak.

LEO It's a big booty with a big thrashing.

LIB Even if all people formed an alliance and gathered tor-
ments, I have a comrade, I think . . . my back, no need to
look for any outside.[18]

LEO If you hold on to that firmness of mind, we're safe. 320

LIB Well, if I have to pay with my back, I'm keen to plunder
the treasury: then I'll deny it and stick to it, and I'll even
give a false oath.

him immobile so that he cannot fight back when he is beaten. In this in-
consistent double simile, the weight is also used for weighing the slave.

    [18] It was normally the back that was beaten. Libanus' back will bear
the brunt of the suffering for him.

LEO   em istaec uirtus est, quando usust qui malum fert forti-
      ter;

      fortiter malum qui patitur, idem post patitur bonum.

325 LIB   quin rem actutum edisseris? cupio malum nanciscier.

LEO   placide ergo unumquicquid rogita, ut acquiescam. non
      uides

      me ex cursura anhelitum etiam ducere?

LIB   age age, mansero
      tuo arbitratu, uel adeo usque dum peris.

LEO   ubinam est erus?

LIB   maior apud forum est, minor hic est intus.

LEO   iam satis est mihi.

330 LIB   tum igitur tu diues es factus?

LEO   mitte ridicularia,
    ⟨Libane⟩.

LIB   mitto. istuc quod affers aures exspectant meae.

LEO   animum aduorte, ut aeque mecum haec scias.

LIB   taceo.

LEO   beas.

      meministine asinos Arcadicos mercatori Pelleo

334–
 5   nostrum uendere atriensem?

LIB   memini. quid tum postea?

LEO   em ergo is argentum huc remisit quod daretur Saureae
      pro asinis. adulescens uenit modo, qui id argentum at-
      tulit.

LIB   ubi is homo est?

    331 Libane *add. Lindsay in apparatu*, ⟨quid sit⟩ *add. Ritschl post*
istuc

LEO   There you go, that's manly behavior, if someone bears a
      thrashing bravely when necessary. He who submits to a
      thrashing bravely can afterwards submit to a good time.

LIB   Why don't you expound the matter to me immediately? 325
      I'm keen to get my thrashing.

LEO   (*pretending to be still panting*) Then ask me each ques-
      tion gently, so that I can calm down. Can't you see that
      I'm still out of breath from running?

LIB   All right, all right, I'll wait just as you wish, or even until
      you die.

LEO   Where on earth is master?

LIB   The old one's in the market, the young one's in here.
      (*points to Cleareta's house*)

LEO   Enough for me now.

LIB   So you've become rich? 330

LEO   Stop your jokes, Libanus.

LIB   All right. My ears are waiting for what you're bringing
      with you.

LEO   Pay attention so that you know about it as well as I do.

LIB   I'm silent.

LEO   You're making me happy. Do you remember that our
      steward sold donkeys from Arcadia[19] to a merchant from
      Pella?

LIB   I do. What next?

LEO   Well then, he sent money back here to be given to Saurea 336
      for the donkeys. A young man's just come who has
      brought this money with him.

LIB   Where is he?

[19] Arcadian donkeys were famous throughout Greece (Varro *rust*.
2. 1. 14).

LEO	iam deuorandum censes, si conspexeris?
LIB	ita enim uero. sed tamen tu nempe eos asinos praedicas
340	uetulos, claudos, quibus suptritae ad femina iam erant
	ungulae?
LEO	ipsos, qui tibi subuectabant rure huc uirgas ulmeas.
LIB	teneo, atque idem te hinc uexerunt uinctum rus.
LEO	memor es probe.
	uerum in tonstrina ut sedebam, me infit percontarier
	ecquem filium Stratonis nouerim Demaenetum.
345	dico me nouisse extemplo et me eius seruom praedico
	esse, et aedis demonstraui nostras.
LIB	quid tum postea?
LEO	ait se ob asinos ferre argentum atriensi Saureae,
	uiginti minas, sed eum se non nosse hominem qui siet,
	ipsum uero se nouisse callide Demaenetum.
350	quoniam ille elocutus haec sic—
LIB	quid tum?
LEO	ausculta ergo, scies.
	extemplo facio facetum me atque magnuficum uirum,
	dico med esse atriensem. sic hoc respondit mihi:
	"ego pol Sauream non noui nec qua facie sit scio.
	te non aequom est suscensere. si erum uis Demaenetum,
355	quem ego noui, adduce: argentum non morabor quin
	feras."
	ego me dixi erum adducturum et me domi praesto fore;
	ille in balineas iturust, inde huc ueniet postea.
	quid nunc consili captandum censes? dice.
LIB	em istuc ago
	quo modo argento interuortam et aduentorem et Sau-
	ream.

348 sese *P*, se *Acidalius*   356 dixeram *P*, dixi erum *Acidalius*

LEO   You think he ought to be swallowed immediately if you set eyes on him?

LIB   Precisely. But are you talking about those old, lame donkeys whose hooves had been worn away up to the thighs?

LEO   Exactly, the ones which used to carry elm-rods from the country here for you.   341

LIB   I get you, and the same ones carried you from here to the country in fetters.

LEO   You remember it well. But while I was sitting at the barber's he began to ask me if I knew a certain Demaenetus, the son of Strato. I said immediately that I knew him and   345
told him that I was his slave, and I showed him our house.

LIB   What next?

LEO   He said he was bringing money as payment for donkeys to the steward Saurea, twenty minas, but he didn't know who this chap was, but he knew the master Demaenetus well. When he'd said this—   350

LIB   (*interrupting*) What then?

LEO   Well, listen and you'll know. Immediately I turned into a clever and grand man and I said that I am the steward. He answered me like this: "I don't know Saurea or what he looks like. It wouldn't be fair of you to be angry. Do bring along your master Demaenetus, whom I do know,   355
if you please. I won't delay you getting the money." I said I'd bring master along and would be at home waiting. He's going to go to the baths, then he'll come here afterwards. What plan do you think we should go for now? Tell me.

LIB   (*in deep thought*) Well, I'm at it, how I can swindle both the newcomer and Saurea out of the money. This scheme   360

179

360		iam hoc opus est exasceato; nam si ille argentum prius
		hospes huc affert, continuo nos ambo exclusi sumus.
		nam me hodie senex seduxit solum seorsum ab aedibus,
		mihi tibique interminatust nos futuros ulmeos,
365		ni hodie Argyrippo argenti essent uiginti minae;
		iussit uel nos atriensem uel nos uxorem suam
		defrudare, dixit sese operam promiscam dare.
		nunc tu abi ad forum ad erum et narra haec ut nos acturi
		sumus:
		te ex Leonida futurum esse atriensem Sauream,
		dum argentum afferat mercator pro asinis.
	LEO	faciam ut iubes.
370	LIB	ego illum interea hic oblectabo, prius si forte aduenerit.
	LEO	quid ais?
	LIB	quid uis?
	LEO	pugno malam si tibi percussero,
		mox quom imitabor Sauream, caueto ne suscenseas.
	LIB	hercle uero tu cauebis ne me attingas, si sapis,
		ne hodie malo cum auspicio nomen commutaueris.
375	LEO	quaeso, aequo animo patitor.
	LIB	patitor tu item quom ego te referiam.
	LEO	dico ut usust fieri.
	LIB	dico hercle ego quoque ut facturus sum.
	LEO	ne nega.
	LIB	quin promitto, inquam, hostire contra ut merueris.
	LEO	ego abeo, tu iam, scio, patiere. sed quis hic est? is est,

364 essent uiginti argenti *P*, argenti essent uiginti *Fleckeisen*, uiginti essent argenti *Pylades*

366 promissam *P*, promiscam *Palmer*

372 Sauream imitabor *P, transp. Fleckeisen*

needs to be roughed out immediately: if he, the stranger, brings the money here before, we're both shut out immediately. Today, when I was alone, the old man took me aside, away from the house, and he threatened me and you, saying that we were going to be elmy[20] unless Argyrippus had twenty silver minas today. He told us to 365 cheat the steward or his wife, and he said he would give us support either way. Now go to the market to master and tell him how we're going to sort this out: you'll turn from Leonida into the steward Saurea while the merchant is bringing the money for the donkeys.

LEO   I'll do as you command. (*turns away*)

LIB   In the meantime I'll divert him here if by chance he arrives earlier.   370

LEO   (*turns back to Libanus*) What do you say?

LIB   What do you want?

LEO   If I deliver a blow to your cheek with my fist while playing Saurea in a moment, make sure you aren't angry.

LIB   God, you will make sure that you don't touch me, if you're wise, so that you don't find your name changed under a bad omen today.

LEO   Come on, bear it patiently.   375

LIB   And you bear it the same way when I hit back.

LEO   I'm telling you how it has to be done.

LIB   And I'm telling you how I'm going to behave.

LEO   Stop refusing.

LIB   I'm not refusing—on the contrary, I'm promising, I insist, to give you tit for tat as you deserve.

LEO   *I* am off and *you*, I know, will put up with it in a moment.

---

20 A joke; since slaves are beaten with elm rods, they can be said to consist of elm wood.

            ille est ipsus. iam ego recurro huc. tu hunc interea hic
              tene.

380   uolo seni narrare.

LIB   quin tuom officium facis ergo ac fugis?

II. iii: MERCATOR. LIBANVS

MER ut demonstratae sunt mihi, hasce aedis esse oportet
       Demaenetus ubi dicitur habitare. i, puere, pulta
       atque atriensem Sauream, si est intus, euocato huc.

LIB   quis nostras sic frangit fores? ohe, inquam, si quid audis.

385 MER nemo etiam tetigit. sanun es?

LIB   at censebam attigisse
       propterea huc quia habebas iter. nolo ego fores con-
            seruas
       meas a te uerberarier. sane ego sum amicus nostris [aedi-
            bus].

MER pol hau periclum est cardines ne foribus effringantur,
       si istoc exemplo omnibus qui quaerunt respondebis.

390 LIB ita haec morata est ianua: extemplo ianitorem
       clamat, procul si quem uidet ire ad se calcitronem.
       sed quid uenis? quid quaeritas?

MER   Demaenetum uolebam.

LIB   si sit domi, dicam tibi.

MER   quid eius atriensis?

LIB   nihilo mage intus est.

MER   ubi est?

LIB   ad tonsorem ire dixit.

387 aedibus *P, del. Gulielmus*

---

[21] A pun. It is Leonida's duty to run away (a) because he needs to
speak to Demaenetus and (b) because bad slaves are always on the run.

    (*looking around*) But who is this here? That's him, that 379
man there is him in person. I'll rush back here in a mo-
ment. You keep him here in the meantime. I want to tell
the old man.

LIB Why don't you do your job then and run away?[21]

Exit LEONIDA to the right.
*Enter a MERCHANT with a young servant; they stop in front of
Demaenetus' house.*

MER The way it was described to me, it ought to be this house
here where Demaenetus is said to live. Go, boy, knock,
and call out here the steward Saurea if he's inside.

LIB (*rushing toward them*) Who's breaking our door like this?
Stop, I say, if you can hear me.

MER No one has even touched it yet. Are you in your right 385
mind?

LIB But I thought you'd touched it because you were heading
this way. I don't want my fellow slave, the door, to be
beaten by you. I am truly a friend of my colleagues.

MER There's no danger that the hinges will broken off the door
if you answer all callers this way.

LIB This is the way with this door: it calls for the porter imme- 390
diately if it sees some ruffian approaching from a dis-
tance. But why have you come? What are you looking
for?

MER I wanted to see Demaenetus.

LIB If he was at home, I'd tell you.

MER How about his steward?

LIB He's not inside either.

MER Where is he?

LIB He said he was going to the barber's.

395	MER	quom uenisset, post non redit?
	LIB	non edepol. quid uolebas?
	MER	argenti uiginti minas, si adesset, accepisset.
	LIB	qui pro istuc?
	MER	asinos uendidit Pellaeo mercatori mercatu.
	LIB	scio. tu id nunc refers? iam hic credo eum affuturum.
	MER	qua facie uoster Saurea est? si is est, iam scire potero.
400	LIB	macilentis malis, rufulus aliquantum, uentriosus, truculentis oculis, commoda statura, tristi fronte.
	MER	non potuit pictor rectius describere eius formam.
	LIB	atque hercle ipsum adeo contuor, quassanti capite incedit.
		quisque obuiam huic occesserit irato, uapulabit.
405	MER	siquidem hercle Aeacidinis minis animisque expletus cedit,
		si med iratus tetigerit, iratus uapulabit.

II. iv: LEONIDA. MERCATOR. LIBANVS

	LEO	quid hoc sit negoti neminem meum dictum magni facere?
		Libanum in tonstrinam ut iusseram uenire, is nullus uenit.
		ne ille edepol tergo et cruribus consuluit hau decore.
410	MER	nimis imperiosust.
	LIB	uae mihi!
	LEO	hodie saluere iussi
		Libanum libertum? iam manu emissu's?
	LIB	opsecro te.

---

[22] The legendary hero of Homer's *Iliad*.

184

MER After he'd gone, he didn't return later?   395
LIB No, he didn't. What did you want?
MER If he were here, he'd have received twenty silver minas.
LIB What for?
MER He sold donkeys to a merchant from Pella at the market.
LIB I know. Are you bringing this money now? I believe he'll
     be here in a moment.
MER What does your Saurea look like? (*aside*) In a second I'll
     be able to know if it's him.
LIB A chap with hollow cheeks, reddish hair, a belly, savage   400
     eyes, average height, and stern face.
MER (*aside*) Not even a painter could sketch his appearance
     more exactly.
LIB Yes, and what's more, I can see him in person, he's walk-
     ing along, shaking his head. Anyone who gets in his way
     when he's angry will get a thrashing.
MER Even if he's walking along full of the threats and fury of 405
     an Achilles,[22] if in his anger he then touches me, he will
     get a thrashing in his anger.

Enter LEONIDA from the right, with a cane.

LEO (*shouting*) What's going on here? No one can be both-
     ered about what I say? When I had ordered Libanus to
     come to the barber's, he didn't come at all. Damn it, he
     hasn't given suitable attention to his back and his shins.
MER (*aside*) He's excessively domineering.   410
LIB (*feigning fear*) Dear me!
LEO (*in a sarcastic tone*) Did I give greetings to the freedman
     Libanus today? Have you already been set free?
LIB I entreat you!

LEO   ne tu hercle cum magno malo mihi obuiam occessisti.

         quor non uenisti, ut iusseram, in tonstrinam?

LIB   hic me moratust.

LEO   siquidem hercle nunc summum Iouem te dicas detinuisse

415   atque is precator assiet, malam rem effugies numquam.

         tu, uerbero, imperium meum contempsisti?

LIB   perii, hospes.

MER   quaeso hercle noli, Saurea, mea causa hunc uerberare.

LEO   utinam nunc stimulus in manu mihi sit—

MER   quiesce quaeso.

LEO   —qui latera conteram tua, quae occalluere plagis.

420   apscede ac sine me hunc perdere, qui semper me ira incendit,

         quoi numquam unam rem me licet semel praecipere furi,

         quin centiens eadem imperem atque ogganniam, itaque iam hercle

         clamore ac stomacho non queo labori suppeditare.

         iussin, sceleste, ab ianua hoc stercus hinc auferri?

425   iussin columnis deici operas araneorum?

         iussin in splendorem dari bullas has foribus nostris?

         nihil est: tamquam si claudus sim, cum fusti est ambulandum.

         quia triduom hoc unum modo foro operam assiduam dedo,

430   dum reperiam qui quaeritet argentum in faenus, hic uos

         dormitis interea domi atque erus in hara, haud aedibus, habitat.

         em ergo hoc tibi.

430 aedibus habitat *P* (*contra legem Hermann-Lachmann*), aedibus
habet *Pylades* (*uix melius, contra legem Ritschelii*)

LEO   Crossing my path will cost you a good thrashing. Why
      didn't you come to the barber's, as I'd told you?

LIB   (*pointing to the merchant*) This chap delayed me.

LEO   Even if you were to say now that Jupiter above had kept
      you and if he were to be here to plead for you, still, you'll   415
      never escape a thrashing. You despised my orders, good-
      for-nothing?

LIB   (*to the merchant, in a pleading voice*) I'm done for,
      stranger.

MER   Saurea, I beg you, don't beat him, for my sake.

LEO   I wish I had a cattle-prod in my hand now—

MER   (*interrupting*) Please calm down. (*steps in between Li-
      banus and Leonida*)

LEO   —so that I could pound your ribs to pieces with it, the
      skin of which has become so thick from blows. (*shoves
      the merchant aside*) Get out of my way and let me kill this   420
      chap, who always sets me on fire with rage. Not a single
      thing can I ever order this thief to do just once; no, a hun-
      dred times I have to command and bark the same things
      at him. Despite all my shouting and anger I am no longer
      fit for the job. (*points to the ground with his cane*) Didn't
      I tell you to remove this dung from here from the door,
      you criminal? (*points to the columns of the house*) Didn't   425
      I tell you to remove the cobwebs from the columns?
      (*points to the door*) Didn't I tell you to make those door-
      knobs of ours shiny? It's no use. As if I were lame I have to
      walk around with a cane. Just because I have business at
      the market which cannot be interrupted for a mere three
      days, trying to find someone looking for money on inter-
      est, you servants in the meantime sleep here at home and
      master has to live in a pig-sty, not a house. Take that now!   431
      (*gives Libanus a blow*)

187

LIB   hospes, te opsecro, defende.

MER   Saurea, oro
mea causa ut mittas.

LEO   eho, ecquis pro uectura oliui
rem soluit?

LIB   soluit.

LEO   quoi datum est?

LIB   Sticho uicario ipsi
tuo.

LEO   uah, delenire apparas, scio mi uicarium esse,
435   neque eo esse seruom in aedibus eri qui sit pluris quam
           ille est.
        sed uina quae heri uendidi uinario Exaerambo,
        iam pro is satis fecit Sticho?

LIB   fecisse satis opinor,
nam uidi huc ipsum adducere tarpezitam Exaerambum.

LEO sic dedero. prius quae credidi, uix anno post exegi;
440   nunc sat agit: adducit domum etiam ultro et scribit num-
           mos.
        Dromo mercedem rettulit?

LIB   dimidio minus opinor.

LEO quid relicuom?

LIB   aibat reddere quom extemplo redditum esset;
nam retineri, ut quod sit sibi operis locatum efficeret.

LEO scyphos quos utendos dedi Philodamo, rettulitne?
445 LIB non etiam.

LEO   hem non? si uelis, da, commoda homini amico.

MER perii hercle, iam hic me abegerit suo odio.

LIB   heus iam satis tu.
audin quae loquitur?

---

437 proiis *B¹DE*, pro his *B³JK*, pro is *Pareus*

LIB (*to the merchant*) My friend, I beg you, protect me.

MER Saurea, I ask you to let him off for my sake.

LEO (*ignoring him*) Hey, did anyone pay for shipping the oil?

LIB Yes.

LEO Who received the money?

LIB Stichus himself, your deputy.

LEO (*in a slightly calmer voice*) Well, well, well, you're trying
      to appease me. I know that I have a deputy and that   435
      there's no slave in master's house who is worth more than
      him. But the wine I sold to the wine-merchant Exaeram-
      bus yesterday, has he settled with Stichus for it now?

LIB I think he has: I saw Exaerambus bring the banker here
      himself.

LEO That's how I like it. When I allowed him credit before, I
      barely managed to get the money out of him a year later.
      Now he's busying himself: he even brings him here on his   440
      own account and orders payment. Has Dromo brought
      home his wages?

LIB Less than half I think.

LEO What about the rest?

LIB He said he'd return it as soon as it was returned to him;
      now it's held back so that he'd finish the job he's been
      hired for.

LEO And the goblets I lent to Philodamus, has he returned
      them?

LIB He still hasn't.   445

LEO What, he hasn't? Give things away if you like, "lend"
      them to a friend.

MER (*aside, but not very quietly*) I can't handle it! This chap
      will drive me off with his disgusting behavior in a mo-
      ment.

LIB (*to Leonida, in a soft voice*) Hey, enough now, you. Can't
      you hear what he's saying?

LEO   audio et quiesco.

MER   tandem, opinor,
conticuit. nunc adeam optumum est, prius quam incipit
    tinnire.
quam mox mi operam das?

LEO   ehem, optume. quam dudum tu aduenisti?

450   non hercle te prouideram (quaeso, ne uitio uortas),
ita iracundia opstitit oculis.

MER   non mirum factum est.
sed si domi est, Demaenetum uolebam.

LEO   negat esse intus.
uerum istuc argentum tamen mihi si uis denumerare,
repromittam istoc nomine solutam rem futuram.

455   MER   sic potius ut Demaeneto tibi ero praesente reddam.

LIB   erus istunc nouit atque erum hic.

MER   ero huic praesente reddam.

LIB   da modo meo periculo, rem saluam ego exhibebo;
nam si sciat noster senex fidem non esse huic habitam,
suscenseat, quoi omnium rerum ipsus semper credit.

460   LEO   non magni pendo. ne duit, si non uolt. sic sine astet.

LIB   da, inquam. uah, formido miser ne hic me tibi arbitretur
suasisse sibi ne crederes. da, quaeso, ac ne formida:
saluom hercle erit.

MER   credam fore, dum quidem in manu ipse habebo.
peregrinus ego sum, Sauream non noui.

LIB   at nosce sane.

463 ipse in manu *P, transp. Acidalius*

LEO (*to Libanus, in a soft voice*) I can hear it and I'm calming
down.

MER (*aside*) At last he's fallen silent, I think. It's best to go up
to him now before he begins to rattle again. (*to Leonida*)
How soon will you give me your attention?

LEO Oh, very good. How long ago did you come? I really 450
hadn't noticed you before—please don't take any offense
—so much did my anger block my eyesight.

MER That's no surprise. But if he's at home, I'd like a word with
Demaenetus.

LEO He (*points to Libanus*) says he's not in. Still, if you want to
pay down this money to me, I shall guarantee that your
debt with us will be settled.

MER No, I prefer it like this: I'll return it to you when your 455
master Demaenetus is present.

LIB (*to the merchant, in a pleading voice*) Master knows him
and he knows master.

MER (*firmly*) I will return it to him when his master is present.

LIB Just give it to him at my risk, I'll vouch for its safety; if our
old man was to know you didn't trust him (*points to
Leonida*), he'd be angry—he himself always trusts him in
everything.

LEO (*to Libanus*) It doesn't matter. No need to give it to me if 460
he doesn't want to. Let him stand there like this.

LIB (*to the merchant*) Give it to him, I say. Dear me! I'm
afraid he might think I advised you not to trust him.
Please, give it to him and stop being afraid. It'll be safe
and sound.

MER I'm sure it will be so long as I have it in my hand myself.
I'm a foreigner, I don't know Saurea.

LIB Well, then get to know him. (*points to Leonida*)

191

465	MER	sit, non sit, non edepol scio. si is est, eum esse oportet.
		ego certe me incerto scio hoc daturum nemini homini.
	LEO	hercle istum di omnes perduint. uerbo caue supplicassis.
		ferox est uiginti minas meas tractare sese.
		nemo accipit, te aufer domum, apscede hinc, molestus
		ne sis.
470	MER	nimis iracunde. non decet superbum esse hominem
		seruom.
	LEO	malo hercle iam magno tuo, ni isti nec recte dicis.
	LIB	impure, nihili. non uides irasci?
	LEO	perge porro.
	LIB	flagitium hominis. da, opsecro, argentum huic, ne male
		loquatur.
	MER	malum hercle uobis quaeritis.
	LEO	crura hercle diffringentur,
475		ni istum impudicum percies.
	LIB	perii hercle. age, impudice,
		sceleste, non audes mihi scelesto subuenire?
	LEO	pergin precari pessumo?
	MER	quae res? tun libero homini
		male seruos loquere?
	LEO	uapula.
	MER	id quidem tibi hercle fiet
		ut uapules, Demaenetum simul ac conspexero hodie.
480		in ius uoco te.
	LEO	non eo.
	MER	non is? memento.
	LEO	memini.

469 aufer te *P*, te aufer *Enger*, te *del. F. Skutsch* (aufer *sc.* minas)

MER It might be him, it might not be him; I really don't know. 465
If it's him, it ought to be him. I know for sure that I won't
give this to anyone I'm not sure about.

LEO *(loudly)* May all the gods confound him. *(to Libanus)*
Don't you dare entreat me with one word! He's being
arrogant because he's handling my twenty minas. *(to the
merchant)* No one's taking it, get yourself home, go away
from here, don't be a nuisance.

MER Too angry. A slave ought not to be haughty. 470

LEO *(to Libanus)* Be prepared for a good beating if you don't
abuse him.

LIB *(to the merchant, loudly)* You scumbag, good-for-noth-
ing. *(softly)* Can't you see that he's angry?

LEO *(to Libanus)* Continue further.

LIB You disgraceful creature, give him the money, please, so
that he won't revile you.

MER You're looking for a thrashing. 474

LEO *(still to Libanus)* Your shins will be crushed unless you
get this shameless individual to act.

LIB *(to the merchant, softly)* I'm done for. *(loudly)* Go on, you
shameless person, you wretch, don't you want to help me,
poor wretch that I am?

LEO *(to Libanus)* Are you continuing to entreat this worthless
person?

MER *(to Leonida)* What? Are you, a slave, insulting a free
man?

LEO Get beaten!

MER That'll happen to you, getting beaten, as soon as I set eyes
on Demaenetus today. I'm calling you to court. 480

LEO I'm not going.

MER You're not going? Remember.

LEO I do.

MER dabitur pol supplicium mihi de tergo uostro.

LEO   uae te!

tibi quidem de nobis, carnufex, detur supplicium?

MER   atque etiam

pro dictis uostris maledicis poenae pendentur mi hodie.

484– LEO quid, uerbero? ain tu, furcifer? erum nos[met] fugitare
5   censes?

i nunciam ad erum, quo uocas, iam dudum quo uolebas.

MER nunc demum? tamen numquam hinc feres argenti num-
                mum, nisi me

dare iusserit Demaenetus.

LEO   ita facito, age ambula ergo.

tu contumeliam alteri facias, tibi non dicatur?

490   tam ego homo sum quam tu.

MER   scilicet. ita res est.

LEO   sequere hac ergo.

praefiscini hoc nunc dixerim: nemo etiam me accusauit

merito meo, nec me alter est Athenis hodie quisquam

quoi credi recte aeque putent.

MER   fortassis. sed tamen me

numquam hodie induces ut tibi credam hoc argentum
                ignoto.

495   lupus est homo homini, non homo, quom qualis sit non
                nouit.

LEO iam nunc secunda mihi facis. scibam huic te capitulo
                hodie

facturum satis pro iniuria; quamquam ego sum sordi-
                datus,

482 supplicium carnufex de nobis detur atque etiam *P, transp.*
Bothe, datur *Lindsay in apparatu (secutus ordinem uerborum quem
uidemus in P)*   484–5 -met *del.* ς, erum *del. Lindsay in apparatu*

MER   I'll be given compensation from your backs.

LEO   Bad luck to you! Compensation should be given to *you* from *us*, you thug?

MER   And for your bad words I'll see you two punished today.

LEO   What, you thug? Do you say so, you villain? Do you think   484 we're running away from master? Go to our master   –5 now, which is where you're calling us and where you've wanted to go for some time now.

MER   Now at last? Still, you won't ever get so much as one silver coin from here unless Demaenetus asks me to give it to you.

LEO   (*more calmly*) All right, come on, go then. Should you insult another man and not be insulted yourself? I am a   490 human being as much as you.

MER   (*also more calmly*) Of course. Quite so.

LEO   Then follow me this way. Touch wood,[23] I could say this now: no one's accused me deservedly yet and there isn't any other man in Athens these days who people believe can be trusted equally well.

MER   Perhaps. Still, you'll never get me to entrust you with this money today because I don't know you. Man is a wolf and   495 not a man toward a man when he doesn't know what he's like.

LEO   Now you're obliging me already. I knew you'd give satisfaction to this chap here today for the injustice. Even

[23] *Praefiscini* is a formula used to avoid *fascinum* (witchcraft) (Char. *gramm.* 306. 9–11 Barwick).

---

487 nisi *P*, ni *Lindsay*
492 me Athenis alter est *P, transp. Bentley*

frugi tamen sum, nec potest peculium enumerari.
MER fortasse.
LEO   etiam [nunc dico] Periphanes Rhodo mercator diues
500   apsente ero solus mihi talentum argenti soli
annumerauit et credidit mihi, nec deceptust in eo.
MER fortasse.
LEO   atque etiam tu quoque ipse, si esses percontatus
me ex aliis, scio pol crederes nunc quod fers.
MER   hau negassim.

ACTVS III

III. i: CLEARETA. PHILAENIVM

CLE nequeone ego ted interdictis facere mansuetem meis?
505   an ita tu es animata ut qui expers matris imperio sies?
PHIL ubi piem Pietatem, si istoc more moratam tibi
postulem placere, mater, mihi quo pacto praecipis?
CLE an decorum est aduorsari meis te praeceptis?
PHIL   quid est?
CLE hoccine est pietatem colere, imperium matris minuere?

499 nunc dico *P, del. Lindsay*
509 matris imperium *P, transp. Pylades*

though I look shabby I'm decent, and my money can't be counted.

MER Perhaps.   499

LEO Even Periphanes, the rich merchant from Rhodes, counted out a silver talent to me and entrusted me with it when master was absent and we were alone, and he wasn't deceived in this.

MER Perhaps.

LEO And you yourself too, if you'd enquired about me from others, I know you'd entrust me with what you're carrying now.

MER I wouldn't want to deny it.

Exeunt LEONIDA, LIBANUS, and the MERCHANT with his servant to the right.

ACT THREE

Enter PHILAENIUM from her mother's house, followed by CLEARETA herself.

CLE (*angrily*) Can't I tame you with my prohibitions? Are   505
you determined to behave as if you were free from your mother's authority?

PHIL (*tartly*) How could I fulfill my duty toward Filial Duty, mother, if I wanted you to like me endowed with such a character as you're prescribing for me?

CLE Is it honorable for you to oppose what I prescribe?

PHIL What do you mean?

CLE Do you call that having regard for your filial duty, to abolish your mother's authority?

510 PHIL nec quae recte faciunt culpo nec quae delinquont amo.
    CLE satis dicacula es amatrix.
    PHIL   mater, is quaestus mihi est:
         lingua poscit, corpus quaerit; animus orat, res monet.
    CLE ego te uolui castigare, tu mi accusatrix ades.
    PHIL neque edepol te accuso neque id me facere fas existumo.
515   uerum ego meas queror fortunas, quom illo quem amo
            prohibeor.
    CLE ecqua pars orationis de die dabitur mihi?
    PHIL et meam partem loquendi et tuam trado tibi;
        ad loquendum atque ad tacendum tute habeas portiscu-
            lum.
        quin pol si reposiui remum, sola ego in casteria
520   ubi quiesco, omnis familiae causa consistit tibi.
    CLE quid ais tu, quam ego unam uidi mulierem audacissu-
            mam?
        quotiens te uotui Argyrippum filium Demaeneti
        compellare aut contrectare, colloquiue aut contui?
        quid dedit? quid iussit ad nos deportari? an tu tibi
525   uerba blanda esse aurum rere, dicta docta pro datis?
        ultro amas, ultro expetessis, ultro ad te accersi iubes.
        illos qui dant eos derides; qui deludunt deperis.
        an te id exspectare oportet, si quis promittat tibi
        te facturum diuitem, si mater moriatur sua?
530   ecastor [nobis] periclum magnum [et] familiae porten-
            ditur,
        dum eius exspectamus mortem, ne nos moriamur fame.

529 moritur mater *P*, moriatur mater *Pylades*, mater moriatur
scripsi rhythmi causa
    530 nobis *et* et *del. Bothe*, magnum *del. Pylades*

PHIL I don't accuse mothers who do what's right and I don't 510
love those who do what's wrong.

CLE You're quite a glib little hussy.

PHIL That's my job, mother. My tongue asks, my body earns,
my mind prompts, the circumstances urge.

CLE I wanted to scold you and now you're here to accuse me!

PHIL I'm not accusing you and I don't think it would be right
for me to do so. But I do moan about my fate since I'm 515
kept away from the one I love.

CLE Will any part of the speechmaking be given to me while
it's still day?

PHIL I grant you both my share of speaking and yours; you'll
give the signal[24] for speaking and being silent. But if I put
down the oar, resting alone in the cabin,[25] the progress of
your whole household comes to a halt.

CLE What are you saying? You're the most impudent girl I've 521
ever seen! How often did I forbid you to speak to Ar-
gyrippus, the son of Demaenetus, or to fondle him, to
chat with him or to look at him? What did he give? What
did he have brought to us? Do you think flattery is gold
for you, witty words instead of gifts? Of your own accord 526
you make love to him, of your own accord you run after
him, of your own accord you have him brought to you.
You laugh at those who give, and those who trick you you
love. Should you wait if someone promises to make you
rich if his mother dies? Heavens above, while we're wait- 530
ing for her death a great peril appears for the household:

---

[24] The *portisculus* is a kind of hammer used in beating time for the
rowers (Non. p. 221 Lindsay).   [25] The meaning of *casteria*, here
translated as "cabin," is not entirely clear. Nonius (p. 121 Lindsay) de-
scribes it as a place where the crew of a ship can rest.

nunc adeo nisi mi huc argenti affert uiginti minas,
ne ille ecastor hinc trudetur largus ... lacrumarum foras.
hic dies summust ⟨quo est⟩ apud me inopiae excusatio.

535 PHIL   patiar, si cibo carere me iubes, mater mea.

CLE   non uoto ted amare qui dant quoia amentur gratia.

PHIL   quid si hic animust occupatust, mater, quid faciam? mone.

CLE   em,
      meum caput contemples, si quidem ex re consultas tua.

539– PHIL   etiam opilio qui pascit, mater, alienas ouis,
40   aliquam habet peculiarem qui spem soletur suam.
      sine me amare unum Argyrippum animi causa, quem
      uolo.

CLE   intro abi, nam te quidem edepol nihil est impudentius.

PHIL   audientem dicto, mater, produxisti filiam.

III. ii: LIBANVS. LEONIDA

545 LIB   Perfidiae laudes gratiasque habemus merito magnas,
      quom nostris sycophantiis, dolis astutiisque,
      scapularum confidentia, uirtute ulnorum freti,

            *   *   *

      qui aduorsum stimulos, lamminas crucesque compe-
      desque,

549–   neruos, catenas, carceres, numellas, pedicas, boias,
50   inductoresque acerrumos gnarosque nostri tergi,
      [qui saepe ante in nostras scapulas cicatrices indiderunt,]

553   *   *   *

534 quo est *add. Leo*   547 ulnorum *Nonius*, ulmorum P
547ᵃ *lacunam exstare putat Fleckeisen*
552 *uersum sed. Bothe* scaplas *Lindsay hanc uix esse formam Plautinam fassus*
553 *lacunam exstare putat Fleckeisen*

the peril that we might die of starvation. And now unless
he brings me twenty minas here, he'll be kicked out from
here, that bloke who is so generous . . . with his tears. This
is the last day on which I accept the excuse that he is poor.

PHIL (*tearfully*) If you tell me to go without food, I'll bear it,   535
my mother.

CLE I don't forbid you to love those who give something that
makes them worth loving.

PHIL What if my heart isn't free, mother, what should I do? Advise me.

CLE Look here! (*points to her grey hair*) Watch *my* head if you
are really considering what's good for you.

PHIL But mother, even the shepherd who pastures other peo-   539–
ple's sheep has some lamb of his own with which he con-   40
soles his hopes. Let me only love Argyrippus, for my joy,
the one I want.

CLE Go inside! Nothing's more shameless than you.

PHIL You brought up an obedient daughter, mother.

*Exit PHILAENIUM into her mother's house, followed by
CLEARETA.
Enter LIBANUS and LEONIDA from the right, the latter car-
rying a wallet.*

LIB (*cheerfully*) Great praise and thanks be to Perfidy as she   545
deserves, since by our swindles, tricks, and clever moves,
relying on the daring of our shoulder blades and the ex-
cellence of our forearms *** who went against cattle-
prods, hot iron-blades, crosses and shackles, neck-irons,   550
chains, prisons, collars, fetters, and yokes, the fiercest
painters fully acquainted with our backs [who have often
before put scars on our shoulder blades] *** now these

eae nunc legiones, copiae exercitusque eorum
555 ui pugnando, periuriis nostris fugae potiti.
id uirtute huius collegai meaque comitate
factum est. qui me est uir fortior ad sufferundas plagas?
LEO edepol uirtutes qui tuas non possis collaudare
sicut ego possim, quae domi duellique male fecisti.
560 ne illa edepol pro merito [nunc] tuo memorari multa pos-
sunt:
ubi fidentem fraudaueris, ubi ero infidelis fueris,
ubi uerbis conceptis sciens lubenter peiieraris,
ubi parietes perfoderis, in furto ubi sis prehensus,
ubi saepe causam dixeris pendens aduorsus octo
565 artutos, audacis uiros, ualentis uirgatores.
LIB fateor profecto ut praedicas, Leonida, esse uera;
uerum edepol ne etiam tua quoque malefacta iterari
multa
et uero possunt: ubi sciens fideli infidus fueris,
ubi prensus in furto sies manufesto et uerberatus,
570 ubi peiieraris, ubi sacro manus sis ammolitus,
ubi eris damno, molestiae et dedecori saepe fueris,
ubi creditum quod sit tibi datum esse pernegaris,
ubi amicae quam amico tuo fueris magis fidelis,
ubi saepe ad languorem tua duritia dederis octo
575 ualidos lictores, ulmeis affectos lentis uirgis.
num male relata est gratia? ut collegam collaudaui?
LEO ut meque teque maxume atque ingenio nostro decuit.
LIB iam omitte istaec, hoc quod rogo responde.

556 collegae *P*, collegai *Seyffert*
557 me uir fortior est *P, transp. Lindsay*, me uir fortior *Merula*
560 nunc *del. Guyet*   565 astutos *P*, artitos *T*, artutos *Fleckeisen*
578 quid uis *D*, quod uis *BJE*

legions, troops and armies of theirs have been put to
flight by fierce fighting and our perjuries. This was done 556
through this colleague's valor and my kind assistance.
Who is braver than me when it comes to suffering blows?

LEO (*with a sneer*) You couldn't praise your brave deeds as
I could, praise the bad things you did at home and in
the field. Your list of achievements is too long to be re- 560
counted: occasions where you cheated someone trusting
you, where you were unfaithful to master, where you
knowingly and happily gave a false oath with solemn
words, where you dug holes through walls, where you
were caught stealing, where you often had to plead your
cause hanging before eight hefty, bold men, valiant rod-
wielders.

LIB Yes, I admit that it's correct as you state, Leonida; but 566
your list of villainies is also a long one: occasions where
you were knowingly unfaithful to someone who trusted
you, where you were caught stealing in flagrante and
beaten, where you gave a false oath, where you laid your 570
hands on something sacred, where you often created
damage, embarrassment, and shame for your masters,
where you denied receiving what you had been entrusted
with, where you were more faithful to your female friend
than to your male, where you often exhausted eight
strong lictors[26] with your toughness, even though they
had flexible elm rods. Have I returned my thanks badly? 576
How did I praise my colleague?

LEO As was most appropriate for me and you and our nature.

LIB (*abruptly*) Stop that now and answer my question.

26 Attendants of magistrates who enforce their orders.

LEO   rogita quid uis.

LIB   argenti uiginti minas habesne?

LEO   hariolare.

580   edepol senem Demaenetum lepidum fuisse nobis:

ut assimulabat Sauream med esse quam facete!

nimis aegre risum contini, ubi hospitem inclamauit,

quod se⟨se⟩ apsente mihi fidem habere noluisset.

ut memoriter me Sauream uocabat atriensem!

585 LIB   manedum.

LEO   quid est?

LIB   Philaenium estne haec quae intus exit atque

una Argyrippus?

LEO   opprime os, is est. subauscultemus.

LIB   lacrumantem lacinia tenet lacrumans. quidnam esse

dicam?

taciti auscultemus.

LEO   attatae, modo hercle in mentem uenit,

nimis uellem habere perticam.

LIB   quoi rei?

LEO   qui uerberarem

590   asinos, si forte occeperint clamare hinc ex crumina.

III. iii: ARGYRIPPVS. PHILAENIVM. LIBANVS. LEONIDA

ARG   quor me retentas?

PHIL   quia tui amans abeuntis egeo.

583 se *BDEK*, sese *Gruterus*

LEO   Ask what you like.

LIB   Do you have twenty silver minas?

LEO   You're prophesying. Old Demaenetus was witty to us: 580
how cleverly he pretended that I'm Saurea! I could
barely suppress my laughter when he shouted at the
stranger because he didn't want to trust me in his ab-
sence. How well he remembered to call me his steward
Saurea!

LIB   (*looking around*) Wait for a moment. 585

LEO   What is it?

*PHILAENIUM and ARGYRIPPUS appear in the door of
Cleareta's house.*

LIB   Isn't that Philaenium who's coming out from in there, to-
gether with Argyrippus?

LEO   Shut your mouth, it's him. Let's listen in. (*drags Libanus
out of view*)

LIB   Both are crying and she's holding him at the lappet of his
cloak. What on earth should I say this means? Let's listen
in silence.

LEO   Well, well, well, it's just come to my mind, I'd really love
to have a pole.

LIB   What for?

LEO   To beat the donkeys with if they begin to bray out of this 590
wallet.

*Enter ARGYRIPPUS from Cleareta's house, followed by PHI-
LAENIUM, who is clinging on to him. They do not notice the
slaves.*

ARG   (*dramatically*) Why are you holding me back?

PHIL   (*in tears*) Because I pine away for you when you go away,
I love you so.

	ARG	uale ⟨uale⟩.
	PHIL	aliquanto amplius ualerem, si hic maneres.
	ARG	salue.
	PHIL	saluere me iubes, quoi tu abiens offers morbum?
	ARG	mater supremam mihi tua dixit, domum ire iussit.
595	PHIL	acerbum funus filiae faciet, si te carendum est.
	LIB	homo hercle hinc exclusust foras.
	LEO	ita res est.
	ARG	mitte quaeso.
	PHIL	quo nunc abis? quin tu hic manes?
	ARG	nox, si uoles, manebo.
	LIB	audin hunc opera ut largus est nocturna? nunc enim esse
		negotiosum interdius uidelicet Solonem,
600		leges ut conscribat quibus se populus teneat. gerrae!
		qui sese parere apparent huius legibus, profecto
		numquam bonae frugi sient, dies noctesque potent.
	LEO	ne iste hercle ab ista non pedem discedat, si licessit,
		qui nunc festinat atque ab hac minatur sese abire.
605	LIB	sermoni iam finem face tuo, huius sermonem accipiam.
	ARG	uale.
	PHIL	quo properas?
	ARG	bene uale: apud Orcum te uidebo.
		nam equidem me iam quantum potest a uita abiudicabo.
	PHIL	quor tu, opsecro, immerito meo me morti dedere optas?

592 uale *P Nonius*, uale uale *Lindsay*
597 mox *P*, nox *Lipsius*

---

[27] The "last hour" alludes to suicide, but also to the formula used by the praetor to announce the end of an audience.

[28] Athenian politician and lawgiver around 600 BC, famous for his frugality.

206

ARG   Farewell, farewell.

PHIL I'd fare somewhat better if you were to stay here.

ARG   Be well.

PHIL You're telling me to be well? By going away you make
      me ill.

ARG   Your mother said this would be my last hour, she told me
      to go home.[27]

PHIL She'll celebrate a dire funeral for her daughter if I have   595
      to be without you.

LIB   (*in a soft voice, to Leonida*) The chap's been shut out
      from here.

LEO   (*to Libanus*) Indeed.

ARG   Let me go please. (*pulls away from Philaenium*)

PHIL Where are you off to now? Why don't you stay here?

ARG   I'll stay at night if you want me to.

LIB   (*quietly*) Can you hear how he's generous with his night-
      shift? Now in daytime our Solon[28] is of course busy writ-   600
      ing the laws the people should keep. Nonsense! Those
      prepared to obey his laws would never be good for any-
      thing and would drink day and night.

LEO   (*quietly*) He wouldn't go one foot away from her if he
      were allowed to stay, but now he's in a hurry and threat-
      ening to leave her.

LIB   (*quietly*) Put an end to your talk now, I'll listen to his.   605

ARG   Farewell.

PHIL Where are you rushing?

ARG   Fare very well: I'll see you in the Underworld: I'll now
      deprive myself of life as quickly as possible.

PHIL Why, I entreat you, do you wish to hand me over to death
      even though I don't deserve it?

ARG   ego te? quam si intellegam deficere uita, iam ipse

610   uitam meam tibi largiar et de mea ad tuam addam.

PHIL quor ergo minitaris mihi te uitam esse amissurum?

       nam quid me facturam putas, si istuc quod dicis faxis?

       [mihi] certum est efficere in me omnia eadem quae tu in

         te faxis.

ARG   oh melle dulci dulcior [mihi] tu es.

PHIL   certe enim tu uita es mi.

615   complectere.

ARG   facio lubens.

PHIL   utinam sic efferamur.

LEO   o Libane, uti miser est homo qui amat!

LIB   immo hercle uero

       qui pendet multo est miserior.

LEO   scio qui periclum feci.

       circumsistamus, alter hinc, hinc alter appellemus.

       ere, salue. sed num fumus est haec mulier quam am-

         plexare?

620 ARG   quidum?

LEO   quia oculi sunt tibi lacrumantes, eo rogaui.

ARG   patronus qui uobis fuit futurus, perdidistis.

LEO   equidem hercle nullum perdidi, ideo quia numquam ul-

       lum habui.

LIB   Philaenium, salue.

PHIL   dabunt di quae uelitis uobis.

LIB   noctem tuam et uini cadum uelim, si optata fiant.

   609 ego *P*, egon *Loman*
   611 tibi *P*, mihi *Loman*
   613 mihi *P*, del. *Lachmann*
   614 mihi *del. Fleckeisen*

THE COMEDY OF ASSES

ARG Me do such a thing? If I were to see you running out of 609
life, I'd immediately donate my life to you and add from
mine to yours.

PHIL Then why are you threatening me with throwing away
your life? What do you think I'll do if you do what you
say? I've set my mind on doing to me everything you do
to yourself.

ARG Oh, you're sweeter than sweet honey.

PHIL Certainly you are sweeter than my life to me. Embrace 615
me.

ARG I do so with pleasure. (*embraces her*)

PHIL I wish we could be carried to the grave like this.

LEO (*quietly*) O Libanus, how miserable a chap is when he's in
love!

LIB (*quietly*) No, a chap is much more miserable when he's
hanging.[29]

LEO (*quietly*) I know it, I've tried it. Let's surround them and
address them, one on this side, the other on that side.
(*loudly, approaching Argyrippus*) Hello, master. But is
the girl you're embracing smoke?

ARG How so? 620

LEO Because your eyes are shedding tears, that's why I asked.

ARG (*angrily*) You've lost a man who was going to be your pa-
tron.

LEO I for one haven't lost any such man because I've never
had one.

LIB Hello, Philaenium.

PHIL The gods will grant you two what you wish for.

LIB I'd wish for a night with you and a jar of wine if my wishes
came true.

[29] A typical punishment for slaves.

625	ARG	uerbum caue faxis, uerbero.
	LIB	tibi equidem, non mihi opto.
	ARG	tum tu igitur loquere quod lubet.
	LIB	hunc hercle uerberare.
	LEO	quisnam istuc accredat tibi, cinaede calamistrate?
		tun uerberes, qui pro cibo habeas te uerberari?
	ARG	ut uostrae fortunae meis praecedunt, Libane, longe,
630		qui hodie numquam ad uesperum uiuam.
	LIB	quapropter, quaeso?
	ARG	quia ego hanc amo et haec med amat, huic quod dem
		nusquam quicquam est,
		hinc med amantem ex aedibus deiecit huius mater.
		argenti uiginti minae med ad mortem appulerunt,
		quas hodie adulescens Diabolus ipsi daturus dixit,
635		ut hanc ne quoquam mitteret nisi ad se hunc annum
		totum.
		uidetin uiginti minae quid pollent quidue possunt?
		ill' qui illas perdit saluos est, ego qui non perdo pereo.
	LIB	iam dedit argentum?
	ARG	non dedit.
	LIB	bono animo es, ne formida.
	LEO	secede huc, Libane, te uolo.
	LIB	si quid uis.
	ARG	opsecro uos,
640		eadem istac opera suauiust complexos fabulari.
	LIB	non omnia eadem aeque omnibus, ere, suauia esse scito:
		uobis est suaue amantibus complexos fabulari,

631 amo et haec me amat *P*, amo et haec med amat *Lindsay*, amo et
med haec amat *Ritschl*, amo atque haec med amat *Kaempf*

210

ARG   *(turning to Libanus, in an angry voice)* Not one more 625
word, you rascal.

LIB   *(innocently)* But I'm wishing them for you, not for my-
self.

ARG   In that case you can say anything you like.

LIB   I'd like to beat this chap here. *(points to Leonida)*

LEO   *(to Libanus)* Who on earth would believe you in this, you
curly-haired catamite? *You* would beat *me*, you, whose
food it is to be beaten?

ARG   *(tragically)* How much your lot is preferable to mine, 629
Libanus; I'll never live till the evening today.

LIB   Why, if I may ask?

ARG   Because *I* love *her* *(points to Philaenium)* and *she* loves
me, and I don't have anything anywhere to give her;
her mother's thrown me out of her house here, me, her
daughter's lover. Twenty silver minas has driven me to my
death; young Diabolus said he'd give it to her today so
that she wouldn't send her anywhere except to him for a
whole year. Can you see what power and what might 636
twenty minas has? The one who loses it is safe, and I don't
lose it, yet I am lost.

LIB   Has he given the money already?

ARG   No, he hasn't.

LIB   Take heart, stop being afraid.

LEO   Step aside here, Libanus, I want to speak to you.

LIB   If there's anything you want. *(moving away with Leon-
ida)*

ARG   Come on, you two! You might as well hug each other 640
while chatting.

LIB   *(playfully)* Master, you should know that not everything
is equally sweet for everyone. Since you're in love, it's
sweet for you to hug each other while chatting. But *I* can't

ego complexum huius nil moror, meum autem hic asper-
natur.

proinde istuc facias ipse quod faciamus nobis suades.

645 ARG ego uero, et quidem edepol lubens. interea, si uidetur,
concedite istuc.

LEO   uin erum deludi?

LIB   dignust sane.

LEO uin faciam ut me Philaenium praesente hoc amplexetur?

LIB cupio hercle.

LEO   sequere hac.

ARG   ecquid est salutis? satis locuti.

LEO auscultate atque operam date et mea dicta deuorate.

650   primum omnium seruos tuos nos esse non negamus;
sed tibi si uiginti minae argenti proferentur,
quo nos uocabis nomine?

ARG   libertos.

LEO   non patronos?

ARG id potius.

LEO   uiginti minae hic insunt in crumina,
has ego, si uis, ⟨nunc⟩ tibi dabo.

ARG   di te seruassint semper,

655   custos erilis, decus popli, thesaurus copiarum,
salus interior corporis amorisque imperator.
hic pone, hic istam colloca cruminam in collo plane.

LEO nolo ego te, qui erus sis, mihi onus istuc sustinere.

  654 nunc *add. Fleckeisen*

  656 interioris corporis *DJE*, interioris hominis *B*, interior corporis
Bothe

212

.be bothered about *his* (*points to Leonida*) hugs, while *he* despises *mine*. So you should practise yourself what you're preaching to us.

ARG   I will indeed, and with pleasure. In the meantime, if it   645
seems good to you, step aside there.

The two slaves move off so that they cannot be overheard by the couple.

LEO   Do you want master to be made fun of?

LIB   He really deserves it.

LEO   Do you want me to make Philaenium embrace me while he's present?

LIB   Yes, I'm keen on it.

LEO   Follow me this way. (*approaches Argyrippus*)

ARG   (*addressing the slaves*) Is there any salvation? You've talked enough.

LEO   Listen, you two, pay attention, and devour my words. First of all we don't deny that we're your slaves. But if you   650
get twenty silver minas, by what name will you call us?

ARG   Freedmen.

LEO   Not patrons?

ARG   That rather.

LEO   There is twenty minas here in this wallet. (*holds it up*) I'll give it to you now if you want to.

ARG   May the gods prosper you always, guardian of your mas-   655
ter, glory of the people, storehouse of riches, inner salva-
tion of the body and commander of love. Put it here,
place this wallet here plainly on my neck.

LEO   I don't want you to bear this burden for me, since you're my master.

ARG   quin tu labore liberas te atque istam imponis in me?
660 LEO   ego baiulabo, tu, ut decet dominum, ante me ito inanis.
ARG   quid nunc?
LEO   quid est?
ARG   quin tradis huc cruminam pressatum umerum?
LEO   hanc, quoi daturu's hanc, iube petere atque orare me-
         cum.
         nam istuc procliue est quo iubes me plane collocare.
PHIL   da, meus ocellus, mea rosa, mi anime, mea uoluptas,
665   Leonida, argentum mihi, ne nos diiunge amantis.
LEO   dic me igitur tuom passerculum, gallinam, coturnicem,
         agnellum, haedillum me tuom dic esse uel uitellum,
         prehende auriculis, compara labella cum labellis.
ARG   ten osculetur, uerbero?
LEO   quam uero indignum uisum est?
670   atqui pol hodie non feres, ni genua confricantur.
ARG   quiduis egestas imperat: fricentur. dan quod oro?
PHIL   age, mi Leonida, opsecro, fer amanti ero salutem,
         redime istoc beneficio te ab hoc, et tibi eme hunc isto ar-
         gento.
LEO   nimis bella es atque amabilis, et si hoc meum esset, hodie
675   numquam me orares quin darem: illum te orare meliust,

---

³⁰ I.e., the wallet will get lost.

ARG   Why don't you free yourself from the strain and put this onto me?

LEO   *I* will carry it, *you*, as is appropriate for a master, should 660
go in front of me empty-handed.

ARG   What now?

LEO   What's the matter?

ARG   Why don't you hand over the wallet here so that it weighs down my shoulder?

LEO   Tell the woman you're going to give it to to ask for it and to plead with me: the place you tell me to put it on plainly is not a plain, but a slope.[30]

PHIL   (*walking toward Leonida*) Give the money to me, apple 664
of my eye, my rose, my soul, my joy, Leonida, stop separating us lovers.

LEO   Then call me your little sparrow, your hen, your quail; call me your little lamb, your kid, or your little calf; grab me by the ears and put your lips on mine. (*she embraces him*)

ARG   (*angrily*) She should kiss you, you thug?

LEO   (*to Argyrippus, coldly*) Well, how inappropriate did it seem? But seriously, you won't get it today unless my 670
knees get a rub.

ARG   Beggars can't be choosers; a rub they shall get. (*kneels down and massages Leonida's legs*) Will you give me what I ask for?

PHIL   Come on, my dear Leonida, I beg you, bring rescue to your lovesick master, buy yourself free from him with this act of kindness, and buy him for yourself with this money.

LEO   (*to Philaenium*) You're terribly pretty and lovely, and if 674
this were mine you'd never be asking me today without me giving it. But it's better if you ask that chap there (*points to Libanus*), he gave it to me to keep it safe. Do

215

illic hanc mi seruandam dedit. i sane bella belle.
cape hoc sis, Libane.

ARG   furcifer, etiam me delusisti?

LEO   numquam hercle facerem, genua ni tam nequiter frica-
res.

age sis tu in partem nunciam hunc delude atque am-
plexare hanc.

680 LIB   taceas, me spectes.

ARG   quin ad hunc, Philaenium, aggredimur,
uirum quidem pol optumum et non similem furis huius?

LIB   inambulandum est: nunc mihi uicissim supplicabunt.

ARG   quaeso hercle, Libane, sis erum tuis factis sospitari,
da mi istas uiginti minas. uides me amantem egere.

685 LIB   uidebitur. factum uolo. redito huc conticinno.
nunc istanc tantisper iube petere atque orare mecum.

PHIL amandone exorarier uis ted an osculando?

LIB   enim uero utrumque.

PHIL   ergo, opsecro, et tu utrumque nostrum serua.

ARG   o Libane, mi patrone, mi trade istuc. magis decorum est

690   libertum potius quam patronum onus in uia portare.

PHIL mi Libane, ocellus aureus, donum decusque amoris,
amabo, faciam quod uoles, da istuc argentum nobis.

LIB   dic igitur med aneticulam, columbam uel catellum,
hirundinem, monerulam, passerculum putillum,

695   fac proserpentem bestiam me, duplicem ut habeam lin-
guam,
circumda torquem bracchiis, meum collum circum-
plecte.

---

31 I am following the interpretation of *conticinium* given by Nonius
(p. 87 Lindsay). Censorinus (24. 2), however, believes that the time re-
ferred to is the early morning.

216

go prettily, my pretty girl. Take this, Libanus, will you. (*throws the wallet to Libanus, who catches it*)

ARG (*getting up, addressing Leonida*) You villain, you've fooled me?

LEO I'd never have done it if you hadn't rubbed my knees so appallingly. (*to Libanus, quietly*) Go on, will you, it's your turn to make fun of him now and to hug her.

LIB (*quietly*) Be quiet and watch me.   680

ARG Why don't we try to influence this one (*points to Libanus*), Philaenium, a really excellent man and not at all like this thief?

LIB (*aside*) I have to parade around; now they will entreat me in turn.

ARG Libanus, I beg you, if you want your master to be saved through your deeds, give me those twenty minas. You can see that I'm in love and need it.

LIB It shall be seen to. I want it done. Return here at dusk.[31]   685 Now in the meantime tell your girl to ask for it and plead with me.

PHIL (*to Libanus*) Do you want to be persuaded by caressing or by kissing?

LIB Both, to be sure.

PHIL Then, I beg you, you should also save us both.

ARG O Libanus, my patron, hand this over to me. It's more ap-   689 propriate that a freedman rather than his patron should carry a burden in the street.

PHIL My dear Libanus, my golden eye, love's gift and glory, please, I'll do what you like, but give us this money.

LIB Then call me your little duck, your dove, your puppy, your swallow, your jackdaw, your teeny-weeny sparrow, turn me into a reptile so that I have a double tongue. Put   695 a chain around me with your arms, embrace my neck. (*she walks toward him*)

217

ARG ten complectatur, carnufex?

LIB   quam uero indignus uideor?
ne istuc nequiquam dixeris in me tam indignum dictum,
uehes pol hodie me, si quidem hoc argentum ferre
    speres.

700 ARG ten ego ueham?

LIB   tun hoc feras ⟨hinc⟩ argentum aliter a me?

ARG perii hercle. si uerum quidem et decorum erum uehere
    seruom,
inscende.

LIB   sic isti solent superbi subdomari.
asta igitur, ut consuetus es puer olim. scin ut dicam?
em sic. abi, laudo, nec te equo magis est equos ullus
    sapiens.

705 ARG inscende actutum.

LIB   ego fecero. hem quid istuc est? ut tu incedis?
demam hercle iam de hordeo, tolutim ni badizas.

ARG amabo, Libane, iam sat est.

LIB   numquam hercle hodie exorabis.
nam iam calcari quadrupedo agitabo aduorsum cliuom,
postidea ad pistores dabo, ut ibi cruciere currens.

710 asta ut descendam nunciam in procliui, quamquam ne-
    quam es.

ARG quid nunc, amabo? quoniam, ut est lubitum, nos delusis-
    tis,
datisne argentum?

LIB   si quidem mi statuam et aram statuis
atque ut deo mi hic immolas bouem: nam ego tibi Salus
    sum.

698 tam indignum dictum in me *P, transp. Bothe hiatum fugiens*
700 hinc *add. Lindsay*   702 istuc *P,* isti *Lambinus,* istic *Pylades*

ARG (*angrily, approaching Libanus*) She should embrace you, you thug?

LIB How undeserving do I seem? So that you won't have made this entirely inappropriate remark against me without any consequences, you'll carry me on your back, at least if you hope to get this money.

ARG *I* should carry *you* on my back?   700

LIB *You* should get this money from *me* here in any other way?

ARG I'm done for. Well, if it is right and proper that a master should carry his servant on his back, climb onto me.

LIB This is how those proud ones are normally tamed. Stand still, then, just as you used to as a boy long ago. Do you know how I mean? (*Argyrippus bends over*) Yes, like that. That's it, well done, there's no horse that's cleverer than you.

ARG Climb onto me straight away.   705

LIB So I will. (*climbs onto Argyrippus, who begins to walk along*) Hello, what's that supposed to be? How are you jogging along? I'll take you off the barley immediately if you don't get into a trot.

ARG Please, Libanus, it's enough now.

LIB You'll never soften me with your entreaties today: with my spurs I'll drive you uphill galloping, and then I'll give you to the millers so that you're tortured there by being forced to work at the double. Stand still so that I can   710 climb down on the slope now, even though you're useless.

ARG What now, please? Now that you two have had your fun with us as you liked, are you giving us the money?

LIB If you erect a statue and an altar for me and sacrifice an ox for me as your god here; because I am Salvation for you.

219

	LEO	etiam tu, ere, istunc amoues aps te atque me ipse aggre- dere
715		atque illa sibi quae hic iusserat mi statuis supplicasque?
	ARG	quem te autem diuom nominem?
	LEO	Fortunam, atque Opsequentem.
	ARG	iam istoc es melior.
	LIB	an quid est [olim] homini Salute melius?
	ARG	licet laudem Fortunam, tamen ut ne Salutem culpem.
	PHIL	ecastor ambae sunt bonae.
	ARG	sciam ubi boni quid dederint.
720	LEO	opta id quod ut contingat tibi uis.
	ARG	quid si optaro?
	LEO	eueniet.
	ARG	opto annum hunc perpetuom mihi huius operas.
	LEO	impetrasti.
	ARG	ain uero?
	LEO	certe inquam.
	LIB	ad me adi uicissim atque experire.
		exopta id quod uis maxume tibi euenire: fiet.
	ARG	quid ego aliud exoptem amplius nisi illud quoius inopia est,
725		uiginti argenti commodas minas, huius quas dem matri?
	LIB	dabuntur, animo sis bono face, exoptata optingent.
	ARG	ut consueuere, homines Salus frustratur et Fortuna.
	LEO	ego caput huic argento fui ⟨tibi⟩ hodie reperiundo.
	LIB	ego pes fui.

714 ipse me *P, transp. Pylades,* ips' med *Lindsay in apparatu,*
fortasse ipsus me   717 olim homini *BDE,* homini *JK*
728 tibi *add. Fleckeisen*

---

32 Lit. "foot."

LEO   Master, will you move that chap away from you and ap-   714
      proach me in person, and will you then erect for me what
      he ordered and make your prayers to me?

ARG   And as which of the gods should I address *you*?

LEO   Fortune, the Obliging.

ARG   You're already better than that chap. (*points to Libanus*)

LIB   Is anything better for a man than Salvation?

ARG   I can praise Fortune without finding any fault with Salva-
      tion.

PHIL Yes, both are good.

ARG   I'll know it as soon as they've given us something good.

LEO   (*approaching Argyrippus*) Wish for what you want to   720
      happen to you.

ARG   What if I do?

LEO   It'll come true.

ARG   I wish that throughout this entire year I have this girl's at-
      tentions.

LEO   You've achieved it.

ARG   Do you really say so?

LEO   Certainly, I'm telling you.

LIB   Now it's your turn to come to me and try. Wish for what
      you want to happen to you most: it'll take place.

ARG   What other thing should I wish for more than that which   724
      I lack, the full twenty minas I can give to (*points to
      Philaenium*) her mother?

LIB   It will be given to you, do take heart, your wishes will
      come true.

ARG   As usually, Salvation and Fortune are deluding man.

LEO   I was the head when it came to finding this money for you
      today.

LIB   I was the tail.[32]

	ARG	quin nec caput nec pes sermoni apparet.
730		nec quid dicatis scire nec me quor ludatis possum.
	LIB	satis iam delusum censeo. nunc rem ut est eloquamur.
		animum, Argyrippe, aduorte sis. pater nos ferre hoc iussit
		argentum ad te.
	ARG	ut temperi opportuneque attulistis!
	LIB	hic inerunt uiginti minae bonae, mala opera partae;
735		has tibi nos pactis legibus dare iussit.
	ARG	quid id est, quaeso?
	LIB	noctem huius et cenam sibi ut dares.
	ARG	iube aduenire, quaeso:
		meritissumo eius quae uolet faciemus, qui hosce amores
		nostros dispulsos compulit.
	LEO	⟨patierin, Argyrippe,⟩
		patrem hanc amplexari tuom?
	ARG	haec faciet facile ut patiar.
740		Leonida, curre opsecro, patrem huc orato ut ueniat.
	LEO	iam dudum est intus.
	ARG	hac quidem non uenit.
	LEO	angiporto
		illac per hortum circum iit clam, ne quis se uideret
		huc ire familiarium: ne uxor resciscat metuit.
		de argento si mater tua sciat ut sit factum—
	ARG	heia,
745		bene dicite.
	LIB	ite intro cito.
	ARG	ualete.
	LEO	et uos amate.

730 scire *ante* possum *P, transp. Hermann*   738 haec faciet facile ut patiar *P ex insequente uersu*, patierin Argyrippe *Fleckeisen*

ARG Well, I can't make head or tail of your talk. I can't under- 730
stand what you're saying or why you're fooling me.

LIB (*to Leonida*) I think he's been made fun of enough. Now
let's tell him how things stand. (*to Argyrippus*) Argyrip-
pus, pay attention, will you? Your father told us to bring
this money to you. (*hands over the wallet*)

ARG How you brought it just in time and just at the right mo-
ment!

LIB There will be twenty good minas in here, acquired
through a bad job; he told us to give it to you on terms 735
agreed upon.

ARG What's that, please?

LIB You are to give him a night with her (*points at Philae-
nium*) and a dinner.

ARG (*after a brief hesitation*) Tell him to come, please. He's
fully deserved it and we'll do what he wants; he pulled
our love together again, which had been pulled apart.

LEO Will you bear it, Argyrippus, that your father embraces
her?

ARG This here (*lifts up the wallet*) will easily make me bear it.
Leonida, run, will you, and ask my father to come here. 740

LEO He's already been inside for a long time.

ARG Well, he didn't come this way.

LEO He secretly went around by the alley that way (*points*)
through the garden so that no one from our household
could see him come here. He's afraid his wife could find
out. If your mother knew about the money, how it hap-
pened—

ARG Dear me, only speak good omens!   745

LIB (*waving at Argyrippus and the girl*) Go inside quickly.

ARG Good-bye to you.

LEO And you two make love.

ACTVS IV

IV. i: DIABOLVS. PARASITVS

DIA agedum istum ostende quem conscripsti syngraphum
inter me et amicam et lenam. leges pellege.
nam tu poeta es prorsus ad eam rem unicus.

PAR horrescet faxo lena, leges quom audiet.

750 DIA age, quaeso, mi hercle translege.

PAR   audin?

DIA   audio.

PAR "Diabolus Glauci filius Clearetae
lenae dedit dono argenti uiginti minas,
Philaenium ut secum esset noctes et dies
hunc annum totum."

DIA   nec cum quiquam alio quidem.

755 PAR addone?

DIA   adde, et scribas uide plane et probe.

PAR "alienum hominem intro mittat neminem.
quod illa aut amicum aut patronum nominet,
aut quod illa amicai ⟨eum⟩ amatorem praedicet,
fores occlusae omnibus sint nisi tibi.

760 in foribus scribat occupatam esse se.
aut quod illa dicat peregre allatam epistulam,
ne epistula quidem ulla sit in aedibus
nec cerata adeo tabula; et si qua inutilis
pictura sit, eam uendat: ni in quadriduo

758 amica *P*, amicai ⟨eum⟩ *Lindsay*, amicae ⟨suae⟩ *Gulielmus*

*Exeunt ARGYRIPPUS and PHILAENIUM into Cleareta's
house, and LIBANUS and LEONIDA into Demaenetus'.*

ACT FOUR

*Enter DIABOLUS from the right, together with his HANGER-
ON.*

DIA Go on, show me that contract you've written, the one be-
tween me and my lady and the madam. Read over the
terms: you are the one and only artist for this sort of
thing.

HAN (*taking out a document*) I'll make sure that the madam
will shudder when she hears the terms.

DIA Go on now, please, read through it for me!   750

HAN Are you listening?

DIA I am.

HAN "Diabolus, the son of Glaucus, has given twenty silver
minas as a gift to the madam Cleareta in order that Phi-
laenium should be with him night and day for this entire
year."

DIA And not with anyone else.

HAN Should I add that?   755

DIA Yes, and mind that you write clearly and properly.

HAN "She shall not let any male outsider in. In case she de-
scribe him as a friend or patron, or in case she say that he
is the lover of a female friend of hers, the door shall be
shut for everyone except you. She shall write on the door 760
that she is engaged. Or in case she say a letter has been
delivered from abroad, there shall not even be any letter
in the house, nor as much as a wax tablet. And should
there be any useless picture, she shall sell it. If she has

765   abalienarit, quo aps te argentum acceperit,
                tuos arbitratus sit, comburas, si uelis,
                ne illi sit cera ubi facere possit litteras.
                uocet conuiuam neminem illa, tu uoces;
                ad eorum ne quem oculos adiciat suos.
770   si quem alium aspexit, caeca continuo siet.
                tecum una postea aeque pocla potitet:
                aps ted accipiat, tibi propinet, tu bibas,
                ne illa minus aut plus quam tu sapiat."
DIA   satis placet.
PAR   "suspiciones omnis ab se segreget.
775   neque illaec ulli pede pedem homini premat,
                quom surgat: nec ⟨quom⟩ in lectum inscendat proxu-
                      mum,
                nec quom descendat inde, det quoiquam manum:
                spectandum ne quoi anulum det nec roget.
                talos ne quoiquam homini ammoueat nisi tibi.
780   cum iaciat, 'te' ne dicat: nomen nominet.
                deam inuocet sibi quam lubebit propitiam,
                deum nullum; si magis religiosa fuerit,
                tibi dicat: tu pro illa ores ut sit propitius.
                neque illa ulli homini nutet, nictet, annuat.
785   post si lucerna exstincta sit, ne quid sui
                membri commoueat quicquam in tenebris."

776 quom[2] *add. Mueller*
785 postid si lucerna exstincta est *DJE*, post si lucerna exstincta est *B*, post si lucerna exstincta sit *Merula*, postid lucerna si exstincta est *Lindsay*

not got rid of it after three days of receipt of the money
from you, you may act as you see fit, you can burn it if you   766
so wish, lest she should have wax she could write on.[33]
She shall not invite any guest; you shall invite them. She
shall not glance at any of them. If she sets her eyes on an-   770
other, she shall be blind immediately. From now on she
shall drink her glasses together with you, glass for glass.
She shall take it from you, make a toast to you, and then
you shall drink, lest she have more or less taste than you."

DIA   I really like it.

HAN   "She shall keep herself above all suspicion. Nor shall she   775
push her foot against anyone else's foot when she is get-
ting up.[34] Neither when she is getting into the adjoining
couch nor when she is getting up from there shall she
give her hand to anyone. She shall not give her ring to
anyone to look at, nor shall she ask to look at anyone
else's. She shall not pass on the dice to anyone save you.
When she is throwing them she shall not say 'you';[35] she   780
shall name your name. She shall invoke any goddess she
likes for a favor, but no god. Should she be under any fur-
ther religious obligation, she shall tell you: *you* shall pray
for that favor for her. She shall not nod, wink, or make
any signs to any man. Later, if the lamp is put out, she   785
shall not move any of her limbs in the darkness."

[33] The passage may refer either to encaustic painting or to wax
being used to preserve a picture.

[34] She is occupying the middle part of the dining-couch, which was
typically designed for three people.

[35] It was common to invoke one's sweetheart before throwing the
dice.

DIA   optume est.
      ita scilicet facturam. uerum in cubiculo—
      deme istuc—equidem illam moueri gestio.
      nolo illam habere causam et uotitam dicere.
790 PAR scio, captiones metuis.
      DIA   uerum.
      PAR   ergo ut iubes
      tollam.
      DIA   quidni?
      PAR   audi relicua.
      DIA   loquere, audio.
      PAR "neque ullum uerbum faciat perplexabile,
      neque ulla lingua sciat loqui nisi Attica.
      fort' si tussire occepsit, ne sic tussiat
795 ut quoiquam linguam in tussiendo proserat.
      quod illa autem simulet quasi grauedo profluat,
      hoc ne sic faciat: tu labellum apstergeas
      potius quam quoiquam sauium faciat palam.
      nec mater lena ad uinum accedat interim,
800 neque ulli uerbo male dicat. si dixerit,
      haec multa ei esto, uino uiginti dies
      ut careat."
      DIA   pulchre scripsti. scitum syngraphum!
      PAR "tum si coronas, serta, unguenta iusserit
      ancillam ferre Veneri aut Cupidini,
805 tuos seruos seruet Venerine eas det an uiro.
      si forte pure uelle habere dixerit,
      tot noctes reddat spurcas quot pure habuerit."
      haec sunt non nugae, non enim mortualia.

228

DIA   Perfect. Of course she will act like this. But in the bedroom—take that out—I'm really keen on her moving. I don't want her to have an excuse and to say she's been forbidden to do so.

HAN   I know, you're afraid of loopholes. 790

DIA   Exactly.

HAN   So as you tell me I'll remove it.

DIA   Naturally.

HAN   Listen to the rest.

DIA   Speak up, I'm listening.

HAN   "She shall not use any ambiguous word and she shall not know how to speak any language save Attic. If by chance 794 she begins to cough, she shall not cough in such a way that she sticks out her tongue to anyone while coughing. But in case she pretend she has a running nose, she shall not do it like this (*demonstrates*): you shall wipe clean her lip rather than that she should openly blow anyone a kiss. And her mother, the madam, shall not come to the wine meanwhile, and she shall not say one abusive word to 800 anyone. If she does, then this shall be her punishment: she shall not have wine for twenty days."

DIA   You've written it beautifully. A fantastic contract!

HAN   "Next point: if she orders her maid to bring garlands, wreaths, or perfumes to Venus or Cupid, your slave shall 805 watch whether she is giving them to Venus or to a man. If by chance she says she wants to spend some nights chastely, she shall give you as many unchaste nights as she had chaste ones." This is no nonsense: these are no dirges.[36]

---

[36] Funerary dirges were silly (Non. p. 212 Lindsay), presumably for apotropaeic reasons.

DIA   placent profecto leges. sequere intro.

PAR   sequor.

IV. ii: DIABOLVS. PARASITVS

810 DIA   sequere hac. egone haec patiar aut taceam? emori
me malim quam haec non eius uxori indicem.
ain tu? apud amicam munus adulescentuli
fungare, uxori excuses te et dicas senem?
praeripias scortum amanti atque argentum obicias

815   lenae? suppiles clam domi uxorem tuam?
suspendam potius me quam tacita haec tu auferas.
iam quidem hercle ad illam hinc ibo, quam tu prope-
    diem,
nisi quidem illa ante occupassit te, effliges scio,
luxuriae sumptus suppeditare ut possies.

820 PAR   ego sic faciundum censeo: me honestiust
quam te palam hanc rem facere, ne illa existumet
amoris causa percitum id fecisse te
magis quam sua causa.

DIA   at pol qui dixti rectius.
tu ergo fac ut illi turbas, litis concias,

825   cum suo sibi gnato unam ad amicam de die
potare, illam expilare.

PAR   iam ⟨iam⟩. ne mone.
ego istuc curabo.

DIA   at ego te opperiar domi.

826 iam emone *P*, iam ⟨iam⟩. ne mone *Lindsay*, clam PAR ne me
mone *Ritschl*

DIA   I do like your terms. Follow me in.

HAN   I'm following you.

Exit DIABOLUS into Cleareta's house, followed by his
HANGER-ON.
Noise. Enter DIABOLUS from Cleareta's house, followed by his
HANGER-ON.

DIA   (*angrily*) Follow me this way. Should I bear this or keep 810
quiet? I'd rather die than not reveal this to his wife.
(*shouting into the house*) You say so? At your mistress's
place you want to do a young man's job, and to your wife
you want to make excuses and say you're an old bloke?
You want to snatch a prostitute from her lover and throw
money at the madam? You want to filch things from your
wife at home? (*muttering to himself*) I'd rather hang my- 816
self than let you get away with this untold. This instant I'll
go to her from here, to the woman you will shortly, I know
it, murder—unless of course she manages to murder you
first—just so that you can supply the funds for your luxu-
rious lifestyle!

HAN   (*calmly, judiciously*) I think one should act like this: it's 820
more honorable for me to reveal this matter than it is for
you to do so, so that she doesn't think you were upset and
did it out of love rather than for her sake.

DIA   Yes, you're right. So make sure you stir up chaos and 824
strife for him; would he be drinking at the same mistress's
place with his own son in broad daylight, and would he
rob his wife?

HAN   Immediately; stop lecturing me. I'll take care of that.

DIA   And I'll wait for you at home.

ACTVS V

V. i: ARGYRIPPVS. DEMAENETVS

ARG age decumbamus sis, pater.

DEM ut iusseris,
mi gnate, ita fiet.

ARG pueri, mensam apponite.

830 DEM numquidnam tibi molestum est, gnate mi, si haec nunc
mecum accubat?

ARG pietas, pater, oculis dolorem prohibet. quamquam ego is-
tanc amo,
possum equidem inducere animum ne aegre patiar quia
tecum accubat.

DEM decet uerecundum esse adulescentem, Argyrippe.

ARG edepol, pater,
merito tuo facere possum.

DEM age ergo, hoc agitemus conuiuium
835 uino ut sermone suaui. nolo ego metui, amari mauolo,
mi gnate, me aps te.

ARG pol ego utrumque facio, ut aequom est filium.

DEM credam istuc, si esse te hilarum uidero.

ARG an tu [ess'] me tristem putas?

DEM putem ego, quem uideam aeque esse maestum ut quasi
dies si dicta sit?

839– ARG ne dixis istuc.
40 DEM ne sic fueris: ilico ego non dixero.

ARG em aspecta: rideo.

837 esse[2] *del. Bothe*

Exit HANGER-ON into Demaenetus' house, exit DIABOLUS to the right.

ACT FIVE

Enter ARGYRIPPUS, DEMAENETUS, and PHILAENIUM from Cleareta's house, all wearing garlands, followed by servants with all that is necessary to continue the banquet outside.

ARG   (*sounding very depressed*) Go on, let's recline, father, if you please.

DEM   My son, it'll be done as you command.

ARG   (*to servants*) Lads, bring the table.

DEM   Do you have any harsh feelings about this, my son, if she's 830
now reclining with me?

ARG   Father, my sense of filial duty removes the sting from the sight. Even though I love her, I can persuade myself not to be upset at her reclining with you.

DEM   It's appropriate for a young man to be respectful, Argyrippus.

ARG   Father, I can do it because you deserve it.

DEM   Go on then, let's hold this banquet with sweet wine as 835
well as sweet talk. I don't want to be feared, I prefer to be loved by you, my son.

ARG   Well, I'm doing both, as befits a son.

DEM   I'll believe this if I see you cheerful.

ARG   Do you think I'm depressed?

DEM   Do I think so? I can see that you're as sad as if you were in for trial.

ARG   Don't say that.   839

DEM   Don't be like that: immediately I won't say it any more.   –40

ARG   There, look: I'm laughing.

233

DEM	utinam male qui mihi uolunt sic rideant.
ARG	scio equidem quam ob rem me, pater, tu tristem credas
	nunc tibi:
	quia istaec est tecum. atque ego quidem hercle ut uerum
	tibi dicam, pater,
	ea res me male habet; at non eo quia tibi non cupiam
	quae uelis;

845   uerum istam amo. aliam tecum esse equidem facile pos-
                         sum perpeti.

DEM	at ego hanc uolo.
ARG	ergo sunt quae exoptas: mihi quae ego exoptem uolo.
DEM	unum hunc diem perpetere, quoniam tibi potestatem
	dedi
	cum hac annum ut esses, atque amanti argenti feci co-
	piam.

849–
50

ARG	em istoc me facto tibi deuinxti.
DEM	quin te ergo hilarum das mihi?

V. ii: ARTEMONA. PARASITVS. ARGYRIPPVS.
DEMAENETVS. PHILAENIVM

ART	ain tu meum uirum hic potare, opsecro, cum filio
	et ad amicam detulisse argenti uiginti minas
	meoque filio sciente id facere flagitium patrem?
PAR	nec diuini nec mi humani posthac quicquam accreduas,

855   Artemona, si huius rei me ess' mendacem inueneris.

ART	at scelesta ego praeter alios meum uirum frugi rata,
	siccum, frugi, continentem, amantem uxoris maxume.
PAR	at nunc dehinc scito illum ante omnis minimi mortalem
	preti,
	madidum, nihili, incontinentem atque osorem uxoris
	suae.

856 frugi *P*, fui (*spondaicum*) *Pylades quia* frugi *et hic et* 857
positum displicet, fueram *dubitanter Leo*

DEM   I wish my enemies laughed liked that.

ARG   I know of course why you think I'm upset with you now, father: because she's with you. And to tell you the truth, father, that does make me feel down; but not because I wouldn't wish you to have what you want; but I love her. I 845 can easily handle it if another girl is with you.

DEM   But I want this one.

ARG   Well, you have what you wish for. And I want to have what I wish for.

DEM   Put up with it for this one day, since I've given you the power to be with her for a year, and since I've given you, the lover, the funding for it.

ARG   Here you go! With this deed you've bound me to your 849 service. –50

DEM   Then why don't you put on a cheerful face for me?

Enter ARTEMONA with the HANGER-ON from Demaenetus' house.

ART   I beg you, are you saying that my husband's drinking here together with his son? And that he's brought twenty silver minas to a mistress? And that he, the father, is committing such an outrage with the full knowledge of my son?

HAN   Artemona, don't trust me ever after when I swear by the 854 gods or men if you find that I've lied to you about this matter.

ART   But I'm such an idiot! I used to think my husband was better than others, sober, good, moderate, full of love for his wife.

HAN   But from now on you should know that he's the most worthless of men, a drunkard, useless, immoderate, and full of hatred for his wife.

860   ART   pol ni istaec uera essent, numquam faceret ea quae nunc
          facit.

      PAR   ego quoque hercle illum antehac hominem semper sum
          frugi ratus,

          uerum hoc facto sese ostendit, qui quidem cum filio

          potet una atque una amicam ductet, decrepitus senex.

      ART   hoc ecastor est quod ille it ad cenam cottidie.

865   ait sese ire ad Archidemum, Chaeream, Chaerestratum,

          Cliniam, Chremem, Cratinum, Diniam, Demosthenem:

          is apud scortum corruptelae est liberis, lustris studet.

      PAR   quin tu illum iubes ancillas rapere sublimem domum?

      ART   tace modo. nc illum mecastor miserum habebo.

      PAR   ego istuc scio,

870   ita fore illi dum quidem cum illo nupta eris.

      ART   ego censeo.

          eum etiam hominem ⟨aut⟩ in senatu dare operam aut
          cluentibus,

          ibi labore delassatum noctem totam stertere!

          ille operi foris faciendo lassus noctu ⟨ad me⟩ aduenit;

          fundum alienum arat, incultum familiarem deserit.

875   is etiam corruptus porro suom corrumpit filium.

      PAR   sequere hac me modo, iam faxo ipsum hominem manu-
          festo opprimas.

      ART   nihil ecastor est quod facere mauelim.

      PAR   manedum.

      ART   quid est?

      PAR   possis, si forte accubantem tuom uirum conspexeris

          cum corona amplexum amicam, si uideas, cognoscere?

880   ART   possum ecastor.

      871 aut *add. Camerarius*
      873 opere *BDJ*, operis *E*, operi *Lindsay*   ad me *add. Fleckeisen*

ART If what you say weren't true, he'd never be doing what 860
   he's doing now.

HAN Previously I too always used to think that he was a good
   man, but in this deed he reveals himself, drinking to-
   gether with his son and renting a mistress together with
   him, that old fart!

ART Yes, that explains why he has to go to dinner every day.
   He says he's going to Archidemus, Chaerea, Chaerestra- 865
   tus, Clinia, Chremes, Cratinus, Dinia, Demosthenes: in
   reality he corrupts his son at a prostitute's and frequents
   the brothels.

HAN Why don't you order your maids to pick him up and drag
   him home?

ART Just be quiet. Yes, I will give him a tough time.

HAN I know that he'll have one so long as you're married to 870
   him.

ART I should think so. The idea of this person being busy
   in the senate or with his clients, and then snoring the
   whole night, worn out by his work there! He comes to
   me at night, worn out from doing business outside. He's
   ploughing someone else's field and leaves his own uncul-
   tivated. And this corrupt person then corrupts his son. 875

HAN Just follow me this way, I'll make sure that you'll catch the
   chap himself in flagrante in a moment.

ART Yes, there's nothing I'd prefer to do.

HAN (*stops near Cleareta's house*) Wait for a moment.

ART What's the matter?

HAN If you were to see your husband lying there with a gar-
   land embracing his mistress, could you recognize him if
   you were to see him?

ART I could indeed. 880

PAR	em tibi hominem.
ART	perii.
PAR	paullisper mane.

aucupemus ex insidiis clanculum quam rem gerant.

ARG	quid modi, pater, amplexando facies?
DEM	fateor, gnate mi—
ARG	quid fatere?
DEM	me ex amore huius corruptum oppido;
PAR	audin quid ait?
ART	audio.
DEM	egon ut non domo uxori meae

885   surrupiam in dcliciis pallam quam habet atque ad te
     deferam,

     non edepol conduci possum uita uxoris annua.

PAR	censen tu illum hodie primum ire assuetum esse in ga-
	neum?
ART	ille ecastor suppilabat me, quod ancillas meas
	suspicabar atque insontis miseras cruciabam.
ARG	pater,

890   iube dari uinum; iam dudum factum est quom primum
     bibi.

DEM	da, puere, ab summo. age tu interibi ab infumo da
	sauium.
ART	perii misera, ut osculatur carnufex, capuli decus!
DEM	edepol animam suauiorem aliquanto quam uxoris meae.
PHIL	dic amabo, an foetet anima uxoris tuae?
DEM	nauteam

895   bibere malim, si necessum sit, quam illam oscul"arier.

---

[37] I translate "puke" because of Greek *nautia* (seasickness, disgust).
Nautea could also refer to bilgewater if there is a connection with the
first Greek meaning. Paul the Deacon thinks of a plant used in tanning
hides (p. 165 Lindsay).

HAN   *(points at the banquet)* Here's the chap for you.

ART   *(agitated)* I'm done for.

HAN   *(holding Artemona back)* Wait for a bit. Let's catch from a hiding place, secretly, what they're up to.

ARG   When will you stop hugging her, father?

DEM   I admit it, my son—

ARG   *(interrupting)* What do you admit?

DEM   —that I'm utterly corrupted because of my love for this girl.

HAN   *(quietly)* Can you hear what he's saying?   884

ART   *(quietly)* I can.

DEM   *(to Philaenium)* I couldn't be hired not to steal my wife's favorite mantle from home and not to bring it to you, not even if my reward were that my wife should live only one more year.

HAN   *(quietly)* Do you think he first got used to go to the brothel today?

ART   *(quietly)* Good god, he's the one who was robbing me! And I suspected my maids and tortured the poor creatures even though they were innocent.

ARG   Father, tell them to give us wine. It's a long time since I   890 had my first drink.

DEM   *(to a servant)* Boy, send it round from the head of the couch. *(to Philaenium)* Go on, meanwhile you give me a kiss from the lower end.

ART   *(quietly)* Poor me, I'm done for! How the villain is kissing her, an old fart fit for the coffin!

DEM   Yes, much sweater breath than that of my wife!

PHIL   Tell me, please, does your wife's breath smell?

DEM   I'd rather drink puke,[37] if necessary, than kiss her.

ART   ain tandem? edepol ne tu istuc cum malo magno tuo
      dixisti in me. sine, reuenias modo domum, faxo ut scias
      quid pericli sit dotatae uxori uitium dicere.

PHIL miser ecastor es.

ART   ecastor dignus est.

ARG   quid ais, pater?

900   ecquid matrem amas?

DEM   egone illam? nunc amo, quia non adest.

ARG   quid quom adest?

DEM   periisse cupio.

PAR   amat homo hic te, ut praedicat.

ART   ne illa ecastor faenerato funditat: nam si domum
      redierit hodie, osculando ego ulciscar potissumum.

ARG   iace, pater, talos, ut porro nos iaciamus.

DEM   maxume.

905   te, Philaenium, mihi atque uxoris mortem. hoc Venerium
        est.
      pueri, plaudite et mi ob iactum cantharo mulsum date.

ART   non queo durare.

PAR   si non didicisti fulloniam,
      non mirandum est, ⟨Artemona⟩; in oculos inuadi optu-
        mum est.

ART   ego pol uiuam et tu istaec hodie cum tuo magno malo
910   inuocasti.

PAR   ecquis currit pollinctorem accersere?

ARG   mater, salue.

---

897 uenias *P*, reuenias *Ritschl*   908 Artemona *add. Havet*

---

[38] The highest throw. Each of the four dice shows a different
number.   [39] A double pun. Artemona uses *durare* in the meaning

ART   (*quietly*) Do you say so? Saying that against me will land   896
you in big trouble. Well then! Just come home, I'll make
sure that you know what danger there is in speaking
badly about a wife with a dowry.

PHIL   You really are a poor wretch.

ART   (*quietly*) And he really deserves it.

ARG   What do you say, father? Do you love mother?   900

DEM   I her? Now I love her because she's not around.

ARG   What when she is around?

DEM   Then I wish she were dead.

HAN   (*quietly, with sarcasm*) This man's in love with you, judg-
ing from his words.

ART   (*quietly*) He's pouring out this stuff on interest: if he re-
turns home today, I'll take the best possible revenge on
him: I'll kiss him.

ARG   Throw the dice, father, so that I can take my turn.

DEM   I will. You for me, Philaenium, and my wife's death.   905
(*throws the dice*) That's the Venus throw![38] (*to the ser-
vants*) Lads, your applause, and give me honey-wine
from the jug for my throw.

ART   (*quietly*) I can't endure it.

HAN   (*quietly*) If you didn't learn the fullers' trade, that's no
surprise, Artemona.[39] It's best to scratch out his eyes.

ART   (*rushing toward them*) I will live, and invoking these
things today will cost *you* a big thrashing.

HAN   (*to the audience*) Is anyone running to fetch the under-
taker?

ARG   (*feebly*) Hello, mother.   911

"endure"; the hanger-on understands it as "harden (cloth)." By likening
her to a fuller, he also says that she is experiencing something disgust-
ing.

241

ART   sat salutis.

PAR   mortuost Demaenetus.

tempus est subducere hinc me; pulchre hoc gliscit proe-
lium.

ibo ad Diabolum, mandata dicam facta ut uoluerit,

atque interea ut decumbamus suadebo, hi dum litigant.

915   poste demum huc cras adducam ad lenam, ut uiginti
minas

ei det, in partem hac amanti ut liceat ei potirier.

Argyrippus exorari spero poterit ut sinat

sese alternas cum illo noctes hac frui. nam ni impetro,

regem perdidi: ex amore tantum est homini incendium.

920 ART   quid tibi hunc receptio ad te est meum uirum?

PHIL   pol me quidem
miseram odio enicauit.

ART   surge, amator, i domum.

DEM   nullus sum.

ART   immo es, ne nega, omnium ⟨hominum⟩ pol
nequissumus.

at etiam cubat cuculus. surge, amator, i domum.

DEM   uae mihi!

ART   uera hariolare. surge, amator, i domum.

925 DEM   apscede ergo paullulum istuc.

ART   surge, amator, i domum.

DEM   iam opsecro, uxor—

ART   nunc uxorem me esse meministi tuam?

modo, quom dicta in me ingerebas, odium, non uxor,
eram.

DEM   totus perii.

911 mortuus est *P*, mortuost *Lindsay in apparatu*
922 hominum *add. Fleckeisen*

ART   Enough of your hello.

HAN   (*to the audience*) Demaenetus is dead. It's time for me to disappear from here. This battle is growing beautifully. I'll go to Diabolus and say that his orders have been executed as he wished. I'll advise that we should recline to dinner in the meantime while these people here are fighting. Then finally I'll bring him here to the madam to- 915 morrow so that he can give her the twenty minas in order to get permission to get his share of the girl. I hope Argyrippus can be persuaded to go shares and let him enjoy her every other night: if I don't achieve it, I've lost my patron; the man is all aflame because of his love.

Exit HANGER-ON to the right.

ART   (*to Philaenium*) Why did you receive this husband of   920 mine at your place?

PHIL   Honestly, he killed me with his tedium, poor woman that I am.

ART   (*to Demaenetus*) Get up, lover, go home.

DEM   I am no more.

ART   O yes, you are—you are the most wicked of men. But the cuckoo is still lying there! Get up, lover, go home.

DEM   Bad luck to me!

ART   You're prophesying the truth. Get up, lover, go home.

DEM   Then draw back a little.   925

ART   Get up, lover, go home.

DEM   I beg you now, my dear wife—

ART   Now you remember that I'm your dear wife? Just before, when you were throwing bad words against me, I was your abomination, not your wife.

DEM   (*tonelessly*) I'm completely dead.

ART   quid tandem? anima foetetne uxoris tuae?

DEM   murram olet.

ART   iam surrupuisti pallam quam scorto dares?

930 PHIL   ecastor qui surrupturum pallam promisit tibi.

DEM   non taces?

ARG   ego dissuadebam, mater.

ART   bellum filium!
istoscin patrem aequom est mores liberis largirier?
nilne te pudet?

DEM   pol, si aliud nil sit, tui me, uxor, pudet.

ART   cano capite te cuculum uxor ex lustris rapit.

935 DEM   non licet manere (cena coquitur) dum cenem modo?

ART   ecastor cenabis hodie, ut dignus es, magnum malum.

DEM   male cubandum est: iudicatum me uxor abducit domum.

ARG   dicebam, pater, tibi ne matri consuleres male.

PHIL   de palla memento, amabo.

DEM   iuben hanc hinc apscedere?

940 ART   i domum.

PHIL   da sauium etiam prius quam abitis.

DEM   i in crucem.

PHIL   immo intus potius. sequere hac me, mi anime.

ARG   ego uero sequor.

936 dignum est *P*, dignus es *Gruterus*, dignu's *Lindsay* (*cum hiatu post* hodie)

ART   What now? Does your wife's breath stink?

DEM   It smells of myrrh.

ART   Have you already stolen a cloak that you can give to the prostitute?

PHIL   Yes, he promised to steal a cloak from you.   930

DEM   (*to Philaenium*) Won't you be quiet?

ARG   I advised him against it, mother.

ART   (*to Argyrippus*) A lovely son! (*to Demaenetus*) Should a father endow his children with that kind of behavior? Don't you have any shame?

DEM   If there were nothing else, I'd be ashamed before you, my dear wife.

ART   When your head is grey your dear wife has to drag you, the cuckoo, from a brothel.

DEM   Can't I stay (dinner is being cooked) just until I've dined?   935

ART   Seriously, your dinner today will consist of a good thrashing, as you deserve it.

DEM   (*aside*) I'll have to recline wretchedly: my wife has sentenced me and is dragging me home.

ARG   I told you, father, not to play tricks on mother.

PHIL   (*to Demaenetus*) Remember about the cloak please.

DEM   (*to Argyrippus*) Won't you tell her to get away from here?

ART   (*to Demaenetus*) Go home.   940

PHIL   (*to Demaenetus*) Give me a kiss before you two go.

DEM   Go and be hanged.

PHIL   No, inside instead. (*to Argyrippus*) Follow me this way, my darling.

ARG   I'm following you indeed.

Exeunt ARTEMONA and DEMAENETUS to their house; exeunt PHILAENIUM and ARGYRIPPUS into Cleareta's house. Enter the whole TROUPE.

v. iii

GREX hic senex si quid clam uxorem suo animo fecit uolup,
  nec nouom nec mirum fecit nec secus quam alii solent;
  nec quisquam est tam ingenio duro nec tam firmo pec-
    tore
945 quin ubi quicque occasionis sit sibi faciat bene.
  nunc si uoltis deprecari huic seni ne uapulet,
  remur impetrari posse, plausum si clarum datis.

TROUPE If this old man got some pleasure behind his wife's back, he didn't do anything new or out of the ordinary, or anything different from what others normally do. Nobody has such a strong character or such a hard heart that he wouldn't enjoy himself when the occasion presents itself. Now if you want to intercede for this old man so that he shouldn't get a beating, we believe that this can be achieved if you give us loud applause. 944

AVLVLARIA,

OR

THE POT OF GOLD

INTRODUCTORY NOTE

The *Aulularia* is one of Plautus' best-known plays. Its main character is Euclio, a man who has been plunged into a personal crisis by finding a pot of gold. Euclio is not a bad person, but he cannot cope with his fortune. Instead of putting the money to good use, he is so afraid of losing it that he spends all his time concealing his find, even from his daughter Phaedrium. He becomes paranoid and begins to look at his neighbors as potential thieves.

Being so preoccupied with his gold, he fails to realize that Phaedrium is also going through a personal crisis. A young man, Lyconides, raped her when he was drunk. She did not recognize her assailant, but he knew who she was. Phaedrium kept her pregnancy secret from everyone except for her old nurse. She is close to giving birth when Lyconides' mother, Eunomia, manages to persuade her brother Megadorus, a confirmed bachelor, to marry. The wealthy Megadorus does not want the equally wealthy and elderly woman whom his sister has in mind, but prefers the young and poor Phaedrium.

Euclio is still unaware of his daughter's situation when Megadorus proposes his match. Suspicious that Megadorus just wants his gold, Euclio agrees to give his daughter in marriage on condition that no dowry be given to Megadorus.

Megadorus sends cooks to Euclio's house to prepare the wedding banquet. This is why Euclio is looking for a different place to hide his gold. But Lyconides' slave has realized what he is doing and manages to steal it. Euclio is in despair.

Meanwhile, Lyconides has understood that he cannot delay any longer. He confesses his deed to his mother and says that he wants to marry Phaedrium. Eunomia now persuades Megadorus to give up his wedding plans. Lyconides then repeats his words to Euclio, who at first believes that Lyconides is admitting to stealing the gold. This misunderstanding results in one of the funniest scenes of ancient comedy. When Euclio finally sees what happened, he accepts the marriage, but asks Lyconides to help him to find the gold again.

Lyconides' slave meets his master, tells him that he stole Euclio's gold, and demands his freedom. The ending of the play is lost. However, the ancient plot summaries and the fragments allow us to understand how the comedy ended. Lyconides returns the gold to Euclio and frees his slave. The marriage takes place, and Euclio, who has realized that the gold cannot make him happy, gives it to the young couple.

Even though this is one of Plautus' most famous comedies, we do not know for certain who wrote the original and when the Latin work was performed first. It is generally assumed that the *Aulularia* is based on a play by Menander, but of course there are other possibilities as well. In the Latin play there are several references to the luxurious lifestyle of women (ll. 167–69, ll. 478–535). It may well be the case that the *Aulularia* was written after the *Lex Oppia* was repealed in 195, a law that severely restricted expenditure on goods considered unnecessary. There is also a fairly lengthy reference to festivals of Bacchus (ll. 406–14), so one can assume that the play was written around the time the *Senatus consultum de Bacchanalibus* was decreed. This regulation from 186 made it much more difficult to hold such celebrations. We cannot go very wrong if we date the *Aulularia* to around 190.

Only the Palatine manuscripts have preserved the *Aulularia*. The Ambrosian palimpsest does not contain it. Nevertheless, the extant text is relatively certain. Two problems, however, deserve to be mentioned. The first is the identity of Lyconides' slave. Megadorus has a slave called Strobilus. Later in the play (l. 697) the manuscripts refer to Lyconides' slave as Strobilus as well. It is inconceivable that we are dealing with only one slave, because Lyconides' slave and Megadorus do not even know each other when they meet. Since in Roman comedy two people have the same name only if confusions are intended, as in the *Menaechmi*, we must be dealing with a manuscript corruption. Lyconides' slave must remain unnamed.

The second problem is the question where Lyconides, his slave, and Eunomia live. In l. 727 Lyconides refers to Megadorus' house as "our house." This has sometimes been taken as an indication that the three of them live with Megadorus. But as Lyconides' slave and Megadorus do not know each other, it is better to assume that Eunomia and her family live in a separate house. Lyconides' expression is not unusual: in Terence's *Adelphoe* (l. 910), Demea speaks of "our household" when referring to his brother's place.

SELECT BIBLIOGRAPHY

Editions and Commentaries

Nicastri, L. (1970), *Aulularia: Introduzione e commento* (Naples).

Stace, C. (1971), *A Commentary on the Aulularia of Plautus (v. 1–586)* (diss., London).

Stockert, W. (1983), *T. Maccius Plautus: Aulularia* (Stuttgart).

Thomas, E. J. (1913), *T. Macci Plauti Aulularia: Introduction, Text, Notes* (Oxford).

Criticism

Hofmann, W. (1977), "Zur Charaktergestaltung in der *Aulularia* des Plautus," *Klio* 59: 349–58.

Ludwig, W. (1961), "Aululariaprobleme," *Philologus* 105: 44–71 and 247–62.

Raffaelli, R., and A. Tontini (eds.) (2000), *Lecturae Plautinae Sarsinates III: Aulularia (Sarsina, 11 settembre 1999)* (Urbino).

AVLVLARIA

ARGVMENTVM I

senex auarus uix sibi credens Euclio
domi suae defossam multis cum opibus
aulam inuenit, rursumque penitus conditam
exsanguis amens seruat. eius filiam
5 Lyconides uitiarat. interea senex
Megadorus a sorore suasus ducere
uxorem auari gnatam deposcit sibi.
durus senex uix promittit atque aulae timens
domo sublatam uariis apstrudit locis.
10 insidias seruos facit huius Lyconidis
qui uirginem uitiarat; atque ipse opsecrat
auonculum Megadorum sibimet cedere
uxorem amanti. per dolum mox Euclio
cum perdidisset aulam, insperato inuenit
15 laetusque natam collocat Lyconidi.

ARGVMENTVM II

Aulam repertam auri plenam Euclio
Vi summa seruat, miseris affectus modis.
Lyconides istius uitiat filiam.
Volt hanc Megadorus indotatam ducere

254

THE POT OF GOLD

PLOT SUMMARY 1

Euclio, a stingy old man who would barely trust himself, finds a
pot with great wealth buried in his house. He hides it deep
down again and watches over it, pale with fear and full of anxi-
ety. Lyconides had violated his daughter's chastity. Meanwhile
old Megadorus, persuaded to marry by his sister, asks for the
hand of the miser's daughter. The austere old man consents at   7
last. Afraid for his pot, he removes it from home and hides it in
various places. The slave of Lyconides, the man who had done   10
violence to the girl, lies in ambush. Lyconides entreats his uncle
Megadorus to yield her as wife to him because he loves her.
Soon after, when Euclio had lost the pot by a trick, he finds it
again, against his hopes, and happily betroths his daughter to   15
Lyconides.

PLOT SUMMARY 2

Euclio watches very carefully over a pot full of gold that he
found, feeling great anxiety. Lyconides violates his daughter's
chastity. Megadorus wants to marry her without dowry, and in   5

5 Lubensque ut faciat dat coquos cum opsonio.
  Auro formidat Euclio, apstrudit foris.
  Re omni inspecta compressoris seruolus
  Id surpit. illic Euclioni rem refert.
  Ab eo donatur auro, uxore, et filio.

order that Euclio should accept willingly, he sends cooks with provisions. Euclio fears for his gold and hides it outside. After witnessing everything, the rapist's slave steals it. Lyconides informs Euclio of it. He is presented by him with the gold, a wife, and a son.

PERSONAE

LAR FAMILIARIS prologus
EVCLIO senex
STAPHYLA anus
EVNOMIA matrona
MEGADORVS senex
STROBILVS seruos
ANTHRAX coquos
CONGRIO coquos
SERVOS Lyconidis
LYCONIDES adulescens
PHAEDRIVM uirgo
PHRYGIA tibicina
ELEVSIVM tibicina

SCAENA

Athenis

THE POT OF GOLD

CHARACTERS

GUARDIAN SPIRIT[1] speaker of the prologue; does not appear later on

EUCLIO an old man; the main character of our play

STAPHYLA an old woman; Euclio's housekeeper

EUNOMIA a married woman; of high status

MEGADORUS an old man; Eunomia's wealthy brother

STROBILUS a slave; works for Megadorus

ANTHRAX a cook; clever and witty

CONGRIO a cook; somewhat slow

LYCONIDES' SERVANT without name in the play

LYCONIDES a young man; Eunomia's son

PHAEDRIUM a young woman; Euclio's daughter

PHRYGIA a flute-girl; overweight and ugly

ELEUSIUM a flute-girl; slim and attractive

STAGING

The stage represents a street in Athens. In the middle we find a shrine of Good Faith with an altar. To its left there is Euclio's house and to its right there is Megadorus'. The exit to the left leads to the countryside; the exit to the right leads to the city center. Eunomia's house is not on stage. It is in the city.

[1] The *Lar familiaris* is a deity protecting the house and its inhabitants.

PROLOGVS

LAR FAMILIARIS

ne quis miretur qui sim, paucis eloquar.
ego Lar sum familiaris ex hac familia
unde exeuntem me aspexistis. hanc domum
iam multos annos est quom possideo et colo

5 patri auoque iam huius qui nunc hic habet.
sed mihi auos huius opsecrans concredidit
auri thesaurum clam omnis: in medio foco
defodit, uenerans me ut id seruarem sibi.
is quoniam moritur (ita auido ingenio fuit),

10 numquam indicare id filio uoluit suo,
inopemque optauit potius eum relinquere
quam eum thesaurum commonstraret filio;
agri reliquit ei non magnum modum,
quo cum labore magno et misere uiueret.

15 ubi is obiit mortem qui mi id aurum credidit,
coepi opseruare, ecqui maiorem filius
mihi honorem haberet quam eius habuisset pater.
atque ille uero minus minusque impendio
curare minusque me impertire honoribus.

20 item a me contra factum est, nam item obiit diem.
is ex se hunc reliquit qui hic nunc habitat filium,
pariter moratum ut pater auosque huius fuit.
huic filia una est. ea mihi cottidie
aut ture aut uino aut aliqui semper supplicat,

25 dat mihi coronas. eius honoris gratia

THE POT OF GOLD

PROLOGUE

Enter the GUARDIAN SPIRIT from Euclio's house.

In case anyone wonders who I am, I'll tell you briefly. I'm the
Guardian Spirit of this household which you saw me coming out
from. For many years already I've been occupying this house
and protecting it for the father and grandfather of the man who
lives here now. Now this man's grandfather entrusted me, on 6
bended knee, behind everyone's back, with a treasure of gold.
He buried it in the middle of the hearth, entreating me to guard
it for him. When he died, he didn't even want to make this
known to his own son—he was so greedy. He wished to leave 11
him penniless rather than show this treasure to his son. He did
leave him a piece of land, not a big one, though, so that he could
live on it with great toil and miserably. When the man who'd en- 15
trusted the gold to me died, I began to observe whether his son
would in any way hold me in greater honor than his father had.
He took less and less trouble over me and showed me less re-
spect. I returned the favor: he also died poor. He left a son be- 20
hind, the one who lives here now, a man of the same character
as his father and grandfather. He has one daughter. *She* wor-
ships me every single day with incense or wine or something
else and gives me garlands. It's in order to honor her that I let 25

---

7 th. auri *P, transp. Camerarius*

feci thesaurum ut hic reperiret Euclio,
quo illam facilius nuptum, si uellet, daret.
nam compressit eam de summo adulescens loco.
is scit adulescens quae sit quam compresserit,
30 illa illum nescit, nec compressam autem pater.
eam ego hodie faciam ut hic senex de proxumo
sibi uxorem poscat. id ea faciam gratia
quo ille eam facilius ducat qui compresserat.
et hic qui poscet eam sibi uxorem senex,
35 is adulescentis est illius auunculus,
qui illam stuprauit noctu, Cereris uigiliis.
sed hic senex iam clamat intus ut solet.
anum foras extrudit, ne sit conscia.
credo aurum inspicere uolt, ne surruptum siet.

ACTVS I

I. i: EVCLIO. STAPHYLA

40 EVC   exi, inquam, age exi: exeundum hercle tibi hinc est foras,
        circumspectatrix cum oculis emissiciis.
STA   nam quor me miseram uerberas?
EVC   ut misera sis
        atque ut te dignam, mala, malam aetatem exigas.
STA   nam qua me nunc causa extrusisti ex aedibus?

---

28 compressit eam *P, transp. Bothe*
35 illius est *P, transp. Leo*

---

2 In Greek the Eleusinian mysteries or the Thesmophoria. The Roman audience may have thought of a Roman festival; Cicero (*leg.* 2. 21) mentions rites of Ceres, which he describes as Greek and as an initiation.

this man here, Euclio, find the treasure, so that he might give her more easily in marriage should he wish to do so: a young man of very high rank has raped her. This young man knows who the girl he raped is, but she doesn't know him, and her fa- 30
ther doesn't even know that she's been raped. I'll make this old man from next door ask for her hand today. My reason for doing this is so that the man who's raped her may marry her all the more easily. And this old man who's going to ask for her hand, he's the uncle of that young fellow who violated her chastity by 35
night during the vigil held in honor of Ceres.[2] (*sound of shouting from Euclio's house*) But now this old man's shouting inside as usual. He's throwing out the old woman so that she can't learn his secret. I think he wants to look at his gold and check that it hasn't been stolen.

Exit the GUARDIAN SPIRIT into the house.

ACT ONE

EUCLIO is shouting in his house.

EUC   Get out, I say! Go on, get out! You really must get out of 40
here, you spy with eyes sent on a mission.

Enter STAPHYLA from Euclio's house, followed by EUCLIO himself, who is pushing and beating her.

STA   Why on earth are you hitting me, miserable thing that
I am?
EUC   So that you're miserable and lead the wretched life you
deserve, you wretch.
STA   Why on earth have you forced me out of the house now?

263

45 EVC   tibi ego rationem reddam, stimulorum seges?
        illuc regredere ab ostio. illuc sis uide,
        ut incedit. at scin quo modo tibi res se habet?
        si hercle hodie fustem cepero aut stimulum in manum,
        testudineum istum tibi ego grandibo gradum.
50 STA   utinam me diui adaxint ad suspendium
        potius quidem quam hoc pacto apud te seruiam.
  EVC   at ut scelesta sola secum murmurat!
        oculos hercle ego istos, improba, effodiam tibi,
        ne me opseruare possis quid rerum geram.
55   apscede etiam nunc . . . etiam nunc . . . etiam . . . ohe,
        istic astato. si hercle tu ex istoc loco
        digitum transuorsum aut unguem latum excesseris
        aut si respexis, donicum ego te iussero,
        continuo hercle ego te dedam discipulam cruci.
60   scelestiorem me hac anu certo scio
        uidisse numquam, nimisque ego hanc metuo male
        ne mi ex insidiis uerba imprudenti duit
        neu persentiscat aurum ubi est apsconditum,
        quae in occipitio quoque habet oculos pessuma.
65   nunc ibo ut uisam, estne ita aurum ut condidi,
        quod me sollicitat plurumis miserum modis.
  STA   noenum mecastor quid ego ero dicam meo
        malae rei euenisse quamue insaniam
        queo comminisci; ita me miseram ad hunc modum
70   deciens die uno saepe extrudit aedibus.
        nescio pol quae illunc hominem intemperiae tenent:
        peruigilat noctes totas, tum autem interdius
        quasi claudus sutor domi sedet totos dies.
        nec iam quo pacto celem erilis filiae

---

[3] Cobblers are "lame" because they sit all day.

EUC   I should be accountable to *you*, you crop of cattle-prods? 45
Go over there, away from the door! (*she obeys*) Look at
that, how she proceeds! But have you any idea what your
situation is? If I lay my hand on a club or a cattle-prod, I'll
accelerate that tortoise pace of yours!

STA   (*aside*) If only the gods would drive me to hang myself in- 50
stead of being your servant in this way.

EUC   (*aside*) How this crook keeps muttering to herself,
though! (*aloud*) I'll tear out those eyes of yours, you crim-
inal, so that you can't observe what I'm doing. Get back 55
still further (*she begins to move away*) . . . still further . . .
still . . . all right! Stand there! Well, if you leave your place
by just a finger's or a nail's breadth or if you look back be-
fore I've told you, I'll immediately put you on the cross,
and that'll teach you your lesson. (*aside*) I know for sure 60
that I've never seen a more wicked person than this old
hag and I'm terribly afraid that she might lie in wait and
play a trick on me when I'm not suspecting it, or that she
might get wind of where the gold is hidden; this woman
has eyes even in the back of her head, she's so evil! Now 65
I'll go and see if the gold is still as I buried it. Poor me!
This worries me dreadfully.

Exit EUCLIO into his house.

STA   I simply cannot imagine what misfortune or what mad-
ness I should say has come over my master: he drives a
poor woman like myself out of the house like this, and of-
ten ten times in a single day. I just don't know what sort of 71
delusions hold that man in their grip. He stays up entire
nights and then, in daytime, he sits at home like some
lame cobbler[3] for entire days. And I have no idea how I 74

265

75   probrum, propinqua partitudo quoi appetit,
    queo comminisci; nec quicquam meliust mihi,
    ut opinor, quam ex me ut unam faciam litteram
    longam ‹meum› laqueo collum quando opstrinxero.

I. ii: EVCLIO. STAPHYLA

EVC   nunc defaecato demum animo egredior domo,
80   postquam perspexi salua esse intus omnia.
    redi nunciam intro atque intus serua.

STA   quippini?
    ego intus seruem? an ne quis aedis auferat?
    nam hic apud nos nihil est aliud quaesti furibus,
    ita inaniis sunt oppletae atque araneis.
85 EVC mirum quin tua me causa faciat Iuppiter
    Philippum regem aut Dareum, triuenefica.
    araneas mi ego illas seruari uolo.
    pauper sum; fateor, patior; quod di dant fero.
    abi intro, occlude ianuam. iam ego hic ero.
90   caue quemquam alienum in aedis intro miseris.
    quod quispiam ignem quaerat, exstingui uolo,
    ne causae quid sit quod te quisquam quaeritet.
    nam si ignis uiuet, tu exstinguere extempulo.
    tum aquam aufugisse dicito, si quis petet.
95   cultrum, securim, pistillum, mortarium,
    quae utenda uasa semper uicini rogant,
    fures uenisse atque apstulisse dicito.
    profecto in aedis meas me apsente neminem

---

78 longum *P*, longam *Scutarius*   meum *add. Camerarius*, mihi *add.*
Lambinus

---

[4] What is known as *I longum* nowadays, a longer shape of the letter
used to indicate vowel length, first appeared around 100 BC. Long let-

can conceal the disgrace of master's daughter any longer, now that her time's coming close. The best thing for me, I suppose, is to tie a good tight noose around my neck and to stretch myself into one long letter.[4]

Enter EUCLIO from his house.

EUC   (*to the audience*) Now that I've regained a clear mind at last I'm leaving the house, after seeing that everything's   80 safe and sound inside. (*to Staphyla*) Go back in now and keep watch inside.

STA   Of course! I am to keep watch inside, am I? Presumably so that nobody takes away the house? Because here at our place there's nothing else to be gained for thieves; it's completely full of emptiness and cobwebs.

EUC   It's quite extraordinary that Jupiter doesn't turn me into   85 King Philip or Darius[5] for your sake, you evil witch. I want those cobwebs watched over for me. I'm poor. I admit it; I bear it; I put up with what the gods give me. Go in and lock the door. I'll be back here in a moment. Mind   90 you don't let any stranger into the house. In case anyone should request fire, I want it to be extinguished so that there's no reason why anyone should ask you: if the *fire* continues to burn, *you* will be extinguished immediately. Next point: say the water's run away if anyone wants some. As for knife, axe, pestle, mortar, the utensils neigh-   95 bors always want to borrow, say thieves have come and taken them away. In short, I don't want anybody to be let

ters refer to wall inscriptions; Staphyla is making an open display of her suffering.

   5 Philip II of Macedon (382–336) and Darius I of Persia (died in 486) were famous for their wealth.

		uolo intro mitti. atque etiam hoc praedico tibi:
100		si Bona Fortuna ueniat, ne intro miseris.
	STA	pol ea ipsa credo ne intro mittatur cauet,
		nam ad aedis nostras nusquam adit quaquam prope.
	EVC	tace atque abi intro.
	STA	taceo atque abeo.
	EVC	occlude sis

fores ambobus pessulis. iam ego hic ero.
105 discrucior animi, quia ab domo abeundum est mihi.
nimis hercle inuitus abeo. sed quid agam scio.
nam noster nostrae qui est magister curiae
diuidere argenti dixit nummos in uiros;
id si relinquo ac non peto, omnes ilico
110 me suspicentur, credo, habere aurum domi.
nam non est ueri simile hominem pauperem
pauxillum parui facere quin nummum petat.
nam nunc quom celo sedulo omnis ne sciant,
omnes uidentur scire et me benignius
115 omnes salutant quam salutabant prius;
adeunt, consistunt, copulantur dexteras,
rogitant me ut ualeam, quid agam, quid rerum geram.
nunc quo profectus sum ibo; postidea domum
me rursum quantum potero tantum recipiam.

102 adit (*praesens aut perfectum contractum*) B¹, adiit B² *et cett.*
111 non est ueri simile P, u. s. n. e. *Pylades*

into my house in my absence. There's another point I
want to make: if Good Fortune herself comes, don't let   100
her in.

STA I think she herself avoids being let in, because she's never
come anywhere near our house.

EUC Be quiet and go inside.

STA Yes, I *am* quiet and I *am* going.

Exit STAPHYLA into Euclio's house.

EUC (*shouting after her*) Mind you lock the door with both
bolts. I'll be here in a moment. (*to himself*) It's mental   105
torture having to go away from my house. I don't want to
go out at all. But I know what I'm doing: the chairman of
our ward said he was distributing silver coins among the
men.[6] If I let this pass and don't demand my share, I think   109
everybody would immediately suspect that I have gold at
home: it doesn't look natural if a poor man cares little
about money, be it ever so tiny a sum, and doesn't ask for
it; now that I'm concealing it painstakingly from all and
sundry so that they don't know, all and sundry do seem to
know and all and sundry greet me more warmly than they
used to. They come up to me, they stop, they shake   116
hands; they ask me how I'm feeling, how I'm doing, what
I'm up to. Now I'll go where I meant to. Afterwards I'll
return home again as quickly as I possibly can.

Exit EUCLIO to the right.

[6] In Athens public profits were regularly distributed among the citizens. However, *argenti nummi* probably refers to Roman sesterces.

ACTVS II

II. i: EVNOMIA. MEGADORVS

120 EVN   uelim te arbitrari med haec uerba, frater,
       meai fidei tuaique rei
       causa facere, ut aequom est germanam sororem.
       quamquam hau falsa sum nos odiosas haberi;
       nam multum loquaces merito omnes habemur,
125   nec mutam profecto repertam nullam esse
       ⟨aut⟩ hodie dicunt mulierem ⟨aut⟩ ullo in saeclo.
       uerum hoc, frater, unum tamen cogitato,
       tibi proxumam me mihique esse item te;
       ita aequom est quod in rem esse utrique arbitremur
130   et mi te et tibi me consulere et monere;
       neque occultum id haberi nec per metum mussari
       quin participem pariter ego te et tu me [ut] facias.
       eo nunc ego secreto ted huc foras seduxi,
       ut tuam rem ego tecum hic loquerer familiarem.
135 MEG   da mi, optuma femina, manum.
    EVN   ubi ea est? quis ea est nam optuma?
    MEG   tu.
    EVN   tune ais?
    MEG   si negas, nego.
    EVN   decet tequidem uera proloqui;
       nam optuma nulla potest eligi:
140   alia alia peior, frater, est.
    MEG   idem ego arbitror,
       nec tibi aduorsari certum est de istac re umquam, soror.

    120 me *P*, med *Guyet ut sit integer tetrameter*
    125 ⟨n⟩ullam *Lindsay*   126 aut . . . aut *add. Leo*
    132 ut *del. Lambinus*   141 re *P*, red *Ritschl*

ACT TWO

Enter EUNOMIA and MEGADORUS from his house.

EUN   Dear brother, I'd like you to understand that I'm saying   120
this out of my loyalty and for your benefit, as is appropri-
ate for a true sister. Still, I'm well aware that we women
are considered a pain in the neck. Yes, we're all consid-
ered very gossipy, and deservedly so. In fact, people say a   125
silent woman has never been found now or in any genera-
tion. However, my brother, keep this one thing in mind: I
am your closest relative, and you are mine. So it's only
fair that you should advise and counsel me—and that I
should do the same for you—as to what we think benefits
each of us; this shouldn't be kept secret or quiet out of   131
fear, but rather I should share it with you and you should
equally share it with me. That's why I've taken you out
here alone now, so I can talk with you here about a pri-
vate matter concerning you.

MEG   Give me your hand, best of women.   135

EUN   (*looking around*) Where is she? Who on earth is she, this
best one?

MEG   It's you.

EUN   Do you say so?

MEG   Well, if you deny it, I also deny it.

EUN   At least *you* ought to speak the truth: there is no best one
to be chosen. One is worse than the other, dear brother.   140

MEG   I think so too, and I'll definitely never contradict you on
this issue, dear sister.

142 –2ᵃ	EVN MEG	da mihi operam amabo. tua est, utere at-

EVN   da mihi operam amabo.

MEG   tua est, utere at-
que impera, si quid uis.

EVN   id quod in rem tuam optumum esse arbitror,

145   ted id monitum aduento.

MEG   soror, more tuo facis.

EVN   facta uolo.

MEG   quid est id, soror?

EVN   quod tibi sempiternum
salutare sit: liberis procreandis—

MEG   ita di faxint!

EVN   uolo te uxorem

150   domum ducere.

MEG   ei occidi!

EVN   quid ita?

MEG   quia mi misero cerebrum excutiunt
tua dicta, soror: lapides loqueris.

EVN   heia, hoc face quod te iubet soror.

MEG   si lubeat, faciam.

EVN   in rem hoc tuam est.

MEG   ut quidem emoriar prius quam ducam.

155   sed his legibus si quam dare uis, ducam:
quae cras ueniat, perendie, soror, foras feratur;
his legibus quam dare uis? cedo: nuptias adorna.

EVN   cum maxuma possum tibi, frater, dare dote;
sed est grandior natu: media est mulieris aetas.

160   eam si iubes, frater, tibi me poscere, poscam.

MEG   num non uis me interrogare te?

EVN   immo, si quid uis, roga.

---

150 occidi *P*, occidis *Weise*
159 sed . . . natu *attribuit Euclioni sororem interroganti Stockert*

EUN Give me your attention please.

MEG It's yours, use it and command me if there's anything you wish.

EUN I've come to recommend to you what I consider to be in 144
your best interest.

MEG Dear sister, you are following your custom.

EUN I want it done.

MEG What's this, dear sister?

EUN Something that should be for your everlasting well-being. In order to beget children—

MEG (*interrupting*) May the gods grant it! 149

EUN —I want you to take home a wife.

MEG Oh no! This is the end of me!

EUN How so?

MEG Because, dear sister, your words are knocking out my brains, poor chap that I am. Your words are stones.

EUN Now now, do what your sister tells you.

MEG If it appealed to me I'd do it.

EUN It's for your own good.

MEG Certainly, that I die before I marry. (*pauses*) But if you'll 155
get me a woman on the following terms, I'll marry her: one who comes tomorrow, dear sister, and is buried the day after. Will you get me one on these terms? Get her here, prepare the wedding.

EUN I can get you one with an enormous dowry, my brother. But she's a bit on the old side. Actually, she is middle-aged. If you want me to ask for her hand for you, dear 160
brother, I'll do so.

MEG You don't mind if I ask you something, do you?

EUN Of course not. Ask whatever you like.

	MEG	post mediam aetatem qui media ducit uxorem domum,
		si eam senex anum praegnatem fortuito fecerit,
		quid dubitas quin sit paratum nomen puero Postumus?
165		nunc ego istum, soror, laborem degam et deminuam tibi.
		ego uirtute deum et maiorum nostrum diues sum satis.
		istas magnas factiones, animos, dotes dapsilis,
		clamores, imperia, eburata uehicla, pallas, purpuram
		nil moror, quae in seruitutem sumptibus redigunt uiros.
170	EVN	dic mihi, si audes, quis ea est quam uis ducere uxorem?
	MEG	eloquar.
		nostin hunc senem Euclionem ex proxumo paupercu-
		lum?
	EVN	noui, hominem hau malum mecastor.
	MEG	eius cupio filiam
		uirginem mi desponderi. uerba ne facias, soror.
		scio quid dictura es: hanc esse pauperem. haec pauper
		placet.
175	EVN	di bene uortant.
	MEG	idem ego spero.
	EVN	quid me? num quid uis?
	MEG	uale.
	EVN	et tu, frater.
	MEG	ego conueniam Euclionem, si domi est.
		sed eccum ⟨uideo⟩. nescio unde sese homo recipit
		domum.

170 dic . . . uxorem *attribuit Eunomiae Pius*   si audes *Priscianus et scholia in Persium*, quaeso *P*   175 quid me nunc quid uis *P*, quid me? num quid uis? *Leo*, num quid me, me nunc uis? *O. Skutsch*   177 uideo *add. Klett*

---

[7] Caesellius (see Gell. 2. 16. 5) says that this is the name for the last child that is born. The meaning "child born after the father's death"

MEG   Suppose a man has passed middle age and marries a woman in her middle age; if such an old fellow gets his old lady pregnant by chance, do you have any doubt that the name in store for the boy is Postumus?[7] Now I'll save   165 and spare you that trouble, dear sister. Thanks to the gods and our ancestors I'm rich enough. I don't care about those great social connections, their pride, their sumptuous dowries, their shouting, their commands, their carriages decked with ivory, their mantles, and their purple clothing; such women drive their husbands into slavery with their expenses.

EUN   Tell me, please, who is this woman you want to marry?   170

MEG   I'm going to tell you. Do you know this old neighbor of ours, a somewhat poor chap, Euclio?

EUN   I do; not a bad person at all.

MEG   I want his daughter, a virgin, to be betrothed to me. Don't give me a lecture, dear sister. I know what you're going to say: that she's poor. But I like this poor one.

EUN   May the gods bless your plan.   175

MEG   I hope so too.

EUN   What about me? Is there anything else I can do for you?

MEG   Be well.

EUN   You too, dear brother.

Exit EUNOMIA to the right.

MEG   I'm going to meet Euclio, if he's at home. (*looks down the street*) Oh look! I can see him. He's just coming back home from somewhere or other.

arose later, because one can only be certain that a child will be the last if a parent dies and because of a popular etymology involving *humus* (earth) (cf. English "posthumous").

II. ii: EVCLIO. MEGADORVS

EVC praesagibat mi animus frustra me ire, quom exibam
domo;

itaque abibam inuitus; nam nec quisquam curialium
180 uenit nec magister quem diuidere argentum oportuit.

nunc domum properare propero, nam egomet sum hic,
animus domi est.

MEG saluos atque fortunatus, Euclio, semper sies.

EVC di te ament, Megadore.

MEG   quid tu? recten atque ut uis uales?

EVC non temerarium est ubi diues blande appellat pauperem.
185 iam illic homo aurum scit me habere, eo me salutat blan-
dius.

MEG ain tu te ualere?

EVC   pol ego hau perbene . . . a pecunia.

MEG pol si est animus aequos tibi, sat habes qui bene uitam co-
las.

EVC anus hercle huic indicium fecit de auro, perspicue palam
est,

quoi ego iam linguam praecidam atque oculos effodiam
domi.

190 MEG quid tu solus tecum loquere?

EVC   meam pauperiem conqueror.

uirginem habeo grandem, dote cassam atque illocabi-
lem,

neque eam queo locare quoiquam.

MEG   tace, bonum habe animum, Euclio.

dabitur, adiuuabere a me. dic, si quid opust, impera.

EVC nunc petit, quom pollicetur; inhiat aurum ut deuoret.

Enter EUCLIO from the right, speaking to himself.

EUC   I had a feeling I was going in vain when I left the house. That's why I went unwillingly. And indeed, none of the ward members came along, nor did the chairman, who ought to have distributed the money. Now I'm in a hurry 181 to hurry home, because I myself am here, but my mind is at home.

MEG   *(loudly)* May you always be well and blessed, Euclio.

EUC   May the gods love you, Megadorus.

MEG   Well then? Are you in good health, just as you wish?

EUC   *(aside)* It's not by chance when a rich man addresses a poor one in such an ingratiating way. Now he knows I 185 have the gold, that's why he's greeting me more politely.

MEG   You say you're well?

EUC   Not terribly well . . . financially speaking.

MEG   If you have peace of mind, what you have is enough to live on.

EUC   *(aside)* The old woman has denounced me as having gold, it's completely out in the open! But I'll cut off her tongue and tear out her eyes immediately when I'm home.

MEG   Why are you talking to yourself? 190

EUC   I'm moaning about my poverty. I have a grown-up virgin daughter, without dowry and without prospects, and I can't give her in marriage to anyone.

MEG   Calm down and cheer up, Euclio. You'll receive money, you'll be helped by me. Tell me if you need anything, command me.

EUC   *(aside)* Now he's trying to get something by making promises. He's gaping after the money in order to swal-

195   altera manu fert lapidem, panem ostentat altera.
        nemini credo qui large blandust diues pauperi:
        ubi manum inicit benigne, ibi onerat aliquam zamiam.
        ego istos noui polypos qui ubi quicquid tetigerunt tenent.

MEG   da mi operam parumper; paucis, Euclio, est quod te uolo
200   de communi re appellare mea et tua.

EVC   ei misero mihi,
        aurum mi intus harpagatum est. nunc hic eam rem uolt,
          scio,
        mecum adire ad pactionem. uerum interuisam domum.

MEG   quo abis?

EVC   iam reuortar ad te: nam est quod inuisam domum.

MEG   credo edepol, ubi mentionem ego fecero de filia,
205   mi ut despondeat, sese a me derideri rebitur;
        neque illo quisquam est alter hodie ex paupertate par-
          cior.

EVC   di me seruant, salua res est. saluom est si quid non perit.
        nimis male timui. prius quam intro redii, exanimatus fui.
        redeo ad te, Megadore, si quid me uis.

199 paucis euclio est quod te uolo *P*, si opera est euclio id quod te uolo *Nonius*

low it. In one hand he's carrying a stone, with the other 195
he's holding out bread. I don't trust any rich man who is
over-polite to a poor one. When he puts his hand on you
in a kind way, he burdens you with some loss. I know
those octopuses: as soon as they've touched something,
they hold on to it.

MEG Give me your attention for a moment; there's something
I want to talk to you about briefly, concerning our com-
mon good, mine and yours, Euclio.

EUC (*aside*) Oh dear me, my gold inside has been stolen. Now 201
he wants to make a deal about it with me, I know. But I'll
go and have a look at home.

EUCLIO moves toward his house.

MEG Where are you going?
EUC I'll come back to you in a moment; there's something I
want to check at home.

Exit EUCLIO into his house.

MEG I do believe that as soon as I mention his daughter and 205
ask him to betroth her to me, he'll think I'm pulling his
leg. No one's more tight-fisted than him today because of
poverty.

Re-enter EUCLIO.

EUC (*aside*) The gods protect me, my possessions are safe. A
thing is safe if it doesn't disappear. I was terribly scared.
Before I returned inside, I was practically dead. (*loudly*)
I'm coming back to you, Megadorus, if there's anything
you want of me.

	MEG	habeo gratiam.
210		quaeso, quod te percontabor, ne id te pigeat proloqui.
	EVC	dum quidem ne quid perconteris quod non lubeat prolo-
		qui.
	MEG	dic mihi, quali me arbitrare genere prognatum?
	EVC	bono.
	MEG	quid fide?
	EVC	bona.
	MEG	quid factis?
	EVC	nec malis neque improbis.
	MEG	aetatem meam scis?
	EVC	scio esse grandem, item ut pecuniam.
215	MEG	certe edepol equidem te ciuem sine mala omni malitia
		semper sum arbitratus et nunc arbitror.
	EVC	aurum huic olet.
		quid nunc me uis?
	MEG	quoniam tu me et ego te qualis sis scio—
		quae res recte uortat mihique tibique tuaeque filiae—
		filiam tuam mi uxorem posco. promitte hoc fore.
220	EVC	heia, Megadore, hau decorum facinus tuis factis facis,
		ut inopem atque innoxium aps te atque aps tuis me irri-
		deas.
		nam de te nec re nec uerbis merui ut faceres quod facis.
	MEG	neque edepol ego te derisum uenio nec derideo,
		nec dignum arbitror.
	EVC	quor igitur poscis meam gnatam tibi?
225	MEG	ut propter me tibi sit melius mihique propter te et tuos.
	EVC	uenit hoc mi, Megadore, in mentem, ted esse hominem
		diuitem,

MEG Thank you. Please don't grudge giving me answers to my 210
      questions.

EUC (*suspiciously*) So long as you don't ask any question I
      don't want to answer.

MEG Tell me, what kind of family do you think I come from?

EUC A good one.

MEG What about my reputation?

EUC It's good.

MEG What about my behavior?

EUC Neither bad nor disreputable.

MEG Do you know my age?

EUC I know it's high, just like your assets.

MEG I've certainly always considered you a citizen without any 215
      bad side, and I do so now.

EUC (*aside*) He can smell the gold. (*loudly*) What do you want
      from me now?

MEG Since you know what I am like and I know what you are
      like—may this turn out well for me, you, and your daugh-
      ter—I'm asking for your daughter's hand. Promise me
      that it'll happen.

EUC Really now, Megadorus, you aren't doing the decent 220
      thing by behaving like this, laughing at me, a poor man
      who's never done anything wrong to you and your family:
      I haven't said or done anything to deserve that you should
      do to me what you're doing now.

MEG I haven't come to laugh at you, and I'm not laughing at
      you, and I don't think you'd deserve it.

EUC Then why are you asking for my daughter's hand?

MEG So you can benefit from me and I can benefit from you 225
      and your family members.

EUC This is what comes to my mind, Megadorus: *you* are a
      rich man with a great following, but *I* am the poorest man

factiosum, me autem esse hominem pauperum pauper-
    rumum;
nunc si filiam locassim meam tibi, in mentem uenit
te bouem esse et me esse asellum: ubi tecum coniunctus
    siem,
230   ubi onus nequeam ferre pariter, iaceam ego asinus in
    luto,
tu me bos magis hau respicias gnatus quasi numquam
    siem.
et te utar iniquiore et meus me ordo irrideat,
neutrubi habeam stabile stabulum, si quid diuorti fuat:
asini me mordicibus scindant, boues incursent cornibus.
235   hoc magnum est periclum, ab asinis ad boues transcen-
    dere.

MEG quam ad probos propinquitate proxume te adiunxeris,
tam optumum est. tu condicionem hanc accipe, ausculta
    mihi,
atque eam desponde mi.

EVC   at nihil est dotis quod dem.

MEG   ne duas.
dum modo morata recte ueniat, dotata est satis.

240 EVC eo dico, ne me thesauros repperisse censeas.

MEG noui, ne doceas. desponde.

EVC   fiat. sed pro Iuppiter,
num ego disperii?

MEG   quid tibi est?

EVC   quid crepuit quasi ferrum modo?

MEG hic apud me hortum confodere iussi. sed ubi hic est
    homo?

244
–5   abiit nec me certiorem fecit. fastidit mei,

227 me item *P*, me autem *Brix*

of the poor. Now if I were to give my daughter in marriage to you, it springs to mind that *you* are an ox and *I* am just a donkey. When I'm hitched up with you and can't 230 carry my burden the same way, I, the donkey, would lie in the mud; you, the ox, would take no more notice of me than if I'd never been born. I wouldn't have you as my equal and the people of my class would laugh at me. On neither side would I have a stable stable if there should be a divorce: the donkeys would tear me up with their teeth, the oxen would run into me with their horns. There's a great danger in crossing over from the donkeys 235 to the oxen.

MEG   The more closely you connect yourself with honorable men through family ties, the better it is. Accept this match of mine, listen to me, and betroth her to me.

EUC   But there's no dowry I could give you.

MEG   No need to give anything. As long as she comes with the right sort of character, she has dowry enough.

EUC   I'm telling you so you don't think I've found any trea- 240 sures.

MEG   I know, no need to lecture me. Betroth her.

EUC   So be it. (*there is a noise*) But good heavens, am I ruined?

MEG   What's wrong with you?

EUC   What made a clink like iron just now?

Exit EUCLIO into his house.

MEG   I had people dig up the garden here at my place. (*realizes that Euclio is gone*) But where is he? He went away and 245

quia uidet me suam amicitiam uelle: more hominum fa-
    cit;
nam si opulentus it petitum pauperioris gratiam,
pauper metuit congrediri, per metum male rem gerit.
idem, quando occasio illaec periit, post sero cupit.

250 EVC si hercle ego te non elinguandam dedero usque ab radi-
    cibus,
impero auctorque ⟨ego⟩ sum ut tu me quoiuis castran-
    dum loces.

MEG uideo hercle ego te me arbitrari, Euclio, hominem ido-
    neum,
quem senecta aetate ludos facias, hau merito meo.

EVC neque edepol, Megadore, facio, nec, si cupiam, copia est.

255 MEG quid nunc? etiam mihi despondes filiam?

EVC   illis legibus,
cum illa dote quam tibi dixi.

MEG   sponden ergo?

EVC   spondeo.

MEG istuc di bene [uortant]—

EVC   ita di faxint. illud facito ut memineris,
conuenisse ut ne quid dotis mea ad te afferret filia.

MEG memini.

EVC   at scio quo uos soleatis pacto perplexarier:

260 pactum non pactum est, non pactum pactum est, quod
    uobis lubet.

251 ego *add. Guyet*
257 uortant *del. Lindsay*, istuc *del. Pylades*

284

didn't tell me his decision. He scorns me because he can see I want his friendship. He is acting as human beings usually do: if a wealthy man goes out of his way to get a poorer one's regard, the poor one is afraid to approach him and harms his own interests out of fear. After that opportunity is gone, that same man wishes for it, but too late.

Re-enter EUCLIO, shouting in the direction of his house.

EUC If I don't have your tongue torn out by the very roots, I 250
order and command you to hand me over to anyone you like for castration.

MEG I can see that you consider me a suitable person to make fun of in my old age, Euclio, even though I don't deserve it.

EUC Megadorus, I'm not making fun of you and even if I wanted to, I wouldn't have the means.

MEG Well then? I ask again: are you betrothing your daughter 255
to me?

EUC Under those conditions and with that dowry I told you about.

MEG Are you betrothing her then?

EUC I am.

MEG May the gods—

EUC (*interrupting*) May the gods do so. Make sure you remember that we agreed that my daughter wouldn't bring you any dowry.

MEG I do remember it.

EUC But I know how you people always twist the facts: what 260
has been agreed is no longer agreed, what hasn't been agreed is now agreed, as you fancy.

MEG   nulla controuorsia mihi tecum erit. sed nuptias
       num quae causa est quin faciamus hodie?
EVC   immo edepol optuma.
MEG   ibo igitur, parabo. num quid me uis?
EVC   istuc. i [et] uale.
MEG   heus, Strobile, sequere propere me ad macellum
       strenue.
265 EVC   illic hinc abiit. di immortales, opsecro, aurum quid ualet!
       credo ego illum iam indaudisse mi esse thesaurum domi.
       id inhiat, ea affinitatem hanc opstinauit gratia.

II. iii: EVCLIO. STAPHYLA

EVC   ubi tu es quae deblaterauisti iam uicinis omnibus
       meae me filiae daturum dotem? heus, Staphyla, te uoco.
270   ecquid audis? uascula intus pure propera atque elue:
       filiam despondi ego: hodie huic nuptum Megadoro dabo.
STA   di bene uortant. uerum ecastor non potest, subitum est
       nimis.
EVC   tace atque abi. curata fac sint quom a foro redeam
       domum;
       atque aedis occlude; iam ego hic adero.

   262 hodie quin faciamus num quae causa est *P*, num quae cau. quin
fac. hod. *Brix*, num quae cau. est hod. quin fac. *Lindsay*
   263 fiet *P*, ei et *Mueller*, et del. *Lebreton*
   266 inaudisse *P*, inaudiuisse *Nonius*, indaudisse *Goeller*

MEG I won't have any argument with you. But is there any reason why we shouldn't have the wedding today?

EUC No, that's perfect.

MEG All right then, I'll go and prepare. Anything else?

EUC No, only this. Go and be well.

MEG (*calling for his servant*) Hello, Strobilus, follow me quickly and speedily to the market.

Strobilus appears from Megadorus' house. Exeunt both to the right.

EUC He's gone. Immortal gods, I beseech you! What power 265 money has! I believe he's already heard that I have a treasure at home. That's what he's gaping after, that's why he's set his mind on this marriage.

EUCLIO goes to the door of his house and calls.

EUC Where are you, you who have already babbled out to all the neighbors that I'm going to give my daughter a dowry? Hey! Staphyla! It's you I'm calling! Are you 270 listening at all?

Enter STAPHYLA from Euclio's house.

EUC Hurry up and wash the dishes inside properly. I've betrothed my daughter. I'll give her in marriage to Megadorus here today.

STA Good luck to them! But good heavens, it's impossible, it's too sudden.

EUC Be quiet and go off. Make sure things are ready when I return home from the market. And lock up the house. I'll be here soon.

Exit EUCLIO to the right.

STA   quid ego nunc agam?
275   nunc nobis prope adest exitium, mi atque erili filiae,
          nunc probrum atque partitudo prope adest ut fiat palam;
          quod celatum atque occultatum est usque adhuc, nunc
              non potest.
          ibo intro, ut erus quae imperauit facta, quom ueniat,
              sient.
          nam ecastor malum maerore metuo ne mixtum bibam.

II. iv: STROBILVS. ANTHRAX. CONGRIO

280 STRO postquam opsonauit erus et conduxit coquos
           tibicinasque hasce apud forum, edixit mihi
           ut dispertirem opsonium hic bifariam.
     ANTH mequidem hercle, dicam ‹tibi› palam, non diuides;
           si quo tu totum me ire uis, operam dabo.
285 CON   bellum et pudicum uero prostibulum popli.
           post si quis uellet, te hau non uelles diuidi.
     STRO atque ego istuc, Anthrax, aliouorsum dixeram,
           non istuc quod tu insimulas. sed erus nuptias
           meus hodie faciet.
     ANTH   quoius ducit filiam?
290 STRO uicini huius Euclionis ‹hinc› e proxumo.
           ei adeo opsoni hinc iussit dimidium dari,
           coquom alterum itidemque alteram tibicinam.
     ANTH nempe huc dimidium dicis, dimidium domum?

283 ‹tibi› palam *Ussing*, ‹pro›palam *Bothe*
290 hinc *add. Pylades*, senis *add. Camerarius*

---

8 A comical name for a cook: Anthrax means "charcoal."
9 *Edixit* parodies official language.   10 Congrio deliberately
misunderstands Anthrax. He takes "split" as a euphemism for anal in-
tercourse; Anthrax's "I'll oblige" thus gets a different meaning as well.

STA   What am I to do now? Now our end is near, the end of   275
myself and master's daughter. Now the time is drawing
near when her disgrace and her giving birth must be re-
vealed. What's been concealed and kept secret up until
now can't be kept quiet any longer. I'll go inside so that
what master ordered will be ready when he comes. Dear
me! I'm afraid I'll have a drink of trials mixed with tribu-
lations.

Exit STAPHYLA into Euclio's house.
Enter STROBILUS from the right, bringing with him the cooks
ANTHRAX[8] *and CONGRIO, two flute-girls, a few attendants*
carrying the shopping, and two sheep.

STRO   After master did the shopping and hired cooks and these   280
flute-girls in the market, he decreed[9] that I should split
the shopping here in two parts.

ANTH   I'll tell you openly, you won't split me. If you want me to
go somewhere complete, I'll oblige.

CON   (*to Anthrax*) What a charming and chaste common   285
whore indeed! If anyone wanted to do so afterwards, you
wouldn't say no to being split.[10]

STRO   Now now, Anthrax! I said this in a different sense, not the
one you allege. Anyway, my master will get married to-
day.

ANTH   Whose daughter is he marrying?

STRO   Our neighbor Euclio's from next door here. He said half   290
of the provisions from here should be given to him, one
of the two cooks, and also one of the two flute-girls.

ANTH   Well then, you're saying half goes here and half goes
home?

289

STRO nemp' sicut dicis.

ANTH   quid? hic non poterat de suo

295   senex opsonari filiai nuptiis?

STRO uah!

ANTH   quid negoti est?

STRO   quid negoti sit rogas?

        pumex non aeque est ardus atque hic est senex.

ANTH ain tandem?

CON   ita esse ut dicis!

STRO   tute existuma:

298ᵃ   *** ⟨existumat⟩

        suam rem periisse seque eradicarier.

300   quin diuom atque hominum clamat continuo fidem,

        de suo tigillo fumus si qua exit foras.

        quin, quom it dormitum, follem opstringit ob gulam.

ANTH quor?

STRO   ne quid animae forte amittat dormiens.

ANTH etiamne opturat inferiorem gutturem,

305   ne quid animai forte amittat dormiens?

STRO haec mihi te ut tibi med aequom est, credo, credere.

ANTH immo equidem credo.

STRO   at scin etiam quo modo?

        aquam hercle plorat, quom lauat, profundere.

---

298 ANTH ain tandem STRO ita . . . dicis ANTH tute existuma *BDV*¹
(dicas *D*) *et Wagner cui* dixi *placet*, ANTH ain . . . dicis STRO tute
existuma *V*² *J et Klingner* (*del.* ut) *et Acidalius* (*scribit* est *potius quam*
esse *et indicat interrogationem*), ANTH ain tandem CON ita . . . dicis
STRO tute existuma *Seyffert*

    298ᵃ *lacunam indicat Havet,* existumat *add. Lindsay*

STRO Well then, just as you say.

ANTH What, couldn't that old fellow buy stuff out of his own
pocket for his daughter's wedding?

STRO Bah!   296

ANTH What's the matter?

STRO You're asking what's the matter? A pumice stone is not as
dry as this old fellow.

ANTH Do you really say so?

CON Can it be as you say?

STRO Judge for yourself: *** then he thinks his property is lost
and he's being destroyed completely. What's more, he   300
immediately implores gods and men if smoke somehow
manages to escape from his roof[11] to the outside. And
what's more, when he goes to sleep, he ties a bag over his
windpipe.

ANTH Why?

STRO So he doesn't lose any vital spirit by accident while sleep-
ing.

ANTH Does he also block his lower windpipe so that he doesn't   305
lose any vital spirit by accident while sleeping?

STRO It's only fair, I believe, if you believe me in all this, just as
it's fair if I believe you.

ANTH No worries, I believe you.

STRO But you know what? When he washes, he cries over the
wasted water.

11 *Tigillum* normally means "beam." The Oxford Latin Dictionary
s.v. translates this passage as "beam over the hearth," but without paral-
lels. Nonius (p. 194 Lindsay) describes a *ligellum* (*sic*) as a hut. If we are
dealing with a *pars pro toto*, the word can stand for "roof."

ANTH censen talentum magnum exorari pote[st]
310 ab istoc sene, ut det qui fiamus liberi?
STRO famem hercle utendam si roges, numquam dabit.
 quin ipsi pridem tonsor unguis dempserat:
 collegit, omnia apstulit praesegmina.
ANTH edepol mortalem parce parcum praedicas.
315 STRO censen uero adeo ess' parcum et misere uiuere?
 pulmentum pridem eripuit ei miluos:
 homo ad praetorem deplorabundus uenit;
 infit ibi postulare plorans, eiulans,
 ut sibi liceret miluom uadarier.
320 sescenta sunt quae memorem, si sit otium.
 sed uter uostrorum est celerior? memora mihi.
ANTH ego, ut multo melior.
STRO   coquom ego, non furem rogo.
ANTH coquom ergo dico.
STRO   quid tu ais?
CON   sic sum ut uides.
ANTH coquos ille nundinalest, in nonum diem
325 solet ire coctum.
CON   tun, trium litterarum homo,
 me uituperas? fur.
ANTH   etiam fur, trifurcifer.

  II. v: STROBILVS. ANTHRAX. CONGRIO
STRO tace nunciam tu, atque agnum hinc uter est pinguior
 ⟨cape atque abi intro ad nos.⟩
ANTH   licet.

309 potest *P, corr. Kampmann*   328 *suppl. Leo*

---

[12] I.e., an Attic talent.   [13] This translation reflects the standard interpretation of *in nonum diem*. Congrio's services are asked for

ANTH Do you think this old man could be persuaded to give us
      a great talent[12] so we might become free?

STRO If you asked him to lend you his hunger, he'll never give it   311
      to you. In fact, the barber trimmed his nails not long ago;
      he collected all the clippings and took them away.

ANTH You describe him as a miserly miser.

STRO Would you believe anyone could actually be so thrifty   315
      and live so wretchedly? Once a kite snatched away a
      piece of meat he had. He goes to the magistrate, full of
      tears. There he begins to demand, crying and wailing,
      that he should be allowed to prosecute the kite. There   320
      are hundreds of things I could tell you if I had time on my
      hands. (*to Anthrax*) But which of you is faster? Tell me.

ANTH I am, just as I'm a lot better.

STRO I'm asking for a cook, not a thief.

ANTH Yes, and I mean as a cook.

STRO (*to Congrio*) What do *you* say?

CON I'm just as you see me.

ANTH (*to Strobilus*) That one's a cook for market-days only, he   324
      goes cooking once every eight days.[13]

CON Are you criticizing me, man of five[14] letters? You thief.

ANTH Thief yourself, triple-felon!

STRO (*to Anthrax*) Be quiet now, you, and grab whichever of
      these two lambs is fatter and go inside to us.

ANTH Certainly.

Exit ANTHRAX into Megadorus' house with a lamb.

---

only on market-days when there is the greatest need for cooks. Stockert
(1983: 102) suggests the translation "for the eighth day," which implies
that Congrio needs more than a week to prepare a meal.

  [14] The thief has only three letters in Latin (*fur*).

STRO   tu, Congrio,
        hunc sume atque abi intro illo, et uos illum sequimini.

330   uos ceteri ite huc ad nos.

CON   hercle iniuria
        dispertiuisti: pinguiorem agnum isti habent.

STRO   at nunc tibi dabitur pinguior tibicina.
        i sane cum illo, Phrygia. tu autem, Eleusium,
        huc intro abi ad nos.

CON   o Strobile subdole,

335   hucin detrusti me ad senem parcissumum?
        ubi si quid poscam, usque ad rauim poscam prius
        quam quicquam detur.

STRO   stultu's, et sine gratia est
        ibi recte facere, quando quod facias perit.

CON   qui uero?

STRO   rogitas? iam principio in aedibus

340   turba istic nulla tibi erit: siquid uti uoles,
        domo aps te afferto, ne operam perdas poscere.
        hic autem apud nos magna turba ac familia est,
        supellex, aurum, uestis, uasa argentea:
        ibi si perierit quippiam (quod te scio

345   facile apstinere posse, si nihil obuiam est),
        dicant: "coqui apstulerunt, comprehendite,
        uincite, uerberate, in puteum condite."
        horum tibi istic nihil eueniet (quippe qui
        ubi quid surrupias nihil est). sequere hac me.

CON   sequor.

STRO You, Congrio, take this one and (*pointing to Euclio's house*) go inside to them, and you (*addressing some of the attendants*) follow him. You, the rest, go this way to our place. (*some of the servants go into Megadorus' house*)   330

CON Your distribution is unfair. They have the fatter lamb.

STRO But now you'll be given the fatter flute-girl. (*turning to the girls*) Go with him now, Phrygia. But you, Eleusium, go in here to us. (*they obey*)

CON Strobilus, you sly fellow, you've shoved me off here to the incredibly stingy old man, haven't you? If I were to ask for anything there, I'd ask myself hoarse before anything was given away.   335

STRO You're a fool, and there's no benefit in doing the right thing, because what one does perishes.

CON How so?

STRO You're asking me? Well, for a start you won't have a noisy crowd in the house there. If you want to use anything, just fetch it from home from your place; no need to waste your energy asking. But here at our place there's a great crowd of servants, tableware, gold, clothing, silver vessels; if anything got lost there—and I know you can easily keep away from it, if nothing's within reach—people would say: "the cooks took it away. Get hold of them, bind them, beat them, throw them into the dungeon." None of this will happen to you there, since there's no opportunity for you to steal anything. (*turning to Euclio's house*) Follow me this way.   341   346

CON All right.

II. vi: STROBILVS. STAPHYLA. CONGRIO

350 STRO heus, Staphyla, prodi atque ostium aperi.

STA   qui uocat?

STRO Strobilus.

STA   quid uis?

STRO   hos ut accipias coquos

      tibicinamque opsoniumque in nuptias.

      Megadorus iussit Euclioni haec mittere.

STA Cererin, Strobile, has sunt facturi nuptias?

355 STRO qui?

STA   quia temeti nihil allatum intellego.

STRO at iam afferetur, si a foro ipsus redierit.

STA ligna hic apud nos nulla sunt.

CON   sunt asseres?

STA sunt pol.

CON   sunt igitur ligna, ne quaeras foris.

STA quid, impurate? quamquam Volcano studes,

360   cenaene causa aut tuae mercedis gratia

      nos nostras aedis postulas comburere?

CON hau postulo.

STRO   duc istos intro.

STA   sequimini.

---

[15] The "wedding for Ceres" is the *sacrum anniuersarium Cereris*, mysteries celebrated by women in memory of the wedding of Pluto and Proserpina.

[16] Alcohol was forbidden at these mysteries.

[17] The Latin imitates the language of tragedy. Cooks are "devoted to Vulcan" because they work with fire.

STROBILUS and CONGRIO go to Euclio's door, with Phrygia, some servants, and a lamb.

STRO (*knocking at Euclio's door*) Hey, Staphyla, come and 350
open the door.

STA (*from inside*) Who's calling?

STRO Strobilus.

STA (*opening the door*) What do you want?

STRO That you take these cooks, the flute-girl, and the provisions for the wedding. Megadorus had them sent here to Euclio.

STA Are they going to hold the wedding for Ceres,[15] Strobilus?

STRO How so? 355

STA Because I can't see that any alcohol's been brought along.[16]

STRO But some will be brought in a moment when master himself returns from the market.

STA There's no firewood here at our place.

CON Are there rafters?

STA Yes, of course there are.

CON Then there is firewood, no need to look for it outside.

STA What, you beast? However much you're devoted to Vulcan,[17] do you expect us to burn down our house for the 360
sake of a dinner or your payment?

CON No, I don't.

STRO (*to Staphyla*) Take them in.

STA (*to Congrio, Phrygia, and the attendants*) Follow me.

Exeunt STAPHYLA, CONGRIO, Phrygia, attendants, and the sheep into the house.

PLAUTUS

II. vii: STROBILVS

STRO curate. ego interuisam quid faciant coqui;
   quos pol ut ego hodie seruem cura maxuma est.
365 nisi unum hoc faciam, ut in puteo cenam coquant:
   ind' coctam sursum subducemus corbulis.
   si autem deorsum comedent si quid coxerint,
   superi incenati sunt et cenati inferi.
   sed uerba hic facio, quasi negoti nil siet,
370 rapacidarum ubi tantum sit in aedibus.

II. viii: EVCLIO. CONGRIO

EVC uolui animum tandem confirmare hodie meum,
   ut bene me haberem filiai nuptiis.
   uenio ad macellum, rogito piscis: indicant
   caros; agninam caram, caram bubulam,
375 uitulinam, cetum, porcinam: cara omnia.
   atque eo fuerunt cariora, aes non erat.
   abbito iratus illinc, quom nihil est qui emam.
   ita illis impuris omnibus adii manum.
   deinde egomet mecum cogitare interuias
380 occepi: festo die si quid prodegeris,
   profesto egere liceat, nisi peperceris.
   postquam hanc rationem uentri cordique edidi,
   accessit animus ad meam sententiam,
   quam minimo sumptu filiam ut nuptum darem.

  363–70 fitodicus seruus *BVJ*, Pythodicus *Z, corruptum pro* Strobilus

  372 haberem *B^{ac} DVJ*, haberem me *B^{pc}, transp. Scaliger*

  377 abeo iratus illinc quoniam (qm) *P*, abbito iratus illinc quom *Lindsay in apparatu*

STRO (*as the others are going in*) Take care of it. (*to the audience, while walking toward Megadorus' house*) I'll check what the cooks are doing. It's my greatest worry that I can keep watch over them today. Unless I do this 365 one thing: have them cook dinner in the dungeon. Then, when it's cooked, we'll haul it up from there in baskets. But if they've cooked something and then eat it up down there, the ones in Heaven go without dinner and the ones in the Underworld with.[18] But I'm waffling here as if there weren't any business at hand, with so many pilfer- 370 ers in the house.

Exit STROBILUS into Megadorus' house.
Enter EUCLIO from the right.

EUC I finally wanted to give myself the courage today to have a good time at my daughter's wedding. I went to the market and asked for fish. They told me it's expensive. Lamb: expensive; beef: expensive; veal, tunny, pork: expensive, 375 everything. And they were more expensive for this reason: I didn't have money. I went away from there, angry, since I don't have the money to buy things with. This way I tricked that whole dirty pack. Then I began to think on my way: if you waste something on a feast day, you could well be in need on a workday, unless you economize. After I put this case[19] to my stomach and my heart, 382 my mind seconded my motion to give my daughter in marriage with a minimum of expenses. Now I bought a

---

[18] This is a jocular comparison of those in the house with the Olympian gods, and of the cooks in the dungeon with the gods of the Underworld.

[19] Euclio uses legal terminology common in sessions of the senate.

385   nunc tusculum emi et hasc' coronas floreas:
        haec imponentur in focum nostro Lari,
        ut fortunatas faciat gnatae nuptias.
        sed quid ego apertas aedis nostras conspicor?
        et strepitust intus. numnam ego compilor miser?
390 CON aulam maiorem, si potest, uicinia
        pete: haec est parua, capere non quit.
    EVC   ei mihi,
        perii hercle. aurum rapitur, aula quaeritur.
        nimirum occidor, nisi ego intro huc propere propero cur-
            rere.
        Apollo, quaeso, subueni mi atque adiuua,
395   confige sagittis fures thesaurarios,
        qui in re tali iam subuenisti antidhac.
        sed cesso prius quam prorsus perii currere.

                    II. ix: ANTHRAX
    ANTH Dromo, desquama piscis. tu, Machaerio,
        congrum, murenam exdorsua quantum potest.
400   ego hinc artoptam ex proxumo utendam peto
        a Congrione. tu istum gallum, si sapis,
        glabriorem reddes mihi quam uolsus ludiust.
        sed quid hoc clamoris oritur hinc ex proxumo?
        coqui hercle, credo, faciunt officium suom.
405   fugiam intro, ne quid turbai hic itidem fuat.

        386 foco *P, corr. Havet*
        390 potes *P*, potest *Heckmann*, pote ex *Lambinus*
        393 *uersum secl. Langen, post 242 posuit Ritschl*
        396 cui *P*, qui *Koch*, ⟨si⟩ cui *Ussing*
        405 turbae hic itidem *P, transp. Lindsay*, turbai hic itidem *Stockert*
    in commentario

little incense and these flower garlands. They'll be placed 386
on the hearth for our Guardian Spirit so he may make
my daughter's wedding a happy one. (*pauses and looks
around*) But why can I see our house wide open? And
there's noise inside! Am I being robbed? Poor me!

CON (*from inside*) Ask for a bigger pot from next door, if possi- 390
ble. This one's small and cannot hold anything.

EUC Dear me, I'm done for! My gold's being stolen, a pot's be-
ing looked for. Surely I'm being murdered unless I hast-
ily make haste to run in here. Apollo,[20] I ask you, come to
my assistance and help me, pierce the treasure thieves 395
with your arrows. You've already helped in such a situa-
tion before. But I'm delaying running before I'm done
for completely.

Exit EUCLIO into his house.
Enter ANTHRAX from Megadorus' house.

ANTH (*to those inside*) Dromo, scale the fish. You, Machaerio,
remove the backbone from the conger-eel and the lam-
prey as quickly as possible. I'm asking Congrio to lend me 400
a bread-pan from next door here. You there, you'll pluck
this cock cleaner for me than a depilated dancer, if you
have any sense. (*stops and listens*) But what rumpus be-
gins here next door? I think the cooks are doing their job.
I'll escape inside so there won't be any chaos at our place 405
as well.

Exit ANTHRAX into Megadorus' house.

[20] God of prophecy and song, but also an athletic deity with bow and
arrows.

PLAUTUS

ACTVS III

III. i: CONGRIO

CON attatae! ciues, populares, incolae, accolae, aduenae
omnes,
date uiam qua fugere liceat, facite totae plateae pateant.
neque ego umquam nisi hodie ad Bacchas ueni in bac-
chanal coquinatum,
ita me miserum et meos discipulos fustibus male contu-
derunt.

410   totus doleo atque oppido perii, ita me iste habuit senex
gymnasium;
411   attat, perii hercle ego miser,
411ᵃ   aperit bacchanal, adest,
412   sequitur. scio quam rem geram: hoc
412ᵃ   ipsus magister me docuit.
nec ligna ego usquam gentium praeberi uidi pulchrius,
itaque omnis exegit foras, me atque hos, onustos fus-
tibus.

III. ii: EVCLIO. CONGRIO

415 EVC redi. quo fugis nunc? tene, tene.
CON   quid, stolide, clamas?
EVC quia ad trisuiros iam ego deferam nomen tuom.
CON   quam ob rem?
EVC quia cultrum habes.

417 quid *P*, qui *Ussing*, quia *Bothe*

---

21 Festivals of Bacchus involved heavy drinking and sometimes vio-
lent behavior. The Roman senate suppressed the cult in 186.

302

ACT THREE

Enter CONGRIO and associates from Euclio's house.

CON   Ah! Ah! Ah! Citizens, compatriots, inhabitants, neigh-
bors, immigrants, all of you, make way for me to flee,
clear all the streets! I've never visited Bacchants at a Bac-
chanalian festival[21] to cook, except for today: poor me,
they pounded away at me and my disciples with their
clubs. I'm all in pain and have perished completely, be-   410
cause that old man treated me like a gymnasium. (*spot-
ting Euclio in the door*) Oh no! I'm as good as dead, poor
me! The shrine's opening, here he is, he's following me. I
know what I'll do: my master's taught me this himself.[22]
I've never seen firewood being given out so freely any-
where: he drove us all out, me and them, laden with
clubs.

Enter EUCLIO from his house.

EUC   Come back! Where are you running to now? Stop him,   415
stop him!
CON   What are you shouting for, idiot?
EUC   Because I'll report your name to the Board of Three[23]
now.
CON   Why?
EUC   Because you have a knife.

---

[22] Unclear; perhaps Euclio's behavior has taught Congrio, and he is
taking out his knife to defend himself; or perhaps his teacher had ad-
vised him to flee in such situations.

[23] The *tresuiri capitales*, responsible for administering justice, im-
prisoning suspects, and executing criminals.

CON   coquom decet.

EVC   quid comminatu's
mihi?

CON   istuc male factum arbitror, quia non latus fodi.

EVC   homo nullust te scelestior qui uiuat hodie,

420   nec quoi ego de industria amplius male plus lubens
faxim.

CON   pol etsi taceas, palam id quidem est: res ipsa testest;
ita fustibus sum mollior magis quam ullus cinaedus.
sed quid tibi nos tactio est, mendice homo?

EVC   quae res?
etiam rogitas? an quia minus quam aequom ‹me› erat
feci?

425 CON   sine, at hercle cum magno malo tuo, si hoc caput sentit.

EVC   pol ego hau scio quid post fuat: tuom nunc caput sentit.
sed in aedibus quid tibi meis nam erat negoti
me apsente, nisi ego iusseram? uolo scire.

CON   tace ergo.
quia uenimus coctum ad nuptias.

EVC   quid tu, malum, curas

430   utrum crudum an coctum ego edim, nisi tu mi es tutor?

CON   uolo scire, sinas an non sinas nos coquere hic cenam?

EVC   uolo scire ego item, meae domi mean salua futura?

CON   utinam mea mi modo auferam, quae attuli, salua:
me hau paenitet, tua ne expetam.

EVC   scio, ne doce, noui.

435 CON   quid est qua prohibes nunc gratia nos coquere hic ce-
nam?
quid fecimus, quid diximus tibi secus quam uelles?

---

424 aequom ereat *P*, aequom ‹me› erat *Seyffert*, erat aequom *Reiz*
433 adtuli (at- *VJ*) *P* (*spat. sequ. B*), ad ‹te› tuli *Studemund*,
adtuli‹mus› *Brix*

CON   As a cook should.

EUC   Why did you threaten me?

CON   I think it's a shame I didn't stab you in the side.

EUC   There isn't a greater criminal alive today than you, or   420
      anyone I'd be happier to hurt more with full intention.

CON   Even if you were silent it would be obvious: the facts
      speak for themselves; thanks to your clubs I'm softer than
      any catamite. But why did you touch us, beggar?

EUC   What? You dare ask? Is it because I did less than was fair?

CON   Stop it! You'll get a good thrashing as truly as my head has   425
      any sense.

EUC   I don't know what'll happen later on, but now your head
      must sense something. But what business did you have in
      my house in my absence, if I hadn't ordered you to come?
      I'd like to know.

CON   Be quiet then. Because we came to cook for the wedding.

EUC   Why the hell do you care whether I eat my food raw or   430
      cooked, unless you're my guardian?

CON   I would like to know, are you letting us cook dinner here
      or not?

EUC   And *I* would like to know, will my things be safe in my
      house?

CON   All I hope for is that I can take away unbroken my own
      things which I brought here. Then I'm content, without
      hankering for yours.

EUC   I know, stop lecturing me. I've got your point.

CON   Why is it that you won't allow us to cook dinner here   435
      now? What have we said or done against your wishes?

EVC   etiam rogitas, sceleste homo, qui angulos omnis
          mearum aedium et conclauium mihi peruium facitis?
          ibi ubi tibi erat negotium, ad focum si adesses,
440   non fissile auferres caput: merito id tibi factum est.
          adeo ut tu meam sententiam iam noscere possis:
          si ad ianuam huc accesseris, nisi iussero, propius,
          ego te faciam miserrumus mortalis uti sis.
          scis iam meam sententiam.
CON   quo abis? redi rursum.
445   ita me bene amet Lauerna, te ‹iam› iam, nisi reddi
          mihi uasa iubes, hic pipulo te differam ante aedis.
          quid ego nunc agam? ne ego edepol ueni huc auspicio
             malo.
          nummo sum conductus: plus iam medico mercedest
          opus.

III. iii: EVCLIO. CONGRIO

EVC   hoc quidem hercle, quoquo ibo, mecum erit, mecum
             feram,
450   neque isti id in tantis periclis umquam committam ut
             siet.
          ite sane nunc[iam] intro omnes, et coqui et tibicinae,
          etiam ‹iam› intro duce, si uis, uel gregem uenalium,
          coquite, facite, festinate nunciam quantum lubet.

    445 te iam *P* (*cum Nonio*), te ‹iam› iam *Hare*, uti ‹iam› iam *Goetz*
    446 populo (-os *D*) hic *P*, pipulo te hic *Nonius*, pipulo te *Nonius alibi et Varro*, hic pipulo te *Reiz*
    451 nunciam *P*, nunc *Linge*
    452 iam *add. Sedgwick* (*uide etiam 451*), ‹ite› etiam *Leo* (*dubitanter*)

EUC   You dare ask, you thug? You're turning every nook and cranny of my house and rooms into a thoroughfare. If you'd stayed at the oven, where your business was, you 440 wouldn't have carried away a split head. That serves you right. And just to let you learn my decision now: if you come any closer to this door without my orders, I'll make sure you're the most wretched mortal on earth. Now you know my decision.

Exit EUCLIO into his house.

CON   (*shouting after him*) Where are you going? Come back again! So help me Laverna,[24] if you don't have my vessels 445 brought back to me, I'll tear up your reputation with my shrill voice here and now, right in front of your house.[25] (*Euclio shuts the door*) What should I do now? I've really come here under a bad omen. I was hired for one sesterce, but the doctor is going to need more than that.

Enter EUCLIO from his house, with the pot of gold under his cloak.

EUC   (*aside, pointing to the pot*) Wherever I go, this here will be with me, I'll carry it with me, and I won't ever allow it 450 to be in such great dangers there. (*to Congrio and assistants*) Go inside now, all of you, cooks and flute-girls. (*to Congrio*) You can even bring in a whole flock of slaves, if you wish. (*to all*) Cook, work, busy yourselves now as much as you like.

---

[24] Laverna protects criminals and thieves, and thus cooks (cf. the prayer in Hor. *epist.* 1. 16. 60–62).

[25] This is the *uagulatio*, the act of publicly voicing accusations; cf. the Twelve Tables (Fest. p. 514 Lindsay).

CON   temperi, postquam impleuisti fusti fissorum caput.
455 EVC   intro abi: opera huc conducta est uostra, non oratio.
CON   heus, senex, pro uapulando hercle ego aps te mercedem
        petam.
    coctum ego, non uapulatum, dudum conductus fui.
EVC   lege agito mecum. molestus ne sis. i [et] cenam coque,
    aut abi in malum cruciatum ab aedibus.
CON   abi tu modo.

III. iv: EVCLIO

460 EVC   illic hinc abiit. di immortales, facinus audax incipit
    qui cum opulento pauper [homine] coepit rem habere
        aut negotium.
    ueluti Megadorus temptat me omnibus miserum modis,
    qui simulauit mei honoris mittere huc causa coquos:
    is ea causa misit, hoc qui surruperent misero mihi.
465   condigne etiam meus med intus gallus gallinacius,
    qui erat anu peculiaris, perdidit paenissume.
    ubi erat haec defossa, occepit ibi scalpurrire ungulis
    circumcirca. quid opust uerbis? ita mi pectus peracuit:
    capio fustem, optrunco gallum, furem manufestarium.
470   credo edepol ego illi mercedem gallo pollicitos coquos,
    si id palam fecisset. exemi ex manu †manubrium†.
    quid opust uerbis? facta est pugna in gallo gallinacio.

458 i et *B*, et *DVJ*, ei *Brix*
461 homine *del. Acidalius*, habere *del. Brix*
466 anui *P*, anu *Stockert*
471 manubrium *suspectum propter antepaenultimam productam*,
manupretium *Leo*

CON   A good time for it, after you've filled my head with cracks with your club.

EUC   Go inside. You were hired for your work here, not for   455 your talk.

CON   Hey, old boy! I'll demand compensation from you for the beating. I was hired for cooking a while ago, not for getting a beating.

EUC   Take me to court. Don't be a nuisance. Go cook dinner, or go away from the house and be hanged.

CON   You go and be hanged yourself.

Exeunt CONGRIO and assistants into Euclio's house.

EUC   He's gone away. Immortal gods, a poor man who begins   460 dealings or some business with a wealthy one begins a daring undertaking. Take Megadorus. He tries to catch a wretch like myself in all sorts of ways, he who's pretended to send the cooks here to honor me. He sent them for one reason only: that they should steal this *(points to his pot)* from me, poor wretch that I am. And likewise even my   465 cock inside, which belonged to the old maid, came within an inch of ruining me. It began to scrape around with its claws, round about, at the place where the gold had been buried. What need is there for words? My heart got so bitter, I took a club and knocked the cock dead, the flagrant thief. I do believe the cooks promised a reward   470 to that cock if it revealed this. But I took the handle out of their hands.[26] What need is there for words? A fight was fought against the cock. *(stops and looks down the street)*

---

[26] The handle of a knife or sword; the cock is the cooks' weapon, as it were, the means to steal Euclio's money.

sed Megadorus meus affinis eccum incedit a foro.
iam hunc non ausim praeterire quin consistam et collo-
    quar.

III. v: MEGADORUS. EVCLIO

475 MEG narraui amicis multis consilium meum
de condicione hac. Euclionis filiam
laudant: "sapienter factum et consilio bono."
nam meo quidem animo si idem faciant ceteri
opulentiores, pauperiorum filias
480 ut indotatas ducant uxores domum,
et multo fiat ciuitas concordior,
et inuidia nos minore utamur quam utimur,
et illae malam rem metuant quam metuont magis,
et nos minore sumptu simus quam sumus.
485 in maxumam illuc populi partem est optumum;
in pauciores auidos altercatio est,
quorum animis auidis atque insatietatibus
nec lex nec sutor capere est qui possit modum.
namque hoc qui dicat, "quo illae nubent diuites
490 dotatae, si istud ius pauperibus ponitur?"
quo lubeant nubant, dum dos ne fiat comes.
hoc si ita fiat, mores meliores sibi
parent, pro dote quos ferant, quam nunc ferunt.
ego faxim muli, pretio qui superant equos,
495 sint uiliores Gallicis cantheriis.
EVC ita me di amabunt ut ego hunc ausculto lubens.
nimis lepide fecit uerba ad parsimoniam.

---

[27] The engagement with Euclio's daughter suffices to make Mega-
dorus Euclio's relation.

[28] Geldings, though useful, were generally not appreciated.

But look, here comes my relation[27] Megadorus from the market. Now I wouldn't dare to walk past him without stopping and accosting him.

EUCLIO steps aside, but remains on stage. Enter MEGADORUS from the right, without seeing Euclio.

MEG   I've told many friends about my plan for this match. They   475
       praise Euclio's daughter: "a sensible thing to do and a
       good plan." Well, at least in my opinion, if other people
       who are well off did the same, marrying the daughters of
       poorer people without dowry, the city would become   481
       much more harmonious, we would suffer less from envy
       than we do now, women would be much more afraid of a
       hard time than they are now, and we would spend less
       than we do now. For the vast majority of people this is   485
       best. There's a fight only with a handful of greedy men;
       neither law nor cobbler can take the measure for their
       greedy hearts and grasping natures. Well then, someone
       might say: "who are those rich women with a dowry going
       to marry, if this rule is laid down for the poorer ones?"
       Let them marry anyone they wish, so long as no dowry   491
       accompanies them. In that case they'd acquire a better
       character for themselves, which they could bring instead
       of a dowry, which is what they're bringing now. I'd make
       those mules which cost more than horses cheaper than
       Gallic geldings.[28]

EUC   As truly as the gods will love me, I enjoy listening to him.   496
       He's spoken so beautifully in favor of economizing.

MEG   nulla igitur dicat, "equidem dotem ad te attuli
        maiorem multo quam tibi erat pecunia;
500   enim mi quidem aequom est purpuram atque aurum
           dari,
       ancillas, mulos, muliones, pedisequos,
       salutigerulos pueros, uehicla qui uehar."
EVC   ut matronarum hic facta pernouit probe!
       moribus praefectum mulierum hunc factum uelim.
505 MEG   nunc quoquo uenias plus plaustrorum in aedibus
       uideas quam ruri, quando ad uillam ueneris.
       sed hoc etiam pulchrum est praequam ubi sumptus
          petunt.
       stat fullo, phyrgio, aurufex, lanarius;
       caupones patagiarii, indusiarii,
510   flammarii, uiolarii, carinarii;
       aut manulearii, aut †murobatharii†,
       propolae linteones, calceolarii;
       sedentarii sutores, diabathrarii,
       solearii astant, astant molocinarii;
515   petunt fullones, sarcinatores petunt;
       strophiarii astant, astant simul zonarii.
       iam hosce apsolutos censeas: cedunt, petunt
       treceni, quom stant thylacistae in atriis
       textores limbularii, arcularii.
520   ducuntur, datur aes. iam [hosce] apsolutos censeas,

    511 murobatharii *P*, malobathrarii *Lambinus*, myrobaptarii *Leo in apparatu*, myrobrecharii *Z*
     515 *uersum secl. Francken*
     516 semisonarii *P*, semul sonarii *Leo*
     518 phylacistae *P*, thylacistae *Wilamowitz*
     520 hosce *del. Bothe*

MEG So no woman could say: "I brought a dowry to you which
     is far greater than the money you had. So it's only fair that   500
     I should be given purple and gold, maids, mules, mule-
     drivers, manservants, pages to greet people, and car-
     riages to drive in."

EUC How well he knows the behavior of married women!
     I wish he were made supervisor of morals[29] among
     women.

MEG Wherever you go nowadays you can see more wagons in   505
     front of a city house than in the countryside when you
     go to a farmhouse. But this is still pleasant compared
     with when the women demand that you should pay their
     bills. There stands the launderer, the embroiderer, the
     goldsmith, and the woollen worker; the dealers in
     flounces and tunics; those who dye garments in flaming   510
     red, violet, and brown; or those who make garments with
     sleeves, or those who sell exotic perfumes; retailers in
     linen and shoemakers; squatting cobblers and producers
     of slippers; sandal-makers are standing there, and pro-
     ducers of mallow garments are standing there; the laun-   515
     derers are demanding pay, and the menders of clothes
     are demanding pay; sellers of women's breast-bands[30]
     are standing there, and sellers of girdles are also stand-
     ing there. Now you may think you've paid these off.
     Again and again hundreds are coming and demanding
     their pay, while the hem-weavers and the chest-makers
     with their money-bags are standing in the halls. They're   520
     brought in and given money. Now you may think you've

29 This office is not made up; some Greek cities had such super-
visors.

30 This is the ancient equivalent of today's bras.

313

quom incedunt infectores corcotarii,
aut aliqua mala crux semper est quae aliquid petat.

EVC compellarem ego illum, ni metuam ne desinat
memorare mores mulierum: nunc sic sinam.

525 MEG ubi nugiuendis res soluta est omnibus,
ibi ad postremum cedit miles, aes petit.
itur, putatur ratio cum argentario;
miles impransus astat, aes censet dari.
ubi disputata est ratio cum argentario,

530 etiam [plus] ipsus ultro debet argentario:
spes prorogatur militi in alium diem.
haec sunt atque aliae multae in magnis dotibus
incommoditates sumptusque intolerabiles.
nam quae indotata est, ea in potestate est uiri;

535 dotatae mactant et malo et damno uiros.
sed eccum affinem ante aedis. quid agis, Euclio?

III. vi: EVCLIO. MEGADORVS

EVC nimium lubenter edi sermonem tuom.

MEG an audiuisti?

EVC   usque a principio omnia.

MEG tamen [e] meo quidem animo aliquanto facias rectius,

540 si nitidior sis filiai nuptiis.

EVC pro re nitorem et gloriam pro copia
qui habent, meminerunt sese unde oriundi sient.

525 nugiuendis *Nonius*, nugigerulis *P* (-us *B^ac D^ac J*)
530 plus *del. Lambinus*
539 e *del. Gulielmus*

paid them off, when in come the saffron-dyers, or there's always some pain in the neck demanding something.

EUC I'd accost him if I weren't afraid that he might stop talking about the ways of women. Now I'll let him go on like this.

MEG When all the sellers of useless decoration are paid, at 525 last a soldier comes and demands his money.[31] You go and reckon up accounts with the banker. The soldier stands around without lunch and thinks he'll be given the money. When the accounts have been discussed with the banker, you owe him money too. The soldier's hope is put 530 off until another day. These and many other disadvantages, together with unbearable expenses, lie in large dowries: a wife without dowry is in her husband's power; those with a dowry afflict their husbands with misery and 535 loss. (*looks around*) But look, there's my relation in front of the house. How are you, Euclio?

EUCLIO comes forward.

EUC I devoured your talk with great pleasure.
MEG You heard it?
EUC Everything right from the beginning.
MEG Still, to my mind you'd behave somewhat more appropriately if you were a bit more elegant at your daughter's 540 wedding.
EUC People who have splendor corresponding to their wealth and a reputation corresponding to their abundance re-

---

31 Respectable people had to pay soldiers the so-called *aes militare*; this came from the government, so one merely had to pass it on (cf. Varro *ling*. 5. 181). It was a big embarrassment if one could not pay.

nec pol, Megadore, mihi nec quoiquam pauperi
opinione melius res structa est domi.
545 MEG immo est ⟨quod satis est⟩, et di faciant ut siet
plus plusque, ⟨et⟩ istuc sospitent quod nunc habes.
EVC illud mihi uerbum non placet, "quod nunc habes."
tam hoc scit me habere quam egomet. anus fecit palam.
MEG quid tu te solus e senatu seuocas?
550 EVC pol ego ut te accusem merito meditabar.
MEG   quid est?
EVC quid sit me rogitas? qui mihi omnis angulos
furum impleuisti in aedibus misero mihi,
qui mi intro misti in aedis quingentos coquos
cum senis manibus, genere Geryonaceo;
555 quos si Argus seruet, qui oculeus totus fuit,
quem quondam Ioni Iuno custodem addidit,
is numquam seruet. praeterea tibicinam,
quae mi interbibere sola, si uino scatat,
Corinthiensem fontem Pirenam potest.
560 tum opsonium autem—
MEG   pol uel legioni sat est.
etiam agnum misi.
EVC   quo quidem agno sat scio
magis curiosam nusquam esse ullam beluam.

545 *suppl. Ussing*   546 plusque ⟨et⟩ *Leo*, ⟨et⟩ plus *Lindsay*
550 te ut *P, transp. Acidalius*

---

[32] Euclio is saying that he has no status and hence no reason to make
an effort.

[33] Geryon was a monster with three bodies and six hands—the ideal
thief in Euclio's imagination.

member where they come from.[32] Megadorus, neither
for myself nor for any other poor man have possessions
been piled up more lavishly than people think.

MEG Well, well, you have enough, and may the gods make sure 545
that you have more and more, and may they preserve
what you have now.

EUC (*aside*) I don't like this phrase, "what you have now." He
knows as well as I do that I have (*pointing at the pot*) this.
The old woman made it known.

MEG Are you the only one to keep away from the senate?

EUC Well, I was thinking about how to accuse you, and rightly 550
so.

MEG What's the matter?

EUC You're asking me what's the matter? You've filled every
nook and cranny of my house with thieves, poor me, by
sending hundreds of cooks into my house, with six hands
each, of Geryon's race.[33] If Argus were to try watching 555
over them, who was completely covered with eyes and
whom Juno once assigned to be Io's guard, he would
never succeed.[34] Then there's the flute-girl, who could
drink dry the fountain of Pirene at Corinth[35] without any
help if it gushed with wine. And as for the provisions— 560

MEG (*interrupting*) Surely they're enough even for a legion.[36]
I've even sent you a lamb.

EUC I know for sure that I haven't seen a beast that takes more
care to find out what's going on than this lamb anywhere.

---

[34] Jupiter loved Io. In order to protect her, he turned her into a cow.
Juno was still jealous and appointed Argus with his many eyes as guardian over her.

[35] This was the main water supply of the city.

[36] A legion normally comprised between 4,200 and 6,000 men.

MEG uolo ego ex te scire qui sit agnus curio.
EVC quia ossa ac pellis totust, ita cura macet.
565 quin exta inspicere in sole ei uiuo licet:
ita is pellucet quasi lanterna Punica.
MEG caedundum conduxi ego illum.
EVC   tum tu idem optumum est
loces efferendum; nam iam, credo, mortuost.
MEG potare ego hodie, Euclio, tecum uolo.
570 EVC non potem ego quidem hercle.
MEG   at ego iussero
cadum unum uini ueteris a me afferrier.
EVC nolo hercle, nam mi bibere decretum est aquam.
MEG ego te hodie reddam madidum, si uiuo, probe,
tibi quoi decretum est bibere aquam.
EVC   scio quam rem agat:
575 ut me deponat uino, eam affectat uiam,
post hoc quod habeo ut commutet coloniam.
ego id cauebo, nam alicubi apstrudam foris.
ego faxo et operam et uinum perdiderit simul.
MEG ego, nisi quid me uis, eo lauatum, ut sacruficem.
580 EVC edepol ne tu, aula, multos inimicos habes
atque istuc aurum quod tibi concreditum est.
nunc hoc mihi factu est optumum, ut ted auferam,
aula, in Fidei fanum: ibi apstrudam probe.
Fides, nouisti me et ego te: caue sis tibi
585 ne tu immutassis nomen, si hoc concreduo.
ibo ad te fretus tua, Fides, fiducia.

---

[37] The Latin pun involves *curiosus* (curious), *curio* (priest presiding over a *curia*, a ward), and *cura* (care).

[38] Lanterns were normally made of horn. Punic ones were made of glass.

318

MEG I'd like to know from you how the lamb can be a care-
taker.

EUC Because it's entirely skin and bones, it's so thin from its
cares.[37] In fact, you can inspect its innards against the sun 565
while it's still alive: it's transparent like a Punic lantern.[38]

MEG I bought it to be slaughtered.

EUC Then you'd best buy a funeral for it as well because I
think it's dead already.

MEG I want to drink with you today, Euclio.

EUC *I* certainly won't drink. 570

MEG But I'll have a jug of old wine brought here from my
place.

EUC I refuse, because I've decided to drink water.

MEG I'll get you properly soaked today, as truly as I live, you
with your decision to drink water.

EUC (*aside*) I know what he's up to: knocking me out with 575
wine, that's the route he's taking, and afterwards what I
have will change its place. But I'll take measures against
it, because I'll bury it somewhere outside. I'll make sure
he wastes both his efforts and his wine.

MEG Unless you want anything from me, I'm going to bathe so
I can sacrifice.

Exit MEGADORUS into his house.

EUC My dear pot, you really do have many enemies, you and 580
the gold that's been entrusted to you. Now this is the best
thing for me to do, my pot: to carry you off into the shrine
of Good Faith; there I'll conceal you well. Good Faith,
you know me and I know you. Make sure you don't 585
change your name if I entrust this to you. I'll go to you,
Good Faith, with trust in your faithfulness.

ACTVS IV

IV. i: LYCONIDIS SERVOS

SER   hoc est serui facinus frugi, facere quod ego persequor,
ne morae molestiaeque imperium erile habeat sibi.
nam qui ero ex sententia seruire seruos postulat,
590   in erum matura, in se sera condecet capessere.
sin dormitet, ita dormitet seruom sese ut cogitet.
nam qui amanti ero seruitutem seruit, quasi ego seruio,
si erum uidet superare amorem, hoc serui esse officium
   reor,
retinere ad salutem, non enim quo incumbat eo impel-
   lere.
595   quasi pueri qui nare discunt scirpea induitur ratis,
qui laborent minus, facilius ut nent et moueant manus,
eodem modo seruom ratem esse amanti ero aequom
   censeo,
ut ⟨eum⟩ toleret, ne pessum abeat tamquam ⟨rete abit in
   mari⟩.
eri ille imperium ediscat, ut quod frons uelit oculi sciant;
600   quod iubeat citis quadrigis citius properet persequi.
qui ea curabit apstinebit censione bubula,
nec sua opera rediget umquam in splendorem compedis.
nunc erus meus amat filiam huius Euclionis pauperis;

592–8 *uersus secl. Brix*
598 ut ⟨eum⟩ toleret *Hare*   rete abit in mari *Stockert in apparatu*
(*cum* ⟨eum⟩), ⟨reticulum in mari⟩ *Langen* (*cum* ⟨eum⟩), ⟨catapirate-
ria⟩ *Lambinus* (*sine* ⟨eum⟩)

EUCLIO goes to the shrine in the middle of the stage.

ACT FOUR

Enter LYCONIDES' SERVANT from the right.

SER   This is the job of a deserving servant, to do what I'm mak-
ing it my aim to do: not to think of master's command as a
botheration and a nuisance; a slave who wants to serve his
master according to his wishes must give first place to his 590
master and second place to himself. And if he sleeps, he
should sleep in such a way that he doesn't forget that he's
a slave: someone who serves a lovesick master, just as I do
now, if he can see that love is gaining the upper hand over
his master, well then, I think it's the servant's duty to re-
strain him for his own good, and not to push him further
in the direction he inclines to. Just as a raft of bulrushes is 595
put under boys who are learning to swim so that they
don't find it so difficult and swim and move their hands
more easily, the same way I think it fair that a slave should
be a raft for a lovesick master, to support him so that he
doesn't sink to the bottom as a fishing net does in the sea.
Let him have a perfect understanding of what his master
commands so that his eyes can read what his face wishes;
let him be in a hurry to execute his orders faster than fast 600
chariots. A man who minds this will avoid a censor's pun-
ishment[39] with ox-hide whips and will never make the
shackles shine at his own expense. Now my master's in
love with the daughter of this poor chap here, Euclio.

[39] Roman censors were responsible for far more than the census.
They also exerted moral supervision.

eam ero nunc renuntiatum est nuptum huic Megadoro
dari.

605 is speculatum huc misit me, ut quae fierent fieret parti-
ceps.

nunc sine omni suspicione in ara hic assidam sacra;

hinc ego et huc et illuc potero quid agant arbitrarier.

IV. ii: EVCLIO. LYCONIDIS SERVOS

EVC tu modo caue quoiquam indicassis aurum meum esse is-
tic, Fides:

non metuo ne quisquam inueniat, ita probe in latebris si-
tum est.

610 edepol ne illic pulchram praedam agat, si quis illam inue-
nerit

aulam onustam auri; uerum id te quaeso ut prohibessis,
Fides.

nunc lauabo, ut rem diuinam faciam, ne affinem morer

quin ubi accersat [me] meam extemplo filiam ducat do-
mum.

uide, Fides, etiam atque etiam nunc, saluam ut aulam aps
te auferam:

615 tuae fide concredidi aurum, in tuo luco et fano [modo]
est situm.

SER di immortales, quod ego hunc hominem facinus audiui
loqui?

se aulam onustam auri apstrusisse hic intus in fano Fide.

caue tu illi fidelis, quaeso, potius fueris quam mihi.

atque hic pater est, ut ego opinor, huius erus quam amat
⟨uirginis⟩.

613 me *del. Hare*   615 modo *del. Pylades*
616 audio *P*, audiui *Bothe*
619 ⟨uirginis⟩ *Mueller*, ⟨meus⟩ *Luchs*, ⟨Euclio⟩ *Goetz*

322

Now it's been reported to master that she'll be given in
marriage to Megadorus here. He sent me here to watch 605
out so that he'd have his share in knowledge of what's
happening. Now I'll sit down on this sacred altar without
arousing any suspicion. (*sits down*) From here I'll be able
to observe in this direction as well as in that what they're
doing.

EUCLIO comes out of the shrine without seeing the slave.

EUC You, Good Faith, make sure you don't tell anyone that my
gold is in your place. I'm not afraid that anyone might
find it, it's placed in the dark so well. Well, if anyone were 610
to find that pot laden with gold, he'd carry off beautiful
spoils. But I ask you to prevent this, Good Faith. Now I'll
wash so I can sacrifice and won't keep my relation from
immediately taking my daughter home as soon as he
claims her. Good Faith, look out again and again so I can
carry off my pot from you safe and sound. I entrusted the 615
gold to your good faith, it's placed in your grove and
shrine.

Exit EUCLIO into his house.

SER Immortal gods, what did I hear this chap talk about do-
ing? He's buried a pot laden with gold here inside, in the
shrine of Good Faith. Please make sure you aren't faith-
ful to him rather than me. I think this is the father of the

620   ibo hinc intro, perscrutabor fanum, si inueniam uspiam
          aurum, dum hic est occupatus. sed si repperero, o Fides,
          mulsi congialem plenam faciam tibi fideliam.
          id adeo tibi faciam; uerum ego mi bibam, ubi id fecero.

IV. iii: EVCLIO

EVC   non temere est quod coruos cantat mihi nunc ab laeua
          manu;
625   simul radebat pedibus terram et uoce croccibat sua:
          continuo meum cor coepit artem facere ludicram
          atque in pectus emicare. sed ego cesso currere.

IV. iv: EVCLIO. LYCONIDIS SERVOS

EVC   <i> foras, lumbrice, qui sub terra erepsisti modo,
          qui modo nusquam comparebas, nunc quom compares
          peris.
630   ego [ede]pol te, praestrigiator, miseris iam accipiam
          modis.
SER   quae te mala crux agitat? quid tibi mecum est commerci,
          senex?
          quid me afflictas? quid me raptas? qua me causa uer-
          beras?
EVC   uerberabilissume, etiam rogitas, non fur, sed trifur?
SER   quid tibi surrupui?
EVC   redde huc sis.
SER   quid tibi uis reddam?
EVC   rogas?

---

628 <i> foras *Lambinus*, <foras> foras *Camerarius*
630 ego edepol *P*, ede- *del.* ς, ego *del. Lindsay inusitate*

---

[40] A *congius* is six *sextarii*, and a *sextarius* is slightly more than half a
liter.

324

girl my master loves. I'll go inside and search the shrine,   620
to see if I can find the gold anywhere while he's busy. But
if I do find it, dear Good Faith, I'll offer you a six-pint[40]
pot filled to the brim with honey-wine. Yes, I'll offer it to
you; (*aside*) but I'll drink it myself as soon as I've done so.

LYCONIDES' SERVANT goes into the shrine.
Enter EUCLIO from his house.

EUC   It's not by chance that a raven was cawing to my left now;
at the same time it was scraping the ground with its claws   625
and croaking with its voice. Immediately my heart began
to jump like a dancer and leap up into my chest. But I'm
delaying running.

EUCLIO rushes to the shrine.
EUCLIO is dragging out LYCONIDES' SERVANT.

EUC   Get out, earthworm! Creeping out from underneath the
earth just now! A moment ago you were nowhere to be
seen, but now that you are to be seen you're finished! I'll   630
give you a dire welcome now, you trickster. (*beats him*)
SER   What grievance is driving you out of your mind? What
business have you with me, old boy? What are you hitting
me for? What are you dragging me for? What are you
beating me for?
EUC   You deserve a beating more than anyone, and yet you
dare ask? You're not just a thief, but a triple-thief!
SER   What did I steal from you?
EUC   Give it back, will you!
SER   What do you want me to give back to you?
EUC   You're asking?

325

635 SER   nil equidem tibi apstuli.
   EVC   at illud quod tibi apstuleras cedo.
       ecquid agis?
   SER   quid agam?
   EVC   auferre non potes.
   SER   quid uis tibi?
   EVC   pone.
   SER   id quidem pol te datare credo consuetum, senex.
   EVC   pone hoc sis, aufer cauillam, non ego nunc nugas ago.
   SER   quid ergo ponam? quin tu eloquere quicquid est suo
       nomine.
640   non hercle equidem quicquam sumpsi nec tetigi.
   EVC   ostende huc manus.
   SER   em tibi, ostendi, eccas.
   EVC   uideo. age ostende etiam tertiam.
   SER   laruae hunc atque intemperiae insaniaeque agitant se-
       nem.
       facin iniuriam mi [an non]?
   EVC   fateor, quia non pendes, maxumam.
       atque id quoque iam fiet, nisi fatere.
   SER   quid fatear tibi?
645 EVC   quid apstulisti hinc?
   SER   di me perdant, si ego tui quicquam apstuli . . .
       niue adeo apstulisse uellem.

     643 an non *del. Langen*

---

[41] The servant uses *auferre* with a dative specifying the person be-
ing robbed; Euclio deliberately misunderstands the dative as an adjunct
specifying the beneficiary.   [42] Euclio uses *pone* as the imperative
of *ponere*, but the servant deliberately misunderstands him and takes
pone as an adverb (behind), i.e., as an invitation to anal sex.

SER I really didn't take away anything, so far as you are con- 635
     cerned.

EUC Then let me have what you've taken away so far as *you* are
     concerned.[41] Well, get on with it!

SER Get on with what?

EUC You can't take it away.

SER What do you want?

EUC Let me have it.

SER I'm sure you've learnt to love providing that service, old
     boy.[42]

EUC Let me have the thing, will you, and stop your witticisms.
     I'm not joking now.

SER So what should I let you have? Why don't you call what-
     ever it is by its proper name. I didn't take or touch any- 640
     thing.

EUC Show me your hands.

SER (*obeying*) Here you go, I'm showing them to you, look.

EUC I can see them. Go on, show me the third one as well.

SER (*aside*) Evil spirits,[43] madness, and insanity are troubling
     this old chap. (*to Euclio*) Aren't you doing me an injus-
     tice?

EUC Yes, I admit it, an enormous injustice, because you aren't
     hanging. And that too will soon happen unless you ad-
     mit it.

SER What should I admit?

EUC What did you take away from here?   645

SER May the gods destroy me if I carried away anything be-
     longing to you . . . (*aside*) and if I wouldn't have wanted to.

---

[43] The *laruae* (evil spirits) were believed to cause madness. They
are connected with the *lares*: the *laruae* are bad, the *lares* are good
(Apul. *Socr.* 152–53).

EVC	agedum, excutedum pallium.
SER	tuo arbitratu.
EVC	ne inter tunicas habeas.
SER	tempta qua lubet.
EVC	uah, scelestus quam benigne, ut ne apstulisse intellegam!

noui sycophantias. age rursum. ostende huc manum

650 dexteram.

SER	em.
EVC	nunc laeuam ostende.
SER	quin equidem ambas profero.
EVC	iam scrutari mitto. redde huc.
SER	quid reddam?
EVC	a, nugas agis,

certe habes.

SER	habeo ego? quid habeo?
EVC	non dico, audire expetis.

id meum, quicquid habes, redde.

SER	insanis: perscrutatus es

tuo arbitratu, nec tui me quicquam inuenisti penes.

655 EVC mane, mane. quis illic est? quis hic intus alter erat tecum
simul?

perii hercle: ill' nunc intus turbat, hunc si amitto, hic
abierit.

postremo hunc iam perscrutaui, hic nihil habet. abi quo
lubet.

SER	Iuppiter te dique perdant.
EVC	hau male egit gratias.

ibo intro atque illi socienno tuo iam interstringam gulam.

660 fugin hinc ab oculis? abin [hinc] an non?

658 male agit *P*, m. egit *Mueller*, m. agit ⟨hic⟩ *Koch*

EUC   Go on, shake out your cloak.

SER   (*complying*) As you like it.

EUC   You might have it under your tunic.

SER   Touch me wherever you wish.

EUC   (*searching him*) Bah, how obliging the thug is, so I won't realize he's taken it. I know your tricks. Go on, again. Show me your right hand, here.

SER   (*showing it*) Here you go.

EUC   Now show me your left.

SER   (*showing the other one as well*) Here you go, I'm showing you both.

EUC   I'm giving up my search now. Give it back to me.   651

SER   What should I give back?

EUC   Oh! You must be joking. Of course you have it.

SER   I have it? What do I have?

EUC   I'm not telling you, you just want to hear it. Give back this thing of mine, whatever you have.

SER   You must be mad. You've searched me just as you wished, and you didn't find anything belonging to you on me.

EUC   Wait, wait. (*turns to the shrine*) Who's that? What other   655 man was in here together with you? (*aside*) I'm really done for. That one's running amok inside now, and if I let go of this one here, he'll disappear. But then I've already searched this one here and he doesn't have a thing. (*to Lyconides' servant*) Go away, wherever you like.

SER   May Jupiter and the gods destroy you.

EUC   (*aside*) Nice way of saying thank you. (*to the slave*) I'll go in and throttle your partner's throat. Get out of my sight   660 now, will you! Go away now, will you!

---

660 hinc² *del. Pylades ut septenarius fiat*   te uideam *P*, recipias *Stockert*, reuideam *Bothe*, reuideas *Goetz*, reuenias *Brix*

SER	abeo.
EVC	caue sis recipias.

IV. V: LYCONIDIS SERVOS

SER emortuom ego me mauelim leto malo
quam non ego illi dem hodie insidias seni.
nam hic iam non audebit aurum apstrudere:
credo efferet iam secum et mutabit locum.

665   attat, foris crepuit. senex eccum aurum effert foras.
tantisper huc ego ad ianuam concessero.

IV. Vi: EVCLIO. LYCONIDIS SERVOS

EVC Fide censebam maxumam multo fidem
esse, ea subleuit os mihi paenissume:
ni subuenisset coruos, periissem miser.

670   nimis hercle ego illum coruom ad me ueniat uelim
qui indicium fecit, ut ego illic aliquid boni . . .
dicam; nam quod edit tam duim quam perduim.
nunc hoc ubi apstrudam cogito solum locum.
Siluani lucus extra murum est auius,

675   crebro salicto oppletus. ibi sumam locum.
certum est, Siluano potius credam quam Fide.

SER eugae, eugae, di me saluom et seruatum uolunt.
iam ego illuc praecurram atque inscendam aliquam in ar-
       borem

ind'que opseruabo aurum ubi apstrudat senex.

680   quamquam hic manere me erus sese iusserat,

---

671 illi *P*, illic *Bothe*

---

[44] This is the benign Roman god of the countryside.

SER (*retreating somewhat*) I'm going.

EUC Do make sure you won't come back.

EUCLIO rushes into the shrine.

SER I'd rather die a horrible death than not catch the old
man out today. Well, he won't dare bury his gold here
any longer. I think he'll take it out with him now and
change location. (*stops and listens*) Ah, the door has 665
creaked. Look, the old chap's taking the gold outside.
Meanwhile I'll step aside here to the door. (*moves to-
ward Megadorus' house*)

EUCLIO leaves the shrine with his pot.

EUC I used to think Good Faith was by far the most faithful
goddess, but she came ever so close to tricking me. If that
raven hadn't come to my help, I'd have perished. Poor
me! I do wish that raven came to me, the one that warned 670
me, so that I could . . . say something nice to it; well, I'd
be as likely to feed it as to destroy its food. Now I'm think-
ing of some lonely spot where I can bury this pot. (*pauses
for a moment*) There's a grove of Silvanus[44] outside the
wall, difficult to reach and full of willow thickets. I'll pick 675
a place there. It's settled now: I'll trust Silvanus rather
than Good Faith.

Exit EUCLIO to the left.

SER Hurray, hurray, the gods want me safe and sound. Now
I'll run there first and climb up some tree, and from there
I'll observe where the old chap buries the gold. Even 680
though master had ordered me to wait for him here, I'm

331

certum est, malam rem potius quaeram cum lucro.

IV. vii: LYCONIDES. EVNOMIA. (PHAEDRIVM)

LYC   dixi tibi, mater, iuxta mecum rem tenes,
     super Euclionis filia. nunc te opsecro
     resecroque, mater, quod dudum opsecraueram:
685   fac mentionem cum auunculo, mater mea.
EVN   scis tute facta uelle me quae tu uelis,
     et istuc confido ⟨a⟩ fratre me impetrassere;
     et causa iusta est, siquidem ita est ut praedicas,
     te eam compressisse uinolentum uirginem.
690 LYC egone ut te aduorsum mentiar, mater mea?
PHAE perii, mea nutrix. opsecro te, uterum dolet.
     Iuno Lucina, tuam fidem!
LYC   em, mater mea,
     tibi rem potiorem uerbo: clamat, parturit.
EVN   i hac intro mecum, gnate mi, ad fratrem meum,
695   ut istuc quod me oras impetratum ab eo auferam.
LYC   i, iam sequor te, mater. sed seruom meum
     †Strobilum† miror ubi sit, quem ego me iusseram
     hic opperiri. nunc ego mecum cogito:
     si mihi dat operam, me illi irasci iniurium est.
700   ibo intro, ubi de capite meo sunt comitia.

687 a *add. Pylades*
693 uideo *P,* uerbo *Leo*
697 *huic seruo uix idem nomen esse potest ac Megadori*

resolved, I'd rather look for a thrashing that comes with a profit.

Exit LYCONIDES' SERVANT to the left.
Enter LYCONIDES and EUNOMIA from the right.

LYC   I've told you, mother, you know about Euclio's daughter
      as well as I do. Now I entreat and implore you, mother,
      do what I'd entreated you to do before. Mention this to   685
      my uncle, my mother.

EUN   You know I want done what you want done, and I'm sure
      I'll achieve it from my brother. And it's a fair cause, if it is
      as you tell me and you did violence to this girl when you
      were drunk.

LYC   Would I lie to you, my mother?   690

PHAE *(from inside Euclio's house)* I'm done for, my nurse. I en-
      treat you, my womb hurts. Juno, goddess of childbirth,
      help me!

LYC   There, mother! There's better proof for you than mere
      words: she's screaming, she's giving birth.

EUN   Come inside with me to my brother, my son, so I can per- 694
      suade him to do the thing you want the way you ask for.

LYC   Do go, I'll follow you in a moment, mother.

Exit EUNOMIA into her brother's house.

LYC   Well, I wonder where my slave is. I told him to wait for
      me here. Now I'm thinking, if he's doing something for
      me, it wouldn't be fair of me to be angry with him. I'll go 700
      inside, where the assembly is taking place which decides
      over my life.

Exit LYCONIDES into Megadorus' house.
Enter LYCONIDES' SERVANT from the left.

IV. viii: LYCONIDIS SERVOS

SER picis diuitiis, qui aureos montis colunt,
ego solus supero. nam istos reges ceteros
memorare nolo, hominum mendicabula:
ego sum ille rex Philippus. o lepidum diem!
705 nam ut dudum hinc abii, multo illo adueni prior
multoque prius me collocaui in arborem
ind'que exspectabam, aurum ubi apstrudebat senex.
ubi ille abiit, ego me deorsum duco de arbore,
effodio aulam auri plenam. inde ex eo loco
710 uideo recipere se senem; ill' me non uidet,
nam ego [non] declinaui paullulum me extra uiam.
attat, eccum ipsum. ibo ut hoc condam domum.

IV. ix: EVCLIO. LYCONIDES

EVC perii, interii, occidi. quo curram? quo non curram? tene,
tene. quem? quis?
nescio, nil uideo, caecus eo atque equidem quo eam aut
ubi sim aut qui sim
715 nequeo cum animo certum inuestigare. opsecro ego uos,
mi auxilio,
oro, optestor, sitis et hominem demonstretis, quis eam
apstulerit.
718 quid ais tu? tibi credere certum est, nam esse bonum ex
uoltu cognosco.
719 quid est? quid ridetis? noui omnis, scio fures esse hic
compluris,

711 non *del. Pylades*   715 uos ego *P, transp. Peters*

---

45 *Pix* is the Latinized form of Greek *sphinx*, or rather the Boeotian
dialect form *phix*. But the creatures watching over the mountains of

SER   I alone surpass the griffins in wealth, those creatures in-
habiting the mountains of gold.[45] Well, I won't even men-
tion those other kings, those poor beggars. I am that
famous King Philip. O what a wonderful day! Well, after   705
going away from here, I got there long before him and I
positioned myself in a tree. From there I observed where
the old boy buried the gold. After he'd gone, I climbed
down from the tree and dug up the pot full of gold. Then
I saw the old bloke coming back from the place, but he
didn't see me because I kept off the road a little. *(looks*   710
down the street) Aha! Look, here he comes. I'll go and
hide this at home.

Exit LYCONIDES' SERVANT *to the right, in the direction of
Eunomia's house.*
Enter EUCLIO *from the left.*

EUC   I'm done for, I'm killed, I'm murdered. Where should I
run? Where shouldn't I run? Stop him, stop him! Whom?
And who? I don't know, I can't see, I trod along blindly. I   714
can't find any certainty in my mind as to where I'm going
or where I am or who I am. *(to the audience)* I beg you, I
entreat you, I beseech you: help me and show me the
man who's taken it away. *(turning to someone in the audi-
ence)* What do *you* say? I've decided to believe you, be-
cause I can see from your face that you're a good man.
(addressing the whole audience) What is it? What are
you laughing for? I know you all; I know there are plenty

gold are the griffins and not the sphinges, and the griffins must be
meant here (Non. p. 222 Lindsay). Plautus seems to have confused
the two.

717   qui uestitu et creta occultant sese atque sedent quasi sint
        frugi.

720   hem, nemo habet horum? occidisti. dic igitur, quis ha-
        bet? nescis?

721   heu me miserum, misere perii,

721a   male perditus, pessume ornatus eo:

722   tantum gemiti et mali maestitiae-

722a   que hic dies mi optulit, famem et pauperiem.

723   peritissumus ego sum omnium in terra;

723a   nam quid mi opust uita, [qui] tantum auri

724   perdidi, quod concustodiui

724a   sedulo? egomet me defruda-

725   ui animumque meum geniumque meum;

725a   nunc eo alii laetificantur

726   meo malo et damno. pati nequeo.

727   LYC   quinam homo hic ante aedis nostras

727a   eiulans conqueritur maerens?

728   atque hicquidem Euclio est, ut opinor.

728a   oppido ego interii: palam est res,

729   scit peperisse iam, ut ego opinor,

729a   filiam suam. nunc mi incertum est

730   abeam an maneam an adeam an fugiam.

730a   quid agam? edepol nescio.

IV. X: EVCLIO. LYCONIDES

·EVC   quis homo hic loquitur?

LYC   ego sum ‹miser›.

EVC   immo ego sum [miser], et misere perditus,
quoi tanta mala maestitudoque optigit.

LYC   animo bono es.

EVC   quo, opsecro, pacto esse possum?

of thieves here who are hiding under smart clothes and
sitting still as if they were decent. (*returning to the previ-
ous person*) What, none of them has it? You've ruined   720
me. Tell me, then, who has it? You don't know? O, I'm
wretched, I've perished wretchedly, I walk along, de-
stroyed wickedly and rigged out awfully. This day's
brought me so much groaning and trouble and sadness,
hunger and poverty. Of all men on earth I'm the most ex-
perienced in suffering. What point is there in life? I've
lost so much gold, which I guarded carefully. I denied
myself, heart and soul, any joy. Now others are having a   725a
good time with it, while I am having a bad time and loss. I
can't handle it.

Enter LYCONIDES from Megadorus' house.

LYC   Who on earth is lamenting here in front of our house,
with wailing and sadness? (*looks around*) And this here is
Euclio, I think. I'm done for completely. It's all out, he al-
ready knows his daughter's given birth, I think. Now I'm
uncertain whether I should go away or stay or go up to   730
him or run away. What should I do? I really don't know.
EUC   (*not seeing Lyconides*) Who's talking here?
LYC   (*stepping forward, speaking half aside*) I'm a poor
wretch.
EUC   No, I am, and I'm destroyed wretchedly; such great trou-
bles and sadness have come over me.
LYC   Cheer up.
EUC   Please, how can I possibly do that?

---

717 *post*   719 *posuit Hermann*   723 perditissumus *P*, peritissu-
mus *Lindsay*   723a qui *del. Spengel*   731 *transp. Acidalius*

LYC   quia istuc facinus quod tuom
       sollicitat animum, id ego feci et fateor.

EVC   quid ego ex te audio?

735 LYC   id quod uerum est.

EVC   quid ego ‹ de te d ›emerui, adulescens, mali,
       quam ob rem ita faceres meque meosque perditum ires
          liberos?

LYC   deus mihi impulsor fuit, is me ad illam illexit.

EVC   quo modo?

LYC   fateor peccauisse ‹ me › et me culpam commeritum scio;
       id adeo te oratum aduenio ut animo aequo ignoscas mihi.

740 EVC   quor id ausu's facere ut id quod non tuom esset tangeres?

LYC   quid uis fieri? factum est illud: fieri infectum non potest.
       deos credo uoluisse; nam ni uellent, non fieret, scio.

EVC   at ego deos credo uoluisse ut apud me te in neruo eni-
         cem.

LYC   ne istuc dixis.

EVC   quid tibi ergo meam me inuito tactio est?

745 LYC   quia uini uitio atque amoris feci.

EVC   homo audacissume,
       cum istacin te oratione huc ad me adire ausum, impu-
         dens!
       nam si istuc ius est ut tu istuc excusare possies,
       luci claro deripiamus aurum matronis palam,
       postid si prehensi simus, excusemus ebrios

750   nos fecisse amoris causa. nimis uile est uinum atque
         amor,
       si ebrio atque amanti impune facere quod lubeat licet.

---

735 emerui (*lac. ind.*) BDE, *sine spatio* JV, ‹ de te d ›emerui *Lindsay*
737 mihi impulsor DEVJ, impulsor mihi B
738 me[1] *add. Bentley*

LYC	Because that deed which is upsetting you, well, I did it and I admit it.	
EUC	What do I hear from you?	
LYC	The truth.	735
EUC	Young man, what harm have I done you to deserve that you'd behave like this and go about ruining me and my offspring?	
LYC	Some god urged me to do it; he led me on.	
EUC	How so?	
LYC	I admit that I've done wrong and that I've deserved your reproach. And so I've come to ask you to forgive me calmly.	
EUC	Why did you dare to do it, to touch what isn't yours?	740
LYC	What do you want to happen? It's done. It can't be undone. I believe it is the will of the gods: if they hadn't wanted it, it wouldn't have happened, I know that.	
EUC	But I believe it is the will of the gods that I kill you at my place in shackles.	
LYC	Don't say that.	
EUC	Then why did you touch what was mine without my agreement?	
LYC	Because I did so through the fault of wine and love.	745
EUC	You utterly reckless individual, how dare you come here to me with that sort of story, you shameless rascal! Well then, if it's legal to use your kind of excuse, we might as well snatch jewellery from married women openly and in broad daylight, and then, if we were caught, we could say as an excuse that we did so while drunk and out of love. Wine and love are too cheap if a man can do what he wants when he's drunk and in love.	750

	LYC	quin tibi ultro supplicatum uenio ob stultitiam meam.
	EVC	non mi homines placent qui quando male fecerunt puri-
		gant.
		tu illam scibas non tuam esse: non attactam oportuit.
755	LYC	ergo quia sum tangere ausus, hau causificor quin eam
		ego habeam potissumum.
	EVC	tune habeas me inuito meam?
	LYC	hau te inuito postulo; sed meam esse oportere arbitror.
		quin tu iam inuenies, inquam, meam illam esse oportere,
		Euclio.
	EVC	nisi refers—
	LYC	quid tibi ego referam?
	EVC	—quod surrupuisti meum,
760		iam quidem hercle te ad praetorem rapiam et tibi scri-
		bam dicam.
	LYC	surrupio ego tuom? unde? aut quid id est?
	EVC	ita te amabit Iuppiter,
		ut tu nescis.
	LYC	nisi quidem tu mihi quid quaeras dixeris.
	EVC	aulam auri, inquam, te reposco, quam tu confessu's mihi
		te apstulisse.
	LYC	neque edepol ego dixi nec feci.
	EVC	negas?
765	LYC	pernego immo. nam neque ego aurum neque istaec aula
		quae siet
		scio nec noui.
	EVC	illam, ex Siluani luco quam apstuleras, cedo.
		i, refer. dimidiam tecum potius partem diuidam.
		tam etsi fur mihi es, molestus non ero. i uero, refer.

LYC Yes, but I've come to you of my own accord to ask you to forgive me for my stupidity.

EUC I don't like people who apologize after behaving badly. You knew that what I wanted wasn't yours; you shouldn't have touched it.

LYC Well, now that I did dare to touch it, I have no objection   755
to keeping it for myself.

EUC You should keep it against my will?

LYC I don't insist on it against your will. But I do think that it ought to be mine: I assure you, in a moment you'll find out that it ought to be mine, Euclio.

EUC If you don't return—   759

LYC (*interrupting*) What should I return to you?

EUC —my property you stole, I'll drag you to the praetor[46] this instant and prosecute you.

LYC I am stealing your property? Where from? Or what is it?

EUC (*with irony*) As truly as Jupiter will love you, you don't know.

LYC Unless you tell me what you're asking for.

EUC I'm demanding the pot of gold back, I say, which you confessed you'd stolen from me.

LYC No, I didn't say or do this at all.

EUC You deny it?

LYC More than that, I deny it absolutely: I don't know about   765
the gold at all, or what pot this is.

EUC The one you'd stolen from the grove of Silvanus. Give it back. Go, return it. I'd rather divide it half and half with you. Even though you're a thief, I won't make a fuss. Do go and return it.

[46] The main function of the praetor was to hear law cases.

LYC   sanus tu non es qui furem me uoces. ego te, Euclio,
770   de alia re resciuisse censui, quod ad me attinet;
         magna est [res] quam ego tecum otiose, si otium est, cu-
            pio loqui.
EVC   dic bona fide: tu id aurum non surrupuisti?
LYC   bona.
EVC   neque ⟨eum⟩ scis qui apstulerit?
LYC   istuc quoque bona.
EVC   atque id si scies
         qui apstulerit, mihi indicabis?
LYC   faciam.
EVC   nec partem tibi
775   ab eo quisque est indipisces nec furem excipies?
LYC   ita.
EVC   quid ⟨si⟩ fallis?
LYC   tum me faciat quod uolt magnus Iuppiter.
EVC   sat habeo. age nunc loquere quid uis.
LYC   si me nouisti minus,
         genere quo sim gnatus: hic mihi est Megadorus aun-
            culus,
         meus fuit pater Antimachus, ego uocor Lyconides,
780   mater est Eunomia.
EVC   noui genus. nunc quid uis? id uolo
         noscere.
LYC   filiam ex te tu habes.
EVC   immo eccillam domi.
LYC   eam tu despondisti, opinor, meo aunculo.
EVC   omnem rem tenes.
LYC   is me nunc renuntiare repudium iussit tibi.

LYC You aren't in your right mind, calling me a thief. Euclio, I thought you'd found out about another matter that concerns me. It's an important matter which I'd like to discuss with you at your leisure, if you have leisure. 771

EUC Give me your word of honor: you didn't steal this gold?

LYC Upon my honor, no.

EUC And you don't know the man who took it away?

LYC Upon my honor, it's no again.

EUC And if you find out who took it away, you'll inform me?

LYC I will.

EUC And you won't take a share from that man, whoever he is, or give shelter to the thief?

LYC No.

EUC What if you deceive me? 776

LYC Then may great Jupiter deal with me as he sees fit.

EUC That'll do. Go on now, say what you want.

LYC In case you don't know what family I come from, Megadorus here is my uncle, my father was Antimachus, and I'm called Lyconides; my mother is Eunomia. 780

EUC I know the family. So what do you want now? That's what I'd like to find out about.

LYC Well, you have a daughter.

EUC Yes, at home there.

LYC You've betrothed her to my uncle, I think.

EUC Absolutely correct.

LYC Well, he's told me to inform you now that he's breaking off the engagement.

---

771 res *del. Hare*   773 eum *add. Langen*   775 cuiquam est *P*, cui sit *Nonius*, cui uis *Nonius (alibi)*, quisque est *Langen*
776 id *B² EVJ*, it *B¹ D*, id ‹si› *Valla*, quid ‹si› *Camerarius*

EVC   repudium rebus paratis, exornatis nuptiis?
785   ut illum di immortales omnes deaeque quantum est per-
         duint,
     quem propter hodie auri tantum perdidi infelix, miser.
LYC   bono animo es, [et] bene dice. nunc quae res tibi et
         gnatae tuae
     bene feliciterque uortat . . . "ita di faxint" inquito.
EVC   ita di faciant.
LYC   et mihi ita di faciant. audi nunciam.
790   qui homo culpam ammisit in se, nullust tam parui preti
     quin pudeat, quin purget sese. nunc te optestor, Euclio,
     ut si quid ego erga te imprudens peccaui aut gnatam
         tuam,
     ut mi ignoscas eamque uxorem mihi des, ut leges iubent.
     ego me iniuriam fecisse filiae fateor tuae
795   Cereris uigiliis per uinum atque impulsu adulescentiae.
EVC   ei mihi, quod ego facinus ex te audio?
LYC   quor eiulas,
     quem ego auom feci iam ut esses filiai nuptiis?
     nam tua gnata peperit, decumo mense post: numerum
         cape;
     ea re repudium remisit aunculus causa mea.
800   i intro, exquaere sitne ita ut ego praedico.
EVC   perii oppido,
     ita mihi ad malum malae res plurumae se agglutinant.
     ibo intro, ut quid huius uerum sit sciam.

787 et *del. Pylades*

EUC   Breaking off the engagement now that everything is
ready and the wedding is prepared? May all the immortal 785
gods and goddesses confound him, the whole lot of them!
Because of *him* I lost such a large amount of gold today.
Poor, unhappy me!

LYC   Cheer up, don't curse. And now, may this turn out well
and happily for you and your daughter . . . say "may the
gods do so."

EUC   May the gods do so.

LYC   And may the gods do so for me. Now listen. No man 790
who's stained himself with guilt is so worthless that he
wouldn't be ashamed and wouldn't apologize. Now I be-
seech you, Euclio, that, if I've done something bad to you
or your daughter without thinking about it, that you for-
give me and that you give her to me as my wife, as the
laws command. I admit that I wronged your daughter at
the vigil held for Ceres, because of wine and the impulse
of youth.

EUC   Oh no! What villainy must I hear from you? 796

LYC   Why are you wailing? I've made you a grandfather on
your daughter's wedding: your daughter's given birth,
nine months later.[47] Calculate for yourself. It's for that
reason that my uncle has broken off the engagement,
for my sake. Go inside and ask if it isn't the way I'm tell- 800
ing you.

EUC   I'm done for completely: so many bad things glue them-
selves to my already bad situation. I'll go inside in order
to find out how much of this is true.

Exit EUCLIO into Megadorus' house.

[47] Ten months in the Latin, because these are lunar months.

LYC   iam te sequor.

haec propemodum iam esse in uado salutis res uidetur.

nunc seruom esse ubi dicam meum †Strolum† non re-
perio:

805   nisi etiam hic opperiar tamen paullisper; postea intro

hunc supsequar. nunc interim spatium ei dabo exqui-
rendi

meum factum ex gnatae pedisequa nutrice anu: ea rem
nouit.

ACTVS V

V. i: LYCONIDIS SERVOS. LYCONIDES

SER   di immortales, quibus et quantis me donatis gaudiis!

quadrilibrem aulam auro onustam habeo. quis me est
ditior?

810   quis me Athenis nunc magis quisquam est homo quoi di
sint propitii?

LYC   certo enim ego uocem hic loquentis modo mi audire ui-
sus sum.

SER   hem,

erumne ego aspicio meum?

LYC   uideone ego hunc [Strobilum] seruom meum?

SER   ipsus est.

LYC   haud alius est.

SER   congrediar.

LYC   contollam gradum.

814–   credo ego illum, ut iussi, eampse anum adiisse, huius nu-
15   tricem uirginis.

---

804 strolum *B*[1] *E*[1] *V*[1], strobolum *B*[2], strobilum *cett.*, *sed Lyconidis*
serui nomen uix idem esse potest ac Megadori
    812 Strobilum *del. Brix*

LYC (*calling after Euclio*) I'm following you in a moment. (*to the audience*) This matter seems to be almost in the shallows of safety now. (*pauses*) I have no idea where I should say my slave is at the moment; but I'll wait for a bit longer 805 here. After that I'll follow Euclio inside. Meanwhile I'll give him an opportunity to find out about my deed from his daughter's maid, the old nurse. She knows everything.

ACT FIVE

Enter LYCONIDES' SERVANT from the right.

SER (*not seeing Lyconides*) Immortal gods, what great joys you bless me with! I have a four-pound pot brimful of gold. Who's richer than me? What man is there in Athens 810 now who the gods are more well-disposed to than me?

LYC (*not seeing his servant*) I'm sure I heard the voice of someone speaking here just now.

SER Hm! Isn't this my master I'm looking at?

LYC Isn't this my slave I'm seeing?

SER It's he himself.

LYC It's no one else.

SER I'll go toward him.

LYC I'll step up. I believe he's been to the old woman herself, 814–as I told him, the nurse of my girl. 15

SER quin ego illi me inuenisse dico hanc praedam atque elo-
          quor?
     igitur orabo ut manu me emittat. ibo atque eloquar.
     repperi—
LYC   quid repperisti?
SER   non quod pueri clamitant
     in faba se repperisse.
LYC   iamne autem, ut soles? deludis.
820 SER ere, mane, eloquar iam, ausculta.
LYC   age ergo loquere.
SER   repperi hodie,
     ere, diuitias nimias.
LYC   ubinam?
SER   quadrilibrem, inquam, aulam auri plenam.
LYC quod ego facinus audio ex te?
SER   Euclioni huic seni surrupui.
LYC ubi id est aurum?
SER   in arca apud me. nunc uolo me emitti manu.
LYC egone te emittam manu,
825   scelerum cumulatissume?
SER abi, ere, scio quam rem geras.
     lepide hercle animum tuom temptaui. iam ut eriperes
          apparabas:
     quid faceres, si repperissem?
LYC   non potes probasse nugas.
     i, redde aurum.
SER   reddam ego aurum?
LYC   redde, inquam, ut huic reddatur.
SER   unde?
830 LYC quod modo fassu's esse in arca.

SER   Why don't I say to him and tell him that I've found this booty? Then I'll ask him to set me free. I'll go and tell him. (*to Lyconides*) I've found—

LYC   (*interrupting*) What have you found?

SER   Not what boys shout out they've found in a bean.[48]

LYC   Your usual jokes? You're making fun of me. (*turns to go*)

SER   Master, wait, I'm going to tell you this instant, listen.   820

LYC   Go on, then, speak.

SER   Today, master, I've found enormous riches.

LYC   Where?

SER   A four-pound pot, I'm telling you, full of gold.

LYC   What villainy must I hear from you?

SER   I nicked it from this old chap, Euclio.

LYC   Where is this gold?

SER   In a chest at my home. Now I want to be set free.

LYC   I should set you free, you heap of infamy?   825

SER   Come, come, master, I know what you're getting at. I tested your attitude really nicely. You were already preparing to snatch it away. What would you be doing if I'd found it?

LYC   You can't convince me that you were joking. Go now, return the gold.

SER   I should return the gold?

LYC   Return it, I say, so it can be returned to Euclio.

SER   Where from?

LYC   The gold you just admitted was in the chest.   830

48 Unclear reference. What children find could be a worm; alternatively, Plautus could refer to a game, or there could be an allusion to beans used as stage money; perhaps we are even dealing with an obscene joke of unclear meaning (cf. the rude joke the slave made in l. 637).

SER   soleo hercle ego garrire nugas.
      ita loquor.

LYC   at scin quo modo?

SER   uel hercle enica, numquam hinc feres a me

                *   *   *

The ending of the Aulularia *was already missing in the arche-type of the Palatine family because none of the extant manu-scripts has it. Unfortunately, the Ambrosian Palimpsest does not contain our play at all. Still, the ancient plot summaries and a few fragments quoted by ancient scholars in order to illustrate grammatical points allow us to reconstruct the ending.*[49] *Ly-conides manages to get the pot of gold from his slave and returns it to Euclio. Euclio is touched by Lyconides' honesty and con-sents to the marriage. He realizes that the gold cannot make him happy and gives it as a dowry to Lyconides, whose bride has given birth to a son. Lyconides' slave is presumably set free, like the slave Gripus in the* Rudens, *who was equally unwilling to part with the treasure he found.*

---

[49] Fr. i: Non. p. 863 Lindsay, a *strophium* is a "short bandage that keeps the swelling breasts of girls in place." Fr. ii is quoted by Gellius (6. 9. 6) to show that the original reduplication vowel was -*e*-. Fr. iii: Non. p. 333 L., *scrobes* can be masculine. Fr. iv: Non. p. 140 L., *diu* can mean "by day." Fr. v: Non. p. 172 L., *hallec* is neuter. Fr. vi: Non. p. 13–14 L., *caperrare* means "frown." Fr. vii: Non. p. 523 L., *legere* can mean "snatch away."

SER   I'm not used to talking serious stuff. It's my way of speaking.

LYC   But you know what? (*grabs him*)

SER   You can even kill me! You'll never carry it away from me.

Fragment i comes from another speech about women's spending; the speaker is probably Megadorus, but it could also be Euclio. Fragment ii describes the behavior of Lyconides' servant, who stole the gold. Fragments iii and iv, both spoken by Euclio, come from the scene in which he gives the gold to the young couple; he describes his paranoid behavior when he still had the gold and his hope that he will now enjoy inner peace. Fragment v is more problematic. It could be assigned to Lyconides' slave, who in addition to his freedom (the raw vegetables) wants some payment (the fish sauce), just as Epidicus expects more than merely his freedom.

Fragments vi and vii probably do not belong here at all. Fragment vi, quoted by Nonius as coming from Varro's Eumenides, *has sometimes been assigned to our play because of the name Strobilus. Nonius is also the source of fragment vii, which he says is from the* Aulularia. *However, he must be wrong because neither the extant play itself nor the plot summaries mention a pimp, a person that would be out of place in this comedy.*

PLAUTUS

FRAGMENTA

i   pro illis corcotis, strophiis, sumptu uxorio
ii   ut ammemordit hominem!
iii   EVC   ego effodiebam in die denos scrobes
iv   EVC   nec noctu nec diu quietus umquam eram; nunc dor-
             miam.
v   SER   qui mi holera cruda ponunt, hallec adduint.

FRAGMENTA DVBIA

vi   quin mihi caperratam tuam frontem, Strobile, omittis?
vii   sed leno egreditur foras,
        hinc ex occulto sermonatus sublegam.

THE POT OF GOLD

FRAGMENTS

	instead of those saffron dresses, breast bands, and expenditures of wives	i
	How he fleeced the chap!	ii
EUC	I used to dig ten ditches a day.	iii
EUC	Neither at night nor by day was I ever calm; now I'll be able to sleep.	iv
SER	Those who serve me raw vegetables should add fish sauce.[50]	v

FRAGMENTS OF UNCERTAIN ORIGIN

| | Why don't you stop frowning at me, Strobilus? | vi |
| | But the pimp's coming out. I'll take in his conversation from here from a hidden spot. | vii |

[50] Pliny the Elder (*nat. hist.* 31. 93–95) describes what *hallec* is. Guts of fish and other refuse are mixed with salt and fermented. The liquid coming out is *garum*. The sediment is *hallec*.

BACCHIDES,

OR

THE TWO BACCHISES

INTRODUCTORY NOTE

It has been known for a long time that Plautus' *Bacchides* is based on Menander's *Dis exapaton* (The Double Deceiver). Even though only a few lines of Menander's work were known, in 1836 Ritschl was able to prove this relationship beyond reasonable doubt by establishing three links between the plays. The first is the correspondence between a line from Menander's piece (cited by Stobaeus, *Eclogae* 4. 52b. 27) and ll. 816–17 from the *Bacchides*: ὃν οἱ θεοὶ φιλοῦσιν ἀποθνῄσκει νέος (he whom the gods love dies young) is the model for *quem di diligunt adulescens moritur*. Second, Ritschl noted that another quotation of Menander's play (fr. 5 Sandbach) must come from a passage similar to the one in which Plautus' slave invents a story about the priest of Diana of Ephesus (ll. 306–13). And finally, he pointed out that Plautus' comedy contains references to a double deception (ll. 975, 1090ᵃ, 1128).

More than a hundred years later, a dream of all students of Plautus became true: in 1968 Handley identified thirteen broken fragments of the Oxyrhynchus papyri as constituting some sixty lines of Menander's *Dis exapaton*, and the *Bacchides* suddenly assumed a degree of importance it had never had before. Now it was possible for the first time to put Menander next to Plautus and to compare how the

Roman poet used his Greek sources. Scholars could see more clearly than ever how Plautus at times translated relatively literally, while at other times he left out parts of the original or expanded it and added his own flavor. More on this topic can be found in the introduction to this volume; now we should turn to the plot itself.

Unfortunately, the beginning of the play has been lost. None of the Palatine manuscripts contains it, which means that already the archetype of this family lacked it. The Ambrosian palimpsest is available for some sections, but sadly not for the beginning. However, various Roman scholars have preserved quotations from the *Bacchides*, and some of these quotations come from the lost part. These, together with the remainder of the play, enable us to reconstruct the background to the story and the lost opening. Mnesilochus, a young Athenian, went to Ephesus to bring back a large sum of gold belonging to his father, Nicobulus. On Samos, he met the courtesan Bacchis and fell in love with her. Bacchis was then hired by a soldier as his mistress. The contract states that she has to provide her services to him for a whole year or pay him back. Mnesilochus knew that she was on her way to Athens, so he sent a letter to his friend Pistoclerus, who was to find out about her whereabouts. Pistoclerus has indeed found Bacchis. She is staying at her sister's place in Athens but is afraid that she might have to leave with the soldier. For reasons no longer clear to us, this sister is also called Bacchis.

At this point the manuscripts are available again. The Athenian Bacchis, henceforth just Bacchis, persuades a reluctant Pistoclerus to help her protect the Samian Bacchis, who in discussions of the play is normally just referred to as

Sister. Pistoclerus falls in love with Bacchis and goes to buy food for Sister's welcome dinner. On his way back he is followed by Lydus, his old tutor, who is upset at his pupil's debauchery but nevertheless enters Bacchis' house with him.

When Pistoclerus leaves the house again, he meets Chrysalus, a cunning slave who had accompanied Mnesilochus to Ephesus. He tells Chrysalus that he has managed to find Bacchis. Chrysalus wants to trick Nicobulus out of his money so that his son can pay off the soldier. After this, Nicobulus meets Chrysalus, who tells him that Mnesilochus has returned home, but only with a small part of the money. Chrysalus claims that he does not know how small the sum is. This is intended to enable Mnesilochus to take as much money as he needs.

Mnesilochus is happy about his slave's trick and his friend's reliability. However, this happiness does not last for long. He overhears Lydus scolding Philoxenus, Pistoclerus' father, for being so lenient and allowing him to see Bacchis. Mnesilochus wants to defend his friend and says that Pistoclerus was helping someone else. But Lydus reports that Pistoclerus has made love to Bacchis. Mnesilochus is shocked because he does not know that there are two Bacchises and that Pistoclerus loves the Athenian, while he himself loves the Samian. Lydus and Philoxenus misjudge the situation and think that Mnesilochus is upset at Pistoclerus' debauchery. Philoxenus asks Mnesilochus to bring his son back to the path of virtue. Mnesilochus promises to do so. He returns all the money to his father, begs him to spare Chrysalus, and then goes to reproach Pistoclerus. Pistoclerus is annoyed and explains to him that there are two Bacchises.

Mnesilochus finds out that his friend has spoken the

truth and is depressed because he did not trust him and returned the money to his father. The situation deteriorates further when the soldier's hanger-on comes and announces that the soldier will take Sister to Elatia unless she can pay him back. Chrysalus promises to help. He dictates a letter from Mnesilochus to Nicobulus, warning him of more tricks masterminded by Chrysalus himself. Then he tells the two young men to go in and hold a banquet with the courtesans. Chrysalus brings the letter to Nicobulus, who has him tied up immediately. But Chrysalus convinces Nicobulus that he is being fooled by his son. They go to Bacchis' house and see the banquet, without being seen themselves. Chrysalus says to Nicobulus that the woman his son is with is a soldier's wife. The soldier comes. Nicobulus agrees to buy his son off, and Chrysalus arranges the deal and sends the soldier away. Chrysalus then goes in to the two young men, claiming that he will scold them. Soon he reappears with a second letter from Mnesilochus. In the letter, Mnesilochus expresses remorse and asks for more money to fulfill a promise he had made to the woman. Nicobulus gives this second sum to Chrysalus and leaves in order to pay the soldier.

On his return he is very angry because the soldier has told him that the woman is not his wife. He meets Philoxenus, and the two go to Bacchis' house to take revenge. The two sisters come out, ridicule the old men, and try to seduce them in order that they should forgive their sons. Philoxenus succumbs almost immediately, just like his son did earlier, while Nicobulus gives in less quickly, also like his son. The play ends with a somewhat apologetic epilogue that tells the audience that they should not be angry with the poet since he is only depicting reality.

When was the first performance of Plautus' play? In l. 53 there is a pun on Bacchis and Bacchants. Bacchants were becoming notorious around 190, and in 186 the senate severely curtailed the activities of the cult. However, the allusion is so general that it cannot help us to date the comedy, and since Plautus introduced the name Bacchis, the presence of the pun is less surprising than its absence would be. In l. 214 Plautus refers to his play *Epidicus*. Clearly, the *Bacchides* is later than *Epidicus*, but the latter is not so easy to date. The most helpful internal reference is in ll. 1072–73. Chrysalus says that he does not want to hold a triumph because that would be too common a thing to do. This could well be a reference to the year 189, when four triumphs were held, by Scipio Asiaticus, Aemilius Regillus, Fabius Labeo, and Aemilius Paullus. If this is correct, the *Bacchides* is a late work. This is in keeping with the use of *cantica*. It is generally acknowledged that the later plays contain more sung passages, and our play is especially rich in song.

SELECT BIBLIOGRAPHY

Editions and Commentaries

Barsby, J. A. (1991), *Plautus: Bacchides; Edited with Translation and Commentary* (3rd corr. repr. Warminster).

Questa, C. (2008), *Titus Maccius Plautus: Bacchides* (Sarsina).

THE TWO BACCHISES

Criticism

Bader, B. (1970), "Der verlorene Anfang der plautinischen Bacchides," *Rheinisches Museum für Philologie* NS 113: 304–23.

Gaiser, K. (1970), "Die plautinischen 'Bacchides' und Menanders 'Dis Exapaton,'" *Philologus* 114: 51–87.

Jocelyn, H. D. (1969), "Chrysalus and the Fall of Troy (Plautus, *Bacchides* 925–978)," *Harvard Studies in Classical Philology* 73: 135–52.

Law, H. (1929), "The Metrical Arrangement of the Fragments of the *Bacchides*," *Classical Philology* 24: 197–201.

Raffaelli, R., and A. Tontini (eds.) (2001), *Lecturae Plautinae Sarsinates IV: Bacchides (Sarsina, 9 settembre 2000)* (Urbino).

Schönbeck, H.-P. (1981), *Beiträge zur Interpretation der plautinischen "Bacchides"* (Düsseldorf).

Skutsch, O. (1982), "Notes on Plautus' *Bacchides*," *Harvard Studies in Classical Philology* 86: 79–80.

Tränkle, H. (1975), "Zu zwei umstrittenen Stellen der plautinischen Bacchides,"*Museum Helveticum* 32: 115–23.

BACCHIDES

PERSONAE

BACCHIS meretrix
ANCILLA
PISTOCLERVS adulescens
PVER
SOROR BACCHIDIS meretrix
LYDVS paedagogus
CHRYSALVS seruos
NICOBVLVS senex
MNESILOCHVS adulescens
PHILOXENVS senex
PARASITVS
ARTAMO lorarius
CLEOMACHVS miles

THE TWO BACCHISES

CHARACTERS

BACCHIS a prostitute; from Athens
SLAVE-GIRL OF BACCHIS only appears in the first scene
PISTOCLERUS a young man; reliable friend of
   Mnesilochus, falls in love with the Athenian Bacchis
BOY serves Cleomachus
SISTER OF BACCHIS also a prostitute; from Samos
LYDUS a slave-tutor; tried to bring up Pistoclerus strictly
CHRYSALUS a slave; serves Mnesilochus
NICOBULUS an old man; father of Mnesilochus
MNESILOCHUS a young man; just returned from Ephesus,
   loves the Bacchis from Samos
PHILOXENUS an old man; father of Pistoclerus
HANGER-ON follows Cleomachus
ARTAMO a slave overseer; serves Nicobulus
CLEOMACHUS a soldier; also loves the Bacchis from
   Samos

SCAENA

Athenis

The stage represents a street in Athens. There are two houses on it, with an altar of Apollo in between: the house on the left belongs to Bacchis; the one on the right belongs to Mnesilochus and his father. The street leads to the harbor on the left and to the city center on the right. The house of Pistoclerus and his father is not on stage but presumably lies on the way to the forum.

---

¹ Fr. i: Fest. p. 168 Lindsay, a *nassiterna* is a type of vessel with handles for water. Fr. ii: Char. *gramm.* 283. 24–27 Barwick, *strenuus* has *strenue* as adverb. Fr. iii: Pomp. *gramm.* v. 199. 10–17 Keil: *lacte* is an alternative form for *lac*. Fr. iv: Serv. *ad Aen.* 6. 383, *cognominis* can be masculine or feminine. Fr. v: Serv. Dan. *ad Aen.* 10. 493, *quidquid* stands for *quodcumque*. Fr. vi: Char. *gramm.* 260. 7–10 B. quotes this passage because of the old form *gratiis*. Fr. vii: Char. *gramm.* 261. 27–262. 3 B., *ilico* can stand for *in loco*. Fr. viii: Serv. Dan. *ad Aen.* 12. 7, *latro* means "soldier." Fr. ix: Non. p. 541 Lindsay, *modicus* can mean "modest." Fr. x: Non. p. 254 L., *saeuitudo* is an alternative form for *saeuitia*. Fr. xi: Non. p. 761 L. cites part of this passage because of the active *opino*; Prisc. *add. gramm.* ii. 575 Keil cites the full text because of *cuias* "where from," but has the modernized *opinor*. Fr. xii: Non. p. 254 L., *suauitudo* is an alternative form for *suauitas*. Fr. xiii: Don. *ad Eun.* 641: *amare* can mean "make love." Fr. xiv: Non. p. 681 L., *cupido* is uncontrollable love, *amor* is rational. Fr. xv: Non. p. 9 L., *exercitus* means "exhausted." Fr. xvi: Non. p. 525 L., *limare* can mean "to connect." Fr. xvii: Non. p. 525 L., *limax* is the adjective of *limare* (since the word is normally a noun meaning "snail," this must be a pun). Fr. xviii: Don. *ad And.* 205 cites this passage in a discussion of double and triple nega-

STAGING

The beginning of the play has been lost, together with a plot summary. Nevertheless, it is quite clear what the beginning must have contained (see the general introduction to this play). It is also relatively certain that the lost passage can hardly have been longer than two hundred to three hundred verses, otherwise the play would have been excessively long.

Not only do we have a good idea of the contents and the length of the lost passage, but we can also reconstruct some of its structure. The Codex uetus Camerarii has preserved traces of an algebraic notation of speakers; the first speaker to appear is A, the second B, and so on. Since Bacchis is abbreviated A, we can assume that she was the first to appear in the play. Interestingly, she was also the first person to appear in Menander's original, of which we know half of the opening line (fr. 1 Sandbach). The second speaker in the Bacchides *was Bacchis' servant, so the first scene was probably a dialogue between the two. The third speaker in Plautus' play was Pistoclerus. Since he is the character who knows most of the background to the play, he presumably delivered a delayed prologue. The fourth speaker was the soldier's servant, who is likely to have accompanied the fifth speaker, Bacchis' sister.*

Various Roman scholars have preserved quotations from the lost beginning of our play because they are interesting to grammarians or lexicographers.[1] The traditional arrangement

---

tions. Fr. xix: Non. p. 145 L., *excantare* means "to take out." Fr. xx: Char. *gramm.* 157. 10–15 B., *Arabus* is an alternative form for *Arabs*. Fr. xxi: Gloss. Plaut. gramm. iii. 58. 2, *noenum* is an alternative form for *non*.

of these fragments can be inferred from the numbers in brack-
ets; it is also the arrangement adhered to by Lindsay and the
most recent editor of the play, Cesare Questa. Questa does not
actually believe that the traditional order of the fragments re-
flects the order in the text as Plautus wrote it, but he prefers to
leave it unchanged because there are too many uncertainties.

Some uncertainties will always remain, but we can at least
establish a modest amount of order. We know that most Plautine
plays begin in senarii, followed by a sung passage, which in its
turn is followed by a recitative in long verses. Even if the lost
passage was three hundred lines long, there is room only for a
single passage in senarii, a single song, and a single passage in
long verses. Thus we can at least arrange the fragments into
three groups, although some fragments are metrically unclear
and the order within the three groups is not without problems
either.

The arrangement of fragments in this edition presumes the
following structure: in the first scene Bacchis and her servant

FRAGMENTA

i (iv)		ecquis euocat	
		cum nassiterna et cum aqua istum impurissumum?	
ii (iii)		conuerrite * scopis, agite strenue	
iii (v)		sicut lacte lactis simile est	
iv (vi)	BAC	illa mea cognominis fuit	5
v (xvi)		quicquid est nomen sibi	
vi (xix)	BAC	sin lenocinium forte collibitum est tibi,	
		uideas mercedis quid tibi est aequom dari,	
		ne istac aetate me sectere gratiis.	

have the house cleaned in preparation for Sister's arrival (fr. i–ii); in this scene the reason for the identical names is also discussed (fr. iii–v). Then Pistoclerus arrives but gets a cool reception from Bacchis (fr. vi). He is the speaker of the prologue (fr. vii–viii). The soldier's servant appears with Sister and delivers a "good slave's speech" in which he praises himself and speaks of the punishments in store for bad slaves (fr. ix–x); this is the beginning of the first song. What follows is a dialogue between this servant and Sister, who dismisses the soldier and speaks of her love for Mnesilochus (fr. xi–xiv). Pistoclerus overhears the conversation and realizes that Sister is the woman he was looking for (fr. xv). The soldier's servant recites part of Sister's contract; contracts are always in senarii, so the abrupt change of metre from song to senarii is not problematic. Sister mocks him (fr. xi). When she meets Bacchis, long verses begin. Sister praises Athens (fr. xviii) and asks Bacchis for help (fr. xviii). The last two fragments consist of one word each, which means that their place in the lost passage is unclear.

FRAGMENTS

		Is anyone calling out that most filthy wretch with a bucket and water?	i (iv)
		sweep it up with your brooms, be strenuous	ii (iii)
		just as alike as milk is to milk	iii (v)
5	BAC	that sister of mine had the same name	iv (vi)
		whatever his[2] name is	v (xvi)
	BAC	But if perhaps you've developed an interest in pandering, you should see what pay you ought to be given, so you don't follow me for nothing at *your* age.	vi (xix)

[2] Or "her name"; reflexive pronouns are unmarked for gender in Latin.

vii (xv)	PIS	Vlixem audiui fuisse aerumnosissumum,	10
		quia annos uiginti errans a patria afuit;	
		uerum hic adulescens multo Vlixem anteit ‹malis›,	
		qui ilico errat intra muros ciuicos.	
viii (vii)	PIS	(latro) suam qui auro uitam uenditat	
ix (i)	PVER	quibus ingenium in animo utibile est, modicum et sine	15
		uernilitate	
x (ii)	PVER	uincla, uirgae, molae: saeuitudo mala	
		fit peior	
xi (viii)	PVER	scio spiritum eius maiorem esse multo	
		quam folles taurini habent, quom liquescunt	
		petrae, ferrum ubi fit.	20
	SOR	quoiatem esse aiebant?	
		Praenestinum opino esse, ita erat gloriosus.	
xii (xii)	SOR	cor meum, spes mea,	
		mel meum, suauitudo, cibus, gaudium.	
xiii (xiii)	SOR	sine te amem	
xiv (xiv)	PVER	‹-› Cupidon tecum saeuit anne Amor?	25
xv (xvii)	PIS	quae sodalem atque me exercitos habet	
xvi (x)	PVER	neque a quoquam acciperes alio mercedem annuam	
		nisi ab sese, nec cum quiquam limares caput.	
xvii (xi)	SOR	limaces uiri	
xviii (ix)	SOR	neque ‹id› hau subditiua gloria oppidum arbitror.	30
xix (xviii)	SOR	nam credo quoiuis excantare cor potes.	
xx (xx)		Arabus	
xxi (xxi)		noenum	33

12 malis *add. O. Skutsch*, fide *add. Leo*

20 cuiatem esse aiebat *in Prisciani ms.* Z, quoiatis tibi uisust *suppl.*
Ritschl

30 id *add. Ritschl*

10	PIS	I've heard that Ulysses was terribly afflicted by troubles because he was away from his home for twenty years, going astray; but this young man (*points to himself*) by far surpasses Ulysses in his misfortunes, a chap who is going astray here inside the city walls.	vii (xv)
	PIS	(a mercenary) who sells his life for gold	viii (vii)
15	BOY	those who have a useful mind in their heads, modest and without slavishness	ix (i)
	BOY	shackles, rods, the mill: bad savagery gets worse	x (ii)
20	BOY	I know that his breath is much stronger than the puffs which ox-hide bellows let out, when boulders are melting, when iron is being produced.	xi (viii)
	SIS	Where did they say he is from? I think he is from Praeneste, to judge from his pompous behavior.	
	SIS	my heart, my hope, my honey, sweetness, nourishment, delight	xii (xii)
	SIS	let me make love to you	xiii (xiii)
25	BOY	Is Cupid or Love venting his anger on you?	xiv (xiv)
	PIS	the girl who has exhausted my friend and me	xv (xvii)
	BOY	you wouldn't take a yearly fee from anyone other than him, and you wouldn't rub heads with anyone else.	xvi (x)
	SIS	rubbing men	xvii (xi)
30	SIS	And I don't think this town has its fame for nothing.	xviii (ix)
	SIS	I think you can charm anyone's heart out.	xix (xviii)
		Arabian	xx (xx)
		not at all	xxi (xxi)

ACTVS I

I. i: BACCHIS. SOROR. PISTOCLERVS

*　　*　　*

35　BAC　quid si hoc potis est ut tu taceas, ego loquar?

SOR　　　　　　　　　　　　　　　　　lepide, licet.

BAC　ubi me fugiet memoria, ibi tu facito ut subuenias, soror.

SOR　pol magis metuo ne defuerit mi in monendo oratio.

BAC　pol ego metuo lusciniolae ne defuerit cantio.
　　　sequere hac.

PIS　　　　quid agunt duae germanae meretrices cognomines?

40　　quid in consilio consuluistis?

BAC　　　　　　　　　　　　　bene.

PIS　　　　　　　　　　　　　　pol hau meretricium est.

BAC　miserius nihil est quam mulier.

PIS　　　　　　　　　　　　　quid esse dicis dignius?

BAC　haec ita me orat sibi qui caueat aliquem ut hominem re-
　　　periam,
　　　ut istunc militem—ut, ubi emeritum sibi sit, se reuehat
　　　domum.
　　　id, amabo te, huic caueas.

PIS　　　　　　　　　　　quid isti caueam?

BAC　　　　　　　　　　　　　ut reuehatur domum,

45　　ubi ei dediderit operas, ne hanc ille habeat pro ancilla
　　　sibi;
　　　nam si haec habeat aurum quod illi renumeret, faciat lu-
　　　bens.

PIS　ubi nunc is homo est?

38 pol quoque *B*, pol ego quoque *CD*, pol ego *Reiz*

370

ACT ONE

BACCHIS is in front of her house, talking to her SISTER.
PISTOCLERUS is standing at a distance.

*   *   *

BAC	How about you keeping quiet and me doing the talking?	35
SIS	Lovely, by all means.	
BAC	When my memory fails me, then mind you come to my help, dear sister.	
SIS	Heavens, I am more afraid that words might fail me when giving you advice.	
BAC	Heavens, and *I* am afraid that song might fail the nightingale. Follow me this way. (*moves toward Pistoclerus*)	
PIS	(*aside*) What are the two sisters doing, prostitutes with the same name? (*to them*) What counsel did you take in your council?	40
BAC	Good counsel.	
PIS	Well, that's unusual for prostitutes.	
BAC	Nothing is more wretched than a woman.	
PIS	What do you say deserves it more?	
DAC	This girl asks me to find her someone to take care that this soldier—that he takes her back home when he's received her services. Please, do take care of this for her.	
PIS	What should I take care of for her?	
BAC	That she's taken back home when she's given him her services, so he doesn't keep her as his slave-girl. Well, if she had the money to pay him back now she'd do so happily.	45
PIS	Where is this person now?	

BAC   iam hic credo aderit. sed hoc idem apud nos rectius
poteris agere; atque is dum ueniat sedens ibi opperibere.
eadem biberis, eadem dedero tibi ubi biberis sauium.

50 PIS   uiscus merus uostra est blanditia.
     BAC   quid iam?
     PIS   quia enim intellego,
duae unum expetitis palumbem, peri, harundo alas uer-
     berat.

non ego istuc facinus mi, mulier, conducibile esse arbi-
     tror.
     BAC qui, amabo?
     PIS   quia, Bacchis, Bacchas metuo et bacchanal tuom.
     BAC quid est? quid metuis? ne tibi lectus malitiam apud me
     suadeat?

55 PIS   magis illectum tuom quam lectum metuo. mala tu es bes-
     tia.

nam huic aetati non conducit, mulier, latebrosus locus.
     BAC egomet, apud me si quid stulte facere cupias, prohibeam.
sed ego apud me te esse ob eam rem, miles quom ueniat,
     uolo,
quia, quom tu aderis, huic mihique hau faciet quisquam
     iniuriam:

60   tu prohibebis, et eadem opera tuo sodali operam dabis;
et ille adueniens tuam med esse amicam suspicabitur.
quid, amabo, opticuisti?
     PIS   quia istaec lepida sunt memoratui:
eadem in usu atque ubi periclum facias aculeata sunt,
animum fodicant, bona distimulant, facta et famam sau-
     ciant.

64 distimulant *CD*, destimulant *uel* destimalant *BT*

BAC He'll be here soon, I believe. But you'll be able to deal
with this matter better at our place. And until he comes
you'll be sitting there waiting. You'll have a drink too, and
I'll give you a kiss too when you've had your drink.

PIS Your flattery is pure birdlime. 50

BAC How so?

PIS Because I understand you two are trying to catch one
pigeon.[3] (*aside*) I'm done for, the twig[4] is hitting my
wings. (*to Bacchis*) Madam, I don't think that that kind of
behavior is good for me.

BAC How so, please?

PIS Because, Bacchis, I'm afraid of Bacchants and your
shrine of Bacchus.

BAC What's that? What are you afraid of? That my bed could
persuade you to do something naughty at my place?

PIS I'm more afraid of your bidding than your bed. You're a 55
bad beast: woman, a shady place is no good for someone
of my age.

BAC If you wanted to do anything stupid at my place, I myself
would prevent you from doing it. But when the soldier
comes, I'd like you to be with me for the simple reason
that when you're there, no one will wrong her (*points to
her sister*) or me. Your presence will prevent it, and at the 60
same time you'll support your friend. And when the sol-
dier comes here he'll suspect I'm your girlfriend. Please,
why have you fallen silent?

PIS Because these things are pleasant to talk about; the very
same things are thorny in practice, when you try them
out: they hurt your heart, torture your possessions, and
wound character and reputation.

---

[3] Also a term for a simpleton, with an obscene double meaning
("penis"). [4] The twig with the birdlime on it.

65	SOR	quid ab hac metuis?
	PIS	quid ego metuam, rogitas, adulescens homo?

penetrem ‹me› huius modi in palaestram, ubi damnis
    desudascitur?

ubi pro disco damnum capiam, pro cursura dedecus,

69   ubique imponat in manum alius mihi pro cestu cantha-
      rum?

68   BAC lepide memoras.

      PIS   ubi ego capiam pro machaera turturem,

70   pro galea scaphium, pro insigni sit corolla plectilis,

pro hasta talos, pro lorica malacum capiam pallium,

ubi mi pro equo lectus detur, scortum pro scuto accubet?

apage a me, apage.

      BAC   ah, nimium ferus es.

      PIS   mihi sum.

      BAC   malacissandus es.

equidem tibi do hanc operam.

      PIS   ah, nimium pretiosa es operaria.

75   BAC simulato me amare.

      PIS   utrum ego istuc iocon assimulem an serio?

      BAC heia, hoc agere meliust. miles quom huc adueniat, te
        uolo

me amplexari.

      PIS   quid eo mihi opust?

      BAC   ut ille te uideat uolo.

scio quid ago.

      PIS   et pol ego scio quid metuo. sed quid ais?

      BAC   quid est?

66 penetrare *P*, penetrem ‹me› *Bothe*
68–9 *transp. Langen*

SIS What do you fear from her?   65

PIS What do I fear, you ask, I, a young man? I should enter a
     gymnasium of this sort where one sweats losses? Where
     I'd take to debt instead of the discus, to shame instead of
     running? Where someone else would place a jug in my
     hand instead of a boxing-glove?

BAC You speak in such a lovely way.

PIS Where I'd take a turtle-dove instead of the sword, where   70
     I'd have a cup instead of a helmet and a plaited garland
     instead of a soldier's crown,[5] where I'd take dice instead
     of the spear and an effeminate cloak instead of my cui-
     rass, where I'd be given a bed instead of a horse, and
     where a sheila would be lying with me instead of a shield?
     Away from me, away!

BAC Ah, you're too wild.

PIS For my own benefit.

BAC You need to be softened. I'll do this work for *you*.

PIS Oh, you're too expensive a worker.

BAC Pretend to love me.   75

PIS Should I pretend this in jest or in earnest?

BAC Well now! You'd better pay attention. When the soldier
     comes here, I want you to embrace me.

PIS What do I need to do that for?

BAC I want him to see you. I know what I'm doing.

PIS God, and I know what I'm fearing. But what do you say?

BAC What is it?

---

[5] Garlands are worn at banquets; the soldier's crown is a decoration
for bravery.

PIS	quid si apud te eueniat desubito prandium aut potatio
80	forte aut cena, ut solet in istis fieri conciliabulis,
	ubi ego tum accubem?
BAC	apud me, mi anime, ut lepidus cum lepida accubet.
	locus hic apud nos, quamuis subito uenias, semper liber est.
	ubi tu lepide uoles esse tibi, "mea rosa," mihi dicito,
	"dato qui bene sit": ego ubi bene sit tibi locum lepidum dabo.
85 PIS	rapidus fluuius est hic, non hac temere transiri potest.
BAC	atque ecastor apud hunc fluuium aliquid perdundum est tibi.
	manum da et sequere.
PIS	aha, minime.
BAC	quid ita?
PIS	quia istoc illecebrosius
	fieri nil potest, nox, mulier, uinum, homini adulescentulo.
BAC	age igitur, equidem pol nihili facio nisi causa tua.
90	ill' quidem hanc abducet; tu nullus affueris, si non lubet.
PIS	sumne autem nihili qui nequeam ingenio moderari meo?
BAC	quid est quod metuas?
PIS	nihil est, nugae. mulier, tibi me emancupo:
	tuos sum, tibi dedo operam.
BAC	lepidu's. nunc ego te facere hoc uolo.
	ego sorori meae cenam hodie dare uolo uiaticam:
95	eo tibi argentum iubebo iam intus efferri foras;
	tu facito opsonatum nobis sit opulentum opsonium.

81 accumbem *B*, accubam *B²C*, accubiam *D*, accubem *Camerarius*

PIS   What if by any chance a lunch or a drinks party or a din-
ner suddenly took place at your establishment, as it nor-
mally happens in those resorts, where would I lie then?   81

BAC   With me, my darling, so that a lovely lover is lying with a
lovely lady. However suddenly you might come, here at
our place there's always a free space. When you want to
have a lovely time, say to me, "my rose, give me some
fun"; I'll give you a lovely place where you can have some
fun.

PIS   (*half aside*) This is a rapid stream, it can't be crossed care-   85
lessly here.

BAC   (*aside*) And, good god, you'll have to lose something at
this river. (*to Pistoclerus*) Give me your hand and fol-
low me.

PIS   No, not a bit of it.

BAC   Why not?

PIS   Because nothing more enticing can happen to a young
man than that: night, a woman, and wine.

BAC   Go on now, it's not important to me, except for your sake.
The soldier will take her away. Don't help me if you don't   90
want to.

PIS   (*aside*) Aren't I useless, being unable to control myself?

BAC   What is it that you're afraid of?

PIS   (*after a pause*) It's nothing, nonsense. Madam, I surren-
der myself to you. I'm yours, I'm giving you my attention.

BAC   You're a sweetie. Now I'd like you to do this: I want
to give my sister a welcome dinner today. I'll have the   95
money brought out to you in a moment. You mind that a
rich meal is bought for us.

PIS ego opsonabo, nam id flagitium meum sit, mea te gratia
et operam dare mi et ad eam operam facere sumptum de
tuo.

BAC at ego nolo dare te quicquam.

PIS   sine.

BAC   sino equidem, si lubet.

100   propera, amabo.

PIS   prius hic adero quam te amare desinam.

SOR bene me accipies aduenientem, mea soror.

BAC   quid ita, opsecro?

SOR quia piscatus meo quidem animo hic tibi hodie euenit
bonus.

BAC meus illequidem est. tibi nunc operam dabo de Mnesilo-
cho, soror,

ut hic accipias potius aurum quam hinc eas cum milite.

105 SOR cupio.

BAC   dabitur opera. aqua calet: eamus hinc intro ut laues.

106   nam uti naui uecta es, credo, timida es.

SOR   aliquantum, soror.

107   simul huic nescioquoi, turbare qui huc it, decedamus
⟨hinc⟩.

[106ᵃ BAC nam uti naui uecta es, credo, timida es.

SOR   aliquantum, soror.]

BAC sequere hac igitur me intro in tectum ut sedes lassitu-
dinem.

106ᵃ *uersum delent plerique edd.*
107 hinc *add. Ritschl*
108 in lectum *P,* in tectum *Tränkle*

378

PIS   I'll do the buying myself, because it would be a disgrace
for me if you were making an effort for my sake and had
to spend money of your own for that effort.

BAC   But I don't want you to give me anything.

PIS   Let me do it.

BAC   Yes, I'll let you do it if you like. Hurry, please.   100

PIS   I'll be back here before I stop loving you.

Exit PISTOCLERUS to the right.

SIS   You'll be giving me a good welcome on my arrival, my
sister.

BAC   What do you mean, please?

SIS   Because at least to my mind you've made a good catch of
fish here today.

BAC   Yes, that boy's mine. Now I'll help you out with Mnesilo-
chus, my sister, so you can receive some gold here instead
of going away with the soldier.

SIS   I'm keen.   105

BAC   I'll help you out. The water's hot; let's go inside so you can
wash. Well, after travelling on ship you're shaky, I think.

SIS   A bit, my sister. (*looks into the distance*) At the same time
let's get away from here from this stranger who is coming
here to cause trouble.

[BAC   Well, after travelling on ship you're shaky, I think.

SIS   A bit, my sister.]

BAC   Then follow me this way into the house so you can relax
from your exhaustion.

Exeunt BACCHIS and SISTER into her house.
*Enter PISTOCLERUS and LYDUS from the right, followed by
servants carrying provisions.*

I. ii: LYDVS. PISTOCLERVS

LYD	iam dudum, Pistoclere, tacitus te sequor,
110	exspectans quas tu res hoc ornatu geras.
	namque ita me di ament, ut Lycurgus mi quidem
	uidetur posse hic ad nequitiam adducier.
	quo nunc capessis ted hinc aduorsa uia
	cum tanta pompa?
PIS	huc.
LYD	quid "huc"? quis istic habet?
115 PIS	Amor, Voluptas, Venus, Venustas, Gaudium,
	Iocus, Ludus, Sermo, Suauisauiatio.
LYD	quid tibi commerci est cum dis damnosissumis?
PIS	mali sunt homines qui bonis dicunt male;
	tu dis nec recte dicis: non aequom facis.
120 LYD	an deus est ullus Suauisauiatio?
PIS	an non putasti esse umquam? o Lyde, es barbarus;
	quem ego sapere nimio censui plus quam Thalem,
	is stultior es barbaro poticio,
	qui tantus natu deorum nescis nomina.
125 LYD	non hic placet mi ornatus.
PIS	nemo ergo tibi
	haec apparauit: mihi paratum est quoi placet.
LYD	etiam me aduorsus exordire argutias?
	qui si decem habeas linguas, mutum esse addecet.
PIS	non omnis aetas, Lyde, ludo conuenit.
130	magis unum in mentem est mihi nunc, satis ut commode
	pro dignitate opsoni haec concuret coquos.

123 poticio *BCD*³, potio *D*¹, putitium Plautus dixit pro stulto *Paul.*
Fest. 241 Lindsay

---

6 Spartan lawgiver, famous for his temperance and self-control.
7 One of the Seven Sages, a polymath developing several sciences.

LYD   I've been following you silently for a long time already, Pistoclerus, waiting to see what you were up to with this   110 gear. Why, as truly as the gods may love me, it seems to me that Lycurgus[6] himself could be led astray here. Where are you betaking yourself up the street now, with such a train?

PIS   Here. (*points to Bacchis' house*)

LYD   What, "here"? Who lives there?

PIS   Love, Pleasure, Charm, Grace, Joy, Wit, Playfulness,   115 Chit-chat, Sweetikiss.

LYD   What business have you with such harmful gods?

PIS   People who talk badly about the good are bad. You are talking badly about the gods. You aren't doing what's right.

LYD   Since when is there any god called Sweetikiss?   120

PIS   You've never thought there is such a god? O Lydus, you're a barbarian. I used to think you're far smarter than Thales,[7] but you're more stupid than a barbarian child.[8] At *your* age you don't know the names of the gods!

LYD   I don't like this outfit.   125

PIS   Well, no one's prepared these things for you: they've been prepared for me, and I like them.

LYD   Are you actually beginning to give me smart replies? Even if you had ten tongues, you still ought to be silent.

PIS   Not every age is fit for the school, Lydus. This one thing   130 weighs much more heavily on my mind, that the cook should take care of this stuff pleasantly enough, in accordance with the excellence of the comestibles.

[8] The meaning of *poticius* is unclear; the interpretation "child" was first advocated by Buecheler. Paul the Deacon thinks that the word means "idiot" (p. 241 Lindsay).

	LYD	iam perdidisti te atque me atque operam meam,
		qui tibi nequiquam saepe monstraui bene.
	PIS	ibidem ego meam operam perdidi, ubi tu tuam:
135		tua disciplina nec mihi prodest nec tibi.
	LYD	o praeligatum pectus!
	PIS	odiosus mihi es.
		tace atque sequere, Lyde, me.
	LYD	illuc sis uide,
		non "paedagogum" iam me, sed "Lydum" uocat.
	PIS	non par uidetur nec sit consentaneum,
140		quom haec ‹qui emit› intus sit et cum amica accubet
		quomque osculetur et conuiuae alii accubent,
		†praesentibus illis "paedagogus" una ut siet.†
	LYD	an hoc ad eas res opsonatum est, opsecro?
	PIS	sperat quidem animus: quo eueniat dis in manu est.
145	LYD	tu amicam habebis?
	PIS	quom uidebis, tum scies.
	LYD	immo neque habebis nec sinam. i prorsus domum.
	PIS	omitte, Lyde, ac caue malo.
	LYD	quid? "caue malo?"
	PIS	iam excessit mi aetas ex magisterio tuo.
	LYD	o barathrum, ubi nunc es? ut ego te usurpem lubens!
150		uideo nimio iam multo plus quam uolueram;
		uixisse nimio satiust iam quam uiuere.
		magistron quemquam discipulum minitarier?
		nil moror discipulos mi ess' tam plenos sanguinis:
		ualens afflictat me uaciuom uirium.

140 haec intus sit et *B*, haec intus intus sit et *CD*, hic intus sit et *S*, haec ‹qui emit› intus sit et *Leo*   142 una *secl. Lindsay (sed metrum nihilo minus displicet, nisi* illis praesente *scribas, cf. Amph. 400*), illis ut una paedagogus assiet *Trappes-Lomax per litteras*

LYD Now you've wasted yourself and me and my efforts; I of-
ten showed you the right way, but in vain.

PIS I've wasted my own efforts in the same place where
you've wasted yours. Your instruction helps neither me 135
nor you.

LYD O what an obstinate breast!

PIS You're getting on my nerves. Shut up and follow me,
Lydus.

LYD Just look at that! He isn't calling me "tutor" any longer,
but "Lydus."

PIS When the one who bought this is inside and lying with his 139
girlfriend, and when he's kissing her and other guests are
lying beside them, it wouldn't be appropriate or accept-
able for a "tutor" to be there in their presence.

LYD Please, was this food bought for these purposes?

PIS I do hope so; but the outcome is in the gods' hands.

LYD You will have a girlfriend? 145

PIS When you see her then you'll know.

LYD (*grabs him*) No, you won't have one and I won't allow it.
Go straight home!

PIS Drop it, Lydus, and watch out for trouble.

LYD (*obeying reluctantly*) What? "Watch out for trouble?"

PIS I'm too old now for having you as my tutor.

LYD O pit, where art thou now? How willingly would I use
thee! I'm already seeing far more than I ever wanted to. 150
Now it would be far better to have lived than to go on liv-
ing. Is it possible that any pupil is threatening his tutor? I
don't care for having such full-blooded pupils: a strong
one is bullying me, a man devoid of strength.

---

146 iturus sum *P*, i prorsus *Ritschl*, ituru's *Bothe*
153 iam *P*, tam *Bothe*

155 PIS fiam, ut ego opinor, Hercules, tu autem Linus.

LYD pol metuo magis ne Phoenix tuis factis fuam
teque ad patrem esse mortuom renuntiem.

PIS satis historiarum est.

LYD   hic uereri perdidit.
compendium edepol haud aetati optabile
160 fecisti quom istanc nactu's impudentiam.
occisus hic homo est. ecquid in mentem est tibi
patrem tibi esse?

PIS   tibi ego an tu mihi seruos es?

LYD peior magister te istaec docuit, non ego.
nimio es tu ad istas res discipulus docilior
165 quam ad illa quae te docui, ubi operam perdidi.
edepol fecisti furtum in aetatem malum
quom istaec flagitia me celauisti et patrem.

PIS istactenus tibi, Lyde, libertas data est
orationis. satis est. sequere hac me ac tace.

ACTVS II

II. i: CHRYSALVS

170 CHRY erilis patria, salue, quam ego biennio,
postquam hinc in Ephesum abii, conspicio lubens.
saluto te, uicine Apollo, qui aedibus
propinquos nostris accolis, ueneroque te
ne Nicobulum me sinas nostrum senem

171 abii *P*, abiui *Reiz*

---

[9] Linus was Hercules' music teacher and died at his hands.

[10] Phoenix accompanied Achilles to the Trojan war as a kind of tutor.
He brought the news of Achilles' death to his father, Peleus.

PIS   I'll become Hercules, I think, and you Linus.[9]   155

LYD   I'm more afraid that I might become Phoenix because of your behavior and that I might bring the word to your father that you've died.[10]

PIS   That's enough of those old stories.

LYD   (*as if addressing the audience*) He's lost his sense of shame. (*to Pistoclerus*) You didn't make an acquisition one would wish to see in a man of your age when you got your impudence. (*to the audience*) He's been killed. (*to* 161 *Pistoclerus*) Do you have it in your mind anywhere that you have a father?

PIS   Am I your slave or are you mine?

LYD   A worse tutor taught you these things, not I. You are a much more docile student of those subjects than of the ones I taught you, where I've wasted my effort. You prac- 166 tised bad deceit at your age when you concealed those misdeeds from me and your father.

PIS   Lydus, you've been given freedom of speech until now. It's enough. Follow me this way and shut up.

Exeunt PISTOCLERUS, LYDUS, and servants into Bacchis' house.

ACT TWO

Enter CHRYSALUS from the harbor.

CHRY   Greetings, land of my master; two years after going away 170 to Ephesus I see you with joy. (*turning to the altar*) I give my greetings to you, neighbor Apollo, you who dwell next to our house, and I beseech you, do not let Nicobu-

175   prius conuenire quam sodalem uiderim
    Mnesilochi Pistoclerum, quem ad epistulam
    Mnesilochus misit super amica Bacchide.

     II. ii: PISTOCLERVS. CHRYSALVS

PIS mirum est me ut redeam te opere tanto quaesere,
180   qui abire hinc nullo pacto possim, si uelim:
    ita me uadatum amore uinctumque attines.
CHRY pro di immortales, Pistoclerum conspicor.
    o Pistoclere, salue.
PIS   salue, Chrysale.
CHRY compendi uerba multa iam faciam tibi.
185   uenire tu me gaudes: ego credo tibi;
    hospitium et cenam pollicere, ut conuenit
    peregre aduenienti: ego autem uenturum annuo.
    salutem tibi ab sodali solidam nuntio:
    rogabis me ubi sit: uiuit.
PIS   nemp' recte ualet?
190 CHRY istuc uolebam ego ex te percontarier.
 PIS qui scire possum?
 CHRY   nullus plus.
 PIS   quemnam ad modum?
 CHRY quia si illa inuenta est quam ille amat, [uiuit] recte [et]
     ualet;
    si non inuenta est, minus ualet moribundusque est.
    anima est amica amanti: si abest, nullus est;
195   si adest, res nulla est: ipsus est . . . nequam et miser.
    sed tu quid factitasti mandatis super?
 PIS egon ut, quod ab illo attigisset nuntius,
    non impetratum id aduenienti ei redderem?
    regiones colere mauellem Accherunticas.

   192 uiuit, et *del. Bothe*   197 illo *P*, illoc *Ritschl*

lus, our old man, find me until I have seen Pistoclerus,   175
Mnesilochus' friend, to whom Mnesilochus sent a letter
about his girlfriend Bacchis.

Enter PISTOCLERUS from Bacchis' house.

PIS   (*calling back into the house*) It's strange that you ask me
so earnestly to come back; I couldn't go away from here   180
in any way even if I wanted to. You hold me fast, bonded
and bound by love.

CHRY   (*aside*) Immortal gods, I can see Pistoclerus. (*loudly*)
Hello, Pistoclerus.

PIS   Hello, Chrysalus.

CHRY   I'll save you a lot of words now. You're happy I've re-   185
turned. I believe you. You're promising me hospitality
and a dinner, as is appropriate for someone arriving from
abroad. And I nod in approval that I'll come. As a mes-
sage I give you hearty greetings from your friend. You'll
ask me where he is. He's alive.

PIS   And kicking, too?

CHRY   I wanted to ask *you* about that.   190

PIS   How can *I* know?

CHRY   No one can know better.

PIS   How so?

CHRY   Because if the girl he loves has been found, he's alive and
kicking; if she hasn't been found, he's unwell and close to
death. To a lover his girlfriend is his life. If she's away, he's
lost. If she's around, his money's lost and he himself is . . .   195
useless and miserable. But what have you done about his
instructions?

PIS   Would I not have sorted out for him on his arrival what
his message mentioned? I'd rather inhabit the nether re-
gions.

387

200   CHRY eho, an inuenisti Bacchidem?

       PIS   Samiam quidem.

     CHRY uide quaeso ne quis tractet illam indiligens;

               scis tu ut confringi uas cito Samium solet.

       PIS iamne ut soles?

     CHRY   dic ubi ea nunc est, opsecro.

       PIS hic, exeuntem me unde aspexisti modo.

205   CHRY ut istuc est lepidum! proxumae uiciniae

               habitat. ecquidnam meminit Mnesilochi?

       PIS   rogas?

          immo unice unum plurumi pendit.

     CHRY   papae!

       PIS immo ut eam credis? misera amans desiderat.

     CHRY scitum istuc.

       PIS   immo, Chrysale, em, non tantulum

210   umquam intermittit tempus quin eum nominet.

     CHRY tanto hercle melior [Bacchis].

       PIS   immo—

     CHRY   immo hercle abiero

          potius.

       PIS   num inuitus rem bene gestam audis eri?

     CHRY non res, sed actor mihi cor odio sauciat.

          etiam Epidicum, quam ego fabulam aeque ac me ipsum

            amo,

215   nullam aeque inuitus specto, si agit Pellio.

         sed Bacchis etiam fortis tibi uisa est?

       PIS   rogas?

         ni nanctus Venerem essem, hanc . . . Iunonem dicerem.

211 Bacchis *secl. Bentley*

---

[11] Samian pottery was the cheapest and of low quality.

CHRY Tell me, have you found Bacchis?   200

PIS Yes, the one from Samos.

CHRY Please, mind that no one handles her carelessly. You know how quickly a vessel from Samos gets broken.[11]

PIS Back at your usual jokes?

CHRY Tell me where she is now, please.

PIS (*pointing to Bacchis' house*) Here, where you just saw me come out from.

CHRY How lovely that is! She lives right next door. Does she re- 205
member Mnesilochus at all?

PIS You ask? Yes, she has the highest opinion of him and him alone.

CHRY Wow!

PIS Yes, what do you think she's like? The poor girl's in love and is missing him.

CHRY That's wonderful.

PIS Yes, Chrysalus, there you go, she never lets ever so tiny an amount of time pass without mentioning him.

CHRY All the better of her.   211

PIS Yes—

CHRY (*interrupting*) Yes, I'd better go.

PIS Don't you enjoy hearing about your master's success?

CHRY It's not the success, but the actor that's wounding my heart with tedium. Even the *Epidicus*, a play I love as much as myself—well, there's no play I enjoy watching less if Pellio is acting in it. But did Bacchis seem attrac- 216
tive to you?

PIS You ask? If I hadn't met Venus, I'd call her . . . Juno.[12]

---

[12] A joke with unexpected ending. Venus is the goddess of love; we expect Pistoclerus to say that he would call the girl a second Venus. Instead he calls her Juno, who is not only not Venus' sister, but also a less desirable goddess revered by matrons.

CHRY   edepol, Mnesiloche, ut hanc rem natam [esse] intellego,
          quod ames paratum est: quod des inuento est opus.
220   nam istic fortasse auro est opus.
  PIS   Philippeo quidem.
  CHRY   atque eo fortasse iam opust.
  PIS   immo etiam prius:
          nam iam huc adueniet miles—
  CHRY   et miles quidem?
  PIS   —qui de amittenda Bacchide aurum hic exiget.
  CHRY   ueniat quando uolt, atque ita ne mihi sit morae.
225   domi est: non metuo neque ⟨ego⟩ quoiquam supplico,
          dum quidem hoc ualebit pectus perfidia meum.
          abi intro, ego hic curabo. tu intus dicito
          Mnesilochum adesse Bacchidi.
  PIS   faciam ut iubes.
  CHRY   negotium hoc ad me attinet aurarium.
230   mille et ducentos Philippum attulimus aureos
          Epheso, quos hospes debuit nostro seni.
          inde ego hodie aliquam machinabor machinam,
          unde aurum efficiam amanti erili filio.
          sed foris concrepuit nostra: quinam exit foras?

         II. iii: NICOBVLVS. CHRYSALVS
235 NIC   ibo in Piraeum, uisam ecquae aduenerit
          in portum ex Epheso nauis mercatoria.
          nam meus formidat animus, nostrum tam diu
          ibi desidere nec redire filium.

    218 esse *del. Bentley*
    220 istoc *P*, istic *GS*
    223 exigit *P*, exiget *Bothe*
    225 ego *add. Bothe*
    235 ecquae *P*, ecquaen *Lindsay*

CHRY Well, Mnesilochus, as I see the situation, you've got someone to love. You need to find something to give her; because perhaps she needs gold.   220

PIS Yes, of King Philip.

CHRY And perhaps she needs it soon.

PIS No, even earlier: soon the soldier will come here—

CHRY (*interrupting*) A soldier, too?

PIS —who'll demand money here for letting Bacchis go.

CHRY (*confidently*) Let him come when he wants to, but he mustn't keep me waiting. I have the money. I'm not   225 afraid and I'm not begging anyone for it so long as this breast of mine is strong with perfidy. Go in, I'll be in charge here. Tell Bacchis inside that Mnesilochus is here.

PIS I'll do as you command.

Exit PISTOCLERUS into Bacchis' house.

CHRY This gold business is *my* concern. We brought one thou-   230 sand two hundred gold Philippics from Ephesus, which a friend owed our old man. From this I'll machinate some machination today to procure the gold for master's love-sick son. (*looks around*) But our door has creaked. Who's coming out?

Enter NICOBULUS from his house.

NIC (*to the audience*) I'll go to the Piraeus[13] and check if any   235 merchant ship from Ephesus has arrived in the harbor: it frightens me that our son's been sitting there for so long and isn't coming back.

13 The Athenian harbor.

CHRY extexam ego illum pulchre iam, si di uolunt.
240   hau dormitandum est: opus est chryso Chrysalo.
    adibo hunc, quem quidem ego hodie faciam hic arietem
    Phrixi, itaque tondebo auro usque ad uiuam cutem.
    seruos salutat Nicobulum Chrysalus.
NIC pro di immortales, Chrysale, ubi mi est filius?
245 CHRY quin tu primum salutem reddis quam dedi?
NIC salue. sed ubinam est Mnesilochus?
CHRY   uiuit, ualet.
NIC uenitne?
CHRY   uenit.
NIC   euax, aspersisti aquam.
    benene usque ualuit?
CHRY   pancratice atque athletice.
NIC quid hoc? qua causa eum ⟨hinc⟩ in Ephesum miseram,
250   accepitne aurum ab hospite Archidemide?
CHRY heu, cor meum et cerebrum, Nicobule, finditur,
    istius hominis ubi fit quomque mentio.
    tun hospitem illum nominas hostem tuom?
NIC quid ita, opsecro hercle?
CHRY   quia edepol certo scio,
255   Volcanus, Luna, Sol, Dies, di quattuor,
    scelestiorem nullum illuxere alterum.
NIC quamne Archidemidem?
CHRY   quam, inquam, Archidemidem.

  245 primum salutem *P*, *transp. Bothe*
  249 hinc *add. Camerarius*
  252 quaque *P*, quomque *Lambinus*

CHRY (*aside*) I'll undo him nicely now if the gods are willing.
  I mustn't be sleepy: Chrysalus, the golden boy, needs 240
  gold.[14] I'll go up to the man whom I'll turn into Phrixus'
  ram[15] here today and whom by the same token I'll fleece
  out of his gold, down to the quick skin. (*loudly*) The slave
  Chrysalus is greeting Nicobulus.

NIC (*anxiously*) Immortal gods, Chrysalus, where is my son?

CHRY Why don't you first return the greeting I gave you? 245

NIC Hello. But where on earth is Mnesilochus?

CHRY He's alive and kicking.

NIC Has he come?

CHRY Yes, he has.

NIC Excellent, you've sprinkled water onto me. Has he been
  well throughout?

CHRY Like a sportsman and an athlete.

NIC What about this? Did he get the gold from my friend
  Archidemides, which is why I'd sent him off to Ephesus
  in the first place?

CHRY (*with sadness*) Dear me, my heart and brains are being 251
  split, Nicobulus, whenever there's mention of that man.
  Do you call that fiend of yours your friend?

NIC How so, please?

CHRY Because I know for sure that the four gods Vulcan,[16] 255
  Moon, Sun, and Day have never shone on any greater
  criminal.

NIC Than Archidemides?

CHRY Yes, than Archidemides.

---

14 A Greek pun; I have added "the golden boy" because the name
Chrysalus is derived from Greek *chrysos* (gold).

15 Phrixus owned the ram with the golden fleece.

16 The god of fire.

NIC quid fecit?

CHRY quid non fecit? quin tu id me rogas?
primumdum infitias ire coepit filio,
260 negare se debere tibi triobulum.
continuo antiquom hospitem nostrum sibi
Mnesilochus aduocauit, Pelagonem senem;
eo praesente homini extemplo ostendit symbolum,
quem tute dederas, ad eum ut ferret, filio.

265 NIC quid ubi ei ostendit symbolum?

CHRY infit dicere
adulterinum et non eum esse symbolum.
quotque innocenti ei dixit contumelias!
adulterare eum aibat rebus ceteris.

NIC habetin aurum? id mihi dici uolo.

270 CHRY postquam quidem praetor recuperatores dedit,
damnatus demum, ui coactus reddidit
mille et ducentos Philippum.

NIC tantum debuit.

CHRY porro etiam ausculta pugnam quam uoluit dare.

NIC etiamne est quid porro?

CHRY em, accipitrina haec nunc erit.

275 NIC deceptus sum, Autolyco hospiti aurum credidi.

CHRY quin tu audi.

NIC immo ingenium auidi haud pernoram hospitis.

272 ducentos et mille *P, transp. Pareus*

NIC What has he done?

CHRY What has he not done? Why don't you ask me that question? First he began to deny everything before your son, to say that he doesn't owe you a farthing. Mnesilochus 261 immediately called on our longstanding friend, old Pelago, for help. In his presence he promptly showed him the token, the one you yourself had given your son to bring to him.[17]

NIC And when he showed him the token? 265

CHRY He began to say it was a forgery and not that token. And how many insults he heaped on this innocent chap! He said he was a forger in other business affairs as well.

NIC Do you two have the gold? That's what I want to be told.

CHRY Well, after the praetor[18] appointed arbitrators, he was 270 finally convicted and forced to return the one thousand two hundred Philippics.

NIC That's as much as he owed.

CHRY But listen further what fight he wanted to put up.

NIC Is there anything further?

CHRY (aside) There! This will now be hawkery.[19]

NIC I've been deceived, I've entrusted the gold to an Autoly- 275 cus[20] of a friend.

CHRY Listen.

NIC No, I didn't know the true nature of my greedy friend.

---

[17] Recognition token; typically a ring was broken into two parts, and each party kept a half.

[18] A Roman official with judicial functions.

[19] The word *accipitrina* occurs only here; its meaning is presumably "rapacity typical of a hawk."

[20] The grandfather of Ulysses, a well-known thief.

CHRY postquam aurum apstulimus, in nauem conscendimus
        domi cupientes. forte ut assedi in stega,
        dum circumspecto, atque ego lembum conspicor
280   longum, strigorem maleficum exornarier.
NIC   perii hercle, lembus ille mihi laedit latus.
CHRY is erat communis cum hospite et praedonibus.
NIC   adeon me fuisse fungum ut qui illi crederem,
        quom mi ipsum nomen eius Archidemides
285   clamaret dempturum esse, si quid crederem?
CHRY is nostrae naui lembus insidias dabat.
        occepi ego opseruare eos quam rem gerant.
        interea e portu nostra nauis soluitur.
        ubi portu eximus, homines remigio sequi,
290   neque aues nec uenti citius. quoniam sentio
        quae res gereretur, nauem extemplo statuimus.
        quoniam uident nos stare, occeperunt ratem
        tardare in ponto.
NIC   edepol mortalis malos!
        quid denique agitis?
CHRY   rursum in portum recipimus.
295 NIC sapienter factum a uobis. quid illi postea?
CHRY reuorsionem ad terram faciunt uesperi.
NIC   aurum hercle auferre uoluere: ei rei operam dabant.
CHRY non me fefellit, sensi, eo exanimatus fui.
        quoniam uidemus auro insidias fieri,
300   capimus consilium continuo; postridie

278 domum *P*, domi *Ritschl*
280 longum st rigorem *B*, longum est rigorem *CD*
286 lembus nostrae naui *P, transp. Pylades*
293 turbare *P*, tardare *Haupt* portu *P*, ponto *Barsby*

CHRY   After we took the gold away, we went onto the ship, wishing to go home. As I sat down on the deck by chance, I saw, while I was looking around, a long fast-sailer, solid[21] and evil, being prepared.

NIC   I'm done for! That fast-sailer is ramming me amidships.   281

CHRY   It was shared between your friend and pirates.

NIC   How can I have been so weak in the head as to trust him, when his very name Archidemides was shouting at me that if I entrusted him with anything, he'd dematerialize[22] it?

CHRY   That fast-sailer was lying in wait for our ship. I began to   286 observe what they were doing. Meanwhile our ship set sail from the harbor. As we were leaving the harbor, these people were rowing after us: neither birds nor winds   290 are faster. When I realized what was going on, we immediately brought the ship to a standstill. When they saw us halted, they began to slow down their boat on the open sea.

NIC   Bad people they are! What did you do in the end?

CHRY   We returned to the harbor.

NIC   Wise of you. What did they do after this?   295

CHRY   They returned to the shore in the evening.

NIC   They wanted to steal the gold; that's what they were after.

CHRY   It didn't take me in, I saw through it, that's why I was beside myself. Since we saw that a trap was being set for the gold, we made a plan at once. The next day we took all the   300

---

[21] Uncertain text. Paul the Deacon (p. 415 Lindsay) glosses *strigor* as "man of solid strength"; applied to a ship, this is an unusually bold metaphor.   [22] A bilingual pun; the name Archidemides contains the Greek word *demos* (people), which sounds similar to Latin *demere* (take away).

auferimus aurum omne illis praesentibus,
palam atque aperte, ut illi id factum sciscerent.

NIC scite hercle. cedo quid illi?

CHRY   tristes ilico,
quoniam extemplo a portu ire nos cum auro uident,
305 subducunt lembum capitibus quassantibus.
nos apud Theotimum omne aurum deposiuimus,
qui illic sacerdos est Dianai Ephesiae.

NIC quis istic Theotimust?

CHRY   Megalobuli filius,
qui nunc in Epheso est Ephesiis carissumus.

310 NIC ne ille hercle mihi sit multo tanto carior,
si me illoc auro tanto circumduxerit.

CHRY quin in eapse aede Dianai conditum est;
ibidem publicitus seruant.

NIC   occidistis me;
nimio hic priuatim seruaretur rectius.

315 sed nilne ⟨huc⟩ attulistis inde auri domum?

CHRY immo etiam. uerum quantum attulerit nescio.

NIC quid? nescis?

CHRY   quia Mnesilochus noctu clanculum
deuenit ad Theotimum, nec mihi credere
nec quoiquam in naui uoluit: eo ego nescio
320 quantillum attulerit; uerum hau permultum attulit.

NIC etiam dimidium censes?

CHRY   non edepol scio;
uerum haud opinor.

NIC   fertne partem tertiam?

301 omne ⟨illim⟩ *Ritschl*
304 q(uonia)m *C*, qum *B*, qvm *D*
315 huc *add. Hermann*

gold ashore in their presence, openly and publicly, to let them know that this had been done.

NIC Clever indeed. Tell me, what did they do?

CHRY They were cast down as soon as they saw us coming with the gold from the harbor, and they put their swift-boat 305 on shore with shaking heads. We left all the gold with Theotimus, who is a priest of Diana of Ephesus there.[23]

NIC Who is that Theotimus?

CHRY The son of Megalobulus, who is now the dearest man in Ephesus to the Ephesians.

NIC He'd be much dearer to me if he tricked me out of that 310 enormous sum of gold.

CHRY No, it's stored in the temple of Diana itself. There they guard it publicly.

NIC You've killed me. It would have been guarded much better here in private. But didn't you two bring any gold 315 home here from there?

CHRY We did. But I don't know how much he brought.

NIC What? You don't know?

CHRY Because Mnesilochus went to Theotimus at night in secret, and he didn't want to trust me or anyone else on the ship. That's why I don't know how little he brought. He 320 didn't bring terribly much, though.

NIC Do you think as much as half?

CHRY I really don't know; but I don't think so.

NIC Is he bringing a third?

[23] Diana, the Greek Artemis, had a famous temple at Ephesus.

CHRY   non hercle opinor; uerum uerum nescio.
        profecto de auro nil scio nisi "nescio."
325   nunc tibimet illuc naui capiundum est iter,
        ut illud reportes aurum ab Theotimo domum.
        atque heus tu.

NIC   quid uis?

CHRY   anulum gnati tui
        facito ut memineris ferre.

NIC   quid opust anulo?

CHRY   quia id signum est cum Theotimo, qui eum illi afferet,
330   ei aurum ut reddat.

NIC   meminero, et recte mones.
        sed istic Theotimus diucsne est?

CHRY   etiam rogas?
        qui habeat auro soccis suppactum solum?

NIC   quor ita fastidit?

CHRY   tantas diuitias habet;
        nescit quid faciat auro.

NIC   mi dederit uelim.
335   sed qui praesente id aurum Theotimo datum est?

CHRY   populo praesente: nullust Ephesi quin sciat.

NIC   istuc sapienter saltem fecit filius,
        quom diuiti homini id aurum seruandum dedit;
        ab eo licebit quamuis subito sumere.

340 CHRY   immo em tantisper numquam te morabitur
        quin habeas illud quo die illuc ueneris.

NIC   censebam me effugisse a uita marituma,
        ne nauigarem tandem hoc aetatis senex;
        id mi haud utrum uelim licere intellego:
345   ita bellus hospes fecit Archidemides.
        ubi nunc est ergo meus Mnesilochus filius?

CHRY   deos atque amicos iit salutatum ad forum.

NIC   at ego hinc ad illum, ut conueniam quantum potest.

CHRY I honestly don't think so; but in truth, I don't know the
      truth. In fact, as far as the gold is concerned, all I know is:
      "I don't know." Now you have to take the ship there your- 325
      self so as to get that gold home from Theotimus. (*after a
      brief pause*) Oh, one more thing.

NIC   What do you want?

CHRY Make sure you remember to bring along your son's ring.

NIC   What's the ring needed for?

CHRY Because that's the sign with Theotimus: he is to return
      the gold to the man who'll bring it.

NIC   I'll remember, and it's a good thing you're mentioning it.
      But is that Theotimus rich?   331

CHRY You even ask? He has the soles nailed to his shoes with
      gold!

NIC   Why is he so high and mighty?

CHRY He has such great wealth, he doesn't know what to do
      with the gold.

NIC   I wish he'd given it to me. But in whose presence was this 335
      gold given to Theotimus?

CHRY In the presence of the whole populace; there's no one in
      Ephesus who doesn't know.

NIC   That at least my son did wisely, giving the gold to a rich
      man to guard; from him we'll be able to collect it even
      without giving him notice.

CHRY Yes, he'll never delay you ever so slightly; you'll have it 340
      the day you get there.

NIC   I thought I'd escaped life at sea so that I wouldn't go on
      ship any more at *this* age, as an old man. I understand I'm
      not allowed a choice, thanks to what my charming friend   345
      Archidemides did. So where's my son Mnesilochus now?

CHRY He went to the market to greet the gods and his friends.

NIC   But I'll go to him so I can meet him as quickly as possible.

401

CHRY ille est oneratus recte et plus iusto uehit.
350 exorsa haec tela non male omnino mihi est:
ut amantem erilem copem facerem filium,
ita feci ut auri quantum uellet sumeret,
quantum autem lubeat reddere ut reddat patri.
senex in Ephesum ibit aurum arcessere,
355 hic nostra agetur aetas in malacum modum,
siquidem hic relinquet nec secum abducet senex
med et Mnesilochum. quas ego hic turbas dabo!
sed quid futurum est, quom hoc senex resciuerit,
quom se excucurrisse illuc frustra sciuerit
360 nosque aurum abusos? quid mihi fiet postea?
credo hercle adueniens nomen mutabit mihi
facietque extemplo Crucisalum me ex Chrysalo.
aufugero hercle, si magis usus uenerit.
si ero reprehensus, macto ego illum infortunio:
365 si illi sunt uirgae ruri, at mihi tergum domi est.
nunc ibo, erili filio hanc fabricam dabo
super auro amicaque eius inuenta Bacchide.

ACTVS III

III. i: LYDVS

LYD pandite atque aperite propere ianuam hanc Orci, op-
secro.
nam equidem haud aliter esse duco, quippe quo nemo
aduenit,

354 Ephesum ⟨hinc⟩ *Camerarius*
369 qui *B*[1], cui *BcCD*, quo *Lambinus*

Exit NICOBULUS to the right.

CHRY That chap's been loaded up nicely and is carrying more
than is fair. This web hasn't begun badly for me at all. So   350
as to make master's lovesick son rich, I made sure he
could take as much gold as he wishes and return to his fa-
ther as much as he wants to return. The old man will go to
Ephesus to fetch the gold. Here our lives will be led in   355
sumptuous style, if indeed the old man leaves me and
Mnesilochus here and doesn't take us with him. What
trouble I'll stir up here! But what's going to happen when
the old man finds out, when he learns he's run there for
nothing and we've squandered the gold? What'll hap-   360
pen to me then? I believe on his return he'll change
my name and immediately turn me from Chrysalus into
Crossalus.[24] I'll run away if necessary. If I'm caught, I'll
present him with a hard time: if he has rods in the coun-   365
try, I have a back at home. Now I'll go. I'll present this
trick about the gold to master's son and about his girl-
friend Bacchis having been found.

Exit CHRYSALUS to the left.

ACT THREE

LYD *(from inside Bacchis' house)* Open up and unclose this
door to the Underworld quickly, please.

Enter LYDUS from Bacchis' house.

Well, I cannot form a different opinion of it, since no one

---

[24] *Crucisalus*, lit. "cross-jumper"; the cross is the most cruel method
of putting a slave to death.

370 nisi quem spes reliquere omnes esse ut frugi possiet.
Bacchides non Bacchides, sed Bacchae sunt acerrumae.
apage istas a me sorores, quae hominum sorbent sangui-
nem.
omnis ad perniciem instructa domus opime atque opi-
pare.
quae ut aspexi, me continuo contuli protinam in pedes.
375 egone ut haec conclusa gestem clanculum? ut celem pa-
trem,
Pistoclere, tua flagitia aut damna aut desidiabula?
quibus patrem et me teque amicosque omnis affectas
tuos
ad probrum, damnum, flagitium appellere una et per-
dere.
nec mei nec te tui intus puditum est factis quae facis,
380 quibus tuom patrem meque una, amicos, affinis tuos
tua infamia fecisti gerulifigulos flagiti.
nunc prius quam malum istoc addis, certum est iam di-
cam patri,
de me hanc culpam demolibor iam et seni faciam palam,
uti eum ex lutulento caeno propere hinc eliciat foras.

III. ii: MNESILOCHVS

385 MNE multimodis meditatus egomet mecum sum, et ita esse
arbitror:
homini amico, qui est amicus ita uti nomen possidet,
nisi deos ei nil praestare; id opera expertus sum esse ita.

377–8 *uersus secl. Ritschl*
381 geruli figulos *P, unam uocem effecit Saracenus*

comes here unless all hopes of being able to be any good 370
have deserted him. The Bacchises are not Bacchises, but
the wildest Bacchants. Away with those sisters from me!
They sip the blood of men. The entire house is set up lux-
uriously and sumptuously for ruin. As soon as I saw these
things, I fled immediately. (*as if addressing Pistoclerus*)
Should I carry this around shut up within me, in secret? 375
Pistoclerus, should I conceal your shameful deeds, your
financial losses, or your indolent resorts from your fa-
ther? With this behavior you strive to drive your father, 380
me, yourself, and all your friends to shame, loss, and dis-
grace together, and to ruin us. Inside you were not
ashamed before me or yourself of the deeds you are
doing, for which you have made your father together
with me, your friends, and your relatives accomplices
and partners[25] in your shameful behavior through your
infamy. Now before you add some misdeed to that, I've
decided to tell your father instantly. (*to the audience*) I'll
clear myself from blame in this matter now and reveal it
all to the old man, so that he gets him out of here from
this filthy dirt-hole quickly.

Exit LYDUS to the right.
*Enter MNESILOCHUS from the left, followed by baggage-
carriers.*

MNE   I've thought about this a lot, and I think it's like this: ex- 385
cept for the gods there's nothing better than a friend, I
mean a friend who deserves that name. I've found this

[25] The compound *gerulifigulus*, attested only here, is ultimately
based on the verbs *gerere* (carry out) and *fingere* (instigate).

nam ut in Ephesum hinc abii (hoc factum est ferme ab-
   hinc biennium)
ex Epheso huc ad Pistoclerum meum sodalem litteras
390   misi, amicam ut mi inueniret Bacchidem. illum intellego
inuenisse, ut seruos meus mi nuntiauit Chrysalus.
condigne is quam techinam de auro aduorsum meum
   fecit patrem,
ut mi amanti copia esset. [sed eccum uideo incedere.]
nam pol meo quidem animo ingrato homine nihil impen-
   siust;
395   malefactorem amitti satius quam relinqui beneficum;
nimio impendiosum praestat te quam ingratum dicier:
illum laudabunt boni, hunc etiam ipsi culpabunt mali.
qua me causa magis cum cura esse aequom, obuigilato
   est opus.
nunc, Mnesiloche, specimen specitur, nunc certamen
   cernitur
400   sisne necne ut esse oportet, malus, bonus quoiuis modi,
iustus iniustus, malignus largus, †commodus incommo-
   dus†.
caue sis te superare seruom siris faciundo bene.
utut eris, moneo, hau celabis. sed eccos uideo incedere
patrem sodalis et magistrum. hinc auscultabo quam rem
   agant.

III. iii: LYDVS. PHILOXENVS. MNESILOCHVS
405 LYD   nunc experiar sitne aceto tibi cor acre in pectore.
sequere.

393 sed . . . incedere *secl. Langen*
394 quidem meo *P, transp. Bothe*

out from my own experience: after I went away to Eph-
esus (that was roughly two years ago), I sent a letter from
Ephesus to my friend Pistoclerus here, telling him
he should find my girlfriend Bacchis. I understand he's   391
found her: so my slave Chrysalus has told me. Splendid
of Chrysalus, what a trick he played on my father about
the gold, so that I, the lover, would have the supplies.
[But look, I can see him walking along.] To my mind
there's nothing more worthless than an ungrateful man.
It's better to let off a malefactor than to leave a benefac-   395
tor in the lurch. It's far better for you to be called prodigal
than ungrateful; the good will praise the first, and even
the bad themselves will find fault with the second. For
that reason I need to be all the more careful and keep my
eyes open. Now, Mnesilochus, the test is being tested,
now the fight is being fought, whether or not you are as
you ought to be, bad or good, whatever way, just or un-   401
just, mean or generous, pleasant or unpleasant. Be care-
ful, will you, that you don't let a slave outdo you in doing
good. Whatever you're like, I remind you, you won't keep
it secret. (*spotting people in the distance*) But look, I can
see the father and the tutor of my friend walk along. I'll
eavesdrop from here what they're up to. (*withdraws a
little*)

Enter LYDUS and PHILOXENUS from the right.

LYD Now I'll test whether you have a heart sharp as vinegar in   405
your chest. Follow me.

---

401 commodus incommodus *C*, com incomodus *B*, comodus inco-
modus *B*[3], commodus incommodis *D*, comincommodus *Bergk*

PHIL   quo sequar? quo ducis nunc me?

LYD   ad illam quae tuom
perdidit, pessum dedit tibi filium unice unicum.

PHIL heia, Lyde, leniter qui saeuiunt sapiunt magis.
minus mirandum est illaec aetas si quid illorum facit

410   quam si non faciat. feci ego istaec itidem in adulescentia.

LYD ei mihi, ei mihi, istaec illum perdidit assentatio.
nam apsque te esset, ego illum haberem rectum ad inge-
        nium bonum:
nunc propter te tuamque prauos factus est fiduciam
Pistoclerus.

MNE   di immortales, meum sodalem hic nominat.

415   quid hoc negoti est Pistoclerum Lydus quod erum tam
        ciet?

PHIL paullisper, Lyde, est lubido homini suo animo opsequi;
iam aderit tempus quom sese etiam ipse oderit. morem
        geras;
dum caueatur praeter aequom ne quid delinquat, sine.

LYD non sino, neque equidem illum me uiuo corrumpi sinam.

420   sed tu, qui pro tam corrupto dicis causam filio,
eademne erat haec disciplina tibi, quom tu adulescens
        eras?
nego tibi hoc annis uiginti fuisse primis copiae,
digitum longe a paedagogo pedem ut efferres aedibus.
ante solem exorientem nisi in palaestram ueneras,

425   gymnasi praefecto hau mediocris poenas penderes.
id quoi optigerat, hoc etiam ad malum accersebatur ma-
        lum:
et discipulus et magister perhibebantur improbi.
ibi cursu, luctando, hasta, disco, pugilatu, pila,

430   saliendo sese exercebant magis quam scorto aut sauiis:
ibi suam aetatem extendebant, non in latebrosis locis.
inde de hippodromo et palaestra ubi reuenisses domum,

PHIL   Where should I follow you? Where are you taking me now?

LYD   To that woman who's destroyed and annihilated your one and only son.

PHIL   Easy, easy, Lydus! Those who restrain their anger are wiser. It's less of a surprise if a man of that age does some of those things than if he doesn't. I too did this in my youth.

LYD   Dear me, dear me, your constant compliance has de-   411 stroyed him: if it weren't for you, I would have turned him into a decent man. Now because of you and your trust in him Pistoclerus has become debauched.

MNE   (*aside*) Immortal gods, he's naming my friend. What's   415 this business, Lydus running down his master Pistoclerus so much?

PHIL   For a short while, Lydus, a man desires to enjoy himself. Soon enough the time will come when he'll even hate himself. Humor him. So long as precautions are taken that he doesn't go over the top, let it be.

LYD   No, I won't, and I won't let him be corrupted while I'm   420 alive. But you, who are defending such a corrupt son, was there the same sort of education when you were a teenager? I say no, in your first twenty years you didn't have the chance to put your foot out of the house one finger's breadth away from your tutor. If you didn't come to the sports ground before sunrise, you'd pay a heavy price to   425 the head of the gymnasium. If this happened to anyone, this trouble would be added to the other trouble: both pupil and tutor would be considered worthless. There they'd train themselves by running, wrestling, throwing the spear and the discus, boxing, playing ball, and jumping, rather than with a prostitute or kisses. There they'd   430 spend their lives, not in dark dens. When you came home

cincticulo praecinctus in sella apud magistrum assideres:
quom librum legeres, si unam peccauisses syllabam,
fieret corium tam maculosum quam est nutricis pallium.

435 MNE propter me haec nunc meo sodali dici discrucior miser;
innocens suspicionem hanc sustinet causa mea.

PHIL alii, Lyde, nunc sunt mores.

LYD   id equidem ego certo scio.
nam olim populi prius honorem capiebat suffragio
quam magistro desinebat esse dicto oboediens;

440 at nunc, prius quam septuennis est, si attingas eum
manu,
extemplo puer paedagogo tabula dirrumpit caput.
quom patrem adeas postulatum, puero sic dicit pater:
"noster esto, dum te poteris defensare iniuria."
prouocatur paedagogus: "eho senex minimi preti,

445 ne attigas puerum istac causa, quando fecit strenue."
it magister quasi lucerna uncto expretus linteo.
itur illinc iure dicto. hocine hic pacto potest
inhibere imperium magister, si ipsus primus uapulet?

MNE acris postulatio haec est. quom huius dicta intellego,
450 mira sunt ni Pistoclerus Lydum pugnis contudit.

LYD sed quis hic est quem astantem uideo ante ostium? o Phi-
loxene,
deos propitios me uidere quam illum <haud> mauellem
mihi.

---

452 haud *add. Hermann*

---

[26] The boy would be beaten black-and-blue.

[27] The meaning of *expretus* is unclear; I have interpreted it as "ex-
tinguished." The image is that of the teacher being wounded and drip-
ping with blood, just as a lamp can drip with oil.

from there, the race court and the sports ground, you'd
sit down on a chair by your teacher, clad in a loincloth;
when you were reading your book, if you got a single syl-
lable wrong, your skin would become as spotted as a
nurse's shawl.[26]

MNE   (*aside*) Dear me, I'm deeply upset that these things are   435
now being said against my friend on my account. Though
innocent, he's being subjected to this suspicion for my
sake.

PHIL   Lydus, ways are different now.

LYD   That I know for sure. Yes, in the olden days a man would
hold an office by popular vote before ceasing to obey his
tutor. But now, before a boy is seven years old, if you lay a   440
hand on him, he immediately cracks the tutor's head with
his tablet. When you go to the father to complain, the fa-
ther speaks to his boy like this: "Be ours so long as you can
defend yourself against abuse." The tutor is summoned:
"Hey, you worthless old fogey, don't you touch the boy for   445
this, since he's acted spiritedly." The teacher goes like a
lamp, extinguished, when the wick is still drenched.[27]
They go away from there after the judgment has been
pronounced. Can a teacher exert authority here under
such conditions, if he himself is the first to get a thrash-
ing?

MNE   (*aside*) This is a harsh complaint. Judging from his words,
I'd be surprised if Pistoclerus hadn't punched Lydus with   450
his fists.

LYD   (*spotting Mnesilochus*) But who's this I can see standing
in front of the door? O Philoxenus, I wouldn't prefer see-
ing the gods favorably disposed to me to seeing him.

PHIL   quis illic est?

LYD   Mnesilochus, gnati tui sodalis ⟨hic quidem est⟩.
        hau consimili ingenio atque ille est qui in lupanari ac-
          cubat.

455   fortunatum Nicobulum, qui illum produxit sibi!

PHIL   saluos sis, Mnesiloche, saluom te aduenire gaudeo.

MNE   di te ament, Philoxene.

LYD   hic enim rite productust patri:
        in mare it, rem familiarem curat, custodit domum,
        opsequens oboediensque est mori atque imperiis patris.

460   hic sodalis Pistoclero iam puer puero fuit;
        triduom non interest aetatis uter maior siet:
        uerum ingenium plus triginta annis maiust quam alteri.

PHIL   caue malum et compesce in illum dicere iniuste.

LYD   tace,
        stultus es qui illi male aegre patere dici qui facit.

465   nam illum meum malum promptare malim quam pecu-
          lium.

PHIL   quidum?

LYD   quia, malum si promptet, in dies faciat minus.

MNE   quid sodalem meum castigas, Lyde, discipulum tuom?

LYD   periit tibi sodalis.

MNE   ne di sirint.

LYD   sic est ut loquor.
        quin ego quom peribat uidi, non ex audito arguo.

470 MNE   quid factum est?

LYD   meretricem indigne deperit.

MNE   non tu taces?

    453 Pistocleri *P in fine uersus*, del. *Hermann*, hic quidem est *add.*
Ritschl
    465–6 *uersus secl. Guyet*

412

PHIL Who is that?

LYD Mnesilochus; he's a friend of your son. He has a completely different nature from that chap who is lying in the brothel. O happy Nicobulus, who brought up that son for himself! 455

PHIL (*approaching Mnesilochus*) Hello, Mnesilochus, I'm glad you've arrived safely.

MNE May the gods love you, Philoxenus.

LYD (*to Philoxenus*) Yes, this chap's been brought up properly by his father: he goes to sea, looks after the family assets, guards the home, and follows and obeys his father's ways and commands. He was Pistoclerus' friend already when 460 the two were boys. The age difference between them, which one's older, isn't even three days, but one has a maturity that's more than thirty years above that of the other.

PHIL Watch out for trouble and stop maligning him.

LYD Be quiet, it's stupid of you to find it hard to bear that someone is talked about badly who behaves badly. Well, 465 I'd rather have him give me my punishment than my money.

PHIL How so?

LYD Because if he were to give me my punishment, he'd decrease it each day.

MNE Lydus, what are you scolding my friend for, your pupil?

LYD Your friend has died.

MNE May the gods forbid.

LYD It's just as I tell you. I even saw him when he was dying, I'm not blaming him on account of rumors.

MNE What's happened? 470

LYD He's shockingly in love with a harlot.

MNE (*trying to interrupt*) Won't you be quiet?

413

LYD atque acerrume aestuosam: apsorbet ubi quemque attigit.

MNE ubi ea mulier habitat?

LYD   hic.

MNE   unde eam esse aiunt?

LYD   ex Samo.

MNE quae uocatur?

LYD   Bacchis.

MNE   erras, Lyde: ego omnem rem scio
quem ad modum est. tu Pistoclerum falso atque insontem arguis.

475 nam ille amico et beneuolenti suo sodali sedulo
rem mandatam exsequitur. ipsus ncquc amat nec tu creduas.

LYD itane oportet rem mandatam gerere amici sedulo,
ut ipsus osculantem in gremio mulierem teneat sedens?
nullon pacto res mandata potest agi, nisi identidem

480 manus ferat ‹ei› ad papillas, labra a labris nusquam auferat?
nam alia memorare quae illum facere uidi dispudet:
quom manum sub uestimenta ad corpus tetulit Bacchidi
me praesente, nec pudere quicquam. quid uerbis opust?
mihi discipulus, tibi sodalis periit, huic filius;

485 nam ego illum periisse dico quoi quidem periit pudor.
quid opust uerbis? si opperiri uellem paullisper modo,
ut opino, illius inspectandi mi esset maior copia,
plus uiderem quam deceret, quam me atque illo aequom foret.

480 ei *add. Leo*
487 opinor Ω, opino *Lindsay*
488 uideerem *A*, uidissem *P*

LYD And a wild whirlpool at that: she swallows anyone as soon as she touches him.

MNE Where does this woman live?

LYD Here. (*points to Bacchis' house*)

MNE Where do people say she's from?

LYD From Samos.

MNE What's she called?

LYD Bacchis.

MNE You're mistaken, Lydus: I know how the whole story goes. You're accusing Pistoclerus wrongly—he's innocent. Yes, he's eagerly carrying out a charge for a close 475 friend of his, his chum. He himself is not in love and you shouldn't believe that he is.

LYD Should he eagerly fulfill his friend's charge in such a way that he himself is sitting there and holding the woman in his lap while she is kissing him? Can't a charge be fulfilled in any other way than by moving his hands to her breasts again and again and on no occasion removing his lips from hers? Indeed, I'm ashamed of telling you the other 481 things I saw him doing: when he put his hand under Bacchis' clothes onto her body, in my presence, and without feeling any shame. What need is there for words? My 485 pupil, your friend, and this man's son has died. Yes, I say that he has died whose sense of shame has died. What need is there for words? If I'd wanted to wait for just a bit more, I think I'd have had a greater opportunity to watch him, and I'd have seen more than would have been right, more than would have been appropriate for me and him.

MNE   perdidisti me, sodalis. egone ut illam mulierem
490   capitis non perdam? perire me malis malim modis.
       satin ut quem tu habeas fidelem tibi aut quoi credas nes-
         cias?

LYD   uiden ut aegre patitur gnatum esse corruptum tuom,
       suom sodalem, ut ipsus sese cruciat aegritudine?

PHIL   Mnesiloche, hoc tecum oro ut illius animum atque inge-
       nium regas;
495   serua tibi sodalem et mi filium.

MNE   factum uolo.
499 PHIL   in te ego hoc onus omne impono. Lyde, sequere hac me.

LYD   sequor.
496   melius multo, me quoque una si cum hoc reliqueris.
497 PHIL   affatim est. Mnesiloche, cura, i, concastiga hominem
       probe,
498   qui dedecorat te, me, amicos, [atque] alios flagitiis suis.

III. iv: MNESILOCHVS

500 MNE   inimiciorem nunc utrum credam magis
       sodalemne esse an Bacchidem incertum admodum est.
       illum exoptauit potius? habeat. optume est.
       ne illa illud hercle cum malo fecit . . . meo;
       nam mihi diuini numquam quisquam creduat,
505   ni ego illam exemplis plurumis planeque . . . amo.
       ego faxo hau dicet nactam quem derideat.
507   nam iam domum ibo atque . . . aliquid surrupiam patri.
507ᵃ   id isti dabo. ego istanc multis ulciscar modis.
       adeo ego illam cogam usque ut mendicet . . . meus pater.
       sed satine ego animum mente sincera gero,

499 *uersum hic habet P ut in Menandri comoedia, post 498 A*
    496 hoc A, illo P   498 amicos P, amicum A atque *del. Trappes-*
    Lomax (per litteras)   503 suo A, suo meo PT, meo *Pylades*

MNE (*talking to himself*) You've ruined me, my friend. Won't I
destroy that woman completely? I'd rather die a horrible
death myself. Is it really possible that you don't know   491
who to regard as reliable and who to trust?

LYD (*to Philoxenus*) Can you see how upset he is that your
son's been corrupted, his friend, so much that he's tor-
menting himself in his grief?

PHIL Mnesilochus, I ask you to control his impulses and incli-
nations; save a friend for yourself and a son for me.   495

MNE Yes, that's what I want done.

PHIL I put this whole load onto you. Lydus, follow me this way.
(*points to the exit on the right*)

LYD Yes, I'm following you. (*after a brief pause*) It would be
much better for you to leave me together with him as
well.

PHIL It's enough. Mnesilochus, take care of it, go, scold him
properly for bringing shame on you, me, his friends, and
others through his monstrous behavior.

Exeunt PHILOXENUS and LYDUS to the right.

MNE It's completely unclear whether I should believe that my   500
friend is more of an enemy now or Bacchis. She pre-
ferred him? She can have him. That's fine. Seriously,
there will be a price to pay for doing that . . . and I'll pay it.
Yes, let no one ever believe me when I swear by the gods
if I don't pay her back in every conceivable way by . . . lov-   505
ing her. I'll take care that she won't say she's found some-
one to make fun of: I'll go straight home and . . . steal
something from my father. That I'll give her. I'll take a
dreadful revenge on her. I'll give her such a hard time
that . . . my father has to go begging. But am I really in

510 qui ad hunc modum haec hic quae futura fabulor?
 amo hercle opino, ut pote quod pro certo sciam.
 uerum quam illa umquam de mea pecunia
 ramenta fiat plumea propensior,
 mendicum malim mendicando uincere.
515 numquam edepol uiua me irridebit. nam mihi
 decretum est renumerare iam omne aurum patri.
 igitur mi inani atque inopi subblandibitur
 tum quom mihi <illud> nihilo pluris [blandiri] referet,
519 quam si ad sepulcrum mortuo narret logos.
[519ᵃ sed autem quam illa umquam meis opulentiis
519ᵇ ramenta fiat grauior aut propensior,
519ᶜ mori me malim excruciatum inopia.]
520 profecto stabile est me patri aurum reddere.
 eadem exorabo Chrysalo causa mea
 pater ne noceat neu quid ei suscenseat
 mea causa de auro quod eum ludificatus est;
 nam illi aequom est me consulere, qui causa mea
525 mendacium ei dixit. uos me sequimini.

III. v: PISTOCLERVS

PIS rebus aliis anteuortar, Bacchis, quae mandas mihi:
 Mnesilochum ut requiram atque ut eum mecum ad te
  adducam simul.
 nam illud animus meus miratur, si a me tetigit nuntius,
 quid remoretur. ibo ut uisam huc ad eum, si forte est
  domi.

518 illud *add. Camerarius* blandiri *A, sed non inuenitur in P*
519ᵃ–519ᶜ *uersus simillimos uersuum 512–14 secl. Guyet, non inue-niuntur in A*

possession of my senses, since I'm talking about the future in this way? Yes, I believe I'm in love, as sure as I can 511 be. But I'd rather outdo a beggar in begging than let her ever become the tiniest bit heavier out of my money. So 515 long as she lives she'll never laugh at me: I've decided to pay back all the gold to my father immediately. Then she'll coax me when I'm empty and poor, at a time when this has no more effect on me than if she were prattling to a dead man at his tomb. [But I'd prefer dying, tormented by poverty, to her ever becoming one tiny bit heavier or weightier through my wealth.] In fact, it's my firm deci- 520 sion to return the gold to my father. At the same time I'll persuade my father not to harm Chrysalus for my sake and not to be angry with him for my sake because he fooled him about the gold. Yes, it's only fair if I look after the man who told him a lie for my sake. (*to his assistants*) Follow me.

Exit MNESILOCHUS to the right, followed by the baggage-carriers.
Enter PISTOCLERUS from Bacchis' house.

PIS   (*calling those inside*) I'll give priority to your orders over 526 everything else, Bacchis: I am to look for Mnesilochus and to bring him back with me. Well, I do wonder why he's dawdling if my message has reached him. I'll go look here at his place to see if by any chance he's at home. (*walks over to Mnesilochus' house*)

III. vi: MNESILOCHVS. PISTOCLERVS

530 MNE   reddidi patri omne aurum. nunc ego illam me uelim
           conuenire, postquam inanis sum, contemptricem meam.
           sed ueniam mi quam grauate pater dedit de Chrysalo!
           uerum postremo impetraui ut ne quid ei suscenseat.

PIS   estne hic meus sodalis?

MNE   estne hic hostis quem aspicio meus?

535 PIS   certe is est.

MNE   is est.

PIS   adibo contra.

MNE   [et] contollam gradum.

PIS   saluos sis, Mnesiloche.

MNE   salue.

PIS   saluos quom peregre aduenis,
           cena detur.

MNE   non placet mi cena quae bilem mouet.

PIS   numquae aduenienti aegritudo obiecta est?

MNE   atque acerruma.

PIS   unde?

MNE   ab homine quem mi amicum esse arbitratus sum antid-
          hac.

540 PIS   multi more isto atque exemplo uiuont, quos quom cen-
          seas
           esse amicos, reperiuntur falsi falsimoniis,
           lingua factiosi, inertes opera, sublesta fide.
           nullus est quoi non inuideant rem secundam optingere;
           sibi ne inuideatur, ipsi ignaui recte cauent.

545 MNE   edepol ne tu illorum mores perquam meditate tenes.
           sed etiam unum hoc: ex ingenio malo malum inueniunt
          suo:

535 *partes sic distribuit Acidalius et del.* et

Enter MNESILOCHUS from the right.

MNE (*speaking to himself*) I've returned all the gold to my   530
     father. Now I'd like her to meet me, now that I have noth-
     ing, that woman who despises me. But how unwilling my
     father was to give me a pardon for Chrysalus! Well, in the
     end I got him to agree not to be angry with him.

PIS (*spotting Mnesilochus*) Isn't this my friend?

MNE (*spotting Pistoclerus*) Isn't this my enemy I see?

PIS (*aside*) It's certainly him.   535

MNE (*aside*) It's him.

PIS (*aside*) I'll walk toward him.

MNE (*aside*) I'll confront him.

PIS Hello, Mnesilochus.

MNE Hello.

PIS Since you've returned from abroad safe and sound, you'll
     be given a dinner.

MNE I don't like a dinner that stirs my bile.

PIS Did you have some unpleasant experience on your re-
     turn?

MNE Yes, a most unpleasant one.

PIS What's the reason?

MNE A man whom I used to believe to be my friend till now.

PIS There are many people that fit this type and descrip-   540
     tion: when you think they're friends, they turn out to
     be treacherous through their treachery, busy with their
     tongues, lazy in their actions, with little reliability. There's
     no one they don't envy for a success; but being such lazy-
     bones, they take good care themselves that no one envies
     them.

MNE Yes, you definitely know their characteristics pretty thor- 545
     oughly. But there's one more thing: through their cursed

421

nulli amici sunt, inimicos ipsi in sese omnis habent.
atque i se quom frustrant, frustrare alios stolidi existu-
    mant.
sicut est hic quem esse amicum ratus sum atque ipsus
    sum mihi:
550   ill', quod in se fuit, accuratum habuit quod posset mali
faceret in me, inconciliaret copias omnis meas.

PIS   improbum istunc esse oportet hominem.
MNE   ego ita esse arbitro.
PIS   opsecro hercle loquere, quis is est.
MNE   beneuolens uiuit tibi.
nam ni ita esset, tecum orarem ut ei quod posses mali
555   facere faceres.

PIS   dic modo hominem qui sit: si non fecero
ei male aliquo pacto, me esse dicito ignauissumum.
MNE   nequam homo est, uerum hercle amicus est tibi.
PIS   tanto magis
dic quis est; nequam hominis ego parui pendo gratiam.
MNE   uideo non potesse quin tibi eius nomen eloquar.
560   Pistoclere, perdidisti me sodalem funditus.
PIS   quid istuc est?
MNE   quid est? misine ego ad te ex Epheso epistulam
super amica, ut mi inuenires?
PIS   fateor factum, et repperi.
MNE   quid? tibi non erat meretricum aliarum Athenis copia
quibuscum haberes rem, nisi cum illa quam ego mandas-
    sem tibi,
565   occiperes tute ⟨ipse⟩ amare et mi ires consultum male?

---

548 frustrantur *P*, frustrant *Acidalius* frustrari *P*, frustrare *scripsi*
concinnitatis causa   552 arbitro *A*, arbitror *P*
   565 ipse *add. Ritschl*, eam *add. Lindsay*

character they find their own curse; they're friends to nobody, they themselves have all people as their enemies. And these idiots think they're fooling others, when they're just fooling themselves. This is what the man is like whom I believed to be as much a friend to me as I am to myself. He took as much care as he could to do as 550 much bad to me as he was able to and to trick me out of all I had.

PIS   He must be a reprobate.

MNE   I think so.

PIS   Please tell me who it is.

MNE   He lives on good terms with you. If it weren't like this, I'd 554 ask you to do him every bad turn you could.

PIS   Just tell me who he is. If I don't do him a bad turn somehow, call me a complete loser.

MNE   He is a crook, but yes, he is your friend.

PIS   Tell me all the more who he is. I care little for the favor of a crook.

MNE   I see that I can't help telling you his name. Pistoclerus, 560 you've utterly destroyed me, your friend.

PIS   What's that?

MNE   What is it? Didn't I send you a letter about my girlfriend from Ephesus, telling you that you should find her for me?

PIS   I admit that this has happened and I've found her.

MNE   Well then? Didn't you have a whole range of other prostitutes in Athens who you could have an affair with, without yourself beginning to make love to the one I had entrusted to you and without stabbing me in the back?

PIS   sanun es?

MNE   rem repperi omnem ex tuo magistro. ne nega.
perdidisti me.

PIS   etiamne ultro tuis me prolectas probris?

MNE   quid amas—

PIS   Bacchidem? duas ergo hic intus eccas Bacchides.

MNE   quid? duae—

PIS   atque ambas sorores.

MNE   loqueris nunc nugas sciens.

570 PIS   postremo, si pergis paruam mihi fidem arbitrarier,
tollam ego ted in collum atque intro hinc auferam.

MNE   immo ibo, mane.

PIS   non maneo, nec tu me habebis falso suspectum.

MNE   sequor.

ACTVS IV

IV. i: PARASITVS

PAR   parasitus ego sum hominis nequam atque improbi,
militis qui amicam secum auexit ex Samo.

575   nunc me ire iussit ad eam et percontarier
utrum aurum reddat anne eat secum simul.
tu dudum, puere, cum illac usque isti simul:
quae harum sunt aedes, pulta. adi actutum ad fores.

568 Bacchidem *Mnesilocho dedit Camerarius*
570 paruam *T*, parum *P*

PIS   Are you in your right mind?   566

MNE   I've learnt the whole story from your teacher. Stop deny-
ing it. You've destroyed me.

PIS   Are you still provoking me with your abuse for no good
reason?

MNE   Why are you having an affair with—

PIS   (*interrupting*) Bacchis? Well, look, in here there are two
Bacchises.

MNE   What? Two?

PIS   And both of them sisters.

MNE   Now you're talking nonsense and you know it.

PIS   (*grabbing Mnesilochus*) Well then, if you continue to be-   570
lieve that I deserve little trust, I'll lift you up onto my
neck and carry you inside.

MNE   No, I'll go myself, wait.

PIS   I'm not waiting, and you won't wrongly have me under
suspicion either.

MNE   I'm following you.

*Exeunt PISTOCLERUS and MNESILOCHUS into Bacchis'
house.*

ACT FOUR

Enter HANGER-ON from the left, accompanied by a boy.

HAN   (*to the audience*) I'm the hanger-on of a bad and wicked
man, of the soldier who carried off his girlfriend from
Samos with him. Now he's told me to go to her and to ask   575
whether she's giving the money back or accompanying
him. (*turning to the boy*) Boy, you came with her to this
place not long ago. Whichever of these houses is theirs,

recede hinc dierecte. ut pulsat propudium!
580 comesse panem tris pedes latum potes,
fores pultare nescis. ecquis [his] in aedibust?
heus, ecquis hic est? ecquis hoc aperit ostium?
ecquis exit?

IV. ii: PISTOCLERVS. PARASITVS

PIS   quid istuc? quae istaec est pulsatio?
〈quid?〉 quae te mala crux agitat, qui ad istunc modum
585 alieno uiris tuas extentes ostio?
fores paene effregisti. quid nunc uis tibi?
PAR adulescens, salue.
PIS   salue. sed quem quaeritas?
PAR Bacchidem.
PIS   utram ergo?
PAR   nil scio nisi Bacchidem.
paucis: me misit miles ad eam Cleomachus,
590 uel ut ducentos Philippos reddat aureos
uel ut hinc in Elatiam hodie eat secum simul.
PIS non it. negat esse ituram. abi et renuntia.
alium illa amat, non illum. duc te ab aedibus.
PAR nimis iracunde.
PIS   at scin quam iracundus siem?
595 ne tibi hercle hau longe est os ab infortunio,
ita dentifrangibula haec meis manibus gestiunt.
PAR quom ego huius uerba interpretor, mihi cautio est
ne nucifrangibula excussit ex malis meis.
tuo ego istaec igitur dicam illi periculo.

581 his *del. Scaliger*
584 quid *add. Ritschl*, 〈male〉 mala *Lindsay*
592 negato *P*, negat *Acidalius*

426

knock. Go to the door now. (*the boy goes to the door and knocks softly*) Get away from there and be hanged! How the shameless rascal knocks! You can eat a loaf of bread 580 three feet wide, but you don't know how to knock on a door. (*goes up and knocks himself, making much noise*) Is anyone in the house? Hey, is anyone here? Is anyone answering this door? Is anyone coming out?

Enter PISTOCLERUS from Bacchis' house.

PIS What's that? What does that frantic knocking mean? Well then? What evil torment is driving you, trying out your strength on someone else's door in this way? You almost 586 broke the door out of its frame. What do you want now?

HAN Hello, young man.

PIS Hello. But who are you looking for?

HAN BACCHIS.

PIS Which one now?

HAN I only know Bacchis. In short: the soldier Cleomachus 589 has sent me to her; she must either return the two hundred gold Philippics, or she must accompany him from here to Elatia today.

PIS She isn't going. She says she won't go. Go away and tell him. She loves someone else, not him. Remove yourself from the house. (*pushes him away*)

HAN You're acting too angrily.

PIS Do you actually know how angry I am? Disaster is not 595 far away from your face: (*shaking his fists*) these tooth-crackers of my hands are itching to spring into action.

HAN (*aside*) Judging from his words, I have to be careful that he doesn't knock my nutcrackers out of my jaws. (*to Pistoclerus*) I'll tell him about this at your own risk.

427

600	PIS	quid ais tu?
	PAR	ego istuc illi dicam.
	PIS	dic mihi,

quis tu es?

	PAR	illius sum integumentum corporis.
	PIS	nequam esse oportet quoi tu integumentum improbu's.
	PAR	sufflatus ille huc ueniet.
	PIS	dirrumptum uelim.
	PAR	numquid uis?
	PIS	abeas. celeriter facto est opus.
605	PAR	uale, dentifrangibule.
	PIS	et tu, integumentum, uale.

in eum [nunc] haec reuenit res locum, ut quid consili
dem meo sodali super amica nesciam,
qui iratus renumerauit omne aurum patri,
nec nummus ullust qui reddatur militi.
610 sed huc concedam, nam concrepuerunt fores.
Mnesilochus eccum maestus progreditur foras.

IV. iii: MNESILOCHVS. PISTOCLERVS

MNE	petulans, proteruo, iracundo animo, indomito, incogi-
tato,

sine modo et modestia sum, sine bono iure atque honore,
incredibilis imposque animi, inamabilis, illepidus uiuo,
615 maleuolente ingenio natus. postremo id mi est quod uolo
616 ego esse aliis. credibile hoc est?
616a nequior nemo est neque indignior quoi
di bene faciant nec quem quisquam
homo aut amet aut adeat.

606 nunc *del.* Bothe

PIS   What are you saying?   600

HAN   I'll tell him about this.

PIS   Tell me, who are you?

HAN   I'm his body shield.

PIS   He must be a good-for-nothing, having a thug like you for his shield.

HAN   He'll come here, all puffed up.

PIS   I'd like him to burst.

HAN   Do you want anything?

PIS   Yes, go away. You need to do so quickly. (*advances*)

HAN   Goodbye, toothcracker.   605

Exit HANGER-ON to the left.

PIS   (*calling after him*) And goodbye to you, shield. (*to the audience*) We're back to square one: I don't know what advice to give my friend about his girlfriend. In his anger he paid back all the gold to his father and there isn't a single coin to be returned to the soldier. (*listening*) But I'll step 610 aside here: the door has creaked. (*observing from a distance*) There, Mnesilochus is coming out with a sad look on his face.

Enter MNESILOCHUS from Bacchis' house.

MNE   (*speaking to himself*) I'm unruly, I have an uncontrollable, irascible, untameable, thoughtless mind, I have no moderation or modesty, no sense of right or honor, I'm unreliable and without self-control, disagreeable and graceless, born with an evil character. In short, I have 615 what I wish only others had. Can you believe it? No one is more useless or deserves less that the gods should do him a good turn or that anyone should love him or approach

		inimicos quam amicos aequom est med habere,
620		malos quam bonos par magis me iuuare.
		omnibus probris, quae improbis uiris
		digna sunt, dignior nullus est homo;
		qui patri reddidi omne aurum amans,
624		quod fuit prae manu. sumne ego homo miser?
624a		perdidi me atque operam Chrysali.
625	PIS	consolandus hic mi est, ibo ad eum.
626		Mnesiloche, quid fit?
	MNE	perii.
626a	PIS	di melius faciant.
	MNE	perii.
627	PIS	non taces, insipiens?
	MNE	taceam?
627a	PIS	sanus satis non es.
	MNE	perii.
628		multa mala mi in pectore nunc
628a		acria atque acerba eueniunt,
629		criminin me habuisse fidem?
629a		immerito tibi iratus fui.
630	PIS	heia, bonum habe animum.
	MNE	unde habeam?
630a		mortuos pluris preti est quam ego sum.
631	PIS	militis parasitus modo
631a		uenerat aurum petere hinc,
632		eum ego meis dictis malis
632a		his foribus atque hac ‹muliere›
		reppuli, reieci hominem.
	MNE	quid mihi id prodest?
634		quod faciam nil habeo miser.
634a		illequidem hanc abducet, scio.

him. It would be fair if I had enemies rather than friends,
it would be more appropriate if the bad were helping
me rather than the good. Nobody is more deserving of all 621
the infamy infamous men deserve. Despite being in love
I returned all the gold to my father, the gold I had in
hand. Aren't I a miserable man? I've ruined myself and
Chrysalus' efforts.

PIS (*to the audience*) He needs my consolation, I'll go to him. 625
(*turning to Mnesilochus*) Mnesilochus, how are you?

MNE I'm dead.

PIS May the gods have something better in store.

MNE I'm dead.

PIS Won't you be quiet, idiot?

MNE I should be quiet?

PIS You aren't in your right mind.

MNE I'm dead. Many bad feelings are springing up in my heart
now, harsh and bitter ones; how could I have found fault
with your reliability? I was angry with you and you didn't
deserve it.

PIS Come on, take heart. 630

MNE Where should I take it from? A dead man is worth more
than I am.

PIS The soldier's hanger-on came a moment ago to demand
the money from here. With my harsh words I drove and
chased him away from this door and this woman.

MNE How does that help me? There's nothing I can do, poor
me. He'll take her away, I know it.

---

628 pectore *P*, pectori *Lindsay 628–628a pro trochaico octonario habens*

632a muliere *add. Ritschl*

634 quid *P*, quod *Lindsay*

635	PIS	si mihi sit . . . non pollicear.
	MNE	scio, dares, noui.
		sed nisi ames, non habeam . . . tibi fidem tantam;
		nunc agitas sat tute tuarum rerum;
		egone ut opem mi ferre putem posse inopem te?
639	PIS	tace modo: deus respiciet nos aliquis.
	MNE	nugae!
639ª	PIS	mane.
	MNE	quid est?
	PIS	tuam copiam
639ᵇ		eccam Chrysalum uideo.

IV. iv: CHRYSALVS. MNESILOCHVS. PISTOCLERVS

640	CHRY	hunc hominem decet auro expendi, huic decet statuam
		statui ex auro;
		nam duplex hodie facinus feci, duplicibus spoliis sum af-
		fectus.
		erum maiorem meum ut ego hodie lusi lepide, ut ludi-
		ficatust!
		callidum senem callidis dolis
		compuli et perpuli mi omnia ut crederet.
645		nunc amanti ero filio senis,
		quicum ego bibo, quicum edo et amo,
		regias copias aureasque optuli,
		ut domo sumeret neu foris quaereret.
		non mihi isti placent Parmenones, Syri,
650		qui duas aut tris minas auferunt eris.

638 opem mi . . . te *P*, opem . . . te mi *Lindsay* (*ut duos dochmios habeat*)

641 hodie facinus feci *P*, facinus feci hodie *Lindsay*

PIS   If I had money, I . . . wouldn't promise it to you.[28]   635

MNE   I know, you'd give it to me, I understand. But if you
       weren't in love, I . . . wouldn't have such faith in you.[29]
       Now you have enough on your hands with your own
       problems. Should I believe that you could bring me help,
       you who are helpless yourself?

PIS   Just be quiet: some god will look after us.

MNE   Nonsense! *(turns to go)*

PIS   Wait.

MNE   What is it?

PIS   Look, I can see Chrysalus, your cash resource.

Enter CHRYSALUS from the left.

CHRY   *(cheerfully, patting his chest)* This man is worth his   640
       weight in gold, for this man a statue of gold ought to be
       set up: I did a double deed today, I'm carrying off double
       spoils. How beautifully I tricked my elder master today,
       how he was made fun of! With my clever tricks I com-
       pelled and coerced the clever old boy to believe me in ev-
       erything. To my lovesick master, the old man's son, with   645
       whom I drink, with whom I eat and love, I have now
       brought the golden wealth of a king, so that he can take
       from his own pocket and doesn't have to look outside. I
       don't like those Parmenos and Syruses,[30] who take two   650
       or three minas away from their masters. Nothing is more

28 A joke with unexpected ending.

29 Another joke with unexpected ending; men in love are consid-
ered unreliable, so we would expect Mnesilochus to say, "If you weren't
in love, I would actually have faith in you."

30 Typical slave names in comedy; Syrus is in fact the name of
Chrysalus' counterpart in Menander's original.

651		nequius nil est quam egens
651a		consili seruos, nisi habet
		multipotens pectus:
		ubiquomque usus siet, pectore expromat suo.
		nullus frugi esse potest homo,
655		nisi qui et bene facere et male tenet.
		improbis cum improbus sit, harpaget furibus,
		furetur quod queat;
		uorsipellem frugi conuenit esse hominem,
		pectus quoi sapit,
660– 1		bonus sit bonis, malus sit malis;
		utquomque res sit, ita animum habeat.
		sed lubet scire quantum aurum erus sibi
		dempsit et quid suo reddidit patri.
665		si frugi est, Herculem fecit ex patre:
		decumam partem ei dedit, sibi nouem apstulit.
		sed quem quaero optume eccum obuiam mihi est.
668		numqui nummi exciderunt, ere, tibi,
668a		quod sic terram optuere?
		quid uos maestos tam tristisque esse conspicor?
670		non placet nec temere est etiam. quin respondetis mihi?
	MNE	Chrysale, occidi.
	CHRY	fortassis tu auri dempsisti parum?
	MNE	quam, malum, parum? immo uero nimio minus multo [quam] parum.
	CHRY	quid igitur ‹tu› stulte, quoniam occasio ad eam rem fuit
		mea uirtute parta ut quantum uelles tantum sumeres,
675		sic hoc digitulis duobus sumebas primoribus?

656 sit *del. Lindsay ut quaternarius fiat*
657 furetur *del. Lindsay*
670 mihi respondetis Ω, *transp. Acidalius*

worthless than a slave who lacks intelligence, if he
doesn't have a versatile mind; whenever necessary, he
should draw a plan from his own mind. Nobody can be
any good unless he knows how to do both good and bad.   655
Let him be a rascal with rascals, let him grab and steal
with thieves as much as he can; a man who has cleverness
in his heart should be able to change his spots. Let him be   660
good to the good, let him be bad to the bad. Whatever the
situation is like, he should adapt to it. But I'd like to know
how much gold master took for himself and what he re-
turned to his father. If he's any good, he's made a Hercu-   665
les out of his father: he's given him a tithe and carried off
nine-tenths for himself.[31] (*spotting Mnesilochus and
Pistoclerus*) But look, excellent, the man I'm looking for
is coming my way. (*pauses, then addresses Mnesilochus*)
Did you lose the money, master, since you're staring at
the ground like this? Why must I see you two so sad and
depressed? I don't like it and there must be some reason   670
for it. Why don't you answer me?

MNE Chrysalus, I'm dead.

CHRY Perhaps you took too little of the gold?

MNE Damn it, how do you mean, too little? No, far less than
too little.

CHRY Then why did you just take it like this, with your two
fingertips, you idiot, when I'd provided you with the op-
portunity to take as much as you wanted? Or didn't you   676

---

[31] Tithes given to Hercules as thank-offerings were very common.

672 quam[2] A, *om.* P
673 tu *add. Bothe*

an nescibas quam eius modi homini raro tempus se
    daret?

MNE erras.

CHRY   at quidem tute errasti, quom parum immersti ampliter.

MNE pol tu quam nunc med accuses magis, si magis rem noue-
    ris.

    occidi.

CHRY   animus iam istoc dicto plus praesagitur mali.

680 MNE perii.

CHRY   quid ita?

MNE   quia patri omne cum ramento reddidi.

CHRY reddidisti?

MNE   reddidi.

CHRY   omnene?

MNE   oppido.

CHRY   occisi sumus.

    qui in mentem uenit tibi istuc facinus facere tam malum?

MNE Bacchidem atque hunc suspicabar propter crimen,
    Chrysale,

    mi male consuluisse: ob eam rem omne aurum iratus
    reddidi

685   meo patri.

CHRY   quid, ubi reddebas aurum, dixisti patri?

MNE me id aurum accepisse extemplo ab hospite Archide-
    mide.

CHRY   em,

    istoc dicto ⟨tu⟩ dedisti hodie in cruciatum Chrysalum;

    nam ubi me aspiciet, ad carnuficem rapiet continuo
    senex.

684 male *B*, me male *CD*, mi male *Lambinus*
687 tu *add. Fleckeisen*

know how rarely an opportunity of this kind presents it-
self to anyone?

MNE You're getting it wrong.

CHRY No, you got it wrong yourself because you didn't delve in
deeply enough.

MNE How much more you'd accuse me now if you knew the
facts better. I'm dead.

CHRY Because of that word I can already feel more trouble
coming.

MNE I'm done for.   680

CHRY How so?

MNE Because I've returned everything to my father, including
the last scrap.

CHRY You've returned it?

MNE Yes, I have.

CHRY All?

MNE Yes.

CHRY We're dead. How did it occur to you to commit such a
horrible crime?

MNE Because of an accusation I suspected that Bacchis and
this chap had done me an injustice, Chrysalus; for that
reason I returned all the gold to my father in my anger.

CHRY What did you say to your father when you were returning
the gold to him?

MNE That I received that gold from our friend Archidemides 686
without delay.

CHRY There you go, with that word you handed Chrysalus over
to crucifixion today: as soon as he sees me, the old man
will drag me to the executioner.

MNE   ego patrem exoraui.

CHRY   nempe ergo hoc ut faceret quod loquor?

690 MNE   immo tibi ne noceat neu quid ob eam rem suscenseat;
       atque aegre impetraui. nunc hoc tibi curandum est,
          Chrysale.

CHRY   quid uis curem?

MNE   ut ad senem etiam alteram facias uiam.
       compara, fabricare, finge quod lubet, conglutina,
       ut senem hodie doctum docte fallas aurumque auferas.

695 CHRY   uix uidetur fieri posse.

MNE   perge, ac facile effeceris.

CHRY   quam, malum, facile, quem mendaci prendit manufesto
          modo?
       quem si orem ut mihi nil credat, id non ausit credere.

MNE   immo si audias quae dicta dixit me aduorsum tibi . . .

CHRY   quid dixit?

MNE   si tu illum solem sibi solem esse diceres,

700   se illum lunam credere esse et noctem qui nunc est dies.

CHRY   emungam hercle hominem probe hodie, ne id nequi-
          quam dixerit.

PIS   nunc quid nos uis facere?

CHRY   enim nil est, nisi ut ametis impero.
       ceterum quantum lubet me poscitote aurum: ego dabo.
       quid mi refert Chrysalo esse nomen, nisi factis probo?

705   sed nunc quantillum usust auri tibi, Mnesiloche? dic
          mihi.

MNE   militi nummis ducentis iam usus est pro Bacchide.

---

[32] Another Greek pun on the name Chrysalus and Greek *chrysos*
(gold); the "golden boy" is not in the Latin.

438

MNE   I persuaded my father.

CHRY You mean, to do what I'm talking about?

MNE   No, not to harm you and not to be angry with you for this.   690
And I barely achieved it. (*after a brief pause*) Now you
have to take care of this, Chrysalus.

CHRY What do you want me to take care of?

MNE   That you have a second go yet at the old man. Plan, de-
vise, invent whatever you like, glue together a plot so that
you deceive the clever man cleverly today and take away
the gold.

CHRY It hardly seems possible.   695

MNE   Go on and you'll achieve it easily.

CHRY Damn it, how easily? Just now he caught me red-handed
in a lie. If I were to ask him not to believe me in anything,
he wouldn't even dare to believe me in that.

MNE   Well, if you were to hear the things he said to me about
you . . .

CHRY What did he say?

MNE   That if you told him that the sun up there is the sun, he'd
believe that it's the moon and that what's now day is the
night.

CHRY I'll trick the chap properly today so he hasn't said this for   701
nothing.

PIS   What do you want us to do now?

CHRY There's absolutely nothing for you to do, except that I
command you to make love to the girls. As for the rest,
demand as much gold from me as you like. I'll give it to
you. What's the point of me being called Chrysalus, the
golden boy, unless I prove it through my actions?[32] But   705
how little gold do you need now, Mnesilochus? Tell me.

MNE   The soldier needs two hundred Philippics for Bacchis
now.

CHRY ego dabo.

MNE   tum nobis opus est sumptu.

CHRY   ah, placide uolo
     unumquicque agamus: hoc ubi egero, tum istuc agam.
     de ducentis nummis primum intendam ballistam in
         senem;

710   ea ballista si peruortam turrim et propugnacula,
     recta porta inuadam extemplo in oppidum antiquom et
         uetus:
     si id capso, geritote amicis uostris aurum corbibus,
     sicut animus sperat.

PIS   apud te est animus noster, Chrysale.

CHRY nunc tu abi intro, Pistoclere, ad Bacchidem, atque effer
         cito—

715 PIS   quid?

CHRY   stilum, ceram et tabellas, linum.

PIS   iam faxo hic erunt.

MNE quid nunc es facturus? id mi dice.

CHRY   coctum est prandium?
     uos duo eritis atque amica tua erit tecum tertia?

MNE sicut dicis.

CHRY   Pistoclero nulla amica est?

MNE   immo adest.
     alteram ille amat sororem, ego alteram, ambas Bacchi-
         des.

720 CHRY quid tu loquere?

MNE   hoc, ut futuri sumus.

CHRY   ubi est biclinium
     uobis stratum?

MNE   quid id exquaeris?

CHRY   res ita est, dici uolo.
     nescis quid ego acturus sim nec facinus quantum exor-
         diar.

CHRY I'll produce them.

MNE Then we need spending money.

CHRY Oh, I'd like us to do one thing at a time; when I've done 709
this, I'll do that. First I'll point my catapult toward the
old man for the two hundred minas. If I knock down the
tower and ramparts with that catapult, I'll instantly storm
into the old and ancient town right through the gate. If I
conquer it, you two can bring gold to your girlfriends in
baskets, to your hearts' content.

PIS Our hearts are with you, Chrysalus.

CHRY Now go inside to Bacchis, Pistoclerus, and quickly bring
out—

PIS (*interrupting*) What? 715

CHRY A pen, wax and tablets, and thread.

PIS I'll make sure that they will be here in a moment.

Exit PISTOCLERUS into Bacchis' house.

MNE What are you going to do now? Tell me.

CHRY Has the lunch been cooked? Will it be the two of you,
and your girlfriend will be with you as number three?

MNE Just as you're saying.

CHRY Doesn't Pistoclerus have a girlfriend?

MNE He does, she's here. He loves one sister, I the other, both
Bacchises.

CHRY What are you saying? 720

MNE I'm telling you how we're going to be.

CHRY Where's your double couch set?

MNE What are you asking this for?

CHRY Business, I want to be told. You don't know what I'm
going to do and what great deed I'm beginning.

441

PLAUTUS

MNE cedo manum ac supsequere propius me ad fores. intro
          inspice.
724 CHRY euax, nimis bellus<t> atque ut esse maxume optabam
–5   locus.
PIS quae imperauisti, imperatum bene bonis factum ilico est.
CHRY quid parasti?
PIS   quae parari tu iussisti omnia.
CHRY cape stilum propere et tabellas tu has tibi.
MNE   quid postea?
CHRY quod iubebo scribito istic. nam propterea <te> uolo
730   scribere ut pater cognoscat litteras quando legat.
          scribe—
MNE   quid scribam?
CHRY   salutem tuo patri uerbis tuis.
PIS quid si potius morbum, mortem scribat? id erit rectius.
CHRY ne interturba.
MNE   iam imperatum in cera inest.
CHRY .   dic quem ad modum.
MNE .“Mnesilochus salutem dicit suo patri.”
CHRY   ascribe hoc cito:
735   “Chrysalus mihi usque quaque loquitur nec recte, pater,
          quia tibi aurum reddidi et quia non te defrudauerim.”
PIS mane dum scribit.
CHRY   celerem oportet esse amatoris manum.

724–5 bellus . . . locus *P*, bellus<t> . . . locus *Barsby*, bellum . . . lo-
cum *Studemund*
729 te *add. Camerarius*

442

MNE Give me your hand and follow me nearer to the door. (*takes him there*) Look inside.

CHRY Fantastic! The spot is terribly pretty and just what I really wanted.   724–5

Enter PISTOCLERUS from Bacchis' house with writing materials.

PIS What you commanded, a good command for good people, was carried out immediately.

CHRY What have you brought?

PIS All that you ordered to be brought.

CHRY You there (*points to Mnesilochus*), take the pen and those tablets quickly.

MNE (*taking them*) What next?

CHRY Write there what I'll tell you. I want you to write for the simple reason that your father may recognize your handwriting when he's reading it. Write—   731

MNE (*interrupting*) What should I write?

CHRY —a hearty greeting to your father in your own words. (*Mnesilochus obeys*)

PIS What if he's writing a greeting of illness and death to him instead? That'll be more to the point.

CHRY Stop interrupting.

MNE What's been commanded is already in the wax.

CHRY Tell me how.

MNE "Mnesilochus heartily greets his father."

CHRY Add to it quickly: "Chrysalus is reviling me all the time, father, because I returned the money to you and because I didn't cheat you." (*Mnesilochus obeys*)   735

PIS Wait while he's writing.

CHRY A lover's hand ought to be fast.

PIS   at quidem hercle est ⟨ad⟩ perdundum magis quam ad
        scribundum cito.

MNE   loquere. hoc scriptum est.

CHRY   "nunc, pater mi, proin tu ab eo ut caueas tibi:

740   sycophantias componit, aurum ut aps ted auferat;
        et profecto se ablaturum dixit." plane ascribito.

MNE   dic modo.

CHRY   "atque id pollicetur se daturum aurum mihi
        quod dem scortis quodque in lustris comedim, [et] con-
           graecem, pater.
        sed, pater, uide ne tibi hodie uerba det: quaeso caue."

745 MNE   loquere porro.

CHRY   ascribedum etiam—

MNE   loquere quid scribam modo.

CHRY "sed, pater, quod promisisti mihi, te quaeso ut memi-
          neris,
        ne illum uerberes; uerum apud te uinctum asseruato
          domi."
        cedo tu ceram ac linum actutum. age obliga, opsigna cito.

MNE   opsecro, quid istis ad istunc usust conscriptis modum,

750   ut tibi ne quid credat atque ut uinctum te asseruet domi?

CHRY quia mi ita lubet. potin ut cures te atque ut ne parcas
          mihi?
        mea fiducia opus conduxi et meo periclo rem gero.

MNE   aequom dicis.

CHRY   cedo tabellas.

MNE   accipe.

CHRY   animum aduortite.
        Mnesiloche et tu, Pistoclere, iam facite in biclinio

---

738 em *B*, hem *CD*, est *Camerarius* ad *add. Camerarius*
743 et *P, om. Nonius*

PIS   Faster at wasting money than at writing.

MNE   Speak. That's written.

CHRY   "Now, my father, you should be careful of him. He's com-   740
ing up with tricks in order to take the money away from
you. And he said that he really would take it." Write that
down explicitly. (*Mnesilochus complies*)

MNE   Just tell me.

CHRY   "And he promises he'll give that gold to me so I can give
it to prostitutes and eat it up and waste it in Greek style in
brothels, father. But, father, mind he doesn't trick you to-
day. Please be careful." (*Mnesilochus keeps writing*)

MNE   Speak further.   745

CHRY   Write down—

MNE   (*interrupting*) Just tell me what I should write.

CHRY   "But, father, I ask you to remember what you promised
me: don't beat him. But do guard him at your place at
home in fetters." (*Mnesilochus finishes, Chrysalus turns
to Pistoclerus*) Give me the wax and thread immediately,
you there. (*passes the items on to Mnesilochus*) Go on,
fasten it and seal it quickly.

MNE   Please, what's the point of having it written in this way,
telling him not to believe you in anything and to put you
in irons and keep watch over you at home?

CHRY   Because I like it this way. Can't you mind your own busi-   751
ness instead of sparing me? I was relying on myself when
I took on the job and I'm conducting my business at my
own risk.

MNE   Fair enough.

CHRY   Give me the tablets.

MNE   Take them. (*hands them over*)

CHRY   Pay attention, you two. Mnesilochus and you, Pistocle-
rus, make sure now that you go to lie down, each of you in

755   cum amica sua uterque accubitum eatis, ita negotium
              est,
        atque ibidem ubi nunc sunt lecti strati potetis cito.
PIS   numquid aliud?
CHRY   hoc atque etiam: ubi erit accubitum semel,
        ne quoquam exsurgatis, donec a me erit signum datum.
PIS   o imperatorem probum!
CHRY   iam bis bibisse oportuit.
760 MNE fugimus.
CHRY   uos uostrum curate officium, ego efficiam meum.

IV. V: CHRYSALVS

CHRY insanum magnum molior negotium,
        metuoque ut hodie possiem emolirier.
        sed nunc truculento mi atque saeuo usus sene est;
        nam non conducit huic sycophantiae
765   senem tranquillum esse ubi me aspexerit.
        uorsabo ego illum hodie, si uiuo, probe.
        tam frictum ego illum reddam quam frictum est cicer.
        adambulabo ad ostium, ut, quando exeat,
        extemplo aduenienti ei tabellas dem in manum.

IV. vi: NICOBVLVS. CHRYSALVS

770 NIC nimio illaec res est magnae diuidiae mihi,
        supterfugisse sic mihi hodie Chrysalum.
CHRY saluos sum, iratus est senex. nunc est mihi
        adeundi ad hominem tempus.
NIC   quis loquitur prope?
        atque hicquidem, opinor, Chrysalust.
CHRY   accessero.

765 <mi> esse *Hermann*
766 illum *P*, illunc *Camerarius*

a double couch with his girlfriend, that's your job, and 756
make sure that you quickly start drinking there where the
couches have been laid out now.

PIS   Anything else?

CHRY Just this, and one more thing: once you've reclined, don't
get up to go anywhere, until you get a sign from me.

PIS   What an excellent commander!

CHRY You ought to have had two drinks already.

MNE   We're running off. 760

CHRY You take care of your duty, I'll sort out mine.

*Exeunt MNESILOCHUS and PISTOCLERUS into Bacchis'
house.*

CHRY I have an insanely big task in hand and I am afraid that I
won't be able to carry it through today. But now I need
the old man in a savage and wild state; it isn't any good for
this trick if the old boy is at peace with me when he sees
me. As truly as I live, I'll turn him over properly today. I'll 766
have him as roasted as a roasted chickpea. I'll walk to the
door so that when he comes out I can give him the tablets
into his hand the minute he arrives.

Enter NICOBULUS from the right.

NIC   It distresses me very much that Chrysalus got away with 770
this today.

CHRY (*aside*) I'm saved, the old man's angry. Now is my time to
approach him.

NIC   (*aside*) Who's talking close by? This is Chrysalus, I think.

CHRY (*aside*) I'll approach him.

447

775	NIC	bone serue, salue. quid fit? quam mox nauigo
		in Ephesum, ut aurum repetam ab Theotimo domum?
		taces? per omnis deos adiuro ut, ni meum
		gnatum tam amem atque ei facta cupiam quae is uelit,
779–80		ut tua iam uirgis latera lacerentur probe
		ferratusque in pistrino aetatem conteras.
		omnia resciui scelera ex Mnesilocho tua.
	CHRY	men criminatust? optume est: ego sum malus,
		ego sum sacer, scelestus. specta rem modo;
785		ego uerbum faciam ‹nullum›.
	NIC	etiam, carnufex,
		minitare?
	CHRY	nosces tu illum actutum qualis sit.
		nunc hasc' tabellas ferre me iussit tibi.
		orabat, quod istic esset scriptum ut fieret.
	NIC	cedo.
	CHRY	nosce signum.
	NIC	noui. ubi ipse est?
	CHRY	nescio.
790		nil iam me oportet scire. oblitus sum omnia.
		scio me esse seruom. nescio etiam id quod scio.
		nunc ab transenna hic turdus lumbricum petit;
		pendebit hodie pulchre, ita intendi tenus.
	NIC	manedum parumper; iam exeo ad te, Chrysale.
795	CHRY	ut uerba mihi dat, ut nescio quam rem gerat!
		seruos arcessit intus qui me uinciant.
		bene nauis agitur, pulchre haec confertur ratis.
		sed conticiscam, nam audio aperiri fores.

785 faciam ‹nullum› *Brachmann*, ‹nullum› faciam *Ritschl*

---

[33] The image is that of one boat ramming another.

NIC Hello, my good slave. What's up? How soon shall I sail to 775
Ephesus so as to take my money back home from Theoti-
mus? You're silent? I swear by all the gods, if I didn't love
my son so much and didn't wish to see done what he
wishes, your sides would be cut up properly with rods 780
now and you'd spend the rest of your life in the mill in
irons. I've found out about all your crimes from Mnesilo-
chus.

CHRY Has he accused me? Excellent: *I* am bad, *I* am wicked
and evil. Just watch out. I won't utter a single word. 785

NIC Are you even threatening me, you thug?

CHRY You'll get to know what he's like in no time. Now he's told
me to bring you this letter. He asked that what's written
there should be done.

NIC Give it to me.

CHRY (*hands it over*) Take note of the seal.

NIC (*seeing it intact*) I've done so. But where is he himself?

CHRY I don't know. I ought not to know anything any more. 790
I've forgotten everything. I know I'm a slave. I don't
know even what I do know. (*aside*) Now this thrush is
picking up the worm from the net. He'll hang nicely to-
day, the way I've set my snare.

NIC Wait for a moment. I'm coming out to you in a second,
Chrysalus.

Exit NICOBULUS into his house.

CHRY How he's fooling me, how I don't know what he's up 795
to! He's summoning slaves from inside to bind me. The
ship's well on course, my boat's approaching it beauti-
fully.[33] (*listening*) But I'll be quiet: I can hear the door
opening.

IV. vii: NICOBVLVS. CHRYSALVS. LORARIVS

NIC   constringe tu illi, Artamo, actutum manus.
800 CHRY quid feci?
NIC   impinge pugnum, si muttiuerit.
       quid hae loquontur litterae?
CHRY   quid me rogas?
       ut ab illo accepi, ad te opsignatas attuli.
NIC   eho tu, ‹scelus,› loquitatusne es gnato meo
       male per sermonem, quia mi id aurum reddidit,
805   et te dixisti id aurum ablaturum tamen
       per sycophantiam?
CHRY   egone istuc dixi?
NIC   ita.
CHRY quis homo est qui dicat me dixisse istuc?
NIC   tace,
       nullus homo dicit: hae tabellae te arguont,
       quas tu attulisti. em hae te uinciri iubent.
810 CHRY aha, Bellorophontem [iam] tuos me fecit filius:
       egomet tabellas tetuli ut uincirer. sine.
NIC   propterea hoc facio ut suadeas gnato meo
       ut pergraecetur tecum, teruenefice.
CHRY o stulte, stulte, nescis nunc uenire te;
815   atque in eopse astas lapide, ut praeco praedicat.

799 illi *P*, illic *Ritschl*   803 scelus *add. Ritschl*
810 Bellorophontem *CD*, Bellerophantem *B*, Bellorophantam
Ritschl iam *del. Bothe*

---

[34] The queen of Argos tried to seduce Bellerophon, but he resisted.
She denounced him to her husband for attempted rape. The king sent
him to his father-in-law with a letter telling him to put Bellerophon to
death.

Enter NICOBULUS from his house, followed by slaves with straps.

NIC   Bind his hands immediately, Artamo. (*the slave obeys*)

CHRY   What have I done?   800

NIC   (*to Artamo*) Smash him with your fist if he mutters. (*to Chrysalus*) What does this letter say?

CHRY   Why do you ask me? I brought it to you sealed just as I received it from him.

NIC   Hey, you criminal, so you gave my son bad words for returning that gold to me, and you said that you were nev-   805 ertheless going to take away that gold through a trick, didn't you?

CHRY   I said that?

NIC   Yes.

CHRY   Who is the man who says that I said that?

NIC   Be quiet, no man says so; these tablets are accusing you, the ones you brought. (*showing them*) Here, they command that you should be bound.

CHRY   I see, your son's turned me into a Bellerophon: I myself   810 have brought the tablets telling you that I should be bound.[34] So be it.

NIC   (*with irony*) I'm merely doing this so you can advise my son to live in Greek style with you, you triple-dyed poisoner.

CHRY   O you poor, poor fool, you don't know that you're being   814 sold now. And yet you're standing on the same block on which the auctioneer proclaims.[35]

[35] Slaves exhibited for sale stood on elevated platforms so that everybody could examine them.

NIC   responde: quis me uendit?

CHRY   quem di diligunt
        adulescens moritur, dum ualet, sentit, sapit.
        hunc si ullus deus amaret, plus annis decem,
        plus iam uiginti mortuom esse oportuit:

820   terrai ‹iam› odium ambulat, iam nil sapit
        nec sentit, tanti est quanti est fungus putidus.

NIC   tun terrae me odium esse autumas? abducite hunc
        intro atque astringite ad columnam fortiter.
        numquam auferes hinc aurum.

CHRY   atqui iam dabis.

825 NIC   dabo?

CHRY   atque orabis me quidem ultro ut auferam,
        quom illum rescisces criminatorem meum
        quanto in periclo et quanta in pernicie siet.
        tum libertatem Chrysalo largibere;
        ego adeo numquam accipiam.

NIC   dic, scelerum caput,

830   dic, quo in periclo est meus Mnesilochus filius?

CHRY   sequere hac me, faxo iam scies.

NIC   quo gentium?

CHRY   tris unos passus.

NIC   uel decem.

CHRY   agedum tu, Artamo,
        forem hanc pauxillulum aperi; placide, ne crepa;
        sat est. accede huc tu. uiden conuiuium?

835 NIC   uideo exaduorsum Pistoclerum et Bacchidem.

CHRY   qui sunt in lecto illo altero?

NIC   interii miser.

---

820 terrae *B*, terre *CD*, terrai ‹iam› *Leo cum hiatu*

NIC   Answer me: who's selling me?

CHRY (*not speaking to Nicobulus directly*) He whom the gods
      love dies young, while he has his strength, senses, and
      wits. If any god loved this man here, he ought to have
      died more than ten, more than twenty years ago. He's   820
      now walking around as the scum of the earth, he doesn't
      have his wits or his senses any more, and he's worth as
      much as a rotten mushroom.

NIC   Are you calling me the scum of the earth? (*to the slaves*)
      Take him inside and tie him tightly to a column. (*to
      Chrysalus*) You'll never take the gold away from here.

CHRY And yet you will give it to me in a moment.

NIC   I will give it to you?   825

CHRY And you'll beg me of your own accord to take it away
      when you find out what danger and what peril that ac-
      cuser of mine is in. Then you'll give freedom to Chrysa-
      lus; but I shall never accept it.

NIC   Tell me, you hardened criminal, tell me, what danger is 830
      my son Mnesilochus in?

CHRY Follow me this way, I'll make sure that you'll know.
      (*walks toward Bacchis' house*)

NIC   Where on earth?

CHRY Only three steps.

NIC   Ten if you want. (*follows him with Artamo*)

CHRY (*stops in front of Bacchis' house*) Go on, Artamo, open
      this door a tiny bit. (*Artamo obeys*) Gently, don't make a
      noise. That's enough. (*to Nicobulus*) You, come here. Can
      you see the party?

NIC   (*peering in*) I can see Pistoclerus and Bacchis right oppo- 835
      site.

CHRY Who are the ones on that other couch?

NIC   Dear me, I'm dead.

453

CHRY nouistine hominem?

NIC noui.

CHRY dic sodes mihi,
bellan uidetur specie mulier?

NIC admodum.

CHRY quid illam, meretricemne esse censes?

NIC quippini?

840 CHRY frustra es.

NIC quis igitur opsecro est?

CHRY inueneris.
ex me quidem hodie numquam fies certior.

IV. viii: CLEOMACHVS. NICOBVLVS. CHRYSALVS

CLEO meamne hic Mnesilochus, Nicobuli filius,
per uim ut retineat mulierem? quae haec factio est?

NIC quis ille est?

CHRY per tempus hic uenit miles mihi.

845 CLEO non me arbitratur militem sed mulierem,
qui me meosque non queam defendere.
nam nec Bellona mi umquam nec Mars creduat,
ni illum exanimalem faxo, si conuenero,
niue exheredem fecero uitae suae.

850 NIC Chrysale, quis ille est qui minitatur filio?

CHRY uir hic est illius mulieris quacum accubat.

NIC quid, uir?

CHRY uir, inquam.

NIC nuptan est illa, opsecro?

CHRY scies hau multo post.

NIC oppido interii miser.

---

[36] The goddess and god of war, respectively.

CHRY Do you know the man?

NIC I do.

CHRY Tell me, if you will, does that woman seem to be good-looking?

NIC Very much so.

CHRY What about her, do you think she's a prostitute?

NIC Why not?

CHRY You're mistaken.   840

NIC Who is she then, please?

CHRY You'll find out. But you'll never get any information out of me today.

Enter CLEOMACHUS from the left.

CLEO (*to himself*) Should Mnesilochus, the son of Nicobulus, hold back my girl here by force? What sort of behavior is this?

NIC (*to Chrysalus*) Who's that?

CHRY (*aside*) This soldier is coming in the nick of time.

CLEO (*to himself*) He doesn't consider me a soldier, but a   845
woman, thinking I can't defend myself and mine: may
neither Bellona nor Mars[36] ever trust me if I don't exter-
minate him if I meet him and if I don't disinherit him of
his life.

NIC Chrysalus, who is that man threatening my son?   850

CHRY He's the husband of that woman your son is lying with.

NIC What, husband?

CHRY Yes, husband.

NIC Is she married, please?

CHRY You'll know it in no time.

NIC Dear me, I'm absolutely dead.

CHRY quid nunc? scelestus tibi uidetur Chrysalus?
855 age nunc uincito me, auscultato filio.
dixin tibi ego illum inuenturum te qualis sit?
NIC quid nunc ego faciam?
CHRY iube sis me exsolui cito;
nam ni ego exsoluor, iam manufesto hominem opprimet.
CLEO nihil est lucri quod me hodie facere mauelim,
860 quam illum cubantem cum illa opprimere, ambo ut
necem.
CHRY audin quae loquitur? quin tu me exsolui iubes?
NIC exsoluite istum. perii, pertimui miser.
CLEO tum illam, quae corpus publicat uolgo suom,
faxo se hau dicat nactam quem derideat.
865 CHRY pacisci cum illo paullula pecunia
potes.
NIC pacisce ergo, opsecro, quid tibi lubet,
dum ne manufesto hominem opprimat neue enicet.
CLEO nunc nisi ducenti Philippi redduntur mihi,
iam illorum ego animam amborum exsorbebo oppido.
870 NIC em illoc pacisce, si potest; perge, opsecro,
pacisce quiduis.
CHRY ibo et faciam sedulo.
quid clamas?
CLEO ubi erus tuos est?
CHRY nusquam. nescio.
uis tibi ducentos nummos iam promittier,
ut ne clamorem hic facias neu conuicium?

CHRY What now? Does Chrysalus seem to be the criminal to you? Go on now, bind me, listen to your son. Didn't I tell 855 you you'd find out about his character?

NIC What am I to do now?

CHRY Have me unbound quickly, if you will; unless I'm unbound, he'll surprise him in flagrante in a moment.

CLEO (*still not noticing anyone*) There isn't any profit I'd prefer making today to surprising him lying with her, so that I can kill both.

CHRY Can you hear what he's saying? Why don't you have me 861 unbound?

NIC (*to slaves*) Unbind him. (*to Chrysalus*) I'm done for, I got such a shock, poor me.

CLEO (*gradually coming closer*) Then I'll make sure that that woman who prostitutes her body to all and sundry won't say that she's found someone to laugh at.

CHRY (*to Nicobulus*) You can settle the issue with him for a 865 small sum.

NIC Settle the issue, then, please, on any terms you like, so long as he doesn't surprise the chap in flagrante and kill him.

CLEO (*still to himself*) Now unless I'm given back two hundred Philippics, I'll swallow up their lives this instant.

NIC (*to Chrysalus*) Well, settle it for that sum if possible. Go 870 on, please, settle it for any price you wish.

CHRY (*to Nicobulus*) I'll go and do my best. (*going up to Cleomachus, who is still at a distance*) What are you shouting for?

CLEO Where's your master?

CHRY Nowhere. I don't know. Do you want to be promised two hundred Philippics now on condition that you won't shout around or pick an argument?

457

875 CLEO nihil est quod malim.

CHRY   atque ut tibi mala multa ingeram?

CLEO tuo arbitratu.

NIC   ut subblanditur carnufex!

CHRY pater hic Mnesilochi est; sequere, is promittet tibi.
      tu aurum rogato; ceterum uerbum sat est.

NIC   quid fit?

CHRY   ducentis Philippis rem pepigi.

NIC   ah, salus
880   mea, seruauisti me. quam mox dico: "dabo"?

CHRY roga hunc tu, tu promitte huic.

NIC   promitto, roga.

CLEO ducentos nummos aureos Philippos probos
      dabin?

CHRY   "dabuntur," inque. responde.

NIC   dabo.

CHRY quid nunc, impure? numquid debetur tibi?
885   quid illi molestu's? quid illum morte territas?
      et ego te et ill' mactamus infortunio.
      si tibi est machaera, at nobis ueruina est domi:
      qua quidem te faciam, si tu me irritaueris,
      confossiorem soricina nenia.
890   iam dudum hercle equidem sentio suspicio
      quae te sollicitet: eum esse cum illa muliere.

CLEO immo est quoque.

---

[37] This is the typical form of an oral, binding contract.

CLEO There's nothing I'd prefer.   875

CHRY And on condition that I can heap many insults onto you?

CLEO At your discretion.

NIC (*to himself, from a distance*) How the rascal fawns on him!

CHRY This is Mnesilochus' father. (*points at him*) Follow me, he'll promise it to you. You should ask for the gold. As for the rest, we've had enough words. (*they go up to him*)

NIC (*to Chrysalus*) What's happening?

CHRY I've made an agreement for two hundred Philippics.

NIC Ah, my salvation, you've saved me. How soon shall I say, "I'll give them to you"?

CHRY (*to Cleomachus*) You ask him. (*to Nicobulus*) You prom-   881
ise him.[37]

NIC (*to Cleomachus*) I promise it, ask.

CLEO Will you give me two hundred genuine gold Philippics?

CHRY (*to Nicobulus*) Say, "they shall be given." Answer him.

NIC I'll give them to you.

CHRY (*to Cleomachus*) What now, you scumbag? Do we owe you anything? Why are you bothering that man? Why are you threatening him with death? Both I and he will give   886
you a tough time. If you have a sword, we have a spit at home. With that I'll make you fuller of holes than the in-testines of a shrew-mouse[38] if you provoke me. I've been   890
feeling for a while already what suspicion is troubling you: that he is with that woman.

CLEO Yes, he *is* with her.

[38] The image is not entirely clear. The reference seems to be to a shrew-mouse being stabbed to death and squeaking. *Nenia* can also mean "gut," and the spit may point to a culinary reference, although it is hard to see what reference this could be.

CHRY   ita me Iuppiter, Iuno, Ceres,
        Minerua, Lato, Spes, Opis, Virtus, Venus,
        Castor, Polluces, Mars, Mercurius, Hercules,
895   Summanus, Sol, Saturnus dique omnes ament,
        ut ille cum illa nec cubat neque ambulat
        neque osculatur neque illud quod dici solet.
NIC   ut iurat! seruat me ille suis periuriis.
CLEO   ubi nunc Mnesilochus ergo est?
CHRY   rus misit pater.
900   illa autem in arcem abiit aedem uisere
        Mineruae. nunc aperta est. i, uise estne ibi.
CLEO   abeo ad forum igitur.
CHRY   uel hercle in malam crucem.
CLEO   hodie exigam aurum hoc?
CHRY   exige, ac suspende te:
        ne supplicare censeas <tibi>, nihili homo.
905   ille est amotus. sine me (per te, ere, opsecro
        deos immortalis) ire huc intro ad filium.
NIC   quid eo introibis?
CHRY   ut eum dictis plurumis
        castigem, quom haec sic facta ad hunc faciat modum.
NIC   immo oro ut facias, Chrysale, et ted opsecro,
910   caue parsis in eum dicere.

893 Latona *P*, Lato *Ussing*
900 abiit *P*, abiuit *Camerarius*
904 tibi *add. Leo*

---

[39] Jupiter: the highest god; Juno: his wife; Ceres: the goddess of
growth and vegetation; Minerva: the goddess of handicrafts; Latona: a
titaness, mother of Apollo and Diana; Ops/Rhea: goddess of abun-

CHRY As truly as Jupiter, Juno, Ceres, Minerva, Latona, Hope,
       Ops, Bravery, Venus, Castor, Pollux, Mars, Mercury,
       Hercules, Summanus, Sun, Saturn, and all the gods[39] 895
       may love me, he is not lying with her, not walking with
       her, not kissing her, not doing the thing that is usually
       said.

NIC   (*aside*) How he's swearing! He's saving me with his false
       oaths.

CLEO Then where is Mnesilochus now?

CHRY His father's sent him to the country, while she has gone 900
       to the acropolis to visit the temple of Minerva. It's open
       now. Go and see if she isn't there.

CLEO I'll go to the market then.

CHRY Or to be hanged.

CLEO Will I get that gold out of him today?

CHRY Get it out of him and get hanged. Don't expect us to suck
       up to you, you good-for-nothing. *Exit CLEOMACHUS to
       the right.* (*turning to Nicobulus*) That chap's been re- 905
       moved. Master, I beg you by the immortal gods, allow me
       to go in here to your son.

NIC   Why will you go in there?

CHRY So as to scold him with a flood of words for doing these
       deeds in this way.

NIC   Yes, I ask you to do so, Chrysalus, and I entreat you, don't 910
       refrain from speaking up against him.

dance, wife of Saturn/Cronus; Venus: the goddess of love; Castor and
Pollux: divine helpers, sons of Jupiter; Mars: the god of war; Mercury:
the god of business; Hercules: a great hero; Summanus: the god of
thunderbolts; Saturn/Cronus: the father of Jupiter.

CHRY   etiam me mones?
      satin est si plura ex me audiet hodie mala
      quam audiuit umquam Clinia ex Demetrio?
NIC   lippi illic oculi seruos est simillimus:
      si non est, nolis esse nec desideres;
915   si est, apstinere quin attingas non queas.
      nam ni illic hodie forte fortuna hic foret,
      miles Mnesilochum cum uxore opprimeret sua
      atque optruncaret moechum manufestarium.
      nunc quasi ducentis Philippis emi filium,
920   quos dare promisi militi: quos non dabo
      temere etiam prius quam filium conuenero.
      numquam edepol quicquam temere credam Chrysalo;
      uerum lubet etiam mi has pellegere denuo:
      aequom est tabellis consignatis credere.

IV. ix: CHRYSALVS

925 CHRY Atridae duo fratres cluent fecisse facinus maxumum,
        quom Priami patriam Pergamum diuina moenitum
        manu

913 ille *P*, illic *Aldus*
922 quicquam temere *P*, temere quicquam *A*

---

[40] An unclear reference, probably to two characters in a play staged shortly before this one.

[41] This passage is a comparison between Chrysalus' deeds and the Trojan war. The parallels are fairly loose. Plautus puts emphasis on the individual image rather than on a coherent narrative; thus he compares himself to Agamemnon as well as to Ulysses. The background to this passage is as follows: Agamemnon and Menelaus, the sons of Atreus, started the Greek (Achaean) expedition against Troy (also called Ilium and Pergamum here, although the latter term strictly refers to the cita-

CHRY Are you even telling me what to do? Isn't it enough if he's
      going to hear more harsh words from me today than
      Clinia ever heard from Demetrius?[40]

Exit CHRYSALUS into Bacchis' house.

NIC   That slave is very similar to a bleary eye; if you don't have
      one, you don't want or desire to have one. If you do have   915
      one, you can't refrain from touching it. Indeed, if he
      hadn't happened to be here today, the soldier would have
      caught Mnesilochus with his wife and would have butch-
      ered the adulterer caught in flagrante. Now I've bought
      my son, as it were, for two hundred Philippics, which I   920
      promised to give to the soldier. I won't give them away
      rashly until I've met my son. Never will I believe Chrysa-
      lus in anything rashly. But I want to read through these
      here again (*looks at the tablets*): it's only fair to believe
      sealed tablets.

Exit NICOBULUS into his house.
Enter CHRYSALUS from Bacchis' house.

CHRY The two Atrid brothers[41] are said to have done an enor-   925
      mous deed when they overthrew Priam's city, Perga-

del of Troy). The purpose of this expedition was to get back Helen, the
wife of Menelaus, who had run off with Paris (also called Alexander),
one of the fifty sons of Priam, the king of Troy (naturally, he did not have
all these sons with Hecuba, the queen). Since at first the Greeks were
unsuccessful, Ulysses devised a strategy: he had Epius build a huge
wooden horse filled with Greek soldiers; Sinon, pretending to be a de-
serter, entered Troy and claimed that this horse was a gift to the gods;
once the horse was inside the city, the Greeks came out of the horse and
let the remaining Greeks into the city, which was subsequently sacked.

armis, equis, exercitu atque eximiis bellatoribus

milli cum numero nauium decumo anno post subege-
runt.

non pedibus termento fuit praeut ego erum expugnabo
meum

930   sine classe sineque exercitu et tanto numero militum.

[cepi, expugnaui amanti erili filio aurum ab suo patre.]

nunc prius quam huc senex uenit, lubet lamentari dum
exeat.

o Troia, o patria, o Pergamum, o Priame periisti senex,

qui misere male mulcabere quadrigentis Philippis au-
reis.

935   nam ego has tabellas opsignatas, consignatas quas fero

936   non sunt tabellae, sed equos quem misere Achiui lig-
neum.

941   tum quae hic sunt scriptae litterae, hoc in equo insunt
milites

942   armati atque animati probe. ita res successit mi usque
adhuc.

943   atque hic equos non in arcem, uerum in arcam faciet im-
petum:

944   exitium, excidium, elecebra fiet hic equos hodie auro
senis.

937   Epiust Pistoclerus: ab eo haec sumptae; Mnesilochus
Sino est

938   relictus, ellum non in busto Achilli, sed in lecto accubat;

939   Bacchidem habet secum: ille olim habuit ignem qui sig-
num daret,

940   hic ipsum exurit; ego sum Vlixes, quoius consilio haec
gerunt.

945   nostro seni huic stolido, ei profecto nomen facio ego Ilio;

miles Menelaust, ego Agamemno, idem Vlixes Lartius,

464

mum, fortified by divine hand, after ten years with their
weapons, horses, army, renowned warriors, and a thou-
sand-strong fleet of ships. That wasn't worth a blister on
one's feet compared with how I shall conquer my master
without a fleet and without an army and such a great
number of soldiers. [I took the gold by storm for master's   931
lovesick son from his father.] Now before the old man
comes here, I wish to lament until he comes out. O Troy,
o father-land, o Pergamum, o aged Priam, you have per-
ished; you'll be balefully and badly beaten and punished
with the loss of four hundred gold Philippics: these tab-   935
lets, which I'm carrying signed and sealed, aren't tablets,
but the wooden horse which the Achaeans sent. The
letters which are written here are the well-armed and
courageous soldiers in this horse. So far my plan's been
successful. And this horse will attack not a stronghold,
but a strongbox. This horse will turn into the death,   944
destruction, dislodgement of the old man's gold today.
Pistoclerus is Epius: the tablets were taken from him.
Mnesilochus is Sinon the abandoned, he isn't lying on the
tomb of Achilles, but on a couch.[42] He has a Bacchis with
him. That one of old once had a fire to give a sign, but this
one burns himself. I am Ulysses, according to whose plan
they're doing this. This stupid old man of ours, I'll defi-   945
nitely give him the name Ilium. The soldier is Mene-
laus, I am Agamemnon, but also Ulysses, son of Laertes.

---

[42] Sinon gave the Greeks who had remained outside Troy a fire sig-
nal from the tomb of Achilles.

---

931 *secl. Kiessling*   937–40 *transp. Questa*
940 hunc *P*, hic *Lambinus*

Mnesilochust Alexander, qui erit exitio rei patriae suae;
is Helenam auexit, quoia causa nunc facio opsidium Ilio.
nam illi itidem Vlixem audiui, ut ego sum, fuisse et auda-
cem et malum:

950 ⟨in⟩ dolis ego prensus sum, ill' mendicans paene inuen-
tus interit,

dum ibi exquirit facta Iliorum; assimiliter mi hodie opti-
git.

uinctus sum, sed dolis me exemi: item se ille seruauit
dolis.

953 Ilio tria fuisse audiui

953a fata quae illi forent exitio:

954 signum ex arce si periisset;

954a alterum etiam est Troili mors;

955 tertium, quom portae Phrygiae

955a limen superum scinderetur:

956 paria item tria is tribus sunt

956a fata nostro huic Ilio.

nam dudum primo ut dixeram nostro seni mendacium
et de hospite et de auro et de lembo, ibi signum ex arce
iam apstuli.

iam duo restabant fata tunc, nec magis id ceperam oppi-
dum.

960 post ubi tabellas ad senem detuli, ibi occidi Troilum,
quom censuit Mnesilochum cum uxore esse dudum mi-
litis.

ibi uix me exsolui: atque id periclum assimilo, Vlixem ut
praedicant

cognitum ab Helena esse proditum Hecubae; sed ut olim
ille se

blanditiis exemit et persuasit se ut amitteret,

965 item ego dolis me illo extuli e periclo et decepi senem.

466

Mnesilochus is Alexander, who will be the end for his father's wealth. He carried off Helen, for whose sake I'm now besieging Ilium. Well, I've heard that Ulysses there was bold and bad, just as I am. I was caught in my tricks, while he almost got killed when he was discovered as a beggar while spying on the Trojans' plans; I had a very similar experience today. I was tied up, but I freed myself with my tricks; in the same way he saved his skin with his tricks. I've heard that Ilium had three fates which would mark its end: if the statue was taken from the citadel;[43] the second is the death of Troilus;[44] the third, when the upper lintel of the Phrygian gate was split open.[45] For this Ilium of ours there are also three fates, parallel to the other three: first, when a while ago I told our old man a lie about his friend, the gold, and the boat, I took away the statue from the citadel. Two fates still remained then and I hadn't taken the city yet. Next, when I brought the letter to the old man, I killed Troilus, when a while ago he believed Mnesilochus was with the soldier's wife. I barely escaped on that occasion; and for this danger I find a parallel in people saying that Ulysses was recognized by Helen and betrayed to Hecuba. But just as he once escaped through flattering words and persuaded her to let him go, so I got myself out of that danger by tricks and

950

955

960

---

[43] The statue was an image of Pallas (Minerva), the goddess guarding the city; it was stolen by Ulysses and Diomedes.   [44] One of Priam's sons.   [45] "Phrygian" is a synonym for "Trojan"; the horse was so big that part of the wall had to be dismantled to get it in.

---

950 in *add. Lambinus* prensus *A*, depransus *P*
951 facta *BD¹D⁴*, fata *ABᶜCDᶜ*   962–65 *secl. Leo*

post cum magnufico milite, urbis uerbis qui inermus
    capit,
conflixi atque hominem reppuli; dein pugnam conserui
    seni:
eum ego adeo uno mendacio deuici, uno ictu extempulo
cepi spolia. is nunc ducentos nummos Philippos militi,
970   quos dare se promisit, dabit.
nunc alteris etiam ducentis usus est, qui dispensentur
Ilio capto, ut sit mulsum qui triumphent milites.
sed Priamus hic multo illi praestat: non quinquaginta
    modo,
quadrigentos filios habet atque equidem omnis lectos
    sine probro:
975   eos ego hodie omnis contruncabo duobus solis ictibus.
nunc Priamo nostro si est quis emptor, comptionalem
    senem
uendam ego, uenalem quem habeo, extemplo ubi oppi-
    dum expugnauero.
sed Priamum astantem eccum ante portam uideo. adibo
    atque alloquar.

979	NIC	quoianam uox prope me sonat?
	CHRY	o
979a		Nicobule.
	NIC	quid fit? ***
980		quid quod te misi, ecquid egis-
980a		ti?
	CHRY	rogas? congredere.
	NIC	gradior.
981	CHRY	optumus sum orator. ad lacrumas
981a		hominem coegi castigando
982		maleque dictis, quae quidem quiui
982a		comminisci.

468

deceived the old man. Then I fought with the boastful 966
soldier, who sacks cities with his words and without arms,
and I beat him off. Next I began a fight with the old man:
I conquered him with one single lie, I immediately took
the spoils with one single blow. Now he'll give the soldier
the two hundred Philippics which he'd promised to give.
Now we need another two hundred, which will be dis- 971
tributed when Ilium is taken, so that there is honey-wine
for the soldiers to triumph. But this Priam here is far su-
perior to the mythical one: he doesn't just have fifty sons,
but four hundred, and all of them genuine and without
blemish. I'll slay all of them today with only two blows.
Now if there is any buyer for our Priam, I'll sell him at a 976
reduced rate; I'll put him on sale as soon as I've con-
quered the city.

Enter NICOBULUS from his house.

But there I can see Priam standing in front of the gate. I'll
approach and address him.

NIC Whose voice can I hear near me?

CHRY Hello Nicobulus.

NIC What's happening? *** What about my mission for you, 980
have you achieved anything?

CHRY You ask? Come here.

NIC (*obeying*) I'm coming.

CHRY I'm an excellent speaker. I brought the chap to tears with
my scolding and my harsh words, such as I could think of.

469

	NIC	quid ait?
	CHRY	uerbum

983 nullum fecit: lacrumans tacitus
983a auscultabat quae ego loquebar;
984 tacitus conscripsit tabellas,
984a opsignatas mi has dedit.
985 tibi me iussit dare, sed metuo ne idem cantent quod
    priores.
    nosce signum. estne eius?

NIC   noui. lubet pellegere has.

CHRY   pellege.
nunc superum limen scinditur, nunc adest exitium ⟨illi⟩
    Ilio,
988 turbat equos lepide ligneus.

NIC   Chrysale, ades dum ego has pellego.

988a CHRY quid me tibi adesse opus est?

NIC   uolo ut quod iubeo facias,
989 ut scias quae hic scripta sient.

989a CHRY nil moror nec scire uolo.

990 NIC tamen ades.

CHRY   quid opust?

NIC   taceas:
990a quod iubeo id facias.

CHRY   adero.

NIC eugae litteras minutas!

CHRY   qui quidem uideat parum;
uerum qui satis uideat, grandes satis sunt.

NIC   animum aduortito igitur.

CHRY nolo inquam.

NIC   at uolo inquam.

CHRY   quid opust?

NIC   at enim id quod te iubeo facias.

NIC What did he say?

CHRY He didn't utter a single word. He was listening in tears
and quietly to what I was saying. (*producing a document*)
Quietly he wrote this letter, sealed it, and gave it to me.
He told me to give it to you, but I'm afraid it might sing 985
the same song as the last one. (*hands it over*) Take notice
of the seal. Is it his?

NIC Yes. I wish to read through it.

CHRY Do. (*aside*) Now the upper lintel is being split open, now
the end is here for that Ilium. The wooden horse is creat-
ing trouble beautifully.

NIC Chrysalus, stay while I'm reading through this.

CHRY What do you need me to stay for?

NIC I want you to do what I tell you, so you know what's writ-
ten here.

CHRY I don't care and I don't want to know.

NIC Still, stay. 990

CHRY What's the point?

NIC Be quiet. Do what I tell you.

CHRY I'll stay.

NIC (*opening the letter*) Goodness, such tiny letters!

CHRY Tiny for someone who doesn't see well enough. But for
someone who does see well enough they're big enough.

NIC Well then, pay attention.

CHRY I don't want to, I tell you.

NIC But I want you to, I tell you.

CHRY What's the point?

NIC Well, just do what I tell you.

---

987 illi *add. Lindsay*

	CHRY	iustum est ⟨ut⟩ tuos tibi seruos tuo arbitratu seruiat.
995	NIC	hoc age sis nunciam.
	CHRY	ubi lubet,
995ᵃ		recita: aurium operam tibi dico.
996	NIC	cerae quidem hau parsit nec stilo;
996ᵃ		sed quicquid est, pellegere certum est.

"pater, ducentos Philippos quaeso Chrysalo
da, si esse saluom uis me aut uitalem tibi."
malum quidem hercle magnum.

	CHRY	tibi . . . dico.
	NIC	quid est?
1000	CHRY	non prius salutem scripsit?
	NIC	nusquam sentio.
	CHRY	non dabis, si sapies; uerum si das maxume,

ne ille alium gerulum quaerat, si sapiet, sibi:
nam ego non laturus sum, si iubeas maxume.
sat sic suspectus sum, quom careo noxia.

1005	NIC	ausculta porro, dum hoc quod scriptum est pellego.
	CHRY	inde a principio iam impudens epistula est.
	NIC	"pudet prodire me ad te in conspectum, pater:

tantum flagitium te scire audiui meum,
quod cum peregrini cubui uxore militis."

| 1010 | | pol hau derides; nam ducentis aureis |

Philippis redemi uitam ex flagitio tuam.

	CHRY	nihil est illorum quin ego illi dixerim.
	NIC	"stulte fecisse fateor. sed quaeso, pater,

ne me, in stultitia si deliqui, deseras.

| 1015 | | ego animo cupido atque oculis indomitis fui; |

persuasum est facere quoius me nunc facti pudet."
prius [te] cauisse ergo quam pudere aequom fuit.

994 ut *add. Hermann*   1017 te *del. Acidalius*

472

CHRY (*reluctantly*) It's only fair if your slave serves you accord-
ing to your wishes.

NIC Now pay attention, will you?   995

CHRY Whenever you wish to, read it out. I put my ears under
your command.

NIC He didn't spare wax or the pen. But whatever it is, I'm re-
solved to read through it. (*begins to read*) "Father, please
give two hundred Philippics to Chrysalus, if you want me
to be safe or alive." No, a big thrashing.

CHRY To you . . . I'm speaking.

NIC What is it?

CHRY Didn't he write a greeting first?   1000

NIC I can't see one anywhere.

CHRY You won't give it to him if you have any sense; but if you
do give it to him, let him find himself another carrier if he
has any sense: I'm not going to take it, even if you order
me to. I'm already suspected enough when I'm free of
guilt.

NIC Keep listening while I'm reading through what's written.   1005

CHRY The letter is shameless right from the beginning.

NIC "I'm ashamed to meet you face to face, father; I've heard
that you know about this great misdeed of mine, that I
slept with the foreign soldier's wife." True, you're not   1010
joking: for two hundred gold Philippics I bought back
your life from your crime.

CHRY There isn't a single word of this that I haven't told him.

NIC "I admit that I've behaved stupidly. But I beg you, father,
don't desert me if I've gone astray in my stupidity. I had a   1015
passionate heart and untameable eyes. I was persuaded
to do a deed which I now feel ashamed of." Well then,
you should have watched out before feeling ashamed.

473

CHRY eadem istaec uerba dudum illi dixi omnia.

NIC "quaeso ut sat habeas id, pater, quod Chrysalus
1020 me obiurigauit plurumis uerbis malis,
  et me meliorem fecit praeceptis suis,
  ut te ei habere gratiam aequom sit bonam."

CHRY estne istuc istic scriptum?

NIC   em specta, tum scies.

CHRY ut qui deliquit supplex est ultro omnibus!

1025 NIC "nunc si me fas est opsecrare aps te, pater,
  da mihi ducentos nummos Philippos, te opsecro."

CHRY ne unum quidem hercle, si sapis.

NIC   sine pellegam.
  "ego ius iurandum uerbis conceptis dedi,
  daturum id me hodie mulieri ante uesperum,
1030 prius quam a me abiret. nunc, pater, ne peiierem
  cura atque abduce me hinc ab hac quantum potest,
  quam propter tantum damni feci et flagiti.
  caue tibi ducenti nummi diuidiae fuant;
  sescenta tanta reddam si uiuo tibi.
1035 uale atque haec cura." quid nunc censes, Chrysale?

CHRY nil ego tibi hodie consili quicquam dabo,
  neque ego hau committam ut, si quid peccatum siet,
  fecisse dicas de [me] mea sententia.
  uerum, ut ego opinor, si ego in istoc sim loco,
1040 dem potius aurum quam illum corrumpi sinam.
  duae condiciones sunt: utram tu accipias uide:
  uel ut aurum perdas uel ut amator peiieret.
  ego nec te iubeo nec uoto nec suadeo.

NIC miseret me illius.

1038 me *del. Merula*

CHRY I said exactly all the same words to him a while ago.

NIC "I beg you to consider it enough, father, that Chrysalus
has scolded me with a great deal of harsh words and 1021
made me a better man through his admonitions, so that
you ought to be grateful to him."

CHRY Is that written there?

NIC (*showing him the letter*) There, look, then you'll know.

CHRY How the delinquent is willing to fawn on everyone!

NIC "Now if it's right for me to ask you for a favor, father, give 1025
me two hundred Philippics, I beg you."

CHRY No, not even a single one if you're in your right mind.

NIC Let me read through it. "I've given a solemn oath that I
would give this to the woman today before the evening,
before she leaves me. Now, father, take care that I'm not 1030
perjuring myself and drag me away as quickly as possible
from here from this woman because of whom I've in-
curred such great loss and disgrace. Don't agonize over
the two hundred Philippics; I'll give it back to you a thou-
sand times over if I live. Farewell and do take care of 1035
this." What do you think now, Chrysalus?

CHRY I won't give you any advice at all today and I won't take
the risk that if anything goes wrong you might say you
acted according to my verdict. But, the way I see it, if I
were in your place I'd give him the gold rather than let 1040
him be ruined. There are two options; see which one you
choose: either you lose the gold or the lover becomes a
perjurer. I don't command, forbid, or advise you at all.

NIC I'm feeling sorry for him.

CHRY   tuos est, non mirum facis.

1045   si plus perdundum sit, periisse suauiust
          quam illud flagitium uolgo dispalescere.

NIC   ne ille edepol Ephesi multo mauellem foret,
          dum saluos esset, quam reuenisset domum.
          quid ego istic? quod perdundum est properem perdere.

1050   binos ducentos Philippos iam intus efferam,
          et militi quos dudum promisi miser
          et istos. mane istic, iam exeo ad te, Chrysale.

CHRY fit uasta Troia, scindunt proceres Pergamum.
          sciui ego iam dudum fore me exitio Pergamo.

1055   edepol qui me esse dicat cruciatu malo
          dignum, ne ego cum illo pignus haud ausim dare;
          tantas turbellas facio. sed crepuit foris:
          effertur praeda ex Troia. taceam nunciam.

NIC   cape hoc tibi aurum, Chrysale, i, fer filio.

1060   ego ad forum autem hinc ibo, ut soluam militi.

CHRY non equidem accipiam. proin tu quaeras qui ferat.
          nolo ego mi credi.

NIC   cape uero, odiose facis.

CHRY non equidem capiam.

NIC   at quaeso.

CHRY   dico ut res se habet.

NIC   morare.

1054 exitium *P*, exitio *Ritschl*

CHRY   He's your son, it's not surprising. If more had to be lost, it   1045
       would be more agreeable if it were lost than if that dis-
       grace were disclosed to every Tom, Dick, and Harry.
NIC   Honestly, I would much prefer him being in Ephesus,
       so long as he were well, to him returning home. What
       should I do in this situation? (*after a pause*) Let me rush
       to lose what has to be lost. I'll bring out two piles of two   1050
       hundred Philippics each from inside now: those that I
       promised the soldier a while ago, poor me, and the other
       ones. Wait there, I'm coming out to you soon, Chrysalus.

Exit NICOBULUS into his house.

CHRY   Troy is being levelled, the chiefs are sacking the city. I've
       known for a long time already that I'd be the end of
       Pergamum. Yes, if anyone were to say that I deserved   1055
       horrible torture, I wouldn't dare to bet against him. I'm
       creating such chaos. (*listening*) But the door has creaked:
       the booty's being carried out from Troy. I'll be quiet now.

Enter NICOBULUS from his house with two bags.

NIC   (*trying to hand one bag over*) Take this gold, Chrysalus,
       go, bring it to my son. As for me, I'll go to the market to   1060
       pay off the soldier.
CHRY   I won't take it. So look for someone to bring it to him. I
       don't want it to be entrusted to me.
NIC   Take it, do, you're getting on my nerves.
CHRY   I won't take it.
NIC   But I ask you to.
CHRY   I'm telling you how things are.
NIC   You're delaying me.

CHRY   nolo, inquam, aurum concredi mihi.

1065   uel da aliquem qui seruet me.

NIC   ohe, odiose facis.

CHRY cedo, si necesse est.

NIC   cura hoc. iam ego huc reuenero.

CHRY curatum est . . . esse te senem miserrumum.

hoc est incepta efficere pulchre: ueluti mi

euenit ut ouans praeda onustus cederem;

1070   salute nostra atque urbe capta per dolum

domum redduco integrum omnem exercitum.

sed, spectatores, uos nunc ne miremini

quod non triumpho: peruolgatum est, nil moror;

uerum tamen accipientur mulso milites.

1075   nunc hanc praedam omnem iam ad quaestorem de-
feram.

IV. x: PHILOXENVS

PHIL quam magis in pectore meo foueo quas meus filius turbas
turbet,

quam se ad uitam et quos ad mores praecipitem inscitus
capessat,

magis curae est magisque afformido ne is pereat neu cor-
rumpatur.

scio, fui ego illa aetate et feci illa omnia, sed more mo-
desto;

1081   duxi, habui scortum, potaui, dedi, donaui, sed enim id
raro.

1080   nec placitant mores quibus uideo uolgo ⟨in⟩ gnatos esse
parentes:

1068 ueluti mihi *P*, ueluti mi *Lindsay*, uti nunc mihi *Guyet*
1071 redduco ⟨iam⟩ *Ritschl*   1080–81 traiecit *Scaliger*
1081 et *P*, sed *Acidalius*   1080 in *add. Seyffert*

CHRY I'm telling you, I don't want to be entrusted with the
    gold. Or give me someone to watch over me.   1065
NIC   Hey, you're getting on my nerves.
CHRY Give it to me if it can't be helped. (*takes it*)
NIC   Take care of it. I'll be back soon.

Exit NICOBULUS to the right.

CHRY Care has been taken . . . that you should be a most miser-
    able old man. This is what it means to see one's undertak-
    ings through beautifully: just as it has become my lot
    to be marching along rejoicing and weighed down with
    booty. Now that the city's been taken through a trick   1070
    without losses on our side, I'm leading the whole army
    home intact. But, my audience, don't be surprised now
    that I'm not holding a triumph: that's too common, I
    don't care for it. Still, my soldiers will be given a recep-
    tion with honeyed wine. Now I'll immediately bring this   1075
    entire booty to the quaestor.[46]

Exit CHRYSALUS into Bacchis' house.
Enter PHILOXENUS from the right.

PHIL The more I ponder in my heart what trouble my son's
    stirring up, what sort of life and what sort of habits he's
    throwing himself into without thinking, the more wor-
    ried I am and the more I fear that he might perish or go
    astray. I know, I was of that age too and I did all those
    things, but in moderation. I did hire a prostitute, I did   1081
    enjoy her, I did drink, I did give money, I did give pres-
    ents, but rarely. I dislike the attitude I can see fathers

---

[46] A magistrate responsible for finances.

1082	ego dare me [ludum] meo gnato institui, ut animo opse-
	quium sumere possit;
	aequom esse puto, sed nimis nolo desidiae ei dare
	ludum.
1084	nunc Mnesilochum, quod mandaui,
1084ᵃ	uiso ecquid eum ad uirtutem aut ad
1085	frugem opera sua compulerit, sic
1085ᵃ	ut eum, si conuenit, scio fe-
1086	cisse: eo est ingenio natus.

ACTVS V

v. i: NICOBVLVS. PHILOXENVS

	NIC	quiquomque ubi sunt, qui fuerunt quique futuri sunt
		posthac
		stulti, stolidi, fatui, fungi, bardi, blenni, buccones,
1089		solus ego omnis longe antideo
1089ᵃ		stultitia et moribus indoctis.
1090		perii, pudet: hoccin me aetatis
1090ᵃ		ludos bis factum esse indigne?
1091		magis quam id reputo, tam magis uror
1091ᵃ		quae meus filius turbauit.
1092		perditus sum atque [etiam] eradicatus
1092ᵃ		sum, omnibus exemplis excrucior.
1093		omnia me mala consectantur,
1093ᵃ		omnibus exitiis interii.
1094		Chrysalus med hodie lacerauit,
1094ᵃ		Chrysalus me miserum spoliauit:
1095		is me scelus auro usque attondit
1095ᵃ		dolis doctis indoctum ut lubitum est.
1096		ita miles memorat meretricem es-
1096ᵃ		se eam quam ille uxorem esse aiebat,

commonly having toward their sons. I've made a practice
of giving money to my son so that he can enjoy himself. I
think that's only fair, but I don't want to indulge his idle-
ness too much. Now I'll go and see if Mnesilochus has
done what I asked him to do, if he's brought the boy back
to proper conduct and sobriety through his efforts, as I   1085
know he has done if he's found him; that's his nature.

ACT FIVE

Enter NICOBULUS from the right, not noticing anyone.

NIC   All the weakheads, thickheads, fatheads, mushrooms, id-
iots, drongos, cretins, wherever they are, were, or will be
hereafter, all these I alone surpass by far in idiocy and
stupid habits. I'm lost and I'm ashamed: is it possible that   1090
I was made fun of twice in outrageous fashion, at my age?
The more I think about it, the more I'm getting hot under
the collar because of the trouble my son's stirred up. I've
been destroyed and annihilated, I'm being tormented in
every conceivable way. Every kind of trouble's following
me, I've died every kind of death. Chrysalus has butch-
ered me today, Chrysalus has robbed me, poor me. That   1095
rascal continuously fleeced me, the dim-wit, of my gold
with bright tricks, as he liked: the soldier tells me that the
woman whom that fellow said was his wife is a prostitute;

1082 ludum *del. Buecheler*
1092 etiam *del. Hermann*

1097		omnia ut quicque actum est memorauit,
1097a		eam sibi ⟨in⟩ hunc annum conductam,
1098		relicuom id auri factum quod ego ei
1098a		stultissumus homo promisissem: hoc,
1099		hoc est quod ⟨cor⟩ peracescit;
1099a		hoc est demum quod percrucior,
1100		med hoc aetatis ludifica-
1100a		ri, immo edepol bis ludos factum
1101		cano capite atque alba barba
1101a		miserum me auro esse emunctum.
		perii, hoc seruom meum non nauci facere esse ausum! atque ego, si alibi
		plus perdiderim, minus aegre habeam minusque id mihi damno ducam.
	PHIL	certo hic prope me mihi nescioquis loqui uisust; sed quem uideo?
1105		hicquidem est pater Mnesilochi.
	NIC	eugae, socium aerumnai et mei mali uideo. Philoxene, salue.
	PHIL	et tu. unde agis?
	NIC	unde homo miser atque infortunatus.
	PHIL	at pol ego ibi sum, esse ubi miserum hominem decet atque infortunatum.
	NIC	igitur pari fortuna, aetate ut sumus, utimur.
	PHIL	sic est. sed tu, quid tibi est?
	NIC	pol mihi par, idem est quod tibi.
1110	PHIL	numquidnam ad filium haec aegritudo attinet?
	NIC	admodum.
	PHIL	idem mihi morbus in pectore est.

he told me how everything was done, that he hired her
for himself for this year, and that the money which I, like
a complete idiot, had promised him was the rest. This,
this really makes my heart bitter. This, above all, is why I
feel tormented, because I'm being fooled at my age, or   1100
rather, because I was fooled twice and cleaned out of my
gold, wretched me, despite my grey head and my white
beard. I'm done for! The idea that my slave dared to hold
this cheaper than rubbish! If I'd lost more elsewhere, I'd
be less upset and would consider it less of a loss.

PHIL (*looking around*) Definitely someone seemed to be talk-
ing here near me; but who do I see? This is Mnesilochus'   1105
father.

NIC (*noticing Philoxenus*) Hurray, I can see a companion in
my suffering and my trouble. (*addressing him*) My greet-
ings to you, Philoxenus.

PHIL And mine to you. Where are you coming from?

NIC Where a miserable and wretched man should come
from.

PHIL But *I* am in the very place where a miserable and
wretched man should be.

NIC Then we have the same fortune, just as we have the same
age.

PHIL Precisely. But how about you, what's your problem?

NIC Exactly the same as yours.

PHIL Does this grief have anything to do with your son?   1110

NIC Indeed.

PHIL I have the same illness in my breast.

1097 omnia *B*, omniaque *B⁴CD* (*sed* memorauit *trisyllabicum
displicet*)   1097ᵃ in *add. Müller*   1099 cor *add. Seyffert*
1100ᵃ sic *P*, bis *O. Skutsch*

NIC   at mihi Chrysalus optumus homo
        perdidit filium, me atque rem omnem meam.

PHIL   quid tibi ex filio nam, opsecro, aegre est?

NIC   scies:

1115   id, perit cum tuo: [atque] ambo aeque amicas habent.

PHIL   qui scis?

NIC   uidi.

PHIL   ei mihi, disperii.

NIC   quid dubitamus pultare atque huc euocare ambos foras?

PHIL   hau moror.

NIC   heus Bacchis, iube sis actutum aperiri fores,
        nisi mauoltis fores et postis comminui securibus.

V. ii: BACCHIS. NICOBVLVS. SOROR. PHILOXENVS

1120   BAC   quis sonitu ac tumultu tanto [nomine] nominat me at-
1120a   que pultat aedis?
1121   NIC ego atque hic.

BAC   quid hoc est negoti?
1121a   nam, amabo, quis has huc ouis adegit?

NIC   ouis nos uocant pessumae.

SOR   pastor harum
        dormit, quom haec eunt sic a pecu balitantes.

BAC   at pol nitent, hau sordidae uidentur ambae.

1125   SOR   attonsae hae quidem ambae usque sunt.

PHIL   ut uidentur
        deridere nos!

NIC   sine suo usque arbitratu.

BAC   rerin ter in anno tu has tonsitari?

1115 atque *del. Acidalius*
1120 nomine *del. Pylades*
1123 sic *P, om. Charisius*

NIC   But this excellent chap Chrysalus has ruined my son, myself, and my entire possessions.

PHIL What upsets you about your son, please?

NIC   You shall know. It's that he's perished together with 1115
yours; both alike have girlfriends.

PHIL How do you know?

NIC   I've seen it.

PHIL Dear me, I'm dead.

NIC   Why are we hesitating to knock and call both boys out here?

PHIL I'm not delaying.

NIC   (*knocking on Bacchis' door*) Hey, Bacchis, have this door opened immediately, will you? Unless you prefer your door and the doorposts to be cut to shreds with axes.

Enter BACCHIS and her SISTER from inside their house.

BAC   Who is calling me and banging at the house with such 1120
great noise and uproar?

NIC   He and I.

BAC   (*to her sister*) What's the matter? Please, who drove these sheep here?

NIC   (*to Philoxenus*) They're calling us sheep, the crooks.

SIS   (*to Bacchis*) Their shepherd's taking a nap, since they are wandering away from the flock like this, bleating.

BAC   But, my word, they are shiny, the two of them don't seem dirty at all.

SIS   Yes, both have been fleeced thoroughly. 1125

PHIL (*to Nicobulus*) How they seem to be making fun of us!

NIC   (*sourly*) Let them do so just as they see fit.

BAC   (*to her sister*) Do you think they're shorn three times a year?

	SOR	pol hodie altera iam bis detonsa certo est.
	BAC	uetulae sunt, †thimiamae†.
	SOR	at bonas fuisse credo.
1130	BAC	uiden limulis, opsecro, ut intuentur?
	SOR	ecastor sine omni arbitror malitia esse.
	PHIL	merito hoc nobis fit, qui quidem huc uenerimus.
	BAC	cogantur quidem intro.
	SOR	hau scio quid eo opus sit,
		quae nec lact' nec lanam ullam habent. sic sine astent.
1135		exsoluere quanti fuere, omnis fructus
1136–7		iam illis decidit. non uides, ut palantes [solae, liberae]
1138		grassentur? quin aetate credo esse mutas:
1138ª		ne balant quidem, quom a pecu cetero apsunt.
		stultae atque hau malae uidentur.
1140	BAC	reuortamur intro, soror.
	NIC	ilico ambae
1140ª		manete: haec oues uolunt uos.
	SOR	prodigium hoc quidem est: humana nos uoce appellant oues.
	NIC	haec oues uobis malam rem magnam quam debent dabunt.
	BAC	si quam debes, te condono: tibi habe, numquam aps te petam.
		sed quid est quapropter nobis uos malum minitamini?
1145	PHIL	quia nostros agnos conclusos istic esse aiunt duos.
	NIC	et praeter eos agnos meus est istic clam mordax canis:
		qui nisi nobis producuntur iam atque emittuntur foras,
		arietes truces nos erimus, iam in uos incursabimus.

1136–7 solae liberae *del. Hermann*

SIS   One of them has certainly already been fleeced twice to-day.

BAC   They're old, *   *   *.

SIS   But I believe they used to be good.

BAC   Please, can you see how they're casting sidelong glances?   1130

SIS   Yes, but I think they're without any wickedness.

PHIL   (*to Nicobulus*) This serves us right for coming here.

BAC   (*to her sister*) They really ought to be driven inside.

SIS   I don't know what that would be good for: they have nei-ther milk nor wool. Let them stand there like this. They've yielded what they were worth, all their produce   1135 is finished. Can't you see how they're wandering around, dispersed [lonely, free]? I even think that they're dumb because of their age. They aren't even bleating despite being away from the rest of the flock. They seem silly, but not bad.

BAC   Let's go back in, my sister.   1140

NIC   (*to the girls*) Stay where you are, both of you: these sheep want to speak to you.

SIS   (*to Bacchis*) This is an omen: the sheep are addressing us with human voice.

NIC   These sheep will give you the good thrashing they owe you.

BAC   If you owe us one, I'll let you off the hook. Have it for yourself, I'll never demand it from you. But what's the reason for threatening us with a thrashing?

PHIL   Because they say our two lambs are locked up there.   1145 (*points to Bacchis' house*)

NIC   And besides these lambs my dog is secretly in there, a real biter. Unless these are produced for us immediately and let out, we'll be ferocious rams and attack you this in-stant.

	BAC	soror, est quod te uolo secreto.
	SOR	eho, amabo.
	NIC	quo illaec abeunt?
1150	BAC	senem illum tibi dedo ulteriorem, lepide ut lenitum red-
		das;
		ego ad hunc iratum aggrediar, ⟨si⟩ possumus nos hos in-
		tro illicere huc.
	SOR	meum pensum ego lepide accurabo, quam⟨quam⟩ odio
		est mortem amplexari!
	BAC	facito ut facias.
	SOR	taceas. tu tuom facito: ego quod dixi hau mutabo.
	NIC	quid illaec illic in consilio duae secreto consultant?
1155	PHIL	quid ais tu, homo?
	NIC	quid me uis?
1155ᵃ	PHIL	pudet dicere me tibi quiddam.
	NIC	quid est quod pudeat?
	PHIL	sed amico homini tibi quod uolo credere certum est.
		nihili sum.
	NIC	istuc iam pridem scio. sed qui nihili es? id memora.
	PHIL	tactus sum uehementer uisco;
1159		cor stimulo foditur.
	NIC	pol tibi mul-
1159ᵃ		to aequius est coxendicem.
1160		sed quid istuc est? etsi iam ego ipsus quid sit prope scire
		puto me;
		uerum audire etiam ex te studeo.
	PHIL	uiden hanc?
	NIC	uideo.

1151 si *add. Ritschl*
1152 quam odiosum est *P,* quamquam odio est *Bergk*
1160 ipse *P,* ipsus *Ritschl* prope *P,* probe *Leo*

BAC   My sister, there's something I'd like to talk to you about in secret.

SIS   Over there, please. (*they move away*)

NIC   Where are they going?

BAC   (*to her sister*) I'm handing that old chap over to you,   1150
the one further away (*points to Philoxenus*), so that you
soften him up beautifully; I will go up to this angry one
(*points to Nicobulus*) to see if we can entice them in here.

SIS   I'll take care of my task beautifully, although it's tedious
to embrace a corpse!

BAC   Do do it.

SIS   Be quiet. You do your part; I won't change what I said.

NIC   What are those two there discussing in their secret discussion?

PHIL   What do you say, my chap?   1155

NIC   What do you want from me?

PHIL   I'm ashamed to tell you something.

NIC   What is it you're ashamed of?

PHIL   Anyway, I've decided to entrust to you, my friend, what I
want. I'm worthless.

NIC   I've known that for a long time. But in what way are you
worthless? Tell me that.

PHIL   I'm completely caught in bird-lime; my heart's being
pierced with a cattle-prod.

NIC   Heavens, it would be much more appropriate if your hip
were. But what is it? Well, I think I myself am already   1160
close to knowing what it is. But I'm keen to hear it from
you.

PHIL   Can you see this woman? (*points to Bacchis' sister*)

NIC   Yes, I can.

	PHIL	hau mala est mulier.
	NIC	pol uero ista mala et tu nihili.
	PHIL	quid multa? ego amo.
	NIC	an amas?
	PHIL	ναὶ γάρ.
	NIC	tun, homo putide, amator istac fieri aetate audes?
	PHIL	qui non?
	NIC	quia flagitium est.
	PHIL	quid opust uerbis? meo filio non sum iratus,
1165		nec te tuo est aequom esse iratum: si amant, sapienter
		faciunt.
	BAC	sequere hac.
	NIC	eunt eccas tandem
1167		probripellecebrae et persuastrices.
1167a		quid nunc? etiam redditis nobis
1168		filios et seruom? an ego experior
1168a		tecum uim maiorem?
	PHIL	abin hinc?
		non homo tuquidem es, qui istoc pacto tam lepidam ille-
		pide appelles.
1170	BAC	senex optume quantum est in terra, sine ⟨me⟩ hoc exo-
		rare aps te,
		ut istuc delictum desistas tanto opere ire oppugnatum.
1171a	NIC	ni abeas, quamquam tu bella es,
1172		malum tibi magnum dabo iam.
	BAC	patiar,
1172a		non metuo ne quid mi doleat
1173		quod ferias.
	NIC	ut blandiloqua est!
		ei mi, metuo.

1170 me *add. Ritschl*

490

PHIL The woman's not bad.

NIC Oh yes, she *is* bad, and you are worthless.

PHIL To cut a long story short, I'm in love.

NIC You're in love?

PHIL Yes indeed.[47]

NIC You, you rotten creature, dare become a lover at your age?

PHIL Why not?

NIC Because it's a disgrace.

PHIL What need is there for words? I'm not angry with my son, and it wouldn't be fair of you to be angry with yours. If they're in love, they're acting wisely.

BAC (*to her sister*) Follow me this way.   1166

NIC (*to Philoxenus*) Look, at last these persuasive seductresses are coming. (*to the girls*) What now? Are you giving us back our sons and my slave? Or am I to try more forceful measures with you?

PHIL Won't you go away from here? You aren't a human being, addressing such a lovely girl in that way, the opposite of lovely.

BAC (*to Nicobulus*) Best of all old men on earth, let me persuade you to give up opposing your son's naughtiness so much.   1170

NIC If you don't go away, I'll give you a good thrashing this instant, even though you're pretty.

BAC I'll bear it, I'm not afraid that your spanking will hurt me.

NIC (*aside*) How coaxing she is! Dear me, I'm scared.

[47] Philoxenus replies in Greek like an oracle.

491

	SOR	hic magis tranquillust.
1175	BAC	i hac mecum intro atque ibi si quid uis
1175ᵃ		filium concastigato.
	NIC	abin a me, scelus?
	BAC	sine, mea Pietas, te exorem.
	NIC	exores tu me?
	SOR	ego quidem ab hoc certe exorabo.
	PHIL	immo ego te oro ut me intro abducas.
	SOR	lepidum te!
	PHIL	at scin quo pacto me ad te intro abducas?
	SOR	mecum ut sis.
1179	PHIL	omnia quae cupio commemoras.
1179ᵃ	NIC	uidi ego nequam homines, uerum te
1180		neminem deteriorem.
	PHIL	ita sum.
	BAC	i hac mecum intro, ubi tibi sit lepide uictibus, uino atque
		unguentis.
1182	NIC	satis, satis iam uostri est conuiui:
1182ᵃ		me nil paenitet ut sim acceptus:
1182ᵇ		quadrigentis Philippis filius me et
1183		Chrysalus circumduxerunt.
1183ᵃ		quem quidem ego ut non excruciem
1184		alterum tantum auri non meream.
1184ᵃ	BAC	quid tandem si dimidium auri
1185		redditur, in' hac mecum intro? atque ut e-
1185ᵃ		is delicta ignoscas.
	PHIL	faciet.
1186	NIC	minime, nolo. nil moror, sine sic.
1186ᵃ		malo illos ulcisci ambo.

SIS   (*to Bacchis, pointing to Philoxenus*) This one's more peaceful.

BAC   (*to Nicobulus*) Come inside with me this way and scold   1175 your son there if you wish.

NIC   Won't you go away from me, you criminal?

BAC   Let me persuade you, my little saint.

NIC   You persuade me?

SIS   I for one will definitely persuade this man. (*points to Philoxenus*)

PHIL   Yes, I beg you to take me inside.

SIS   How lovely you are!

PHIL   But do you know on which condition you should take me inside to you?

SIS   On condition that you're together with me.

PHIL   You're saying everything I desire.

NIC   (*to Philoxenus*) I've seen useless people, but no one worse than you.

PHIL   That's what I'm like.

BAC   (*to Nicobulus*) Come inside with me, this way, where   1181 you'll have a lovely time with food, wine, and perfumes.

NIC   I've already had more than enough of your party. I don't care about how I've been received. My son and Chrysalus have swindled me out of four hundred Philippics. I wouldn't forgo torturing him, not for the same amount of gold again.

BAC   And what if half the gold is returned to you, won't you go   1184a inside with me? And you must forgive them for their naughtiness.

PHIL   He'll do it.

NIC   No, I don't want to. I couldn't care less, let it be like this. I prefer to take revenge on those two.

PHIL etiam tu, homo nihili? quod di dant boni caue culpa tua
    amissis:
    dimidium auri datur: accipias potesque et scortum ac-
    cumbas.

1189 NIC egon ubi filius corrumpatur meus, ibi potem?
–90 PHIL   potandum est.

NIC age iam, id ut ut est, etsi est dedecori, patiar, facere indu-
    cam animum:

1192   egon quom haec cum illo accubet inspectem?
BAC   immo equidem pol tecum accumbam,

1192ª   te amabo et te amplexabor.
1193 NIC caput prurit, perii, uix negito.
1193ª BAC non tibi uenit in mentem, amabo,
1194   si dum uiuas tibi bene facias
1194ª   tam pol id quidem esse hau perlonginquom,
1195   nec, si hoc hodie amiseris, post in
1195ª   morte id euenturum esse umquam?

NIC quid ago?
PHIL   quid agas? rogitas etiam?
NIC   lubet et metuo.
BAC   quid metuis?
NIC ne obnoxius filio sim et seruo.
BAC   mel meum, amabo, istaec fiant.
    tuost: unde illum sumere censes, nisi quod tute illi de-
    deris?
    hanc ueniam illis sine te exorem.

1197 fiunt *P*, fiant *Ussing*
1198 censes sumere *P, transp. Ritschl*

494

PHIL What is it with you, idiot? Don't lose through your own
fault what good the gods are giving you. You're given half
the gold; you should take it, drink, and sleep with a pros-
titute.

NIC I should be drinking in the place where my son's being
corrupted?

1189–
90

PHIL You have to drink.

NIC Go on now, whatever it's like, even if it's a disgrace, I'll
bear it, I'll bring myself to do it. But should I look on
when she's lying with him?

BAC No, of course not. I'll be lying with *you*, I'll make love to
you and embrace *you*.

NIC (*aside*) My head's itching, I'm done for, I can barely keep
refusing.

BAC (*to Nicobulus*) Please, doesn't it occur to you that if you
do yourself a good turn while you're alive, that's not a
terribly long time anyway, and that if you let go of this
opportunity today, it'll never come to you when you're
dead?

NIC (*to Philoxenus*) What am I to do?

1196

PHIL What are you to do? You even ask?

NIC I'd like to, and I'm scared.

BAC What are you scared of?

NIC Of being vulnerable in front of my son and my slave.

BAC My honey, please, let this happen now: he's yours; where
do you think he's taking it from unless you yourself give it
to him? Let me persuade you to forgive them for this.

	NIC	ut terebrat! satin offirmatum
1200		quod mihi erat, id me exorat?
		tua sum opera et propter te improbior?
	BAC	neminis quam mea mauellem.
		satin ego istuc habeo offirmatum?
	NIC	quod semel dixi hau mutabo.
	BAC	it dies, ite intro accubitum,
		filii uos exspectant intus.
	NIC	quam quidem actutum emoriamur.
1205	SOR	uesper hic est, sequimini.
	NIC	ducite nos quo lubet tamquam quidem addictos.
	BAC	lepide ipsi hi sunt capti, suis qui filiis fecere insidias.
	GREX	hi senes nisi fuissent nihili iam inde ab adulescentia,
		non hodie hoc tantum flagitium facerent canis capitibus;
		neque adeo haec faceremus, ni antehac uidissemus fieri
1210		ut apud lenones riuales filiis fierent patres.
		spectatores, uos ualere uolumus; [et] clare applaudite.

1201 ne is *P*, neminis *Leo*
1211 et *del. Bergk* applaudere *P*, applaudite *Bergk*

NIC How she's drilling a hole into me! Is she persuading me to give up what was my firm resolution? (*to Bacchis*) Am I 1201 less respectable now because of your effort and because of you?

BAC I'd prefer it through my effort rather than anyone else's. Do I have this as your firm resolution?

NIC I won't change what I've said once.

BAC The day is going, go inside to lie down, your sons are waiting for you.

NIC Waiting for how soon we die.

SIS It's evening, follow us. 1205

NIC Take us where you like as if we were your bond slaves.

BAC (*to the audience*) They're caught in a lovely way themselves, and they wanted to set a trap for their sons!

Exeunt BACCHIS and her SISTER into their house, followed by PHILOXENUS and NICOBULUS.
Enter the whole TROUPE.

TROUPE If these old men hadn't been worthless already from their youth onwards, they wouldn't have committed such a great offence now that their heads are grey. And we wouldn't have put on this play if we hadn't seen it happen before that fathers turn into their sons' rivals at 1210 the pimps' places. Spectators, we wish you well; applaud loudly!

CAPTIVI,

OR

THE CAPTIVES

INTRODUCTORY NOTE

The *Captiui* was praised by Lessing as one of the finest plays ever put on the stage. Dousa, the great Dutch scholar, said that whenever he opened the *Captiui*, he himself became a captive of the play. The driving force behind the action is not passionate love as in other comedies, but the touching devotion of a slave, Tyndarus, to his master, Philocrates.

Philocrates is a young man from Elis. The Eleans are at war with the Aetolians, and Philocrates and Tyndarus have been taken prisoners. They are sold to an old Aetolian called Hegio.

Hegio has already bought a number of Elean captives, but not in order to make money as a slave-dealer. His aim is a noble one: his son Philopolemus was taken prisoner by the Eleans, and Hegio is trying to exchange one of his captives for his son.

Philopolemus is not Hegio's only child. We learn that he had a second son. When this second son was four years old, he was kidnapped by Hegio's own slave Stalagmus, and both slave and son disappeared for good. Hegio has long since given up all hope of ever finding his kidnapped son again. But he is all the keener to retrieve Philopolemus.

Hegio has found out that Philocrates belongs to a

wealthy family, and he hopes that he will be able to exchange Philopolemus for him. What he cannot know is that Philocrates and Tyndarus have exchanged their clothes; Philocrates pretends to be Tyndarus, and Tyndarus pretends to be Philocrates. In this way they want to trick Hegio and set Philocrates free. They manage to persuade Hegio to send Philocrates, whom he believes to be the slave, to Elis to bring back Philopolemus. Meanwhile, Tyndarus is to stay at Hegio's place.

The scheme does not work for long. Aristophontes, another of Hegio's captives, is at Hegio's brother's place. When he hears that Philocrates is also a prisoner, he asks if he can speak to him and is brought to Tyndarus. Aristophontes, who does not know about the captives' trick, reveals the truth to Hegio, who is deeply upset at having lost a captive who would have been invaluable for getting his son back. Tyndarus gets punished very severely. He will have to do the hardest kind of slave labor until he dies. Nevertheless, he remains defiant and does not regret saving his master.

But Philocrates returns soon and brings with him not only Philopolemus but also Stalagmus, Hegio's slave. Hegio is sorry for punishing Tyndarus so hard. He questions Stalagmus about his other son's fate and finds out that Stalagmus sold this other son to Philocrates' family. Tyndarus turns out to be Hegio's other son. Both sons are restored to Hegio, and Stalagmus gets the punishment he deserves.

Since the *Captiui* is such an unusual comedy, it would be interesting to know something about the Greek original. Plautus mentions neither the name of the original play nor its author, and other potential sources of information such as papyrus finds or comments in later literature are equally unhelpful in this respect; we do know that a certain Posidippus wrote a play of the same name, but in the absence of more detailed information, it is impossible to draw any conclusions. At least we have some indications as to when Plautus' play was first performed. In l. 90, Ergasilus speaks of going to the *Porta Trigemina* to earn money, presumably as a porter. A market at this place existed as early as 193. The other pieces of evidence are less clear-cut, but perhaps convincing when considered in their entirety rather than one by one. In l. 888, there is a pun on *boia*, a forked stick used to punish slaves, and the Celtic Boii. The Boii were finally defeated in the battle of Mutina in 193, and when Scipio Nasica held a triumph in 191, he presumably had Boii in his train. The *Captiui* is likely to have been staged after this event. Can we be more precise? In l. 162 there is a pun on soldiers from Placentia in Etruria. This need not be a topical reference, but if it is, it may refer to the resettlement of the town in 190 at Scipio Nasica's command (Placentia was attacked by the Boii in 200). Similarly, the pun on naval troops in l. 164 might refer to Regillus' naval triumph in 189. It is possible that Tyndarus is punished by being sent to the quarry, because this is what happened to the Aetolian leaders in 190 (Livy 37. 3. 8). Rome defeated the Aetolians in 189, and that may well be the year when *The Captives* were first performed; a positive portrayal of Aetolians while they were still fighting with Rome is unlikely.

For the text of the *Captiui* we by and large have to rely on the Palatine manuscripts. The Ambrosian palimpsest has only preserved traces of this play.

SELECT BIBLIOGRAPHY

Editions and Commentaries

Brix, J., and M. Niemeyer (1910), *Ausgewählte Komödien des T. Maccius Plautus für den Schulgebrauch erklärt*, vol. 2: *Captivi* (6th ed. Leipzig).

Lindsay, W. M. (1900), *The Captivi of Plautus: Edited with Introduction, Apparatus Criticus and Commentary* (London).

Criticism

Benz, L., and E. Lefèvre (eds.) (1998), *Maccus barbarus: Sechs Kapitel zur Originalität der* Captivi *des Plautus* (Tübingen).

Franko, G. F. (1995), "*Fides*, Aetolia, and Plautus' *Captivi*," *Transactions of the American Philological Association* 125: 155–76.

Hough, J. N. (1942), "The Structure of the *Captivi*," *American Journal of Philology* 63: 26-37.

Konstan, D. (1976), "Plautus' *Captivi* and the Ideology of the Ancient City-State," *Ramus* 5: 76–91.

Lowe, J. C. B. (1991), "Prisoners, Guards, and Chains in Plautus' *Captivi*," *American Journal of Philology* 112: 29–44.

Raffaelli, R. (2006), "Una commedia anomala: i *Captivi*," in G. Petrone and M. M. Bianco (eds.), *La commedia di Plauto e la parodia: il lato comico dei paradigmi tragici* (Palermo), 25–52.

Raffaelli, R., and A. Tontini (eds.) (2002), *Lecturae Plautinae Sarsinates V: Captivi (Sarsina, 8 settembre 2001)* (Urbino).

Wellesley, K. (1955), "The Production Date of Plautus' *Captiui*," *American Journal of Philology* 76: 298–305.

CAPTIVI

ARGVMENTVM

Captust in pugna Hegionis filius;
Alium quadrimum fugiens seruos uendidit.
Pater captiuos commercatur Aleos,
Tantum studens ut natum ‹captum› recuperet;
5 Et inibi emit olim amissum filium.
Is suo cum domino ueste uersa ac nomine
Vt amittatur fecit; ipsus plectitur;
Et is reduxit captum, et fugitiuom simul,
Indicio cuius alium agnoscit filium.

arg. 4 captum *add. Bothe*
arg. 5 inibi *P*, in ibus *Gulielmus*

THE CAPTIVES

PLOT SUMMARY

Hegio's son was taken prisoner in battle. A runaway slave sold
his other son when he was four years old. The father bought
Elean captives, being very keen on recovering the son who was
taken prisoner. And among them he bought the son he had lost 5
long ago. This one exchanged clothes and names with his mas-
ter and brought it about that the master was sent off. He himself
was punished. And the master brought back the captive son and
the runaway slave together. With information provided by this
slave, Hegio recognizes his other son.

PERSONAE

ERGASILVS parasitus
HEGIO senex
LORARIVS
TYNDARVS seruos captiuos
PHILOCRATES adulescens captiuos
ARISTOPHONTES adulescens
PVER
PHILOPOLEMVS adulescens
STALAGMVS seruos

SCAENA

in Aetolia

THE CAPTIVES

CHARACTERS

ERGASILUS a hanger-on; Philopolemus' friend
HEGIO an old man; a very dignified Aetolian
SLAVE-OVERSEER works for Hegio
TYNDARUS a slave, prisoner of war; serves Philocrates, but
    turns out to be Hegio's son
PHILOCRATES a young prisoner of war; from Elis
ARISTOPHONTES a young man; Philocrates' friend from
    Elis
SLAVE-BOY works in the kitchen
PHILOPOLEMUS a young man; Hegio's other son, prisoner
    of war in Elis
STALAGMUS a slave; of bad character

STAGING

We are in a city in Aetolia. The stage represents a street in it. On
the street there is Hegio's house. To the left, the street leads to
the harbor; to the right, to the city center. The house of Hegio's
brother is off-stage, in the direction of the city center.

PROLOGVS

   hos quos uidetis stare hic captiuos duos,
   illi quia astant, hi stant ambo, non sedent;
   hoc uos mihi testes estis me uerum loqui.
4 senex qui hic habitat Hegio est huius pater.
21 hic nunc domi seruit suo patri, nec scit pater;
22 enim uero di nos quasi pilas homines habent.
5 sed is quo pacto seruiat suo sibi patri,
   id ego hic apud uos proloquar, si operam datis.
   seni huic fuerunt filii nati duo;
   alterum quadrimum puerum seruos surpuit
   eumque hinc profugiens uendidit in Alide
10 patri huiusce ⟨hominis⟩. iam hoc tenetis? optume est.
   negat hercle illic ultumus. accedito.
   si non ubi sedeas locus est, est ubi ambules,
   quando histrionem cogis mendicarier.
   ego me tua causa, ne erres, non rupturus sum.
15 uos qui potestis ope uostra censerier
   accipite relicuom: alieno uti nil moror.
   fugitiuos ille, ut dixeram ante, huius patri

     2 illi qui astant *BD*, illi qui stant *VEJ*, illi quia astant *Lindsay*
     21, 22 *hic posuit Niemeyer*
     10 patri huiusce ⟨hominis⟩ *Lindsay in apparatu*

---

   1 The censors classified and registered citizens according to their property. Those who had enough to pay taxes were on the censor's list and were called *assidui* (permanent residents), a word connected with

THE CAPTIVES

PROLOGUE

Tyndarus and Philocrates are standing in front of Hegio's house, chained together. Enter the SPEAKER OF THE PROLOGUE.

Those two prisoners you can see standing here, they're both standing, not sitting, because the people back there are standing (*points to some spectators standing at the back*). You're my witnesses that I'm speaking the truth. The old man who lives here, Hegio, is this one's (*points to Tyndarus*) father. Now this chap (*points to Tyndarus*) is his own father's slave at home, and his father doesn't know it. Yes, the gods really treat us humans like footballs. But how it happened that he's his own father's slave, that I'll tell you here, if you give me your attention. This old man had two sons. A slave snatched one of them when he was a four-year-old boy, and on his flight from here he sold him in Elis to the father of this man (*points to Philocrates*). Do you get it now? Excellent. (*looks around*) That one at the very back says no. Step forward. (*a spectator comes to the stage*) If there's no room for you to sit, there's room for you to walk (*points to the exit*), since you force an actor to turn beggar. Don't be fooled, I'm not going to crack my lungs for your sake. (*to the rest of the audience*) You who have enough property to be on the censor's list,[1] receive the instalment that's still due; I don't much like to be in debt. As I said before, that runaway slave sold his master (*points to Tyndarus*) to the father of this chap here (*points to*

4

7

11

15

sedere (sit), hence the jocular contrast between the man who cannot sit and those who are on the censor's list.

domo quem profugiens dominum apstulerat uendidit.
is postquam hunc emit, dedit eum huic gnato suo
20   peculiarem, quia quasi una aetas erat.
23   rationem habetis, quo modo unum amiserit.
postquam belligerant Aetoli cum Aleis,
25   ut fit in bello, capitur alter filius.
medicus Menarchus emit ibidem in Alide.
coepit captiuos commercari hic Aleos,
si quem reperire posset qui mutet suom,
illum captiuom: hunc suom esse nescit qui domi est.
30   et quoniam heri indaudiuit de summo loco
summoque genere captum esse equitem Aleum,
nil pretio parsit, filio dum parceret:
reconciliare ut facilius posset domum,
emit hosc' de praeda ambos de quaestoribus.
35   hisce autem inter sese hunc confinxerunt dolum,
quo pacto hic seruos suom erum hinc amittat domum.
itaque inter se commutant uestem et nomina;
illic uocatur Philocrates, hic Tyndarus:
huius illic, hic illius hodie fert imaginem.
40   et hic hodie expediet hanc docte fallaciam,
et suom erum faciet libertatis compotem,
eodemque pacto fratrem seruabit suom
reducemque faciet liberum in patriam ad patrem
imprudens: itidem ut saepe iam in multis locis
45   plus insciens quis fecit quam prudens boni.
sed inscientes sua sibi fallacia
ita compararunt et confinxerunt dolum
itaque hi commenti de sua sententia
ut in seruitute hic ad suom maneat patrem:

34 hosce e *Studemund dubitanter*

Philocrates), the master he'd snatched when he was running
away from home. After this man bought him, he gave him to his
son here (*points to Philocrates*) as his own because their age was 20
roughly the same. Well, you understand how he lost one son.
Now that the Aetolians are fighting with the Eleans, his other 25
son's taken prisoner, as so happens in a war. A doctor, Menar-
chus, bought him in the same place, in Elis. This man here be-
gan to buy Elean prisoners of war in the hope of finding some-
one he could exchange his son for, I mean the prisoner; he
doesn't know that this chap here at home (*points to Tyndarus*) is
his son as well. And since he heard yesterday that an Elean 30
knight of the highest rank and the highest family connections
had been taken prisoner, he didn't spare his wallet so long as he
could spare his son. In order to be able to get him back home
more easily, he bought these two from among the spoils from
the quaestors.[2] But they've come up with a scheme among 35
themselves how this slave here (*points to Tyndarus*) can send
his master home. So they interchange clothes and names among
each other. That one (*points to Tyndarus*) calls himself Philo-
crates, this one (*points to Philocrates*) Tyndarus. That one's pos-
ing as this one and this one as that one today. And this chap here 40
(*points to Tyndarus*) will carry out this trick brilliantly today;
he'll set his master free and by the same stroke he will, unknow-
ingly, save his brother and let him return home to his father as a
free man: just as often before in many places a person's done 45
more good unknowingly than knowingly. But in their scheme
they've unknowingly prepared, contrived, and devised their
trick in such a way, all at their own suggestion, that this chap
here (*points to Tyndarus*) is remaining in slavery at his father's.

[2] The quaestors were Roman officials whose main duties were
money-related. They sold booty in auctions.

50 ita nunc ignorans suo sibi seruit patri;
   homunculi quanti sunt, quom recogito!
   haec res agetur nobis, uobis fabula.
   sed etiam est paucis uos quod monitos uoluerim.
   profecto expediet fabulae huic operam dare:
55 non pertractate facta est neque item ut ceterae:
   nec spurcidici insunt uorsus immemorabiles;
   hic nec periurus leno est nec meretrix mala
   nec miles gloriosus; ne uereamini
   quia bellum Aetolis esse dixi cum Aleis:
60 foris illic extra scaenam fient proelia.
   nam hoc paene iniquom est, comico choragio
   conari desubito agere nos tragoediam.
   proin si quis pugnam exspectat, litis contrahat:
   ualentiorem nactus aduorsarium
65 si erit, ego faciam ut pugnam inspectet non bonam,
   adeo ut spectare postea omnis oderit.
   abeo. ualete, iudices iustissumi
   domi duellique duellatores optumi.

ACTVS I

I. i: ERGASILVS

ERG   iuuentus nomen indidit "Scorto" mihi,
70   eo quia inuocatus soleo esse in conuiuio.
       scio apsurde dictum hoc derisores dicere,
       at ego aio recte. nam scortum in conuiuio
       sibi amator, talos quom iacit, scortum inuocat.
       estne inuocatum ⟨scortum⟩ an non? planissume;
75   uerum hercle uero nos parasiti planius,

60 illic *P*, illi *Lindsay*   74 scortum *add. Bentley*

So now he's his own father's slave and doesn't know him. Of 50
what little importance humans are when I think about it! For us
this will be fact, for you it will be fiction. But there's still some-
thing else I'd like to point out to you briefly. It'll definitely be
worth paying attention to this play: it hasn't been composed in 55
the hackneyed fashion or the same way as the others; there are
no dirty lines in it that are unfit to be repeated. Here there's no
pimp perjuring himself, no bad prostitute, no boastful soldier.
Don't be afraid because I said that the Aetolians are at war with
the Eleans: the battles will take place out there, off-stage. Well, 60
it would almost be unfair if we were suddenly to try staging a
tragedy with our comedy get-up. So if anyone's looking for a
battle scene, he'd better pick some quarrels. If he picks on a
stronger opponent, I bet he'll watch such an unpleasant battle
scene that he'll hate watching all of them afterwards. Now I 66
leave the stage. Farewell, most just of judges at home and best
of warriors in war.

*Exit the SPEAKER OF THE PROLOGUE off the stage; exeunt
Tyndarus and Philocrates into the house.*

ACT ONE

Enter ERGASILUS from the right.

ERG   The young people have given me the name "The Prosti-
       tute" because people shout out when I'm at a banquet. I 70
       know the mockers say that's an absurd nickname, but I
       claim it has a point; well, when a lover throws the dice at a
       banquet, he shouts out his prostitute's name. Is the pros-
       titute's name shouted out or not? It clearly is. But when it 75
       comes to us hangers-on, people shout "out" even more

515

quos numquam quisquam nec uocat neque inuocat.
quasi mures semper edimus alienum cibum;
ubi res prolatae sunt, quom rus homines eunt,
simul prolatae res sunt nostris dentibus.
80   quasi, quom caletur, cocleae in occulto latent,
suo sibi suco uiuont, ros si non cadit,
item parasiti rebus prolatis latent
in occulto miseri, uictitant suco suo,
dum ruri rurant homines quos ligurriant.
85   prolatis rebus parasiti uenatici
[canes] sumus, quando res redierunt, Molossici
odiosicique et multum incommodestici.
et hic quidem hercle, nisi qui colaphos perpeti
potes parasitus frangique aulas in caput,
90   uel ire extra Portam Trigeminam ad saccum licet.
quod mihi ne eueniat nonnullum periculum est.
nam postquam meus rex est potitus hostium—
ita nunc belligerant Aetoli cum Aleis;
nam Aetolia haec est, illi est captus [in] Alide
95   Philopolemus, huius Hegionis filius
senis qui hic habitat, quae aedes lamentariae
mihi sunt, quas quotiensquomque conspicio fleo;
nunc hic occepit quaestum hunc fili gratia
inhonestum et maxume alienum ingenio suo:
100   homines captiuos commercatur, si queat
aliquem inuenire, suom qui mutet filium.
quod quidem ego nimis quam cupio ‹et opto› ut impe-
          tret;

86 canes *del. Pylades, ante* Molossici *posuit Niemeyer*
89 potes *P,* potes‹t› *Brix*   94 illic *P,* illi *Lindsay in del. Brix*
102 cupio ‹et opto› ut *Niemeyer*

clearly; no one ever calls on us or calls out our names.
Like mice we're constantly eating other people's food.
When it's vacation and people go to the countryside, it's
also vacation for our teeth. Just as snails hide in a secret   80
place when it's hot and live on their own juice if no dew
falls, hangers-on hide in a secret place during vacation,
poor devils, and live on their own juice while the people
they sponge on live a country life in the countryside.
During vacation we hangers-on are hunting dogs;[3] after   85
vacation we are Molossian dogs,[4] Molestian dogs, and
veritable Labra-bores. And here at any rate, unless as a
hanger-on you can bear blows, and pots being broken on
your head, you can just as well go outside the Three-Arch   90
Gate[5] to carry a porter's bag. There's quite some danger
that this will happen to me. Well, after my patron fell into
the enemy's hands—you see, the Aetolians are at war
with the Eleans now; this is Aetolia, and Philopolemus   94
was taken prisoner there, in Elis; he's the son of Hegio,
the old man living here, whose house makes me lament
—every time I see it I have to cry. Now for his son's sake
he began this degrading business here, which is com-
pletely out of keeping with his character: he's buying   100
prisoners in the hope of finding someone he could ex-
change his son for. I really wish and desire very much that

[3] I.e., thin as greyhounds and hunting for meals.

[4] A famous breed of dog, similar to modern mastiffs, strongly built.

[5] The *Porta Trigemina* was between the Aventine Mount and the
river; the road through the gate led to Ostia.

nam ni illum recipit, nihil est quo me recipiam.
n⟨eque⟩ ulla est spes iuuentutis, sese omnes amant;
105 ill' demum antiquis est adulescens moribus,
quoius numquam uoltum tranquillaui gratiis.
condigne pater est eius moratus moribus.
nunc ad eum pergam. sed aperitur ostium,
und' saturitate saepe ego exii ebrius.

I. ii: HEGIO. LORARIVS. ERGASILVS

110 HEG aduorte animum sis: tu istos captiuos duos,
heri quos emi de praeda de quaestoribus,
is indito catenas singularias
istas, maiores, quibus sunt iuncti, demito;
sinito ambulare, si foris, si intus uolent,
115 sed uti asseruentur magna diligentia.
liber captiuos auis ferae consimilis est:
semel fugiendi si data est occasio,
satis est, numquam postilla possis prendere.
LOR omnes profecto liberi lubentius
120 sumus quam seruimus.
HEG non uidere ita tu quidem.
LOR si non est quod dem, mene uis dem ipse . . . in pedes?
HEG si dederis, erit extemplo mihi quod dem tibi.
LOR auis me ferae consimilem faciam, ut praedicas.
HEG ita ut dicis: nam si faxis, te in caueam dabo.
125 sed satis uerborum est. cura quae iussi atque abi.

104 nulla *P*, nec ulla *Brix*, non ulla *Lindsay in apparatu*
111 a quaestoribus *Fleckeisen*

[6] He implies that the overseer did not save any money to buy his freedom.

he succeeds in it: if he doesn't get him back, there's
nowhere for me to go. There's no hope in the young
people, they all love only themselves. Only that young   105
chap belongs to the old school: I've never lightened his
countenance without some tangible reward. His father
has the same good character. Now I'll call on him. (*moves
toward the door, then stops*) But there opens the door I
often came out of, tipsy from having filled myself so well.
(*steps aside*)

Enter HEGIO from his house, followed by a SLAVE-OVER-
SEER.

HEG   Pay attention, will you? Those two prisoners I bought   110
from among the spoils from the quaestors yesterday, put
one of these separate chains on each of them and take off
the heavier ones they're bound with now. Let them walk
around outside or inside if they wish, provided they're   115
watched over very carefully. A free man taken prisoner is
like a wild bird: once he's given a chance of escape, it's
enough, you can never catch him afterwards.

OVER   Well, we'd all rather be free than slaves.   120

HEG   You at any rate don't seem to be like that.[6]

OVER   If I don't have anything to give you, do you want me to
give you . . . the slip?

HEG   If you give me the slip, there will immediately be some-
thing I can give you.

OVER   I'll be like a wild bird, just as you tell me.

HEG   Just as you say: if you do so, I'll give you a cage to be in.
But enough small talk. Do take care of what I ordered   125

ego ibo ad fratrem ad alios captiuos meos,
uisam ne nocte hac quippiam turbauerint.
ind' me continuo recipiam rursum domum.

ERG aegre est mi hunc facere quaestum carcerarium
130   propter sui gnati miseriam miserum senem.
sed si ullo pacto ille huc conciliari potest,
uel carnuficinam hunc facere possum perpeti.

HEG quis hic loquitur?

ERG   ego, qui tuo maerore maceror,
macesco, consenesco et tabesco miser;
135   ossa atque pellis sum misera . . . macritudine;
neque umquam quicquam me iuuat quod edo domi:
foris aliquantillum etiam quod gusto id beat.

HEG Ergasile, salue.

ERG   di te bene ament, Hegio.

HEG ne fle.

ERG   egone illum non fleam? egon non defleam
140   talem adulescentem?

HEG   semper sensi filio
meo te esse amicum et illum intellexi tibi.

ERG tum denique homines nostra intellegimus bona,
quom quae in potestate habuimus ea amisimus.
ego, postquam gnatus tuos potitust hostium,
145   expertus quanti fuerit nunc desidero.

HEG alienus quom eius incommodum tam aegre feras,
quid me patrem par facere est, quoi ille est unicus?

---

135 miser (miseri B¹) amacritudine *P*, miser macritudine *Nonius*

and go away. I'll go to my brother's to my other prisoners. I'll check that they didn't create any trouble last night. From there I'll return home immediately.

Exit the SLAVE-OVERSEER into Hegio's house; ERGASILUS approaches, but is not yet fully visible.

ERG (*loudly enough for Hegio to hear*) I'm sad that this unfor- 129
tunate old man has to do prison business because of his son's unfortunate circumstances. (*aside*) But if the son can be got back here in any way, I could even bear it if the father were doing executions.

HEG (*looking around*) Who's speaking here?

ERG (*comes to Hegio and starts crying*) I, a wretched man who is growing weary, thin, old, and weak because of my grief for you. (*aside*) I'm skin and bones from miserable . . . 135
thinness. (*to Hegio*) And nothing I eat at home ever pleases me. (*aside*) But the tiniest morsel I taste outside makes me happy.

HEG Hello, Ergasilus.

ERG May the gods love you dearly, Hegio.

HEG Stop crying.

ERG Should I not cry for him? Should I not weep without re-
straint for such a man? 140

HEG I always felt that you were close to my son and I saw that he was close to you.

ERG Only when we've lost what we once had in our power do we understand our blessings. After your son fell into the enemy's hands I realized how much he meant to me and 145
now I long for his return.

HEG Since you as an outsider find it so hard to bear his misfor-
tune, what must I as his father do, for whom he is the only son?

521

	ERG	alienus? ego alienus illi? aha, Hegio,
		numquam istuc dixis neque animum induxis tuom;
150		tibi ille unicust, mi etiam unico magis unicus.
	HEG	laudo, malum quom amici tuom ducis malum.
		nunc habe bonum animum.
	ERG	eheu, huic illud dolet,
		quia nunc remissus est edendi exercitus.
	HEG	nullumne interea nactu's, qui posset tibi
155		remissum quem dixti imperare exercitum?
	ERG	quid credis? fugitant omnes hanc prouinciam,
		quoi optigerat postquam captust Philopolemus tuos.
	HEG	non pol mirandum est fugitare hanc prouinciam.
		multis et multigeneribus opus est tibi
160		militibus: primumdum opus est Pistorensibus;
		eorum sunt aliquot genera Pistorensium:
		opus Panicis est, opus Placentinis quoque;
		opus Turdetanis, opust Ficedulensibus;
		iam maritumi omnes milites opus sunt tibi.
165	ERG	ut saepe summa ingenia in occulto latent!
		hic qualis imperator nunc priuatus est.
	HEG	habe modo bonum animum, nam illum confido domum
		in his diebus me reconciliassere.
		nam eccum hic captiuom adulescentem Aleum,
170		prognatum genere summo et summis ditiis:
		hoc illum me mutare—

169 eccum ⟨intus⟩ *Redslob*

---

[7] *Pistorenses* = inhabitants of Pistorium, pun on *pistor* (miller/baker); *Panici* = *Punici* (Phoenicians?), pun on *panis* (bread); *Placentini* = inhabitants of Placentia (modern Piacenza), pun on *placenta* (cake);

ERG   Outsider? I an outsider to him? No, no, Hegio, never say
that, and never believe that. To you he's the only one, but   150
to me he's even more of an only one than an only one.
(*starts crying again*)

HEG   I praise you for considering a friend's misfortune to be
your own misfortune. Now take heart.

ERG   Oh, oh, oh, this one (*points to his stomach*) is in pain
about the eating force having been dismissed now.

HEG   Haven't you found anyone in the meantime who could
mobilize the force for you again which you said has been   155
dismissed?

ERG   Would you believe it? All and sundry have been shying
away from this task ever since your Philopolemus was
captured, who it had been allotted to.

HEG   Well, it's not strange that they've been shying away from
this task. You need many soldiers of different kinds:[7] first
you need the ones from Bakerville. There are several   161
types of soldiers from Bakerville: you need those from
Breading and you also need those from the Cake Dis-
trict. You need soldiers from Thrushia and you need sol-
diers from Puerto Fico. Then you also need all the sol-
diers from the coast.

ERG   How often the greatest talents lie hidden! So great a   165
commander is a private citizen today.

HEG   Do cheer up: I am confident that I shall get him back
home in a few days. Look here (*points to his house*),
there's a young prisoner from Elis, from a great family
and with great wealth. Exchanging him for my son—   171

Turdetani = a Spanish tribe, pun on *turdus* (thrush); *Ficedulenses* =
comic formation, pun on *ficedula* (beccafico, a bird considered a deli-
cacy).

<ERG>   confido fore.
[ERG] ita di deaeque faxint. sed num quo foras
   uocatus <es> ad cenam?
HEG   nusquam, quod sciam.
   sed quid tu id quaeris?
ERG   quia mi est natalis dies;
175   propterea <a> te uocari ad te ad cenam uolo.
HEG   facete dictum! sed si pauxillo potes
   contentus esse.
ERG   ne perpauxillum modo,
   nam istoc me assiduo uictu delecto domi;
   age sis, roga emptum: "nisi qui meliorem afferet
180   quae mi atque amicis placeat condicio magis,"
   quasi fundum uendam, meis me addicam legibus.
HEG   profundum uendis tu quidem, hau fundum, mihi.
   sed si uenturu's, temperi.
ERG   em, uel iam otium est.
HEG   i modo, uenare leporem: nunc erim tenes;
185   nam meus scruposam uictus commetat uiam.
ERG   numquam istoc uinces me, Hegio, ne postules:
   cum calceatis dentibus ueniam tamen.
HEG   asper meus uictus sane est.
ERG   sentisne essitas?
HEG   terrestris cena est.
ERG   sus terrestris bestia est.
190 HEG   multis holeribus.
ERG   curato aegrotos domi.
   numquid uis?
HEG   uenias temperi.

171–2 *partes sic distribuit Lindsay*   173 es *add.* ς
175 a *add. Schoell*   176 pauxillum *P*, pauxillo *Lambinus*

524

ERG   (*interrupting*) I trust it's going to work out. May the gods and goddesses bring it about. (*after a pause*) But have you been asked out for dinner anywhere?

HEG   (*cautiously*) No, nowhere as far as I know. But why do you ask?

ERG   Because it's my birthday. That's why I want to be invited 175
by you to a dinner at your place.[8]

HEG   Wittily said! But only if you can be content with little.

ERG   So long as it's not too little: with that kind of meal I constantly entertain myself at home. Go on, will you; demand to buy:[9] (*very formally*) "It's settled unless anyone offers a better deal, which I and my associates like more." As if I were selling a plot by auction, I'll award myself to 181
you, on my own terms.

HEG   You're not selling me your plot, but your plight. But if you're going to come, come early.

ERG   There you go, I'm free even now.

HEG   No, do go and hunt for the hare: at present you have the hedgehog; my food comes and goes on a stony path. 185

ERG   You'll never get the better of me that way, Hegio, don't expect to do so: I'll still come, with shoes on my teeth.

HEG   My food is very rough.

ERG   Do you eat briars?

HEG   It's a dinner that grows on the ground.

ERG   The pig's an animal that grows on the ground.

HEG   With many vegetables. 190

ERG   Then look after the sick at home. (*turning to go*) Is there anything you want?

HEG   Come early.

---

[8] Under normal circumstances Ergasilus would have to invite Hegio to the birthday dinner.   [9] Parody of an auction.

ERG   memorem mones.

HEG   ibo intro atque intus subducam ratiunculam,
       quantillum argenti mi apud tarpezitam siet.
       ad fratrem, quo ire dixeram, mox iuero.

ACTVS II

II. i: LORARII. TYNDARVS. PHILOCRATES

195   LOR   si di immortales id uoluerunt, uos hanc aerumnam exse-
           qui,
        decet id pati animo aequo: si id facietis, leuior labos erit.
        domi fuistis, credo, liberi:
        nunc seruitus si euenit, ei uos morigerari mos bonust
        et erili imperio eamque ingeniis uostris lenem reddere.
200   indigna digna habenda sunt, erus quae facit.
200ᵃ   TYN + PHILOC   oh! oh! oh!
       LOR   eiulatione haud opus est, [multa] oculis aciem minuitis;
        in re mala animo si bono utare, adiuuat.
       TYN   at nos pudet, quia cum catenis sumus.
       LOR   at pigeat postea
        nostrum erum, si uos eximat uinculis,
205   aut solutos sinat quos argento emerit.
206   TYN   quid a nobis metuit? scimus nos
206ᵃ   nostrum officium quod est, si solutos sinat.

     201 multa oculis multa mira clitis *P*, [multa] oculis aciem minuitis
Niemeyer
     204 uinculis *P*, uinclis *Lindsay (qui duo cola esse putat)*

THE CAPTIVES

ERG   You're reminding someone who remembers.

Exit ERGASILUS to the right.

HEG   I'll go in and reckon up my balance inside, how little
       money I have at the banker's. Soon I'll go to my brother,
       where I said I was going.

Exit HEGIO into his house.

ACT TWO

*Enter two SLAVE-OVERSEERS from Hegio's house, followed
by slaves and by PHILOCRATES and TYNDARUS, who have
exchanged clothes. They are in light fetters.*

OVER   (*in a patronizing tone*) If it is the will of the immortal   195
       gods that you should undergo this affliction, you ought to
       bear it patiently. If you do so, your burden will be lighter.
       I believe you were free at home; if slavery has now been
       inflicted on you, it's a good idea to comply with it and with
       your master's authority and to soften slavery through
       your attitude toward it. The wrongs a master does must   200
       be deemed right.

TYN + PHILOC   No, no, no!

OVER   There's no need for wailing; you're merely diminishing
       your eyes' sharpness. In a bad situation it helps to keep a
       stiff upper lip.

TYN   But we're ashamed of being in chains.

OVER   But our master would be annoyed later if he took the fet-
       ters off you, or if he let you loose, since he bought you for   205
       good money.

TYN   (*with indignation*) What does he fear from us? We know
       what our duty is if he lets us loose.

527

| | LOR | at fugam fingitis: sentio quam rem agitis. |

LOR   at fugam fingitis: sentio quam rem agitis.
PHILOC nos fugiamus? quo fugiamus?
LOR   in patriam.
PHILOC   apage, hau nos id deceat,
        fugitiuos imitari.
      LOR   immo edepol, si erit occasio, hau dehortor.

210 TYN unum exorare uos sinite nos.
      LOR   quidnam id est?
      TYN ut sine hisce arbitris
         atque uobis nobis detis locum loquendi.
      LOR fiat. apscedite hinc: nos concedamus huc.
         sed breuem orationem incipisse.
215 TYN em istuc mihi certum erat. concede huc.
215a LOR abite ab istis.
      TYN   obnoxii ambo
         uobis sumus propter hanc rem, quom quae uolumus nos
218–   copia est; ea facitis nos compotes.
19 PHILOC secede huc nunciam, si uidetur, procul,
220   ne arbitri dicta nostra arbitrari queant
         neu permanet palam haec nostra fallacia.
         nam doli non doli sunt, ni astu colas,
         sed malum maxumum, si id palam prouenit.
         nam si erus tu mi es atque ego me tuom esse seruom assi-
           mulo,
225   tamen uiso opus est, cauto est opus, ut hoc sobrie sineque
           arbitris
         accurate [hoc] agatur, docte et diligenter;
         tanta incepta res est: hau somniculose hoc
         agendum est.

215a abite *P*, ite *Lindsay* (*qui credit 215 + 215a esse octonarium trochaicum*)   217 ea ‹fide› *Niemeyer*

OVER But you're planning to flee: I can feel what you're up to.

PHILOC We should flee? Where should we flee?

OVER To your country.

PHILOC Nonsense, that wouldn't be appropriate for us, imitating runaway slaves.

OVER Oh no, I'm not discouraging you if there's a chance.

TYN Let us persuade you to do us one favor. 210

OVER What's that?

TYN Give us the opportunity to speak without being overheard by these people (*points to the slaves*) or by you.

OVER All right. (*to the slaves*) Go away from here. (*to the other overseer*) We should move here. (*to Tyndarus*) But don't start a long talk.

TYN Well, I hadn't planned it. (*to Philocrates*) Move over 215 here.

OVER (*to the slaves*) Go away from them.

TYN (*to the overseers*) We're both obliged to you for this, since we have the opportunity to say what we want; you give it to us.

PHILOC (*to Tyndarus*) Now step aside here, far away, please, so 220 that no witnesses can witness our words and this scheme of ours doesn't leak out into the public. (*they walk away*) Unless you manage it cleverly, trickery isn't trickery, but greatest torture, if it ceases to be secret; if you're my master and if I pretend to be your slave, still, we have to 225 watch out, we have to be cautious that this is done soberly, without witnesses, and precisely, cleverly, and carefully. Such a great task's been begun: it mustn't be carried out in a dozy way.

---

222 ni *P*, ni⟨si⟩ *Lindsay*
226 hoc *del. Guyet*

TYN	ero ut me uoles esse.
PHILOC	spero.

TYN nam tu nunc uides pro tuo caro capite
230   carum offerre ⟨me⟩ meum caput uilitati.
PHILOC scio.
TYN   at scire memento, quando id quod uoles habebis;
       nam fere maxuma pars morem hunc homines habent:
         quod sibi uolunt,
       dum id impetrant, boni sunt;
       sed id ubi iam penes sese habent,
235   ex bonis pessumi et fraudulentissumi
       fiunt.
PHILOC   nunc ut mihi te uolo esse autumo.
       quod tibi suadeam, suadeam meo patri.
       pol ego si te audeam, meum patrem nominem:
       nam secundum patrem tu es pater proxumus.
240 TYN audio.
PHILOC   et propterea saepius ted ut memineris moneo:
       non ego erus tibi, sed seruos sum; nunc opsecro te hoc
         unum—
       quoniam nobis di immortales animum ostenderunt
         suom,
       ut qui erum me tibi fuisse atque ess' nunc conseruom ue-
         lint,
       quod antehac pro iure imperitabam meo, nunc te oro per
         precem—
245   per fortunam incertam et per mei te erga bonitatem pa-
         tris,
       perqu' conseruitium commune, quod hostica euenit
         manu,
       ne me secus honore honestes quam quom seruibas mihi,
       atque ut qui fueris et qui nunc sis meminisse ut memine-
         ris.

TYN   I will be as you want me to be.

PHILOC I hope so.

TYN   Now you can see that for *your* dear life I'm holding *my*   229
own dear life cheap.

PHILOC I know.

TYN   But remember to know when you have what you want:
most people have the habit of being good while they're
trying to achieve what they want for themselves, but of   235
turning from good to very bad and treacherous once they
have attained it.

PHILOC Now I'm telling you how I want you to be toward me.
What I'm advising you I'd advise my own father. Well, if I
had a choice I'd call *you* my father: next to my real father
you are the closest thing to a father I have.

TYN   I'm attending to you.   240

PHILOC And that's why I remind you more often to remember:
I'm not your master, but your slave. Now I beg you for
this one thing—since the immortal gods have shown us
their will, namely that I've *been* your master and that I'm
now your fellow servant; what I used to order you to do
before, as was my right, I'm now asking you by way of
entreaty—by our uncertain fortune, by my father's good-   245
ness toward you, and by our shared slavery, which the
enemy's power has inflicted on us: don't honor me less
than when you were my slave and remember carefully
who you were and who you are now.

---

230 me *add. Hermann*
231 scire memento *P, transp. Fleckeisen*
244 quod *P,* quom *Fleckeisen*

TYN   scio equidem me te esse nunc et te esse me.

PHILOC   em istuc si potes

250   memoriter meminisse, inest spes nobis in hac astutia.

II. ii: HEGIO. PHILOCRATES. TYNDARVS

HEG   iam ego reuortar intro, si ex his quae uolo exquisiuero.

        ubi sunt isti quos ante aedis iussi huc produci foras?

PHILOC edepol tibi ne in quaestione essemus cautum intelle-
        go,

        ita uinclis custodiisque circummoeniti sumus.

255 HEG   qui cauet ne decipiatur uix cauet quom etiam cauet;

        etiam quom cauisse ratus est saepe is cautor captus est.

        an uero non iusta causa est ut uos seruem sedulo,

        quos tam grandi sim mercatus praesenti pecunia?

PHILOC nec pol tibi nos, quia nos seruas, aequom est uitio uor-
        tere,

260   nec te nobis, si abeamus hinc, si fuat occasio.

HEG   ut uos hic, itidem illic apud uos meus seruatur filius.

PHILOC captus est?

HEG   ita.

PHILOC   non igitur nos soli ignaui fuimus.

HEG   secede huc. nam sunt quae ‹ego› ex te solo scitari uolo.

        quarum rerum te falsiloquom mi esse nolo.

PHILOC   non ero

265   quod sciam. si quid nescibo, id nescium tradam tibi.

        263 quae ex te *P*, ego *add. Fleckeisen*, ex te quae *Camerarius*
        265 nesciui *P*, nescibo *Acidalius*

TYN I know that *I* am *you* now and that *you* are *me*.

PHILOC Well then, if you can remember this carefully, there's 250
    hope for us in this scheme.

Enter HEGIO from his house.

HEG (*loudly, to those inside*) I'll come back in in a moment if I
    find out from these men what I want. (*to the overseers*)
    Where are the ones I had brought out here in front of the
    house?

PHILOC (*approaching Hegio*) Well, I can see that you took pre-
    cautions that we shouldn't require looking for: we're
    completely surrounded by fetters and guards.

HEG He who takes precautions against being deceived is 255
    hardly cautious even when he *is* cautious; even when he
    thinks that he's been cautious such a cautious person has
    often been caught out. But don't I have good reason to
    guard you carefully, since I paid such a high price for you
    cash down?

PHILOC It wouldn't be fair of us to blame you for guarding us;
    (*cheekily*) and it wouldn't be fair of you to blame us if we 260
    clear out from here if we get a chance.

HEG My son's being held prisoner there at your place, just as
    you are here.

PHILOC Has he been captured?

HEG Yes.

PHILOC So we were not the only cowards.

HEG (*leads him further away from Tyndarus*) Step over here:
    there are things I'd like to ask you in private. I don't want
    you to lie to me about these issues.

PHILOC I won't lie about what I know. If I don't know about 265
    something, I'll give it to you as unknown.

TYN   nunc senex est in tonstrina, nunc iam cultros attinet.
      ne id quidem, inuolucrum inicere, uoluit, uestem ut ne
        inquinet.
      sed utrum strictimne attonsurum dicam esse an per pec-
        tinem
      nescio; uerum, si frugi est, usque ammutilabit probe.
270 HEG   quid tu? seruosne esse an liber mauelis, memora mihi.
PHILOC   proxumum quod sit bono quodque a malo longissume,
      id uolo; quamquam non multum fuit molesta seruitus,
      nec mi secus erat quam si essem familiaris filius.
TYN   eugepae! Thalem talento non emam Milesium,
275   nam ad sapientiam huius ‹hominis› nimius nugator fuit.
      ut facete orationem ad seruitutem contulit!
HEG   quo de genere natust illic Philocrates?
PHILOC   Polyplusio:
      quod genus illi est unum pollens atque honoratissumum.
HEG   quid ipsus hic? quo honore est illic?
PHILOC   summo, atque ab summis uiris.
280 HEG   tum igitur ei quom †in Aleis tanta† gratia est, ut prae-
        dicas,
      quid diuitiae, suntne opimae?
PHILOC   unde excoquat sebum senex.
HEG   quid pater? uiuitne?
PHILOC   uiuom, quom inde abimus, liquimus;
      nunc uiuat‹ne› necne, id Orcum scire oportet scilicet.

    267 inuolucre *P*, inuolucrum *Turnebus*
    275 hominis *add. Niemeyer*
    280 in Aleis tam gratia *Niemeyer*
    283 uiuat *P*, uiuatne *Bothe*

TYN (*aside, with joy*) Now the old man's at the barber's, now
he's already holding the razor near him.[10] He didn't even
want to put a cover over him so as not to make his clothes
dirty. But whether I should say he's going to give him a
close shave or one through the comb I don't know. Yet if
he does a decent job, he'll fleece him properly.

HEG How about you? Tell me, do you prefer to be a slave or a 270
free man?

PHILOC What's closest to good and furthest from evil, that's
what I want; but slavery wasn't very troublesome for me,
and I wasn't in a different situation from being a son of
the house.

TYN (*aside*) Bravo! I wouldn't buy Thales of Miletus[11] for a
talent: compared with this man's wisdom he was a mere 275
amateur. How brilliantly he's adapted his way of speaking
to being a slave!

HEG What family does Philocrates belong to there?

PHILOC The Moneybag family; that family has the greatest
influence and the highest standing there.

HEG How about himself? How's his standing?

PHILOC Very high, and he's of most distinguished ancestry.

HEG Well then, since he has such great influence among the 280
Eleans, as you're saying, how about his wealth; is it fat?

PHILOC So fat that the old man could get dripping out of it.

HEG What about his father? Is he alive?

PHILOC When we went away from there, we left him alive;
whether or not he's alive now the Underworld should
know of course.

---

[10] Cutting someone's hair is a metaphor for tricking him; cf. English
"fleece."   [11] Famous pre-Socratic philosopher, engineer, and sci-
entist; one of the Seven Sages.

TYN   salua res est, philosophatur quoque iam, non mendax
        modo est.
285 HEG   quid erat ei nomen?
PHILOC   Thesaurochrysonicochrysides.
HEG   uidelicet propter diuitias inditum id nomen quasi est.
PHILOC immo edepol propter auaritiam ipsius atque auda-
        ciam.
        nam illi quidem Theodoromedes fuit germano nomine.
HEG   quid tu ais? tenaxne pater est eius?
PHILOC   immo edepol pertenax;
290   quin etiam ut magis noscas: Genio suo ubi quando sacru-
        ficat,
        ad rem diuinam quibus opus est, Samiis uasis utitur,
        ne ipse Genius surrupiat: proinde aliis ut credat uide.
HEG   sequere hac me igitur. eadem ego ex hoc quae uolo ex-
        quaesiuero.
        Philocrates, hic fecit hominem frugi ut facere oportuit.
295   nam ego ex hoc quo genere gnatus sis scio, hic fassust
        mihi;
        haec tu eadem si confiteri uis, tua ⟨ex⟩ re feceris:
        quae tamen sci scire me ex hoc.
TYN   fecit officium hic suom,
        quom tibi est confessus uerum, quamquam uolui sedulo
        meam nobilitatem occultare et genus et diuitias meas,
300   Hegio; nunc quando patriam et libertatem perdidi,
        non ego istunc me potius quam te metuere aequom cen-
        seo.
        uis hostilis cum istoc fecit meas opes aequabilis;

288 illi *EV*, illic *BD*, ille *Camerarius*
291 est opus *P*, opus est ς   296 ex *add. Valla*
297 scio *P* (scito V²), sci *Lindsay in apparatu*

TYN (*aside*) The situation's safe: he's even philosophizing now, not just lying.

HEG What was his name?   285

PHILOC Goldtreasure-Goldwinson.

HEG I take it that that name, so to speak, was given to him for his wealth.

PHILOC No, for his greed and audacity. (*aside*) His real name there was Theodoromedes.

HEG What do you say? Is his father stingy?

PHILOC No, more than that, incredibly stingy; well, to give you 290
a better idea of him: when he's sacrificing to his Guardian Spirit, he uses Samian earthenware[12] as vessels needed for the ceremony so his Guardian Spirit himself cannot steal them. So you can see for yourself how he trusts others.

HEG (*walks toward Tyndarus*) Well then, follow me this way. (*aside*) I'll find out from this one (*points to Tyndarus*) what I want to know in the same way. (*turning to Tyndarus*) Philocrates, this chap did the decent thing for a decent man to do: I know from him what family you 295
come from, he admitted it to me; if you want to confess these same things, it'll be to your own advantage. Still, you should know that I know them from him.

TYN (*in a sad, dignified voice*) He did his duty when he confessed the truth to you, however keen I was to conceal my noble birth, my family connections, and my wealth from you, Hegio; now that I've lost home and freedom, I don't 300
think it's fair that he should fear me rather than you. The power of the enemy has put my lot on an equal footing

---

[12] The cheapest vessels available, of very low quality.

memini, quom dicto haud audebat: facto nunc laedat li-
cet.

sed uiden? fortuna humana fingit artatque ut lubet:

305   me qui liber fueram seruom fecit, e summo infumum;

qui imperare insueram, nunc alterius imperio opsequor.

et quidem si, proinde ut ipse fui imperator familiae,

habeam dominum, non uerear ne iniuste aut grauiter mi
imperet.

Hegio, hoc te monitum, nisi forte ipse non uis, uoluerim.

310 HEG loquere audacter.

TYN   tam ego fui ante liber quam gnatus tuos,

tam mihi quam illi libertatem hostilis eripuit manus,

tam ille apud nos seruit quam ego nunc hic apud te ser-
uio.

est profecto deus, qui quae nos gerimus auditque et ui-
det:

is, uti tu me hic habueris, proinde illum illic curauerit;

315   bene merenti bene profuerit, male merenti par erit.

quam tu filium tuom tam pater me meus desiderat.

HEG memini ego istuc. sed faterin eadem quae hic fassust
mihi?

TYN ego patri meo esse fateor summas diuitias domi

meque summo genere gnatum. sed te optestor, Hegio,

320   ne tuom animum auariorem faxint diuitiae meae:

ne patri, tam etsi sum unicus, decere uideatur magis,

me saturum seruire apud te sumptu et uestitu tuo

potius quam illi, ubi minime honestum est, mendican-
tem uiuere.

309 uolueram *P*, uoluerim *Brix*
321 unicus sum *P*, sum unicus *Mueller*

with his. I remember the time when he didn't dare to
hurt me by word: now he can do so by deed. But can you
see? Fortune moulds and pinches human life as she likes.
She turned me, who'd been free, into a slave, from the   305
highest into the lowest. I, who was used to issuing com-
mands, now obey another's command. And if I were to
have a master like the one I was when I was commander
of our family, I shouldn't be afraid that he would order
me around in an unjust or harsh way. (*pauses*) Hegio, I'd
like to remind you of one thing, unless you object.

HEG Speak boldly.   310

TYN Once I was just as free as your son; the enemy's armed
force has taken freedom away from me just as it did from
him; and he's a slave at our place just as I'm now a slave at
yours. There really is a god who hears and sees what we
are doing. He will look after him there the way you treat
me here. The man deserving well he will reward well, the   315
man deserving badly he will treat in the same way.[13] My
father's missing me just as you're missing your son.

HEG I remember that. But do you admit the same things this
chap has admitted to me?

TYN I do admit that my father has great wealth at home and
that I come from a great family. But I entreat you, Hegio,
do not let my riches make you greedier; otherwise it   320
might seem more appropriate to my father that even
though I'm his only son, I should be a well-fed slave at
your place, nourished and clothed at your expense,
rather than live as a beggar back there, where it would be
most disgraceful.

[13] Here and in the following passages there is much dramatic irony:
the truth of Tyndarus' words is greater than he himself knows.

HEG   ego uirtute deum et maiorum nostrum diues sum satis.

325   non ego omnino lucrum omne esse utile homini exis-
        tumo:

    scio ego, multos iam lucrum lutulentos homines reddidit;

    est etiam ubi profecto damnum praestet facere quam lu-
        crum.

    odi ego aurum: multa multis saepe suasit perperam.

    nunc hoc animum aduorte, ut ea quae sentio pariter
        scias.

330   filius meus illic apud uos seruit captus Alide:

    eum si reddis mihi, praeterea unum nummum ne duis,

    et te et hunc amittam hinc. alio pacto abire non potes.

TYN   optumum atque aequissumum oras optumusque homi-
       num es homo.

    sed is priuatam seruitutem seruit illi an publicam?

335 HEG priuatam medici Menarchi.

PHILOC   pol isquidem huius est cluens.

    tam hoc quidem tibi in procliui quam imber est quando
        pluit.

HEG   fac is homo ut redimatur.

TYN   faciam. sed te id oro, Hegio—

HEG   quiduis, dum ab re ne quid ores, faciam.

TYN   ausculta, tum scies.

    ego me amitti, donicum ille huc redierit, non postulo.

340   uerum te quaeso [ut] aestumatum hunc mihi des, quem
        mittam ad patrem,

    ut is homo redimatur illi.

HEG   immo alium potius misero

    hinc, ubi erunt indutiae, illuc, tuom qui conueniat pa-
        trem,

    qui tua quae tu iusseris mandata ita ut uelis perferat.

340 ut *del. Bosscha*

HEG Thanks to the gods and our ancestors I'm rich enough. I 325
don't think that all sorts of profit are useful for a man un-
der all circumstances; I know that profit has already cor-
rupted many men. In some cases, in fact, it's better to
make a loss than a profit. I hate gold: it has often led many
people to act badly on many issues. Now pay attention so
that you know what I think as well as I do. My son was 330
taken prisoner and is a slave there, at your place, in Elis.
If you return him to me, you needn't give me a single ses-
terce in addition and I'll send you and this chap (*points to
Philocrates*) away from here. On no other terms can you
get away.

TYN What you say is absolutely fine and fair and you're the
finest man of all. But is he the slave of a private citizen or
of the state?

HEG Of a private citizen, the doctor Menarchus. 335

PHILOC (*interrupting*) That man is this one's (*points to Tyn-
darus*) client! That requires as little effort as water when
it's raining. (*moves out of earshot after a stern gesture
from Tyndarus*)

HEG Have him ransomed.

TYN I will. But I ask you for this, Hegio—

HEG (*eagerly*) I'll do anything you like so long as you don't ask
for anything that upsets my plan.

TYN Listen, then you'll know. I don't demand to be sent away
until your son's returned. But I do ask you to give me this 340
man (*points to Philocrates*) on bail to send him to my fa-
ther so that that chap is ransomed there.

HEG No, I'd rather send someone else there when there's a
truce; he can go to your father and carry out your instruc-
tions according to your wishes.

TYN   at nihil est ignotum ad illum mittere: operam luseris.
345   hunc mitte, hic transactum reddet omne, si illuc uenerit.
         nec quemquam fideliorem nec quoi plus credat potes
         mittere ad eum nec qui magis sit seruos ex sententia,
         neque adeo quoi suom concredat filium hodie audacius.
         ne uereare, meo periclo huius ego experiar fidem,
350   fretus ingenio eius, quod me ess' scit erga sese beniuo-
           lum.
HEG   mittam equidem istunc aestumatum tua fide, si uis.
TYN   uolo;
         quam citissume potest, tam hoc cedere ad factum uolo.
HEG   num quae causa est quin, si ille huc non redeat, uiginti minas
         mihi des pro illo?
TYN   optuma immo.
HEG   soluite istum nunciam,
355   atque utrumque.
TYN   di tibi omnes omnia optata offerant,
         quom me tanto honore honestas quomque ex uinclis eximis.
         hoc quidem hau molestum est iam, quod collus collari caret.
HEG   quod bonis bene fit beneficium, gratia ea grauida est bonis.
         nunc tu illum si illo es missurus, dice, [de]monstra, prae-
           cipe
360   quae ad patrem uis nuntiari. uin uocem huc ad te?
TYN   uoca.

359 monstra *Camerarius* (*cf. Mil. 256*)

TYN   But there's no point in sending him someone he doesn't know; you'll waste your effort. Send this one (*points to*   345 *Philocrates*), he'll sort out everything once he gets there. You can't send him anyone more faithful, anyone he trusts more, any slave who conforms more to his wishes, in short, anyone he would entrust his son to more readily today. Don't be afraid, I'll put his faithfulness to the test at my own risk; I trust in his character because he knows   350 that I wish him well.

HEG   All right, I'll send him on bail on your guarantee, if you want to.

TYN   I do; I want this matter to come to pass as quickly as possible.

HEG   Do you have any objection to giving me twenty minas for him if he doesn't return here?

TYN   No, that's perfectly fine.

HEG   (*to overseers*) Release that one (*points to Philocrates*) now; both, actually. (*the overseers are taking off the fet-*   355 *ters*)

TYN   May all the gods fulfill all your wishes since you're honoring me with such great honor and since you're releasing me from the fetters. Yes, that's not disagreeable at all now, having a neck that doesn't have a necklet on.

HEG   A good deed done to good people brings gratitude full of good things. Now if you're going to send him there, tell him, show him, teach him what you want to be reported   360 to your father. Do you want me to call him over here to you?

TYN   Yes, do.

II. iii: HEGIO. PHILOCRATES. TYNDARVS

HEG   quae res bene uortat mihi meoque filio
uobisque, uolt te nouos erus operam dare
tuo ueteri domino, quod is uelit, fideliter.
nam ego te huic dedi aestumatum uiginti minis,
365   hic autem te ait mittere hinc uelle ad patrem,
meum ut illic redimat filium, mutatio
inter me atque illum ut nostris fiat filiis.

PHILOC   utroque uorsum rectum est ingenium meum,
ad ted atque illum; pro rota me uti licet:
370   uel ego huc uel illuc uortar, quo imperabitis.

HEG   tute tibi [ea] tuopte ingenio prodes plurumum,
quom seruitutem ita fers ut <eam> ferri decet.
sequere. em tibi hominem.

TYN   gratiam habeo tibi,
quom copiam istam mi et potestatem facis,
375   ut ego ad parentes hunc remittam nuntium,
qui me quid rerum hic agitem et quid fieri uelim
patri meo ordine omnem rem illuc perferat.
nunc ita conuenit inter me atque hunc, Tyndare,
ut te aestumatum in Alidem mittam ad patrem,
380   si non rebitas huc, ut uiginti minas
dem pro te.

PHILOC   recte conuenisse sentio.
nam pater exspectat aut me aut aliquem nuntium
qui hinc ad se ueniat.

TYN   ergo animum aduortas uolo
quae nuntiare hinc te uolo in patriam ad patrem.
385 PHILOC   Philocrates, ut adhuc locorum feci, faciam sedulo
ut potissumum quod in rem recte conducat tuam,
id petam id persequarque corde et animo atque auribus.

HEG (*approaching Philocrates*) May this turn out well for me,
and for my son, and for you two: your new master wants
you to devote yourself faithfully to your old master's
wishes: I've given you to him on a bail of twenty minas,
and he says he wants to send you off to his father so that   365
he, the father, can ransom my son there, so that an ex-
change of our sons can take place between me and him.

PHILOC My efforts are directed in both directions, toward you
and him. You can use me as a wheel: I will turn here or   370
there, where you command.

HEG You benefit greatly from your own character since you're
bearing your slavery as one ought to bear it. Follow me.
(*leads him to Tyndarus*) Here's the man for you.

TYN (*to Hegio*) I'm grateful to you for giving me the chance
and opportunity to send him back to my parents as a mes-   375
senger. He'll bring a full and detailed account to my fa-
ther there, how I'm doing here and what I wish to be
done. (*to Philocrates*) Now the agreement between me
and him, Tyndarus, is that I can send you to Elis to my fa-
ther on bail; if you don't return here, I have to give him   380
twenty minas for you.

PHILOC I think that's a good agreement: your father is expect-
ing either me or some other messenger who is coming to
him from here.

TYN Well then, I'd like you to pay attention to what I want you
to report home to my father from here.

PHILOC Philocrates, as I've done so far, I'll continue to do this   385
eagerly: with heart, mind, and ears I will look for and
strive after what benefits you most.

---

364 aestumatum huic dedi *P, transp. Bothe*
371 ea *del. Fleckeisen*   372 eam *add. Schoell ex 371*
380 huc *P,* huic *Loman*   387 petam *P,* petam‹que› *Niemeyer*

TYN	facis ita ut te facere oportet. nunc animum aduortas uolo:
	omnium primum salutem dicito matri et patri
390	et cognatis et si quem alium beneuolentem uideris;
	me hic ualere et seruitutem seruire huic homini optumo,
	qui me honore honestiorem semper fecit et facit.
PHILOC	istuc ne praecipias, facile memoria memini tamen.
TYN	nam equidem, nisi quod custodem habeo, liberum me
	esse arbitror.
395	dicito patri quo pacto mihi cum hoc conuenerit
	de huius filio.
PHILOC	quae memini, mora mera est monerier.
TYN	ut eum redimat et remittat nostrum huc amborum ui-
	cem.
PHILOC	meminero.
HEG	at quam primum pote: istuc in rem
	utrique est maxume.
PHILOC	non tuom tu magis uidere quam ille suom gnatum
	cupit.
400 HEG	meus mihi, suos quoique est carus.
PHILOC	numquid aliud uis patri
	nuntiari?
TYN	me hic ualere et (tute audacter dicito,
	Tyndare) inter nos fuisse ingenio hau discordabili,
	nec te commeruisse culpam (nec me aduorsatum tibi)
	beneque ero gessisse morem in tantis aerumnis tamen;
405	nec med umquam deseruisse te nec factis nec fide,
	rebus in dubiis, egenis. haec pater quando sciet,
	Tyndare, ut fueris animatus erga suom gnatum atque se,

---

[14] Tyndarus is Philocrates' guardian, so he has some authority despite being a slave.

TYN   You're acting as you ought to. Now I'd like you to pay at-
tention: first of all give my regards to my mother and fa-
ther and relatives and if you see anyone else who wishes   390
me well. Say that I'm doing well here and that I'm a slave
of this excellent man, who's always honored me with his
respect, and is doing so now.

PHILOC   Don't instruct me about that; I remember it easily all
the same.

TYN   Well, except for having a guard, I consider myself to be
free. Tell my father about my agreement with this man   395
regarding his son.

PHILOC   It's mere delay to be reminded of what I remember.

TYN   He is to ransom him and send him back here in exchange
for the two of us.

PHILOC   I'll remember.

HEG   But as quickly as possible: that's of the highest impor-
tance to each of us two.

PHILOC   *You* don't want to see *your* son more than *he* wants to
see *his*.

HEG   My son is dear to me, his own son is dear to everybody.   400

PHILOC   (*turning back to Tyndarus*) Do you want your father to
be told anything else?

TYN   Yes, that I'm doing well here and—you should say so
boldly, Tyndarus—that we got on with each other with-
out the least disagreement; that you haven't committed
any offense (and that I didn't oppose you);[14] that you
obeyed your master well, even in such great trials and
tribulations; and that you never deserted me in word or   405
deed, in dangers and in need. When my father knows
what your attitude was toward his son and himself, Tyn-

numquam erit tam auarus quin te gratiis emittat manu:
et mea opera, si hinc rebito, faciam ut faciat facilius.
410 nam tua opera et comitate et uirtute et sapientia
fecisti ut redire liceat ad parentes denuo,
quom apud hunc confessus es et genus et diuitias meas:
quo pacto emisisti e uinclis tuom erum tua sapientia.
PHILOC feci ego ista ut commemoras, et te meminisse id gra-
tum est mihi.
415 merito tibi ea euenerunt a me; nam nunc, Philocrates,
si ego item memorem quae me erga multa fecisti bene,
nox diem adimat; nam quasi seruos [meus] esses, nihilo
setius
<tu> mihi opsequiosus semper fuisti.
HEG   di uostram fidem,
hominum ingenium liberale! ut lacrumas excutiunt mihi!
420 uideas corde amare inter se. <quibus et> quantis laudi-
bus
suom erum seruos collaudauit!
PHILOC   pol istic me hau centesumam
partem laudat quam ipse meritust ut laudetur laudibus.
HEG ergo quom optume fecisti, nunc adest occasio
bene facta cumulare, ut erga hunc rem geras fideliter.
425 PHILOC magis non factum possum uelle quam opera experiar
persequi;
id ut scias, Iouem supremum testem laudo, Hegio,
me infidelem non futurum Philocrati—
HEG   probus es homo.

---

408 gratus *P*, gratiis *plurimi edd*.   414 ista *P*, ita *Bothe*
417 si *P*, quasi *Fleckeisen* meus *del. Guyet*, mi *Bentley*
418 tu *add. Fleckeisen*   420 quibus et *add. Gertz*, <erus hunc>
laudibus *Lindsay in apparatu*

darus, he'll never be so greedy as not to make you a free
man at his own expense. And if I return from here, I'll use
my own efforts to make him do so more readily; well,   410
through *your* efforts, kindness, noble spirit, and wisdom
you've let me return to my parents again, when you ad-
mitted my family and my riches to this man (*points to
Hegio*). By this stroke you released your master from the
fetters through your wisdom.

PHILOC I did as you say and I'm thankful that you remember it.
You deserved that I did these things for you: if I were now 415
to say in the same way, Philocrates, how many good turns
you did *me*, the day wouldn't be long enough; you were
always no less obedient to me than if you'd been my
slave.

HEG (*half aside*) Immortal gods, I implore your faith! The no-
ble character of the men! How they bring tears to my
eyes! You can see that they love each other from the   420
heart. With what great praises did the slave praise his
master!

PHILOC The praise he's giving me is not one per cent of how
he's deserved to be praised himself.

HEG (*to Philocrates*) Well then, since you behaved very well,
you now have the opportunity to crown your good deeds
by acting faithfully toward this man (*points to Tyn-
darus*).

PHILOC I'm just as keen on trying to follow it through in deed 425
as I am on wanting it done. To assure you, I'll call upon
great Jupiter as my witness, Hegio, that I shan't be un-
faithful to Philocrates—

HEG (*interrupting*) You're a decent fellow.

PHILOC nec me secus umquam ei facturum quicquam quam
memet mihi.

TYN istaec dicta; te experiri et opera et factis uolo;

430 et, quo minus dixi quam uolui de te, animum aduortas
uolo,
atque horunc uerborum causa caue tu mi iratus fuas;
sed, te quaeso, cogitato hinc mea fide mitti domum
te aestumatum, et meam esse uitam hic pro te positam
pignori,
ne tu me ignores, quom extemplo meo e conspectu aps-
cesseris,

435 quom me seruom in seruitute pro ted hic reliqueris
tuque te pro libero esse ducas, pignus deseras
nec des operam pro me ut huius huc reducem facias
filium;
scito te hinc minis uiginti aestumatum mittier.
fac fidele sis fidelis, caue fidem fluxam geras:

440 nam pater, scio, faciet quae illum facere oportet omnia;
serua tibi in perpetuom amicum me, atque hunc inuen-
tum inueni.
haec per dexteram tuam te dextera retinens manu
opsecro, infidelior mi ne fuas quam ego sum tibi.
tu hoc age. tu mihi erus nunc es, tu patronus, tu pater,

445 tibi commendo spes opesque meas.

PHILOC   mandauisti satis.
satin habes, mandata quae sunt facta si refero?

TYN   satis.

PHILOC et tua et tua huc ornatus reueniam ex sententia.
numquid aliud?

TYN   ut quam primum possis redeas.

439 fidelis sis fideli *P, sed* fidele *aduerbium testatur Nonius*

PHILOC —and that I shan't treat him any differently from how I'd treat myself.

TYN These are words; I want to test you in your efforts and deeds. And insofar as I said less about you than I wanted, 430 I want you to pay attention. Don't be angry with me because of these words. But please consider that you're being sent home on my pledge on bail and that my life is put down here as a security for you; so don't forget me as soon as you get out of sight, while leaving me here as a 435 slave in slavery instead of you; and don't consider yourself free and desert your pledge without making an effort to save me by getting this man's son back here. Remember that you're being sent off on a bail of twenty minas. Make sure you're absolutely faithful, take care you don't have fluctuations in your faithfulness: I know my father 440 will do everything he ought to; save me as your friend for good and find this man (*points to Hegio*) as your friend, the one you've already found to be so. I entreat you by your right hand, holding you back with my right hand: don't be less faithful to me than I am toward you. Pay attention. Now *you* are my master, *you* are my patron, *you* are my father. I commend my hopes and my fortunes 445 to you.

PHILOC Enough commands. Is it enough for you if I bring back your commands as accomplishments?

TYN It is.

PHILOC I'll return here equipped according to (*turning to Tyndarus*) your wishes and to (*turning to Hegio*) yours. Anything else?

TYN Yes, come back as soon as you can.

PHILOC   res monet.

HEG   sequere me, uiaticum ut dem a tarpezita tibi,

450   eadem opera a praetore sumam syngraphum.

TYN   quem syngraphum?

HEG   quem hic ferat secum ad legionem, hinc ire huic ut liceat
        domum.
        tu intro abi.

TYN   bene ambulato.

PHILOC   bene uale.

HEG   edepol rem meam
        constabiliui, quom illos emi de praeda a quaestoribus;
        expediui ex seruitute filium, si dis placet.

455   at etiam dubitaui, hos homines emerem an non emerem,
        diu.
        seruate istum sultis intus, serui, ne quoquam pedem
        efferat sine custode‹la. iam› ego apparebo domi;
        ad fratrem modo ‹ad› captiuos alios inuiso meos,
        eadem percontabor ecquis hunc adulescentem nouerit.

460   sequere tu, te ut amittam; ei rei primum praeuorti uolo.

ACTVS III

III. i: ERGASILVS

ERG   miser homo est qui ipse sibi quod edit quaerit et id aegre
        inuenit,
        sed ille est miserior qui et aegre quaerit et nihil inuenit;

457 custodela *Gruterus*, iam *add. Bothe*, ego ‹desubito› *Schoell*
458 ad *add. Fleckeisen* (*cf. 126*)

---

[15] Roman official, mainly responsible for jurisdiction.

PHILOC The situation demands it.

HEG (*to Philocrates*) Follow me so I can give you some travel-
ling money from the banker's, and at the same time I'll 450
get a passport from the praetor.[15]

TYN What passport?

HEG (*to Tyndarus*) One to take with him to the army so he gets
permission to go home. You go inside.

TYN (*to Philocrates*) Have a good trip.

PHILOC Goodbye.

Exit TYNDARUS into the house.

HEG (*to the audience*) I really did strengthen my cause when I
bought those people from among the booty from the
quaestors. Gods willing, I've freed my son from slavery.
But I hesitated for a long time whether I should buy 455
these people or not. (*to overseers and slaves*) Slaves,
guard that man inside, will you, so that he doesn't set his
foot outside anywhere without a guard. I'll be home in a
moment. I'm just going to see my other prisoners at my
brother's. At the same time I'll ask if anyone knows this
young man here. (*to Philocrates*) Follow me so that I can 460
send you off; I want to sort out this business first.

*The overseers and slaves go inside. Exeunt HEGIO and PHI-
LOCRATES to the right.*

ACT THREE

Enter ERGASILUS from the right.

ERG Wretched is the man who has to look for his food himself
and has a hard time finding it, but more wretched is the

553

ill' miserrumust, qui quom esse cupit, ⟨tum⟩ quod edit
    non habet.

nam hercle ego huic die, si liceat, oculos effodiam lu-
    bens,

465   ita malignitate onerauit omnis mortalis mihi;

nec ieiuniosiorem nec magis effertum fame

uidi nec quoi minus procedat quicquid facere occeperit,

ita[que] uenter gutturque resident esurialis ferias.

ilicet parasiticae arti maxumam malam crucem,

470   ita iuuentus iam ridiculos inopesque ab se segregat.

nil morantur iam Lacones unisupselli uiros,

plagipatidas, quibus sunt uerba sine penu et pecunia:

eos requirunt qui lubenter, quom ederint, reddant domi;

ipsi opsonant, quae parasitorum ante erat prouincia,

475   ipsi de foro tam aperto capite ad lenones eunt

quam in tribu aperto capite sontes condemnant reos;

nec ridiculos iam terrunci faciunt, sese omnes amant.

nam ⟨ego⟩ ut dudum hinc abii, accessi ad adulescentes in
    foro.

"saluete," inquam. "quo imus una?" inquam [ad pran-
    dium]: atque illi tacent.

480   "quis ait 'hoc' aut quis profitetur?" inquam. quasi muti si-
    lent,

nec me rident. "ubi cenamus?" inquam. atque illi ab-
    nuont.

dico unum ridiculum dictum de dictis melioribus,

463 tum *add. Niemeyer*
468 ita *Pylades*
476 aperto capite sontes *P*, s. a. c. *Brix*
478 ut *P*, ⟨ego⟩ ut *Seyffert*, ut⟨i⟩ *Lindsay*
479 ad prandium *del. Lindsay*

one who has a hard time looking for it and doesn't find
anything. And that one is most wretched who doesn't
have anything to eat when he wishes to eat. Well, if I were
allowed to, I'd happily tear out this day's eyes: it's given all   465
mortals such a supply of meanness. I haven't seen a more
hungriful day than this or one more stuffed with starva-
tion, or one that's less successful in anything it's begun
to do: my stomach and throat are sitting through this
hunger-holiday in complete idleness. The hanger-on's art
can now go and be hanged: the youngsters nowadays   470
keep entertainers without money at a distance from
themselves. They can't be bothered about us Spartan
one-bench[16] men any longer, us blow-bearers, who have
bonmots without food and money. They're looking for
people who willingly return the favor at home when
they've eaten. They themselves go shopping, which used
to be the hangers-on's task before, they themselves go   475
from the market to the pimps, as barefaced as they
condemn guilty defendants in court.[17] They don't care
tuppence[18] for entertainers any longer, they all love only
themselves. When I went away from here some time ago,
I approached young men on the market. "Hello there," I
say. "Where are we going together?" I say. And they fall
silent. "Who says 'here' or who's volunteering?" I say.   480
They're silent as if they were dumb, and they don't give
me a smile. "Where are we dining?" I say. And they shake
their heads. I tell one of my better jokes, for which I used

---

[16] An *unisupsellium* is a bench for a single person, as distinct from
the regular couches where respectable guests would lie together during
dinner.   [17] Reference to the *comitia tributa*, popular assemblies
in which some court cases were decided.   [18] Lit. a *terruncius*, a cop-
per coin of low value weighing three *unciae*, worth a quarter of an *as*.

quibus solebam menstrualis epulas ante adipiscier:
nemo ridet; sciui extemplo rem de compecto geri;
485   ne canem quidem irritatam uoluit quisquam imitarier,
saltem, si non arriderent, dentes ut restringerent.
abeo ab illis, postquam uideo me sic ludificarier;
pergo ad alios, uenio ad alios, deinde ad alios: una res!
omnes ⟨de⟩ compecto rem agunt, quasi in Velabro olea-
    rii.
490   nunc redeo inde, quoniam me ibi uideo ludificarier.
item alii parasiti frustra obambulabant in foro.
nunc barbarica lege certum est ius meum omne perse-
    qui:
qui consilium iniere, quo nos uictu et uita prohibeant,
is diem dicam, irrogabo multam, ut mihi cenas decem
495   meo arbitratu dent, quom cara annona sit. sic egero.
nunc ibo ad portum hinc: est illic mi una spes cenatica;
si ea decollabit, redibo huc ad senem ad cenam asperam.

III. ii: HEGIO

HEG   quid est suauius quam bene rem gerere
bono publico, sicut ego feci heri, quom
500   emi hosce homines: ubi quisque uident,
eunt obuiam gratulanturque eam rem.
ita me miserum restitando
retinendo[que] lassum reddiderunt:
uix ex gratulando miser iam eminebam.

489 de *add. Fleckeisen*   503 que *del. Hermann*

---

[19] A market district in Rome.
[20] I.e., Roman law.
[21] It is to the public good to get a citizen back.

to get banquets lasting a whole month. No one's laugh-
ing. I knew immediately they were acting out a conspir-
acy. No one was even willing to imitate an angry dog and   485
at least bare their teeth if they wouldn't smile at me. I left
them after seeing that I was being made a fool of like this.
I approached others, I came to others, then to others still:
same story! All were acting out a conspiracy, like the oil-
sellers in the Velabrum.[19] Now I'm returning from there   490
since I can see that I'm being made a fool of. Other hang-
ers-on were also wandering around on the market, all for
nothing. Now I've decided to pursue my full rights with
foreign law:[20] I'll summon the people to court who've
come up with the plan to deprive us of livelihood and life,
and as penalty I'll inflict on them that they have to give
me ten dinners at my own discretion, when the price of
food is high. That's how I like it. Now I'll go off to the har-   496
bor; that's where my last hope is, dinner-wise. If that falls
through, I'll return here to the old man and his rough
dinner.

Exit ERGASILUS to the left.
*Enter HEGIO with Aristophontes from the right, accompanied
by slaves.*

HEG   (*joyfully*) What's sweeter than being successful and con-
        tributing to the public good,[21] just as I did yesterday
        when I bought these people? Whenever anyone sees   500
        me, they come toward me and congratulate me on it.
        Poor me! They completely exhausted me by stopping me
        and holding me up. Poor me! I could barely emerge from

505	tandem abii ad praetorem; ibi uix requieui:
506	rogo syngraphum: datur mi ilico:
506a	dedi Tyndaro: ille abiit domum.
	inde ilico praeuortor domum, postquam id actum est;
508	ego protinus ad fratrem inde abii,
508a	mei ubi sunt alii captiui.
509	rogo Philocratem ex Alide
509a	ecquis omnium norit:
510	tandem hic exclamat eum
510a	sibi esse sodalem;
511	dico eum esse apud me hic.
511a	extemplo orat opsecratque
	eum sibi ut liceat uidere:
	iussi ilico hunc exsolui. nunc tu sequere me,
514– 15	ut quod me orauisti impetres, eum hominem uti conue- nias.

III. iii: TYNDARVS

TYN nunc illud est quom me fuisse quam esse nimio mauelim:

nunc spes opes auxiliaque a me segregant spernuntque se.

hic ille est dies quom nulla uitae meae salus sperabilest,

neque exitium exitio est neque adeo spes, quae mi hunc aspellat metum,

520 nec subdolis mendaciis mihi usquam mantellum est meis,

nec sycophantiis nec fucis ullum mantellum obuiam est,

nec deprecatio perfidiis meis nec malefactis fuga est,

nec confidentiae usquam hospitium est nec deuorticu- lum dolis:

operta quae fuere aperta sunt, patent praestigiae,

525 omnis palam est res, nec de hac re negotium est

the flood of congratulations. At last I went away to the 505
praetor. There I could barely calm down: I asked for a
passport; I was given one immediately. I gave it to Tyn-
darus; he went home. After this was done, I immediately
went toward my home first. Straightaway I went to my
brother's, where the other prisoners of mine are. I asked
if anyone among all those people knew Philocrates from
Elis. At last this chap (*points to Aristophontes*) called out 510
that he's his chum. I said he's at my place here. He imme-
diately asked and begged to be allowed to see him. At
once I had him untied. (*to Aristophontes*) Now follow
me (514–15) so you get what you asked me for and meet
the man.

*Exit HEGIO into his house, followed by Aristophontes and the
slaves.*
Exit TYNDARUS from the house.

TYN Now's the time when I'd much prefer *having* lived to
living. Now my hopes, resources, and help are deserting
me and leaving me in the lurch. This is the day when no
rescue for my life can be hoped for, when there's no way
to get out of harm's way, when there's no hope that could
drive out my fear, when there's no cloak for my sly lies 520
anywhere, when there's no cloak at hand for my tricks
and disguises, when there's no begging for pardon for my
falsehoods, no escape for my misdeeds, and when there's
no shelter for my boldness, no resort for my deceptions 525

---

517 spernuntque me *P*, spernuntque se *Gulielmus*
521 *uersum del. Niemeyer*
525 res palam est *P, transp. Bothe*

559

quin male occidam oppetamque pestem eri uicem
   meamque.
perdidit me Aristophontes hic modo qui uenit intro;
is me nouit, is sodalis Philocrati et cognatus est.
nec iam Salus seruare, si uolt, me potest, nec copia est,
530   nisi si aliquam corde machinor astutiam.
quam, malum? quid machiner? quid comminiscar?
   maxumas
nugas ineptus incipisso. haereo.

III. iv: HEGIO. TYNDARVS. ARISTOPHONTES

HEG quo illum nunc hominem proripuisse foras se dicam ex
     aedibus?
TYN nunc enim uero ego occidi: eunt ad te hostes, Tyndare.
535   quid loquar? quid fabulabor? quid negabo aut quid fate-
     bor? [mihi]
     res omnis in incerto sita est. quid rebus confidam meis?
     utinam te di prius perderent quam periisti e patria tua,
     Aristophontes, qui ex parata re imparatam omnem facis.
     occisa est haec res, nisi reperio atrocem mi aliquam astu-
     tiam.
540 HEG sequere. em tibi hominem. adi, atque alloquere.
TYN   quis homo est me hominum miserior?
ARI quid istuc est quod meos te dicam fugitare oculos, Tyn-
     dare,
     proque ignoto me aspernari, quasi me numquam noue-
     ris?
     equidem tam sum seruos quam tu, etsi ego domi liber fui,
     tu usque a puero seruitutem seruiuisti in Alide.

527 hic qui uenit modo *P, transp. Lindsay*, istic q. u. m. *Niemeyer*
532 ineptias *P*, ineptus *Leo*   incipisse *BVE*, incepisse *OJ*, incipisso
Camerarius   535 mihi *del. Lindemann*

anywhere. What was covered is uncovered, my tricks lie
open, the whole thing's out. There's no doubt about it: I'll
die miserably and reach the end on account of master
and myself. Aristophontes here, who just came in, has
destroyed me. He knows me, he's a friend and relative of
Philocrates'. Salvation herself cannot save me any longer,
if she wants to, and there is no opportunity, unless I think   530
up some trick in my heart. But what trick, damn it? What
can I think up? What can I come up with? I'm a fool, I'm
beginning something really stupid. I'm stuck.

Enter HEGIO and ARISTOPHONTES, followed by slaves.

HEG   I wonder where that chap's now rushed out of the house
to?

TYN   (*to himself*) Now I'm truly dead: the enemy's coming to-
ward you, Tyndarus. What will I say? What will I tell   535
him? What will I deny or what will I admit? The whole
matter's on uncertain ground. How could I be confident
about my situation? I wish the gods had destroyed you
before you disappeared from home, Aristophontes;
you're turning the whole thing from settled back to un-
settled. This matter's dead unless I find some shocking
trick for myself.

HEG   (*to Aristophontes*) Follow me. Here's your man. Go and   540
address him.

TYN   (*aside*) Who on earth is more wretched than me? (*pre-
tends not to know Aristophontes*)

ARI   What's the matter? I wonder why you're avoiding eye-
contact with me, Tyndarus, and why you're snubbing me
as if I were a stranger, as if you'd never got to know me?
Yes, I am a slave like you, even if I was free at home and
you were a slave in Elis from childhood.

545 HEG   edepol minime miror, si te fugitat aut oculos tuos,
             aut si te odit, qui istum appelles Tyndarum pro Philo-
                crate.

    TYN   Hegio, hic homo rabiosus habitus est in Alide,
             ne tu quod istic fabuletur auris immittas tuas.
             nam istic hastis insectatus est domi matrem et patrem,
550   et illic isti qui insputatur morbus interdum uenit.
             proin tu ab istoc procul recedas.

    HEG   ultro istum a me!
    ARI   ain, uerbero?
             me rabiosum atque insectatum esse hastis meum memo-
                ras patrem,
             et eum morbum mi esse, ut qui me opus sit insputarier?
    HEG   ne uerere, multos iste morbus homines macerat,
555   quibus insputari saluti fuit atque is profuit.
    ARI   quid tu autem? etiam huic credis?
    HEG   quid ego credam huic?
    ARI   insanum esse me?
    TYN   uiden tu hunc quam inimico uoltu intuetur? concedi op-
                tumum est,
             Hegio: fit quod tibi ego dixi, gliscit rabies, caue tibi.
    HEG   credidi esse insanum extemplo, ubi te appellauit Tynda-
                rum.
560 TYN   quin suom ipse interdum ignorat nomen nec scit qui siet.
    HEG   at etiam te suom sodalem esse aibat.

      550 sputatur *MSS*, insputatur *Pylades ex codice antiquo*
      558 ego *del. Bothe*

---

    [22] People spat out when they saw an epileptic fit; this apotropaeic rite was meant to protect from infection (cf. Plin. *nat*. 28. 35). Hegio goes one step further and humorously treats being spat on as a cure.

HEG   (*to Aristophontes*) Seriously, I'm not surprised at all if 545
he's avoiding you, or eye-contact with you, or if he hates
you, since you address him as Tyndarus instead of Philo-
crates.

TYN   Hegio, this man was considered a lunatic in Elis, so don't
take what he says seriously; at home he chased his
mother and father with spears, and there he sometimes 550
gets the illness that is spat upon.[22] So go far away from
him.

HEG   (*to slaves*) Away with him from me!

ARI   (*to Tyndarus*) Do you say so, you thug? Are you telling
him that I'm a lunatic and chased my own father with
spears? That I have the illness that makes it necessary to
spit on me?

HEG   Stop being afraid, that illness tortures a lot of people for 555
whom being spat on was helpful and beneficial.

ARI   (*to Hegio*) How's this? You too? Do you actually believe
him?

HEG   Believe him in what?

ARI   That I'm mad?

TYN   (*to Hegio*) Can you see how he's looking around with such
a hostile expression on his face? It's best for you to leave,
Hegio: what I told you is happening, his frenzy is increas-
ing; look out for yourself.

HEG   I immediately believed that he's mad when he called you
Tyndarus.

TYN   Well, from time to time he doesn't even know his own 560
name and has no idea who he is.

HEG   But he also said he's your friend.

TYN   hau uidi magis.
    et quidem Alcumeus atque Orestes et Lycurgus postea
    una opera mihi sunt sodales qua iste.

ARI   at etiam, furcifer,
    male loqui mi audes? non ego te noui?

HEG   pol planum id quidem est,

565   non nouisse, qui istum appelles Tyndarum pro Philo-
        crate.
    quem uides, eum ignoras: illum nominas quem non ui-
        des.

ARI   immo iste eum sese ait qui non est esse et qui uero est ne-
        gat.

TYN   tu enim repertu's, Philocratem qui superes ueriuerbio.

ARI   pol ego ut rem uideo, tu inuentu's, uera uanitudine

570   qui conuincas. sed quaeso hercle, agedum aspice ad me.

TYN   em.

ARI   dic modo:
    ⟨tun⟩ negas te Tyndarum esse?

TYN   nego, inquam.

ARI   tun te Philocratem
    esse ais?

TYN   ego, inquam.

ARI   tune huic credis?

HEG   plus quidem quam tibi . . . aut mihi.
    nam illequidem, quem tu hunc memoras esse, hodie hinc
        abiit Alidem
    ad patrem huius.

ARI   quem patrem, qui seruos est?

571 te negas *P*, tun negas te *Bosscha*
573 hunc memoras esse *P*, esse hunc memoras *Bothe*

TYN   A likely story. Then Alcumeus, Orestes, and Lycurgus[23] are my friends just as much as he is.

ARI   You good-for-nothing, you even dare abuse me? Don't I know you?

HEG   Well, it's obvious you don't know him, since you call him   565
Tyndarus instead of Philocrates. You don't know the man you see; you name the man you don't see.

ARI   No, he says he's someone he isn't and he denies being the one he really is.

TYN   (*hinting*) Yes, you've been found to get the better of Philocrates just by telling the truth.

ARI   As I see this matter, you've been found to confute the truth with your falsehood. But I ask you seriously, go on: look at me.

TYN   All right.

ARI   Just tell me: do you deny that you're Tyndarus?   571

TYN   Yes, I do, I assure you.

ARI   Do you say that you're Philocrates?

TYN   Yes, I assure you.

ARI   (*to Hegio*) Do you believe him?

HEG   More than you, surely . . . (*suspiciously*) or myself: well, the one who you say this one here is went to Elis today to this one's father.

ARI   What father? He's a slave.

---

[23] Three famous madmen in Greek mythology. Alcumeus/Alcmaeon and Orestes became mad after killing their mothers. Lycurgus became mad because he had banned the cult of Dionysus and subsequently killed his own son.

PLATUS

PLAUTUS

TYN   et tu quidem
575   seruos es, liber fuisti, et ego me confido fore,
si huius huc reconciliasso in libertatem filium.

ARI   quid ais, furcifer? tun te gnatum ⟨esse⟩ memoras liberum?

TYN   non equidem me Liberum, sed Philocratem esse aio.

ARI   quid est?
ut scelestus, Hegio, nunc iste ⟨te⟩ ludos facit!
580   nam is est seruos ipse, nec praeter se umquam ei seruos fuit.

TYN   quia tute ipse eges in patria nec tibi qui uiuas domi est,
omnis inueniri similis tui uis; non mirum facis:
est miserorum ut maleuolentes sint atque inuideant bonis.

ARI   Hegio, uide sis ne quid tu huic temere insistas credere.
585   atque, ut perspicio, profecto iam aliquid pugnae edidit.
filium tuom quod redimere se ait, id ne utiquam mi placet.

TYN   scio te id nolle fieri; efficiam tamen ego id, si di adiuuant.
illum restituam huic, hic autem in Alidem me meo patri.
propterea ad patrem hinc amisi Tyndarum.

ARI   quin tute is es:
590   nec praeter te in Alide ullus seruos istoc nomine est.

TYN   pergin seruom me exprobrare esse, id quod ui hostili optigit?

ARI   enim iam nequeo contineri.

575 seruos et *P*, s. es *Fleckeisen*
577 te gnatum *P*, te gnatum esse *Pylades*, tete gnatum *Gruterus*
579 te *add. Gruterus*
582 inuenire *P*, inueniri *Camerarius* tibi *P*, tui *Fleckeisen*
585 edidit *P*, dedit *Scioppius*

TYN (*to Aristophontes*) And you're also a slave and were free
before; and I trust I'll be free if I restore this man's son to   576
freedom here.

ARI What are you saying, you thug? Are you telling us that
you are a born free man?

TYN I'm not saying that I'm Freeman,[24] but Philocrates.

ARI What's that? How this thug is now making a fool of you,
Hegio! He himself is a slave and he never had a slave   580
besides himself.

TYN Just because you yourself are a pauper in our country and
don't have anything to live on at home, you want every-
one to be found to resemble you. No big surprise: it's
typical of wretched people to be spiteful and jealous of
respectable ones.

ARI Hegio, do make sure you don't continue to trust this man
blindly. As I can see it, he has indeed already given you   585
some trouble. I'm not at all happy about him saying he'll
ransom your son.

TYN I know you don't want it done; but I'll carry it through
nevertheless if the gods help me. I'll restore that man to
this one here (*points to Hegio*), and this one here will in
turn restore me to my father in Elis. That's why I sent
Tyndarus to my father.

ARI No, you yourself are him. Besides you there isn't any   590
slave with that name in Elis.

TYN Are you continuing to reproach me for being a slave,
which became my lot because of armed conflict?

ARI Seriously, I can't control myself any longer.

---

24 In the Latin there is a pun on *Liber* (Bacchus) and *liber* (free).

TYN   heus, audin quid ait? quin fugis?
iam illic hic nos insectabit lapidibus, nisi illunc iubes
comprehendi.

ARI   crucior.

TYN   ardent oculi: fit opus, Hegio;

595   uiden tu illi maculari corpus totum maculis luridis?
atra bilis agitat hominem.

ARI   at pol te, si hic sapiat senex,
pix atra agitet apud carnuficem tuoque capiti illuceat.

TYN iam deliramenta loquitur, laruae stimulant uirum,
⟨Hegio.⟩

HEG   quid si hunc comprehendi iusserim?

TYN   sapias magis.

600 ARI crucior lapidem non habere me, ut illi mastigiae
cerebrum excutiam, qui me insanum uerbis concinnat
suis.

TYN audin lapidem quaeritare?

ARI   solus te solum uolo,
Hegio.

HEG   istinc loquere, si quid uis, procul. tamen audiam.

TYN namque edepol si adbites propius, os denasabit tibi

605 mordicus.

ARI   nec pol me insanum, Hegio, esse creduis
nec fuisse umquam, neque esse morbum quem istic au-
tumat.
uerum si quid metuis a me, iube me uinciri: uolo,
dum istic itidem uinciatur.

TYN   immo enim uero, Hegio,
istic qui uolt uinciatur.

597 atra pix *P, transp. Lindemann*

TYN   (*to Hegio*) Hey, can you hear what he's saying? Why don't you run away? In a moment he'll chase us with stones here unless you have him arrested.

ARI   I'm being tormented!

TYN   His eyes are ablaze. He's having a fit, Hegio. Can't you 595 see that his whole body is covered with lurid spots? Black bile[25] is driving him mad.

ARI   If this old man did the sensible thing, black pitch would drive *you* mad at the hangman's and would light up your head.

TYN   Now he's raving; evil spirits are driving him, Hegio.

HEG   What if I have him put under restraint?

TYN   You'd be doing the sensible thing.

ARI   I'm in agony because I don't have a stone to smash out 600 the brains of this whipping-post, who's driving me mad with his words.

TYN   Can you hear? He's looking for a stone.

ARI   Hegio, I'd like to speak to you one to one.

HEG   Speak from there, from a distance, if you want anything. I'll listen all the same.

TYN   Yes, because if you get any closer he'll bite your nose off. 604

ARI   Hegio, don't believe that I'm mad, or that I've ever been, or that I have the illness he says. But if you fear anything from me, have me tied up. I want it, so long as this chap is also tied up.

TYN   No, no, no, Hegio, let the one be tied up who wants it.

[25] One of the four humors, responsible for madness and melancholy.

---

599 HEG hercle quid *B*[1]*VEJ*, HEG quid *B*[3], ⟨Hegio⟩ HEG quid *Lindsay*, hercle qui . . . iusseris *Leo* (*qui omnia Tyndaro dat*)

ARI   tace modo. ego te, Philocrates

610   false, faciam ut uerus hodie reperiare Tyndarus.

611–   quid mi abnutas?

12   TYN   tibi ego abnuto?

ARI   quid agat, si apsis longius?

HEG quid ais? quid si adeam hunc insanum?

TYN   nugas! ludificabitur,

garriet quoi nec pes umquam nec caput compareat.

615   ornamenta apsunt: Aiacem, hunc quom uides, ipsum ui-
des.

HEG nihili facio. tamen adibo.

TYN   nunc ego omnino occidi,

nunc ego inter sacrum saxumque sto, nec quid faciam
scio.

HEG do tibi operam, Aristophontes, si quid est quod me uelis.

ARI ex me audibis uera quae nunc falsa opinare, Hegio.

620   sed hoc primum, me expurigare tibi uolo, me insaniam

nec tenere nec mi esse ullum morbum, nisi quod seruio.

at ita me rex deorum atque hominum faxit patriae com-
potem,

ut istic Philocrates non magis est quam aut ego aut tu.

HEG   eho dic mihi,

quis illic igitur est?

ARI   quem dudum dixi a principio tibi.

625   hoc si secus reperies, nullam causam dico quin mihi

et parentum et libertatis apud te deliquio siet.

HEG quid tu ais?

TYN   me tuom esse seruom et te meum erum.

---

[26] Ajax, son of Telamon, a mythological hero driven mad by Athena;
killed the flocks and then committed suicide.

[27] *Saxum*, the flint knife used by priests to kill sacrificial victims.

ARI Just shut up. I'll make sure, you false Philocrates, that
you'll be discovered to be the true Tyndarus today. (*Tyn-*
darus is making signs to Aristophontes) Why are you
shaking your head at me?

611
–12

TYN I'm shaking my head at you?

ARI (*to Hegio*) What would he be doing if you were further
away?

HEG (*to Tyndarus*) What do you say? What if I approach this
lunatic?

TYN Nonsense! He'll make a fool of you, he'll waffle things
you cannot make head or tail of. The stage get-up is miss-
ing, but when you see him, you see Ajax[26] himself.

615

HEG I don't care. I'll approach him all the same. (*moves to-*
ward Aristophontes)

TYN (*aside*) Now I'm done for completely, now I'm standing
between altar and knife[27] and I don't know what to do.

HEG I'm attending to you, Aristophontes, if there's anything
you want to tell me.

ARI You'll hear the truth from me, Hegio, which you're now
believing to be a lie. But first I want to clear myself with
you: I'm not mad and there's nothing wrong with me ex-
cept that I'm a slave. But as truly as the king of gods and
men may restore me to my own country, that man is no
more Philocrates than I or you.

620

HEG Oho! Tell me, who is he then?

ARI The one I told you right from the start. If you find this
otherwise, I have no objection to losing parents and free-
dom at your place.

625

HEG (*to Tyndarus*) What do *you* say?

TYN That I'm your slave and that you're my master.

HEG   haud istuc rogo.
          fuistin liber?

TYN   fui.

ARI   enim uero non fuit, nugas agit.

TYN   qui tu scis? an tu fortasse fuisti meae matri opstetrix,

630   qui id tam audacter dicere audes?

ARI   puerum te uidi puer.

TYN   at ego te uideo maiorem maior: em rursum tibi.
          meam rem non cures, si recte facias. num ego curo tuam?

HEG   fuitne huic pater Thesaurochrysonicochrysides?

ARI   non fuit, neque ego istuc nomen umquam audiui ante
            hunc diem.

635   Philocrati Theodoromedes fuit pater.

TYN   pereo probe.
          quin quiescis . . . dierectum cor meum? ac suspende te.
          tu sussultas, ego miser uix asto prae formidine.

HEG   satin istuc mihi exquisitum est, fuisse hunc seruom in
            Alide
          neque esse hunc Philocratem?

ARI   tam satis quam numquam hoc inuenies secus.

640   sed ubi is nunc est?

HEG   ubi ego minime atque ipsus se uolt maxume.

643   sed uide sis.

ARI   quin exploratum dico et prouisum hoc tibi.

644 HEG   certon?

ARI   quin nihil, inquam, inuenies magis hoc certo certius.

645   Philocrates iam inde usque amicus fuit mihi a puero
          puer.

631 maior maiorem *P, transp. Brix*

HEG That's not what I'm asking. Were you free before?

TYN Yes, I was.

ARI No, he wasn't, he's fooling you.

TYN (*to Aristophontes*) How do *you* know? Were you perhaps my mother's midwife, as you dare to state this so boldly? 630

ARI When I was a boy I saw you as a boy.

TYN And now that I'm a grown-up I see you as a grown-up. There you go, tit for tat! You wouldn't meddle with my business if you did the right thing. I'm not meddling with yours, am I?

HEG Was his father Goldtreasure-Goldwinson?

ARI No, he wasn't, and I've never heard that name before this day. Philocrates' father was Theodoromedes. 635

TYN (*aside*) I'm dying thoroughly. Calm down, my heart . . . damn it all, hang yourself! *You* are jumping up and down, while *I*, poor devil, can barely stand for fear.

HEG Is it absolutely clear that this man was a slave in Elis and that he isn't Philocrates?

ARI So absolutely that you'll never find it to be otherwise. But 640 where is he now?

HEG Where I want him to be least and where he wants to be most. But are you quite sure?

ARI Yes, I'm telling you that this has been investigated and checked for you.

HEG For certain?

ARI Yes, I assure you, you won't find anything more certain that this certainty. Philocrates has been my friend since we were both boys.

HEG   tum igitur ego deruncinatus, deartuatus sum miser

642   huius scelesti techinis, qui me ut lubitum est ductauit
            dolis.
         sed qua facie est tuos sodalis Philocrates?

ARI   dicam tibi;
         macilento ore, naso acuto, corpore albo, oculis nigris,
         subrufus aliquantum, crispus, cincinnatus.

HEG   conuenit.

TYN   ut quidem hercle in medium ego hodie pessume pro-
            cesserim.

650   uae illis uirgis miseris, quae hodie in tergo morientur
            meo.

HEG   uerba mihi data esse uideo.

TYN   quid cessatis, compedes,
         currere ad me meaque amplecti crura, ut uos custodiam?

HEG   satin med illi hodie scelesti capti ceperunt dolo?
         illic seruom se assimulabat, hic sese autem liberum.

655   nuculeum amisi, reliqui pigneri putamina.
         ita mi stolido sursum uorsum os subleuere offuciis.
         hicquidem me numquam irridebit. Colaphe, Cordalio,
            Corax,
         ite istinc, efferte lora.

COL   num lignatum mittimur?

III. v: HEGIO. TYNDARVS. ARISTOPHONTES

HEG   inicite huic manicas ‹maxumas› mastigiae.

660 TYN   quid hoc est negoti? quid ego deliqui?

641–2 *post 645 posuit Brix*
659 maxumas *add. Spengel*

---

28 Pun on the two meanings of *conuenit*. Hegio means that the de-
scription fits; Tyndarus says that there is an agreement between two
parties.

HEG So I've been cut up and dismembered by this rascal's 641
tricks, poor me; he led me on with his tricks as he liked.
But what does your friend Philocrates look like?

ARI I'll tell you. He has a narrow face, a sharp nose, fair com
plexion, dark eyes, and his hair is somewhat reddish,
wavy, and curly.

HEG That agrees.

TYN (*aside*) It does agree[28] . . . with me having come to the 649
fore most inauspiciously today. Bad luck to those
wretched rods that will die on my back today.

HEG I can see I've been fooled.

TYN (*aside*) Shackles, why are you hesitating to rush to me and
embrace my shins so I can guard you?

HEG Haven't those rascals who were caught caught me out
well with their trick today? That one was pretending
to be a slave, and this one to be free. I threw away the 655
nut and kept the shell as a surety. They fooled[29] me in ev-
ery conceivable way, idiot that I am. But this one will
never have the laugh on me. (*shouting into the house*)
Colaphus, Cordalio, Corax, get out from there, bring out
your straps.

Enter three OVERSEERS with whips and chains.

COL Are we being sent to collect firewood?[30]

HEG Put the heaviest handcuffs onto this rascal. (*the overseers
are obeying*)

TYN What's the matter? What have I done wrong? 660

---

[29] Lit. "they smeared my face," a phrase based on the practical joke
of painting the face of someone who is sleeping (Non. p. 65 Lindsay).

[30] A joke; loads of firewood are bound with straps, as are slaves.

	HEG	rogas,

HEG   rogas,
     sator sartorque scelerum et messor maxume?
TYN   non "occatorem" dicere audebas prius?
     nam semper occant prius quam sariunt rustici.
HEG   at‹tat› ut confidenter mihi contra astitit!
665 TYN   decet innocentem seruolum atque innoxium
     confidentem esse, suom apud erum potissumum.
HEG   astringite isti sultis uehementer manus.
TYN   tuos sum, tu has quidem uel praecidi iube.
     sed quid negoti est? quam ob rem suscenses mihi?
670 HEG   quia me meamque rem, quod in te uno fuit,
     tuis scelestis, falsidicis fallaciis
     delacerauisti deartuauistique opes.
     confecisti omnis res ac rationes meas:
     ita mi exemisti Philocratem fallaciis.
675   illum esse seruom credidi, te liberum;
     ita uosmet aiebatis itaque nomina
     inter uos permutastis.
TYN   fateor omnia
     facta esse ita ut ‹tu› dicis, et fallaciis
     abiisse eum aps te mea opera atque astutia;
680   an, opsecro hercle te, id nunc suscenses mihi?
HEG   at cum cruciatu maxumo id factum est tuo.
TYN   dum ne ob male facta peream, parui existumo.
     si ego hic peribo, ast ille ut dixit non redit,
     at erit mi hoc factum mortuo memorabile,
685   ‹me› meum erum captum ex seruitute atque hostibus
     reducem fecisse liberum in patriam ad patrem,
     meumque potius me caput periculo
     praeoptauisse quam is periret ponere.

664 attat *Hermann*, confidenter ‹homo› *Leo in apparatu*
665 seruom *P*, seruolum *Bothe*   678 tu *add. Camerarius*

HEG   You're asking, you sower, hoer, and greatest reaper of crimes?

TYN   Didn't you want to say "harrower" earlier? Farmers always harrow before they hoe.

HEG   Look at that, how boldly he's stood up to me!

TYN   An innocent and blameless slave ought to be bold, especially in front of his master.   665

HEG   (*to overseers*) Tie up his hands tightly, will you.

TYN   I'm yours, you can even have them cut off. But what's the matter? Why are you angry with me?

HEG   Because as far as you could you hacked me and my hopes   670 to pieces and tore my chances to shreds through your wicked and false swindles. You've destroyed all my plans and calculations by snatching Philocrates from me through your swindles. I believed that he is a slave and   675 that you are free; so you said yourselves and interchanged your names.

TYN   I admit that everything was done as you say, and that he left you because of my tricks, my effort, and my cunning. Seriously, I ask you, is that why you're angry with me   680 now?

HEG   You'll pay for doing this with the hardest torture.

TYN   So long as I don't die for bad deeds, I don't care. If I die here and if he doesn't return as promised, this deed of mine will still be worth remembering when I'm dead: that I made it possible for my master, who was a prisoner,   685 to return from slavery and the enemy to his own land and his father as a free man, and that I preferred to put my own life at risk rather than let him die.

---

685 me *add. Pylades*

	HEG	facito ergo ut Accherunti clueas gloria.
690	TYN	qui per uirtutem periit, at non interit.
	HEG	quando ego te exemplis excruciaro pessumis
		atque ob sutelas tuas te morti misero,
		uel te interiisse uel periisse praedicent;
		dum pereas, nihil interdico aiant uiuere.
695	TYN	pol si istuc faxis, hau sine poena feceris,
		si ille huc rebitet, sicut confido affore.
	ARI	pro di immortales! nunc ego teneo, nunc scio
		quid hoc sit negoti. meus sodalis Philocrates
		in libertate est ad patrem in patria ⟨domo⟩.
700		bene est, nec quisquam est mi aeque melius quoi uelim.
		sed hoc mihi aegre est, me huic dedisse operam malam,
		qui nunc propter me meaque uerba uinctus est.
	HEG	uotuin te quicquam mi hodie falsum proloqui?
	TYN	uot[a]uisti.
	HEG	quor es ausus mentiri mihi?
705	TYN	quia uera obessent illi quoi operam dabam:
		nunc falsa prosunt.
	HEG	at tibi oberunt.
	TYN	optume est.
		at erum seruaui, quem seruatum gaudeo,
		quoi me custodem addiderat erus maior meus.
		sed malene id factum ⟨tu⟩ arbitrare?
	HEG	pessume.
710	TYN	at ego aio recte, qui aps te seorsum sentio.
		nam cogitato, si quis hoc gnato tuo

691 pessumis excruciauero *P, transp. Camerarius,* p. cruciauero *Brix*   694 dicant *P,* aiant *Fleckeisen*
699–700 domo *add. Schoell,* neque ⟨usquam⟩ *Lange* qui bene est *in fine uersus* 699 *ponit*

578

HEG   Then make sure that you're famous in the Underworld.

TYN   A man who dies as a result of his noble character does not   690
perish.

HEG   When I've tortured you in the harshest ways and put you
to death for your tricks, they can say that you've perished
or that you've merely died; so long as you die, I don't for-
bid them to say that you're alive.

TYN   If you do that, you won't have done it without suffering   695
for it if that man returns here, as I'm sure he will.

ARI   *(aside)* Immortal gods! Now I grasp it, now I know what's
going on. My friend Philocrates is at home with his father
in freedom. That's good, and there isn't anyone toward   700
whom I'm better disposed. But I'm upset that I did this
chap here a bad turn, who's now in fetters because of me
and my words.

HEG   Didn't I forbid you to tell me any lies today?

TYN   You did.

HEG   Why did you dare lie to me?

TYN   Because the truth would have been an obstacle to the   705
man I was trying to help, whereas lies are useful.

HEG   But they'll be harmful to you.

TYN   Very well. But I saved my master and I'm happy that he's
saved; my old master had made me his guardian. But do
you think this was a bad deed?

HEG   A very bad one.

TYN   But I say it was a good one; my opinion is not the same as   710
yours. Well, think about it, if a slave of yours were to do

---

704 uotuisti *Pareus* (uotuin *in* 703)
709 tu *add. Pylades*

		tuos seruos faxit, qualem haberes gratiam?
		emitteresne necne eum seruom manu?
		essetne apud te is seruos acceptissumus?
715		responde.
	HEG	opinor.
	TYN	quor ergo iratus mihi es?
	HEG	quia illi fuisti quam mihi fidelior.
	TYN	quid? tu una nocte postulauisti et die
		recens captum hominem, nuperum, nouicium,
720		te perdocere ut melius consulerem tibi
		quam illi quicum una ⟨a⟩ puero aetatem exegeram?
	HEG	ergo ab eo petito gratiam istam. ducite
		ubi ponderosas, crassas capiat compedis.
		inde ibis porro in latomias lapidarias.
		ibi quom alii octonos lapides effodiunt, nisi
725		cotidiano sesqueopus confeceris,
		"Sescentoplago" nomen indetur tibi.
	ARI	per deos atque homines ego te optestor, Hegio,
		ne tu istunc hominem perduis.
	HEG	curabitur;
		nam noctu neruo uinctus custodibitur,
730		interdius sub terra lapides eximet:
		diu ego hunc cruciabo, non uno apsoluam die.
	ARI	certumne est tibi istuc?
	HEG	non moriri certius.
		abducite istum actutum ad Hippolytum fabrum,
		iubete huic crassas compedis impingier;
735		inde extra portam ad meum libertum Cordalum
		in lapicidinas facite deductus siet:

720 a *add. Pylades*

this for your son, what gratitude would you feel toward
him? Would you set that slave free or not? Wouldn't that
slave be your favorite? Answer me.   715

HEG I think so.

TYN Then why are you angry with me?

HEG Because you've been more faithful to him than to me.

TYN What? You expected to teach me in one night and one
day, a man taken prisoner recently, a fresh novice, to look
after your interests better than those of a man I'd spent   720
my life with from childhood?

HEG Then ask *him* for thanks for that. (*to overseers*) Take him
to a place where he puts on heavy, hefty shackles. (*to
Tyndarus*) From there you'll go straight to the stone
quarries. While others are digging out eight blocks each
there, they'll call you Beatnik unless you finish half as   725
much work again every day.

ARI I entreat you by the gods and men, Hegio, don't lose that
man.

HEG I'll see to that:[31] at night he'll be guarded bound with a
fetter, and during the day he'll hew out stones under-   730
ground. I'll torture him for a long time, I won't let him off
the hook in a single day.

ARI Is that settled for you?

HEG Death isn't more settled than that. (*to overseers*) Take
him away to the blacksmith Hippolytus immediately, and
have hefty shackles put on him. Have him brought from   735
there to the quarries to my freeman Cordalus outside the

_____

[31] Pun on the two meanings of *perdere*; Aristophontes means "lose"
in the sense of "destroy," while Hegio deliberately understands it as "let
escape."

atque hunc me uelle dicite ita curarier
ne qui deterius huic sit . . . quam quoi pessume est.
TYN quor ego te inuito me esse saluom postulem?
740 periclum uitae meae tuo stat periculo.
post mortem in morte nihil est quod metuam mali.
etsi peruiuo usque ad summam aetatem, tamen
breue spatium est perferundi quae minitas mihi.
uale atque salue, etsi aliter ut dicam meres.
745 tu, Aristophontes, de me ut meruisti, ita uale;
nam mihi propter te hoc optigit.
HEG   abducite.
TYN at unum hoc quaeso, si huc rebitet Philocrates,
ut mi eius facias conueniundi copiam.
HEG periistis, nisi hunc iam e conspectu abducitis.
750 TYN uis haec quidem hercle est, et trahi et trudi simul.
HEG illic est abductus recta in phylacam, ut dignus est.
ego illis captiuis aliis documentum dabo,
ne tale quisquam facinus incipere audeat.
quod apsque hoc esset, qui mihi hoc fecit palam,
755 usque offrenatum suis me ductarent dolis.
nunc certum est nulli posthac quicquam credere.
satis sum semel deceptus. speraui miser
ex seruitute me exemisse filium:
ea spes elapsa est. perdidi unum filium,
760 puerum quadrimum quem mihi seruos surpuit,
neque eum seruom umquam repperi nec filium;

gate. And say that I want him to be looked after in such a way that it should in now way be worse for him . . . than it is for the one for whom it is worst.

TYN Why should I demand to be well against your will? The 740 risk to my life is at your own risk. After death, there is no evil in death for me to fear. Even if I live to a great age, it's still only a short period for me to bear what you're threatening me with. Farewell and be well, even though you deserve that I should say otherwise. You, Aristophontes, 745 may you fare as you've deserved of me: this has happened to me because of you.

HEG (*to overseers*) Take him away.

TYN But I ask you for one thing: give me a chance to meet Philocrates if he comes back here.

HEG (*to overseers*) You're dead if you don't remove him from my sight immediately. (*the overseers are dragging Tyndarus away*)

TYN That's violence, being pulled and pushed at the same 750 time.

Exit TYNDARUS to the left with the overseers.

HEG That man's been taken away into custody directly as he deserves. I'll give those other prisoners a warning example so that nobody dares to begin such a trick. If it hadn't 754 been for the man who revealed it to me they'd have bridled me and led me on with their tricks permanently. Now I definitely won't trust anyone in anything in future. Once bitten, twice shy. Dear me, I was hoping that I'd ransomed my son from slavery; that hope has fallen through. I lost *one* son, a boy of four years, whom a slave 760 snatched away from me, and I've never found that slave

maior potitus hostium est. quod hoc est scelus?
quasi in orbitatem liberos produxerim.
sequere hac. redducam te ubi fuisti. neminis
765   miserere certum est, quia mei miseret neminem.
ARI   exauspicaui ex uinclis. nunc intellego
redauspicandum esse in catenas denuo.

ACTVS IV

IV. i: ERGASILVS

ERG   Iuppiter supreme, seruas me measque auges opes,
maxumas opimitates opiparasque offers mihi,
770   laudem, lucrum, ludum, iocum, festiuitatem, ferias,
pompam, penum, potationes, saturitatem, gaudium,
nec quoiquam homini supplicare nunc‹iam› certum est
      mihi;
nam uel prodesse amico possum uel inimicum perdere,
ita hic me amoenitate amoena amoenus onerauit dies.
775   sine sacris hereditatem sum aptus effertissumam.
nunc ad senem cursum capessam hunc Hegionem, quoi
      boni
tantum affero quantum ipsus a dis optat, atque etiam am-
      plius.
nunc certa res est, eodem pacto ut comici serui solent,
coniciam in collum pallium, primo ex med hanc rem ut
      audiat;

772 nunc *P*, nunc‹iam› *Geppert*

584

or my son again. The *older* one's fallen into the enemy's
hands. What misfortune is this? As if I'd got children only
to be childless again! (*to Aristophontes*) Follow me this   764
way. I'll take you back to where you were before. I'm
definitely not going to have pity on anyone, since no one
has pity on me.

ARI I left the fetters under good omens. Now I understand I
have to enter the chains again under bad omens.

*Exeunt HEGIO and ARISTOPHONTES with slaves to the
right.*

ACT FOUR

Enter ERGASILUS from the left.

ERG Great Jupiter, you save me, prosper my property, and
bring me huge and lavish prosperity, praise, profit, plea-   770
sure, laughter, liveliness, and leisure, a parade of dishes,
provisions, parties for drinking, fullness, joy. I definitely
won't seek anyone's goodwill from now on; I can help a
friend or destroy an enemy: this beautiful day has loaded
me down with beautiful beauty. I've got hold of a stuffed   775
inheritance with no strings attached.[32] Now I'll direct my
course to this old chap Hegio; I'm bringing him as much
good as he himself wishes for from the gods, and even
more. Now I've decided I'll throw my cloak round my
neck the same way slaves in comedy usually do, so he can

[32] Lit. "without sacrifices"; Festus (p. 370 Lindsay) tells us that
people did not just inherit money, but with it the obligation to perform
certain sacrifices.

780 speroque me ob hunc nuntium aeternum adepturum ci-
bum.

IV. ii: HEGIO. ERGASILVS

HEG quanto in pectore hanc rem meo magis uoluto,
tanto mi aegritudo auctior est in animo.
ad illum modum sublitum os esse mi hodie!
neque id perspicere quiui.

785 quod quom scibitur, per urbem irridebor.
quom extemplo ad forum aduenero, omnes loquentur:
"hic ille est senex doctus quoi uerba data sunt."
sed Ergasilus estne hic procul quem uideo?
collecto quidem est pallio. quidnam acturust?

790 ERG moue aps te moram atque, Ergasile, age hanc rem.
eminor interminorque, ne [quis] mi opstiterit obuiam,
nisi quis satis diu uixisse sese homo arbitrabitur.
nam qui opstiterit ore sistet.

HEG hic homo pugilatum incipit.

ERG facere certum est. proinde ut omnes itinera insistant sua:

795 ne quis in hanc plateam negoti conferat quicquam sui.
nam meum est ballista pugnum, cubitus catapulta est
mihi,
umerus aries, tum genu ad quemqu' iecero ad terram
dabo,
dentilegos omnis mortalis faciam, quemque offendero.

HEG quae illaec eminatio est nam? nequeo mirari satis.

800 ERG faciam ut huius diei locique meique semper meminerit.

785 ⟨tum⟩ per *Lindemann ut tetrameter fiat*
791 quis *del. Guyet*
795 hac platea *P,* hanc plateam *Bothe*
796 meus . . . pugnus *P, sed* pugnum *grammaticus testatur* (*Keil 5.*
587. 12)

hear this from me first. I expect that for this message I'll   780
get food forever.

Enter HEGIO from the right.

HEG   The more I'm turning this matter around in my heart, the
more my grief increases inside me. Is it possible that I
was fooled like that today? I couldn't see through it. Once   785
this is known, I'll be a laughing-stock throughout the city.
As soon as I come to the market, everybody will be say-
ing: "This is that clever old man who was tricked." (*looks
around*) But isn't this Ergasilus I can see in the distance?
He's girded up his cloak. What on earth is he going to do?
(*steps aside*)

ERG   Stop delaying and sort this out, Ergasilus. I issue a warn-   790
ing and a threat: let no one stand in my way unless he
believes he's lived long enough: anyone who stands in my
way will stand on his head. (*shadow-boxes*)

HEG   (*aside*) He's beginning a boxing-match.

ERG   I mean what I say. So all should stick to their own paths.
Let no one bring any business of his into this street: 795
my fist is a stone, my elbow is an arrow, my shoulder is a
battering ram, and I'll knock to the ground anyone I di-
rect my knee at. I'll make all mortals tooth-collectors,
whomever I meet.

HEG   (*aside*) What do all those threats mean? I can't help won-
dering.

ERG   I'll make sure that he remembers this day, this place, and   800

qui mi in cursu [opstiterit], faxo uitae is extemplo opstite-
　　rit suae.

HEG quid hic homo tantum incipissit facere cum tantis minis?

ERG prius edico, ne quis propter culpam capiatur suam:
　　continete uos domi, prohibete a uobis uim meam.

805 HEG mira edepol sunt ni hic in uentrem sumpsit confiden-
　　tiam.
　　uae misero illi, quoius cibo iste factust imperiosior!

ERG tum pistores scrofipasci, qui alunt furfuribus sues,
　　quarum odore praeterire nemo pistrinum potest:
　　eorum si quoiusquam scrofam in publico conspexero,

810 　　ex ipsis dominis meis pugnis exculcabo furfures.

HEG basilicas edictiones atque imperiosas habet:
　　satur homo est, habet profecto in uentre confidentiam.

ERG tum piscatores, qui praebent populo piscis foetidos,
　　qui aduehuntur quadrupedanti, crucianti cantherio,

815 　　quorum odos subbasilicanos omnis abigit in forum,
　　eis ego ora uerberabo surpiculis piscariis,
　　ut sciant alieno naso quam exhibeant molestiam.
　　tum lanii autem, qui concinnant liberis orbas ouis,
　　qui locant caedundos agnos et dupla agninam danunt,

820 　　qui Petroni nomen indunt uerueci sectario,
　　eum ego si in uia Petronem publica conspexero,
　　et Petronem et dominum reddam mortalis miserrumos.

801 in cursu *del. Bothe*, opstiterit[1] *del. Lindsay*

---

[33] According to Paul the Deacon (p. 227 Lindsay), *petro* is a term for
a country yokel derived from *petra* (stone). While he is probably right
about usage, the derivation seems wrong. *Petro* is a Sabellian first name
connected with the word for "four," just as the Latin name *Quintus* orig-
inally just meant "child born in the fifth month of the year." *Petro* be-
came a derogatory term, just as Spanish *Diego* became English "dago."

me for good. If anyone stands in my way during my journey, I'll make sure that he'll immediately stand in the way of his own survival.

HEG (*aside*) What great task is he beginning to do with such great threats?

ERG I'm announcing it in advance so that no one comes to grief for failing to take the right measures. Stay at home, keep my violence away from you.

HEG (*aside*) It would be strange if he hasn't put boldness into 805 his belly. Bad luck to the wretched chap whose food has made him all too domineering!

ERG Next point: the millers feeding sows, who raise pigs with the husks, because of whose stench no one can go past the mill; if I see a sow of any one of them in public, I'll 810 knock the husks out of their owners themselves with my fists.

HEG (*aside*) He has royal and imperious proclamations; the man is full, yes, he has boldness in his belly.

ERG Next point: the fishmongers, who ride here on a jogging, jolting gelding and who offer the people stinking fish whose stench drives all loafers in the arcade out into 815 the market, I'll whack their faces with their fish baskets so that they know what a nuisance they are to the public nose. Next point now: the butchers who arrange for sheep to be bereft of their children, who arrange for the lambs to be slaughtered and then sell the meat for double the price, who call the wether followed by the flock their 820 Petro;[33] if I set my eyes on this Petro in a public street, I'll make both Petro and its master the most wretched of mortals.

In our passage, the butchers probably use the name as an affectionate term, while Ergasilus shows contempt.

HEG   eugepae! edictiones aedilicias hicquidem habet,
        mirumque adeo est ni hunc fecere sibi Aetoli agorano-
        mum.

825 ERG   non ego nunc parasitus sum sed regum rex regalior,
        tantus uentri commeatus meo adest in portu cibus.
        sed ego cesso hunc Hegionem onerare laetitia senem,
        qui homine ⟨homo⟩ adaeque nemo uiuit fortunatior.

HEG   quae illaec est laetitia quam illic laetus largitur mihi?

830 ERG   heus ubi estis? ⟨ecquis hic est?⟩ ecquis hoc aperit os-
        tium?

HEG   hic homo ad cenam recipit se ad me.

ERG   aperite hasce ambas fores
        prius quam pultando assulatim foribus exitium affero.

833 HEG   perlubet hunc hominem colloqui.
833a   Ergasile.

ERG   Ergasilum qui uocat?

834 HEG   respice.

ERG   Fortuna quod tibi
834a   nec facit nec faciet, [hoc] me iubes.
835   sed quis est?

HEG   respice ad me, Hegio sum.

ERG   oh mihi,
836   quantum est hominum optumorum optume, in
836a   tempore aduenis.

HEG   nescioquem ad portum nactus es ubi cenes, eo fastidis.

ERG   cedo manum.

HEG   manum?

ERG   manum, inquam, cedo tuam actutum.

   824 Aetoli sibi *Guyet*
   828 homo *add. Lindsay*, qu⟨o mih⟩i homine Niemeyer
   830 ecquis hic est *add. Bothe*   834a hoc *del. Brix*

HEG (*aside*) Bravo! This man has an aedile's edicts,[34] and it
would be a surprise indeed if the Aetolians haven't made
him their market inspector.

ERG Now I'm not a hanger-on, but a regular royal king of 825
kings, if the supply for my stomach in the harbor is any-
thing to go by—food! But I'm delaying weighing old
Hegio here down with joy; no man's luckier than him.

HEG (*aside*) What is that joy this joyful creature is giving me?

ERG (*knocking at the door*) Hello, where are you? Is anyone 830
here? Is anyone opening this door?

HEG (*aside*) He's coming for dinner at my place.

ERG Open this door, both leaves, before I bring destruction to
it by battering it to splinters.

HEG (*aside*) I really want to speak to him. (*loudly*) Ergasilus.

ERG Who's calling Ergasilus?

HEG Kindly look at me.

ERG Look at you kindly?[35] You're telling me to do what Good
Fortune isn't doing for you, or ever will do. But who is it? 835

HEG Kindly look at me. I'm Hegio.

ERG (*looks back*) Oh best man of all best men, you're coming
just in time.

HEG You've found someone at the harbor where you can eat,
that's why you're too proud for me.

ERG Give me your hand.

HEG My hand?

ERG I'm telling you, give me your hand immediately.

---

[34] The aediles were magistrates with police functions, but they also
exercised legal jurisdiction.

[35] Pun on the two meanings of *respicere*: "look back" and "look on
someone with favor."

	HEG	tene.
	ERG	gaude.
	HEG	quid ego gaudeam?
	ERG	quia ego impero, age gaude modo.
840	HEG	pol maerores mi anteuortunt gaudiis.
	ERG	⟨gaude modo.⟩

       iam ego ex corpore exigam omnis maculas maerorum
          tibi.

       gaude audacter.

	HEG	gaudeo, etsi nil scio quod gaudeam.
	ERG	bene facis. iube—
	HEG	quid iubeam?
	ERG	ignem ingentem fieri.
	HEG	ignem ingentem?
	ERG	ita dico, magnus ut sit.
	HEG	quid? me, uolturi,
845		tuan causa aedis incensurum censes?
	ERG	noli irascier.

       iuben an non iubes astitui aulas, patinas elui,
       laridum atque epulas foueri foculis feruentibus?
       alium piscis praestinatum abire?

	HEG	hic uigilans somniat.
	ERG	alium porcinam atque agninam et pullos gallinaceos?
850	HEG	scis bene esse, si sit unde.
	ERG	pernam atque opthalmiam,

       horaeum, scombrum et trygonum et cetum et mollem
          caseum?

	HEG	nominandi istorum tibi erit magis quam edundi copia
		hic apud med, Ergasile.
	ERG	mean me causa hoc censes dicere?

840 noli irascier *P*, gaude modo *Brix* (noli irascier *falso ex 845*)

HEG (*stretches it out*) Take it.

ERG (*grasping it*) Be happy.

HEG What should I be happy for?

ERG Because I'm ordering you to be, go on, just be happy.

HEG Well, sadness has the upper hand over joy in my case.   840

ERG Just be happy! I'll immediately drive all spots of grief out of your body. Rejoice boldly.

HEG I am rejoicing, even if I don't know what I should be rejoicing for.

ERG Thank you. Order—

HEG (*interrupting*) What should I order?

ERG —a huge fire to be made.

HEG A huge fire?

ERG Yes, I'm saying it should be big.

HEG (*angrily*) What? You vulture, do you think I'll set fire to my house for your sake?

ERG Don't be angry. Are you ordering the pots to be set near   846 the fire, yes or no? The pans to be washed, and the lard and titbits to be heated up in burning braziers? Someone else to go and buy fish?

HEG He's sleeping with open eyes.

ERG Another one to buy pork and lamb and spring chicken?

HEG You know how to have a good time if you have the means.   850

ERG Ham and sea-bream, salted fish, mackerel, and sting-ray, and dolphin, and soft cheese?

HEG You'll have more of a chance to name those things than to eat them here at my place, Ergasilus.

ERG Do you think I'm saying this for my own sake?

HEG   nec nil hodie nec multo plus tu hic edes, ne frustra sis.

855   proin tu tui cottidiani uicti uentrem ad me afferas.

ERG   quin ita faciam, ut ⟨tu⟩te cupias facere sumptum, etsi
        ego uotem.

HEG   egone?

ERG   tune.

HEG   tum tu mi igitur erus es.

ERG   immo beneuolens.
      uin te faciam fortunatum?

HEG   malim quam miserum quidem.

ERG   cedo manum.

HEG   em manum.

ERG   di te omnes adiuuant.

HEG   nil sentio.

860 ERG   non enim es in senticeto, eo non sentis. sed iube
      uasa tibi pura apparari ad rem diuinam cito,
      atque agnum afferri proprium pinguem.

HEG   quor?

ERG   ut sacrufices.

HEG   quoi deorum?

ERG   mi hercle, nam ego nunc tibi sum summus Iuppiter,
      idem ego sum Salus, Fortuna, Lux, Laetitia, Gaudium.

865   proin tu deum hunc saturitate facias tranquillum tibi.

HEG   esurire mihi uidere.

ERG   miquidem esurio, non tibi.

HEG   tuo arbitratu, facile patior.

ERG   credo, consuetu's puer.

856 te *P*, tute *Bentley*   862 ⟨album⟩ agnum *Niemeyer*

---

[36] Pun on *sentire* (feel) and *senticetum* (thicket of briars).

HEG   You won't eat nothing here today, but you won't eat much 855
more either, don't be fooled. So bring me a stomach
ready for your everyday fare.

ERG   No, I'll take care that you yourself wish to squander
money, even if I forbade it.

HEG   I?

ERG   Yes, you.

HEG   Then you're my master.

ERG   No, your well-wisher. Do you want me to make you
happy?

HEG   Yes, certainly, rather than unhappy.

ERG   Give me your hand.

HEG   Here's my hand. (*stretches it out*)

ERG   (*grasping it*) All the gods are helping you.

HEG   I don't feel a thing.

ERG   Well, you're not in a thicket, that's why you're too thick to 860
feel anything.[36] But order clean vessels to be prepared
for you for religious rites quickly, and a suitable fat lamb
to be brought here.

HEG   Why?

ERG   So you can sacrifice.

HEG   To what god?

ERG   To me: I'm great Jupiter for you now; I'm also Salvation,
Fortune, Light, Joy, and Happiness. So placate this god 865
by making him full.

HEG   I can feel that you're hungry.

ERG   No, *I* can feel that I'm hungry, *you* can't.

HEG   As you wish, I can easily bear it.

ERG   I believe so, you got used to it as a boy.[37]

---

[37] *Pati* (bear it) is interpreted by Ergasilus as being at the receiving
end in sexual intercourse.

HEG   Iuppiter te dique perdant.

ERG   te hercle . . . mi aequom est gratias
agere ob nuntium; tantum ego nunc porto a portu tibi
    boni:

870   nunc tu mihi places.

HEG   abi, stultu's, sero post tempus uenis.

ERG   igitur olim si aduenissem, magis tu tum istuc diceres;
nunc hanc laetitiam accipe a me quam fero. nam filium
tuom modo in portu Philopolemum uiuom, saluom et
    sospitem
uidi in publica celoce, ibidemque illum adulescentulum

875   Aleum una et tuom Stalagmum seruom, qui aufugit
    domo,
qui tibi surrupuit quadrimum puerum filiolum tuom.

HEG   abi in malam rem, ludis me.

ERG   ita me amabit sancta Saturitas,
Hegio, itaque suo me semper condecoret cognomine,
ut ego uidi.

HEG   meum gnatum?

ERG   tuom gnatum et genium meum.

880 HEG   et captiuom illum Alidensem?

ERG   μὰ τὸν Ἀπόλλω.

HEG   et seruolum
meum Stalagmum, meum qui gnatum surpuit?

ERG   ναὶ τὰν Κόραν.

HEG   iam hodie—

ERG   ναὶ τὰν Πραινέστην.

---

879 meum<ne> *Bentley*   882 diu *P*, hodie *Niemeyer*

---

38 Ergasilus begins with an oath by Apollo, the god of prophecy, mu-

HEG May Jupiter and the gods destroy you.

ERG No, you . . . should thank me for my message; so much good am I now bringing to you from the harbor. Now you should propitiate me. 870

HEG Go away, you're being silly, you're coming too late, behind schedule.

ERG If I'd come before, then you could have said this with better reason; now receive from me the joy I'm bringing: I just saw your son Philopolemus in the harbor, alive, safe, and sound, in a swift-boat belonging to the state, and there I also saw that young man from Elis together with him, and your slave Stalagmus, who fled from home and snatched your son from you when he was a four-year-old boy. 876

HEG Go be hanged, you're pulling my leg.

ERG As truly as holy Fullness will love me, Hegio, and as truly as she may always grace me with her name, I have seen him.

HEG My son?

ERG Your son and my guardian spirit.

HEG And that prisoner from Elis? 880

ERG Yes, by Apollo.

HEG And my slave Stalagmus, who snatched my son away?

ERG Yes, by Cora.[38]

HEG Did he—

ERG (*interrupting*) Yes, by Praeneste.

sic, and many other things. He continues to swear by Proserpina, whose Greek name is Cora/Core, but since Cora is also a Volscian town, he turns to unusual oaths by Italian cities. Praeneste is modern Palestrina. Signea, Frusino, and Alatrium are nowadays better known as Segni, Frosinone, and Alatri.

HEG   uenit?

ERG   ναὶ τὰν Σιγνέαν.

HEG certon?

ERG   ναὶ τὰν Φρουσινῶνα.

HEG   uide sis.

ERG   ναὶ τὸν Ἀλάτριον.

HEG quid tu per barbaricas urbis iuras?

ERG   quia enim item asperae

885   sunt ut tuom uictum autumabas esse.

HEG   uae aetati—

ERG   tuae!

quippe quando mihi nil credis, quod ego dico sedulo.

sed Stalagmus quoius erat tunc nationis, quom hinc abit?

HEG Siculus.

ERG   at nunc Siculus non est, Boius est, boiam terit:

liberorum quaerundorum causa ei, credo, uxor data est.

890 HEG dic, bonan fide tu mi istaec uerba dixisti?

ERG   bona.

HEG di immortales, iterum gnatus uideor, si uera autumas.

ERG ain tu? dubium habebis etiam, sancte quom ego iurem

tibi?

postremo, Hegio, si parua iuri iurando est fides,

uise ad portum.

HEG   facere certum est. tu intus cura quod opus est.

895   sume, posce, prome quiduis. te facio cellarium.

ERG nam hercle, nisi mantiscinatus probe ero, fusti pectito.

885 tuae *Ergasilo dat Lindsay*
888 et *P,* at *Camerarius*

---

39 The "Boian lady" is a neck collar used for torturing slaves.

HEG —come already today?

ERG Yes, by Signea.

HEG Definitely?

ERG Yes, by Frusino.

HEG Are you quite sure?

ERG Yes, by Alatrium.

HEG Why are you swearing by foreign cities?   884

ERG Because they're as rough as you said your food is.

HEG Bad luck to—

ERG (*interrupting*) You! Since you won't believe a word of what I'm saying in earnest. But what was Stalagmus' nationality when he went away from here?

HEG Sicilian.

ERG Now he's not a Sicilian, he's a Boian and embracing a Boian lady.[39] I guess she was given to him in marriage with a view to begetting children.

HEG Tell me, did you tell me about this in good faith?   890

ERG Yes, I did.

HEG Immortal gods, I seem born again if you're speaking the truth.

ERG Do you say so? You'll still doubt it when I'd give you a solemn oath? Well then, Hegio, if you have little faith in my oath, go and look in the harbor.

HEG I'll certainly do so. You take care inside of what's needed. Take, demand, help yourself to anything you like. I   895 hereby make you my butler.

ERG Yes, if I don't tuck in[40] properly, you can comb me down with a club.

---

[40] *Mantiscinari*, of doubtful meaning. Perhaps connected with *mantisa* (sauce), hence my translation. Possibly punning on Greek *mantis* (soothsayer).

	HEG	aeternum tibi dapinabo uictum, si uera autumas.
	ERG	unde id?
	HEG	a me meoque gnato.
	ERG	sponden tu istud?
	HEG	spondeo.
	ERG	at ego tuom tibi aduenisse filium respondeo.
900	HEG	cura quam optume potes.
	ERG	bene ambula et redambula.

IV. iii: ERGASILVS

ERG illic hinc abiit, mihi rem summam credidit cibariam.
di immortales, iam ut ego collos praetruncabo tegoribus!
quanta pernis pestis ueniet, quanta labes larido,
quanta sumini apsumedo, quanta callo calamitas,
905 quanta laniis lassitudo, quanta porcinariis!
nam si alia memorem, quae ad uentris uictum condu-
cunt, mora est.
nunc ibo ut pro praefectura mea ius dicam larido,
et quae pendent indemnatae pernae, is auxilium ut fe-
ram.

IV. iv: PVER

PVER Diespiter te dique, Ergasile, perdant et uentrem tuom,
910 parasitosque omnis, et qui posthac cenam parasitis dabit.
clades calamitasque, intemperies modo in nostram adue-
nit domum.
912 quasi lupus esuriens metui ne in me faceret impetum.

912 metui *P*, timui *A*, *fortasse* mi timui

---

41 Here and in what follows we find a parody of a *sponsio*, a type of
binding agreement. After Hegio makes his promise, the food belongs to

HEG I'll serve you meals for good if you're telling the truth.

ERG Out of whose pocket?

HEG Out of mine and that of my son.

ERG Are you giving me your word?[41]

HEG Yes, I am giving you my word.

ERG And I am giving you this word: your son's arrived.

HEG Attend to it as well as you can.   900

ERG Have a good walk there and a good walk back.

Exit HEGIO to the left.

ERG He's left and he's put me in charge of the food depart-
     ment. Immortal gods, how I will chop the necks off the
     backs in a moment! What havoc will fall on the ham, what
     loss on the lard, what utter consumption on the udder,
     what misfortune on the meat, what sleepiness on the   905
     slaughterers and pork-butchers! Well, if I were to men-
     tion the other things which help toward the stomach's
     sustenance it would just cause delay. Now I'll go in order
     to pass judgment on the lard by virtue of my office and to
     bring help to the ham hanging unsentenced.

Exit ERGASILUS into the house. There is noise inside.
Enter a SLAVE-BOY from Hegio's house.

BOY May Jupiter and the gods destroy you, Ergasilus, and
     your stomach, and all hangers-on, and anyone who gives   910
     a dinner to hangers-on hereafter. Damage, loss, and mis-
     fortune just came into our house. I was afraid that he'd

Ergasilus. Ergasilus in turn puns on *spondere* and *respondere*: he "gives
a reply" and "makes a *sponsio*" to the effect that Hegio's son has come.

912ᵃ   ubi uoltus ⟨e⟩sur⟨ie⟩ntis ********* impetum

nimisque hercle ego illum male formidabam, ita frende-
      bat dentibus.

adueniens deturbauit totum cum carni carnarium:

915   arripuit gladium, praeruncauit tribus tegoribus glandia;

aulas calicesque omnis confregit, nisi quae modiales
      erant.

coquom percontabatur possentne seriae feruescere.

cellas refregit omnis intus recclusitque armarium.

asseruate istunc, sultis, serui. ego ibo ut conueniam se-
      nem,

920   dicam ut sibi penum aliud [ad]ornet, siquidem sese uti
      uolet;

nam hic quidem ut adornat aut iam nihil est aut iam nihil
      erit.

ACTVS V

V. i: HEGIO. PHILOPOLEMVS. PHILOCRATES

HEG   Ioui disque ago gratias merito magnas,

quom te redducem tuo patri reddiderunt

quomque ex miseriis plurumis me exemerunt,

925   quae adhuc te carens dum hic fui sustentabam,

quomque hunc conspicor in potestate nostra,

quomque haec reperta est fides firma nobis.

PHILOP satis iam dolui ex animo, et cura satis me et lacrumis
      maceraui,

912ᵃ *uersus non inuenitur in* P   914 carne Ω, carni *Bothe*

915 praeruncauit A, praetruncauit P   920 adornet A, ornet P

926 conspicio P, conspicor *Geppert*

dash at me like a hungry wolf. When the face of the hungry *** dash. I was terribly scared of him, the way he was gnashing his teeth! When he arrived he threw down the whole meat stand with the meat. He grabbed a sword 915 and chopped the sweet-breads off three meat-joints. He smashed all pots and dishes to pieces, except those that were bucket-sized. He asked the cook if the storage-vats could stand the heat of cooking. He broke open all larders inside and opened up the pantry. (*shouting to those inside*) Watch that man, will you, slaves! I'll go meet master. I'll tell him to get other provisions for himself, if he 920 wants to use any himself: the way this chap here goes about it, there's either nothing left now or there will be nothing left in a moment.

Exit SLAVE-BOY to the left.

ACT FIVE

Enter HEGIO, PHILOPOLEMUS, PHILOCRATES, and STA-LAGMUS from the left, the latter in chains.

HEG (*to Philopolemus*) I give great thanks to Jupiter and the gods, and deservedly so, for bringing you back and returning you to your father, for freeing me from the many miseries which I endured until now while I was here 925 without you, for seeing this man (*points to Stalagmus*) in our power, and for finding that this man's (*points to Philocrates*) promise was a firm one.

PHILOP (*to Hegio*) I've already had enough mental torture, I've worn myself out enough through worry and tears, and

satis iam audiui tuas aerumnas, ad portum mihi quas me-
　　morasti.
930　hoc agamus.

PHILOC　　　　　　quid nunc, quoniam tecum seruaui fidem
tibique hunc reducem in libertatem feci?

HEG　　　　　　　　　　　　　　fecisti ut tibi,
Philocrates, numquam referre gratiam possim satis,
proinde ut tu promeritu's de me et filio.

PHILOP　　　　　　　　　　immo potes,
pater, et poteris et ego potero, et di eam potestatem da-
　　bunt
935　ut beneficium bene merenti nostro merito muneres;
sicut tu huic potes, pater mi, facere merito maxume.

HEG　quid opust uerbis? lingua nulla est qua negem quicquid
　　roges.

PHILOC　postulo aps te ut mi illum reddas seruom, quem hic re-
　　liqueram
pignus pro me, qui mi melior quam sibi semper fuit,
940　pro bene factis eius ut ei pretium possim reddere.

HEG　quod bene fecisti referetur gratia. id quod postulas,
et id et aliud quod me orabis impetrabis. atque te
nolim suscensere quod ego iratus ei feci male.

PHILOC　quid fecisti?

HEG　　　　　　in lapicidinas compeditum condidi,
945　ubi resciui mihi data esse uerba.

PHILOC　　　　　　　　　　uae misero mihi,
propter meum caput labores homini euenisse optumo!

HEG　at ob eam rem mihi libellam pro eo argenti ne duis:
gratiis a me, ut sit liber, ducito.

I've already heard enough about your hard times, which
you told me about at the harbor. Let's turn to this matter.   930

PHILOC Well then; I kept my promise toward you and re-
turned this chap (*points to Philopolemus*) to you in free-
dom.

HEG Philocrates, you've made sure that I'll never be able to
show you enough gratitude for your kindness toward me
and my son.

PHILOP No, father, you are able to, and you will be, and I will
also be, and the gods will give us the ability to reward a   935
man who is kind to us with our kindness; just as you can
be kind to this man for his great kindness, my father.

HEG (*to Philocrates*) What need is there for words? I don't
have any tongue with which I could refuse anything you
ask for.

PHILOC I want you to give me back that slave I left here as se-
curity for myself. He's always been better to me than to
himself. I'd like to reward him for his services.   940

HEG For your kindness toward us you'll receive thanks. What
you're requesting, this and anything else you ask me for,
you'll get it. (*hesitates for a moment*) And I wouldn't want
you to be angry with me for treating him badly in my
rage.

PHILOC What did you do?

HEG I had him wear shackles and put him into the quarries
when I found out that I'd been tricked.   945

PHILOC Oh no, I'm so wretched! Because of me the best of
men had to suffer!

HEG But because of that you shouldn't give me a farthing[42] for
him. Take him from me for free so that he can be free.

---

[42] Lit. a silver *libella*, i.e., a tenth of a *denarius*.

PHILOC   edepol, Hegio,
        facis benigne. sed quaeso hominem ut iubeas arcessi.

HEG   licet.

950   ubi estis uos? ite actutum, Tyndarum huc arcessite.
        uos ite intro. interibi ego ex hac statua uerberea uolo
        erogitare meo minore quid sit factum filio.
        uos lauate interibi.

PHILOP   sequere hac, Philocrates, me intro.

PHILOC   sequor.

V. ii: HEGIO. STALAGMVS

HEG   age tu illuc procede, bone uir, lepidum mancupium
        meum.

955 STA   quid me oportet facere, ubi tu talis uir falsum autumas?
        fui ego bellus, lepidus: bonus uir numquam, nec frugi
           bonae,
        neque ero umquam: ne ⟨in⟩ spem ponas me bonae frugi
           fore.

HEG   propemodum ubi loci fortunae tuae sint facile intellegis.
        si eris uerax, tua ex re facies . . . ex mala meliusculam.

960   recte et uera loquere, sed nec uere nec ⟨tu⟩ recte adhuc
        fecisti umquam.

STA   quod ego fatear, credin pudeat quom autumes?

HEG   at ego faciam ut pudeat, nam in ruborem te totum dabo.

STA   heia, credo ego imperito plagas minitaris mihi.
        tandem istaec aufer, dic quid fers, ut feras hinc quod pe-
           tis.

957 umquam *P*, numquam *Vahlen* in add. *Guyet*
960 tu *add. Schoell hoc loco* (*alii alibi, sed cf. Men. 960*)

---

[43] I.e., he will beat him until he is bleeding everywhere.

PHILOC My sincere thanks, Hegio. But please have him
brought here.

HEG Of course. (*to those inside the house*) Where are you? 950
(*two overseers enter from the house*) Go immediately,
fetch Tyndarus here. (*exeunt overseers to the left*) You
two go in. In the meantime I want to get the information
out of this whipping-post here (*points to Stalagmus*) as to
what's happened to my younger son. You have a bath
meanwhile.

PHILOP Philocrates, follow me in, this way.

PHILOC I'm following you.

Exeunt PHILOPOLEMUS and PHILOCRATES into the house.

HEG Go on, step forward there, my good man, my charming
slave.

STA What should I do when a man like you is telling lies? Yes, 955
I was pretty and charming; but never a good man or of
good character, and I never will be. Don't set your hopes
on me being of good character in future.

HEG You grasp pretty easily what sort of situation you're in. If
you're truthful, you'll turn your situation . . . from a bad
one into a slightly better one. Tell me the honest truth; 960
but so far you've never behaved truthfully or honestly.

STA Do you believe I feel shame just because you're telling
me what I'd admit myself?

HEG But I'll make sure that you will feel shame: I'll make you
blush all over.[43]

STA Goodness, I suppose you are threatening a complete
novice with a beating: me. Stop that now and tell me what
you're proposing, so that you can get from me what you
demand.

965 HEG satis facundu's. sed iam fieri dicta compendi uolo.

STA ut uis fiat.

HEG   bene morigerus fuit puer, nunc non decet.

      hoc agamus. iam animum aduorte ac mihi quae dicam
         edissere.

      si eris uerax, ⟨e⟩ tuis rebus feceris meliusculas.

STA nugae istaec sunt. non me censes scire quid dignus siem?

970 HEG at ea supterfugere potis es pauca, si non omnia.

STA pauca effugiam, scio; nam multa euenient, et merito
      meo,

      quia et fugi et tibi surrupui filium et eum uendidi.

HEG quoi homini?

STA   Theodoromedi in Alide Polyplusio,
      sex minis.

HEG   pro di immortales, is quidem huius est pater

975   Philocratis.

STA   quin melius noui quam te et uidi saepius.

HEG serua, Iuppiter supreme, et me et meum gnatum mihi.

      Philocrates, per tuom te genium opsecro, exi, te uolo!

V. iii: PHILOCRATES. HEGIO. STALAGMVS

PHILOC Hegio, assum. si quid me uis, impera.

HEG   hic gnatum meum
      tuo patri ait se uendidisse sex minis in Alide.

980 PHILOC quam diu id factum est?

STA   hic annus incipit uicesumus.

PHILOC falsa memorat.

965 dictis compendium uolo *P*, d. u. c. *Bothe*, dicta compendi uolo
Guyet
  968 e *add. Camerarius*
  975 Philocratis *B*, Philocrates *EJ*

HEG You're quite eloquent. But I want you to save your words. 965

STA Yes, as you wish.

HEG (*aside*) As a boy he obeyed me well, but now it's inappropriate. (*aloud*) Let's sort this out. Pay attention now and answer my questions. If you're truthful, you'll improve your situation slightly.

STA That's nonsense. Do you think I don't know what I deserve?

HEG But you can escape a little of it, if not all. 970

STA I'll escape precious little, I know: many things will happen, and I deserve them because I ran away and snatched your son and sold him.

HEG To whom?

STA To Theodoromedes Moneybag in Elis, for six minas.

HEG Immortal gods, that's the father of this man here, Philocrates.

STA Well, I even know him better than I know you and I've seen him more often.

HEG Great Jupiter, save me and save my son for me. (*into the* 976
house) Philocrates, I beg you by your guardian spirit, come out, I want to speak to you!

Enter PHILOCRATES from the house.

PHILOC Hegio, here I am. If you want anything from me, I'm at your command.

HEG This man says he sold my son to your father in Elis for six minas.

PHILOC How long ago did this happen? 980

STA Almost twenty years.

PHILOC He's telling lies.

STA   aut ego aut tu. nam tibi quadrimulum
       tuos pater peculiarem paruolo puero dedit.

PHILOC   quid erat ei nomen? si uera dicis, memoradum mihi.

STA   Paegnium uocitatust, post uos indidistis Tyndaro.

985   PHILOC   quor ego te non noui?

STA   quia mos est obliuisci hominibus
       nec nouisse quoius nihili sit faciunda gratia.

PHILOC   dic mihi, isne istic fuit, quem uendidisti meo patri,
       qui mihi peculiaris datus est?

STA   huius filius.

HEG   uiuitne is homo?

STA   argentum accepi, nil curaui ceterum.

990   HEG   quid tu ais?

PHILOC   quin istic ipsust Tyndarus tuos filius,
       ut quidem hic argumenta loquitur. nam is mecum a pue-
          ro puer
       bene pudiceque educatust usque ad adulescentiam.

HEG   et miser sum et fortunatus, si ‹uos› uera dicitis;
       eo miser sum quia male illi feci, si gnatus meust.

995   eheu, quom ego plus minusque feci quam ‹me› aequom
          fuit.
       quod male feci crucior; modo si infectum fieri possiet!
       sed eccum incedit huc ornatus haud ex suis uirtutibus.

V. iv: TYNDARVS. HEGIO. PHILOCRATES. STALAGMVS

TYN   uidi ego multa saepe picta, quae Accherunti fierent
       cruciamenta, uerum enim uero nulla adaeque est Acche-
       runs

982 paruolum *P*, paruolo *Lindemann ex codice*
993 uos *add. Camerarius*
995 me *add. Bentley*

STA   (*to Philocrates*) Either I or you; your father gave you a little four-year-old as your own when you were a little boy.

PHILOC What name did he have? If you're telling the truth, tell me.

STA   He was called Paegnium, and later you gave him the name Tyndarus.

PHILOC Why don't I know you?   985

STA   Because it's people's custom to forget and not to know someone whose goodwill is to be regarded as worthless.

PHILOC Tell me, was the one you sold to my father the one I was given as my own?

STA   Yes, the son of this man here (*points to Hegio*).

HEG   Is he alive?

STA   I received the money, I didn't care about the rest.

HEG   (*to Philocrates*) What do *you* say?   990

PHILOC Well, Tyndarus himself is your son, according to the evidence this man's producing: from a young age till adulthood, he was brought up with me in a good and decent fashion.

HEG   I'm both wretched and lucky if you two are telling the truth. I'm wretched because I treated him badly, if he's my son. Dear me, I did both more and less than I ought 995 to have done. I'm in agony because I treated him badly; if only it could be undone! (*looks down the street*) But look, here he comes, in an outfit that doesn't suit his noble conduct.

Enter overseers with TYNDARUS from the left. He is in chains and has a crowbar in his hands.

TYN   I've often seen many pictures of the tortures taking place in the Underworld, but truly there's no Underworld that

1000   atque ubi ego fui, in lapicidinis. illic ibi demum est locus
             ubi labore lassitudo est exigunda ex corpore.
             nam ubi illo adueni, quasi patriciis pueris aut monerulae
             aut anites aut coturnices dantur, quicum lusitent,
             itidem mi haec aduenienti upupa qui me delectem data
             est.
1005   sed erus eccum ante ostium, et erus alter eccum ex Alide
             rediit.

HEG   salue, exoptate gnate mi.

TYN   hem, quid "gnate mi"?
             attat, scio quor te patrem assimules esse et me filium:
             quia mi item ut parentes lucis das tuendi copiam.

PHILOC   salue, Tyndare.

TYN   et tu, quoius causa hanc aerumnam exigo.
1010 PHILOC   at nunc liber in diuitias faxo uenies. nam tibi
             pater hic est; hic seruos qui te huic hinc quadrimum sur-
               puit,
             uendidit patri meo te sex minis, is te mihi
             paruolum peculiarem paruolo puero dedit
             illi; ⟨hi⟩c indicium fecit; nam hunc ex Alide huc reduci-
               mus.
1015 TYN   quid huius filium?

PHILOC   intus eccum fratrem germanum tuom.

[TYN   quid tu ais? adduxtin illum huius captiuom filium?

PHILOC   quin, inquam, intus hic est.

TYN   fecisti edepol et recte et bene.

1014 illic *P*, ill . . . *A*, illi hic *Lindsay* reduximus *Brix*
1016–22 *uersus desunt in A*

can match the place where I was, in the quarries. That,   1000
then, is the place where weariness has to be driven out of
one's body through hard work: just as patrician boys are
given jackdaws or ducks or quails to play with, I was given
this crow[44] for entertainment (*looks at the crowbar*), as
soon as I arrived there. But look, my master's in front of   1005
the door, and my other master's returned from Elis.

HEG   Greetings, my son; I've been longing for you.

TYN   What do you mean, "my son"? (*pauses*) Oh, I know why
you pretend that you're my father and I'm your son: be-
cause like parents you let me see the light.

PHILOC Greetings, Tyndarus.

TYN   And greetings to you, for whose sake I've been going
through this affliction.

PHILOC But now I'll make sure you come to riches as a free   1010
man: this man here (*points to Hegio*) is your father. This
here (*points to Stalagmus*) is the slave who snatched you
away from him when you were four years old and who
sold you to my father for six minas; when you and I were
little boys, he in turn gave you to me there to be my own.
This man (*points to Stalagmus*) indicated it: we brought
him back from Elis.

TYN   What about his son?   1015

PHILOC In there, look, is your true brother.

[TYN   What do you say? Did you bring back that son of his, the
prisoner?

PHILOC Yes, I assure you, he's in here.

TYN   You did what's right and good.

---

[44] Lit. "hoopoe," a crowbar shaped like this bird's bill.

PLAUTUS

PHILOC nunc tibi pater hic est. hic fur est tuos qui paruom hinc
te apstulit.
TYN at ego hunc grandis grandem natu ob furtum ad car-
nuficem dabo.
1020 PHILOC meritus est.
TYN ergo edepol ‹merito› meritam mercedem dabo.
sed ‹tu› dic oro: pater meus tune es?
HEG ego sum, gnate mi.
TYN nunc demum in memoriam redeo, quom mecum reco-
gito.]
nunc edepol demum in memoriam regredior audisse me
quasi per nebulam, Hegionem meum patrem uocarier.
1025 HEG is ego sum.
PHILOC compedibus quaeso ut tibi sit leuior filius
atque huic grauior seruos.
HEG certum est principio id praeuortier.
eamus intro, ut arcessatur faber, ut istas compedis
tibi adimam, huic dem.
STA quoi peculi nihil est, recte feceris.

V. V: GREX

GREX spectatores, ad pudicos mores facta haec fabula est,
1030 neque in hac subigitationes sunt neque ulla amatio
nec pueri suppositio neque argenti circumductio,
neque ubi amans adulescens scortum liberet clam suom
patrem.
huius modi paucas poetae reperiunt comoedias,
ubi boni meliores fiant. nunc uos, si uobis placet
1035 et si placuimus neque odio fuimus, signum hoc mittite:
qui pudicitiae esse uoltis praemium, plausum date.

1020 merito *add. Gruterus* 1021 tu *add. Havet*
1022 cogito *P*, recogito *Gruterus*

614

PHILOC Now this man (*points to Hegio*) is your father. This
man (*points to Stalagmus*) is the thief who snatched you
from here when you were little.

TYN But now that we're both adults I'll hand him over to the
hangman for the theft.

PHILOC He's deserved it.   1020

TYN Then I'll give him his deserved reward deservedly. (*to
Hegio*) But please do tell me: are you my father?

HEG I am, my son.

TYN Now at last I begin to remember when I think about it.]
Now at last I begin to remember hearing, through a fog,
as it were, that my father's called Hegio.

HEG That's me!   1025

PHILOC (*to Hegio*) Please let your son lose the weight of the
shackles and let him have a slave who gains their weight.

HEG I'll definitely attend to that first. Let's go in so the black-
smith can be sent for, so that I can take these shackles off
you and give them to this chap (*points to Stalagmus*).

STA You will do well, as I have nothing of my own.

Exeunt ALL who are still on stage.
Enter the whole TROUPE.

TROUPE Spectators, this play was written to promote decent
behavior, and in it there is no fondling, no love affair, no   1030
fraudulent introduction of a boy-child into a family, no
cheating someone out of his money, no scene in which a
young lover sets free a prostitute behind his father's back.
Poets come up with few comedies of this kind, where the
good become better. Now if you like it and if you liked us   1035
and if we weren't tedious, give us the following sign: you
who want virtue to be rewarded, give us your applause.

METRICAL APPENDIX

AMPHITRVO

arg. 1 + 2, 1–152 ia^6
153–158 ia^8
159–160 tr^8
161 wil
162 cho^3
163–164^a ?
165 c^r + c^r
166–167 an^4
168–172 ion$^{4\wedge}$
173–176 ba^4
177 an$^{4\wedge}$
178 ba^4
179 ba$^{3\wedge}$
180–218 ia^8
219–221 cr^4
222 tr^7
223 cr^2 + tr$^{4\wedge}$
224–232 cr^4
233 cr^2 + tr$^{4\wedge}$
234–236 cr^4
237 cr^1 + tr^2
238–241 cr^4
242 cr^2 + cr^c

243–244 cr^4
245 cr^2 + thy
246 cr^4
247 sp^2
248–252 ia^8
253–254 tr^7
255–262 ia^8
263–462 tr^7
463–498 ia^6
499–550 tr^7
551–571 ba^4
572 ba^c + ba^c
573 ba^4
574 an$^{4\wedge}$
575–579 tr sy$^{17\text{metr}}$
580–583^a tr sy$^{10\text{metr}}$
584–585^a tr sy$^{8\text{metr}}$
586–632 tr^7
633 ba^6
634 ba^4
634^a–635 ba^c
635^a ba^4
636–637 ba^6

638 ba^4
638^a ba^c
639 ba^4
639^a ba^c
640 ba^6
641 ba^c
641^a ba^4
641^b ba^c
642 ba^6
643 ba^c
644 ba^3
645 ba^4
645^a ba^c
646–647 ba^4
647^a ba^2
648 ba$^{3\wedge}$
649–650 ba^4
650^a ba^c
651 ba^2
652 ba^4
653 ba^c
654–860 tr^7

861–955 ia^6
956–973 tr^7
974–983 ia^6
984–1005 ia^8
1006–1008 ia^6
1009–fr. vi tr^7
fr. vii–x ia^6
fr. xi–1052 tr^7
1053–1061 ia^8
1062 an^8
1063 ia^8
1064–1065 tr^7
1066 ia^8
1067–1068 ia^c
1069–1071 ia^8
1072 tr^7
1073 ia^4
1074–1085 ia^8
1086–1130 tr^7
1131–1143 ia^6
1144–1146 tr^7

ASINARIA

arg., 1–126 ia^6
127–132 cr^4
133 cho^2
133^a wil
134–137 cr^4
138–380 tr^7

381–503 ia^7
504–544 tr^7
545–745 ia^7
746–829 ia^6
830–850 ia^8
851–947 tr^7

AVLVLARIA

arg. 1 + 2, 1–119 ia⁶
120–130 ba⁴
131–134 ba² + ia⁴^
135 ia² + ia²
136–139 ia⁴
140 ia⁶
141 tr⁷
142–142ᵃ cr⁴
143 ith
144 cr⁴
145 ith
146 an⁴
147–148 ba⁴
149–152 an⁴
153 vʳ
154 an⁴^ + cʳ
155 ba² + cʳ
156–158 vʳ
159 ba³ + cʳ
160 vʳ
161–279 tr⁷
280–392 ia⁶
393 tr⁷
394–405 ia⁶
406–409 tr⁸

410 an⁸
411–412ᵃ tr⁴^
413–414 ia⁸
415–446 vʳ
447–474 tr⁷
475–586 ia⁶
587–660 tr⁷
661–712 ia⁶
713–717 an⁸
720 an⁷
721–726 an sy²²ᵐᵉᵗʳ
727–730ᵃ tr sy¹⁶ᵐᵉᵗʳ
731–802 tr⁷
803–807 ia⁷
808–818 tr⁷
819–822 tr⁸
823 tr⁷
824–826 tr⁴^
827–831 tr⁸
fr. i–ii?
fr. iii ia⁶
fr. iv tr⁷
fr. v ia⁶
fr. vi ia⁷
fr. vii ia⁶

BACCHIDES

fr. i–viii ia⁶ (iii, iv, v, viii ?)
fr. ix tr⁸

fr. x cr⁴
fr. xi ba⁴

fr. xii cr^4

fr. xiii cr^1 (?)

fr. xiv–xv cr^2 + cr^c

fr. xvi ia^6

fr. xvii cr^c (?)

fr. xviii tr^7 (?)

fr. xix ia^6 (or part of tr^7?)

fr. xx–xxi ?

35–108 tr^7

109–367 ia^6

368–498 tr^7

500–525 ia^6

526–572 tr^7

573–611 ia^6

612–614 tr^8

615 tr^7

616 an$^{4\wedge}$

616^a–617 an^4

618 ia$^{4\wedge}$

619–620 ba^4

621 cr^c + cr^c

622 cr^2 + cr^c

623 cr^3

624 cr^2 + cr^c

624^a cr^3

625 ba^3

626–631^a wil

632–632^a ia^4

633 wil + cr^c

634–634^a ia^4

635 wil + c^r

636 cho^2 + c^r

637 ar + c^r

638 wil + adon

639 wil + c^r

639^a tr$^{4\wedge}$

639^b wil

640–642 tr^8

643 cr^c + cr^c

644 cr^4

645 cr^c + cr^c

646 thy + thy

647–649 cr^4

650 tr$^{4\wedge}$ + cr^c

651 tr$^{4\wedge}$

651^a wil

652 c^r

653 cr^2 + tr$^{4\wedge}$

654–655 ia^4

656 cr^1 + tr^2 + cr^2

657 cr^2

658 cr^2 + ith

659 cr^c

660–661 ia^4

662 c^r + c^r

663–667 cr^2 + cr^c

668 cr^2 + thy

668^a ia$^{4\wedge}$

669 ia^6

670–760 tr^7

761–924 ia^6

925–952 ia^8

953–956^a tr sy^{16metr}

957–962 ia^8

963–964 tr[7]
965–968 ia[8]
969 tr[7]
970 ia[4]
971–972 ia[c]
973–978 ia[8]
979–984[a] tr sy[24metr]
985 tr[8]
986 tr[7]
987–988 ia[8]
988[a] v[r]
989–990[a] wil
991 tr[7]
992–993 tr[8]
994 tr[7]
995–996 ia[4]
996[a] ia[2] + c[r]
997–1075 ia[6]
1076 an[8]
1077 an[7]
1078 an[8]
1079 an[7]
1081–1082 an[8]
1083 an[7]
1084–1086 an sy[10metr]
1087–1088 an[7]
1089–1091[a] an sy[12metr]
1092–1099 an sy[30metr]
1099[a]–1101[a] an sy[10metr]
1102–1104 an[7]
1105 an[8]
1106–1108 an[7]

1109–1111 cr[4]
1112 cr[2] + thy
1113–1115 cr[4]
1116 an[4]
1117–1119 tr[7]
1120 ba[4]
1120[a] ba[c]
1121 ba[3]
1121[a] ba[2] + ba[c]
1122–1123 ba[4]
1124 v[r]
1125–1126 ba[4]
1127 ba[2] + ba[c]
1128 ba[c] + ia[4∧]
1129 ?
1130 ba[3∧] + ba[c]
1131–1138[a] ba[4]
1139 ba[1] + ba[c]
1140 ba[4]
1140[a] ba[1] + ba[c]
1141–1148 tr[7]
1149–1150 an[7]
1151–1153 an[8]
1154 an[7]
1155–1155[a] an[4∧]
1156–1157 an[7]
1158–1159[a] an sy[6metr]
1160–1165 an[7]
1166 an[4∧]
1167–1168[a] an sy[8metr]
1169–1171 an[7]
1171[a] an[4∧]

1172–1173 an sy^{6metr}
1174–1175^a an sy^{6metr}
1176–1178 an^7
1179–1180 an sy^{6metr}
1181 an^7
1182–1183 an sy^{8metr}
1183^a an$^{4\wedge}$
1184–1186^a an sy^{12metr}
1187–1192 an^7

1192^a an$^{4\wedge}$
1193–1195^a an sy^{12metr}
1196–1199 an^7
1200 an$^{4\wedge}$
1201–1202 an^7
1203 an$^{4\wedge}$
1204–1206 an^7
1207–1211 tr^7

CAPTIVI

1–194 ia^6
195–199 ia^c
200 ia^6
200^a extra metrum
201 tr^7
202 ia^6
203 ia^8
204 cr^c + cr^2
205 cr^4
206 ia^4
206^a cr^4
207 cr^2 + ith
208–209 tr^8
210 cr^4
211 cr^2
212 cr^2 + ith
213 cr^4
214 cr^2 + tr^2
215 an^4
215^a c^r + c^r

216 cr^4
217 cr^c + cr^2
218–221 cr^4
222 cr^2 + cr^c
223 cr^4
224 ia^7
225 ia^8
226–230 ba^4
231 an$^{4\wedge}$ + ia$^{4\wedge}$
232 an$^{4\wedge}$ + ia^4
233 ia$^{4\wedge}$
234 cr^3
235–239 cr^4
240–241 tr^8
242–360 tr^7
361–384 ia^6
385–497 tr^7
498 an^4
499 ba^4
500 an^4

501 ba^4

502–503 tr^4

504–505 ba^4

506–506^a ba^c + ba^c

507 ia$^{4\wedge}$ + c^r

508–508^a an^4

509 tr$^{4\wedge}$

509^a c^r

510 tr$^{4\wedge}$

510^a c^r

511 ith

511^a-512 tr^4

513 ia^6

514–515 ia^7

516–524 ia^8

525 ia^6

526–527 tr^8

528 tr^7

529 ia^8

530 ia^6

531 tr^7

532 ia^6

533 ia^8

534 tr^7

535 tr^8

536–540 ia^8

541–658 tr^7

659–767 ia^6

768–769 tr^7

770–771 ia^8

772 tr^7

773–774 ia^8

775 tr^7

776–780 ia^8

781–783 ba^4

784 ia$^{4\wedge}$

785 ba^c + ba^2

786–787 ba^4

788 ba^2 + ba^c

789 ba^4

790 ba^c + ba^c

791–832 tr^7

833–834^a ia^4

835 cr^4

836 cr^3

836^a cr^c

837 ia^7

838–908 tr^7

909–921 ia^8

922–926 ba^4

927 ba^c + ba^2

928–929 tr^8

930–1036 tr^7

INDEX OF PROPER NAMES

The index is limited to names of characters in the plays and of characters, persons, towns, countries, peoples, stars, deities, and plays mentioned in the plays. Names for which established English forms or translations exist are listed under the English forms—for instance, *Jupiter* or *Underworld*. Comic formations and unusual personifications are listed under the Latin forms—for example, *Thesaurochrysonicochrysides* or *Saturitas*—even in cases where I have translated them in the text itself.

INDEX

INDEX